MARVIN R. GOLDFRIED
State University of New York at Stony Brook

MICHAEL MERBAUM
Adelphi University

— EDITORS

Behavior Change through Self-Control

HOLT, RINEHART AND WINSTON, INC.
New York Chicago San Francisco Atlanta
Dallas Montreal Toronto London Sydney

To our parents

Library of Congress Catalog Card Number: 72–84063
ISBN: 0–03–086046–6
Printed in the United States of America
4 5 6 090 9 8 7 6 5 4 3 2

PREFACE

The study of self-control is currently gaining wide attention in psychology and other social scientific disciplines. In part, this interest reflects a deep concern over the real and potential infringement of personal choice by external agencies that exert substantial control over individual behavior. Under these conditions, certain questions have become especially relevant. What role does the individual play in determining his own future, his fate, his life? Is an individual the product, the prisoner of, or the creative collaborator with his environment? In reality, how actively can each person participate in shaping the world he so intimately represents? The study of self-control grapples directly with these issues.

The dilemmas raised by these questions are not impersonal social considerations, but are salient to various forms of psychological treatment. Behavior therapy, in particular, is now in the midst of an acceleration of conceptual formulations and technical innovations designed to facilitate self-control as an essential ingredient in the treatment of behavior disorders. This is an interesting phenomenon in itself. Why should behavior therapy be so energetically committed to this project? Perhaps part of this interest is a reaction to early criticisms of behavior therapy which have stereotyped its practitioners as robot-like environmentalists who brashly rejected any pretense of inner life. While there might be some creditability to this interpretation, other possibilities are equally reasonable. Eventually, as with any emerging scientific discipline, there is a maturing of scientific curiosity to include all phenomena whether or not they are consistent with traditional lines of inquiry. As studies in this area proceed, it is becoming more apparent that self-control represents an exciting excursion into territory which holds important practical implications for human progress. The purpose of this volume is to highlight some of the most important trends and hopefully to stimulate the advancement of theory, research, and practice in this area.

The present volume is the first of its kind to offer a sampling of theory, research, and clinical applications contained in the self-control literature. The appeal of this book should be broad and appropriate for a variety of advanced undergraduate and graduate courses: abnormal psychology, behavior therapy, clinical psychology, personality theory, mental hygiene, perhaps even education.

For their aid in the preparation of this book, we wish to offer our thanks to a number of people. First, thanks are due to Debby Doty, who was thoroughly supportive, and who offered gentle pressure at the most appropriate times. David L. Rosenhan gave many valuable suggestions and served as an effective reinforcer in guiding our judgment in various areas. Gerald C. Davison graciously examined the manuscript and shared his keen insights with us. We also wish to acknowledge the help and moral support of Anita and Daniel Goldfried, Marta, Tal, and Marc Merbaum, whose understanding, affection, and tolerance have meant so much to us.

Stony Brook, New York — M. R. G.
Garden City, New York — M. M.
May 1972

ORGANIZATION OF THE BOOK

The readings which follow offer a sampling of those significant writings which have attempted to incorporate principles of self-control within a behavioral framework. The basic theme underlying each of these papers is the assumption that self-control, like any other psychological phenomenon, can best be understood within the framework of general psychology.

The organization of the readings included in this volume reflects the interplay between theory, research, and actual clinical application. Thus, Part II on theory and Part III on basic research serve as foundations from which guidelines for the clinical application of self-control procedures have been derived. In Part IV, clinical strategies and practical treatment methods are presented for handling various behavior problems. Part V offers case studies to illustrate the several applications of self-control procedures, and the effectiveness of various treatment programs is evaluated by the controlled outcome studies sampled in Part VI. Consistent with the diversity of problem areas in which self-control procedures have been applied, the collection includes such topics as anxiety reduction, problem solving, pain tolerance, various types of compulsive behaviors, and maladaptive interpersonal relations.

In Part I (Introduction), Goldfried and Merbaum present an overview of self-control. In this paper they outline the background, current status, and practical procedures which have been developed to enhance an individual's ability to modify his own behavior. Also surveyed are those maladaptive behaviors toward which the change process has most frequently been directed.

Part II, on Theoretical Bases for Self-Control, includes the classic work of Skinner, and Bandura and Walters dealing directly with self-control, as well as the theoretical viewpoints of Miller and Dollard, and of Schachter and Singer, which have stimulated subsequent clinical and research activities on self-control.

Part III, dealing with Empirical Studies on Self-Control, presents research evidence confirming the effectiveness—at least within a laboratory setting—of various self-control precedures. Different self-verbalizations have been found to result in varying emotional states (Velten), and anxiety reduction (Valins and Ray) and increased pain tolerance (Davison and Valins) have been shown to be facilitated by differential labeling of physiological states. Tolerance for noxious stimuli has also been found to be modified by an increased motivational state (Orne) and attention to competing cues (Kanfer and Goldfoot). Also included in this section are findings that heart rate can be directly controlled by an individual through biofeedback procedures (Lang). Some of the research findings associated with training in creative problem solving (Meadow and Parnes), though not focusing directly on the topic of self-control, serve as an empirical basis for subsequent work on training in independent coping skills. This section also includes research dealing with the development of standards for self-reinforcement (Bandura and Whalen) and the demonstration that self-reinforcement procedures may be used as a means for influencing behavior (Bandura and Perloff).

In Part IV, Self-Control in Clinical Practice—Extrapolation from Theory and Research, we see the way in which basic psychological principles have been utilized in devising self-control procedures for clinical use. Applying Miller and Dollard's mediational view, Ellis has developed rational (-emotive) therapy as a way of training the individual to control his maladaptive emotional states by carefully identifying and differentially labeling life situations. Also drawing on Miller and Dollard's work and basic research on problem solving, D'Zurilla and Goldfried have outlined procedures for training individuals to cope more independently with problematic situations. Ferster, Nurnberger, and Levitt, and Homme offer innovative variations of operant procedures to facilitate self-control. Also included in this section are Cautela's description of a self-administrated imaginal aversive conditioning procedure, Salter's presentation of the way in which self-hypnotic procedures may be learned and used in controlling physiological and emotional responses, and Goldfried's suggested procedural modifications of systematic desensitization for providing the client with an active coping skill.

The selection of papers included in Part V, Case Studies in the Clinical Application of Self-Control, provides concrete examples of the way in which the various self-control procedures have been used. Included among the problematic behaviors dealt with in this section are homosexuality, marital problems, study problems, alcoholism, obesity, generalized anxiety, heterosexual anxiety, and epileptic seizures.

Despite the fact that many of the self-control procedures have been derived from basic research and theory, the need to confirm their effectiveness when actually employed in clinical settings clearly exists. Part VI, Outcome Studies in the Clinical Application of Self-Control, presents research to determine the utility of various self-control procedures in dealing with such problems as speech anxiety, social anxiety, obesity, smoking, and alcoholism.

Finally, Part VII of the book, Some Reflections on Self-Control, contains an excerpt from a paper by Kanfer, who offers his view on self-control issues central to research and clinical work.

Our purpose has been to construct a format which has a logical continuity that flows easily from one section to the next. Thus, we hope the reader will be able to sample some of the more significant original writings in the area, and to understand the bases for a variety of procedures by which self-control might eventually be learned.

CONTENTS

PREFACE iii

ORGANIZATION OF THE BOOK v

PART I. Introduction

1. A perspective on self-control 3
Marvin R. Goldfried and Michael Merbaum

PART II. Theoretical Bases for Self-Control

2. Higher mental processes 37
Neal E. Miller and John Dollard

3. Cognitive, social, and physiological determinants of emotional state 54
Stanley Schachter and Jerome E. Singer

4. Self-control 58
Burrhus F. Skinner

5. The development of self-control 70
Albert Bandura and Richard H. Walters

PART III. Empirical Studies on Self-Control

6. A laboratory task for induction of mood states 81
Emmett Velten, Jr.

7. Evaluation of training in creative problem solving 92
Arnold Meadow and Sidney J. Parnes

8. The influence of motivation on hypnotic behavior 101
Martin T. Orne

9. Effects of cognitive desensitization on avoidance behavior 106
Stuart Valins and Alice A. Ray

10. Maintenance of self-attributed and drug-attributed behavior change 116
Gerald C. Davison and Stuart Valins

11. Self-control and tolerance of noxious stimulation 130
Frederick H. Kanfer and David A. Goldfoot

12. Transmission of patterns of self-reinforcement through modeling 138
Albert Bandura and Carol Kupers Whalen

13. Relative efficacy of self-monitored and externally imposed reinforcement systems 152
Albert Bandura and Bernard Perloff

14. Fear reduction and fear behavior: Problems in treating a construct 162
Peter J. Lang

PART IV. Self-Control in Clinical Practice: Extrapolations from Theory and Research

15. Rational psychotherapy 171
Albert Ellis

16. Cognitive processes, problem-solving and effective behavior 183
Thomas J. D'Zurilla and Marvin R. Goldfried

17. The control of eating 195
Charles B. Ferster, John I. Nurnberger, and Eugene E. Levitt

18. Control of coverants: The operants of the mind 213
Lloyd E. Homme

19. Covert sensitization 224
Joseph R. Cautela

20. Three techniques of autohypnosis 235
Andrew Salter

21. Systematic desensitization as training in self-control 248
Marvin R. Goldfried

PART V. Case Studies in the Clinical Application of Self-Control

22. A homosexual treated with rational psychotherapy 259
Albert Ellis

23. Self-control procedures in personal behavior problems 268
Israel Goldiamond

24. Treatment of compulsive behavior by covert sensitization 287
Joseph R. Cautela

25. Reduction of generalized anxiety through a variant of systematic desensitization 297
Marvin R. Goldfried

26. Reducing heterosexual anxiety 305
Thomas J. D'Zurilla

27. The conditioned inhibition of uncinate fits 317
Robert Efron

PART VI. Outcome Studies on the Clinical Application of Self-Control

28. Group insight versus group desensitization in treating speech anxiety 331
Donald H. Meichenbaum, J. Barnard Gilmore, and Al Fedoravicius

29. Reduction of social anxiety through modification of self-reinforcement: An instigation therapy technique 348
Lynn P. Rehm and Albert R. Marston

30. Self-directed program for weight control: A pilot study 364
Mary B. Harris

31. Modification of smoking behavior 377
D. Carl Ober

32. Covert sensitization with alcoholics: A controlled replication 387
Beatrice Ashem and Lawrence Donner

PART VII. Some Reflections on Self-Control

33. Self-regulation: Research, issues, and speculations 397
Frederick H. Kanfer

NAME INDEX 431

SUBJECT INDEX 435

PART I

Introduction

1

A PERSPECTIVE ON SELF-CONTROL[1]

Marvin R. Goldfried and Michael Merbaum

Perhaps more openly than any other psychotherapeutic approach, behavior therapy has directly confronted the broad moral and therapeutic issue of control as it exists within the therapeutic relationship. A working assumption in behavior therapy is that the client enters therapy because of behavior problems which he is unable to solve by himself, and, therefore, seeks the assistance and direction of the therapist in order to eliminate these difficulties. This orientation provides a therapeutic atmosphere that endorses the overt manipulation of client behavior and promotes deliberate attempts to create appropriate environments for the purpose of behavior change. As a consequence, behavior therapy has frequently been criticized on the grounds that only minimal attention is given to the role of the client in creating his own conditions and guidelines for self-improvement. It seemed to many that undue emphasis was placed on the therapist as the absolute controller who directly manipulated the conditions he assumed were necessary for personal growth to take place.

Despite these criticisms, however, behavior therapists, like therapists from other orientations, have always recognized that the ultimate goal of therapy is to provide the client with the resources to cope independently with his own life. For example, this recognition may be noted in the writings of Dollard and Miller (1950), who suggest: "It is desirable that the patient have some skill at the deliberate solution of emotional problems which we call self-study. In the ordinary case, this skill is a by-product of

[1] This paper was prepared especially for inclusion in this volume.

the original therapeutic training" (p. 436). In more recent years, behavior therapists have paid greater recognition to this ultimate goal at the outset of treatment, and have begun to develop therapeutic procedures which might more directly facilitate self-control.

In their now classic debate on the control of human behavior, Rogers and Skinner (1956) raise certain questions which are relevant to this issue. Although this debate is usually cited as illustrating the differences between Rogers' and Skinner's orientations, there are certain important points on which they happen to agree. Both acknowledge that the dangers associated with the control of human behavior can indeed be frightening, and both recognize the importance of providing the client with a certain measure of self-direction. The point at which the essential difference occurs between the client-centered and behavioral approaches is with respect to the *means* by which this goal may be achieved. Rather than viewing the client's inner direction as an outcome of some natural, though undefined growth process, the behavior therapist has staunchly maintained that the ultimate achievement of self-control, like any other ability, can be learned through the systematic application of various principles of behavior change. Thus, just as one must provide external control and direction in the initial stages of teaching a child to ride a bicycle, the eventual achievement of self-control may require the active and deliberate efforts of the therapist.

In recent years, the importance of self-control has gained momentum as both therapy and research have helped to illuminate the crucial variables that have been involved. The purpose of this paper is to provide an overview of the work that has been done in this area. We shall begin by discussing at greater length previous interest in the topic of self-control, as it has existed both within the psychoanalytically oriented and behavioral traditions. After providing a working definition of self-control, the remainder of the paper reviews and evaluates the work which has been done on the various mechanisms of self-control.

THE PSYCHOANALYTIC TRADITION

The ingenuity man has developed to consciously regulate his own behavior has fascinated virtually all scholars at one time or another. The philosophical notion of *will* or *willpower* was invented as a conceptual explanation to account for the ability of rational man to assert himself and thereby sustain his integrity with relative immunity from external coercion. For most western philosophers *will* was guided by reason, conscious volition, and the conviction that man is endowed with the capacity to voluntarily suppress base impulses and desires that would otherwise subvert the exercise of wise choice.

A classic version of this position is provided by John Stuart Mill, who reflected:

> He who lets the world, or his own portion of it, choose his plan of life for him, has no need of any other faculty than the ape-like one of imitation. He who chooses his plan for himself, employs all of his faculties. He must use observation to see, reasoning and judgment to foresee, activity to gather materials for decision, discrimination to decide and when he has decided, firmness and self-control to hold to his deliberate decision.

This glorification of reason as a cornerstone of *will* in nineteenth-century Victorian philosophy was seriously challenged by Freud's insights into the irrational forces influencing man's behavior.

The ingenious psychic system which Freud devised comprised an assortment of motivational systems operating in simultaneous conflict and harmony with one another. The maturing of the individual required the harnessing of these forces in order to achieve a balance in personal functioning. Perhaps the most important concept distinguishing psychoanalytic theory from other views was the role of the unconscious in determining behavior. Conscious, willful action was relegated to a subordinate position and the power of reason was dismissed as a deceptive veneer for man's instinctual satisfaction.

At the core of the psyche was the Id, where innate biological drives pressed for immediate and mindless gratification. This was a self-contained world of instinctual strivings that were completely autonomous from environmental control. Within this section of the mind, repressed anxieties and fears were also developmentally superimposed over these intrinsic motivational states. Basically, the Id was thought to serve its own affective self-interest, without any cognitive checks to moderate its consequences on the working of the total organism.

Arising out of the Id, through a process of maturational differentiation, emerged the Ego. The aim of the Ego was to provide a balance between unreasonable affective expression and the demands of external reality. As the antithesis of the Id, the Superego was hypothesized as a specialized division of the Ego. Among other functions, the role of the Superego was to oversee the Id's intentions and to encourage the Ego to suppress, usually because of guilt, all impulse expressions violating moral norms of conduct.

The external environment, society and culture, play a rather ambiguous role in influencing behavior in psychoanalytic theory. Rapaport (1960) points out, for example, that Freud's theoretical views of reality underwent at least three revisions and elaborations. At first Freud considered reality, or actually the mental representation of reality, to be the target of ego defense. It was assumed that early traumatic experiences were the source of pathological disturbance, and the object of ego defense operations was to neutralize their catastrophic effect. Freud's revision of this early theory succeeded in expanding the influence of reality in determining the course of normal development. He went on to postulate a secondary thought process which established a direct and veridical connection between the person and his environment. The "secondary process" has a "broad access to reality over which it exercises selective judgment and choices" (Rapaport, 1960, p. 59). In his final revision, Freud conceived of reality as a real threat to security. Id drive states were conceived of as being the true focus of defense because their free expression had the potential for creating disastrous conflict with the external world. As Rapaport states, "defense against drives came to represent reality and, as constituents of Ego and Superego structure, they became internalized regulators of behavior" (p. 59). Despite some theoretical concessions in recognizing the impact of environmental reality, the external world was viewed by Freud as an antagonist to be feared rather than an ally to be courted.

This sketch of the enormously complicated topology of Freud's psychic system is obviously incomplete. However, insofar as the issue of self-control is concerned, it is the Ego which develops as the clearest internal representative of reality and the coordinator of coherent mental processes from which reason and sanity unfold. The Ego is endowed with energy which is used to achieve psychological equilibrium by neutralizing the force of the Id, Superego, and external reality when their conflicts tend to jeopardize the smooth functioning of the system. This is normally accomplished through defense mechanisms whose function is to delay, subvert, compromise, or block the return of repressed material into conscious control of the person's psychological life. Since most of the Ego is itself unconscious, however, psychic battles usually occur without conscious awareness and without voluntary control.

A creative extension of Freud's Ego concept was offered by Hartmann (1958), who suggested that the Ego does not simply develop out of the Id, but can be conceived of as a separately developing potential readiness for psychological adaptation. This conflict-free Ego apparatus is not directly involved with defensive operations, but is responsive to maturational and learning experiences essential to the acquisition of social competence skills. According to Hartmann, certain important functions such as visual perception, object comprehension, language development, various forms of thinking, as well as important phases of motor development, are not necessarily bound up with aggressive or sexual urges. The Ego, as conceived by Hartmann, is purposive and autonomous from the pressures of internal drive states and from the coercive impact of environmental stimulation. As stated by Hartmann (1958): "in addition to controlling internal impulses, the Ego also functions in assisting the individual to control his behavior so as to adapt to the demands of the real world."

Rapaport (1958) extended Hartmann's observations by attempting to define the balance of psychological ingredients which sustain the autonomy of the Ego. Rapaport assumes that, "while the ultimate guarantees of the Ego's autonomy from the Id are man's constitutionally given apparatuses of reality relatedness, the ultimate guarantees of the Ego's autonomy from the environment are man's constitutionally given drives." Thus, Rapaport insisted on two essential autonomies which provide an intrapsychic balance and which serve to protect the organism against inner or outer violations of personal integrity.

The theorizing by Hartmann, Rapaport, and other contemporary Ego psychoanalytic theorists extended Freud's ideas by emphasizing the value of Ego resources as a prerequisite for healthy psychological growth. This change in focus also produced certain radical revisions in psychoanalytic therapeutic technique. Rather than therapeutic attention exclusively directed toward the control of irrational drive states or repressed conflicts, greater interest developed in areas of reality adaptation and the rearrangement of cognitions that regulate behavior. Nevertheless, even with provocative alterations in some areas of psychoanalytic thinking, the organism is still seen as a closed system, where the behavioral pathologies are usually screens for some underlying inner cause residing exclusively within the person. It follows theoretically that if those causes could be identified and subjected to successful emotional and intellectual scrutiny, the pathology would disappear. Attempts at more direct facilitation of purposeful action are generally dismissed as superficial, or at best supportive.

One additional point is worth noting. The goal of most psychoanalytic therapy is personality change in a global sense. Specific changes in behavior are part of a more general personality change package. Thus, ego control or self-control will in most instances have to be bolstered generally, rather than specifically, to correct a particular problem area. While this overall goal is certainly an admirable one, particularly when self-control is at stake, the path is often too time-consuming and financially costly to cope with the urgent and practical demand for treatment currently existing in society. Fortunately, recent clinical theory and practice in behavior therapy have created a rapidly developing alternative to psychoanalytic therapies, especially within the broad area of cognitive reorganization.

THE BEHAVIORAL TRADITION

In the latter part of the nineteenth century, experimental psychology emerged from the shadows of philosophy and established itself as a separate scientific discipline. Many psychologists, particularly those interested in the process of learning, gravitated toward the natural sciences as a major source of guidance and direction. In keeping with this orientation, the subject matter of psychology became overt behavior rather than subjective private experience, and a rigorous attempt was made to discover methods for generating data that could be observed, recorded, and reliably reproduced by other scientists.

In America, a new psychology found its inspiration through the radical influence of John B. Watson, a young psychologist from the University of Chicago. In 1913, Watson boldly proclaimed that "psychology as the behaviorist views it is a purely objective branch of natural science. Its theoretical goal is the prediction and control of behavior." The term "conditioning" became the rallying ground for those psychologists committed to an experimental psychology based upon objective stimulus-response relationships.

One important feature of this theoretical revolution was a decided preference for subject populations that would yield data to meet stringent standards for scientific purity. For this purpose, animals were much more appropriate than human beings. The reasons for the selection of infrahuman subjects are not difficult to understand. Animals, unlike humans, could be placed in research environments with genetic, early experience and experimental conditions highly controlled. Furthermore, the ethical quandary of subjecting humans to many aversive deprivations could be conveniently bypassed. While most of the learning research was conducted on animals, a general assumption of most learning theorists was that they could eventually extrapolate from the apparent regularities in animal behavior to the realm of human experience.

Despite the interest in extending its findings to human behavior, learning theory has had difficulty in incorporating "private events" such as thoughts, fantasy, imagination and the like within its theoretical framework. Indeed, there was a noticeable reluctance of theorists to speculate in this area, in large part due to the difficulty in specifying and quantifying the physical properties of the internal environment. In recent years, however, with a shift in importance from intrahuman to human experimentation, the relevance of symbolic activity has been revived in behavior theories. This change can be attributed to the kinds of issues being approached, as well as to the evolution of an improved psychological technology. Particularly relevant to understanding some of the unique properties of human learning are studies dealing with the areas of self-control, self-regulation, and self-reinforcement. Bandura (1969) provides a salient restatement of this problem.

> Unlike humans, who continually engage in self-evaluative and self-reinforcing behavior, rats or chimpanzees are disinclined to pat themselves on the back for commendable performances, or to berate themselves for getting lost in culs-de-sac. By contrast, people typically set themselves certain standards of behavior and self-administer rewarding or punishing consequences depending on whether their performances fall short of, match, or exceed their self-prescribed demands. (p. 32)

The concept of self-control as applied to human learning is, for the most part, a contemporary theoretical problem in learning. Many current notions about self-control phenomena, however, are extensions of issues learning theorists have been studying for years. For example, the way in which well-entrenched habits become extinguished, unlearned, or counter-conditioned has always been a popular topic in the learning literature, and the solution to this problem is directly associated with the ultimate purpose of self-control. A variety of learning theorists have approached these provocative problems from their own special vantage points.

Guthrie (1935), for example, was convinced that the breaking of habits could be achieved by learning new responses to the same stimulus situation which previously elicited the old habit. He assumed that this new learning would interfere with the execution of the old habit and the latter would eventually decay as new behavior became tied to the same situational cues. Thus, in order to effectively substitute new responses, the cues which were contiguous to the old habit would have to be carefully identified, and the new behavior inserted at the appropriate point in the sequence. What Guthrie was advocating was a method of treatment based on a program of stimulus control. By continually repeating the maladaptive habit sequence and by introducing adaptive responses at appropriate intervals, a new stimulus complex could be arranged. The crucial feature of what Guthrie was advocating, then, is that the person become more attentive to the stimuli controlling his response. With this information, the individual can learn to manage his own behavior more effectively.

A serious attempt to define theoretically the operation of the higher mental processes in the solution of emotional problems was outlined by Miller and Dollard (1941) and Dollard and Miller (1950) in their classic works *Social Learning and Imitation* and *Personality and Psychotherapy.* In building their system, a distinction was made between two levels of habitual and automatic reflexive behavior. The next level was composed of responses mediated by symbolic internal activity, and represented the "higher mental processes." In the symbolic sphere two forms of behavior were noted. One, labeled "instrumental behavior," included all voluntary motor action functionally intended to produce changes in the relationship between the organism and its environment. This behavior is similar to operant responses described by Skinner. The most complex problem-solving role, however, was reserved for the "cue-producing responses." These are defined as mental operations such as language, thinking, images, and the like, which mediate socially complex behavior. The temporal and spatial patterning of these mediating responses and the inherent flexibility of ideational cues facilitate the deliberate and rational use of mental faculties in the solution of a wide range of intellectual and emotional problems. Reason, foresight, insight, and logic are mental attributes characteristically associated with the effective utilization of cue-producing responses.

Dollard and Miller were very much impressed with man's potential for the creative use of higher mental faculties. In many ways, their work laid the foundation for subsequent work in the area of self-control by Bandura (1969). Bandura conceptualizes self-control phenomena within what he refers to as a reciprocal-interaction framework. This general theory combines both mediational (cognitive) and nonmediational (observable instrumental behavior) concepts in accounting for learning and performance change. Bandura assumes, for example, that reinforcement contingencies can significantly influence behavior without the benefit of cognitive awareness to mediate this action. However, through extensive self-monitoring, individuals are usually capable of identifying the contingency rules which govern their behavior. With this information, they can learn to control subsequent behavior more effectively than if awareness were nonexistent. While giving ample coverage to the obvious significance of operant and classical conditioning in learning, Bandura leans toward a formulation that emphasizes symbolic activity as a special human phenomenon which cannot be duplicated in animal research. This is particularly true of the concept of self-reinforcement, an essential component of the self-control process. Bandura suggests that patterns of self-reinforcement are the product of early childhood learning, powerfully transmitted through contact with parents and other social agents. To a great extent this learning is symbolically acquired through vicarious observational methods. Self-control represents the blending of these previously internalized standards of conduct with current environmental contingencies to produce complex social behavior.

Although frequently regarded as an uncompromising environmentalist, Skinner (1953) has never dismissed the significance of private events in the analysis of behavior. In *Science and Human Behavior* he notes:

> Yet to a considerable extent an individual does appear to shape his own destiny. He is often able to do something about the variables affecting him. Some degree of "self-determination" of conduct is usually recognized in the creative behavior of the artist and scientist, in the self-exploratory behavior of the writer, and in the self-discipline of the ascetic. Humbler versions of self-determination are more familiar. The individual "chooses" between alternative courses of action, "thinks through" a problem while isolated from the relevant environment, and guards his health or his position in society through the exercise of "self-control." (p. 228)

Skinner's theoretical analysis of self-control is essentially an extension of general principles of operant behavior. An individual is said to have exercised self-control when he can effectively influence the variables of which his behavior is a function. Whether the process requires arranging environmental conditions to increase the possibility of receiving positive reinforcement, or manipulating inner emotional states to discipline the emergence of certain desired instrumental behaviors, the purposes and principles involved are generally the same. Skinner regards self-control as behavior like any other behavior. Thus, self-control is a function of personal history variables interacting with current environmental influences to create the conditions for individual action.

Kanfer and Phillips (1970) detail the dimensions of self-control and offer concrete suggestions as to how undesirable response sequences can be disrupted or replaced. Their theoretical and empirical analysis is heavily influenced by Skinner. In reviewing the literature they propose a series of instrumental steps which, if taken properly, appear to facilitate the emergence of successful self-control. Of prime value is the initiation of self-control operations *early* in the response sequence. A further suggestion is the liberal use of environmental support systems designed to restrict the possibility of the emission of the maladaptive target behavior, and the simultaneous encouragement of alternate responses, particularly alternate behavior which will be socially reinforced. Extremely vital is a clear specification of the desired end product of the self-control effort. Finally, they stress the importance of obtaining clear feedback, so that self-corrective measures can be introduced if the program begins to lose momentum.

It is readily apparent from the summaries of different behavior theory approaches to the issues of self-control that both mediational and nonmediational views are represented. From our point of view, a comprehensive theory should account for both components.

A WORKING DEFINITION OF SELF-CONTROL

Self-control can be viewed as a process through which an individual becomes the principal agent in guiding, directing, and regulating those features of his own behavior that might eventually lead to desired positive consequences. Typically, the emphasis in self-control is placed on those variables *beneath the skin* which determine the motivation for change. It is equally important to realize, however, that environmental influences have played a vital role in developing the unique behavioral properties of the self-control sequence. Thus, we assume that self-control is a skill learned through various social contacts, and the repertoire of effective self-control responses is gradually built up through increased experimentation with a complex environment. Once the basic self-control information and techniques have been acquired, however, the environment does not automatically release the form or content of the self-control behavior. Rather, a certain degree of judgmental direction is required, whereby the individual himself must formulate a plan of action, test the efficiency of the personal control operation used, and appraise whether the performance and its outcome have met internalized standards of competence. One might best characterize this aspect of self-control as an exercise in discrimination and problem solving.

In distilling the various approaches to the problem of self-control, we suggest the following definition: *Self-control represents a personal decision arrived at through conscious deliberation for the purpose of integrating action which is designed to achieve certain desired outcomes or goals as determined by the individual himself.* A number of points in this orientation require further clarification.

According to our orientation, we conceive of the act of self-control as being mediated by cognitive processes which are available to conscious recognition. Miller and Dollard (1941) and Dollard and Miller (1950) have labeled these intermediary internal behaviors as "cue-producing responses." Bandura (1969) and Kanfer (1970) have similarly stressed the importance of mediating variables in dealing with the process of self-control. All of these conceptions lean heavily on the importance of thought and language in delaying impulsive action, and for introducing a competing cognitive alternative into the self-regulatory sequence.

It is crucial to point out that attempts at self-management usually appear when the smooth execution of normal response chains are inadequate to cope with current internal or external demands. In many ways this reality poses a particularly difficult task for most people because the behavior to be controlled is often one that results in immediate positive reinforcement, but adverse future consequences. Examples of this phenomenon are legion—smoking, overeating, deviant sexual behavior, unrestrained aggression, and the like. Kanfer and Phillips (1970) suggest:

> The process of self-control always involves the change of the probability of executing a response that has both rewarding and aversive consequences, and the selective initiation of a controlling response by a person even though the tempting response is available and more immediately rewarding. (p. 414)

Realistically, the demand for self-regulation may not initially stem from the individual himself. Social agencies may instigate the process by threatening retaliation if the unacceptable behavior is not brought under appropriate control. Or, due to the availability of new information from an external source, the decision to attempt self-control is initiated. A good example of an external source producing a massive self-controlling response from many was the Surgeon General's report on the relationship between cigarettes and cancer. Another familiar example is the feedback typically gotten from friends about how unattractively obese one is becoming because of poor eating habits. Internal experience may also set the self-control process in motion; guilt, embarrassment, and shame over habitual but irrational acts are powerful incentives for change. The violation of internalized norms of conduct generates exceedingly powerful emotional reactions which can be relieved only when the maladaptive behavior is absolutely controlled, or at least sharply reduced in frequency. For an excellent theoretical analysis of those variables associated with committing oneself to behavior change, the reader is referred to Marston and Feldman (1971) and Kopel (1972).

In summary, our definition of self-control includes the following points:

1. A prerequisite of self-control is that it is the individual himself who determines his own special goal or outcome to be achieved. This is not to say that he may be uninfluenced to adopt a particular goal. In the final analysis, however, the choice remains an individual matter.
2. We assume that the strategies for self-control must be deliberately and consciously arranged to reduce the frequency of the unacceptable target behavior. These strategies may include various degrees of personal self-regulation, or may involve the enlisting of environmental support to enhance the attempts at self-control. Regardless of which strategy is employed, a necessary condition is that the person must both be able to verbalize his goal, and to specify each of the several steps he will take to alter his problematic behavior.
3. We view self-control as a functionally defined concept. That is, whether or not one has demonstrated self-control is determined not so much upon procedures employed as it is on the consequences of the action taken.
4. It is our contention that self-control cannot be regarded as a global personality construct. Instead, self-control may more appropriately be viewed as referring to a specific response, or perhaps class of responses, relevant to the alteration of certain maladaptive behaviors.
5. Finally, it is assumed that self-control does not emerge from any innate potential within the individual, but is acquired through experience, whether it be trial-and-error or more systematic learning.

MECHANISMS OF SELF-CONTROL

In the section which follows, we shall describe some of the self-control procedures which have been used for the modification of various forms of problematic behavior, including maladaptive *emotional-physiological* reactions as well as problematic *instrumental* responses.

While it seems almost like a contradiction in terms to discuss the means by which one can gain control over "involuntary" behaviors, the modification of emotional-physiological reactions has been approached by training the individual to manipulate those voluntary responses which serve as elicitory stimuli for such involuntary reactions (Bijou and Baer, 1961).

The control of maladaptive emotional-physiological reactions has involved autosuggestion and self-administered relaxation techniques, cognitive relabeling, and self-administered aversive conditioning procedures. In the case of maladaptive instrumental behaviors, the self-control procedures have included the manipulation of those environmental stimuli which set the occasion for the behavior, the use of self-verbalizations to initiate and direct more adaptive behaviors, and the employment of self-reinforcement techniques to establish favorable consequences for competing adaptive responses.

Self-Control of Maladaptive Emotional-Physiological Reactions

There are several forms of maladaptive emotional-physiological reactions—such as anxiety, deviant sexual attractions, low pain thresholds, epileptic seizures—which have been the target of self-control procedures. Rather than focusing our discussion on each of these reactions per se, we shall describe the various self-control mechanisms used in dealing with these difficulties—i.e., such procedures as autosuggestion and self-administered relaxation, cognitive relabeling, and self-administered aversive conditioning—illustrating each with the type of maladaptive behavior toward which it typically has been directed.

AUTOSUGGESTION AND SELF-ADMINISTERED RELAXATION. The use of autosuggestive techniques has received widespread attention over the years, with one of the objectives being the attainment of direct control over *physiological* reactions. Within the area of behavior modification, the most popular of these procedures involves Jacobson's (1938) method for training in deep muscular relaxation. Used as one of the essential components of systematic desensitization, Jacobson's procedure, or its abbreviated variations (e.g., Paul, 1966), involves training the individual in alternately tensing and relaxing various muscle groups, until he is capable of voluntarily arriving at a state of deep muscular relaxation. Accompanying this muscular relaxation are various autonomic concomitants, including decrease in pulse rate, blood pressure, and skin conductance (Jacobson, 1938; Paul, 1969a).

Another procedure which has been used for the control of physiological reactions has been Schultz and Luthe's (1959) method for "autogenic training." Bearing some similarities to both Jacobson's method and yoga exercises, autogenic training is a form of autosuggestion in which the individual is given practice in attending to both his physiological sensations and his immediate state of consciousness. The procedure involves daily practice of certain exercises, including complete muscular relaxation, and concentration on subjective sensations of warmth and heaviness. As is the case with Jacobson's procedure, autogenic training has been found to be an effective method for learning to gain control over various aspects of physiological reactivity (Schultz & Luthe, 1959).

A somewhat different approach to the control of autonomic responsivity has been described by Lang (1968). Rather than training the individual in any particular exercises along the lines described by Jacobson or Schultz and Luthe, Lang and his associates found that by providing subjects with continual feedback regarding their cardiac activity, together with instructions to maintain a steady rate, it was possible to get subjects to the point where they could voluntarily control their own heart rate.

The attempt to train individuals to obtain direct control over autonomic activity has also been illustrated in a fascinating case study reported by Efron (1957). After training an epileptic patient to inhibit the onset of seizures by having her inhale an unpleasant odor during the early phases of the aura, Efron conditioned these olfactory stimuli to the *sight* of a specific object (i.e., the patient's bracelet). With repeated practice, the physical presence of the bracelet alone was sufficient for blocking the onset of the fits. Carrying this higher order conditioning procedure one step further, the patient eventually reached the point where by merely *thinking* of the bracelet, she was successfully able to inhibit the seizures.

Closely related to the control of physiological reactivity have been attempts to modify *negative emotional reactions*, particularly anxiety. According to Jacobson (1938), the state achieved through deep muscular relaxation is such that it *directly* (i.e., physiologically) inhibits anxiety reactions. As yet, there has been no empirical confirmation of this hypothesis (Lang, 1969), and competing explanations for the relationship between physiological and emotional responses have been proposed by others (e.g., Schachter & Singer, 1962). Regardless of what the underlying process might entail, training in relaxation—typically, although not necessarily within the context of systematic desensitization—has nonetheless been found to serve as an effective procedure for the reduction of anxiety.

Some attempts have been made to conduct systematic desensitization in such a way so that most of the procedure could be carried out directly by the client himself (e.g., Kahn & Baker, 1968; Migler & Wolpe, 1967). The purpose of most of these reports has been to demonstrate that self-administered desensitization may be used as a way of freeing professional therapeutic time, rather than a means by which the client might be provided with a more general coping technique. By contrast, the use of systematic desensitization as a procedure for training in self-control has been described by Goldfried (1971). On the basis of various research findings, systematic desensitization is presented as a means for providing the individual with an active skill for coping with anxiety-producing situations in general, rather than as a passive desensitization of specific fears. Within this model of desensitization, Goldfried has outlined specific procedural modifications, each of which is likely to facilitate the learning of this self-regulating skill.

Several case studies have been reported in which the attempt was made to instruct the client in anxiety-reducing techniques, the goal of which was training in self-control. Goldfried (1973) has described a case of generalized anxiety, where a multidimensional hierarchy was used to provide the client with the skill of "relaxing away" her anxieties in a multitude of situations. Similarly, Lazarus (1958) has reported the case of a client who was able to prevent severe anxiety attacks by use of autohypnotic techniques. The procedure described by Lazarus was, in essence, very similar to the use of relaxation *in vivo.* Weil and Goldfried (1972) have described the successful use of self-administered relaxation procedures with an eleven-year-old suffering from insomnia. In a deliberate attempt to train a client in self-control procedures for reducing heterosexual anxiety, D'Zurilla (1969) employed one of the procedural modifications outlined by Goldfried (1971). Thus, the client was asked to *maintain* the anxiety-producing image during systematic desensitization while relaxing away this tension, so as to provide a "behavioral rehearsal" for relaxing *in vivo* whenever experiencing feelings of anxiety. Arkowitz (1969) has reported the results of a case in which he trained a client in the technique of self-desensitization to alleviate a problem involving heterosexual anxiety, but where the client was successful in employing the same procedures at a later time in other, unrelated situations (e.g., examination anxiety).

In addition to the control of physiological and emotional responses, autosuggestive procedures have also been employed to increase *tolerance for noxious stimuli.* Salter (1941) has described a self-hypnotic procedure which may be used to raise pain threshold. For each of the training procedures described—which in many ways are similar to the exercises outlined by Schultz and Luthe (1959)—the emphasis is on providing the individual with the ability to be in control of his own physiological and cognitive state.

One area in particular which has received considerable attention by those interested in the application of self-control procedures for tolerance of noxious stimulation has been that of obstetrics. Based on the assumption that the pain associated with labor is due to muscular tension resulting from fear, Read (1944) developed procedures for training in "natural childbirth." The training technique makes use of rapid breathing exercises as well as practice in muscular relaxation, all of which is directed toward breaking the presumed vicious cycle between fear, muscular tension, and pain. A variation of these procedures was developed by Lamaze (1958) and Velvovski and his associates (Velvovski, Platonov, Ploticher, & Csougom, 1960). This technique, which has been referred to as the "psychoprophylactic method," does not accept Read's assumption of the intrinsic relationship between fear, muscular tension, and pain. Instead, the training technique focuses on the attempt to directly raise the pain threshold by having uterine contractions serve as a signal for rapid breathing, which is accompanied by intense concentration on the sensations of breathing, and not the pain. The psychoprophylactic method also incorporates various other principles which are directed at reducing the noxious components of childbirth (e.g., the term "pain" is replaced by "contraction").

The effectiveness of the natural childbirth and psychoprophylactic techniques has been attested to by various clinical studies which, because of the fact that subjects were self-selected and controls were absent, have more the status of a series of case reports than they do controlled investigation (Goodrich & Thomas, 1948; Kline & Guze, 1955; Yahia & Ulin, 1965). The findings of these several reports indicate that women who underwent a training program prior to childbirth typically required less medication or anesthesia during the delivery.

We may note a study by Kanfer and Goldfoot (1966) on the tolerance of noxious stimulation as having direct relevance to self-control training for childbirth—particularly the psychoprophylactic method. In order to determine effective procedures by which an individual might raise his pain threshold, Kanfer and Goldfoot had subjects attend to various stimuli while one hand was immersed in ice water. The results of the study revealed that pain tolerance could be increased by focusing one's attention on non-pain-related stimuli (e.g., slides, a clock). These findings are interpreted by the authors as indicating that the self-control mechanism involved here may entail attending to "cues which compete with the response-produced cues associated with noxious events" (Kanfer & Goldfoot, 1966, p. 84). A follow-up study by Seidner and Kanfer (1972) has indicated that pain tolerance could be increased still further if the subject had direct responsibility for *producing* the competing cues.

Within the context of one of his investigations on hypnosis, Orne (1959) has also reported some findings relevant to self-directed tolerance for noxious events. Orne's working model of hypnosis incorporates not only an altered state of consciousness, but also the person's role-conception of the hypnotized subject, as well as his increased motivation to react in given ways. Orne's study on the motivational component of hypnosis is most relevant here. The noxious task employed by Orne was one which required subjects to hold a heavy weight at arm's length until it became intolerable. Male subjects in a waking state who were motivated to continue as long as possible were able to persist longer on this same task than they could while under the influence of hypnotic suggestion. Within the context of self-control, the important finding in this study is the fact that the individual's motivational state per se can greatly influence his ability to tolerate noxious stimulation.

In summary, it would appear that the use of autosuggestive and self-administered relaxation procedures has an important potential for attaining self-control over physiological reactions, the reduction of anxiety, and increasing one's tolerance for noxious stimulation. However, work in this area is still in its infancy, and a greater refinement of theory and technique may bring about revolutionary changes in clinical practice.

COGNITIVE RELABELING. The behavioral approach has often been criticized on the grounds that it neglects the existence of the individual's cognitive processes. Except perhaps for the most "radical" of behavior therapists, however, the judicious reference to mediational processes in conceptualizing human functioning may be seen as completely consistent with a behavioral viewpoint (cf. Davison, Goldfried, & Krasner, 1970). The two major theoretical sources for the use of cognitive relabeling as a self-control process consists of Miller and Dollard's (1941) and Dollard and Miller's (1950) discussion of labeling and the "higher mental processes," and Schachter and Singer's (1962) description of the interaction between cognitive and physiological factors in determining emotional state.

Although Dollard and Miller (1950) have typically been faulted by behavior therapists for simply translating traditional psychoanalytic procedures into learning theory terminology, rather than suggesting innovative techniques which might stem directly from behavioral principles, they nonetheless have provided one of the most significant theoretical platforms on which certain behavioral techniques have subsequently been based. In particular, their discussion of "cue-producing responses"—whether involving the overt use of language or covert self-statements—as a means of facilitating or inhibiting other responses is highly relevant to the question of self-control.

In describing their mediational view of emotional arousal, Dollard and Miller point out that fear reactions may often be elicited by the individual's cue-producing response (i.e., label) to a given situation, rather than the objective stimulus properties of the situation itself. They argue that by modifying the label one attaches to the situation, it should be possible to alter the individual's maladaptive emotional reaction. Rational psychotherapy (Ellis, 1958), or as it has more recently been called, rational-emotive therapy (Ellis, 1962), is based on a proposition very much like that described by Dollard and Miller. As Ellis states it:

> It would appear, then, that positive human emotions, such as feelings of love or elation, are often associated with or result from thoughts, or internalized sentences, stated in some form or variation of the phrase "This is good!" and that negative human emotions, such as feelings of anger or depression, are frequently associated with or result from thoughts or sentences which are stated in some form or variation of the phrase "This is bad!" (p. 37)

An experimental test of the effects of self-verbalization on mood states has been carried out by Velten (1968). Subjects were asked to read self-referent statements which reflected elation ("This is great—I really do feel good—I *am* elated about things"), depression ("I have too many bad things in my life"), or neutral feelings ("Utah is the Beehive State"). Consistent with his hypothesis, Velten found that mood changed as a function of the statements read. These changes were measured by the subject's verbal report, as well as by such indirect indicators as writing speed, decision time, reaction time on a word-association task, and spontaneous verbalizations.

Rimm and Litvak (1969) similarly tested the effects of self-verbalizations on emotional arousal, and found that a significantly greater emotional reaction (as indicated by breathing rate and depth) was elicited by affect-related statements than by neutral ones. Consequently, the basic assumption that self-statements are capable of eliciting maladaptive emotional responses appears to have empirical support.

In addition to maintaining that a person's internal sentences determine his emotional state, Ellis (1958) additionally assumes that maladaptive emotional reactions stem from self-statements which are, in fact, *irrational* (e.g., "Everyone must love me," "I must be perfect," etc.). The primary goal of therapy from his orientation is to have the client modify these unrealistic internal sentences. Included among the various ways in which an attempt is made to modify these self-verbalizations are instructions given to the client that, whenever he experiences emotional upset in some life situation, he should stop to ask himself whether some irrational internal sentences may be at the root of this feeling (e.g., "I *must* do extremely well on this task"). If so, he is encouraged to replace the irrational statement with a more appropriate one (e.g., "It would be *nice* if I could do very well on this task"). Thus, instead of engaging in what is essentially self-defeating (i.e., emotionally-arousing) labeling activities, the client is trained to understand and control these cue-producing responses.

Although the research findings of Velten (1968) and Rimm and Litvak (1969) corroborate one of the basic assumptions underlying rational-emotive therapy, much of the support comes from case reports. On the basis of uncontrolled case studies with a variety of different problems (e.g., Ellis, 1957b, 1959, 1961), the therapeutic effectiveness of this approach would appear to be promising. In addition, some data based on controlled outcome research, which are just beginning to appear in the literature (e.g., Karst & Trexler, 1970; Meichenbaum, Gilmore, & Fedoravicius, 1971), similarly offer support for the effectiveness of the procedure.

Homme's (1965b) description of the self-generated nature of emotional reactions, while employing Skinnerian terminology, is very much within the spirit of Miller and Dollard. Instead of maintaining that emotional responses may be mediated by "cue-producing responses," Homme discusses the role of "coverants"—a contraction of "covert operant"—in the control of maladaptive emotional reactions. He suggests that the frequency of adaptive coverants may be increased by emitting them immediately prior to some high probability behavior (cf. Premack, 1959). According to Homme, if brushing one's teeth can be made contingent upon telling oneself "I feel great," for example, it should be possible to bring about a more positive mood state. Although the successful use of this technique has been reported in a case study (Johnson, 1971), this approach has not yet been tested by means of controlled outcome studies.

In Schachter and Singer's (1962) discussion of the determinants of emotional state, they maintain that the specific emotion experienced by an individual depends not only upon his state of physiological arousal, but also on the way in which he *interprets* or *labels* this state. They further suggest that this labeling process itself is influenced by what the individual attributes as being at the origin of this arousal. This view has been tested empirically by several studies, some of which have direct implications for providing an individual with control over his maladaptive emotional states, and increasing his tolerance for noxious stimulation.

In Schachter and Singer's (1962) classic study in this area, they began by injecting a number of subjects with epinephrine. Some of the subjects were informed that they would experience certain physiological effects as a result of the drug, while others were left uninformed as to the origin of their state of arousal. Although all subjects were exposed to a confederate displaying considerable anger, the group which was informed as to the effects of the drug reacted with significantly less anger than did the uninformed group. According to Schachter and Singer, the informed subjects had attributed their arousal state to the drug and not the emotional nature of the social situation, and consequently were less influenced by the cues associated with the confederate's emotional state. Essentially the same findings were obtained with subjects exposed to a euphoric confederate, thus supporting the notion that emotional state is greatly influenced by the individual's covert labeling.

The effect of cognitive evaluation of arousal states was also studied by Valins (1966), where male subjects were presented slides of seminude females and were given the opportunity to concomitantly monitor their heart rate. The changes in heart rate fed back to the subjects were in fact bogus, and were provided as a basis by which subjects might attribute certain emotional reactions as resulting from the slides. In comparison to subjects who monitored these same sound changes, but who were led to believe they had nothing to do with their internal reactions, experimental subjects subsequently reported greater attraction to the pictures.

In applying this attribution paradigm to the modification of a maladaptive emotional response, Valins and Ray (1967) have interpreted the anxiety-reduction which occurs during systematic desensitization as being based on the individual having learned to control his physiological state, which he then labels as indicating "I am no longer afraid." To test this hypothesis, Valins and Ray provided snake phobics with false feedback as to their physiological state as they viewed pictures of snakes. To enhance the credibility of the feedback, signs of reactivity were provided when subjects were given the signal they were about to receive a shock. The results of the Valins and Ray study indicated that subjects who were "cognitively desensitized" to fear of snakes showed less avoidance behavior than subjects who were instructed that what they had heard while viewing pictures of snakes consisted of meaningless sounds.

In commenting on the study by Valins and Ray, Bandura (1969) has cautioned against drawing any far-reaching extrapolations which might be based on these findings, primarily because of the fact that no adequate preassessment was obtained on the subjects' initial fear of snakes. In light of a replication of this study by Sushinsky and Bootzin (1970), in which a more stringent preassessment for fear level was employed, this caution was well taken. Using subjects whose avoidance behavior appeared to be stronger than those in the Valins and Ray study, Sushinsky and Bootzin were *unable* to demonstrate the effects of cognitive desensitization.

In a study on the cognitive manipulation of pain, Nisbett and Schachter (1966) gave subjects a placebo and then subjected them to a mild electric shock. Those subjects who were led to believe that the physiological arousal experienced during the shock was due to the *drug*, rather than the shock, were able to tolerate significantly more pain stimulation. These findings failed to hold up in another condition, however, where the shock provided was strong.

The implications of differential attribution, as it directly relates to the self-control of tolerance for noxious stimulation, was investigated by Davison and Valins (1969). In an attempt to manipulate pain tolerance, they administered shock to a group of subjects and then provided them with a drug (actually a placebo) which would presumably increase pain tolerance. So as to reinforce the subjects' expectations regarding the effectiveness of the drug, the shock levels were surreptitiously reduced once the drug had "taken effect." Shortly thereafter, the experimental treatment was introduced, which consisted of telling half of the subjects that the drug had worn off, and informing the remainder of the subjects that it really was a placebo. Subjects who were led to believe that the drug had *no effect* reported having more confidence in their ability to withstand shock on a subsequent trial and, in fact, were found to tolerate more shock in a subsequent experiment. These findings are interpreted as providing a method for facilitating self-control by attributing changes to one's own efforts.

Although the work by Schachter and Singer, as well as subsequent investigators, appear to have relevance for the control of maladaptive emotional reactions and ability to tolerate noxious stimulation, there are certain conflicting findings which suggest limitations to this approach. Sushinsky and Bootzin's (1970) failure to replicate Valins and Ray (1967), as well as Nisbett and Schachter's (1966) finding that cognitive manipulation of pain was successful for mild, but not strong, levels of shock would suggest that a key question which remains unanswered is the effectiveness with which such cognitive manipulations are capable of modifying emotional states at various levels of intensity. In essence, the issue may involve the question of how effectively an individual can "delude" himself into maintaining cognitively that he is no longer afraid, or that he is better able to tolerate noxious stimulation, when so many other aspects of his reaction inform him that he indeed is anxious, or that the shock does indeed hurt.

SELF-ADMINISTERED AVERSIVE CONDITIONING. The use of self-administered aversive conditioning for the modification of maladaptive emotional responses has typically been employed in those instances where there exists a maladaptive positive reaction to certain stimuli. The aversive counterconditioning procedures entail the pairing of an aversive stimulus with those stimuli which serve as attractions for the deviant reactions, the objective of which is to establish a conditioned aversion to these tempting situations.

The typical approach which has been employed in self-administered aversive counterconditioning has involved the implementation of these procedures by means of an *imaginal* pairing of positive and aversive stimuli (Anant, 1967; Cautela, 1967; Davison, 1968a; Gold & Neufeld, 1965; Miller, 1959). Although there have been slight variations in the way in which the technique is implemented, the basic procedure may be exemplified by Cautela's (1967) description of *covert sensitization.* Cautela suggests that the client first be trained in techniques of deep muscular relaxation, the purpose of which is not entirely clear. Once in a relaxed state, the individual is instructed to visualize the situation with which the pleasurable, but maladaptive activity (e.g., drinking, deviant sexual behavior) is typically associated. As the person imagines himself getting closer to actually engaging in the maladaptive behavior, he is asked to imagine himself getting more and more nauseous, until, immediately prior to the behavior itself, he begins to vomit. Upon withdrawing from the situation, the feeling of nausea disappears. The client is instructed to practice covert sensitization at home between sessions, and perhaps most important of all, to *use* the technique when actually tempted to engage in these behaviors in actual life situations.

The use of self-administered, imaginal aversive conditioning has been employed in the treatment of alcoholism (Anant, 1967; Ashem & Donner, 1968; Cautela, 1966; Miller, 1959), obesity (Cautela, 1966b; Harris, 1969; Stuart, 1967), cigarette-smoking (Keutzer, 1968; Tooley & Pratt, 1967), deviant sexual behavior (Barlow, Leitenberg, & Agras, 1969; Cautela, 1967; Davison, 1968a; Gold & Neufeld, 1965), and maladaptive interactions with a parent (Davison, 1969b).

In addition to the success reported in those uncontrolled case reports in which self-administered aversive procedures were employed, the technique has received empirical confirmation in controlled investigations as well. Thus, Ashem and Donner (1968) employed covert sensitization with alcoholics, all of whom had a history of unsuccessfully having undergone various forms of treatment. In comparison with a no-contact control group, those clients who were treated with covert sensitization showed significantly higher abstinence rates after a six-month follow-up. Barlow et al. (1969) studied the effectiveness of covert sensitization in two cases of sexual deviation (homosexuality and pedophilia), in which the acquisition phase of the training was followed by an extinction period and then again by a reacquisition phase. In comparison with base-line data, they found a decline in reported sexual arousal to previously tempting scenes when presented in imagination, as well as a decrease in maladaptive sexual urges experienced *in vivo*. During the extinction phase, in which only the scenes were presented, the clients again reported sexual arousal, but these feelings disappeared again during reacquisition.

The fact that the subjects in Barlow et al.'s study reverted back to their pretreatment state during extinction would suggest that (a) clients should continue employing the self-administered aversive conditioning even though behavior change has presumably taken place, or (b) some attempt should be made to establish more sexually appropriate stimuli as sources of arousal. In this regard, we may note Bandura's (1969) description of conditioned aversion:

> The major value of aversion procedures is that they provide a means of achieving control over injurious behavior for a period of time during which alternative, and more rewarding, modes of response can be established and strengthened. Used by itself, this method may bring about only temporary suppression of deviant tendencies. (p. 509)

The success achieved by Ashem and Donner (1966) and Davison (1968a) who, in addition to employing aversive counterconditioning, made an attempt to build in more adaptive responses, would seem to confirm Bandura's recommendation.

Along these lines, we might note the approach to self-administered aversive conditioning suggested by Homme (1965b). Homme suggests that an individual can learn to gain control by emitting aversive self-statements or "covert operants" (e.g., "Cigarettes cause cancer.") in the presence of stimuli which typically elicit the maladaptive reaction (e.g., desire to smoke). Following this, the person is encouraged to substitute some statement antithetical to the maladaptive behavior (e.g., "I will feel better.") and then engage in some reinforcing activity (e.g., drinking coffee).

In a criticism of Homme's procedures, Mahoney (1970) cautions that by emitting the self-verbalization (e.g., "Cigarettes cause cancer.") for the suppression of some maladaptive behavior, the technique may paradoxically serve to remind the person of the behavior he is trying to eliminate, thereby making self-control more difficult. Another problem noted by Mahoney is that the "aversive" self-statement may lose its noxious quality after a period of time, especially when it is paired with reinforcing activities. These criticisms are well-taken, although there is little data currently available as yet to back them up. In one study on the effectiveness of Homme's suggested treatment procedures, the technique was found to be successful in modifying smoking behavior, but no more effective than treatment with a placebo

(Keutzer, 1968). In many respects, Homme's suggested approach may represent only a weak version of the other procedures for self-administered aversive conditioning.

One more point might be made regarding the use of aversive counterconditioning procedures. Very much within the context of self-control, Bandura (1969) suggests that rather than viewing aversion procedures as resulting in a passive modification of the valence of certain stimuli, it could more appropriately be construed as a means for providing the individual with the technique of aversive self-stimulation, which he may then actively use to counteract the tempting quality of the addictive stimuli. According to this view, then, the training procedure can be construed as a "behavioral rehearsal" for what the individual is to do in the real-life situation, much the same way as systematic desensitization can be interpreted as a means for providing the individual with a strategy for coping with anxiety-producing events (cf. Goldfried, 1971).

Self-Control of Maladaptive Instrumental Responses

Although there is probably no limit to the variety of maladaptive instrumental responses which would be amenable to self-control procedures, the problems which have received most of the attention in the literature consist of overeating and smoking, with a few reports appearing on marital problems and poor study habits. The procedures which have been employed in training individuals to gain control over maladaptive instrumental responses include techniques involving stimulus control, the use of verbal self-directions, and the institution of self-reinforcement following the occurrence of more adaptive, competing behaviors. Although we shall discuss each of these procedures separately in the section which follows, they clearly may be used in combination. Indeed, the combined use of each of these techniques is likely to be most effective in obtaining self-control.

STIMULUS CONTROL. Although instrumental behavior is typically thought of as being maintained primarily by reinforcing consequences, it is also controlled by discriminative stimuli which have been associated with the reinforced behavior. Thus, the pigeon learns to peck at a disk only when the light is on, and the first cup of coffee in the morning serves as a cue for an individual to light up a cigarette. The relevance of stimulus control for self-regulation stems primarily from the fact that an individual is capable of modifying certain maladaptive behaviors by altering the discriminative stimuli associated with these behaviors. Skinner (1953) has described self-directed stimulus control as a means by which the individual can either avoid some temptation by removing discriminative stimuli, or facilitate the occurrence of certain adaptive responses by exposing himself to certain stimuli which will increase its likelihood.

A problem area toward which much of the work on stimulus control has been directed is that of obesity. The attempt to gain control over eating habits by manipulating the discriminative stimuli associated with such behaviors is particularly relevant in light of the findings by Schachter and his associates (Goldman, Jaffa, & Schachter, 1968; Schachter, 1967; Schachter & Gross, 1968) that, in comparison to individuals of normal weight, the eating habits of obese individuals are more likely to be controlled by external factors than by the internal sensations of hunger. Self-directed weight-control programs using techniques of stimulus control have been described by Ferster, Nurnberger, and Levitt (1962), Harris (1969), and Stuart (1967). The procedure used in these programs is similar, and typically involves narrowing the range of situations and times during which eating can occur. In addition, the individual is instructed to avoid eating while engaging in other activities, such as reading or watching TV, the general purpose of which is to have these situations no longer function as discriminative stimuli for eating. Although these programs have typically been shown to be effective in bringing about weight loss, the inclusion of a variety of self-control techniques (e.g., covert sensitization) makes it difficult to isolate the relative effectiveness of this procedure alone.

Other problems to which stimulus control has been applied include the modification of smoking behavior (Nolan, 1968; Ober, 1968; Upper & Meredith, 1970), inefficient study habits (Goldiamond, 1965c), and marital problems (Goldiamond, 1965c). As has been the case with the work done on weight control, the use of stimulus control in each of these other instances involves the narrowing of those discriminative stimuli which are associated with the maladaptive responses.

The use of stimulus control for the elimination of smoking behavior may be illustrated with a case study reported by Nolan (1968). The procedure was implemented by having the individual—Nolan's wife—agree to smoke only when sitting in a certain chair. In addition, things were arranged so that no other activities, such as reading, watching TV, or holding a conversation, could be carried out while sitting in this chair. As a result of following this procedure, she was able to abstain from smoking after a period of one month.

The successful use of stimulus control procedures for the modification of smoking has also been reported by Upper and Meredith (1970). The treatment program consisted of having subjects use a portable timer which was set according to their typical interval between cigarettes. The buzzer which sounded at the end of the interval served as a signal for their smoking. Once their smoking behavior was under control of the buzzer, subjects gradually increased the time between signals. The results of the study indicated that when compared to subjects in attention-placebo and no-contact control groups, those participating in the stimulus control program showed significantly greater decrements in smoking behavior.

Goldiamond (1965c) has described other problematic behaviors for which a stimulus control approach was employed. In the case of a student unable to maintain efficient study behavior, for example, it was recommended that the student's desk be used for study only, and that other activities be carried out elsewhere. Goldiamond also describes a marital problem in which he recommended rearranging the household furniture so as to provide a stimulus situation which had less of an association with the marital arguments. Also associated with this case was the husband's tendency to sulk. Although the individual's privilege to sulk was acknowledged, he was instructed to do so only in a certain place. The fact that sulking decreased after a regime of engaging in this activity while sitting on a "sulking stool" in the garage, however, may be better illustrative of aversive, rather than stimulus control.

For some reason, the range of problems described in the literature toward which stimulus-control has been applied seems to be fairly narrow. Considering the fact that external stimuli mark the occasion for so much of our everyday behavior, principals of stimulus control would seem to have the potential for providing an individual with the means by which he might modify a wide variety of maladaptive behaviors.

VERBAL SELF-DIRECTION. In addition to the external stimulus control of behavior, man's use of language provides him with the ability to generate his own stimuli, which in turn, are capable of directing his actions. This may consist either of simple self-generated verbal commands which instigate certain behaviors (Skinner, 1953), or more complex planning and reasoning which can influence the decision to emit certain behaviors and not others (Dollard & Miller, 1950; Miller & Dollard, 1941).

The role of self-instruction for the control of overt behavior has been studied developmentally by Luria (1961), who concludes that prior to age four, children are typically unable to use self-verbalizations as a means for regulating their behavior. The likelihood that this finding is tied to the specific nature of previous learning history, rather than any innate developmental sequence, is suggested by recent work in this area. For example, in a study by S. L. Bem (1967), it was found that under conditions of specialized training, three-year-olds were brought to the point where they eventually were capable of utilizing self-instruction to control their behavior. Similar findings have been reported by Meichenbaum and Goodman (1971) with impulsive grade-school children.

The use of self-instruction as a means of self-control among children has also been studied by O'Leary (1968), who found it to be effective in providing subjects with the ability to resist the temptation to cheat. In this study, grade-school boys were allowed to work on a task in which the probability of obtaining a prize could be increased by cheating. The cheating consisted of pressing a key at the "wrong" time to obtain marbles which later could be exchanged for a prize. Although all children were aware of what was "right" and "wrong," the frequency of transgressions was significantly less for those boys who were instructed to tell themselves whether they should press or not prior to actually responding.

In conjunction with a description of the way in which an individual can learn to manage his own contingencies, Homme (1965b) describes the use of "coverants" or self-administered verbal contracts, to increase the likelihood that certain behaviors will occur. According to Homme, the individual who wants to facilitate study behavior should tell himself something like: "As soon as I complete this reading assignment, I can reinforce myself by watching TV." In a case report described by Johnson (1971), Homme's coverant technique was successfully employed by a client as an aid in directing adaptive interpersonal behaviors. The likelihood of emitting the appropriate coverant at any given time was insured by having the client carry in his possession index cards containing these verbal statements. This use of the index card procedure may be viewed as a way of gaining some stimulus control over the likelihood of utilizing these self-verbalizations.

In dealing with situations requiring more than simple self-directed statements, Miller and Dollard (1941) and Dollard and Miller (1950) describe the use of cue-producing responses in the process of coping with various situations where the most appropriate response is not apparent. The use of "higher mental processes," argue Miller and Dollard, can eliminate many of the negative consequences which are likely to accompany overt trial and error. Man's ability to reason and plan, particularly when faced with a problematic situation requiring some decision on his part, plays a significant role in the likelihood of his controlling his own fate.

Based in part on some of the suggestions outlined by Miller and Dollard, D'Zurilla and Goldfried (1971; 1973) have outlined procedures for training in problem-solving. Within the context of facilitating self-control, these procedures are directed toward enabling the individual to become better able to decide upon the most effective course of action when confronted with a problematic situation. The training procedures are directed toward providing the individual with the ability to utilize each of the following steps in coping with difficult life situations: (a) being able to recognize problematic situations when they occur and making an attempt to resist the temptation to act impulsively or do nothing to deal with the situation; (b) defining the situation in concrete or operational terms, and then formulating the major issues with which he must cope; (c) generating a number of possible behaviors which might be pursued in this situation; (d) deciding on the course(s) of action most likely to result in positive consequences; and finally (e) acting upon the final decision and verifying the effectiveness of the behavior in resolving the problematic situation.

The effectiveness of some of the techniques outlined by D'Zurilla and Goldfried (1971; 1973) may be illustrated by the work of Parnes and Meadow (1959) and Meadow and Parnes (1959). In an attempt to facilitate creative problem-solving, Parnes and Meadow tested the effectiveness of "brainstorming" instructions. The brainstorming technique emphasizes that the individual generate as many ideas as possible in a given situation, inhibiting any premature evaluation as to their value. When compared with a group who was told to produce only "good" ideas, subjects using brain-storming instructions were able to produce not only more ideas, but also ideas of good quality. Further, subjects who had previously taken part in a course on creative problem-solving (Meadows & Parnes) were better able to generate good ideas under brainstorming conditions than those subjects who had no prior formal training in this procedure.

Although the use of self-verbalized instructions would appear to be an effective way of modifying behavior—whether it consists of relatively simple self-verbalized prods for emitting a given response, or more complex problem-solving processes involved in arriving at an effective course of action—the necessity for a behavior being followed by positive consequences nonetheless exists. This is nicely demonstrated in a token economy program by Ayllon and Azrin (1964), where it was found that instructions, when *combined* with reinforcement, were more effective in modifying behavior than either of the two employed alone. Although the use of self-directions would appear to be particularly useful in instigating certain adaptive behaviors which might otherwise be less likely to occur, once emitted, these responses must be maintained by reinforcing consequences.

SELF-REINFORCEMENT. In its traditional usage the concept of reinforcement has been defined in terms of events which originate outside the person, typically involving the physical act of administering reinforcing consequences by agents other than the person himself. Under these conditions, the behavioral criteria for obtaining reinforcement is determined by a community in which the individual has only marginal control. In contrast, the phenomenon of self-reinforcement highlights the responsibility of each individual in the evaluation of his own behavior and by the presentation of self-initiated reinforcement in symbolic or actual terms.

One of the major hurdles in self-reinforcement research involves devising ways of objectifying and recording the self-reinforcement response itself. It may be sufficient theoretically to assume that self-reinforcement is a viable concept, but it is another matter to demonstrate the actual occurrence of the event, let alone calculate the effect it may have on subsequent behavior. Kanfer and Marston (1963a) have dealt with this problem by first requiring a person to make a judgmental assessment of his personal performance (a cognitive component) and then to link this covert response to an instrumental motor response which produces a specific object (a token) as a material reward. In this study the authors found they could influence self-reinforcement by varying the attitude (positive or negative) of the experimenter who initially dispensed the reward tokens. Their interpretation of this study is that self-reinforcement can be categorically objectified as a response that is subject to the intervention of social reinforcement.

As we have seen by the Kanfer and Marston research, self-reinforcement can be considered a response with properties that are amenable to shaping by behavioral principles common to the maintenance of most operants. In a different line of research, Bandura and his associates (Bandura & Kupers, 1964; Bandura & Perloff, 1967) have examined the growth of self-reinforcement under conditions where no immediate external reinforcement is involved. Their position, which has received considerable support in a number of studies, demonstrates that the matching of a person's standards for self-reinforcement to the observed behavior of a model is a powerful determiner of one's style of self-reinforcement. In the vicarious learning paradigm, the subject observes rather than acts in the presence of a model. Thus, the necessary data for complex social behavior are symbolically absorbed, collated, and assigned appropriate response weights without ever having been actually performed during the acquisition process. Bandura believes that much of our social behavior is generated through such observational learning, and is then externally reinforced at a later date. In terms of economy, if Bandura and Walters (1963) are correct, the vicarious learning paradigm spares an organism the tediousness of learning through stages of successive approximation typically assumed to be necessary in operant conditioning theory.

In an experimental investigation of the origins of varying standards for self-reinforcement, Bandura and Kupers (1964) had grade-school children observe models who displayed varying criteria for self-reinforcement. In one condition, the model rewarded himself with candy and self-approving statements for only high-level performance on a particular game; in the second condition, a low performance standard was sufficient for self-reinforcement. The results of this study clearly indicated that on subsequent performance trials, the standards for self-reinforcement displayed by the children reflected those standards they had observed in the model. Bandura and Kupers also found certain characteristics of the model himself to be important, in that adults constituted more powerful models that did peers.

A later study by Liebert and Allen (1967) demonstrated that the development of self-reinforcement standards may be facilitated by having the model verbalize the particular "rule structure." That is, the child who observed the self-reinforcing pattern of the model, and additionally heard the model verbalize rule structure (e.g., "*That's* a good score . . . that *deserves* a chip.") was more likely to assume the model's self-reinforcement standards than was the child for whom no rule structure was provided.

Although the observational learning and direct reinforcement paradigms have been employed in the investigation of the developmental origins of self-reinforcement, the actual process of socialization typically involves each of these social learning principles. Recognizing this joint influence, Mischel and Liebert (1966) investigated the effect of modeling and direct reinforcement, both when they were consistent and when they were contradictory. The results of their study indicate that children who observed a model displaying a high standard for self-reinforcement, and who additionally were directly rewarded only for their high level of performance, were most consistent in their adoption of this self-reinforcement pattern. This was true in their own subsequent performance, as well as in the transmission of this pattern of self-reinforcement to other children when asked to "demonstrate" how the game worked. Those children who were subjected to inconsistent training procedures—where the model set high standards for himself, but used low standards for rewarding the child, or vice versa—were more likely to adopt the lower standards for self-reinforcement. The results of this study demonstrate quite nicely that the socialization agent who attempts to train children in self-control by having them "do as I say, not as I do," is more likely to be unsuccessful than one who utilizes a more systematic approach based on relevant social learning principles.

In the typical real-life situation, self-reinforcement and external reinforcement are events which exist concurrently, often making it difficult to completely isolate their independent action. Nonetheless, in order to affirm the effect of self-reinforcement, it has been essential to devise "pure" self-reinforcement conditions that are not contaminated by external reinforcement. Thus, Bandura and Perloff (1967) compared children who were given the opportunity to be self-rewarding with children who received externally administered reinforcement, and with a control group who received no apparent reinforcement from either source. The results of this study indicated that the self and external reinforcement treatments were equally effective, and that the children in both of these conditions were more highly productive than those children in the control condition. Subsequent work by Johnson (1970) on self-reinforcement has confirmed these findings.

A prime working assumption underlying self-reinforcement is that internal standards provide the criteria by which behavior is judged to be eligible for reinforcement. If, for example, behavior is simple and habitual, it is rare to find these responses self-reinforced. Kanfer (1969) suggests, on the other hand, that when skills are being formed, or when creative work is being carried out, self-rewards or criticisms are frequently introduced. Under these conditions, self-surveillance probably aids in maintaining an optimum motivational level and in addition provides an ongoing monitoring system to insure that a particular level of competence is being attained. Kanfer and Marston (1963b) found, for example, that self-rewarding responses were more frequent when high competence behavior was emitted on difficult as compared with easy tasks. In addition, the clearer the performance standards were on a specific task, the easier it was for the subject to provide himself with accurate feedback.

From a clinical perspective, Kanfer and Marston suggest that the shaping of self-reinforcement is somewhat analogous to self-confidence training. Following this research direction, Rhem and Marston (1968) initiated a therapy procedure based on a self-reinforcement program for male students who were inhibited in dating. An elaborate procedure was developed in which each client specified for himself a series of interpersonal tasks in which he would like to feel more comfortable. After arranging these tasks in order of increasing difficulty, the client was encouraged to perform them *in vivo* and then to evaluate his own behavior along a prearranged scale of approach or avoidance. Sessions with the therapist reviewed the week's work, and self-administered points were given for success or failure in a given task. For exemplary achievements, the therapist offered positive verbal reinforcement. When the clients rated their performance in the low categories, the therapist asked them "how they might have changed their behavior to increase their self-evaluation." Under no circumstances did the therapist actually suggest alternative behaviors. This therapeutic procedure was compared with a nonspecific therapy group and a no-therapy control composed of individuals with similar social problems. It was found that compared with the nonspecific therapy and control conditions, the self-reinforcement therapy group showed significantly more improvement on measures dealing with self-reports of anxiety as well as overt behavior. The authors contend that self-reinforcement therapy is valuable because the person not only acts as his own therapist, but also because the rearrangement of his own cognitive self-evaluative systems is motivationally self-induced.

In a recent paper, Cautela (1970) has offered a therapeutic procedure based upon principles of self-reinforcement. Unlike most research methods, which generally require a physically palpable self-reinforcement response (acquiring tokens, points, etc.), Cautela's reinforcement response is exclusively mediated and executed in imagination. According to Cautela, "covert reinforcement," as the therapeutic procedure is called, is also inferentially capable of explaining behavior change and maintenance in nonpathological contexts. The first step in the self-reinforcement program is the identification of those mental images representing objects or situations which, if visualized, create a positive emotional reaction. While the client is in a relaxed state, he is asked to imagine current social situations with which he is experiencing difficulties. He is instructed to visualize these situations and imagine himself behaving in a socially effective and nonanxious manner. At various points in the imaginal sequence, the client administers to himself the prearranged reinforcement images, provided he feels he is eligible for the delivery of reinforcement. The client is also instructed to practice the procedure at home.

An important practical approach to the use of self-reinforcement in producing greater self-control was advanced by Homme (1965b, 1966). Homme, theorizing from a Skinnerian frame of reference, has devised an imaginative operant conditioning paradigm that incorporates Premack's differential probability hypothesis (Premack, 1965). Homme assumes that people can be trained to effectively manage their own covert and overt behavior through what he terms "contingency management." Drawing on the Premack principle, "for any pair of responses, the more probable one will reinforce the less probable one," (Premack, 1965, p. 132), Homme has evolved a self-reinforcement paradigm that may be useful in the modification of various troublesome behavior. The sequence of events outlined by Homme requires (a) the identification of stimuli which precede the unwanted act, (b) the interposition of a thought antithetical to the target stimuli, (c) a thought supporting the virtues of an alternative course of action, and (d) a self-induced maneuver which provides reinforcement as a consequence of refraining from the habitual behavior.

In summary, the reality of self-reinforcement as an integral feature of self-control is currently assuming a focal position in theories of behavior. While in no way underestimating the powerful impact of environmental contingencies, the emphasis on covert processes has merely enlarged the picture. Interestingly enough, the shift in emphasis now being introduced by behavioral theorists is anything but original to the dynamicist who has always considered internal states as his primary targets for treatment. What is original, we believe, is the concerted effort to integrate, objectify, and specify the antecedents of self-regulatory processes in scientifically meaningful terms. This demands, among other things, a close connection between theory and research. The extensive research program by Bandura and his co-workers is an excellent case in point. Through his research, the critical influence of models in vicariously transmitting social information without the intervention of immediate environmental consequences has been vividly demonstrated. In addition, Kanfer and his colleagues have begun to conceptualize theoretically the environmental origins and internal determinants associated with self-rewarding and self-critical response styles. Further work in this area has incalculable clinical significance.

SUMMARY AND CONCLUSIONS

In contrast to most other views of self-control, the behavioral orientation stresses the belief that self-control may be facilitated through the process of learning, much the same as any other aspect of human functioning. According to this view, it makes little sense to describe an individual as having "good" or "poor" self-control. Rather than being viewed as a general trait, the behavioral approach to the study of self-control has focused on the different procedures which might be employed in allowing the individual to gain greater control over various forms of problematic behaviors. In the case of deviant emotional-physiological reactions—including anxiety, deviant sexual attractions, low pain threshold, epileptic seizures, and attraction to such potentially maladapted sources of gratification as alcohol and cigarettes—the methods for obtaining greater self-control have involved autosuggestion and self-administered relaxation techniques, cognitive relabeling, and the use of self-administered aversive conditioning procedures. Although there is probably no limit to the various types of maladaptive instrumental responses for which self-control procedures would be relevant, most of the work which has been done in this area has been concerned with overeating, smoking, marital problems, and poor work habits. The procedures which have been typically employed in training individuals to gain control over maladaptive instrumental responses include techniques involving stimulus control, the use of verbal self-directions, and the institution of self-reinforcement following the occurrence of more adaptive, competing behaviors.

Thus, the concept of self-control may best be viewed as a generic term encompassing a variety of different procedures which may be employed to modify various types of maladaptive behaviors. The same is true of the term "behavior modification." When viewed as the therapeutic application of general principles of psychology to individuals manifesting deviant behavior, behavior modification similarly encompasses a number of therapeutic procedures for dealing with a large array of behavior problems. These similarities should not come as too much of a surprise, particularly when one views self-control as involving these same principles of behavior change. However, within the self-control framework, the individual is explicitly taught to function as his own therapist. As is the case with behavior modification procedures in general, the question of which self-control procedure or procedures to use in any given instance may be determined only after a careful assessment of those variables maintaining the maladaptive behavior (cf. Goldfried and Pomeranz, 1968; Mischel, 1968; Peterson, 1968).

The work which has been done up until this point on self-control and behavior modification is clearly in its formative state. Many of the techniques employed have been based on a tenuous extrapolation from behavior theory and research. Although the several procedures have shown to be successful in individual cases, the greatest need at present is for more controlled outcome studies. In much of the research work done in this area, the method employed has typically involved a "treatment package," in which a number of different self-control techniques were included. What is ultimately needed, then, is outcome research to determine the effectiveness of each technique when used alone, as well as their interaction with other self-control procedures (cf. Mahoney, 1972).

One final point before concluding. The increased interest in very recent years on the importance of self-control appears to have paralleled the situation where man is becoming more and more concerned about the dangers of external control (cf. Skinner, 1971). The potential of external control has become more frightening of late, perhaps because we are more aware of its existence, but also because the number of ways in which we can be controlled by others is becoming more pervasive and effective. While acknowledging the crucial need for effective behavior technology, London (1969) has called attention to the moral and ethical questions associated with being controlled. As a means of counteracting this danger, he notes the following:

> In order to defend individual freedom, it is necessary to enhance the power of individuals. If behavior technology endangers freedom by giving refined powers to controllers, then the antidote which promotes freedom is to give more refined power over their own behavior to those who are endangered. Since everyone is endangered, this means facilitating self-control in every one. (pp. 213–214)

Because of the importance of this issue, one of the major contributions the behavioral sciences can make to society is to help convert the promise of self-control into a reality. Our personal and group integrity is likely to depend on this.

PART II

Theoretical Bases for Self-Control

2

HIGHER MENTAL PROCESSES

Neal E. Miller and John Dollard

The higher mental processes are based on elaborations of the simpler innate or instinctive modes of adjustment. The function of the higher mental processes can be brought out more clearly after a brief résumé of the simpler mechanisms. One of the important innate functions is primary drive. The innate mechanism for drive is provided by various nerve endings and receptors so arranged that strong stimulation is produced when the body is injured, starved, cold, etc.[1]

Drives move the individual to respond. But even in the naïve individual, not all responses have an equal probability of occurrence. For each primary drive, there is an innately determined preferential order, which we have called the *innate hierarchy*. In many instances, such as the flexion reflex which produces withdrawal from painful stimuli, the dominant response in the hierarchy is likely to avoid the strong stimulus. Similarly, but less certainly, the crying of a hungry infant is likely to bring the adult with food to terminate hunger. Different strong stimuli have an innate tendency to elicit different responses. Stepping on a thorn with the left foot elicits withdrawal of the left foot and extension of the right, and stepping on a thorn with the right foot elicits withdrawal of the right foot and extension of the left. Thus the

[1] Though drives are often correlated with needs, it should be clearly noted that not every situation in which the body suffers from a need produces strong stimulation which acts as a drive. The body may need more oxygen but die of carbon monoxide poisoning without any stimulation being produced which is certain to rouse the individual to action.

strong drive stimuli also have distinctiveness or cue value. In certain lower animals, the innate hierarchy of responses to a given situation may include one elaborate, patterned response which is definitely dominant over all others. Such responses are called instincts. The particular instinctive response which occurs usually depends not only on the drive stimulus which is present, but also on other weak but distinctive stimuli which act as cues.

As many writers have pointed out, fixed instincts may fail to be adequate for adjustment to a changing environment. In most animals, and particularly in man, the innate hierarchy is subject to modification by learning. The basis for learning is, of course, the innately rewarding value of an escape from strong stimulation, which strengthens the connections to the responses most closely associated with that escape. For learning to occur, the response in the innate hierarchy must be dominant by a narrow enough margin so that its extinction, if not rewarded, will allow the occurrence of other responses.[2]

Even where most final adjustments are the product of learning, the innate hierarchy still plays an important rôle in determining which responses are most likely to occur to certain stimuli and which responses will not be tried at all and hence not learned. When the arrangement of responses in an innate hierarchy consists of combinations which are quite likely, with slight modification, to be rewarded, it may vastly simplify the process of learning. For example, as the infant matures, highly coördinated step and balancing reflexes appear as innate responses to various forms of proprioceptive stimulation. These innately coördinated stepping and balancing patterns form a nucleus of responses which with relatively little modification can be remade into a great variety of habits ranging all the way from walking to running back a punt through a field of opponents for a touchdown. Locomotor habits are learned with infinitely more ease than they would be if the innate hierarchy were not already heavily weighted in favor of response patterns likely to be rewarded.

Learning enables the individual to perfect and modify adjustments based on the innate hierarchy. In man, these modifications may be very great. Cultural activities in particular—those distinctive of a nation, a community, a class, a sect, or other social groups—are characteristically learned.

Learning enables the individual to acquire better adjustments to situations in which he has had experience. But what of new situations? It would be inefficient for the individual to have to fall back upon his innate hierarchy in every new situation. The simplest solution to this problem is provided by the mechanism of *innate generalization*, whereby responses rewarded in one situation tend to transfer to other similar situations. The course of innate generalization is determined by sensory structures which make certain cues seem similar and others different. But just as it is impossible for an innate

[2] It seems that in addition to the factor of sheer strength of response, some types of connections, such as those involved in spinal reflexes, are much less subject to modification by reward than others.

hierarchy to be adapted to changing conditions, so is it impossible for an innate basis of generalization or transfer of training to produce perfect adaptation to new conditions. Two situations which at one time should, for the best interests of the organism, be reacted to similarly may change so that they should be reacted to differently at another time.

ACQUIRED CUE VALUE

One of the adjustments to this dilemma seems to be the capacity of the individual to learn to pay attention to certain relevant aspects of the complex of cues and to base his generalization primarily upon these aspects. Thus a lieutenant may learn to pay attention to the spread eagle on a colonel's shoulder and salute anybody wearing this, irrespective of his physique, style of uniform, or other innately more distinctive cues. To a certain extent, paying attention is a matter of learning to respond by directing the sense organs so that they will be exposed to the relevant cues. Responses of looking at other cues are extinguished; responses of looking at the silver eagle on the shoulder are rewarded; a discrimination is established. To the naïve civilian, the eagle appears in the context of a fat face with a ruddy complexion, or of a lean face with a sallow complexion, and in many other stimulus configurations. The eagle is at first not significant in these contexts, because the other cues are innately more striking, and because civilian training has rewarded noticing faces and their expressions, rather than shoulders and their insignia. If the lieutenant stops to look first at the shape of the face, the facial expression, and other aspects of a new officer whom he meets, he may be reprimanded for not behaving appropriately, e.g., saluting. He learns to escape from the anxiety induced by punishment by looking first at the eagle on the shoulder and then responding appropriately to it. After the lieutenant has learned, upon meeting any new man in uniform, to look first of all at the shoulders, where the insignia are worn, rather than at the face, the eagle will be seen more distinctly than other cues not looked at. Thus the eagle will be more likely to be the basis for either new learning or generalization than the other cues.

In some cases, paying attention may involve more central factors. These have not been investigated in detail, but Lashley's (1941) results seem to indicate that these factors, even if central, are subject to modification by learning, and hence in the present system may be functionally classified as responses. Learning to respond to similar classes of cues in different contexts (circularity, triangularity, twoness) is called *abstraction* and plays an important rôle in the higher mental processes.[3] Not much is known about

[3] It seems likely that one of the factors which makes the mental processes of man so much "higher" than those of animals is a greater capacity to respond selectively to more subtle aspects of the environment as cues. This problem is far beyond the scope of the present investigation.

the intimate details of the processes involved in abstraction. It is known, however, that it can be facilitated by teaching the individual to respond in the same way to a large number of different cue patterns all containing the crucial element (Hull, 1920). The response is always rewarded whenever the crucial element is present and never when this element is absent. Thus the response becomes more and more strongly connected to the relevant cue and extinguished as a response to other cues.

Once the individual has learned in a variety of situations to make a given response to the cue relevant to the category in question, this response may facilitate further reactions to the category abstracted by producing an additional cue common to the different situations, A lieutenant learns to salute every time he sees the eagle on a colonel's shoulder. As he salutes, he stimulates proprioceptors within his own body and feels himself saluting. Thus the act of saluting produces an additional cue which is common to the situation of meeting any colonel, tall or short, fat or thin. Further responses, such as saying, "Yes, Sir," with proper respect, may be attached to the cues produced by just having saluted, as well as to the cue of the eagle. First the lieutenant looks at the shoulder, making the eagle more distinctly visible as an external cue; then he salutes, providing himself with internal cues which are likewise common to all situations involving meeting a colonel. These and other acquired cue-selecting and cue-producing responses form a basis for the lieutenant's concept of a superior officer.

It can be seen that the mechanism of acquired cue value parallels that of acquired reward value. Just as it is possible through learning to connect to a weak stimulus a response which produces a strong stimulus and thus gives the weak stimulus an acquired drive value, so is it also possible to connect to a relatively obscure stimulus a response which produces a distinctive stimulus and thus gives the obscure stimulus an acquired cue value.[4]

Counting is an important cue-producing response. A person who has not learned to count can respond to oneness, twoness, or even fiveness, but he cannot learn to respond with perfectly accurate discriminations to large numbers of objects. A person who has learned the response sequence involved

[4] One form of response-produced cues seems to blend very closely with the stimulus pattern which elicits it. This is the factor which is added to the bare external stimulation and is called perception. That it is the result of response-produced stimulation is suggested by the fact that it is delayed, more influenced by past experience, and more variable than the immediate effects of external stimuli. Closely related to perception is imagery, which can, to a certain extent, mirror the effects of previous cues in the absence of these cues. Although imagery and perception have not been carefully studied from this point of view, it seems probable that they follow the same laws of learning as do other responses, even though the responses producing these cues may possibly occur within the organizing centers of the brain. (See Miller & Dollard, 1941, p. 59, n. 5.) That perceptions are modifiable by learning is indicated by the common observation that members of a strange race tend to look alike until one has learned to respond differently to them.

in counting can learn to discriminate perfectly between small differences in large numbers. Without counting, the grocer cannot tell whether or not he has exactly three dozen oranges; with counting, he can discriminate perfectly. It will be remembered that in an illustrative experiment mentioned in Miller and Dollard (1941), Chapter II, the younger child was unable to learn to find candy under the correct one of a long row of similar black books. Had he been able to count, his responses to these similar books would have given him a quite distinctive cue, the thirteenth book, which could have been the basis for learning exactly where to find the candy.

A cue which would otherwise not be distinctive can acquire greater distinctiveness in two ways: the individual may learn to direct his sense organs toward that cue, or he may learn to react to that obscure cue with a response, such as counting, which produces a more distinctive cue.[5] As the innate distinctiveness of a cue (or pattern of cues) is enhanced, further learned responses are more likely to be attached to that cue, and it is more likely to operate significantly in the transfer of training from one situation in which it is present to others in which it is also present.

ACQUIRED EQUIVALENCE OF CUES

It is sometimes desirable for the individual to be able to learn to generalize from one situation to another despite the fact that these situations have no external cues in common. For example, the various enemies surrounding a tribe may not be distinguished by any single physical cue in common; that is, an enemy may be just as similar to members of the tribe as he is to other enemies. Nevertheless, it may be desirable for a member of a tribe to learn to generalize a given response, say avoidance, to all enemies.

Such generalization can be mediated by response-produced cues. In this example, however, there is no common external cue to which a common response may be connected, like the eagles on the shoulders of colonels. A common response must be connected to each individual enemy; and once such a response is acquired through a number of separate learning situations, cues produced by this common response can serve as the common stimuli necessary for generalization. The tribesman may learn at different times to respond to each of a number of different people with the same word, "enemy."[6] This verbal response produces a cue which is common to all these

[5] Both of these mechanisms are relevant to the process of *copying* as analyzed in Miller and Dollard (1941), Chapter X.

[6] Many children learn to respond to all people with fear, except those whom they have learned to call *friends*. The word "friend" serves as a cue to mediate generalizations in a manner similar to that illustrated in this example. In most cases, both mechanisms probably work at once, so that an enemy is either anyone whom the person has been taught to call "enemy" or anyone whom he has not been taught to call "friend."

enemies. Once this response is learned, the cue which it produces may mediate the transfer of other responses. The tribesman may transfer his various responses of retreating, threatening, fighting, etc., learned as reactions to one enemy, to any other person whom he also calls an enemy.

The details of the mechanism for this transfer may be illustrated briefly. A man is rewarded by social praise for hurling a particularly colorful taunt at some enemy in a minor squabble which does not come to actual blows. This taunt becomes strengthened as a response to the cue of seeing that enemy. Just previously, however, the man has perhaps said aloud or to himself, "He is an enemy." Thus the responses involved in making the taunt are attached not only to the cue of the sight of the particular enemy, but also to the cue of hearing or feeling himself say the word "enemy." On a subsequent occasion, an indivdual who looks quite different, but whom the man has also learned to call an enemy, appears. The cue of hearing or feeling himself call the other person an enemy produces the verbal cue to which the response of hurling a taunt has been attached. Thus the man generalizes the rewarded epithet from one enemy to another. Friends are not so likely to be taunted in this way because they do not elicit the cue-producing response of saying the word "enemy."[7]

Generalizations based upon response-produced cues are more modifiable than those based upon innate similarities. If the man learns to stop calling an individual an enemy and to start calling him a friend, the whole pattern of responses elicited by the word "enemy" will cease to generalize from other enemies to this individual, and a whole new mode of behavior, consisting of responses which have been rewarded in the presence of other people called friends, will tend to appear. It is obvious that this modifiability of response-mediated generalization makes it superior to innate generalization as a means of adjustment to a changing environment.

Response-mediated generalizations play an important rôle in social behavior, where many of the most important categories are culturally rather than innately determined. To begin with a humble example, the Roman numeral *III*, the Arabic numeral *3*, and the written word *three* are innately quite distinctive as cues. But training in our society has attached the same cue-producing responses to each of these patterns of stimulation. The most obvious of these cue-producing responses is the verbal one; but there are a host of other responses, such as holding up three fingers, which tend to occur in minimal form, supply additional cues common to these three stimuli, and mediate generalization from any one to the others.

Murdock (1941) has demonstrated the rôle of kinship terms in the generalization of the incest taboo. National names, class names, local names,

[7] For a more technical discussion of such acquired, or *secondary generalization*, see Hull (1939).

and occupational names, together with many other responses which cluster around each of these verbal designations, provide responses which supply cues affording a basis for partial stimulus equivalence between persons to whom the same responses have been learned. Stereotypes (Lippmann, 1930, pp. 88–94) function in this way. A name, e.g., Negro, mediates the transfer of a whole pattern of responses to any individual called by that name. Lippmann has stressed the point that responses are often maladaptive when so generalized. As long as behavior is cued to the word "Negro," or other parts of the stereotype, discriminations are not made on the basis of personality patterns and social class.

That response-produced cues actually do play the crucial rôle which has been ascribed to them is demonstrated by carefully controlled experiments. Birge (1941) has shown that if young children are taught to call two very different stimulus objects by the same name, other responses (such as reaching for the objects) are more likely to generalize from one to the other than when the two objects have been given different names. She has also shown that such generalization is much more likely to occur when the children say the name aloud, so that it is certain that the cue-producing response is actually present, than when they do not say the name aloud.

The mechanisms involved in facilitating the generalization of responses from one situation to another have been emphasized. One of these is learning to discriminate, single out, and pay attention to obscure cues present as relevant similarities in the external stimulus situation. Another of these mechanisms is learning to react with a response producing a cue which gives two otherwise different situations a degree of acquired similarity. The examples used to illustrate these types of generalization have been simple. It is probable, however, that the generalization of responses to relevant cues, either externally present or response-produced, plays an important rôle in much more complicated and less understood situations—even in the highest forms of intellectual activities.

According to the traditional story, Newton was started on his application of the principle of gravity to celestial mechanics by generalizing a response from a falling apple to the moon. An apple and the moon are different in many respects, but are similar in that both are bodies possessing mass. Newton presumably responded on the basis of this similarity. The response generalized was a verbal one, "pulled toward the earth." Newton is reputed to have said to himself in effect, "If an apple is pulled toward the earth, the moon should be pulled toward the earth."[8] When more is understood about the detailed mechanisms of such generalization and the innate

[8] It will be recognized that similar types of generalization have played important parts in the construction of other scientific theories. According to Einstein (1938, p. 286), "It has often happened in physics that an essential advance was achieved by carrying out a consistent analogy between apparently unrelated phenomena."

capacities which make it possible, a step will be taken toward the better understanding of one of the crucial factors involved in higher mental processes.

FORESIGHT

Sometimes the responses of an individual do not seem to be connected to cues immediately present in the environment, but rather to his knowledge of what is likely to happen next. Such behavior is commonly called *foresightful.* A simple example from an animal experiment may serve as an illustration.

The purpose of the experiment (Miller, 1935) was to see whether animals would combine two separately learned habits in a foresightful manner. In the first stage of the experiment, hungry rats were started at the beginning of a short alley and learned to run the length of the alley, to go through a curtain, and to enter a box where they found a special device consisting of a narrow angular passageway in which, by turning sharply to the right, they got food.

In the second stage, the special device was removed from the box at the end of the alley and taken to another part of the room. Here the animals were placed directly in front of the device and allowed to enter. As soon as they had turned their heads sharply to the right and started to eat, they were given an electric shock. This elicited anxiety and retreat which were rewarded by escape from shock.

In the third stage of the experiment, the animals were placed at the start of the alley. This was to determine whether the two separately learned habits would be combined so that the animals would no longer run down the alley. A curtain at the far end prevented them from seeing the special angular device which, for purposes of additional control, was absent on this trial. The animals started to run down the alley and then stopped.

A control test (in which animals were shocked in a device that had not been associated with the alley) indicated that this tendency for the animals to stop was not produced by emotional upset, primary stimulus generalization, or other such factors. The two habits may thus be said to have been combined in a foresightful manner. The animals had learned that running down the alley led to the special angular device. At another time, without running down the alley, they had learned to avoid the shock in this device. Combining these two separately learned habits, they now refused to go down the alley. How was this foresightful behavior produced?

In the first stage of the experiment the animals learned to run through the alley and into the special device with the narrow angular passageway containing food. Because of the gradient of reward, the last response before eating—turning sharply to the right—was strengthened the most. This response tended to become anticipatory so that the rats started to turn to the right soon after being put into the alley and were observed to run down the right-hand side of the alley. According to the present theoretical analysis, learning that the alley led to the reward device consisted of learning to respond to cues in the alley with anticipatory responses such as turning to the right. Later when the animals were placed directly in front of the reward device in another part of the room, they turned to the right and felt themselves turning immediately before receiving the shock. Thus the responses of anxiety and retreat became connected to the cue produced by the response of turning to the right. When the animals were placed at the start of the alley, the external cues present there elicited similar responses of turning to the right producing internal cues similar to those associated with the shock. Thus anxiety and retreat were generalized from the special device to the alley. That the anticipatory cue-producing response actually played an important rôle in mediating this generalization is indicated by the fact that a previous experimenter (Tolman, 1933), who had not taken pains to see that such a response was present, had failed to secure foresightful behavior.

In human beings some foresight seems to be mediated by nonverbal anticipatory responses similar to those present in the rat. It is often difficult for the individual to explain in words the basis of such foresight. Where the mediating response is a verbal one, it is more easily described. A human subject in an experiment similar to that on the rat might report: "On my way down the alley, I started to say to myself how good the food would taste in the reward device; then I remembered the shock, a cold shudder ran down my spine, and I stopped."

LANGUAGE

Cue-producing responses play an important part in the higher mental processes. In all societies, children are taught a special set of such responses —the language current in the group. Learning a language supplies the child with an enormous arsenal of cue-producing responses and with habits of using those responses in ways which have been found socially valuable.

Words by themselves usually are weak stimuli, serving as cues rather than drives, except on those rare occasions when someone shouts or sings very loudly. During the educational process, the individual learns to make many fine discriminations between words as cues. The sound of a word, though a weak stimulus, may acquire drive value in the same way that any other cue may acquire drive value. The individual may learn to react to the weak stimulus of a softly spoken insult with a response of anger producing a stimulus strong enough to have considerable drive value. Threatening words may become cues eliciting strong anxiety, and words of praise, at first relatively neutral, may, by association with primary rewards, acquire strong reward value.

Because of the extreme importance of language as a product of social learning which, in turn, influences the course of subsequent learning, some of the significant steps in the process of learning to speak will be briefly sketched.

A child's first vocal behavior is crying. This response is high in the innate hierarchy of responses to any exceedingly strong stimulus, such as cold, hunger, or pain. Its dominance may be further increased by learning. Crying is frequently rewarded by the appearance of an adult who covers the cold child with a warm blanket, feeds the hungry child, or removes a stabbing pin. Perhaps as a result of these rewards, a child's later vocalization seems often to have a shrill character like fragmented parts of the crying behavior. If the crying and speaking situations are similar enough so that the effects of these rewards for crying generalize to the vocalizations involved in speaking, it might be expected that children who have been cared for every time they cry would learn to speak more readily than those who have not. Whether these two situations actually are similar enough so that sufficient generalization occurs to have any practical effect is an unsolved problem.

At the same time that the child is practicing his own crying responses, he is learning to respond to the voices of others. Adults who are feeding, fondling, and otherwise caring for infants usually talk to them; thus certain tones of the human voice acquire a reward value and may later be used to soothe the fretful child. It seems possible that this acquired reward value of the sounds in the language generalizes to sounds which the child makes while he is babbling and help to reinforce his babbling behavior.[9]

In general, a child's first contact with the more formal aspects of language is in learning to use words spoken by other people as cues for his responses. A sharp "No!" is followed by punishment, which can only be escaped by stopping or retreating. Eventually, stopping becomes anticipatory and occurs to the word "No" spoken sharply, without the punishment. At the same time, "No" is acquiring an anxiety-arousing value, so that any response which brings an escape from a torrent of "Noes" is rewarded. Exactly which verbal cues a child will learn to respond to and how he will

[9] It would be interesting to compare the babbling behavior of different children after an attempt had been made to give different phonemes a special acquired reward value. One child would be talked to with a certain phoneme while being fed and with a different but equally pronounceable phoneme while being dressed or having some other routine performed which seems to annoy him. A second child would be talked to with the first phoneme while being dressed and the second while being fed. Each child would be talked to with both phonemes for an equal length of time. The babbling behavior of the two children would then be compared. The prediction would be that the child would learn to babble with the phoneme which had been given an acquired reward value more than with the other.

learn to respond to them depends, of course, upon his learning capacity at the particular age and upon what his parents try hardest to teach him.

At the same time that the child is being rewarded for making more responses to words as cues, he is gradually learning another aspect of language, namely, how to make the response of uttering words.[10] If a cooky is out of reach, the response pattern of pointing at it with the body and eyes and reaching for it with the hand is often rewarded by inducing some older person to give the child the cooky. If this gesture is accompanied by a sound, it is more likely to be rewarded. If the sound seems to be some appropriate word, such as "Look-at," reward is still more likely. Eventually, the more effortful parts of the gesture drop out, and the verbal response, which is least effortful and most consistently rewarded, becomes anticipatory and persists. The mechanism of reward gradually differentiates language from its original matrix of other, more clumsy, overt responses. The child learns to talk because society makes that relatively effortless response supremely worthwhile.

The child is given meticulous training in connecting words to objects and connecting acts to words. He is also given careful training in connecting words to other words, in combining words into sequences of stimulus-producing responses. The child must learn to combine words according to the rules of grammar; he is corrected thousands of times for grammatical mistakes. Unfortunately, no one has made a thorough learning analysis of the system of habits involved in combining words into grammatically correct sentences. It must be highly complex since it involves abilities which are not possessed by animals or feeble-minded persons. Precisely what these abilities are is not well understood.

The habits involved in grammar are habits which govern the manner in which other learned responses, words, and phrases are combined. Thus they might be called higher-order habits. But the habits of grammar are not the only high-order habits which the child learns. By combining words and sentences into unsuccessful requests and into successful requests, into inadequate instructions and into adequate instructions, into poor descriptions and into good descriptions, into unsuccessful arguments and into successful arguments, into wrong explanations and into correct explanations, the child receives punishment for certain combinations of words and reward for others.

The child is given careful training in responding to the spoken word as a cue; he is taught to follow directions. He is also given meticulous training in producing the appropriate word as a response. The child first learns to respond with a different word to each of many simple stimulus situations; then he is taught to combine words into larger patterns paralleling complex relationships and sequences of events in the environment. In this way, he

[10] As shown in Miller and Dollard (1941), Chapter XIII, imitation plays an important role in this process.

accumulates a store of different stimulus-producing responses which he can use later in guiding his own behavior.

The child receives a certain amount of social reward for carrying out this final step of using language to guide his own behavior. He is praised if he comes near the glass bookcase, says, "No, no," and then retreats. In being taught to keep his promises, he is also rewarded specifically for using his own words as cues to guide his own responses.

Since speaking is a type of activity which can occur without interfering with most other responses, it is easy for speech to move forward in the sequence of acts and become an anticipatory response. Thus speaking comes to play an important rôle in thinking and reasoning. But a series of spoken words, like any other series of acts, tends to become shortened as anticipatory responses crowd out any dispensable units. Thus the individual quickly learns to think in terms of abbreviated speech; the gross responses of making sounds, useless in thinking though necessary in talking, are omitted. This process is facilitated by a certain amount of punishment for thinking all one's thoughts aloud. Whether or not the responses in the adult are in terms of actual slight speech movements or are in terms of learned neural connections which function as stimulus-producing responses is as yet an unsettled research problem.

REASONING

Although reasoning is very important in social behavior, many of the details of the dynamics of reasoning are not yet well understood. This much seems clear: The function of reasoning is to shorten the process of overt trial and error by causing the individual to avoid responses which would be likely to be errors or to make early in the sequence responses likely to be rewarded. Without reasoning, the responses likely to be rewarded might only occur much later, if at all. If these responses actually are rewarded, they are learned; if not, they tend to become extinguished.

Cue-producing responses are important in the process of reasoning. In the response-mediated generalizations which have already been discussed, two separately acquired habits were combined to produce the generalized response. In one of the examples, a tribesman learned the habit of calling two people enemies. He also learned the habit of taunting one of these people. As a result of a combination of these two separately learned habits, he taunted the other person. Such a combination of two separate items of experience (putting two and two together) is one of the characteristics of simple reasoning.

Most examples of reasoning, however, seem to involve longer sequences of cue-producing responses. Sometimes these progress smoothly with one response rapidly cuing the next; sometimes one sequence after another is abandoned, so that the process resembles overt trial and error.

Since primary rewards and punishments are usually not administered during the episodes of trial and error involved in reasoning, the responses must be selected or rejected by the acquired reward value or acquired anxiety value of the cues which they produce. If a response produces a cue which has been associated with reward, that response and the responses leading to it are strengthened, tend to persist or recur, and thus to become cues for still further responses. If, on the other hand, a response produces a cue to which anxiety-producing responses have been connected, that response and the others leading to it tend to be weakened and not to be cues to further behavior. The individual learns to cease making responses which produce cues arousing anxiety; stopping such responses is rewarded by reduction in anxiety.[11]

In some cases, the cue-producing responses employed in reasoning may be abbreviations of the gross responses which have actually been employed in carrying out the act contemplated. This seems to have been the case with the rat which tended to turn right in the experiment on foresight. With human beings, the sequences of cue-producing responses employed in reasoning have often been learned by the individual as a part of his culture. These may be responses of language or of mathematics. In reasoning out the design of an apparatus, an experimenter may find it desirable to draw diagrams. One part of the diagram becomes a cue which determines the way he will design the rest of the apparatus. After he has made a satisfactory diagram, he will use it as a cue to guide the further responses of building the apparatus. If the apparatus fails, he is likely to abandon it; if it brings him fame and fortune, he may go on designing similar gadgets for the rest of his life.

Some of the dynamics of reasoning may be illustrated in slightly more detail by the analysis of a simple example. An instructor who was working on a paper to read before a research seminar knew that it was conventional to spend approximately an hour reading a paper at that seminar and wondered how many typewritten pages he should write. Having been embarrassed in the past for appearing before seminars with papers that were either too long or too short, he was motivated to white a paper of approximately the correct length.

His initial response in this dilemma was one which had often been rewarded in other similar dilemmas. He said to himself, "I'll ask Professor

[11] Similarly, response sequences are weakened if they produce cues which have been associated with non-reward. In Pavlovian terminology (1927), such cues might be called *conditioned inhibitors*. According to our hypothesis, escape from fatigue is the primary reward teaching the subject to halt responses producing such cues.

Smith."[12] This response, performed either subvocally or centrally (the exact locus is of anatomical rather than functional importance), produced a stimulus pattern which was a cue to a number of further responses. At first, these responses produced a temporary relaxing sense of reassurance, which seemed to reward and strengthen the response of saying to himself, "I'll ask Professor Smith." But in the past experience of this instructor, permanent relaxation after thinking of an idea had never been rewarded. He had learned that one cannot afford to tarry too long at a sub-goal. In such situations he had been rewarded for tensing again to spur himself to greater action. The additional drive produced by this tension, together with the cue of saying to himself, "I'll ask Professor Smith," resulted in a slight tendency to get up out of his chair and go downstairs. As soon as he raised his head, however, he became aware of cues indicating the lateness of the hour. Previously, in the presence of such cues, he had tried to look for people in similar situations and had discovered that persons of professional status, including this professor, were rarely to be found in their offices at night. As a result of these experiences, the responses of pulling at locked doors and saying to himself, "He is not in," had become anticipatory to the cue of lateness of the hour. Instead of continuing downstairs, therefore, he tended to stop, almost before starting, and to say, "He is not in."

The occurrence of these responses, however, produced cues which had been connected with further responses. He had frequently been rewarded by getting information from homes over the telephone when he had found that people were not in their offices. He said to himself, "I'll telephone him." The cue produced by this response immediately touched off a twinge of anxiety. Punishment had long since taught him not to telephone people too late at night. The anxiety was a cue and a drive to terminate this response sequence.

With these responses stopped, the cue of the work on his desk again caused him to say to himself, "How many pages for the paper?" This response produced cues which elicited first the association of a paper for the meetings of the American Psychological Association. Then he said to himself, "An A.P.A. paper is fifteen minutes, and six pages." To these cues were attached in this context strong anticipatory responses originating from experiences of ultimate success with other similar problems; a triumphant instant of anxiety reduction was followed by additional motivation to continue.

Up to this point, symbolic trial and error had played the chief rôle in determining the manner in which his internal stimulus-producing responses followed each other. First, the response occurred which was highest in his initial hierarchy of responses to the momentary context of cues. When this response produced cues with acquired reward value, it persisted and served

[12] This verbal response seemed to come up as automatically as any simple motor habit.

as a cue to still further responses. When, on the other hand, it produced cues with acquired anxiety value or cues to which inhibition had been attached by extinction, it was abandoned and the next dominant response in the hierarchy occurred.

As soon as the succession of stimulus-producing responses had led to the arithmetical formulation of the problem, the subject reached a point where past learning provided not only each of the responses which formed a unit of reasoning, but also the manner in which to combine the responses rapidly in order to cue himself for the final response suitable to problem solution. His arithmetic teacher had taught him all the units of adding, multiplying, and dividing and how to combine them appropriately in various types of problem situations. He therefore said to himself, "If I read six pages in a quarter of an hour, then I will read four times six, or twenty-four pages, in one hour." This became the cue to counting the pages already written and saying to himself, "Five more pages will make it the right length." This last verbal response reduced his anxiety over the danger of possible embarrassment and served as a cue to guide his further writing.

At the end of the seminar, his colleagues congratulated him on his paper. While he was being rewarded, he said to himself, "I am glad I figured out a paper of the right length," and rapidly rehearsed some of the responses which had been successful links in the process. This rehearsal probably strengthened the acquired reward value of the cues produced by these responses.

The function of reasoning in the example analyzed was to cause the instructor to write a paper of appropriate length. Had he proceeded by sheer trial and error unaided by reasoning, he might have been punished for reading a good many papers far too long or too short before finally being rewarded for reading one of the right length. Since the reasoning produced a paper of exactly the right length, he learned the appropriate response in a single trial.

As a result of the acquired reward of solving this problem and the final reward of reading a paper of the correct length, the instructor also learned something about the technique of solving such problems. The connection between the various segments of cue-producing responses involved in the reasoning were strengthened. Should he forget how many pages to read in an hour, it would be easier for him to solve the same problem in the same way a second time. Since most of the units of the reasoning are applicable to other similar problems, it would be easier for him to solve these also. He could, for example, quickly tell how many pages to read in thirty minutes or in two hours.

By being rewarded for using cue-producing responses, the instructor tended to learn to initiate the symbolic process, to stop and think rather than ask somebody else or give up. The dominance of symbolic responses relative to various forms of direct action was probably increased in the resultant hierarchy. In this particular example, such an effect is difficult to demonstrate conclusively. In other instances, it is clear that the habit of stopping overt action and taking time to think can be learned. A tenderfoot is taught[13] that when he is lost in the woods, he must not immediately dash off in some direction that might take him still farther away from the trail, but must sit down, rehearse his last actions, and canvass all possible plans of action before initiating any of them. A person who has acquired this habit is almost certain to behave more adaptively than one who strikes off immediately and without thought.

The tendency to use cue-producing responses in a dilemma can be strengthened by rewards; it can also be weakened by extinction or punishment. Thus, in some people, so much anxiety has been attached to the cue-producing responses involved in mathematics that they never try this mode of problem solution. Often, if such people can be encouraged to try learning mathematics again, they become able to solve problems which have previously been impossible for them. Sometimes it seems that people fail to show the intelligence of which they are capable because they are afraid to express original, unconventional ideas either to others or to themselves. In solving difficult problems, it is advisable not to discard a bad idea too soon; if the sequence of cue-producing responses is allowed to progress further, some element in the obviously impractical idea may supply the cue to further responses leading to an adaptive solution.[14]

The final step in the reasoning process is to respond overtly in some instrumental way to the last cue-producing response. As a result of his experience, the instructor was rewarded not only for figuring out the proper length for his paper, but also for letting this be the cue to write a paper of that length.

Reactions to response-produced cues are not always dominant over competing responses. Sometimes people who have not been rewarded for translating certain types of ideas into action may dismiss them as too theoretical. At the depth of the recent economic depression, one of the authors figured out that if conditions got much worse, so that stocks went appreciably lower, the whole financial structure would be disrupted so much that no

[13] This instruction is usually verbal: The individual is presented with cues arousing anxiety as an acquired drive and rewarded for rehearsing in words what to do when lost. Because the process of socialization has already connected overt responses to these words, they can sometimes lead to the desired behavior.

[14] It may be ventured that one of the capacities which make for better reasoning is the ability to respond with many different cue-producing responses at once so that further responses may be elicited on the basis of a pattern of cues representing many different units of experience. For reasoning to occur at all, according to the present analysis, the individual must respond to some cue with a response producing a further cue and also must respond to that cue-producing response while it is still present. Thus the hypothesis demands that the reasoning individual be able to respond to at least two different cues at once with two different responses.

form of investment would be profitable. He therefore reasoned that one could not lose, but only gain, by buying stocks. The reasoning seemed perfectly sound to him. It was a good idea, but he did not act on it. Others who acted on similar ideas made considerable money; he did not. As might be expected from the foregoing analysis, the reasoning process is a rather tenuous chain which may be readily broken at any link. Often reasoned responses to a drive or an environmental cue are overridden by more direct, unreasoned responses.[15]

[15] For a more rigorous discussion of some of these same problems, with special reference to animal experiments, see a series of articles by Hull (1930; 1931; 1934; 1935).

3

COGNITIVE, SOCIAL, AND PHYSIOLOGICAL DETERMINANTS OF EMOTIONAL STATE[1]

Stanley Schachter and Jerome E. Singer

The problem of which cues, internal or external, permit a person to label and identify his own emotional state has been with us since the days that James (1890) first tendered his doctrine that "the bodily changes follow directly the perception of the exciting fact, and that our feeling of the same changes as they occur *is* the emotion" (p. 449). Since we are aware of a variety of feeling and emotion states, it should follow from James' proposition that the various emotions will be accompanied by a variety of differentiable bodily states. Following James' pronouncement, a formidable number of studies were undertaken in search of the physiological differentiators of the emotions. The results, in these early days, were almost uniformly negative. All of the emotional states experimentally manipulated were characterized by a general pattern of excitation of the sympathetic nervous system but there appeared to be no clear-cut physiological discriminators of the various emotions. This pattern of results was so consistent from experiment to experiment that Cannon (1929) offered, as one of the crucial criticisms of the

[1] This experiment is part of a program of research on cognitive and physiological determinants of emotional state which is being conducted at the Department of Social Psychology at Columbia University under PHS Research Grant M-2584 from the National Institute of Mental Health, United States Public Health Service. This experiment was conducted at the Laboratory for Research in Social Relations at the University of Minnesota.

The authors wish to thank Jean Carlin and Ruth Hase, the physicians in the study, and Bibb Latané and Leonard Weller who were the paid participants.

James-Lange theory, the fact that "the same visceral changes occur in very different emotional states and in non-emotional states" (p. 351).

More recent work, however, has given some indication that there may be differentiators. Ax (1953) and Schachter (1957) studied fear and anger. On a large number of indices both of these states were characterized by a similarly high level of autonomic activation but on several indices they did differ in the degree of activation. Wolff and Wolff (1947) studied a subject with a gastric fistula and were able to distinguish two patterns in the physiological responses of the stomach wall. It should be noted, though, that for many months they studied their subject during and following a great variety of moods and emotions and were able to distinguish only two patterns.

Whether or not there are physiological distinctions among the various emotional states must be considered an open question. Recent work might be taken to indicate that such differences are at best rather subtle and that the variety of emotion, mood, and feeling states are by no means matched by an equal variety of visceral patterns.

This rather ambiguous situation has led Ruckmick (1936), Hunt, Cole, and Reis (1958), Schachter (1959), and others to suggest that cognitive factors may be major determinants of emotional states. Granted a general pattern of sympathetic excitation as characteristic of emotional states, granted that there may be some differences in pattern from state to state, it is suggested that one labels, interprets, and identifies this stirred-up state in terms of the characteristics of the precipitating situation and one's apperceptive mass. This suggests, then, that an emotional state may be considered a function of a state of physiological arousal[2] and of a cognition appropriate to this state of arousal. The cognition, in a sense, exerts a steering function. Cognitions arising from the immediate situation as interpreted by past experience provide the framework within which one understands and labels his feelings. It is the cognition which determines whether the state of physiological arousal will be labeled as "anger," "joy," "fear," or whatever.

In order to examine the implications of this formulation let us consider the fashion in which these two elements, a state of physiological arousal and cognitive factors, would interact in a variety of situations. In most emotion inducing situations, of course, the two factors are completely interrelated. Imagine a man walking alone down a dark alley, a figure with a gun suddenly appears. The perception-cognition "figure with a gun" in some fashion initiates a state of physiological arousal; this state of arousal is interpreted in terms of knowledge about dark alleys and guns and the state of arousal is labeled "fear." Similarly a student who unexpectedly learns that he has made

[2] Though our experiments are concerned exclusively with the physiological changes produced by the injection of adrenalin, which appear to be primarily the result of sympathetic excitation, the term physiological arousal is used in preference to the more specific "excitation of the sympathetic nervous system" because there are indications, to be discussed later, that this formulation is applicable to a variety of bodily states.

Phi Beta Kappa may experience a state of arousal which he will label "joy."

Let us now consider circumstances in which these two elements, the physiological and the cognitive, are, to some extent, independent. First, is the state of physiological arousal alone sufficient to induce an emotion? Best evidence indicates that it is not. Marañon (1924), in a fascinating study, (which was replicated by Cantril & Hunt, 1932, and Landis & Hunt, 1932) injected 210 of his patients with the sympathomimetic agent adrenalin and then simply asked them to introspect. Seventy-one percent of his subjects simply reported their physical symptoms with no emotional overtones; 29% of the subjects responded in an apparently emotional fashion. Of these the great majority described their feelings in a fashion that Marañon labeled "cold" or "as if" emotions, that is, they made statements such as "I feel *as if* I were afraid" or "*as if* I were awaiting a great happiness." This is a sort of emotional "déjà vu" experience; these subjects are neither happy nor afraid, they feel "as if" they were. Finally a very few cases apparently reported a genuine emotional experience. However, in order to produce this reaction in most of these few cases, Marañon (1924) points out:

> One must suggest a memory with strong affective force but not so strong as to produce an emotion in the normal state. For example, in several cases we spoke to our patients before the injection of their sick children or dead parents and they responded calmly to this topic. The same topic presented later, during the adrenal commotion, was sufficient to trigger emotion. This adrenal commotion places the subject in a situation of 'affective imminence' (pp. 307–308).

Apparently, then, to produce a genuinely emotional reaction to adrenalin, Marañon was forced to provide such subjects with an appropriate cognition.

Though Marañon (1924) is not explicit on his procedure, it is clear that his subjects knew that they were receiving an injection and in all likelihood knew that they were receiving adrenalin and probably had some order of familiarity with its effects. In short, though they underwent the pattern of sympathetic discharge common to strong emotional states, at the same time they had a completely appropriate cognition or explanation as to why they felt this way. This, we would suggest, is the reason so few of Marañon's subjects reported any emotional experience.

Consider now a person in a state of physiological arousal for which no immediately explanatory or appropriate cognitions are available. Such a state could result were one covertly to inject a subject with adrenalin or, unknown to him, feed the subject a sympathomimetic drug such as ephedrine. Under such conditions a subject would be aware of palpitations, tremor, face flushing, and most of the battery of symptoms associated with a discharge of the sympathetic nervous system. In contrast to Marañon's (1924) subjects he would, at the same time, be utterly unaware of why he felt this way. What would be the consequence of such a state?

Schachter (1959) has suggested that precisely such a state would lead to the arousal of "evaluative needs" (Festinger, 1954), that is, pressures would act on an individual in such a state to understand and label his bodily feelings. His bodily state grossly resembles the condition in which it has been at times of emotional excitement. How would he label his present feelings? It is suggested, of course, that he will label his feelings in terms of knowledge of the immediate situation.[3] Should he at the time be with a beautiful woman he might decide that he was wildly in love or sexually excited. Should he be at a gay party, he might, by comparing himself to others, decide that he was extremely happy and euphoric. Should he be arguing with his wife, he might explode in fury and hatred. Or, should the situation be completely inappropriate he could decide that he was excited about something that had recently happened to him or, simply, that he was sick. In any case, it is our basic assumption that emotional states are a function of the interaction of such cognitive factors with a state of physiological arousal.

This line of thought, then, leads to the following propositions:

1. Given a state of physiological arousal for which an individual has no immediate explanation, he will "label" this state and describe his feelings in terms of the cognitions available to him. To the extent that cognitive factors are potent determiners of emotional states, it could be anticipated that precisely the same state of physiological arousal could be labeled "joy" or "fury" or "jealousy" or any of a great diversity of emotional labels depending on the cognitive aspects of the situation.

2. Given a state of physiological arousal for which an individual has a completely appropriate explanation (e.g., "I feel this way because I have just received an injection of adrenalin") no evaluative needs will arise and the individual is unlikely to label his feelings in terms of the alternative cognitions available.

Finally, consider a condition in which emotion inducing cognitions are present but there is no state of physiological arousal. For example, an individual might be completely aware that he is in great danger but for some reason (drug or surgical) remain in a state of physiological quiescence. Does he experience the emotion "fear"? Our formulation of emotion as a joint function of a state of physiological arousal and an appropriate cognition, would, of course, suggest that he does not, which leads to our final proposition.

3. Given the same cognitive circumstances, the individual will react emotionally or describe his feelings as emotions only to the extent that he experiences a state of physiological arousal.

[3] This suggestion is not new, for several psychologists have suggested that situational factors should be considered the chief differentiators of the emotions. Hunt, Cole, and Reis (1958) probably make this point most explicitly in their study distinguishing among fear, anger, and sorrow in terms of situational characteristics.

4

SELF-CONTROL

Burrhus F. Skinner

THE "SELF-DETERMINATION" OF CONDUCT

Implicit in a functional analysis is the notion of control. When we discover an independent variable which can be controlled, we discover a means of controlling the behavior which is a function of it. This fact is important for theoretical purposes. Proving the validity of a functional relation by an actual demonstration of the effect of one variable upon another is the heart of experimental science. The practice enables us to dispense with many troublesome statistical techniques in testing the importance of variables.

The practical implications are probably even greater. An analysis of the techniques through which behavior may be manipulated shows the kind of technology which is emerging as the science advances, and it points up the considerable degree of control which is currently exerted. The problems raised by the control of human behavior obviously can no longer be avoided by refusing to recognize the possibility of control. Sections of *Science and Human Behavior* (Skinner, 1953) consider these practical implications in more detail. In Section IV, for example, in an analysis of what is generally called social behavior, we see how one organism utilizes the basic processes of behavior to control another. The result is particularly impressive when the individual is under the concerted control of a group. Our basic processes are responsible for the procedures through which the ethical group controls the behavior of each of its members. An even more effective control is exerted by such well-defined agencies as government, religion, psychotherapy, economics, and education; certain key questions concerning such control are considered in Section V. The general issue of control in human affairs is summarized in Section VI.

First, however, we must consider the possibility that the individual may control his own behavior. A common objection to a picture of the behaving organism such as we have so far presented runs somewhat as follows. In emphasizing the controlling power of external variables, we have left the organism itself in a peculiarly helpless position. Its behavior appears to be simply a "repertoire"—a vocabulary of action, each item of which becomes more or less probable as the environment changes. It is true that variables may be arranged in complex patterns; but this fact does not appreciably modify the picture, for the emphasis is still upon behavior, not upon the behaver. Yet to a considerable extent an individual does appear to shape his own destiny. He is often able to do something about the variables affecting him. Some degree of "self-determination" of conduct is usually recognized in the creative behavior of the artist and scientist, in the self-exploratory behavior of the writer, and in the self-discipline of the ascetic. Humbler versions of self-determination are more familiar. The individual "chooses" between alternative courses of action, "thinks through" a problem while isolated from the relevant environment, and guards his health or his position in society through the exercise of "self-control."

Any comprehensive account of human behavior must, of course, embrace the facts referred to in statements of this sort. But we can achieve this without abandoning our program. When a man controls himself, chooses a course of action, thinks out the solution to a problem, or strives toward an increase in self-knowledge, he is *behaving*. He controls himself precisely as he would control the behavior of anyone else—through the manipulation of variables of which behavior is a function. His behavior in so doing is a proper object of analysis, and eventually it must be accounted for with variables lying outside the individual himself.

It is the purpose of Section III in *Science and Human Behavior* to analyze how the individual acts to alter the variables of which other parts of his behavior are functions, to distinguish among the various cases which arise in terms of the process involved, and to account for the behavior which achieves control just as we account for behavior of any other kind. The present chapter concerns the processes involved in *self-control*, taking that term in close to its traditional sense, while Chapter XVI concerns behavior which would traditionally be described as *creative thinking*. The two sets of techniques are different because in self-control the individual can identify the behavior to be controlled while in creative thinking he cannot. The variables which the individual utilizes in manipulating his behavior in this way are not always accessible to others, and this has led to great misunderstanding. It has often been concluded, for example, that self-discipline and thinking take place in a nonphysical inner world and that neither activity is properly described as behavior at all. We may simplify the analysis by considering examples of self-control and thinking in which the individual manipulates *external* variables, but we shall need to complete the picture by discussing the status of private events in a science of behavior (Skinner, 1953, Chapter XVII). A purely private event would have no place in a study of behavior, or perhaps in any science; but events which are, for the moment at least, accessible only to the individual himself often occur as links in chains of otherwise public events and they must then be considered. In self-control and creative thinking, where the individual is largely engaged in manipulating his own behavior, this is likely to be the case.

When we say that a man controls himself, we must specify who is controlling whom. When we say that he knows himself, we must also distinguish between the subject and object of the verb. Evidently selves are multiple and hence not to be identified with the biological organism. But if this is so, what are they? What are their dimensions in a science of behavior? To what extent is a self an integrated personality or organism? How can one self act upon another? The interlocking systems of responses which account for self-control and thinking make it possible to answer questions of this sort satisfactorily, as we see in Chapter XVIII (Skinner, 1953). We can do this more conveniently, however, when the principal data are at hand. Meanwhile, the term "self" will be used in a less rigorous way.

"SELF-CONTROL"

The individual often comes to control part of his own behavior when a response has conflicting consequences—when it leads to both positive and negative reinforcement. Drinking alcoholic beverages, for example, is often followed by a condition of unusual confidence in which one is more successful socially and in which one forgets responsibilities, anxieties, and other troubles. Since this is positively reinforcing, it increases the likelihood that drinking will take place on future occasions. But there are other consequences—the physical illness of the "hang-over" and the possibly disastrous effects of overconfident or irresponsible behavior—which are negatively reinforcing and, when contingent upon behavior, represent a form of punishment. If punishment were simply the reverse of reinforcement, the two might combine to produce an intermediate tendency to drink, but we have seen that this is not the case. When a similar occasion arises, the same or an increased tendency to drink will prevail; but the occasion as well as the early stages of drinking will generate conditioned aversive stimuli and emotional responses to them which we speak of as shame or guilt. The emotional responses may have some deterrent effect in weakening behavior—as by "spoiling the mood." A more important effect, however, is that any behavior which weakens the behavior of drinking is automatically reinforced by the resulting reduction in aversive stimulation. We have discussed the behavior of simply "doing something else," which is reinforced because it displaces punishable behavior, but there are other possibilities. The organism may make the punished response less probable by altering the variables of which it is a function. Any behavior which succeeds in doing this will automatically be reinforced. We call such behavior self-control.

The positive and negative consequences generate two responses which are related to each other in a special way: one response, the *controlling response*, affects variables in such a way as to change the probability of the other, the *controlled response*. The controlling response may manipulate any of the variables of which the controlled response is a function; hence there are a good many different forms of self-control. In general it is possible to point to parallels in which the same techniques are employed in controlling the behavior of others. A fairly exhaustive survey at this point will illustrate the process of self-control and at the same time serve to summarize the kind of control to be emphasized in the chapters which follow.

TECHNIQUES OF CONTROL

Physical Restraint and Physical Aid

We commonly control behavior through physical restraint. With locked doors, fences, and jails we limit the space in which people move. With strait-jackets, gags, and arm braces we limit the movement of parts of their bodies. The individual controls his own behavior in the same way. He claps his hand over his mouth to keep himself from laughing or coughing or to stifle a verbal response which is seen at the last moment to be a "bad break." A child psychologist has suggested that a mother who wishes to keep from nagging her child should seal her own lips with adhesive tape. The individual may jam his hands into his pockets to prevent fidgeting or nail-biting or hold his nose to keep from breathing when under water. He may present himself at the door of an institution for incarceration to control his own criminal or psychotic behavior. He may cut his right hand off lest it offend him.

In each of these examples we identify a controlling response, which imposes some degree of physical restraint upon a response to be controlled. To explain the existence and strength of the controlling behavior we point to the reinforcing circumstances which arise when the response has been controlled. Clapping the hand over the mouth is reinforced and will occur again under similar circumstances because it reduces the aversive stimulation generated by the cough or the incipient bad break. In the sense of Chapter XII (Skinner, 1953), the controlling response *avoids* the negatively reinforcing consequences of the controlled response. The aversive consequences of a bad break are supplied by a social environment; the aversive consequences of breathing under water do not require the mediation of others.

Another form of control through physical restraint is simply to move out of the situation in which the behavior to be controlled may take place. The parent avoids trouble by taking an aggressive child away from other children, and the adult controls himself in the same way. Unable to control his anger, he simply walks away. This may not control the whole emotional pattern, but it does restrain those features which are likely to have serious consequences.

Suicide is another form of self-control. Obviously a man does not kill himself because he has previously escaped from an aversive situation by doing so. As we have already seen, suicide is not a form of behavior to which the notion of frequency of response can be applied. If it occurs, the components of the behavior must have been strengthened separately. Unless this happens under circumstances in which frequency is an available datum, we cannot say meaningfully that a man is "likely or unlikely to kill himself" —nor can the individual say this of himself (Skinner, 1953, Chapter XVII). Some instances of suicide, but by no means all, follow the pattern of cutting off one's right hand that it may not offend one; the military agent taken by the enemy may use this method to keep himself from divulging secrets of state.

A variation on this mode of control consists of removing the situation, so to speak, rather than the individual. A government stops inflationary spending by heavy taxation—by removing the money or credit which is a condition for the purchase of goods. A man arranges to control the behavior of his spendthrift heir by setting up a trust fund. Non-coeducational institutions attempt to control certain kinds of sexual behavior by making the opposite sex inaccessible. The individual may use the same techniques in controlling himself. He may leave most of his pocket money at home to avoid spending it, or he may drop coins into a piggy bank from which it is difficult to withdraw them. He may put his own money in trust for himself. H. G. Wells's Mr. Polly used a similar procedure to distribute his funds over a walking trip. He would mail all but a pound note to himself at a village some distance along his route. Arriving at the village, he would call at the post office, remove a pound note, and readdress the balance to himself at a later point.

In a converse technique we increase the probability of a desirable form of behavior by supplying physical *aid*. We facilitate human behavior, make it possible, or expand and amplify its consequences with various sorts of equipment, tools, and machines. When the problem of self-control is to generate a given response, we alter our own behavior in the same way by obtaining favorable equipment, making funds readily available, and so on.

Changing the Stimulus

Insofar as the preceding techniques operate through physical aid or restraint, they are not based upon a behavioral process. There are associated processes, however, which may be analyzed more accurately in terms of stimulation. Aside from making a response possible or impossible, we may create or eliminate the occasion for it. To do so, we manipulate either an eliciting or a discriminative stimulus. When a drug manufacturer reduces the probability that a nauseous medicine will be regurgitated by enclosing it in tasteless capsules—or by "sugar-coating the pill"—he is simply removing a stimulus which elicits unwanted responses. The same procedure is available in the control of one's own reflexes. We swallow a medicine quickly and "chase" it with a glass of water to reduce comparable stimuli.

We remove *discriminative* stimuli when we turn away from a stimulus which induces aversive action. We may forcibly look away from a wallpaper design which evokes the compulsive behavior of tracing geometrical patterns. We may close doors or draw curtains to eliminate distracting stimuli or achieve the same effect by closing our eyes or putting our fingers in our ears. We may put a box of candy out of sight to avoid overeating. This sort of self-control is described as "avoiding temptation," especially when the aversive consequences have been arranged by society. It is the principle of "Get thee behind me, Satan."

We also *present* stimuli because of the responses they elicit or make more probable in our own behavior. We rid ourselves of poisonous or indigestible food with an emetic—a substance which generates stimuli which elicit vomiting. We facilitate stimulation when we wear eyeglasses or hearing aids. We arrange a discriminative stimulus to encourage our own behavior at a later date when we tie a string on our finger or make an entry in a date book to serve as the occasion for action at an appropriate time. Sometimes we present stimuli because the resulting behavior displaces behavior to be controlled—we "distract" ourselves just as we distract others from a situation which generates undesirable behavior. We amplify stimuli generated by our own behavior when we use a mirror to acquire good carriage or to master a difficult dance step, or study moving pictures of our own behavior to improve our skill in a sport, or listen to phonograph recordings of our own speech to improve pronunciation or delivery.

Conditioning and extinction provide other ways of changing the effectiveness of stimuli. We arrange for the future effect of a stimulus upon ourselves by pairing it with other stimuli, and we extinguish reflexes by exposing ourselves to conditioned stimuli when they are not accompanied by reinforcement. If we blush, sweat, or exhibit some other emotional response under certain circumstances because of an unfortunate episode, we may expose ourselves to these circumstances under more favorable conditions in order that extinction may take place.

Depriving and Satiating

An impecunious person may make the most of an invitation to dinner by skipping lunch and thus creating a high state of deprivation in which he will eat a great deal. Conversely, he may partially satiate himself with a light lunch before going to dinner in order to make the strength of his ingestive behavior less conspicuous. When a guest prepares himself for an assiduous host by drinking a large amount of water before going to a cocktail party, he uses self-satiation as a measure of control.

Another use is less obvious. In *Women in Love*, D. H. Lawrence describes a practice of self-control as follows:

> A very great doctor . . . told me that to cure oneself of a bad habit, one should force oneself to do it, when one would not do it;—make oneself do it—and then the habit would disappear. . . . If you bite your nails, for example, then when you don't want to bite your nails, bite them, make yourself bite them. And you would find the habit was broken.

This practice falls within the present class if we regard the behavior of "deliberately" biting one's fingernails, or biting a piece of celluloid or similar material, as automatically satiating. The practice obviously extends beyond what are usually called "bad habits." For example, if we are unable to work at our desk because of a conflicting tendency to go for a walk, a brisk walk may solve the problem—through satiation.

A variation on this practice is to satiate one form of behavior by engaging in a somewhat similar form. Heavy exercise is often recommended in the control of sexual behavior on the assumption that exercise has enough in common with sexual behavior to produce a sort of transferred satiation. (The effect is presumed to be due to topographical overlap rather than sheer exhaustion.) A similar overlap may account for a sort of transferred deprivation. The practice of leaving the table while still hungry has been recommended as a way of generating good work habits. Presumably for the same reason the vegetarian may be especially alert and highly efficient because he is, in a sense, always hungry. Self-deprivation in the field of sex has been asserted to have valuable consequences in distantly related fields—for example, in encouraging literary or artistic achievements. Possibly the evidence is weak; if the effect does not occur, we have so much the less to explain.

Manipulating Emotional Conditions

We induce emotional changes in ourselves for purposes of control. Sometimes this means simply presenting or removing stimuli. For example, we reduce or eliminate unwanted emotional reactions by going away for a "change of scene"—that is, by removing stimuli which have acquired the power to evoke emotional reactions because of events which have occurred in connection with them. We sometimes prevent emotional behavior by eliciting incompatible responses with appropriate stimuli, as when we bite our tongue to keep from laughing on a solemn occasion.

We also control the *predispositions* which must be distinguished from emotional *responses* (Skinner, 1953, Chapter X). A master of ceremonies on a television program predisposes his studio audience toward laughter before going on the air—possibly by telling jokes which are not permissible on the air. The same procedure is available in self-control. We get ourselves into a "good mood" before a dull or trying appointment to increase the probability that we shall behave in a socially acceptable fashion. Before asking the boss for a raise, we screw our courage to the sticking place by rehearsing a history of injustice. We reread an insulting letter just before answering it in order to generate the emotional behavior which will make the answer more easily written and more effective. We also engender strong emotional states in which undesirable behavior is unlikely or impossible. A case in point is the practice described vulgarly as "scaring the hell out of someone." This refers almost literally to a method of controlling strongly punished behavior by reinstating stimuli which have accompanied punishment. We use the same technique when we suppress our own behavior by rehearsing past punishments or by repeating proverbs which warn of the wages of sin.

We reduce the extent of an emotional reaction by delaying it—for example, by "counting ten" before acting in anger. We get the same effect through the process of adaptation, described in Chapter X (Skinner, 1953), when we gradually bring ourselves into contact with disturbing stimuli. We may learn to handle snakes without fear by beginning with dead or drugged snakes of the least disturbing sort and gradually moving on to livelier and more frightening kinds.

Using Aversive Stimulation

When we set an alarm clock, we arrange for a strongly aversive stimulus from which we can escape only by arousing ourselves. By putting the clock across the room, we make certain that the behavior of escape will fully awaken us. We *condition* aversive reactions in ourselves by pairing stimuli in appropriate ways—for example, by using the "cures" for the tobacco and alcohol habits already described. We also control ourselves by creating verbal stimuli which have an effect upon us because of past aversive consequences paired with them by other people. A simple command is an aversive stimulus—a threat—specifying the action which will bring escape. In getting out of bed on a cold morning, the simple repetition of the command "Get up" may, surprisingly, lead to action. The verbal response is easier than getting up and easily takes precedence over it, but the reinforcing contingencies established by the verbal community may prevail. In a sense the individual "obeys himself." Continued use of this technique may lead to a finer discrimination between commands issued by oneself and by others, which may interfere with the result.

We prepare aversive stimuli which will control our own future behavior when we make a resolution. This is essentially a prediction concerning our own behavior. By making it in the presence of people who supply aversive stimulation when a prediction is not fulfilled, we arrange consequences which are likely to strengthen the behavior resolved upon. Only by behaving as predicted can we escape the aversive consequences of breaking our resolution. As we shall see later, the aversive stimulation which leads us to keep the resolution may eventually be supplied automatically by our own behavior. The resolution may then be effective even in the absence of other people.

Drugs

We use drugs which simulate the effect of other variables in self-control. Through the use of anesthetics, analgesics, and soporifics we reduce painful or distracting stimuli which cannot otherwise be altered easily. Appetizers and aphrodisiacs are sometimes used in the belief that they duplicate the effects of deprivation in the fields of hunger and sex, respectively. Other drugs are used for the opposite effects. The conditioned aversive stimuli in "guilt" are counteracted more or less effectively with alcohol. Typical patterns of euphoric behavior are generated by morphine and related drugs, and to a lesser extent by caffeine and nicotine.

Operant Conditioning

The place of operant reinforcement in self-control is not clear. In one sense, all reinforcements are self-administered since a response may be regarded as "producing" its reinforcement, but "reinforcing one's own behavior" is more than this. It is also more than simply generating circumstances under which a given type of behavior is characteristically reinforced—for example, by associating with friends who reinforce only "good" behavior. This is simply a chain of responses, an early member of which (associating with a particular friend) is strong because it leads to the reinforcement of a later member (the "good" behavior).

Self-reinforcement of operant behavior presupposes that the individual has it in his power to obtain reinforcement but does not do so until a particular response has been emitted. This might be the case if a man denied himself all social contacts until he had finished a particular job. Something of this sort unquestionably happens, but is it operant reinforcement? It is certainly roughly parallel to the procedure in conditioning the behavior of another person. But it must be remembered that the individual may at any moment drop the work in hand and obtain the reinforcement. We have to account for his not doing so. It may be that such indulgent behavior has been punished—say, with disapproval—except when a piece of work has just been completed. The indulgent behavior will therefore generate strong aversive stimulation except at such a time. The individual finishes the work in order to indulge himself free of guilt (Skinner, 1953, Chapter XII). The ultimate question is whether the consequence has any strengthening effect upon the behavior which precedes it. Is the individual more likely to do a similar piece of work in the future? It would not be surprising if he were *not*, although we must agree that he has arranged a sequence of events in which certain behavior has been followed by a reinforcing event.

A similar question arises as to whether one can extinguish one's own behavior. Simply emitting a response which is not reinforced is not self-control, nor is behavior which simply brings the individual into circumstances under which a particular form of behavior will go unreinforced. Self-extinction seems to mean that a controlling response must arrange the lack of consequence; the individual must step in to break the connection between response and reinforcement. This appears to be done when, for example, a television set is put out of order so that the response of turning the switch is extinguished. But the extinction here is trivial; the primary effect is the removal of a source of stimulation.

Punishment

Self-punishment raises the same question. An individual may stimulate himself aversively, as in self-flagellation. But punishment is not merely aversive stimulation; it is aversive stimulation which is contingent upon a given response. Can the individual arrange this contingency? It is not self-punishment simply to engage in behavior which is punished, or to seek out circumstances in which certain behavior is punished. The individual appears to punish himself when, having recently engaged in a given sort of behavior, he injures himself. Behavior of this sort has been said to show a "need for punishment." But we can account for it in another way if in stimulating himself aversively, the individual escapes from an even more aversive condition of guilt (Skinner, 1953, Chapter XII).

There are other variations in the use of aversive self-stimulation. A man concerned with reducing his weight may draw his belt up to a given notch and allow it to stay there in spite of a strong aversive effect. This may directly increase the conditioned and unconditioned aversive stimuli generated in the act of overeating and may provide for an automatic reinforcement for eating with restraint. But we must not overlook the fact that a very simple response—loosening the belt—will bring escape from the same aversive stimulation. If this behavior is not forthcoming, it is because it has been followed by even more aversive consequences arranged by society or by a physician—a sense of guilt or a fear of illness or death. The ultimate question of aversive self-stimulation is whether a practice of this sort shows the effect which would be generated by the same stimulation arranged by others.

"Doing Something Else"

One technique of self-control which has no parallel in the control of others is based upon the principle of prepotency. The individual may keep himself from engaging in behavior which leads to punishment by energetically engaging in something else. A simple example is avoiding flinching by a violent response of holding still. Holding still is not simply "not-flinching." It is a response which, if executed strongly enough, is prepotent over the flinching response. This is close to the control exercised by others when they generate incompatible behavior. But where another person can do this only by arranging external variables, the individual appears to generate the behavior, so to speak, simply by executing it. A familiar example is talking about something else in order to avoid a particular topic. Escape from the aversive stimulation generated by the topic appears to be responsible for the strength of the verbal behavior which displaces it (Skinner, 1953, Chapter XXIV).

In the field of emotion a more specific form of "doing something else" may be especially effective. Emotions tend to fall into pairs—fear and anger, love and hate—according to the direction of the behavior which is strengthened. We may modify a man's behavior in fear by making him angry. His behavior is not simply doing something else; it is in a sense doing the opposite. The result is not prepotency but algebraic summation. The effect is exemplified in self-control when we alter an emotional predisposition by practicing the opposite emotion—reducing the behavioral pattern in fear by practicing anger on nonchalance, or avoiding the ravages of hatred by "loving our enemies."

THE ULTIMATE SOURCE OF CONTROL

A mere survey of the techniques of self-control does not explain why the individual puts them into effect. This shortcoming is all too apparent when we undertake to engender self-control. It is easy to tell an alcoholic that he can keep himself from drinking by throwing away available supplies of alcohol; the principal problem is to get him to do it. We make this controlling behavior more probable by arranging special contingencies of reinforcement. By punishing drinking—perhaps merely with "disapproval"—

we arrange for the automatic reinforcement of behavior which controls drinking because such behavior then reduces conditioned aversive stimulation. Some of these additional consequences are supplied by nature, but in general they are arranged by the community. This is indeed the whole point of ethical training (Skinner, 1953, Chapter XXI). It appears, therefore, that society is responsible for the larger part of the behavior of self-control. If this is correct, little ultimate control remains with the individual. A man may spend a great deal of time designing his own life—he may choose the circumstances in which he is to live with great care, and he may manipulate his daily environment on an extensive scale. Such activity appears to exemplify a high order of self-determination. But it is also behavior, and we account for it in terms of other variables in the environment and history of the individual. It is these variables which provide the ultimate control.

This view is, of course, in conflict with traditional treatments of the subject, which are especially likely to cite self-control as an important example of the operation of personal responsibility. But an analysis which appeals to external variables makes the assumption of an inner originating and determining agent unnecessary. The scientific advantages of such an analysis are many, but the practical advantages may well be even more important. The traditional conception of what is happening when an individual controls himself has never been successful as an educational device. It is of little help to tell a man to use his "willpower" or his "self-control." Such an exhortation may make self-control slightly more probable by establishing additional aversive consequences of failure to control, but it does not help anyone to understand the actual processes. An alternative analysis of the *behavior* of control should make it possible to teach relevant techniques as easily as any other technical repertoire. It should also improve the procedures through which society maintains self-controlling behavior in strength. As a science of behavior reveals more clearly the variables of which behavior is a function, these possibilities should be greatly increased.

It must be remembered that formulae expressed in terms of personal responsibility underlie many of our present techniques of control and cannot be abruptly dropped. To arrange a smooth transition is in itself a major problem. But the point has been reached where a sweeping revision of the concept of responsibility is required, not only in a theoretical analysis of behavior, but for its practical consequences as well.

5

THE DEVELOPMENT OF SELF-CONTROL

Albert Bandura and Richard H. Walters

As the child becomes physically more mobile and his range of social contacts increases, he spends less and less time in the company of his parents, whose opportunities of directly influencing his behavior consequently decrease. Nevertheless, most children, even in the absence of reinforcement from external agents, maintain many of the response patterns they have acquired through parental training. At this stage, self-generated stimuli may outweigh the influence of external stimuli in governing behavior.

SELF-REACTIONS AS DETERMINANTS OF SOCIAL CONTROL

The process of acquiring self-control has usually been described as one in which parental standards are incorporated, introjected, or internalized, a "superego" is formed, or some inner moral agent that is a facsimile of the parent is developed to hold in check impulses that are "ego-alien." These descriptions are replete with terms that have considerable surplus meaning and that frequently personify the controlling forces. The superfluous character of the constructs becomes evident when one examines laboratory studies in which animals are trained not to exhibit behavior that the experimenter has arbi-

Reprinted with minor editorial changes by permission of the senior author and Holt, Rinehart and Winston from *Social Learning and Personality Development.* New York: Holt, Rinehart and Winston, 1963, pp. 162–172.

trarily selected as deviant. For example, Whiting and Mowrer (1943), using a socialization paradigm, taught rats, as a result of punishment, to take a circuitous route to a food reward instead of a considerably shorter and more direct one; the rats maintained this behavior for some time after punishments were withdrawn. The substitution of less direct, more effortful, and more complicated ways of obtaining reward exhibited by the animals parallels changes in children's behavior that result from social training and are ordinarily regarded as indices of the development of self- or impulse-control. However, no one would say that the rats in the Whiting and Mowrer study had internalized the superego of the experimenters or had introjected their standards.

Numerous attempts have been made to identify differences among fear, guilt, and shame as determinants of social control and even to characterize cultures in terms of the modal inhibitory forces that maintain social conformity (Benedict, 1946; Mead, 1950; Piers and Singer, 1953; Whiting, 1959). Two criteria have been advanced for distinguishing guilt from shame. The first of these assumes a dichotomy between external and internal sanctions and regards shame as a reaction to actual or anticipated disapproval by an audience and guilt as a negative self-evaluation resulting from a deviation from an internalized moral standard. Somewhat similar bases for distinction are Riesman's (1950) contrast between inner-directed and outer-directed persons and the public-private dimension of Levin and Baldwin (1959).

It is reasonable to believe that both external and internal sanctions are instrumental in maintaining social control in almost every society and individual (Ausubel, 1955). Indeed, the requirement that in case of guilt the intrapsychic self-evaluative response should occur without reference to any actual or fantasied reactions of external agents is probably very rarely, if ever, met. This requirement presupposes that guilt is mediated by an internal moral agent, which originated and developed from sanctions imposed by the parents or other primary socializing agents, but which is now completely independent of an individual's current social experiences. To the extent that a person selects a reference group whose members have standards that are similar to his own, his self-evaluations undoubtedly involve an assessment of how these members would react to his behavior. The size of the group by reference to which a particular person evaluates his behavior may vary considerably; when a person's immediate reference group is small and select and does not share the values of the majority of persons of his social class, it may sometimes appear that he is making an independent self-evaluation and displaying "inner-directed" behavior, whereas he may be, in fact, highly dependent on the actual or fantasied approval or disapproval of a few individuals whose judgments he values highly.

A second criterion that has been proposed as a basis for distinguishing guilt and shame assumes that these are a function of degree of responsibility or voluntariness, which may be thought of in terms of a dichotomy between a transgression and a defect (Levin and Baldwin, 1959) or between a motive and an attribute (Piers and Singer, 1953). From this point of view, a person has little or no responsibility for a personal limitation and consequently can feel no guilt, but only shame, on account of his defect. It is true that persons may attempt to conceal intellectual and physical shortcomings in order to avoid negative reactions from others, but these do not necessarily involve a negative self-evaluation that could be described either as guilt or as shame. Let us imagine that a keen swimmer, as a result of an accident, acquires an unsightly scar that invokes reactions, such as staring, from others. He may forego swimming, thereby avoiding displaying his defect in public, but his giving up swimming would in this case be a means of avoiding aversive stimulation and not necessarily a shame, or a self-punitive guilt, reaction. This example highlights the difficulty of distinguishing between shame and fear of aversive responses from others. Of course, the former swimmer could negatively evaluate himself for concealing the defect, or attribute to himself responsibility for the injury.

It is evident that sharp distinctions such as those considered above give rise to semantic difficulties and do little to further the understanding of the acquisition and maintenance of self-control responses, which are undoubtedly a function both of fear of anticipated aversive reactions from others and of self-generated aversive stimulation. On the other hand, it is profitable to attempt to identify social influences that generate or intensify fear of others' disapproval or self-punitive responses for transgressions and defects, and factors that affect the size and nature of the groups that persons permit to influence their behavior.

SOCIAL RESTRICTIONS AND DEMANDS

In all cultures there are social demands, customs, and taboos that require a member to exhibit self-control. Biological gratifications must be regulated in relation to the time schedules of the culture and to prescribed routines. Feeding, elimination, and sleep routines are rigorously imposed by parents and involve delay of gratification of biological needs or interference with other rewarding activities. In conforming to these schedules and demands, the child has often to relinquish behavior that has previously led to immediate and direct reinforcement and to replace this by responses that are less efficient for obtaining immediate reinforcement for the agent. Thus, even the basic socialization processes involve the acquisition of a certain degree of self-control and the observing of social prohibitions and requirements.

Self-control of this kind is demanded for the convenience and well-being of other members of society. Although conformity to schedules involves some delay of reward, gratifications are freely permitted once this is achieved; moreover, since the scheduled gratifications are initially mediated by other family members, they occur in the context of social reinforcements and thus themselves acquire reward value. For example, while enforcing a bedtime routine, most parents give children their undivided attention and associate the observation of the time schedule with events such as story reading or participation in some highly rewarding play activity. Consequently, when children have adapted to such schedules, they have little incentive to deviate.

The situation is different in cases in which attractive rewards are denied to some members of society but are freely available to others. In this case, the problem of maintaining self-control extends beyond childhood years and for most individuals persists throughout their lifetime. Some highly valued rewards are permitted only to those members of society who have attained a certain social status by reason of age, social position, rank, or ethnic background. Barriers to obtaining such rewards may arise from personal limitations, intellectual or physical, and other fortuitous factors, over which the individual has little or no control. They may arise also from a lack of socio-vocational skills, possession of which gives access to the financial resources that are, for the majority of people, the primary means of obtaining highly rewarding goal-objects. Since proficiency in such skills is often dependent on an early commencement of training, which must then continue over a lengthy period of time, persons not infrequently find that lack of opportunities or guidance during their childhood and adolescent years has, in effect, imposed a life-time barrier to their legitimately acquiring possessions and status, or participating in activities that for other persons are evident sources of enjoyment and means for obtaining additional social and material rewards. Thus, both genetic and early-experience factors may create conditions under which persons are tempted to acquire socially acceptable rewards by socially unacceptable means. In fact, many theories of delinquency and crime portray the deviator as one who is oriented toward obtaining rewards that are very highly valued in the culture, but who lacks the opportunities of learning the means of obtaining them in a legitimate way (Cloward and Ohlin, 1960; Merton, 1957).

Social restrictions are not, however, aimed solely at the regulation of means for attaining culturally approved goals. In most, if not all, societies there are certain goals that are strongly prohibited, no matter what means are used to achieve them; yet, for some individuals, the attainment of these goals is a highly effective reinforcer. Sexual perversion and the use of drugs are examples of goals of this kind.

In the generally competitive atmosphere of North American society, achievement demands are made on the majority of children. Cultural achievement norms include the attainment of a level of academic or vocational proficiency that is likely to lead to economic self-sufficiency, and the establishing and maintaining of a home in which a family may be raised. Achievement demands are highly variable among social-class, ethnic, and other subcultural groups; nevertheless, in a society in which upper-mobility is a cultural ideal, parents and other adults in the family usually exert pressures on young people to surpass, or at least equal, the attainments of the previous generation. Nevertheless, as we have already noted, even in competitive societies restrictions are customarily placed on the means by which achievements may be attained. Thus a high degree of social approval in North American society is contingent both on achievement striving and on the observance of social restrictions designed to prevent this striving from having socially harmful consequences.

DISCRIMINATIVE TRAINING IN SELF-CONTROL

Compliance with regulatory social schedules, to which reference was made in an earlier paragraph, involves a considerable amount of discrimination learning in the exercise of self-control. Children must also be taught to discriminate circumstances under which certain classes of behavior may be exhibited from those under which they are not socially acceptable, and to utilize only those forms of response that are appropriate for the occasion. For example, children are expected to refrain from showing physical aggression toward adults or initiating physical attacks on peers; yet, at the same time, boys are expected to relax controls if first attacked by peers and to make efforts to defend themselves, though usually with the restrictions that they do not employ implements that could result in serious injury or use defensive physical aggression against younger or weaker opponents. Moreover, in certain well-defined social contexts, particularly in competitive physical-contact sports, boys are expected not only to defend themselves from attack but also to initiate and maintain physically aggressive behavior. Similar kinds of discrimination are also required in adulthood. For the majority of the population exercise of self-control involves refraining from injurious forms of attack, even in the face of persistent instigation, and the attenuation of the more noxious forms of aggression. However, disciplinary agents, such as parents, police, and armed servicemen, are permitted much freer and more direct expression of aggression in certain well-defined social contexts.

Restraints placed on the expression of sex behavior illustrate demands for self-control which are quite age- and status-specific. A child is required to maintain generalized self-control of sex responses until adolescent years, when some attenuated forms of sexuality are expected toward carefully selected sex objects. When adulthood is reached, demands for self-control are considerably relaxed; indeed, in the case of marital partners, overcontrol is regarded as a symptom of psychosexual maladjustment. Thus, in the case of sexuality the discriminations that are involved are primarily temporal.

There are other response systems over which individuals are expected to develop discriminative self-control, for example, dependency and cooperative–competitive behavior. In these and most of the other cases discussed so far, if the agent does not possess the reward he desires, he must regulate, delay, or renounce socially disapproved but expedient activities and select only culturally approved means and times for attaining his rewards.

SOME BEHAVIORAL MANIFESTATIONS OF SELF-CONTROL

The withholding or delay of social rewards elicits a variety of responses, some of which have already been discussed elsewhere (Bandura and Walters, 1963). Nonaggressive responses to frustration are exceedingly diverse and are highly dependent on the previous training of the individual from whom the rewards are withheld. Moreover, largely because of varying social-learning histories, individuals differ considerably in the extent to which they are able to tolerate self-imposed delay of reward and to persist in the pursuit of a goal, the attainment of which requires self-denial and self-restraint. Reactions to frustration also depend on such factors as the length of time for which reward is delayed (Mischel and Metzner, 1962), on the occurrence or nonoccurrence of partial rewards during the course of achievement striving, and on the confidence with which, at any point in the goal-oriented behavior sequence, a favorable outcome may be forecast (Mahrer, 1956).

When barriers to social and material rewards occur, a frustrated person is ideally expected to maintain his orientation toward the goal objects he is seeking, but to strive to acquire these rewards in socially acceptable ways. This solution, as we have seen, may necessitate the expenditure of considerable time and effort and may not always be possible. Under such circumstances, some persons attempt to overcome barriers by illegitimate or culturally disapproved means which involve little delay or effort before the desired goals are attained. An alternative reaction is to devaluate goal objects that appear to be inaccessible or are not readily attained. This is a relatively easy way of maintaining self-control, especially if the frustrated person selects a reference group, the members of which mutually reinforce the devaluating behavior. This kind of response, which in an extreme and pervasive form is encountered among beatnik and Bohemian groups, occurs from time to time in the history of most persons.

The function of devaluating responses as a means of maintaining self-control is apparent in the results of an experiment by Tallman (1962). Junior college students were administered two tests that supposedly provided highly valid measures of academic aptitude. They were informed that if they passed either of these tests, a letter endorsing them for university admission and scholarship aid would be added to their permanent academic record. Both tasks were insoluble, but opportunities were provided to cheat on one of them. Measures of the students' appraisal of the letter of recommendation were obtained before the administration of the tests, immediately after the completion of the experiment, and again at a later date. Virtually all students initially attempted to achieve the desired object by legitimate means. After they had exhausted the legitimate alternatives, 52 percent of the students who recognized the possibility of cheating and perceived their performance as poor resorted to deviant means for achieving the goal, while students who did not deviate devaluated the previously desired goal object.

Changes in children's evaluation of a toy with which they were forbidden to play were recorded by Aronson and Carlsmith (1963). Provided the threat of punishment for deviation was relatively mild, the children rated the forbidden toy as relatively low in attractiveness following a play period during which they had complied with the prohibition. When the threat of punishment was more severe, the children's evaluations of the toy were not affected, presumably because their conformity behavior was adequately maintained by their anticipation of the painful consequences of deviation. Devaluation may be initially an outcome of successfully maintained self-control; however, to the extent that the reinforcement value of the object in question has been reduced, the person who devaluates should experience less instigation to deviate on future occasions when the formerly desired goal object presents itself.

Other experimental studies suggest that when subjects perceive themselves as voluntarily undertaking arduous tasks in order to achieve a goal, they tend to evaluate the tasks more highly that if they feel themselves to be coerced (Brehm and Cohen, 1962). In one study fraternity pledges were required to serve in an unexpectedly long and boring piece of psychological research under threat of nonacceptance by their immediate reference group, the fraternity, if they refused to cooperate. These pledges expressed high annoyance with the task and regarded themselves as relatively free to refuse their cooperation; nevertheless, all agreed to participate. Compared to a control group of subjects who felt less annoyed with the task and more compelled to cooperate, these pledges expressed a high evaluation of the task as a potential source of satisfaction.

Both devaluation of not readily attainable or forbidden goals and activities and high evaluation of unpleasant means to a goal that is highly desired appear to be learned ways of maintaining self-control. Although no direct evidence is as yet available, one may suspect that responses of this kind can be readily transmitted by parents and other social models.

Although means of *resisting deviation* have received most attention in the literature relating to self-control, there are other equally important ways in which self-control may be exhibited. For example, a person may possess many rewarding resources, but may regulate the manner in which he administers them to himself. One frequently encounters people who make *self-reward contingent on their performing certain classes of responses* which they come to value as an index of personal merit. Such people may set themselves very explicit standards of achievement, failure to meet which is not considered deserving of self-reward and may even elicit *self-punitive responses*; on the other hand, they may reward themselves generously on those occasions on which they attain their self-imposed standards.

There are marked individual differences in the extent to which persons deny themselves rewards that by others are regarded as socially permissible. Two equally wealthy men may differ considerably in the extent to which they utilize their resources to obtain gratifications for themselves; one may lead an extremely frugal life, while the other may be extremely self-indulgent. Cultural forces sometimes influence the frequency and form of self-rewards and the occasions on which these are administered. Extreme self-denial occurs within some religious sects and subcultural groups; for example, austerity is a cultural norm for the Hutterites (Eaton and Weil, 1955; Kaplan and Plaut, 1956), who strive to preserve their way of life in spite of the increasing availability of consumer goods. In this culture not only are material self-reinforcements sparingly administered, but because of the emphasis on personal responsibility for conduct, self-denial and self-punitive reactions occur with high frequency.

> Control of impulses rather than expression is the rule. Enjoyment of food, drink, music, and sex are rather frowned upon, and are not spoken of publicly. No fighting or verbal abuse is permitted. A spirit of compromise, of giving in to one's opponent, is the accepted guide for interpersonal disagreements and frictions. It is expected that a Hutterite man will not get angry, swear, or lose his temper. It is considered wrong to be interested in the outside world, its activities and values. A Hutterite should not be interested in acquiring possessions, or engaging in politics, but instead should devote himself to living his life according to the rules set down by the Bible (Kaplan and Plaut, 1956, pp. 19–20).

In contrast, in Arapesh society (Mead, 1935) self-rewards are freely dispensed and are not made contingent on the meeting or surpassing of social demands and standards, few of which are rigorously imposed upon the members of this society.

Self-control is also exhibited in the *postponement of culturally approved immediate reinforcements in favor of some potentially more rewarding long-term goal.* Professional status can often be achieved only through long hours of arduous study and training; similarly, the attainment of some valued possession, such as a home, may entail the sacrifice of many day-to-day pleasures. Self-control of this kind occurs in the life-histories of most individuals and is, indeed, such a frequently observed occurrence that it has been largely neglected in the literature on the topic.

PART III

Empirical Studies on Self-Control

6

A LABORATORY TASK FOR INDUCTION OF MOOD STATES[1]

Emmett Velten, Jr.

In a famous review of the literature on the effects of psychotherapy, Eysenck (1961a) concluded that only three studies offered even meagre evidence of psychotherapeutic efficacy. Two of these three were by "semantic" psychotherapists, Albert Ellis (1957b) and E. Lakin Phillips (1956), whose methods were highly similar. The third was by Joseph Wolpe (1958), a leading exponent of behavior therapy. Since Eysenck's review, much work has been done and many hypotheses confirmed by investigators of behavior therapy. However, such research productivity has not been forthcoming from the Ellis-Phillips camp.

The theoretical goal of this experiment was to test the central tenet of "semantic" therapy, that the constructions or interpretations people place upon events determine their affective responses. Much evidence from the literature on the determinants of emotions suggests a model of emotion highly congruent with Ellis's (Mandler, 1962). Reviews of hypnosis and autosuggestion methods in psychotherapy (Ellis, 1962; Gordon, 1967; Schultz and Luthe, 1959; Sparks, 1962) lend indirect support to the tenets of the semantic psychotherapists.

Reprinted by permission of the author and Pergamon Press from *Behaviour Research and Therapy*, 1968, *6*, 473–482.

[1] This study is based upon a Dissertation (Velten, 1967) submitted to the University of Southern California in partial fulfillment of the requirements for the PhD degree. Dr. L. Douglas DeNike served as Dissertation committee chairman and rendered invaluable service during the preparation of this article.

METHOD

Subjects

*S*s were 100 unpaid volunteer undergraduate college women who signed up for an experiment in "the autosuggestion of mood states."

Physical Arrangements

Subjects in the group section of the experiment sat at classroom desks. Each *S* in the individual treatment section of the experiment sat in a small room at a 36 × 40 in. table with *S* sitting at a longer side and *E* sitting at a shorter side to *S*'s right.

Group Assessment of Primary Suggestibility

A measure of primary suggestibility (Eysenck and Furneaux, 1945; Stukát, 1958; Weitzenhoffer, 1953) was obtained from each *S* to serve as a covariate in the analysis of treatment effects. The Harvard Group Scale of Hypnotic Susceptibility, (*HGS*), Form A, (Shor and Orne, 1962) provided the measure. All but 17 *S*s received the hypnotic induction scale prior to the individual experimental treatment.

Individual Experimental Treatment

Pre-Measures–Two variables were measured prior to experimental manipulations to assess pre-treatment mood level:

(1) *Decision Time* (DT). This pre-measure involved the use of five pairs of tins, each tin weighing about 1 oz, pre-arranged in parallel columns perpendicular to *S*'s edge of the table. The tins in each pair were equal in weight. The *E* read aloud instructions which indicated that *S* was to pick up the weights in the first pair, decided which was the heavier and so indicate, then to go on to successive pairs.[2]

(2) *Perceptual Ambiguity* (PA). This pre-measure involved presenting *S* with a "vase and faces" ambiguous figure (Osgood, 1953, p. 220, Fig. A) which was drawn in black ink on a lineless index card. The instructions for this pre-measure required *S* to say "Now" whenever she perceived fluctuations in the perspective of the ambiguous figure.

[2] Instructions and other original materials mentioned in this paper are available in Velten (1967).

Mood Induction and Control Group Procedures

Immediately upon completion of the pre-measure *PA* task, each *S* was assigned randomly to one of five treatment groups. She read silently and then aloud either demand characteristics instructions or instructions which prepared her to receive mood or neutral statements. Instructions were in the first person, typed entirely in capitals on lineless index cards, and were placed before *S* by *E* one by one as *S* completed reading the previous card. Instructions for the mood (Elation and Depression) treatments emphasized that *S* should try to feel the mood suggested by the statements, that she could do this, that there was nothing to worry about, and so on. These instructions were read at *S*'s own pace.

Identity and Purpose of the Five Treatments

Immediately upon completion of their appropriate preparatory instructions, the Elation (*EL*), Depression (*DE*), and Neutral (*NU*) *S*s read silently, then aloud, their appropriate mood induction statements. For *EL* and *DE* treatments, two sets of stimuli were used, each composed of 60 self-referent statements. The statements gradually progressed from relative mood neutrality to "elation" for the *EL* group, and from relative mood neutrality to "depression" for the *DE* group. In the *NU* group, they remained affectively neutral and were not self-referent. Subjects in the Elation Demand Characteristics (*EDC*) and Depression Demand Characteristics (*DDC*) treatments had no preparatory instructions, but proceeded directly from the pre-measures to the reading of instructions designed to induce simulated elation and depression, respectively. The mood statements, neutral statements, and demand characteristics instructions were all typed entirely in capitals on lineless index cards, and were presented individually to *S* by *E*. All these statements were exposed to *S* for 20 sec each, while the demand characteristics instructions were read at *S*'s own pace.

Elation Treatment–The tone of the statements exposed to *S*s in the *EL* treatment was one of happiness, cheer, liveliness, efficiency, optimism, and expansiveness. Two sample *EL* statements were: "If your attitude is good, then things are good, and my attitude is good." "This is great—I really do feel good—I *am* elated about things."

Depression Treatment–The tone of the statements exposed to *S*s in the *DE* treatment was one of indecision, tiredness, slowness, unhappiness, inefficiency, and pessimism. Two sample *DE* statements were: "Every now and then I feel so tired and gloomy that I'd rather just sit than do anything." "I have too many bad things in my life."

Neutral Treatment–The purpose of the *NU* treatment was to serve as a control for the possible effects of reading statements and experimental participation per se. Two sample *NU* statements were: "This book or any part thereof must not be reproduced in any form." "Utah is the Beehive State."

Elation Demand Characteristics and Depression Demand Characteristics Treatments–The purpose of the *EDC* and *DDC* treatments was to serve as controls for conscious role-playing or unconscious influence of *S*s by the obvious demand characteristics (Orne, 1962) of the *EL* and *DE* treatments, respectively. *Ss* in both demand characteristics treatments read instructions which explained the procedure used with either the *EL* or *DE* treatment, were provided respectively with a few synonyms for elation or depression, and read instructions to "behave the way I (*S*) estimate other *S*s behave who have been administered all sixty statements representing this mood of (elation) (depression)." They were then shown five samples of the *EL* or *DE* statements, and finally read instructions to "always remember to act as if I were (elated) (depressed)."

Critical Measures

To assess the effects of the treatments on mood, seven critical measures were taken in the following order:

Writing Speed (WS)–Instructions required *S* to write out numbers in descending order from 100. *S*s were stopped after 1 min.

Distance Approximation (DA)–Instructions required *S* to close her eyes and to make certain specified estimations of distance by placing her hands those distances apart.

Decision Time (DT)–Instructions and manner of presentation for this measure were the same as for pre-measure *DT*, although different pairs of weights were used.

Perceptual Ambiguity (PA)–This measure consisted of another ambiguous figure (Osgood, 1953, p. 219, Fig. 81) similar to that of pre-measure *PA*, and presented in the same manner.

Word Association (WA)–Instructions for this measure were typical of those employed in word association tests. There were 16 stimulus words.

Multiple Affect Adjective Check List, Today Form (MAACL)–Instructions required *S*s to check adjectives which applied to them in a long list.

Spontaneous Verbalizations (SV)–The score for this measure was obtained by *E*'s making a record of the number of words uttered by *S* during the course of the critical measures.

The general predictions made were that *EL* and *DE S*s would differ significantly from each other on each critical measure, and that the performance of *NU S*s would fall between those of the two mood treatments. Performances of the two demand characteristics treatments were expected to be significantly different from the respective mood treatments for which they provided controls. Elation *S*s were expected to write more numbers, have larger estimations of distances, to make decisions more quickly, to experience less perceptual ambiguity, to have briefer word association reaction times, to score lower on the *MAACL* "depression scale," and to make more spontaneous verbalizations than the *DE S*s (Fisher and Marrow, 1934; Foulds, 1951; Johnson, 1937; Zuckerman, Lubin, and Robins, 1956).

Post-Experimental Questionnaire

Following the completion of the criterial measures, each *S* was required to fill out a questionnaire designed to indicate her awareness of effects induced by the treatment and her awareness of *E*'s hypotheses regarding the criterial measures.

RESULTS

PRE-TREATMENT EQUATION OF THE EXPERIMENTAL GROUPS. To test for differences in mood level and primary suggestibility among treatment groups prior to treatments, one-way analyses of variance were performed on pre-measure *DT*, pre-measure *PA*, and the *HGS*. The results of the analyses indicated that there were no significant differences among groups prior to treatment.

MOOD-RELEVANT EXPRESSIVE BEHAVIOR. On their post-experimental questionnaires, some *DE S*s made such clear reports as the following: "Sad and lonesome, unhappy—I feel and felt like crying when I think hard about things" (*S* no. 9). "They (the mood-statements) made me feel upset at first because they held a lot of meaning for me. Later on though, I kind of gave up." And: "Everything kept making me think of crummy things and unwanted feelings" (no. 12). "Tired, lonely, unhappy, unloved, homesick, rejected, discontent, wistful, and loving" (no. 22). "When I came into the room, though I felt a bit worried about a coming exam, I was cheerful and rather contented. Apparently the statements did have a result, since I now feel tired and with little ambition to do anything" (no. 24). "Tired, depressed, worrying" (no. 35). Two *DE S*s appeared to be close to tears.

On the questionnaire some *EL S*s made such clear reports as the following: "They (the mood-statements) made me feel happier, wilder, more confident, more desirable, more capable of being a fascinating woman, sexier" (no. 30). "They made me feel very ambitious and I want to get right down to homework" (no. 34). "Good, alive, energetic, confident, more appealing, happier, more ready to get started, more able to work" (no. 77), "I feel more alive, more able to accomplish something today. I also feel more like seeing my friends and talking with them" (no. 89). "They made me feel more optimistic" (no. 90). "They amused me, pleased me, and gave me a confidence I didn't have when I first walked in" (no. 95).

In only a few cases did *S*s in the two demand characteristics treatments appear elated or depressed, and in these cases their behavior was histrionic and easily identifiable as "faking." For example, of the two *DDC* *S*s who engaged in attempts to portray depression, one pouted, shook her head woefully, pulled long faces, and said in response to an example of a *DE* mood-statement provided as part of the *DDC* instructions: "I don't have to read that one; I known that one by heart," in a quavering voice.

Behavior of the *NU* Ss tended to be typically neutral with regard to elation and depression, though several seemed initially to show non-verbal expressions of boredom or perplexity as they read their statements.

In sum then, the mood-relevant expressive behavior of *S*s supported the contention that the mood treatments had induced elation and depression while the corresponding demand characteristics control treatments and the *NU* treatment had not been successful in including similar mood-like behavior. Behavior of the obviously role-playing demand characteristics *S*s suggested that intentional role-playing by mood treatment *S*s would have also been gross and easily identifiable.

RELATION OF PRIMARY SUGGESTIBILITY, PRE-TREATMENT MOOD LEVEL, AND CRITERIAL PERFORMANCE. When correlations of primary suggestibility and pre-treatment mood level with criterial measure performance were calculated, performance on four criterial measures was found significantly related to primary suggestibility for both the *EL* and *DE* treatments. On these measures, the higher the primary suggestibility, the more the respective mood treatment affected *S*. Performance of *S*s in other treatments was essentially unrelated to primary suggestibility, and pre-treatment mood level was essentially unrelated to any treatment *S*'s criterial performance.

PRIMARY SUGGESTIBILITY AND PRE-TREATMENT MOOD LEVEL AS COVARIATES FOR THE FIVE TREATMENTS. Double analyses of covariance were performed using as covariates primary suggestibility and pre-treatment mood level as measured by pre-measure *DT*, and using the seven criterial measures as experimental variables (see Table 1). These analyses revealed that the null hypothesis of equality of treatment group centroids after they had been adjusted for the contributions of the covariates could be rejected at the 0.001 level for four of the seven criterial measures: *WS*, *DT*, *WA*, and the *MAACL*. Thus, treatments produced significant differences among groups even after the control for possible confounding by primary suggestibility and pre-treatment mood level.

MULTIPLE COMPARISONS AMONG ADJUSTED TREATMENT MEANS. To determine which of the differences between individual pairs of the five treatment means were significant after the means had been adjusted for the contributions of pre-treatment mood level and primary suggestibility, Tukey's multiple-range tests were performed (see Table 2).

The *MAACL* produced five significant differences in ten comparisons between pairs of means adjusted for the contributions of the covariates. On

Table 1: Summary of Analyses of Covariance of the Performance of Treatment Groups on the Criterial Measures, Using the Group Scale and Pre-measure Decision Time as Covariates

	Source		Wilks' Lambda	*df*	*F*
Writing speed	Adjusted T	9.23	0.6125	4	14.71*
	Adjusted W	8.74		93	
Distance approximation	Adjusted T	9.13	0.9448	4	1.36
	Adjusted W	9.07		93	
Decision time	Adjusted T	11.12	0.7930	4	6.07*
	Adjusted W	10.89		93	
Perceptual ambiguity	Adjusted T	11.05	0.9255	4	1.87
	Adjusted W	10.97		93	
Word association	Adjusted T	10.28	0.8368	4	4.54*
	Adjusted W	10.10		93	
MAACL	Adjusted T	9.07	0.7088	4	9.55*
	Adjusted W	8.73		93	
Spontaneous verbalizations	Adjusted T	5.22	0.9300	4	1.75
	Adjusted W	5.14		93	

* $P < 0.001$.

this criterial measure, *DE S*s scored further in the predicted direction than all other groups. In addition, *EL S*s scored as more elated than *DDC S*s.

Writing Speed produced three significant differences. *EL S*s wrote significantly more numbers in 1 min than did *DE* and *EDC S*s. Depression *S*s wrote significantly fewer numbers than did *NU S*s. Thus, on this measure, the mood-relevant behavior of *EL* and *DE S*s differed significantly and in the expected direction on an elation–depression continuum.

Decision Time produced three significant differences, with *EL S*s taking significantly less time to make decisions than did *S*s in *DE, NU,* and *EDC* treatments. Thus, according to prediction, the mood-relevant behavior of *EL S*s was such as to indicate that they were more elated than all other treatment groups except, unexpectedly, the *DDC* treatment.

Word Association produced two significant differences. The reaction times of *DE S*s were longer than those of *EL* and *DDC S*s. Thus, on this measure, mood-relevant behavior of *DE S*s differed in such a way as to indicate that they were more depressed than *EL* and *DDC S*s.

Spontaneous Verbalizations produced only one significant difference, and this was between *EL* and *DE* treatment groups.

Distance Approximation produced only one significant difference. The distancc approximations of *NU S*s wcrc significantly largcr than thosc of *DE S*s. Thus, on this measure, the mood-relevant of *NU* and *DE S*s differed in such a way as to indicate as predicted, that the latter were the more depressed.

Table 2: Summary of Tukey's Multiple-Range Test as Applied to Individual Comparisons between Adjusted Treatment Means on the Criterial Measures

Treatment Groups	Means	E	D	N	EDC	DDC
			Writing Speed			
E	50.19	. .	11.88‡	4.42	10.84‡	6.25
D	38.31		. .	7.46*	1.04	5.63
N	45.77			. .	6.42	1.83
EDC	39.35				. .	4.59
DDC	43.94					. .
			Distance Approximation			
E	54.90	. .	8.40	2.09	3.00	0.34
D	46.49		. .	10.50*	5.44	8.15
N	56.99			. .	5.06	2.35
EDC	51.93				. .	2.71
DDC	54.64					. .
			Decision Time			
E	37.83	. .	24.10*	27.10*	21.70*	9.31
D	61.95		. .	2.95	2.45	4.80
N	64.91			. .	5.40	17.80
EDC	59.50				. .	12.40
DDC	47.14					. .
			Perceptual Ambiguity			
E	31.87	. .	5.28	10.99	11.18	7.78
D	37.15		. .	16.27	16.46	13.06
N	20.88			. .	0.17	3.21
EDC	20.69				. .	3.40
DDC	24.09					. .
			Word Association			
E	36.12	. .	18.20†	6.62	7.64	6.33
D	54.32		. .	11.58	10.56	11.87*
N	42.74			. .	1.02	0.29
EDC	43.76				. .	1.31
DDC	42.45					. .
			MAACL			
E	10.55	. .	14.00‡	3.23	2.05	7.65*
D	24.55		. .	10.97‡	11.95‡	6.35*
N	13.78			. .	1.18	4.42
EDC	12.60				. .	5.60
DDC	18.20					. .

Table 2—continued

Treatment Groups	Means	E	D	N	EDC	DDC
			Spontaneous Verbalizations			
E	1.74	..	1.15†	0.57	0.64	0.55
D	0.61		..	0.56	0.49	0.58
N	1.17			..	0.07	0.02
EDC	1.10				..	0.09
DDC	1.19					..

* $P < 0.05$.
† $P < 0.01$.
‡ $P < 0.001$.

Perceptual Ambiguity produced no significant differences.

POST-EXPERIMENTAL QUESTIONNAIRE. Analysis of the questionnaire revealed that a preponderance of *EL* and *DE Ss* reported being significantly affected in elated and depressed directions, respectively, by their experimental manipulations, while *NU, EDC,* and *DDC Ss* preponderantly failed to report any such effects. With very few exceptions, *S*s in *EL*, *DE*, *EDC*, and *DDC* treatments did not report predicted effects on criterial measures significantly more than they reported nonpredicted effects.

DISCUSSION

The results of this experiment largely confirmed predictions made. Elation and *DE* treatments differed significantly from each other on five of seven criterial measures of mood-relevant behavior, and each difference was in the predicted direction. On every measure except *DA, NU* treatment means fell between those of *EL* and *DE* treatment groups, as was predicted. On two of seven measures, *EL* and *EDC* treatment groups differed significantly; and on two of seven, *DE* and *DDC* treatment groups differed significantly. In all cases *EDC* and *DDC* treatment means fell between *DE* and *EL* treatment means. On five criterial measures, means of both demand characteristics treatments were closer to the means of the opposite mood treatment than to the treatments for which they were intended to provide controls. The lack of significant correlations between primary suggestibility and the criterial measure performance of *EDC* and *DDC Ss* implies that *S*s' willingness or ability to respond automatically to demand characteristics of the experiment was not related to primary suggestibility.

The post-experimental questionnaire data supported the conclusion from the behavioral measures that *EL* and *DE* treatments had been successful in inducing elation and depression, respectively, and that the *EL* treatment had been better retained than had the *DE* treatment. Neutral *S*s did not report elation or depression. Elation Demand Characteristics and *DDC* treatments were generally unsuccessful in inducing apparent elation or depression. With a very few exceptions, *S*s were unaware that they were performing on criterial measures in the directions predicted by *E*. Thus, the data consistently indicate that *S*s did not simply respond to the demand characteristics of the experimental situation, that possession of correct hypotheses regarding criterial performance was not responsible for *S*s' behavior, and that differential mood-relevant behavior had been induced.

RESEARCH USE OF THE METHOD. The present method appears to have potential for the experimental induction and study of elation, depression, and perhaps for other moods such as fear or sexual arousal. If appropriate lists of statements could be developed for the induction of these and other moods, the controlled laboratory investigation of mood might be greatly facilitated.

STATEMENT-READING AS A THERAPEUTIC SPECIFIC. The generally positive results of this experiment suggests the possible value of lists of mood or other statements in psychotherapy. The *T* and the patient would develop appropriate statement lists after exploration of the patient's problems. This procedure would be somewhat analogous to the development of anxiety hierarchies in systematic desensitization. The patient would be instructed to practice appropriate lists at or near to the times he becomes aware of undesirable moods and behavior. According to conditioning theory, it might be expected that repeated use of a particular list of statements, particularly if the individual rehearsed them at times when he felt especially bad, would eventually lead to the conditioning of undesirable affect to the statements themselves. To counteract the possibility that the usefulness of the therapy-statements would be reduced either by this means or by simple habituation, alternate sets of statements could be constructed, and the patient could be instructed to begin his use of therapy-statements at the inception of the negative emotion, rather than waiting until it had become full-blown.

IMPLICATIONS FOR PSYCHOLOGICAL INVENTORIES. The results of the present experiment are consistent with the finding that psychological inventories containing a preponderance of negative self-references are likely to be disturbing to those taking them. (Amrine, 1965). To the extent that such disturbance is attributable to depressive mood change as distinct from fear of self-disclosure, it might be possible to lessen objections to such inventories by increasing the number of neutral or positive items.

RELATION TO SEMANTIC PSYCHOTHERAPY. Insofar as the present experiment provided a test of the central tenet of rational-emotive and other semantic psychotherapies, and insofar as the results may be accepted, there is additional evidence that the claims of Ellis (1957b; 1962) and Phillips (1956) regarding the efficacy of their therapies may be taken seriously.

SUMMARY

One hundred female college students were administered the Harvard Group Scale of Hypnotic Susceptibility, Form A, to provide a measure of primary suggestibility. In a 2nd hr, each *S* was randomly assigned to one of five individual treatments of 20 *S*s each. One group read and concentrated upon 60 self-referent statements intended to be elating; a second group read 60 statements intended to be depressing. A third group read 60 statements which were neither self-referent nor pertaining to mood. This group controlled for the effects of reading and experimental participation per se. Fourth and fifth groups received demand characteristics control treatments designed to produce simulated elation and simulated depression, respectively.

Two measures of pre-treatment mood level were obtained from each *S* at the beginning of her individual treatment. Following treatment, as criteria for elation and depression, seven behavioral task measures were obtained. Four of these distinguished significantly among the treatment groups. The comparative performance of *S*s in the three control groups indicated that the obtained mood changes could not be attributed to artificial effects. Moreover, post-experimental questionnaire data strongly supported the conclusion that Elation and Depression treatments had indeed respectively induced elation and depression.

7

EVALUATION OF TRAINING IN CREATIVE PROBLEM SOLVING[1]

Arnold Meadow and Sidney J. Parnes

A training method widely employed in industry, government, and education is the creative problem-solving method outlined by Osborn (1957). The present study was designed to provide a systematic experimental test of the effects of a 30-hour training course in creative problem solving which utilizes Osborn's brainstorming and related methods.

Examination of the literature in the area of creative thinking indicates four groups of relevant studies. A first series comprises studies attempting to differentiate creative from noncreative individuals by means of tests of cognitive functioning, by personality measures, and by biographical data analysis (Creative Education Foundation, 1958).

A second series attempts to determine the effects of various factors postulated to inhibit productive thinking. Among these are studies evaluating the effects of pathological personality syndromes, experimentally induced anxiety, and experimentally induced set (Rapaport, Gill, & Schafer, 1945–46; Youtz, 1955).

Studies comparing individual and group problem-solving procedures (Lindzey, 1954; Taylor, Berry, & Block, 1957; Taylor & McNemar, 1955) and studies evaluating a lecture and a workshop in creative thinking (Gerry,

[1] This study was financed by a grant from the Creative Education Foundation. The IBM Corporation provided the programing and computations required by the statistical analysis.

DeVeau, & Chorness, 1957; True, 1957) comprise the third and fourth bodies of literature.

HYPOTHESES

In the course at the University of Buffalo the procedures in Osborn's textbook (1957) are described, and students are given practice in their application (Parnes, 1958). The brain-storming principle is emphasized throughout the course. The basic thesis of this principle is that creativity is encouraged by the temporal segregation of hypothesis formation and the judicial evaluation of the adequacy of hypotheses.

In the attempt to evaluate the effects of the course in creative problem solving, three hypotheses were proposed for experimental testing: the method employed in the course produces a significant increment (*a*) in quantity of ideas, (*b*) in quality of ideas, and (*c*) in three personality variables—need achievement, dominance, and self-control. The variables embodied in these hypotheses were selected on the basis of a search of the literature for measures reported to discriminate creative from noncreative individuals (Creative Education Foundation, 1958).

METHOD

Experimental Design

The three hypotheses were tested by administering a battery of psychological tests comprised of 11 measures to students taking the Creative Problem Solving courses in the School of Business Administration and to control groups of *S*s taking other courses in the same school. The basic design of the experiment is depicted in Table 1.

The experimental group consisted of a total of 54 students in three Creative Problem Solving courses. Two were evening sections; the other was a day section. Since total pre–post testing time required four hours, it was not practicable to administer all tests to one control group. Two control groups were accordingly employed. Those measures of the battery which were considered to be tests of ability were administered to Control Group A. Control Group B received those tests which were considered to be personality measures. The one exception to this procedure was the Thematic Apperception Test (TAT) Originality ability measure which was included in the Control Group B battery because the total number of ability tests was too great to be administered during one testing period.

Each experimental *S* was matched with an *S* from each of the two control groups on the basis of age, sex, and Wechsler Adult Intelligence Scale

Table 1: Design of Experiment

Pre-Post Test Measures	Experimental Group ($N = 54$)	Control Group A ($N = 54$)	Control Group B ($N = 54$)
1. AC Test of Creative Ability—Other Uses (quantity)	X	X	
2. Plot Titles Low (quantity)	X	X	
3. Guilford Unusual Uses (quality)	X	X	
4. Apparatus Test (quality)	X	X	
5. AC Test of Creative Ability—Other Uses (quality)	X	X	
6. Plot Titles High (quality)	X	X	
7. Thematic Apperception Test—Originality (quality)	X		X
8. Thematic Apperception Test—Need Achievement	X		X
9. California Psychological Inventory—Dominance Scale	X		X
10. California Psychological Inventory—Self-Control Scale	X		X
11. Wechsler Adult Intelligence Scale—Vocabulary[a]	X	X	X

[a] Pretest only—for matching of experimental and control groups.

(WAIS) Vocabulary score (Wechsler, 1955). In order to increase the accuracy of matching, the initial number of control *S*s tested was 200. Completion of the matching yielded a total of 54 *S*s for the experimental group and 54 *S*s for each of the two control groups. The experimental and control groups were closely matched on the selected variables. Ages for the experimental group ranged from 17 to 51 years, for Control Group A, 17 to 50 years, and for Control Group B, 18 to 42 years. For the experimental and control A groups the average of the differences in age for the 54 matched pairs was 3.6 years; the average of the differences in weighted WAIS Vocabulary score was .60. For the experimental and control B groups the average of the differences in age of the 54 matched pairs was 3.8 years, and the average of differences in WAIS Vocabulary score was .68.

Of the final experimental group sample, 42 were male; 12 were female. The final Control Group A and B samples each consisted of 48 male and 6 females *S*s. Of the 54 Experimental versus Control Group A matchings, 38 were of the same sex. The corresponding number of same sex matching for Experimental and Control Group B was 40.

Tests were administered to all *S*s as groups in their regular classes at the beginning and end of the semester. Three class sections were used to obtain the experimental *S*s; ten sections were needed to attain the necessary number of control *S*s.

Experimental Instructions

Each instructor introduced the experiment to his class by describing it as a university research project which would "not have anything to do with your grades." The test administrator was then presented to the class.

> *Instructions given at pretest session at beginning of semester.* I think you will find interesting what you are asked to do. Sometimes the nature of the task may seem strange or silly. Nevertheless, please cooperate to the fullest extent inasmuch as everything you are asked to do is highly significant.
>
> *Instructions read at posttest session at the end of semester.* All of you are subjects in an experiment designed to measure changes which may have occurred in your thinking as a result of all your course work at the University this semester.
>
> During this period you will be given the posttest, consisting of a series of tests similar to the ones given the first time.
>
> Your instructor, Mr. ———, is interested in seeing how well each one of you does. On the other hand, as explained before, the results of these tests will not go on your record, or have anything to do with your grades. It is a serious study which will provide some interesting scientific data, and we would appreciate your sincere cooperation.
>
> In the tests you will now take, you may use any answers which you may have used before and/or any new answers. The important point is to get as high a score as possible on the present test.

Scoring

All measures were scored by two independent raters. Protocols were coded so that no rater was aware of whether he was rating the protocol of a control or an experimental subject.

Pearson correlation coefficients between the scores of these raters were computed for all measures which required qualitative ratings. Computations were based on a randomly selected sample of 50 *S*s. Correlations ranged from .691 on the TAT Need Achievement to .993 on Guilford's Unusual Uses.

Guilford Measures–The Guilford measures were scored in accordance with standard scoring instructions provided by the author of the tests.[2]

AC Test of Creative Ability (AC)–Only one item from Part V of the AC Test was employed because of time limitation (listing all possible uses for a wire coat hanger). The scoring procedure for this test was modified to yield a quantity and *quality* score instead of a quantity and *uniqueness* score. Each response was scored as indicating either good or bad quality.

[2] The authors are indebted to J. P. Guilford and P. R. Merrifield for their assistance in providing the unpublished tests and scoring instructions, and to Robert F. Berner for statistical advice.

The quality score was defined as comprising two dimensions: (*a*) uniqueness—degree to which the response departed from the hanger's conventional use and (*b*) value—the degree to which the response was judged to have social, economic, aesthetic, or other usefulness.

The scorer was instructed to rate each response on a 1 2 3 scale for uniqueness and a 1 2 3 scale for value. The response was finally scored as indicating good quality if assigned a combined uniqueness and value score of at least 5. Final quality score used was the total number of "good quality" responses. Any response which duplicated (in essential meaning) responses already given was eliminated from the scoring.

Need Achievement–This modification of the TAT test was scored according to directions published by McClelland, Atkinson, Clark, and Lowell (1953, pp. 107–138). The Originality measure was derived from story protocols obtained from the same four TAT type cards utilized for deriving the Need Achievement measure. Previous studies employing the Originality measure were based on a global appraisal by scorers (Barron, 1955). In the present investigation an attempt was made to introduce greater objectivity in scoring by adopting a detailed rating method. A four-step rating scale was utilized to define the Originality dimension on each of an *S*'s four stories: (*a*) description or bare story—one point; (*b*) story with some elaboration of characters and/or plot—two points; (*c*) elaborate story—three points; (*d*) story indicating unusual amount of imaginative elaboration—four points. An *S*'s total originality score was the sum of the points for all four stories.

California Psychological Inventory–The CPI Dominance and Self Control Scales were scored according to standard instructions provided by Gough[3] (1957).

Sequence of Tests

In designing the experiment, cognizance was taken of the effect the sequence of the tests might have on results. Test sequence was identical for the experimental group and Control Group A. The comparison of the experimental group with Control Group B, however, introduces an uncontrolled test sequence variable. On the one hand, the experimental group had taken the series of six ability tests prior to the administration of the three personality measures and the TAT Originality measure. On the other hand, Control Group B was administered the personality measures and the TAT Originality measure without prior administration of the series of ability tests.

The primary experimental interest was in testing the effects of the creative problem-solving course on abilities. The decision was therefore

[3] We wish to thank Harrison Gough for providing the individual item keys for the two scales. We also wish to express acknowledgment to the Consulting Psychologists Press, Inc., Palo Alto, California, for permission to use the scales.

made to place six of the seven ability tests before the personality tests, thus leaving the comparison of the ability tests of the expeiimental group with Control Group A uncontaminated by the test sequence effect. *A priori* considerations suggested, moreover, that the ability tests were less likely to influence personality measures than the converse arrangement.

RESULTS

In order to control for possible differences in initial levels of performance, an analysis of covariance was employed for the evaluation of differences between experimental and control groups on all measures. Inspection of the data indicated that the regression was sufficiently linear to meet the assumptions of the covariance model.

The calculation procedure employed is that described by Edwards (1950, pp. 341–348) for a two-variable analysis of covariance design.

Table 2 presents the comparison between the adjusted mean variances of experimental and control groups for the two measures of quantity of ideas. Inspection of the F ratios indicates both measures are significant beyond the 1% level.

A similar comparison is depicted in Table 3 for the five measures of quality of ideas. The results indicate that the AC Other Uses (quality), and the Guilford Apparatus and Unusual scores are significant beyond the 1% level. The Plot Titles High score just fails to reach the 5% level of significance. (Obtained F is 4.01; 4.02 is required for the 5% level.) The TAT Originality measure does not yield a significant difference.

The comparison between experimental and control groups for the three personality measures is presented in Table 4. The results indicate that the

Table 2: Analysis of Covariance between Pre–Post Differences of Matched Experimental and Control Groups Controlled for Initial Score Level—Quantity Creativity Measures

Test	Source of Variation	Sum of Squares Errors of Est.	*df*	Mean Square	*F*	*P*
AC Other Uses Quantity	Between groups plus error	1946.012	53			
	Residual within groups (error)	1057.891	52	20.344		
	Adjusted Means	888.121	1	888.121	43.655	<.01
Guilford Plot Titles Low	Between groups plus error	4382.5275	53			
	Residual within groups (error)	3231.9973	52	62.154		
	Adjusted Means	1150.5302	1	1150.5302	18.511	<.01

Table 3: Analysis of Covariance between Pre–Post Differences of Matched Experimental and Control Groups Controlled for Initial Score Level—Quality Creativity Measures

Test	Source of Variation	Sum of Squares Errors of Est.	*df*	Mean Square	*F*	*P*
AC Other Uses Quality	Between groups plus error	819.5780	53			
	Residual within groups (error)	352.0691	52	6.711		
	Adjusted Means	467.5089	1	467.5089	69.046	<.01
Guilford Apparatus	Between groups plus error	2603.3446	53			
	Residual within groups (error)	1466.6488	52	28.205		
	Adjusted Means	1136.6958	1	1136.6958	40.301	<.01
Guilford Unusual Uses	Between groups plus error	1432.6361	53			
	Residual within groups (error)	795.3507	52	15.295		
	Adjusted Means	637.2854	1	637.2854	41.666	<.01
Guilford Plot Titles High	Between groups plus error	279.4798	53			
	Residual within groups (error)	259.4284	52	4.989		
	Adjusted Means	20.0514	1	20.0514	4.019	>.05
TAT Originality	Between groups plus error	114.5780	53			
	Residual within groups (error)	111.2877	52	2.14		
	Adjusted Means	3.2903	1	3.2903	1.538	>.05

experimental as compared with the control group achieves a significant increase in Dominance. This comparison is significant at the 5% level. The results for the Need Achievement and Self Control variables indicate no significant differences.

DISCUSSION

The comparison between the Experimental and Control Group A indicated significant differences on both quantitative and qualitative measures of ability. On the two measures of idea quantity the experimental group attained a greater increase than the control group. This result suggests the conclusion

Table 4: Analysis of Covariance between Pre–Post Differences of Matched Experimental and Control Groups Controlled for Initial Score Level—Personality Measures

Test	Source of Variation	Sum of Squares Errors of Est.	*df*	Mean Square	*F*	*P*
TAT Need	Between groups plus error	408.5023	53			
Achieve-ment	Residual within groups (error)	401.8881	52	7.729		
	Adjusted Means	6.6142	1	6.6142	.856	>.05
CPI	Between groups plus error	550.0154	53			
Domi-nance	Residual within groups (error)	500.1160	52	9.618		
	Adjusted Means	49.8994	1	49.8994	5.188	<.05
CPI	Between groups plus error	1160.8034	53			
Self Control	Residual within groups (error)	1148.0450	52	22.078		
	Adjusted Means	12.7584	1	12.7584	.578	>.05

that the creative problem-solving students were utilizing the course methods, even though the tests gave no instructions to do so.

Three of the quality measures (the AC Other Uses—Quality, and the Guilford Apparatus and Unusual Uses tests) yielded highly significant differences. In evaluating the results indicated by the AC Other Uses and Guilford Unusual Uses scores, the specified nature of the training employed in the course must be considered. The students did receive practice on the type of problem included on these tests. However, since the instructors carefully avoided practice on any objects even remotely similar to the type of objects which appeared on the tests, the results do indicate generalization of this training. Results of the Apparatus Test probably represent a greater degree of learning generalization inasmuch as problems designed to afford students practice in thinking of improvements for apparatus were deliberately excluded from training.

Of the three personality measures, the CPI Dominance scale was the one measure which yielded a significant difference. This result indicated an increase in Dominance of the Experimental as compared with Control Group B ($P < .05$). This scale was devised by Gough "to assess factors of leadership ability, dominance, persistence, and social initiative. . . . High scorers tend to be seen as: Aggressive, confident, persistent, and planful; as being persuasive and verbally fluent; as self-reliant and independent; and as having leadership potential and initiative. Low scorers tend to be seen as: Retiring, inhibited, commonplace, indifferent, silent and unassuming; as being slow in thought and action; as avoiding of situations of tension and decision; and as lacking in self-confidence" (Gough, 1957, p. 12).

It is interesting that Dominance was the one variable out of the three personality variables which yielded a positive result. The personality type it represents is the very type which the methods of the course were explicitly designed to encourage.

SUMMARY

The experiment was designed to evaluate the effects of a creative problem-solving course on creative abilities and selected personality variables. Three hypotheses were tested: the method employed in the course would produce a significant increment (*a*) in quantity of ideas, (*b*) in quality of ideas, and (*c*) in the three personality variables—need achievement, dominance, and self-control.

A battery of 10 test measures was administered to matched experimental and control groups at the beginning and end of a creative problem-solving course. The following results were obtained: (*a*) The experimental as compared with the control group attained significant increments on the two measures of quantity of ideas; (*b*) the experimental as compared with the control group attained significant increments on three out of five measures of quality of ideas; (*c*) the experimental as compared with the control group showed a significant increment on the California Psychological Inventory Dominance scale.

Results are interpreted to indicate that the creative problem-solving course produces a significant increment on certain ability measures associated with practical creativity and on the personality variable dominance.

8

THE INFLUENCE OF MOTIVATION ON HYPNOTIC BEHAVIOR[1]

Martin T. Orne

In studying the nature of the hypnotic trance, the question arises as to which phenomena are primary and consistent components of the trance state and which are secondary derivatives. Let us postulate that increased motivation is a constant accompaniment of the hypnotic state. The present phase of the research was designed to show that certain phenomena long viewed as part and parcel of the hypnotic state may more parsimoniously be viewed as derivatives of increased motivation, and can be reproduced *pari passu* by other motivational techniques that have no direct relationship to hypnosis.

For years it has been claimed that there is an increase in physical capacity during the trance state. In part this claim has been based on casual observation, the favorite example being that of the stage hypnotist who places a subject in deep trance across two chairs and permits one or more individuals to stand or sit upon him. This "experiment," with variations, is often cited as irrefutable evidence for increased physical capacity. Another group of frequently cited observations are those concerning the ability of the subject to maintain his hand in an outstretched position for extended periods of time without evidence of fatigue. On the basis of this type of data, estimates of greatly increased physical capacity have been made (McDougall, 1926; Moll, 1904).

An early study by Nicholson (1920, p. 89) maintained that "during

Martin T. Orne, abridged from "The Nature of Hypnosis: Artifact and Essence," *Journal of Abnormal and Social Psychology, 58*, 1959, 277–299.

[1] This experiment was originally reported in German (Orne, 1954).

the hypnotic sleep the capacity for work seemed practically endless." Unfortunately, no quantitative data were given, and the study was poorly controlled. In a meticulous investigation, Williams (1930) showed no difference between hypnotic and wake states in the ability to maintain the arm in an outstretched position. However, this study failed to employ suggestions to the effect that the arm would not get tired and could not drop. In another similar investigation, using an ergograph and employing appropriate hypnotic suggestions, Williams (1929) found a 12 to 16% increment in the trance. More recently, Roush (1951) showed an increment in performance in hypnosis significant at better than the .05% level using the arm dynomometer, the hand dynomometer, and hanging by the hands as measures of fatigue.

All the experiments performed by psychologists in the laboratory have followed orthodox scientific methods insofar as a standard set of instructions was given to the *S* to hold a weight, pull an ergograph, or perform a similar task in both the nonhypnotic and hypnotic states. The better experiments used the usual ABBA arrangement to control fatigue or practice effects. Any increment in performance was defined as an increase in capacity due to trance. It is necessary here to question the logic on which the interpretation of these results is based. While these experiments undoubtedly show that instructions given in trance state result in increased performance over that achieved by the same instructions in the wake state, they do not necessarily show an increase in capacity. Alternatively, the *S* may be more willing to exert himself while in hypnosis. The governing factor could be the increase in the *S*'s motivation to comply with the experimenter's request rather than an increased capacity to comply. The instructions, while identical in wording, may be experienced as quite different by the *S* in hypnosis and the waking state. The request to hold a weight at arm's length, given in trance, may be a highly motivating cue or "suggestion," especially if the *S* is told that he is to feel very powerful and not fatigued. The identically worded request in the wake state is perceived as a request by the experimenter and may be followed if good rapport exists between experimenter and *S*. However, as the discomfort of the task increases, the *S* becomes increasingly disinclined to comply. Viewed in this context, the reported experimental results do not necessarily imply that physical capacity is in fact increased in trance but, rather, that the trance state increases performance.

PROCEDURE

Nine *S*s in deep trance were asked to hold a kilogram weight at arm's length. This was done in such a way as to derive maximal benefit from the peculiar nature of the trance state. Thus the *S* was told to hallucinate a table, and only after the table was both seen and felt by the *S* was the suggestion given that the right arm would feel no fatigue and no pain.

All the standard tests of deep trance were met in each *S*. A kilogram weight was placed in the *S*'s right hand, and the *S* was instructed to place it on the imagined table, to continue holding it with his fingers, and under no circumstances to drop it or his arm. Continuous suggestions were given to the effect that he would be able to hold onto the weight, that his arm would not get tired, etc., and that he would continue to see the table. The end point was when the *S* was no longer able to hold up his arm and began to come out of trance. At that point he was reassured, told to drop the weight, and deep trance suggestions were again given. After some minutes, and having made certain deep trance was again established, the *S* was awakened with a carefully induced posthypnotic amnesia. The *S* was not told the length of his performance. For the second part of the experiment, which was done within half an hour of the first, the *S*, not now under hypnosis, was instructed as follows:

> This is a most important part of our experiment. It is very important for us to know your endurance and physical capacity. What I want you to do is a very difficult task. It does not look difficult but it is. I want you to hold this kilogram weight at arm's length. Your hand will get tired and it will take great effort to do this. There is a natural tendency to drop the weight if your hand gets tired. However, it is vital that we get your true capacity. Surprisingly enough, our female subjects have been able to hold the weight for T minutes. [The time T given would be his previous performance during hypnosis rounded off to the nearest half minute.] Our male subjects have been able to hold the weight at least T + ½ minutes. I realize that this is a difficult and painful task. Just to make it interesting we will try a game. At T minus 2 minutes we will start you off at 5 cents. At T minus one and a half, we will double that and make it 10 cents. At T minus one, 20 cents. At T minus one half, 40 cents. At T, 80 cents and at T plus one half, $1.60.

Then the *S* was told that while we could not afford to pay over $1.60, we were, of course, interested in how long he could actually hold the weight. One final point was explained to him:

> While we often feel that we are so tired that we cannot go on, this is not really true. One can rarely be so tired as not to be able to continue for 30 seconds. Accordingly, I would like you to give me one-half minute's notice before you actually drop the weight.

RESULTS

Table 4 gives the results for the nine *S*s tested. All but one *S* in the wake state immediately exceeded hypnotic performance. This *S* held the weight for 6 min. 5 sec. in trance, a very remarkable performance, but in a

Table 4: Comparison of Subjects' Performance in Hypnotic and Wake State

	Hypnosis		Waking	
Subject	Minutes	Seconds	Minutes	Seconds
1	4	05	5	33
2[a]	4	40	6	25
3	4	38	8	06
4(*a*)[b]	6	05	3	29
(*b*)	5	50	10	02
5	7	07	7	57
6	10	05	16	00
7	4	52	5	49
8	5	20	5	32
9[c]	4	57	2(*a*)	10
			5(*b*)	09

[a] This experiment was performed in 1950. In 1957, it came to my attention that this *S* feels that he simulated completely throughout this experiment. At the time, I was totally unaware of this possibility and the *S* was in trance by all the usual criteria.

[b] *S* dropped the weight after 3′ 29″ in the wake state. The next day, care was taken to motivate him adequately. While the hypnotic performance was only 15″ below the previous day, his wake performance now exceeded 10′.

[c] This *S* suddenly dropped the weight without warning in the wake state after 2′ 10″. She was encouraged and after a 20′ time lag again held the weight. This time her performance was 5′ 09″. This performance in itself is better than her hypnotic performance of 4′ 57″; however, it might seem that the waking performance was better than this, as the 2′ 10″ period was not given credit.

subsequent wake state dropped the weight after only 3½ min. The exception demonstrates very clearly that it is necessary to ego-involve the person in the task and to convince him of his ability to do it. He reported that the seven minutes that had been given as an illustration of "average performance" had seemed so long, and his hand became so tired after three minutes that he felt convinced that he would be unable to come even close to the average, so therefore "why bother to try?" The next day the *S* was more carefully motivated and encouraged. He was then able to hold the weight for over 10 minutes.

DISCUSSION

This experiment does not purport to prove that there is no increase in physical capacity in the trance state. Because of the motivating nature of the trance state, and the operational difficulty in obtaining equal motivational states, it becomes a technical impossibility to prove conclusively whether increased physical capacity is produced or not. The data, however, do show that the usually observed increase in performance of trance *S*s may be accounted for by motivational difference.

From a theoretical viewpoint the reinterpretations to which this study had led seem most significant. As long as we believe physical capacity to be in fact increased by the simple expedient of the induced trance, it becomes necessary to look for the focus of the trance in something neurophysiological. If, on the other hand, we can understand the apparent increase in physical capacity observed during the trance state in terms of differences of motivation, we are then led to view hypnosis in psychological terms. It is clear that this study says nothing about why the trance tends to increase motivation nor does it even prove that this is so. It merely shows that adequate motivation in the wake state leads to levels of performance equal or better than those found in the trance.

An objection that might be raised takes the form of the question as to what would happen if similar motivational techniques were used in the trance state to those in the wake state. But this question has little bearing on the essential point. If application of these techniques should produce a trance performance greater than the wake performance, it could be interpreted as the result of combined effects of ego-motivation and the postulated increased motivation associated with hypnosis. If, on the other hand, performance in trance were not greater it could be argued that the type of ego-motivation used is not germane to the trance state.

It may, finally, be argued that the *S* in the wake state is, in fact, still in hypnosis, since the same experimenter who induced hypnosis conducts the second phase. Perhaps *S*s performed better in the wake state because of the demand characteristics of the experiment, i.e., my expectation that they should do so! It is not easy wholly to refute this argument. That all previous studies are open to the same criticism does not answer the question. The clinical observation that the *S* does not look, act, or feel in any way the same in the hypnotic part and the waking part appears much more relevant. Nevertheless, I hope sometime to repeat the study with the aid of another hypnotist who believes in "the power of hypnosis" and who, therefore, expects *S* to do better in hypnosis than in the wake state. If it were possible for me to enable *S*s subsequently to exceed their hypnotic performance, it would go far toward removing this objection, of which I was aware during the collection of data.

9

EFFECTS OF COGNITIVE DESENSITIZATION ON AVOIDANCE BEHAVIOR[1]

Stuart Valins and Alice Allen Ray

Experimental investigations of the modification of avoidance behavior have demonstrated that systematic desensitization procedures are particularly effective. Lang, Lazovik, and Reynolds (1965) and Davison (1968b) have found that the efficacy of these procedures is primarily dependent upon the *gradual exposure* of the feared object (in imagination or otherwise) to a subject who is in a state of *muscle relaxation*. According to Wolpe (1958), muscle relaxation is a response which is incompatible with and which inhibits the physiological correlates of fear. Fear reduction and the extinction of avoidance behavior presumably result from the successful induction of this physiological incompatibility. Since various implications of these theoretical speculations are amenable to experimental investigation, it is rather surprising that no such investigations have been reported. For example, there is as yet no evidence that subjects who are instructed to relax are less physiologically responsive to phobic stimuli than subjects who are not instructed to relax. Such differences are clearly required by the theory. In the absence of evidence supporting these testable physiological speculations, we shall assume, for the moment, that they may be wrong. Why then should the muscle-relaxation procedure be a necessary feature of systematic desensitization?

[1] This research was supported by a faculty research grant from the University of North Carolina School of Medicine and by the Foundations' Fund for Research in Psychiatry. The able assistance of J. Hugh Brian during the first experiment is gratefully acknowledged. Gerald Davison and Richard Nisbett provided helpful comments on an earlier draft of this paper.

Research based on Schachter's theory of emotion has shown that cognitive labeling processes are important determinants of emotional behavior. When experiencing a state of physiological arousal, subjects will behave most emotionally if they identify an emotional stimulus as the source of their arousal (Nisbett & Schachter, 1966; Schachter & Singer, 1962). Similar effects are observed even when this arousal state is more apparent than real. A subject who is induced to think that his heart rate has changed in response to a photograph of a nude female will consider her more attractive and desire a copy of the photograph more than one to which he thinks his heart rate has not changed (Valins, 1966). Thus, regardless of one's actual internal state, the cognition, "That stimulus has affected me internally," will have effects which are markedly different from the cognition, "That stimulus has not affected me internally."

The present investigation is based upon the assumption that the latter cognition is induced during systematic desensitization. Subjects are instructed and instruct themselves to relax while in the presence of stimuli that are ordinarily frightening. To the extent that they are successful in *believing* that they are relaxed in such a situation, they will be able to say, "That stimulus no longer affects me internally." It may thus be irrelevant whether autonomic or somatic relaxation is induced during desensitization therapy so long as the individual feels or thinks that he is relaxed. Although subsequent research may reveal that physiological relaxation does indeed accompany this cognition, the cognition alone may be the important modifier of avoidance behavior.

Two experiments will be reported in which cognitions will be induced concerning physiological reactions to snake stimuli. Subjects will think that such stimuli do not affect their heart rates, whereas other fear-provoking stimuli, electric shocks, do affect their heart rates. They should thus believe that their fear of snakes is not warranted. It is hypothesized that these subjects will manifest more approach behavior when subsequently exposed to a live snake than will suitable control subjects.

EXPERIMENT I

Procedure

The experiment was described as a study of physiological reactions to frightening stimuli. All subjects were told that these reactions were to be measured in response to electric shocks and to slides of snakes. One group of subjects heard what they thought were their heart-rate reactions to these stimuli. A second group of subjects heard the identical sounds, but did not associate them with their heart rates.

Manipulations of Information Concerning Internal Reactions–The experimental subjects (heart-rate feedback) were told that the experimenter was interested in their heart-rate reactions. These reactions were presumably being measured using a microphone, amplifier, signal tracer, and tape recorder. The microphone was attached to each subject's chest from which it ostensibly picked up the major heart sounds. These sounds would then be amplified, made audible, and recorded on the tape recorder. All of the experimental subjects were asked to ignore the "heart sounds." The sounds that the subjects heard were actually prerecorded and consisted of square-wave pulses.

The control subjects (extraneous sounds) were told that the experimenter was interested in their vasomotor or finger-temperature reactions to the slides and shocks. They were told that they would also hear a tape recording of meaningless sounds throughout the experiment. The experimenter was presumably interested in whether these sounds would affect their vasomotor reactions to the fear stimuli. The subjects were asked to ignore these sounds.

After summarizing the procedure, the experimenter attached the suitable electrodes and physiological transducers, started the tape recorder, and left the room. There then followed a 2-minute period during which the subjects heard their "heart beats" or the "extraneous sounds." During this period, the rate of the sounds varied between 66 and 72 beats per minute. Beginning with the third minute, 20 slides were projected, at 1-minute intervals, into the subject's room through a one-way screen. The slide presentation was coordinated with the tape recording so that subjects heard a marked increase in the rate of the sounds to 10 of the slides (from 72 to 90 beats per minute). This rate increase was apparent throughout the duration of the slide (15 seconds) and then gradually subsided. A detailed description of these manipulations may be found elsewhere (Valins, 1966).

Shock and Snake Stimuli–The slides to which the subjects heard an increase in the rate of the sounds consisted of the word "SHOCK." A mild electric shock was delivered to the first and third fingers of the subject's left hand 7 seconds after the stimulus word appeared. These shocks gradually increased in intensity from the first (6 milliamps) to the tenth slide (10 milliamps). Each 500-pulse-per-second shock was presented for .10 second.

Subjects heard no change in the rate of the sounds to 10 slides which depicted various kinds of snakes. These slides, previously rank ordered by judges according to the degree of fear provoked, were shown in increasing order of intensity.

In summary, all subjects were shown 20 slides. Ten of these were of snakes (Slides 2, 4, 5, 7, 10, 12, 14, 15, 17, 20) and 10 of the word "SHOCK" (Slides 1, 3, 6, 8, 9, 11, 13, 16, 18, 19). The experimental subjects heard what they thought were their heart-rate reactions to these slides and heard that their heart rates were not affected by the snake slides, although they were affected by the shock slides. Thus, although their fear of shocks is apparently justified, their fear of snakes is not. Control subjects, exposed to the identical tape recording and fear stimuli, were not given any information about their internal reactions.

Snake-Avoidance Test–To assess whether the manipulation had the predicted behavioral effect, the subject was asked to pick up a live 30-inch boa constrictor. After presenting the last slide, the experimenter returned to the subject's room, removed the electrodes and transducers, and said:

> On this sheet of paper, there is a list of six things that I would like you to try to do. This part of the experiment is optional, but I do want you to do as many of these things as you can. I'll leave the instructions with you for a few minutes so that you can decide what you want to do.

The experimenter left the room and allowed the subject 5 minutes to make his decision. The following was written on the sheet of paper:

> In the next room, there is a small and harmless boa constrictor that is securely enclosed in a glass cage. This snake is tame and does not bite. During the next part of the experiment, you will be asked to:
>
> 1. Enter the room and look at the snake.
> 2. Take the cover off the cage and look down at the snake.
> 3. Reach into the cage and get your hand far enough in so that your wrist is below the top of the cage.
> 4. Touch the snake once.
> 5. Pick the snake up a few inches.
> 6. Pick the snake up and out of the cage, and hold it for as long as you can.
>
> This part of the experiment is completely optional. It is important, however, that you try to do some of the above. Please take a few minutes and give it your full consideration.

The experimenter then returned, asked the subject if he wished to continue, and, if he did, led him into the doorway of the room where the snake was caged. The subject was asked to perform each of the above behaviors, in sequence, upon the experimenter's signal. The experimenter departed to an observation room and knocked on the one-way screen at 30-second intervals. With each signal, the subject was to attempt to perform one of the behaviors. A postexperimental interview followed the avoidance test.[2]

Subjects–The subjects were sophomore and junior undergraduates who were recruited in their dormitories with an incentive of $1.50. These subjects were randomly assigned to the experimental and control conditions. On the basis of their responses to a brief questionnaire administered when they arrived for the experiment, it was apparent that the two groups did not

[2] The snake-avoidance test was adapted from Davison (1968b).

differ with respect to their fear of snakes or shocks. There were 21 female and 7 male subjects in each condition.

Results

Since most of the experimental subjects accepted the bogus heart beats as veridical and could distinguish that the snake slides did not affect their heart rates, the major requirements for a test of the hypothesis were satisfied. However, the data for two female subjects were incomplete. One control subject refused to go beyond the first shock slide, and one experimental subject removed the microphone early in the session because of doubts concerning the veridicality of the sounds.

SNAKE-APPROACH BEHAVIOR. It was hypothesized that cognitions concerning internal reactions will affect avoidance behavior. Subjects who think that snake stimuli do not affect them internally should consider their fear of snakes to be unwarranted. These subjects should manifest more approach behavior when confronted with the live snake than should the control subjects. The data which allow a test of this hypothesis are presented in Table 1. In this table are tabulated the number of subjects whose closest approach behavior corresponded to one of those listed in the left-hand column. Considering all subjects, it can be seen that the experimental ones manifested somewhat more approach behavior than did the controls, but this difference is not significant.

It is reasonable, however, that a more adequate test of the hypothesis could be made if subjects were selected on the basis of their experience with snakes. In this unselected sample of subjects, prior experience with snakes

Table 1: Closest Snake-Approach Behavior

	Heart-rate Feedback		Extraneous Sounds	
Closest Approach Behavior	All *S*s	*S*s Who Never Touched a Snake	All *S*s	*S*s Who Never Touched a Snake
Would not enter room (0)	0	0	3	3
Entered room (1)	2	2	1	1
Took cover off cage (2)	0	0	2	2
Reached into cage (3)	2	2	1	1
Touched snake (4)	6	3	6	4
Picked up snake in cage (5)	0	0	0	0
Held snake for less than 30 sec. (6)	0	0	2	1
Held snake for 30 sec. (7)	17	13	12	4
Mean approach	5.59	5.55	4.74	3.62

may have been a major and undesirable determinant of behavior during the avoidance test. This was obviously so since *all* of the subjects who reported that they had previously touched a snake also touched the boa during the avoidance test, whereas only 69% of the inexperienced subjects touched the boa ($\chi^2 = 5.15$, $p < .05$). When the experienced subjects are eliminated from the sample, it is apparent that the manipulation has had the predicted effect. Considering just those subjects who had never previously touched a snake, closer approach behavior is manifested by the experimental subjects than by the controls (Mann-Whitney test, $z = 2.34$, $p < .02$). Moreover, 65% of the experimental subjects completed the avoidance test by holding the snake for the full 30 seconds, whereas only 25% of the control subjects did ($\chi^2 = 4.21$, $p < .05$).

EXPERIMENT II

The results of the first experiment indicate that cognitions concerning internal reactions can affect avoidance behavior. Subjects who believed that snake stimuli did not affect them internally approached and held a live snake more than did subjects who had no information about their internal reactions. A second experiment was subsequently conducted to determine whether these results could be obtained using a selected sample of subjects who were more frightened of snakes than the average undergraduate. A different snake-avoidance test was also used. It was thought that the first avoidance test, which required subjects to be alone with a snake in a dimly lit room, might be too frightening for these selected subjects. Also, the test was now conducted by an experimenter who had no knowledge of the condition to which the subject had been assigned. This is an improvement over the first experiment, although it is unlikely that the experimenter's behavior had much of an effect during the first avoidance test. The first test was rather mechanical since the major instructions were not presented orally, and the experimenter was in another room observing relatively clear-cut behavior.

Procedure

Subjects participating in this experiment were seen twice. In all respects, the procedure in the first session of this experiment was identical to that in the previous experiment. However, to strengthen the manipulation, a second session was conducted approximately 1 week later. The avoidance test was postponed until the end of the second session. This second session was also identical to the first with the exception that different snake stimuli were used. At those minutes when the subjects had previously seen a slide of a snake, they now saw a live snake. The boa constrictor was in a glass cage on the experimenter's side of a one-way screen. At the appropriate times, a bright light was turned on above the cage, allowing the subject to see the snake.

Snake-Avoidance Test–At the end of the second session, the subjects were given a short questionnaire to complete and told that another experimenter would be in to speak with them. When he arrived, the second experimenter asked the subject if he would like to see the snake. (All subjects answered in the affirmative.) The subject was led into the room where the snake was caged and the experimenter said:

> Snakes really make very nice pets. They are affectionate and become tame and used to people very quickly. This particular species will not bite under any circumstances. Snakes also aren't slimy or wet as many people think. Can you touch him?

If the subject touched the snake, he was asked to pick it up. If he refused either of these requests, he was offered $1 and, if necessary, $2 to perform the behavior. This procedure permits an assessment of the amount of pressure required to induce subjects to touch or pick up the snake. A discussion of the experiment followed the avoidance test.

Subjects–The subjects were male freshmen who had taken a number of questionnaires at the beginning of the semester. One of the questionnaire items concerned the extent to which they were frightened of snakes. Subjects recruited for the experiment had indicated that they were very or extremely frightened of harmless snakes. That these subjects were more frightened of snakes than average was indicated by their responses on a questionnaire completed before the beginning of the first session. Their mean fear of snakes was 67.29 (on a 100-point scale), whereas the mean initial fear of the unselected subjects participating in the first experiment was 58.15 ($t = 2.11$, $p < .05$). The subjects were randomly assigned to the experimental ($N = 23$) and control ($N = 12$) conditions, and these conditions proved comparable with respect to the subjects' initial fear of snakes and shocks. All subjects were paid $3 for their participation.

Results

All of the experimental subjects accepted the sounds as their heart beats. The data of one control subject were eliminated because of his prior knowledge of the details of the experiment.

AVOIDANCE-TEST BEHAVIOR. The avoidance test conducted in this experiment allows a determination of the amount of pressure required to induce subjects to perform a given behavior. The experimental subjects, who presumably believe their fear of snakes is unjustified, should require less pressure than the control subjects. The number of subjects requiring specified amounts of pressure to touch the snake is presented in Table 2. Confirming the hypothesis, these data show that the experimental subjects required less pressure than did the control subjects ($z = 2.03$, $p < .05$).

Table 2: Pressure Applied To Touch Snake

Pressure Applied	Heart-rate Feedback: All *Ss*	Heart-rate Feedback: *Ss* Who Never Touched a Snake	Extraneous Sounds: All *Ss*	Extraneous Sounds: *Ss* Who Never Touched a Snake
Would not touch at all (3)	2	1	2	2
Touched for $2 (2)	0	0	2	1
Touched for $1 (1)	7	4	4	3
Touched without money offered (0)	14	9	3	2
Mean pressure applied	.56	.50	1.27	1.38

That this difference is significant without regard to the subjects' prior experience with snakes suggests that experience may not have been an important determinant of behavior during this avoidance test. Such is indeed the case, since inspection of Table 2 reveals no tendency for experienced subjects to require less pressure than inexperienced ones. Finally, the significance of the group difference in pressure required to touch the snake is not very much affected when just the inexperienced subjects are considered ($z = 1.93$, $p < .06$). These data suggest that, relative to prior experience with snakes, the manipulation was an effective determinant of behavior during the avoidance test. Nevertheless, it was evidently not sufficient to induce subjects to pick up the snake. Although the experimental and control subjects differed in the pressure required to *touch* the snake, there were no group differences in the pressure required to *pick up* the snake.

SUBJECTIVE FEAR REACTIONS. Subjects completed short questionnaires concerned with their fear of snakes and shocks before the first-session manipulation and after the second-session manipulation. On only one of these questions did the two groups differ. After the second manipulation, the experimental subjects said that they were more frightened that the shocks might have harmed them physically ($p < .05$). Since these subjects heard a marked increase in their "heart rates," it is reasonable that they feared the shocks might be a strain on their hearts.

Experimental and control subjects did not differ in their rated fear of snakes or shocks before the first-session manipulation or after the second-session one. It is puzzling, though, that both groups of subjects increased their fear of shocks ($p < .01$) and decreased in the fear of snakes ($p < .01$). Such an effect would be expected for the experimental subjects who could use the bogus feedback as a basis for answering the question: "How frightened are you of ________?" It is not easily explained, however, why the control subjects should rate their fears in this manner. Control subjects in other feedback experiments have never shown any tendency to be affected by the extraneous sounds. A possible explanation is suggested when we consider that two of these control subjects suspected that the sounds were their heart beats, and two others reported that their heart rates increased to the shocks. It is possible, then, that the sound manipulation caused the subjects to introspect and that it induced a weak version of the cognition, "Shocks affect me internally but snakes do not." Such cognitions could result in the control subjects rating their fears in a manner similar to that of the experimental subjects. If this explanation is correct, however, it is evident that the weak cognition was not sufficient to affect avoidance behavior. Control subjects required significantly more pressure to touch the snake.[3]

DISCUSSION

It is clear from the results of these experiments that avoidance behavior can be modified by information concerning internal reactions. Subjects who thought that snake stimuli did not affect them internally were more likely to hold a live snake or required less pressure to touch a live snake than subjects who had no information about their internal reactions. These effects were observed for subjects who were moderately frightened of snakes and for those who were more than moderately frightened.

The similarity between the false heart-rate feedback manipulation and the muscle-relaxation procedure used in desensitization therapy is obvious. Both procedures lead subjects to believe that phobic stimuli are having few internal effects. However, the rationale for the effectiveness of these procedures is quite different. We have assumed that certain cognitions are of prime importance for inducing behavior change and that these cognitions may or may not be veridical. Advocates of desensitization therapy are not very much concerned with cognition but base their rationale upon the induction of physiological incompatibility. Whatever cognitions are induced by muscle relaxation are presumably veridical. Furthermore, these cognitions may result from the successful induction of muscle relaxation to phobic stimuli but are not necessarily important for modifying behavior.

Although our results indicate that cognitions about internal reactions are important modifiers of behavior, it is, of course, not possible to conclude that successful desensitization therapy is based upon the induction of these cognitions. Nevertheless, until it has been demonstrated that a muscularly

[3] It is interesting to note that in the first adequate laboratory investigation of systematic desensitization, Lang and Lazovik (1963) found no differences in subjective fear between their desensitized and control subjects, although desensitized subjects did manifest more snake-approach behavior. Differences in fear were not observed until a 6-month follow-up interview. It is possible that our groups do not differ in fear because we have observed them before their subjective reactions could catch up with actual behavior.

relaxed subject is less physiologically responsive to a phobic stimulus than a subject who is not relaxed, we may continue to question the necessity of physiological incompatibility for desensitization therapy. Even if veridical muscle relaxation is found to be necessary, cognitions relevant to internal reactions may still mediate the behavior change. This is implicit in the arguments of Davison (1967) who has attempted to explain why the relaxation procedure used in desensitization therapy inhibits anxiety, whereas curare-induced relaxation does not. During desensitization therapy the subject consciously and effortfully induces his own relaxation, whereas with curare his muscles are relaxed by an external agent. Such a distinction is reminiscent of Schachter and Singer's manipulation of physiological arousal and information about what caused the arousal. Subjects who thought that they were aroused by an injection did not act emotional, whereas subjects who thought that they were self-aroused did act emotional. In Schachter and Singer's experiment emotion is aroused by the cognition, "*I* have reacted in this situation." Davison's distinction suggests that emotion is inhibited during desensitization therapy by the cognition, "*I* have been able to control my reactions in this situation."

SUMMARY

It was suggested that the modification of avoidance behavior by systematic desensitization is dependent upon the manipulation of cognitions about internal reactions. Two experiments were conducted to determine whether such cognitions could affect snake-avoidance behavior. In both experiments *S*s were led to believe that snake stimuli did not affect them internally. These *S*s, in comparison to suitable control *S*s, were later observed to manifest more approach behavior when confronted with a live snake. This effect was significant for *S*s who were moderately frightened of snakes and for those who were more than moderately frightened.

10

MAINTENANCE OF SELF-ATTRIBUTED AND DRUG-ATTRIBUTED BEHAVIOR CHANGE[1]

Gerald C. Davison and Stuart Valins

This research is concerned with a person's attributions about the causes of a change in his behavior. That is, given that a person is behaving in a particular manner, will the cognitive and behavioral consequences be different if the cause of it is attributed to himself than if it is attributed to an external force or agent? It will be hypothesized that behavior change which is attributed to oneself will persist or be maintained to a greater degree than behavior change which is attributed to an external agent such as a drug.

Although this research is restricted to overt behavior, much of it was stimulated by considerations of covert visceral behavior. If we define behavior as a perceptible physiological reaction, there is good evidence that different attributions about the source of this "internal behavior" will have different effects. Schachter and his associates (Nisbett & Schachter, 1966; Schachter & Singer, 1962) have clearly shown that if this internal behavior is attributed to oneself, the consequences will be different than if the behavior is attributed to an external agent such as a drug. When it is attributed to oneself, the person has some information which can lead to inferences about himself or about stimuli in the external environment. Thus, if *I* have reacted in this anger-inducing situation, then I must be angry. If *I* have reacted in this euphoric

Gerald C. Davison and Stuart Valins, "Maintenance of Self-Attributed and Drug-Attributed Behavior Change," *Journal of Personality and Social Psychology, 11,* 1969, 25–33.

[1] This research was supported by Research Grants MH 12715 and MH 14557 from the National Institute of Mental Health. We are deeply indebted to William Samuel and Michael Weiner for their persistent and expert performance as experimenters. Thanks are also due to James H. Geer for his comments on the manuscript.

situation, then I must be happy. If *I* have reacted to these electric shocks, then they must be painful. The situation is quite different, however, if the physiological reactions or internal behaviors are attributed to an external agent. The person is less able to make inferences about the external situation or about himself if his internal behavior is drug-induced. Thus, subjects do not get angry or happy (Schachter & Singer, 1962) and do not consider shocks painful (Nisbett & Schachter, 1966) if they believe that their internal behavior is drug-induced. In effect, a self-attributed visceral reaction makes us stop, look, and listen, and allows us to make certain inferences about ourselves and the stimulus situation. A drug-attributed visceral reaction provides us with little or no information about ourselves or the world.

These speculations about attribution are relevant to a psychiatric problem which is particularly serious but which unfortunately is far too often ignored. That is, how can psychiatric patients be weaned off tranquilizers? The remarkable effects that the introduction of tranquilizers has had upon the treatment of psychiatric patients is well known. It has been estimated, for example, that the patient population of mental hospitals in New York State, which for some time had been increasing by 2,000 or more every year, dropped by 500 through increased discharges during the first year in which chlorpromazine and reserpine were in general use (White, 1964). Within the hospitals still further consequences could be observed (for example, 75% fewer patients being placed on restraint or in seclusion).

Without denying the importance of these drugs, a curious problem has arisen in that it has become increasingly evident that drugs often cannot be withdrawn without causing patients to relapse (Kamano, 1966). Although drugs produce significant and beneficial behavioral changes, these changes seem to be dependent upon the continued use of the drug. When the drug is terminated, the person's behavior deteriorates. Psychiatrists have not adequately responded to this problem. The general practice is apparently to maintain patients on drugs indefinitely. Apart from the possibly adverse physiological effects of long-term drug usage, the problem is of interest for theoretical reasons. It seems to indicate that little if any relearning occurs on the part of people who take these drugs. That is, if a patient is chronically anxious or frightened by a number of things in his environment, he can be calmed down, perhaps indefinitely, by tranquilizers, but the situations that set him off originally will do so again once the drug is withdrawn. The patient has not learned that the situations are harmless.

A similar problem is evident in the animal literature. A number of studies, in particular those of Neal Miller and his associates (Miller, 1966), have found that drugs will reduce fear as evidenced by the reinstatement of a bar-pressing response which was previously associated with electric shock, but that once the drug is withdrawn, the animals stop the bar pressing. The fear response is evidently suppressed temporarily by the drug, but no relearning is apparent since it reappears once the drug is withdrawn. The animals evidently have not learned that bar pressing is no longer associated with shock. Although the animal literature is by no means consistent (e.g., Miller, Murphy, & Mirsky, 1957; Nelson, 1967), it can be summarized by saying that the transfer of a drug-produced change in behavior to the nondrug state is often difficult to find.

Granted that the problem exists and that it warrants further attention, how can we get a drug-induced change in behavior to persist into the nondrug state? Considering the experiments dealing with the labeling of visceral behavior, the answer may be quite simple. What would happen if we made someone attribute his changed behavior to himself rather than to the drug? Imagine a patient whose persistent fears have diminished due to a tranquilizer that he has been taking for some months. After this period let us convince the patient that we have substituted an inert placebo for the real drug throughout the past month. What should he conclude from this? We believe that the patient would now have to accept the responsibility for his changed behavior and because of this might make three inferences: (*a*) "The world can't be that frightening after all" (he will reevaluate the stimulus situation); (*b*) "I have succeeded and am competent" (he will feel happy and proud of himself); (*c*) "I will subsequently be able to behave differently when in stressful situations" (his expectations and aspirations for improved behavior will be higher). These kinds of inferences would seem to facilitate the maintenance of the behavior change once we have actually terminated the drug. Such subjects should maintain their improved behavior to a greater degree than those who have a drug-attribution for their behavior change.

These attribution notions lead to the following hypothesis: Subjects who are disabused of the cognition that a drug has produced certain significant changes in their behavior will be more likely to maintain these behavior changes than subjects who continue to believe that their changed behavior was due to a drug. A direct way of testing this hypothesis would be to use drugs, but for several reasons we chose not to: they require extensive pretesting; they are relatively unpredictable; and the supervision of a physician would be necessary. Additional difficulties are posed by the necessity to establish a dosage which would be strong enough to change behavior yet weak enough to convince a subject that he had "actually" received a placebo. While all these problems do not appear insurmountable, our primary interest in attribution per se rather than in drugs led to an analogical test of the hypothesis. The experiment was therefore conducted by (*a*) obtaining a premeasure of pain and tolerance thresholds using fingertip-administered electric shocks; (*b*) administering a placebo capsule which was presumably a drug; (*c*) surreptitiously lowering the overall intensities of the shocks during a second threshold procedure so that all subjects believed that they could take more electric shocks before pain was experienced and before they desired to stop than they did during the first threshold procedure; (*d*) telling half the subjects that they had received a placebo; and (*e*) assessing their reactions during a third threshold procedure during which the subjects received no pill. It was predicted that those subjects who were led to attribute their behavior during Threshold II to themselves (because they had received a placebo) would subsequently raise their thresholds more than subjects who attributed their behavior during Threshold II to a drug.

STUDY I

Method

Subjects–Subjects were male undergraduates enrolled in introductory psychology courses. As part of the course requirements, they were offered participation in two separate ½-hour experiments to be run back-to-back. The first was described as an experiment in skin sensitivity and the second as an experiment in intersensory stimulation. Subjects had no expectations about the use of electric shock or drugs.

Apparatus–The shock generator delivered 60 cycle shocks, 500 milliseconds in duration. The shock intensities for the first and third threshold tests began with 0 microamperes and increased by 200 microamperes at each step. The intensities for the second threshold test began with 0 microamperes and increased by 100 microamperes at each step. The electrodes were Grass silver-plated cup-type, 5/16 inch in diameter, taped with electrode paste to the first and third fingertips of the subject's nondominant hand.

Procedure–Structured to the subject as two independent experiments, the procedure actually entailed three shock-threshold tests, the first two administered by one experimenter and the third by another. The procedures were identical for all subjects except where noted below. The design is summarized in Table 1.

After the usual introductions, the experimenter explained that he was studying the possible effects of a vitamin compound, "parataxin," upon skin sensitivity. In order to test this, he would determine, by means of a specially constructed shock apparatus, when the subject first perceived a shock, first felt that it was "painful or unpleasant," and finally perceived it as "so painful or unpleasant that you cannot tolerate any more." A parataxin capsule would then be administered and a second threshold taken a few minutes after ingestion of the "fast-acting drug." The subject was assured that both the pill and the shocks were quite harmless. At this point each subject was asked to sign a "Subject Consent Form," which indicated that a full explanation of the experiment would be given later and that the subject could withdraw at any time. No subject withdrew from the experiment.

After attaching the electrodes the experimenter gave the subject a score sheet on which to check the shocks as they were administered; it was

Table 1: Summary of Experimental Design

Group	Procedure			
Placebo	Threshold I (Experimenter I)	Threshold II (Experimenter I) with pill	Disabuse: "It was a placebo"	Threshold III (Experimenter II)
Drug	same	same	No disabuse: "Now the drug has worn off"	same

intended thereby to make the manipulated changes at Threshold II all the more salient. One hundred shock intensities were listed, and the subject was instructed to circle those corresponding to the three threshold points described above. The first threshold test was then administered. Following this test, the subject was given the parataxin capsule and left alone "while it takes effect." After 2 minutes the experimenter returned and repeated the threshold test, except for a surreptitious manipulation of the actual shock intensities designed to make the subject believe that the capsule had changed his threshold performance. The shock intensities were halved such that, for example, when the subject received Shock Number 5 on this second threshold test, he was actually receiving half of what he had received on Threshold I for "Shock Number 5."

Up to this point the experimenter was "blind" as to experimental condition. He now flipped a card from a hidden pile of group-assignment cards, telling him whether the subject was to be in the "placebo" or "drug" group. At this point instructions varied as follows:

> *Placebo:* Would you be very surprised if I told you that you didn't get a real drug? We really just gave you a placebo pill; that is, the capsule just contained inactive sugar. We had to do this to control for what is called the placebo effect. When you do drug research, sometimes people are affected just because of the attention that you have given them, and regardless of what you have given them. To control for this effect we have divided our subjects into two groups; one group gets the real drug and another group gets the fake pill. To determine whether the drug has had an effect, we have to compare drug people with placebo people. Do you understand?

The subject's questions as to why he had taken more shock were deflected by statements like, "Well, that could happen, I guess." The subject was then sworn to secrecy and thanked for his participation.

> *Drug:* Let me check your eyes to see to what extent your pupils can dilate. This is a measure of the amount of effect the drug has had on you. I am just going to shine a small light in your eye, and there is

> nothing to be afraid of. Just hold your head steady, please. Your pupils are still not constricting completely. The parataxin is beginning to wear off though, and you should be back to normal in another minute or so.

After a second pupillary check, the experimenter said that the parataxin had, in fact, worn off. The subject was then thanked for his participation.

Threshold III–The second experimenter entered shortly after the first had left, but before he could launch into the cover story for "his experiment" the first experimenter returned and asked the subject to fill out a questionnaire which "the Department requires in experiments which use drugs." The second experimenter suggested that the subject do this during a natural pause in the experiment. (This ploy resulted in subject's construing the questionnaire as part of the "first experiment" without, however, his actually seeing it until after Threshold III.) The second experimenter then proceeded to explain that he was studying the effects of intersensory stimulation upon pain sensitivity. He was running his study in tandem with the first experiment simply because of the availability of the apparatus and for convenience of scheduling. For purposes of experimental design, the subject would have to undergo another threshold test "which you probably are already familiar with from the first experiment." After this initial threshold test, the subject would be given another, during which auditory stimulation would be interspersed. The same threshold test as in Threshold I was then administered. Naturally, this experimenter was "blind" as to the subject's condition and performance. Following this, the subject completed the questionnaire. Prior to debriefing, the last nine subjects (five placebo and four drug) were asked for a rating of a sample shock. The shock administered was that which the subject had indicated as "painful or unpleasant" on Threshold I, this bit of information having been surreptitiously left behind by the first experimenter. Several further questions were asked of all subjects before complete debriefing, namely (to placebo subjects): "I see that you took more shocks on Mr. ______'s second threshold test. Since the capsule was actually a placebo, how do you account for this?" To all subjects: "Did you see my experiment related in any way to Mr. ______'s?" "How many shocks did you expect to take on the threshold test I just gave you?" All subjects were then thoroughly debriefed.

Results

SUCCESS OF THE MANIPULATIONS. The questionnaire which the subjects had filled out "for the Department" provided supporting data that the desired effects had been achieved by the various manipulations. All subjects in the placebo group did, in fact, regard the pill they had received as a placebo and, except for two subjects, the drug subjects believed that their capsule was a true drug and that it had produced a change in skin sensitivity. The data of two drug subjects, who suspected that they had gotten a placebo and that the shock intensities had been halved, were excluded. None of the subjects considered the "two experiments" as related.

THRESHOLD PERFORMANCE. It should be noted first that all subjects took more shocks on Threshold II than on Threshold I before announcing pain and tolerance. There were also no differences between placebo and drug groups when Threshold II was compared to Threshold I (t's < 1). Thus, the two groups of subjects behaved similarly through the second threshold test, as one would expect from the random assignment of subjects to the groups.

The data of primary interest are the differences between Threshold III and Threshold I for those points at which subjects reported pain and inability to continue. As can be seen in Table 2, subjects who were disabused of the cognition that they had received a drug (placebo) took an average of 1.77 more shocks at the third threshold test before reporting pain, while subjects who entered the third test still believing that the drug had effected the changes during Threshold II did not, on the average, improve at Threshold III as compared to Threshold I. The difference between the improvement of placebo and drug subjects, however, is marginally significant. More striking are the changes for tolerance. Here placebo subjects endured 1.15 more shocks, while drug subjects took —.73, this difference being statistically reliable.

Perhaps a better way of looking at the data is to consider the improvement from Threshold I to III as a percentage of the improvement from I to II. Analyzing the data in this manner allows us to evaluate the percentage of "drug-improved" behavior which is subsequently maintained. Such an analysis also has the virtue of correcting for different degrees of behavior change from Threshold I to II. It can be seen in Table 2 that placebo subjects maintain a greater percentage of their "drug-improved" behavior than did drug subjects. The principal hypothesis was therefore confirmed: disabusing subjects of the cognition that a drug had effected improvement in their shock-taking behavior leads to greater generalization of this "drug effect" to the "undrugged" state.

Some additional findings are also of interest. It will be recalled that following Threshold III the subject was asked how many shocks he had thought he would take on that threshold. Of the 13 placebo subjects 10 (77%) indicated that they had expected to take more shock on the third threshold than on the first, while of the 11 drug subjects none expressed the expectation of taking more. This difference is highly significant ($p < .001$), suggesting that being disabused of a drug-attribution cognition increases subjects' expectations about the number of shocks they will be able to take on a subsequent test.

It will also be recalled that nine subjects were asked, following Threshold III, to rate a single shock on a scale ranging from 0 (not at all painful or unpleasant) to 100 (extremely painful or unpleasant); the shock given each subject was that rated as painful on Threshold I. Analysis of these

Table 2: Shocks Taken before Announcing Pain and Tolerance, Study I

		Pain					Tolerance				
		No Shocks			Dif-ference	% Improvement	No Shocks			Dif-ference	% Improvement
Condition	*N*	I	II	III	III–I*	III–I/II–I***	I	II	III	III–I***	III–I/II–I**
Placebo	13	6.69	10.31	8.46	1.77	75%	13.08	24.08	14.23	1.15	10%
Drug	11	7.82	13.00	7.82	0	−4%	11.73	19.91	11.00	−.73	−26%

* $p = .12$, two-tailed Placebo versus Drug.
** $p = .06$, two-tailed Placebo versus Drug.
*** $p < .05$, two-tailed Placebo versus Drug.

Table 3: Shocks Taken before Announcing Pain and Tolerance, Study II

		Pain					Tolerance				
		No Shocks			Dif-ference	% Improvement	No Shocks			Dif-ference	% Improvement
Condition	*N*	I	II	III	III–I*	III–I/II–I*	I	II	III	III–I**	III–I/II–I**
Placebo	11	10.40	26.40	14.98	4.54	37%	21.27	48.00	25.27	4.00	15%
Drug	10	10.20	24.90	11.30	1.10	13%	21.60	43.60	20.80	−.80	4%

* $p = .12$, Placebo versus Drug.
** $p < .01$, Placebo versus Drug.

data reveals that placebo subjects considered this shock to be somewhat less painful than did drug subjects ($t = 2.15$, $p < .10$, two-tailed). All subjects also rated the perceived pain of the last shock that they had taken on the final threshold. In spite of the fact that the placebo subjects had taken stronger shocks, they rated their final shocks as being no stronger than did the drug subjects. These two sets of ratings suggest that the placebo subjects reevaluated the painfulness of the shocks.

STUDY II

Method

A replication was conducted with an apparatus which permitted the delivery of shocks in smaller incremental steps. Thresholds I and III now consisted of a series of shocks increasing by 100-microampere steps while Threshold II increased in 50-microampere steps. It was thought that by using smaller increments the dependent measure would more readily reflect the subjects' ability to withstand shock. The electrodes and their placement were the same as in Study I. An added feature was a remote control unit that enabled the experimenter to deliver the shocks at some distance from the subjects, as well as to reduce by one-half the intensities of all shocks for Threshold II. As in the first study, all shocks were 500 milliseconds in duration.

This replication was identical to Study I except for a procedural change designed to improve the deception. The subject was told that *he* would have to set the shock intensities himself under the ruse that the experimenter had to monitor various physiological changes at a console at the other end of the room. It was felt that the deception would thereby be even more compelling since the subjects would now be less likely to think that the experimenter was reducing the intensity of the shocks. Dummy electrodes were taped to the forearm of the subject's nonpreferred hand for this purpose, and the shock box was positioned so that the subject could read and manipulate the decade switches. The instructions were to increase each successive shock by 100 microamperes. In all other respects the procedure followed by the first experimenter was the same as that of the first experiment. With the exception that the subject was setting the shock intensities, the second experimenter also followed the same procedure as in the first experiment.

Results

As in Study I, the manipulations were successful. Placebo subjects regarded their pill as a placebo while drug subjects believed it was a drug and attributed their improvement at Threshold II to it. Furthermore, all subjects noted significant decreases in their pain sensitivity at Threshold II and all believed that the two experiments were unrelated. The data of one drug subject were excluded, however, because he thought that the drug was still active during the third threshold test.

THRESHOLD PERFORMANCE. As in Study I, the first and second thresholds of the two groups did not differ. The placebo and drug groups did differ, however, in their change-scores between Threshold III and Threshold I for reports of pain and of tolerance. It can be seen in Table 3 that once again there is marginal significance for pain, the placebo subjects showing a mean increase of 4.54 shocks as compared to the increase of 1.10 shocks of the drug group. If we combine the probability levels for Studies I and II (cf. Stauffer et al., 1949), the marginal differences for pain are significant at the .03 level. Considering the point at which subjects stopped taking shock, placebo subjects also raised their tolerances significantly more than drug subjects. Analyzing the improvement on Threshold III as a function of the improvement on Threshold II leads to similar data: placebo subjects maintained a greater percentage of their "drug-improved" behavior than did drug subjects.[2]

As in Study I, subjects were asked how many shocks they had expected to take on Threshold III. Of the 11 placebo subjects 9 (82%) expected to take more shock than they had on Threshold I, while of the 10 drug subjects none had this expectation. This difference is highly significant ($p < .001$), replicating the corresponding finding from Study I.

Subjects were also asked to rate a single shock on a scale from 0 to 100, the shock given being that which had been rated as painful by each respective subject on Threshold I. Whereas marginal significance had been found in Study I (placebo subjects tending to rate this as less painful than drug subjects), the difference in this replication was not significant. This finding is also supported by the ratings of the last shock of the third threshold. Placebo subjects rated this shock as significantly *more* painful than did drug subjects ($p < .02$). These data suggest that although placebo subjects took more shock on the third threshold, they may not have reevaluated the painfulness of these shocks.

DISCUSSION

The results of Study I and the replication support the hypothesized importance of attribution in generalizing drug-produced behavior changes to the nondrug state. In our analogue to psychoactive drug therapy, subjects were deceived successfully into believing that a drug had significantly raised their

[2] Moreover, we find within the placebo group a "genuine" effect; that is, relative to their own Threshold I, these subjects took significantly more shocks before announcing pain ($p < .01$) and before stopping ($p < .01$). This "true effect" was not found in Study I, the actual increase for those placebo subjects not being significant, although it *was* significantly greater than the decrease observed for the drug group.

pain thresholds and increased their tolerances for electric shock. The crucial attributions were then differentially manipulated by disabusing some subjects (placebo) of the notion that their behavior change could have been caused by the capsule. Deprived of this drug attribution, subjects evidently attributed their improvement to themselves, subsequently maintaining these changes to a greater degree than manifested by control subjects, who continued to attribute their improvement at the second threshold to the drug.[3]

It is important to distinguish our findings from the well-known "placebo effect" (cf. Frank, 1961; Honigfeld, 1964). The placebo effect refers to the phenomenon whereby individuals change with an inactive substance in a direction in which they think they should change. In our own studies above, this would refer to the improvement that might have been observed at Threshold II over and above the surreptitious halving of all shock intensities. This is for our purposes uninteresting; furthermore, conclusions cannot be drawn from our data because improvement from Threshold I to II could be accounted for by adaptation, for which we did not have a control group. Our main results deal with the differences between Thresholds I and III, that is, with the *persistence* of our analogical drug-produced behavioral change on Threshold II. Our disabusing the placebo subjects of the cognition that they had received a true drug may be seen as using a placebo cognition to effect *superior* behavior change, and not as placebos are generally used, namely, as a control for the administration of a drug and the attendant expectations of gain over and above the actual drug effect.

The mechanism by which attribution effected maintenance of the behavior change has not adequately been isolated in this experiment. It was expected that one or more of three processes would be initiated when a subject observed that his changed behavior (on Threshold II) was due to himself: *reevaluation* (the subject would infer that the shocks were not as painful as he originally thought); *changes in expectations and aspirations* (the subject would infer that his subsequent behavior would resemble his behavior on Threshold II and he would be motivated to take more shock); *generation of positive affect* (the subject would be pleased and proud of his improved performance on Threshold II, and these positive feelings would raise his threshold for pain, perhaps by reducing his anxiety). Of these processes, we have data relevant to reevaluation and changes in expectations.

If reevaluation occurred we would expect that prior to the third threshold the placebo subjects would have inferred or convinced themselves that the shocks were really not as painful as they had originally believed. Their performance on the third threshold would then reflect this reevaluation. In accord with this reasoning, placebo subjects did take more shocks on the

[3] Our distinction between self-attributed and drug-attributed behavior change may seem similar in some ways to Rotter's (1966) distinction between internal and external control. We hesitate to stress this apparent similarity, however, inasmuch as Rotter restricts himself to locus of *reinforcement*, whereas it is difficult to find reinforcement operating meaningfully in our paradigm.

third threshold before announcing pain and before stopping than they did on the first threshold. Drug subjects did not. Although the changes in pain thresholds were not as strong as the changes in tolerance, both may be considered a reflection of reevaluation (the pain threshold data are understandably weaker when one considers that subjects seemed to find this a difficult judgment, one which in fact results in variances more than twice as large as that of the tolerance threshold). However, if reevaluation did occur, we might also expect that the placebo subjects would have rated the shocks lower in painfulness than the drug subjects when given the opportunity to do so after the third threshold. There was a tendency for this to occur in the first experiment but not in the second.

It is the absence of strong effects on this measure that leads us to question whether reevaluation of the shocks accounted for the placebo subjects' third threshold performance. Nevertheless, we believe that reevaluation is still a viable explanation. The fact that the subjective pain ratings do not reflect reevaluation might very well be due to their having been obtained *after* the third threshold. At this point in time, placebo subjects might have considered that, although they took more shock on the second threshold than on the first, their third threshold performance was relatively poor. Their inability to match their Threshold II performance might have then led them to infer that the shocks were more painful than they had thought *prior to* the third threshold. In other words, subjects might have evaluated the shocks as less painful after the second threshold and consequently took more shock on the third threshold, *but*, when considering that this last performance was not as good as on the second threshold, they might have inferred that the shocks really were painful. We have here two reevaluations, the second of which may have cancelled the first.

Considering now the subjects' expectations after the second threshold, it will be recalled that in both experiments placebo subjects expected to tolerate more shocks on the third threshold than on the first, whereas drug subjects did not. Although these differences in expectation were predicted, can they alone account for the differences in third threshold performance? If subjects were motivated to match their expectations to take more shock on Threshold III than on I, then behavior on the third threshold could be explained without reference to reevaluation. This is possible and not at all uninteresting. Since we were apparently successful in dissociating the two experiments, subjects would be matching their own expectations and not those of the second experimenter. We believe, however, that this explanation seems to account better for the tolerance data than for the pain data. Tolerance for shock is something that a subject could raise without deceiving the experimenter, whereas, without reevaluation, the recognition of pain could be changed only by deceiving the experimenter. Experimental subjects do not act in this manner! It seems more likely that they would reevaluate the pain of the shocks than harm an innocent experimenter.

Although this study does not permit us to accurately specify the mechanism by which the evaluation of one's behavior affects subsequent behavior, it should be clear that attitude-change research has produced data consistent with ours. Both dissonance research and the data that D. J. Bem (1967) has gathered supporting his interpretation of that research lead to the conclusion that attitude change is very much influenced by an individual's explanation for his behavior. If an individual believes that he is responsible for engaging in a behavior which is inconsistent with his own attitude, his attitude will more readily change and become consistent with this behavior than if he believes that external forces are responsible for his behavior. Thus, if there is little external justification for engaging in the behavior (e.g., it is effortful, associated with little reward, not very important to the experimenter or science), the individual is likely to interpret the behavior as self-induced. If it is self-induced the individual can best explain his behavior by forming an attitude that can account for it. Thus, in these situations we find more attitude change than in those situations where there are adequate external justifications for engaging in the behavior.

These data and speculation seem also to have interesting implications for the general area of behavior modification. As an extension of general experimental psychology, behavior therapy is essentially environmentalistic, looking to external variables for the alteration of "abnormal" behavior. The literature indicates to us little concern shown to how the individual so manipulated *perceives the reasons for his changing*. If we make what seems to be the reasonable assumption that the behavior therapy client construes agents of change to be *outside* himself, we have a situation analogous to that dealt with above, namely, a change brought about through external influence. It seems that especially the operant approaches would pose problems for the maintenance of behavior change once the artificially imposed contingencies are withdrawn (cf. Davison, 1969b); and the failure thus far to demonstrate *enduring* behavior change via operant procedures might be accounted for at least in part by the notions of attribution proposed here. If a person realizes that his behavior change is totally dependent upon an external reward or punishment, there is no reason for his new behavior to persist once the environmental contingencies change.

Likewise, consider a recent comment (Davison & Valins, 1968) made on the conflicting results obtained with the use of the barbiturate Brevital as a means to induce deep muscle relaxation during systematic desensitization (cf. Brady, 1966, 1967; Friedman, 1966; Reed, 1966). It was suggested that the use of this drug to *impose* relaxation upon an individual might create problems for the generalization of desensitization in imagination to the real life state. It has been observed from experimental studies in desensitization that the transfer of desensitization effects from the imaginal anxiety hierarchy to the life situation is not at all a simple matter (Davison, 1968b). The Brevital-desensitization work seems to be a situation identical to the core of this paper: the relaxation produced by Brevital is likely to be perceived by the person as not of his own doing. The important cognition, "I have been able to control my reactions in this situation," seems more probable when persons relax their *own* muscles than when they are relaxed by a drug (cf. Valins & Ray, 1967). This concern is quite separate from the efficacy of Brevital to enable the client to climb his imaginal anxiety hierarchy, just as the experiments reported above do not concern the changes at Threshold II; rather, we would expect that clients who attribute their relaxation during desensitization to a drug rather than to their own efforts will maintain these gains significantly less when confronted with the real situation.

SUMMARY

It is proposed that behavior changes which are believed to be brought about by oneself will be maintained to a greater degree than behavior changes which are believed to be due to external forces or agents. Within the framework of psychoactive drug therapy, a change in overt behavior which is attributed to one's own efforts should be more persistent than a change in overt behavior which is attributed to a drug. An experimental analogue of drug therapy is reported in which subjects (*a*) underwent a pain threshold and shock tolerance test, (*b*) ingested a drug (really a placebo), and (*c*) repeated the test with the shock intensities surreptitiously halved. All subjects thus believed that a drug had changed their threshold performance. Half of the subjects were then told that they had actually received a placebo, whereas the other half continued to believe that they had received a true drug. It was found that subjects who attributed their behavior change to themselves (i.e., who believed they had ingested a placebo) subsequently perceived the shocks as less painful and tolerated significantly more than subjects who attributed their behavior change to the drug.

11

SELF-CONTROL AND TOLERANCE OF NOXIOUS STIMULATION[1]

Frederick H. Kanfer
and David A. Goldfoot

Tolerance of pain can be modified by changing the stimulational input to an *S*, or by physiological and pharmacological agents which change the threshold for the pain stimulus. When continuing exposure to a pain stimulus is under *S*'s *own* control, the event can be classified under the general paradigm provided by Skinner (1953) for the operation of self-controlling mechanisms. Skinner defines self-control as a process in which a person makes a response that alters the probability of the occurrence of another response. The first of these may be called a controlling response and the second the controlled response. The self-control paradigm characteristically involves either of two types of conflict situations. In the first, *S* has available the means for terminating a noxious stimulus at any time, but continuation of exposure to the noxious stimulus is also associated with reinforcement of high magnitude. In the second, *S* can make a response which leads to immediate reinforcement, but the behavior also has ultimate aversive consequences which tend to inhibit the occurrence of the instrumental response, or to strengthen antagonistic responses.[2]

Reprinted by permission of F. H. Kanfer and D. A. Goldfoot and the Southern Universities Press, "Self-control and tolerance of noxious stimulation," *Psychological Reports*, 1966, 18, 79–85.

[1] This study was supported in part by Research Grant MH 06921-04 from the National Institute of Mental Health, United States Public Health Service, F. H. Kanfer, Principal Investigator.

[2] The first of these conflict situations is illustrated by such widely known dilemmas as that of a brave boy's pain endurance in the presence of peers, or the silence of a military prisoner in the face of physical assaults. The second type is encountered in "resistance to temptation" situations, such as those faced by the alcoholic or the obese excessive eater.

The present study utilized the first type of situation. The purpose of this study was to examine the effectiveness of several different behaviors as self-controlling responses which might alter tolerance of a noxious stimulus.

All *S*s were given the cold pressor test and asked to keep a hand in ice water as long as possible. For two experimental groups the potential self-controlling responses were verbal and related in content to the noxious stimulus. In a *Negative Set* group, emphasis on the aversive aspects of the stimulus was intended to shorten tolerance by increasing *S*'s attention to the ice water effects and arousing a repertoire of motor responses associated with pain stimuli. In a *Talk* group, the availability of competing verbal responses was intended to facilitate pain tolerance. In the remaining two experimental groups, the self-controlling responses involved *ad lib*, use by *S* of environmental objects (a timing clock or a slide projector) not directly related to the pain stimulus. These external stimuli represented potential sources of distraction for *S*.

METHOD

Subjects

*S*s were 60 female undergraduates in business and psychology courses who volunteered and were paid for their participation. Three additional *S*s began the experiment but terminated after discovering the nature of the task. All *S*s were naïve about the purpose of the experiment. *S*s were randomly assigned to five equal groups of 12 *S*s.

The Noxious Stimulus

It is known that phasic vasoconstriction and vasodilatation (Lewis effect) occur during the course of hand immersion in ice water (Lewis, 1929). Various *E*s (Carlson, 1962; Krog, *et al.*, 1960; Kunckle, 1949; Teichner, 1965) have demonstrated that this phasic phenomenon is associated with the perception of pain. Kunckle (1949) hypothesizes that cyclic pain is associated with the Lewis effect. Although this hypothesis has not been thoroughly studied, it is apparent that *S*s not manifesting the Lewis effect find the ice water task exceedingly uncomfortable (Teichner, 1965). In addition, Teichner (1965) has shown that the absence of phasic vasodilatation is in part a function of *S*'s emotional state.

Marked individual differences can be expected in this stimulus situation, then, due to both the physiological and psychological state of *S*. Since the majority of *S*s who experience the Lewis effect do so within 4½ min. (Teichner, 1965), and since Kunckle (1949), and Wolff and Hardy (1941) reported an increasing numbness for *S*s between 4 and 7 min., it was decided to expose *S*s for a maximum of 5 min. to ice water kept at a constant temperature of 1° C.

Design and Procedure

The experiment was conducted in a bare, soundproof room, softly illuminated and containing only *S*'s chair and a low table for holding the ice water pan. Precautions were taken to eliminate any distracting visual or auditory stimuli in the room, since pilot work had shown that the amount of environmental stimulation is a relevant variable in the present experimental procedure.

Each *S* was seated in the experimental room and asked to remove her rings, bracelet and watch. These items were collected and kept in the adjoining room from which *E* monitored the experimental procedure. *S*s in all groups were then told: "We are interested in measuring some physical changes that occur in people under various circumstances. For the first part of this experiment I would like you to wear these electrodes around your arm. They will measure the electrical activity in your skin. Now, when I tell you to, please place your hand in this cold water, and keep it there as long as you can." *S*'s dominant hand was placed in the water and a signal button, activated by *S*'s other hand, was used to permit *S* to make a definite decision and to provide a clear-cut response for terminating the task. In order to increase the plausibility of the stated purpose of the study, *E* excused himself at this point "to take a reading in the adjoining room." He then returned and continued with the instructions appropriate for each *S*'s particular group. Since the instructions describe the experimental treatments of the groups, they are reproduced verbatim:

> *Group I* (Control).—You might find this experience uncomfortable. Keep your hand in the water as long as you can. Be sure to let me know when you take your hand out of the water by pushing this button.
>
> *Group II* (*Verbal*, Negative set).—You will find this water very uncomfortable. Most people experience severe pain and cramping, especially in the area of the back of the hand, the palm, and in the joints of the fingers. The pain is quite severe. Keep your hand in the water as long as you can. Be sure to let me know when you take your hand out of the water by pushing this button.
>
> *Group III* (*Verbal*, Talk).—You might find this experience uncomfortable. To help you keep your hand in the water, please describe aloud your moment-to-moment sensations. Be careful to observe and to verbalize all sensations and thoughts you have pertaining to this situation. This microphone will record what you say. Try to verbalize every thought. Keep your hand in the water as long as you can. Be sure to let me know when you take your hand out of the water by pushing this button.
>
> *Group IV* (*External distraction*, Clock).—You might find this experience uncomfortable. To help keep your hand in the water, you may use this clock. It will be useful for you to know how long you have kept your hand in the water. Most people use the clock to

set goals for themselves to continue for another X amount of time. Please use the clock to help you keep your hand in the water as long as you can. Be sure to let me know when you take your hand out of the water by pushing this button.

Group V (*External distraction*, Slide).—You might find this experience uncomfortable. To help you keep your hand in the water, you may use this slide projector. Please describe aloud each slide which you look at. Press this button with your (nondominant) hand to change slides. You may change slides as often as you wish. Please use the slide projector to help you keep your hand in the water as long as you can. Be sure to let me know when you take your hand out of the water by pushing this button.

For the *Clock* group only, a large wall clock was mounted at *S*'s eye level. For the *Slide* group, a Sawyer 700 projector with remote control was arranged to project a picture in front of *S* at eye level. The projector was loaded with 100 slides of Europe. Slides varied, containing pictures of landscapes, buildings, landmarks, and people. The slides were arranged in random order and started at different points for each *S*.

The electrodes were non-functional, terminating in wires clearly leading into *E*'s monitoring room. A one-way observation screen permitted *E* to observe *S* in the soundproof room. *S* was asked to submerge her hand into the water up to her wrist, palm down, under the floating ice. *E* determined proper positioning of *S*'s hand, began timing, and left the soundproof room.

Each *S* was stopped when her hand had been in the ice water for 5 min. After completion of the cold pressor test, *S* was asked to complete a posttest questionnaire. On this questionnaire, *S* was asked: (1) to rate the discomfort of the water on a scale from 1 (mildly unpleasant) to 8 (absolutely intolerable); (2) to describe what she was thinking about while her hand was in the water; (3) to indicate any mechanisms or tricks which she might have used; (4) to indicate whether she had ever used these tricks before; (5) to predict whether she could have done better if something else were available to help her keep her hand in the water; (6) to indicate whether and how the particular self-controlling response used in her group affected her performance; (7) to rate her everyday sensitivity to pain on a scale from 1 (intolerant) to 5 (very tolerant); (8) to state what made her want to keep her hand in the water; and (9) to estimate the total duration of having kept her hand in the water.

RESULTS

The main measure of the effectiveness of the self-controlling devices was the time *S*s kept their hands in the standard ice water preparation. The mean numbers of seconds for the groups were: *Control*, 174.2; *Negative* set,

Table 1: Analysis of Variance of Toleration Time (in Sec) for All Groups

Source	*df*	*MS*	*F*	*p*
Between	4	32266.0	2.97	.05
Within	55	10869.4		
Total	59			

178.2; *Talk*, 129.0; *Clock*, 196.5; *Slide*, 271.3. An *F* test for the total number of seconds of toleration (Table 1) indicates a significant difference between groups at $p < .05$. The significant *F* value indicates that the various controlling devices differed in their effectiveness in prolonging pain tolerance. The *Slide* group showed the longest tolerance, with least tolerance by the *Talk* group.

A Neuman-Keuls test was carried out to examine further the differences among groups. The greatest difference, significant at $p < .05$, was obtained between the *Slide* group and the *Talk* group. The order of means suggests the superiority of those groups using environmental distraction responses (*Slide* and *Clock* groups) over those using verbal mechanisms, and over the *Control* group.

Several posttest questionnaire data gave frequency distributions and limited ranges which precluded use of statistical comparisons. Therefore, only descriptive statistics are given. Average water discomfort ratings were as follows: *Control*, 4.3; *Negative*, 5.2; *Talk*, 4.1; *Clock*, 4.7; *Slide*, 4.3. Similarly, when *S*s rated their tolerance of pain in everyday life, their average ratings ranged from 2.8 to 3.5, and appeared to be similar in the groups.

All *S*s were asked whether the self-control mechanism they were instructed to use affected their tolerance time. Table 2 summarizes the findings. In addition, *S*s were asked to indicate whether any further external aid would have helped them. Fifty percent of the *S*s in the *Negative, Talk,* and *Clock* groups responded in the affirmative, whereas 58.0% of the *Control* group and only 16.6% of the *Slide* group responded in the affirmative. From these data and from Table 2, it appears that the subjective appraisal of the utility of the self-controlling devices closely paralleled the toleration time data. The *Slide* group indicated the greatest satisfaction with the provided self-controlled mechanism and also performed better than the other groups.

*S*s also reported the mechanisms which they actually employed during the task, in addition to those which they were instructed to use. While 9 *S*s in the *Slide* group and 7 *S*s in the *Clock* group reported that they used no additional mechanisms, 10 *S*s in the *Negative* group, and 6 *S*s in *Control* and *Talk* groups used other self-controlling behaviors. The *Negative* group reported the greatest use of motor mechanisms. Eight *S*s said that they tried "squirming," fist clenching, etc., to reduce their discomfort and increase tolerance. The questionnaire replies suggest that, when the self-control mecha-

Table 2: Responses to the Question, "Did (the Self-Control Mechanism) Affect Your Performance?"

Response	Negative Set	Talk	Clock	Slide
Hindrance	2	3	0	0
Help	4	5	9	12
No effect	6	4	3	0

nism supplied by *E* was effective, no additional mechanisms were employed by *S*.

The results indicate that *S*s in all groups significantly underestimated the length of time they tolerated the ice water. Thirty-five *S*s underestimated this period of time, as opposed to 4 correct estimations and 9 overestimations. The *Clock* group, for obvious reasons, was not included in this analysis. A product-moment correlation between actual time and estimated time of toleration was computed, with $r = .57$ ($p < .005$, 47 *df*).

DISCUSSION

The results of this study support the hypothesis that tolerance of an aversive stimulus can be affected by providing *S* with controlling responses which he can utilize at his own discretion, without further intervention by *E*. The findings further suggest that self-control behaviors which provide some external stimulation, e.g., a clock or slides, effect greater facilitation than verbal devices. Particular parameters of the environmental distraction procedure, e.g., modality of presentation, stimulus complexity, *S*'s interest in the task, etc., remain to be investigated. Since it appears that those cues which compete with the response-produced cues associated with noxious events may further prolong toleration, it would be of interest to explore further effects of direct reduction of the pain-associated cues by self-controlling devices. For instance, if increased muscle tension or irregular breathing characterized response to the cold pressor test, then behaviors which result in normal breathing and reduced muscle tension may be effective responses to be utilized in self-control.

The low tolerance in the *Talk* group is of interest because clinicians often ascribe beneficial "cathartic" effects to verbalized reports of subjective experiences. Under the conditions of the present study, it is more plausible to hypothesize that attention to a noxious stimulus and the labelling of its aversive effects enhanced the tendency toward hand withdrawal because, in *S*'s past history, these additional responses have probably been followed by an escape response from the stimuli which are described or experienced as aversive. In the *Negative Set* group the instructions also may have resulted in increased attention to the aversive stimulus. In addition, anticipation of severe pain would be expected to arouse anticipatory motor responses designed to reduce pain. Further, *S*s indicated on the post-experimental questionnaire that the instructions in this group led them to set a tolerance goal toward longer exposure. These conflicting response tendencies produced by the instructions in the *Negative Set* group could have acted to yield the results for this group. Isolation of the contribution of each of these factors would have to be carried out in a separate experiment.

An inherent problem in research on self-control lies in the fact that most *S*s come to the experiment with well-learned self-controlling mechanisms. If a noxious stimulus must be tolerated in an experiment, and no further instructions are given, *S*s use the particular devices which they had found helpful in their past experience. In the *Control* group, for example, *S*s reported the use of many self-controlling devices including thinking of something else, counting, teeth clenching, and others. Consequently, the experimental groups in this study differed from the *Control* group mainly because *E* provided the same method for control of the tolerance response to all *S*s, or because the controlling response involved some external stimulation. With adult *S*s it would be difficult to eliminate completely the occurrence of self-instructed devices in the study of self-control. The results therefore represent only the relative increase in effectiveness of experimental mechanisms as compared to the uncontrolled and variable effects of pre-experimentally learned self-controlling responses.

The behavioral analysis of self-control reveals yet another set of variables which influence the behavioral outcome. Since the controlled response is usually an element in an approach-avoidance conflict situation, conflict theory suggests that manipulations of any of the variables which change the approach or avoidance tendency in *S* could serve as self-controlling devices. Thus, the probability of occurrence of those approach or avoidance responses could be altered by varying responses on which they are contingent. The present study has served mainly the methodological purpose of testing the utility of the Skinnerian self-control paradigm rather than establishment of substantive knowledge about different forms of self-control. The main advantage of the present approach over the traditional concept of self-control as a "voluntary" act lies in its potential for application of training methods for this behavior. It suggests that a person may learn to manipulate and control his own behavior and that the manner in which he does so is subject to learning as a function of the very same variables which affect other behaviors not commonly considered to be under *S*'s "voluntary" control.

SUMMARY

This study investigated the effects of several behaviors as potential self-controlling devices in the tolerance of a noxious stimulus. In a cold-pressor test, experimental groups were instructed: (1) to expect severe pain; (2) to verbalize aloud their momentary experiences; (3) to use a clock for setting a goal for tolerance; or (4) to view and describe slides, in order to enhance tolerance of the ice water. Duration of tolerance differed significantly, with a descending order of mean tolerance in groups (4), (3), (1), control, (2). Posttest questionnaires revealed varying use of other self-controlling mechanisms in the groups. The utility of Skinner's paradigm for the study of self-control was discussed.

12

TRANSMISSION OF PATTERNS OF SELF-REINFORCEMENT THROUGH MODELING[1]

Albert Bandura
and Carol Kupers Whalen

According to current social-learning theories, new responses are acquired and existing behavioral repertoires are maintained or modified through positive or negative reinforcements administered by external agents. Although the controlling power of external reinforcing stimuli cannot be minimized (Ferster, 1958; Skinner, 1961), self-administered primary and conditioned rewards may frequently outweigh the influence of external stimuli in governing social behavior, particularly in the case of older children and adults.

The latter phenomenon, however, has been virtually ignored both in psychological theorizing and experimentation, perhaps due to the preoccupation with infrahuman learning. Unlike human subjects, rats or chimpanzees are disinclined to pat themselves on the back for commendable performances, or to berate themselves for getting lost in cul-de-sacs. By contrast, people typically make self-reinforcement contingent on their performing certain classes of responses which they have come to value as an index of personal merit. They often set themselves relatively explicit criteria of achievement,

Albert Bandura and Carol Kupers Whalen, "Transmission of Patterns of Self-Reinforcement through Modeling," *Journal of Abnormal and Social Psychology, 69,* 1964, 1–9.

[1] This investigation was supported in part by Research Grant M-5162 from the National Institutes of Health, United States Public Health Service. The study was conducted while the junior author was the recipient of an undergraduate National Science Foundation research fellowship.

The authors are grateful to Robert Grant, Jefferson Union School District, and to Herbert Popenoe, Los Angeles City School Districts, for their assistance in arranging the research facilities.

failure to meet which is considered undeserving of self-reward and may elicit self-denial or even self-punitive responses; on the other hand, they tend to reward themselves generously on those occasions when they attain their self-imposed standards. Since self-administered rewards may serve both as powerful incentives for learning and as effective reinforcers in maintaining behavioral repertoires in humans, it is of considerable interest to determine the manner in which self-reinforcing responses are acquired.

It is likely that self-rewarding responses are to some extent directly conditioned through differential reinforcements administered initially by external agents. In this learning process the agent adopts a criterion of what constitutes a worthy performance and consistently rewards the subject for matching or exceeding the adopted criterion level, while performances that fall short of it are nonrewarded or punished. When subsequently the subject is given full control over the self-administration of reinforcers, he is likely to utilize the rewards in a contingent manner, with achieved performance levels serving as the primary discriminative stimuli.

Some recent evidence for the direct conditioning of self-reinforcing responses is provided by Kanfer and Marston (1963a) who found that when subjects were generously rewarded on an ambiguous noncontingent task they not only increased their rate of self-reinforcement, but also rewarded themselves frequently on a new learning task; in contrast, when subjects participated with an agent who grudgingly parted with limited token rewards and cautioned against excessive self-reward, the subjects exhibited considerably less self-reinforcement on both the training and generalization tasks. In addition, the incidence of self-reinforcement has been found to be partly dependent on the correctness of the subjects' responses, and on the similarity between training and generalization tasks (Kanfer, Bradley, & Marston, 1962; Kanfer & Marston, 1963b; Marston & Kanfer, 1963).

While the studies quoted above demonstrate the role of direct reinforcement in the acquisition of self-rewarding tendencies, it is doubtful that people receive much direct training in self-reinforcement on the majority of tasks they encounter, nor can performances in most situations be evaluated meaningfully independent of the accomplishments of others. Consequently, a person's self-evaluations may be importantly dependent upon the degree to which he matches the behavior of models whom he has chosen for comparison, and the self-reinforcement schedules which the models have adopted with respect to their own achievements. Some evidence for the influential role of vicarious learning is provided in recent demonstrations that social behavior may be rapidly acquired or modified as a function of observing the behavior and attitudes exhibited by models (Bandura, 1962). The present experiment, therefore, studied self-reinforcing responses as products of imitative learning.

Children participated in a task with an adult or a peer model, the scores being controlled by the experimenter. Under one experimental condition the model set a high criterion for self-reinforcement; on trials in which the model obtained or exceeded the standard he rewarded himself, while on trials in which he failed to meet the adopted standard he displayed self-denial and self-critical behavior. In a second experimental condition the model displayed a similar pattern of self-reward and self-disapproval, but adopted a relatively low self-reinforcement criterion. After exposure to their respective models the children received a wide range of scores and the performances for which they rewarded themselves were recorded.

It was predicted that children would imitate the self-reinforcement patterns exhibited by their respective models, whereas control-group subjects who were not exposed to the models would display no consistent pattern of self-reinforcement. On the assumption that children are apt to have been repeatedly positively reinforced for imitating models of the same sex and non-rewarded or negatively reinforced for opposite-sex imitation, it was also predicted that the subjects would match the self-reinforcement patterns of a same-sex model to a greater degree than that of a model of the opposite sex.

Finally, the relative effectiveness of models in shaping self-reinforcing responses may vary as a function of their prestige, competence, age status, or social power (Bandura, Ross, & Ross, 1963; Jakubczak & Walters, 1959; Miller & Dollard, 1941; Rosenbaum & Tucker, 1962). Because of differential competencies, adults are likely to exhibit more successful and rewarding responses than peers and, therefore, to the extent that children are differentially rewarded for matching adult and peer models, adults would eventually become the more powerful modeling stimuli. On the other hand, it might be argued that children would view adults as too divergent in ability to serve as meaningful models for self-evaluation (Festinger, 1954), whereas the self-reinforcement patterns exhibited by peers would be considered more realistic and, therefore, would be adopted more readily. In the present experiment, however, the adults displayed considerable variability in performance and a given subject would readily notice, from his own similarly wide range of scores, that there were little or no adult-child ability level differences on the particular task employed. Consequently, it was predicted that children would match the self-reinforcement patterns of adult models more closely than those of peer models.

METHOD

Subjects

The subjects were 80 boys and 80 girls ranging in age from 7 to 9 years. The children were drawn from six public schools participating in the Los Angeles Board of Education summer recreation program.

A male and female adult and two 9-year-old children served in the role of models. None of the subjects was acquainted with either the adult or the peer models.

Experimental Design

The children were subdivided into male and female subjects and randomly assigned to 16 experimental subgroups of 8 subjects each, and a control group consisting of 16 boys and 16 girls. Half the experimental children observed adult models, and half were exposed to peer models. In addition, half the children in both the adult and peer model conditions observed same-sex models, while the remaining children in each group witnessed models of the opposite sex. The control children had no prior exposure to the models and were tested only on the self-reinforcement task.

Procedure

A male assistant to the experimenter contacted the children individually on the playground and invited them to participate in the study. The assistant escorted each child to the experimental room and introduced him to the female experimenter and to the model, who supposedly had arrived early and was waiting for the session to commence.

In order to enhance the credibility of the experimental situation, the instructions were given to both the child and the model simultaneously, thus creating the set that the model was simply another naïve subject. The experimenter explained that the purpose of the study was to collect normative data on the psychomotor abilities of a large sample of people. In the adult-model conditions, the experimenter added that data from adults as well as from children were desired, and that it was more convenient to test the adults in school than to transport the test apparatus from place to place. The experimenter further explained that subjects were being tested in pairs so as to expedite collection of the normative data. The same explanations were given to children in the peer-model condition, except the subjects were led to believe that their partner was selected at random from the participants in the recreation program. Following these preliminary instructions, the child and the model were introduced to the bowling task that provided a means for modeling self-reinforcement responses.

Apparatus

The bowling apparatus used in this experiment was the one employed by Gelfand (1962). The equipment consisted of a miniature bowling alley with a 3-foot runway at the end of which there were three upright doweled target markers. The middle marker was labeled 10 points while the two adjacent ones were each labeled 5 points. The subjects were informed that whenever a bowling ball hit a target, the corresponding marker would drop. The target area, however, was carefully screened from view by fiberboard shields which covered the end-zone area of the runway and encircled the targets; consequently, the children had no knowledge of whether or not the bowling balls were in fact striking the targets. The experimenter further explained that occasionally the balls might bounce off the sides of the alley and, therefore, there may at times be little correspondence between the observed route of the bowling balls and the markers that drop. Actually, the experimenter sat behind the apparatus and controlled the scores by pulling appropriate strings that dropped the point markers. The models thus obtained identical scores with each subject and, similarly, all children received the same pattern of performance scores. Since the experimenter had to reset the markers after each trial and to return the bowling balls to the children from the back of the apparatus via an inclined trough, her position and activities appeared quite natural and justified.

After acquainting the child and the model with the bowling apparatus, the experimenter explained the rules of the game. The subjects would be allowed three balls per game and each would have a chance to play quite a few games. In the adult-model condition, the experimenter asked the child if he would mind letting the model take the first turn since he had to return to his work shortly, while in the peer-model condition, the experimenter's decision to let the model perform first appeared to be arbitrary.

The experimenter then called the subject's attention to a large bowl of M & M candies positioned beside the starting point of the alley within easy reach of the bowler. The subjects were given highly permissive instructions to help themselves to the candy whenever they wished, but if they did not feel like eating all the M & M's during the session they could save them in the containers provided. M & M candies were selected as reinforcers because of their high attractiveness value and low satiation properties.

Before commencing the trials, the subjects were asked to treat themselves to some candy while the experimenter set the targets. This procedure, in addition to enhancing permissiveness for self-reward, was primarily designed to identify those children who would refuse to take candy because of parental prohibitions or for other reasons. If a child refused to take any candy he was, therefore, excluded from subsequent phases of the experiment. This occurred very infrequently, affecting only approximately 5% of the children.

Patterns of Self-Reinforcement

The model performed for 10 trials of three balls each and obtained scores ranging from 5 to 30 points.

In the *high criterion for self-reinforcement* condition the model rewarded himself with candy and positive self-evaluative verbalizations only when he obtained or exceeded a score of 20. On such trials the model took one or two M & Ms and commented approvingly, "I deserve some M & Ms for that high score." "That's great! That certainly is worth an M & M treat." In contrast, on trials in which he failed to meet the adopted criterion of 20, the model denied himself candy and remarked self-critically, "No M & Ms for that." "That does not deserve an M & M treat."

In the *low criterion for self-reinforcement* condition the model, while exhibiting a similar pattern of self-reward and self-disapproval, adopted a criterion of 10 points, a relatively low level of performance. On trials in which he obtained or exceeded a score of 10, he rewarded himself with candy and made self-approving comments, while on trials in which he failed to meet the adopted standard he took no candy and criticized himself.

There was some minor variation in the magnitude of self-reinforcement; the model generally took one M & M when he performed at or slightly above criterion, and two M & Ms when he scored well above the adopted minimum level.

While the model performed his trials the child, seated next to the bowling apparatus, was engaged to help in the scoring process. The assistant stood at a nearby blackboard, recorded the appropriate number whenever a marker dropped, totaled the scores at the end of each game, and then announced them to the bowler. The child was asked to call out the number each time the marker dropped. His participation was solicited in this manner for two reasons: First, to reinforce the three-balls-per-game set so that his scores would be meaningful to him, and second, to insure that he was attending to the model's performances and self-reinforcing responses.

After completing his 10 trials the model departed, the assistant generously refurnished the candy supply, and the experimenter asked the child to take his turns. The postexposure test was conducted with the models absent in order to remove any situational pressures on the children to adopt the model's patterns of self-reinforcement.

The child then performed 15 trials of three balls each. He received scores similar to those of the model, ranging from 5 to 30 points, according to a prearranged program.

It was found during pretesting that children occasionally forgot their subscores or made errors in addition. Therefore, in the experiment proper the assistant recorded the scores on the blackboard for the child and announced the total number of points at the completion of each trial.

For the purpose of testing our hypotheses the scores were divided into three critical levels: 5, 10–15, and 20–30. Since even the model who adopted a low criterion for self-reinforcement had to reach a minimum level of 10 points before rewarding himself, and since pretest data revealed that children rewarded themselves relatively infrequently when they obtained the lowest possible score, only two 5-point trials were included. Similarly, it was not expected that scores of 20 or higher would elicit differential self-reinforcing behavior from control and experimental children since all subjects would be inclined to reward themselves for such commendably high levels of performance. For this reason, in only 5 of the 15 programed trials did children receive scores of 20 or higher. It was assumed that the 10–15

Table 1: Distribution of Mean Percentage of Self-Reinforcement as a Function of Sex of Subjects, Sex and Age of Models, and the Self-Reinforcement Criteria Exhibited by the Models

	Performance Level					
	Adult Models			Peer Models		
Experimental Treatment	5	10–15	20–30	5	10–15	20–30
High criterion						
Male model						
Boys	0	0	100	0	11	89
Girls	0	13	87	8	25	67
Female model						
Boys	0	8	92	0	23	77
Girls	0	5	95	6	16	78
Total	0	7	93	4	19	77
Low criterion						
Male model						
Boys	3	59	38	7	57	36
Girls	0	67	33	2	58	40
Female model						
Boys	0	75	25	3	67	30
Girls	0	60	40	7	60	33
Total	1	66	33	5	61	34
No model control	24	47	28			
Programed distribution	14	53	33			

performance level would be the most crucial one in differentiating the groups and, therefore, the children obtained a score of 10 or 15 on approximately half of the total trials.

Measures of Self-Reinforcement

The assistant recorded on data sheets the trials for which the child rewarded himself with candy and the total number of M & Ms taken in each self-reinforced trial. The frequency of positive and negative self-evaluative remarks by the child that matched precisely the model's verbal responses was also recorded.

RESULTS

In order to provide a picture of the children's distribution of self-reinforcement as a function of treatment conditions, the number of times each

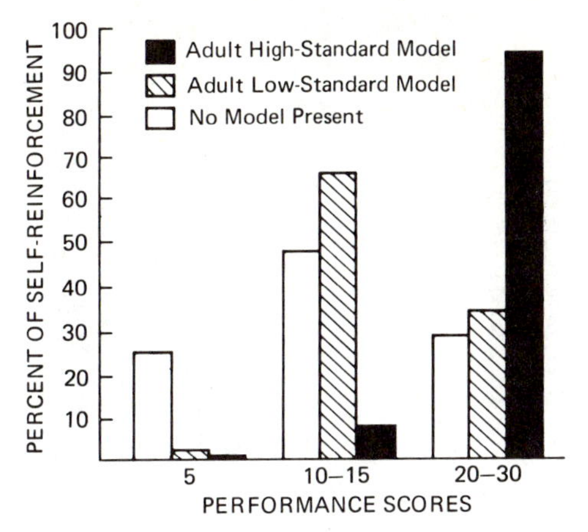

FIGURE 1. The distribution of self-reinforcement as a function of performance level by control children and those exposed to adult models adopting high and low criteria for self-reinforcement.

child rewarded himself with candy for 5, 10–15, and for 20–30 point performances, respectively, was divided by his total number of self-reinforced trials. The mean percentages of self-reinforcing responses displayed by the experimental and control groups at each of the three performance levels are shown in Table 1 and summarized graphically in Figures 1 and 2.

It should be noted that compared to the programed distribution the control children and those exposed to low-criterion models engaged in a slightly disproportionate frequency of self-reinforcement at the low or intermediate performance levels. The reason for this discrepancy is that some of the children displayed midtrial self-reinforcement; e.g., on a 20-point trial in which a child secured a score of 10 on the first roll, he might reward himself immediately rather than wait until he had completed the trial by rolling the two remaining bowling balls. In such cases the children were scored as having rewarded themselves for a 10-point performance and thus some children accumulated more 5- and 10-point trials than had been intended in the original programing.

Midtrial self-reinforcement occurred relatively frequently in the control group (23% of the total self-reinforced trials), but rarely in groups of children who observed a model exhibit either high (5%) or low (9%) standards for reinforcement. The difference between percentages of midtrial self-reinforcement for the control children and those in the combined-model conditions is highly significant ($Z = 2.53$; $p < .02$). Considering that the models consistently postponed self-reward until the completion of a trial, these intergroup differences provide some evidence that the behavior of models is influential in transmitting self-control in the utilization of readily available rewarding resources.

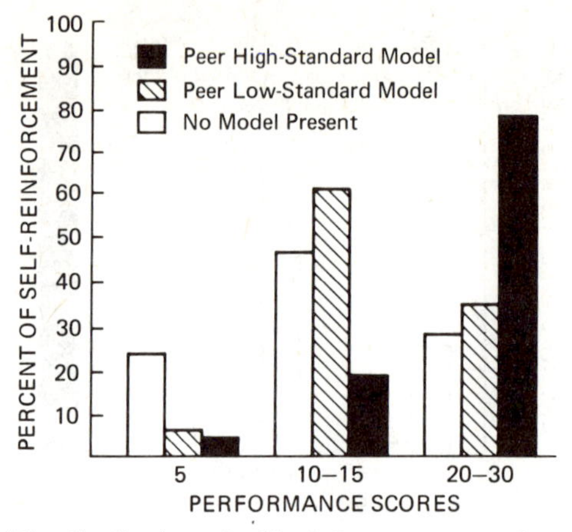

FIGURE 2. The distribution of self-reinforcement as a function of performance level by control children and those exposed to peer models adopting high and low criteria for self-reinforcement.

EVALUATION OF GROUP DIFFERENCES

The fact that the majority of children seldom rewarded themselves following performances that fell short of their model's minimum criteria precluded the use of parametric tests of significance. Consequently, in group comparisons where the obtained frequencies of self-reinforcing responses were relatively low, chi-square tests were employed based on the number of children in a condition who reinforced themselves at all after a given level of performance. The median test was utilized to evaluate the significance of differences at performance levels that resulted in a higher incidence of self-reward.

Since the results failed to reveal any significant sex-of-model or sex-of-subject influences on self-reinforcing responses, the data yielded by these subgroups were combined in testing the principal hypotheses.

AGE STATUS OF THE MODEL

As predicted, children matched the self-reinforcement patterns of the adult models more precisely than their peer counterparts. Relative to the children who observed the high-criterion adult model, children in the high-criterion peer condition displayed a slightly greater tendency to reward themselves for 10–15 point performances ($\chi^2 = 7.06$, $p < .01$). The corresponding percentages of children in these two groups were 10% and 37%, respectively.

For the high-criterion subjects a score of 5 points fell well below the model's minimum standard. Consequently, very few of these children rewarded themselves at this performance level and no significant differences between peer- and adult-model conditions were obtained. On the other hand, in the low-criterion condition, where a score of 5 approached but did not quite reach the model's minimum criterion, more of the children who observed the peer model rewarded themselves at least once for a 5-point performance (37%) than did children who were exposed to the adult model (3%). This difference yielded a chi-square value of 11.68 that is significant beyond the .001 level. At the high performance levels, of course, the children engaged in frequent self-reinforcement regardless of the age status of the model.

Because of the differential influence of the adult and peer models, data from these treatment groups were analyzed separately.

Influence of Modeled Self-Reinforcement Patterns

In order to test the statistical significance of the obtained differences attributable to modeling, separate chi-square analyses were obtained for each of the three performance levels. The chi-square values and their corresponding level of significance appear in Table 2.

These group differences may be summarized as follows: Children exposed to models adopting either low or high standards for self-reinforcement rarely rewarded themselves when performing at the lowest possible level, whereas a relatively high proportion of the control children engaged in self-reinforcement after obtaining identically low scores. At the intermediate performance level most of the children in the control and the low-criterion groups rewarded themselves, while self-reinforcement by children exposed to high-criterion models was relatively infrequent. Finally, at the high performance level children who observed the high-criterion model engaged in an exceedingly high proportion of self-reward relative to the controls and to the low-criterion model groups.

Table 2: Significance of the Difference in Self-Reinforcing Responses between Children in the Modeling Conditions and Those in the Control Group

Performance Level	Adult-Model Condition	Peer-Model Condition
	χ^2	χ^2
5 points	36.50*	15.79*
10–15 points	63.21*	33.33*
20 30 points	49.95*	40.53*

* $p < .001$.

Imitation of Self-Approving and Self-Critical Verbal Responses

Since the incidence of imitative verbal self-reinforcement was essentially the same irrespective of the sex, age status, and criterion level of the models, the experimental subgroup data were combined in the statistical analysis.

Twenty-seven percent of the experimental children reproduced precisely the models' self-approving or self-critical verbalizations in response to their own performances. In contrast, not a single child in the control group expressed any positive or negative self-evaluative statements, imitative or otherwise. This difference yielded a chi-square value of 8.12, which is significant beyond the .01 level.

Magnitude of Self-Reinforcement

The children displayed some variability in the mean number of candies taken per self-reinforced trial. Chi-square analyses revealed that generosity in self-reward was not attributable to sex-of-subjects, sex-of-models, or to differential modeling treatments. The age status of the model, however, appeared to be a significant source of variance ($\chi^2 = 10.10$, $p < .01$). On the average, a higher percentage of the children in the peer-model condition (41%) rewarded themselves in excess of their model's maximum of two candies, than did either the control children (31%) or those who observed adult models (16%).

It will be recalled that the models rewarded themselves with two candies when they obtained high scores relative to their adopted standard, but took only one candy for criterion-level performances. In order to test for any modeling effects in the distribution of magnitude of self-reinforcement the mean number of M & Ms taken per trial after scores of 20 or lower were compared by the Wilcoxon test with the means for scores of 25 and 30 points.

While the control-group children did not engage in differential amounts of self-reinforcement as a function of performance level, subjects in each of the experimental subgroups, irrespective of whether they observed adults or peers modeling high or low standards, displayed greater self-reinforcement at the higher achievement levels. In each experimental condition the Z value was significant well beyond the .01 level.

DISCUSSION

The overall results of this experiment provide strong support for the hypothesis that patterns of self-reinforcement can be acquired imitatively through exposure to models without the subjects themselves being administered any direct differential reinforcements by external agents.

This is shown clearly by the fact that children in the experimental conditions made self-reinforcement contingent on their achieving performance levels that matched the self-reward criteria of their respective models, whereas children in the control group administered rewards to themselves more or less independently of their task accomplishments. The influence of models is further reflected in the finding that a number of the children reproduced precisely the content of their model's self-approving and self-critical verbal behavior. Not only did the children adopt the model's self-rewarding standards and verbal reinforcements, but they even matched the minor variations in magnitude of self-reinforcement exhibited by the models.

There are several possible reasons for the surprisingly precise matching of the models' self-reinforcing response patterns. First, the bowling task scores did not have much absolute value, consequently they provided the subjects little basis for judging what might constitute an inadequate or a superior performance independent of some reference norm. Even if relevant normative data were available, since the subjects' performances varied widely and unpredictably the children still had no basis for evaluating their own abilities. Thus the combination of performance ambiguity and instability would tend to enhance the potency of the model's standard-setting and self-reinforcing behavior. On the other hand, had the subjects' performances been consistently low and markedly discrepant from the model's achievements, the children might very well have rejected the model's relatively high self-reinforcement standards. In order to investigate this variable systematically, a study of imitative learning of self-reinforcement patterns is planned in which groups of children will obtain relatively stable scores at varying degrees of discrepancy from the performance levels and self-reinforcement criteria displayed by the models.

In accord with prediction and findings from other investigations cited earlier, adults served as more powerful modeling stimuli than peers in transmitting both standards and magnitude of self-reinforcement. Contrary to hypothesis, however, the study failed to yield any significantly Sex-of-Model $\times$ Sex-of-Subject interaction effects. This is particularly surprising since bowling might be considered a partially masculine-typed activity and, therefore, boys should at least be more prone than girls to imitate the male model (Bandura, Ross, & Ross, 1961). While the data from the high-standard condition suggest such a trend, the differences are not of statistically significant magnitude, perhaps because of the small number of cases in the cells.

Although the children acquire positive and negative self-reinforcing responses without the mediation of direct external reinforcement, it is probable that the evaluative properties of performances which fall short of, match, or exceed a reference norm are the resultant of past discriminative reinforcements. Through the repeated pairing of performance deficits with aversive consequences and successfully matched behavior with rewards, differential achievement levels per se eventually acquired positive and negative valence. It should be noted, however, that performance-produced cues have relatively little evaluative significance apart from a selected reference norm. Once the evaluative properties of differential accomplishments are well established, adequate or inadequate matches are likely to elicit similar self-evaluative responses irrespective of the specific behavior being compared. At this stage the whole process becomes relatively independent of external reinforcement and the specific contingencies of the original training situations. As demonstrated in the present experiment, subjects will adopt the particular criteria for self-reinforcement exhibited by a reference model, evaluate their own performances relative to that standard, and then serve as their own reinforcing agents.

Theory and research relating to the process of internalization and self-control have generally focused on *resistance to deviation* and the occurrence of *self-punitive responses* following transgression. Perhaps an even more prevalent and important behavioral manifestation of self-control is the manner in which a person regulates the self-administration of highly rewarding resources. Thus in the experiment rewarding resources were readily available and their use was socially permissible; nevertheless, the groups of children differed markedly in the extent to which they utilized the reinforcers to obtain self-gratification. Children presented with low-criterion models were highly self-indulgent, rewarding themselves on the average more than twice as frequently as children in the high-criterion condition who displayed considerable self-denial. In the case of the control children, self-rewards were apparently freely dispensed and not made contingent on meeting or surpassing any minimum standard of achievement. These group patterns may be regarded as prototypic of cultures in which the majority of adults consistently display self-denying (Eaton & Weil, 1955) or self-indulgent (Hughes, Tremblay, Rapoport, & Leighton, 1960) behavior and, having limited opportunity to observe other behavioral examples, the children tend to model themselves after the prevalent self-reinforcement patterns.

In discussions of psychopathology and psychotherapy attention is frequently directed to the presence of behavioral deficits or to anxiety- and guilt-motivated inhibitory tendencies. A large proportion of the clients seeking psychotherapy, however, present relatively competent repertoires and are not excessively inhibited in their social behavior. These clients experience a great deal of self-generated aversive stimulation and self-imposed denial of positive reinforcers stemming from their excessively high standards for self-reinforcement, often supported by comparisons with historical or contemporary models noted for their extraordinary achievement. This process frequently gives rise to depressive reactions, a lessened disposition to perform because of the unfavorable work to self-reinforcement ratio, and efforts to escape the self-generated aversive stimulation through alcoholism, grandiose ideation, and other modes of avoidant behavior. In these cases, the modification of standards for self-reinforcement would clearly constitute a principal psychotherapeutic objective (Bandura, 1969).

SUMMARY

In a test of the hypothesis that patterns of self-reinforcement are acquired imitatively, one group of children observed either peer or adult models who adopted a high criterion for self-reinforcement, a second group was exposed to models who exhibited a similar pattern of self-reward and self-disapproval, except they adopted a relatively low criterion, while children in a control group observed no models. A postexposure test revealed that the children's patterns and magnitude of self-reinforcement closely matched those of the model to whom they had been exposed. Adults generally served as more powerful modeling stimuli than peers in transmitting self-reinforcing responses.

13

RELATIVE EFFICACY OF SELF-MONITORED AND EXTERNALLY IMPOSED REINFORCEMENT SYSTEMS[1]

Albert Bandura
and Bernard Perloff

It has been abundantly documented by research that behavior is governed to some extent by its consequences. However, investigations of reinforcement processes have involved limited forms of reinforcing feedback, characteristically produced by externally controlled operations in which an experimenter imposes a particular contingency upon an organism and delivers reinforcing stimuli whenever the appropriate responses are displayed. While this system of behavioral control may be adequate in accounting for responsivity in infrahuman organisms, it is considerably less efficacious when applied to human functioning which is self-regulated to a greater degree. Unlike rats or chimpanzees, persons typically set themselves certain standards of behavior, and generate self-rewarding or self-punishing consequences depending upon how their behavior compares to their self-prescribed demands.

In recent years there have been numerous investigations of the conditions governing the acquisition of behavioral standards and self-reinforcing responses (Bandura, Grusec, & Menlove, 1967; Bandura & Kupers, 1964; Bandura & Whalen, 1966; Marston, 1965a; Mischel & Liebert, 1966). Although these studies have shown that after persons adopt a self-monitoring system their performances arouse positive and negative self-evaluative reactions, there has been no adequate demonstration that self-administered

Albert Bandura and Bernard Perloff, "Relative Efficacy of Self-Monitored and Externally Imposed Reinforcement Systems," *Journal of Personality and Social Psychology, 7*, 1967, 111–116.

[1] This research was supported by Public Health Research Grant M-5162 and by Predoctoral Fellowship FI-MH-34,248 from the National Institute of Mental Health.

consequences do, in fact, possess reinforcing capabilities. The major purpose of the present study was therefore to test the efficacy of self-monitored reinforcement, and to compare it to that of an externally imposed system of reinforcement.

A self-reinforcing event includes several subsidiary processes, some of which have been extensively investigated in their own right. First, it involves a *self-prescribed standard of behavior* which serves as the criterion for evaluating the adequacy of one's performances. The standard-setting component has received considerable attention in studies of aspiration level.

In the case of most performances, objective criteria of adequacy are lacking and hence, the attainments of other persons must be utilized as the norm against which meaningful self-evaluations can be made. Thus, for example, a student who achieves a score of 120 points on an examination, and whose aspirations are to exceed modal levels, would have no basis for either positive or negative self-reactions without knowing the accomplishments of others. A self-reinforcing event, therefore, often involves a *social comparison process.*

Third, the *reinforcers are under the person's own control*; and fourth, *he serves as his own reinforcing agent.* These various defining characteristics guided both the form of the self-monitored reinforcement system and the types of controls that were instituted.

The capacity to maintain effortful behavior over time is perhaps the most important attribute of a reinforcement operation, and consequently it was this property that was tested in the present investigation. Children performed a task in which they could achieve progressively higher scores by turning a wheel on a mechanical device. Subjects in the self-monitored reinforcement condition selected their own performance standard and rewarded themselves whenever they attained their self-prescribed criterion. Children assigned to an externally imposed reinforcement condition were yoked to the self-reward group so that the same performance standard was set for them and the reinforcers were automatically delivered whenever they reached the predetermined level.

In order to ascertain whether subjects' behavioral productivity was due to the operation of contingent self-reinforcement or to gratitude for the rewards that were made available, children in an incentive-control group performed the task after they had received the supply of rewards on a noncontingent basis. A fourth group worked without any incentives to estimate the response maintenance value of the task itself.

It was predicted that both self-monitored and externally imposed reinforcement systems would sustain substantially more behavior than conditions in which rewards were bestowed noncontingently or were absent altogether. No hypothesis was put forward concerning the relative efficacy of the two systems of reinforcement, since there exists no adequate theoretical basis for a differential prediction.

METHOD

Subjects

The subjects were 40 boys and 40 girls drawn from two elementary schools in a lower middle-class area. The children's ages ranged from 7 to 10 years.

Apparatus

The apparatus consisted of a rectangular box, the front face of which contained a vertical plastic-covered aperture ½ inch wide by 16 inches high divided into four equal sections. Contained within this upright column were four score-indicator lamps, each one capable of illuminating one and only one of the translucent sections. Directly adjacent to the sections were mounted, in ascending order, the corresponding numbers 5, 10, 15, and 20, signifying four performance levels.

The score indicator lamps were activated in an ascending order by turning a wheel located at the bottom of the apparatus. It required eight complete rotations of the wheel to advance 5 points, so that a total of 32 cranking responses was necessary to attain a 20-point score.

A criterion-selector switch, which could be turned to any one of four positions corresponding to the scores next to the lights, was mounted on the front panel of the apparatus. The electrical circuit was so designed that whenever the selected performance standard was attained a chime sounded and the lights were automatically extinguished, signifying the completion of the trial. For example, in the case where a 20-point standard was chosen, the lamps adjacent to the numbers 5, 10, 15, and 20 would be illuminated after 8, 16, 24, and 32 rotations of the wheel, respectively, and then all of them would simultaneously extinguish.

Contained within the upright section was an automatic chip dispenser which delivered plastic tokens into a bowl mounted in front of the apparatus. The bountiful supply of tokens was hidden from view since their public display would not only provide children with a basis for comparing their earned rewards with the maximum possible, but it might also produce erroneous hypotheses about normative performance on this task. These factors, if uncontrolled, could have served as extraneous determinants of responsivity in the contingent-reinforcement conditions.

Located above the chip receptacle was a button which, when pressed, released a token into the bowl. A remote control device was constructed that was capable of performing the same operations as the selector switch and the token delivery button, and when necessary, rendering them inoperative.

Procedure

The introductory phase of the experiment was the same for all subjects. The children were brought individually to a mobile laboratory, ostensibly to test some game equipment. After the experimenter explained and demonstrated the operation of the apparatus, the children were given a practice trial to familiarize themselves with the task.

Small plastic tokens served as the reinforcers or incentives in those treatment conditions that required them. Children who received contingent reinforcement—either self-administered or externally applied—were informed that the tokens would later be exchanged for prizes, and the more tokens they obtained the more valuable the redeemable prizes. The incentive control subjects, who were given tokens on a noncontingent basis, were also informed that the chips they possessed would be traded later for prizes.

Several procedures were instituted in order to remove any extraneous social influences on subjects' responsivity. It was explained to children in all groups that they would perform the task alone in the room because the experimenter had some other work to do, and they might work at it as long as they wished. They were asked to notify the experimenter, who was in another room of the mobile laboratory, after they no longer wished to continue the activity. Moreover, children in the self-reinforcement condition selected their performance standard after the experimenter had departed. To remove any concern that the experimenter might evaluate their behavioral productivity from the number of tokens accumulated, the children were instructed to place the banks in which they deposited their tokens in a sealed paper bag; a second experimenter would collect the banks later that day and return with the prizes in a few weeks. Finally, to control for the possibility that children's response output might be partly determined by the classroom activities they were missing, subjects in all four conditions were tested during the same instructional periods.

Children in the *self-monitored reinforcement* condition were informed that they would have to decide which performance standard they wished to set for themselves, and then to return to selector switch to that level. In addition, they were instructed to treat themselves to tokens whenever they attained their self-imposed standard. Since these subjects had full control over the token rewards, they were free to choose their own magnitude of self-compensation on any given trial.

The children were further told that after they had selected the performance level they desired to attain, they could, if they wished, change it once, but only once, during the remainder of the session. This procedure was employed for two reasons: first, observation of self-reinforcing behavior occurring under naturalistic conditions reveals that individuals rarely shift their behavioral standards capriciously. Rather, persons usually adhere to their adopted standards and change them only as a result of cumulative feedback experiences. Therefore, an effort was made to elicit from children criterion-selection behavior which could be somewhat analogous to that occurring in everyday life.

The second reason for allowing the self-reinforcement group only one modification in their standards was related to the yoking requirement of the experiment. In order to control for the influence of behavioral standards upon responsivity across the four treatments, the performance requirements adopted by a child in the self-reward group were applied to the subject paired with him in each of the remaining conditions. Thus, for example, if a particular child in the self-monitoring group initially selected a criterion of 15 and after 20 trials lowered it to 10, this same pattern of standards was set for his yoked counterpart in each of the three comparison groups.

It is possible that any one of the children in the other conditions might persist longer than the self-reward subject to whom he was matched. If the standard selection had been highly changeable, there would be no basis for deciding what criterion to impose upon him for the remainder of the session. The limitation that standards be modified only once created a situation in which most self-reward children effected their allotted change before terminating the session, thus establishing the final performance requirement. In fact, 16 of 20 subjects had made the change before discontinuing the task. Therefore, it was meaningful to apply the standard last employed by the self-reward subject to children in the other conditions who might display more endurance than their matched partner.

After the instructions were completed, the children were handed a token bank, and left alone to perform the task as long as they wished.

Children in the *externally imposed reinforcement* system were yoked according to the procedure described above, so that the performance standard was fixed for them and the tokens were automatically delivered by the machine whenever they reached the prescribed performance level. They also received the same magnitude of reward as children in the self-reinforcement condition, that is, if a subject in the self-reward group treated himself to two tokens on a given trial, the machine would dispense two chips on the same trial to the paired counterpart in the external-reinforcement condition.

Subjects in this group were told that the machine determined the performance standard, and upon reaching it the tokens were automatically delivered. The token dispenser and the standard setting were, in fact, controlled by the experimenter from a remote console in an adjoining observation room.

Children in the "inheritance" or *incentive-control* condition were given at the beginning of the session the entire amount of tokens accumulated by their partner in the self-reward group. As in the previous treatment, the children were told that the machine regulated the performance standards operative at any given time. Another *control group* of subjects performed the task without receiving any tokens whatsoever to evaluate the response maintenance capacity of the game itself.

There are two important elements within a self-reinforcing event whose independent effects must be assessed before persistence of self-reinforced behavior can be meaningfully interpreted. These are (*a*) the self-imposition of an achievement standard, and (*b*) the self-administration of rewards. In order to examine the performance increments, if any, due to imposing a standard alone, a second study was conducted. The behavioral output of 10 children allowed to select the performance standard for which they endeavored was compared to that of 10 yoked subjects for whom the same standard was externally imposed; neither group, however, received any token rewards.

Dependent Measures

The number of cranking responses performed by the children, which constitutes the major dependent variable, was mechanically recorded. In addition, the experimenter recorded the performance standards selected by the self-reward children, and the number of reinforcers that they administered to themselves on each trial. A second observer, who scored independently the latter responses of 15 subjects, was in perfect agreement with the experimenter.

RESULTS

BEHAVIORAL PRODUCTIVITY

Figure 1 presents the mean number of effortful cranking responses performed by boys and girls in each of the four conditions of the main experiment. Analysis of variance of these data disclosed a highly significant main effect due to reinforcement conditions ($F = 15.56$; $p < .001$).

In order to determine the specific differences contributing to the overall treatment effect, separate t tests were computed for pairs of conditions. These analyses revealed that self-monitored and externally imposed reinforcement were equally efficacious ($t = 1.62$), but both reinforcement systems sustained substantially more behavior than either noncontingent rewards or a nonreward condition. Children who reinforced their own behavior generated significantly more responses than children in the incentive-control group ($t = 3.91$; $p < .001$), or the no-incentive condition ($t = 3.87$; $p < .001$). The corresponding t values for comparisons between external re-

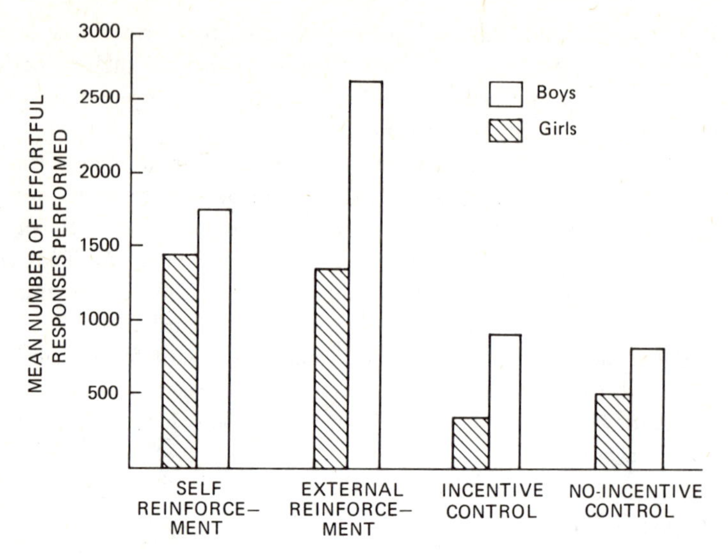

FIGURE 1. Mean number of responses performed as a function of sex and type of reinforcement system.

inforcement and the incentive-control and no-incentive-control groups were $t = 5.53$ ($p < .001$) and $t = 5.49$ ($p < .001$), respectively. It is also interesting to note that rewarding subjects noncontingently did not produce a significant increment in performance as revealed by comparison with the behavior of children who performed the task without any external incentives ($t = 0.04$).

The analysis also revealed that boys generated more responses than girls ($F = 13.09$; $p < .001$). Although no significant interaction effect was obtained between sex and treatment conditions, external reinforcement produced more behavior in boys ($t = 2.45$; $p < .05$) than the self-monitored system.

Children who set their own performance standards without engaging in self-reinforcement produced a mean number of 369 cranking responses, whereas the corresponding mean for the yoked controls was 586. Statistical analysis of these scores yielded no significant difference ($F = 1.56$) between the groups, thus indicating that self-imposition of a standard alone has no response maintenance value.

Self-Imposition of Performance Demands

The four performance standards employed in the present experiment essentially correspond to advancing fixed-ratio schedules of 8, 16, 24, and 32 responses for each self-reinforcement. Table 1 presents the standards ini-

Table 1: Self-Imposed Standards and Associated Magnitude of Self-Reward

*S*s	1st Standard	Mean No. Rewards	2nd Standard	Mean No. Rewards
Boys				
1	10	1.00	No change	
2	10	1.00	5	1.09
3	15	1.00	20	1.18
4	15	1.00	20	1.00
5	15	0.98	No change	
6	20	1.11	5	1.02
7	20	1.00	10	1.06
8	20	1.00	10	0.90
9	20	1.00	15	1.00
10	20	1.00	No change	
Girls				
1	10	1.00	15	1.00
2	10	1.11	20	1.14
3	15	1.00	5	1.04
4	15	1.00	20	1.00
5	15	1.04	20	1.12
6	15	1.00	No change	
7	20	1.00	5	1.05
8	20	1.00	5	0.93
9	20	1.21	5	1.02
10	20	1.00	10	1.00

tially adopted by children in the self-monitoring condition, the performance demands that they imposed upon themselves in later phases of the experiment, and the average magnitude of self-reward associated with the achievement of each standard.

It is apparent from these data that the children did not behave in ways that would maximize rewards. Not a single child chose the lowest ratio schedule, and approximately half the children self-prescribed the most austere schedule of self-reinforcement (i.e., 32 responses for each self-reward). Moreover, a third of the children subsequently altered their initial standard to a higher level, without a significant commensurate increase in amount of self-reward, thereby imposing upon themselves a more unfavorable work-to-reinforcement ratio.

It is also interesting to note that three children occasionally did not reward themselves after attaining their chosen criterion. In two of the three cases this occurred after they had reduced their performance standard drastically. At times these children apparently did not regard their low performances as sufficiently meritorious to warrant self-reward.

DISCUSSION

Results of this study disclose that self-monitored reinforcement possesses considerable behavior maintenance value. Moreover, the high response productivity engendered by this system was not due to merely the self-imposition of a performance standard, or availability of positive incentives.

Although self-regulated and externally imposed reinforcement did not differ in their capacity to sustain behavior, there was some suggestive evidence that, within the age range studied, boys might be more responsive under conditions of externally determined than of self-governed reinforcement, while for girls both systems are equally efficacious. These findings are consistent with those of developmental studies (Sears, Rau, & Alpert, 1965), showing that sex differences in adult-role behavior and various indexes of self-control generally favor the girls. The obtained sex difference in response productivity under all treatment conditions is most likely due to the fact that the task required some physical effort, and consequently the boys' higher output simply reflects their greater strength.

A supplementary finding of considerable interest is the prevalence with which children imposed upon themselves highly unfavorable schedules of reinforcement. This behavior is all the more striking considering that the self-imposition of high performance demands occurred in the absence of any social surveillance and under high permissiveness for self-reward. Evidence obtained from experiments investigating the acquisition of self-reinforcing behavior (Bandura & Kupers, 1964; Bandura & Whalen, 1966; Bandura et al., 1967) throws some light on the probable mechanism governing this apparently irrational behavior.

The above studies demonstrate that after a person has adopted a standard of what constitutes a worthy performance, attainments that fall short of self-prescribed norms generate negative self-evaluative reactions, whereas those that match or exceed the guiding standard give rise to positive self-evaluations. Hence, under conditions where persons are provided with ample opportunities to optimize their material outcomes by engaging in behavior which has low self-regard value, strong conflicting tendencies are likely to be aroused. On the one hand, individuals are tempted to maximize rewards at minimum effort costs to themselves, but on the other hand, low quality performances produce negative self-evaluative consequences which, if sufficiently strong, may inhibit generous self-compensation. Indeed, many of the children in the experiment set themselves performance requirements that incurred high effort costs at minimum material recompense. These findings are at variance with predictions from reward-cost theories unless these formulations are extended to include the self-esteem costs of rewarding devalued behavior.

The foregoing discussion has been primarily concerned with conflicts that might arise between two forms of self-reinforcing tendencies and how their resolution results in selective self-reinforcement under the discriminative control of performance standards. Of equal importance is the recurring phenomenon in which self-generated consequences conflict with externally occurring outcomes, as when certain behaviors are reinforced by particular social agents, but if carried out would give rise to self-critical reactions. Conversely, response patterns may be effectively maintained by self-reinforcement operations under conditions of minimal external support. It is perhaps due to the stabilizing effects of self-reinforcement that persons do not ordinarily behave like weathervanes in the face of conflicting patterns of external contingencies which they repeatedly encounter in their social environment.

In view of the demonstrated efficacy of self-monitored systems, it would be of interest to explore further the extent to which self-reinforcement may substitute for, supplement, or override the effects of externally occurring outcomes. It would likewise be of considerable import to determine the degree to which overt behavior can be regulated by covert self-reinforcing operations which rely upon self-generated symbolic consequences in the form of self-satisfaction, esteem-enhancing reactions, or self-deprecation.

Although many children selected unusually high performance standards for themselves and did not lower them to enhance their fortunes, other children self-imposed equally lofty standards of achievement but later settled for a relatively mediocre level of productivity. Further research is needed to establish the conditions determining both the initial imposition of behavioral requirements for self-reward, and the direction in which self-reinforcement contingencies might subsequently be altered.

SUMMARY

This experiment was designed to test the behavior maintenance capabilities of self-monitored reinforcement and to compare it to that of an externally-imposed system of reinforcement. One group of children selected their own performance standards and rewarded themselves whenever they attained their self-prescribed level. For a 2nd group of children the same behavioral standards were imposed and the reinforcers were externally administered. *S*s in the control groups performed either without any incentives, or received rewards on a non-contingent basis. The results disclose that self-monitored and externally applied reinforcement were equally efficacious, but both reinforcement systems sustained substantially more responsivity than did the control conditions. Contrary to expectation from reward-cost theories, most of the children imposed upon themselves highly unfavorable schedules of reinforcement which incurred high effort costs at minimum self-reward.

14

FEAR REDUCTION AND FEAR BEHAVIOR

PROBLEMS IN TREATING A CONSTRUCT[1]

Peter J. Lang

Despite the fact that most theorists and clinical workers are convinced that autonomic responses are a significant part of fear and anxiety, little effort has been made to directly train this response system.

Programs designed to control these somatic responses have been almost exclusively restricted to drugs. While this approach has proved palliative, it has seldom permanently changed the subject's emotional life. The drug effects generally persist only so long as the drug is taken, and if the initiating circumstances return, the subject's somatic response reappears, unaltered. Efforts at retraining autonomic responses have been few—perhaps because authorities in the field have long argued that the instrumental conditioning of the autonomic nervous system is impossible (Kimble, 1961; Morgan, 1965). Only Jacobson (1938) and Schultz and Luthe (1959) have argued for such training in therapeutic setting, and these workers emphasized the important mediating function of the striate musculature. However, data has been accumulating which suggests that patients could learn to control autonomic responses. Fowler and Kimmel (1962) and Kimmel and Kimmel (1963) have reported that spontaneous GSR's may be treated as free operants, and that their reinforcement leads to a relative increment in their occurrence. These findings have been confirmed by Rice (1964), who nevertheless, signaled the role of

Peter J. Lang, abridged from "Fear Reduction and Fear Behavior: Problems in Treating a Construct," *Research in Psychotherapy, 3*, 1968, 90–102.

[1] This research was supported by Grant No. MH 10993 from the National Institute of Mental Health, United States Public Health Service.

muscle potential changes in the acquisition of the response, and more recently by Crider, Shapiro, and Tursky (1966).

Considerable work has also been done on the operant control of the cardiovascular system. Razran (1961) reported a study by Lisina in which this investigator demonstrated conditioned vasoconstriction and vasodilation of the forearm. More recently Snyder and Noble (1966) reported operant conditioning of digital vasoconstriction. Shearn's (1962) demonstration that cardiac rate accelerations could be brought under operant control has been confirmed, and work extended by Frazier (1966) and Jasper Brener (1966). All three of these latter workers used electric shock as a reinforcing contingency.

In our own laboratory we have been studying the ability of human subjects to stabilize and reduce cardiac rate when they are simply provided with appropriate feedback and given instructions to apply themselves to that task. In a recent study (Hnatiow & Lang, 1965) experimental subjects were instructed to maintain cardiac rate within a target area of six beats per minute (bpm). To facilitate this task, they were presented with a display in which lateral movements of a pointer were synchronized with beat-to-beat acceleration or deceleration of heart rate. The central, six beat range was marked in red, and subjects were told to maintain the pointer within this area. Figure 1 shows the display used in this research and two interpulse interval histograms taken during successive nondisplay and display periods. The marked reduction in variability during display periods was characteristic of the experimental group, who showed a significantly smaller heart rate standard deviation than did a control group that received no meaningful feedback. Analysis of respiration rate, inspiration to total cycle ratio, and depth of respiration revealed no significant relationship between heart rate stabilization and any of these respiratory variables.

An experiment just completed (Lang, Sroufe, & Hastings, 1967) was designed to explore the effects of instruction and task variables on this process. Lacey (1959) and others have noted that continued attention (such as might be required by this task) leads to decrease in cardiac rate and an associated reduction in rate variability. This experiment compared the cardiac feedback display situation with a tracking task, which could be expected to produce the effects suggested above. We also separately evaluated stabilization under the following conditions: (*a*) the display is correctly interpreted to the subject, (*b*) he receives the display but no information about its meaning, and (*c*) the display is interpreted as providing feedback, but it is not actually synchronized with the subject's heart rate.

Subjects for this experiment were 60 male college students, randomly assigned to one of two groups of yoked subjects. Subject pairs were run concurrently in separate, darkened, sound-shielded room, and heart rate and respiration was recorded continuously from both subjects.

After approximately 15 minutes of rest, a meter display was presented

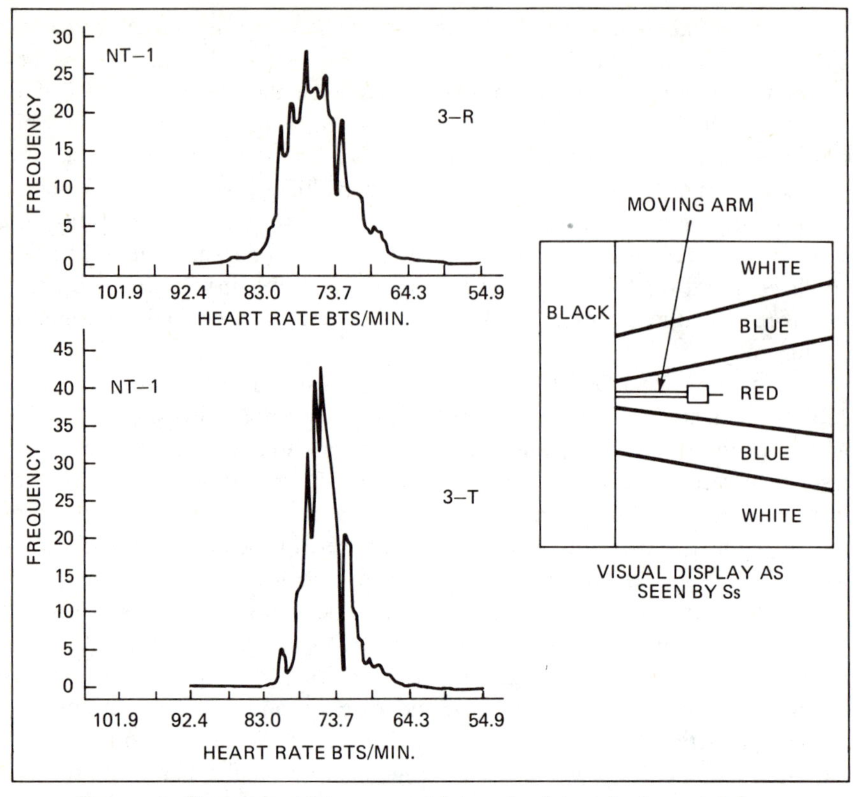

FIGURE 1. Frequency histograms of interpulse intervals (reported in beats per minute) taken from a single subject on consecutive 5-minute test periods. The originals were plotted by a 400B computer of average transients and written out on a Leeds and Northrup recorder. Curve ND-3 shows the pulse distribution when subject received no information about his cardiac rate; Curve D-3 was obtained during the succeeding trial in which subject observed a visual display of his concurrent heart rate. This display is shown at the right side of the figure (Hnatiow & Lang, 1965. © 1965, The Williams & Wilkins Co., Baltimore, Md. 21202, U.S.A.).

for 5 minutes. Two more display periods were presented subsequently with 5-minute nondisplay periods in between. Subjects were selected and instructed in such a fashion that they were unaware that another subject was concurrently participating in the same experiment.

For one member of each yoked pair, the meter display is a representation of his beat-to-beat changes in cardiac rate. The meter is arranged during the initial rest period so that the center area of the meter is the subject's average heart rate. The full range of the meter is approximately 40 bpm. The other member watches exactly the same display as his yokemate (i.e., he watches the other subject's heart rate changes).

The two groups (pair sets) were given different instructions: Group I was told that the display represented beat-to-beat changes in their own cardiac rate. They were further instructed to maintain the meter pointer in the exact center of the dial, so as to keep a steady heart rate. Thus one member of the pair was correctly informed about the task (I-E), while his control was given the same instructions, but did not receive appropriate feedback (I-C).

Group II was given the task of visually tracking the meter display. They were told to press a microswitch (a very small thumb movement) whenever the meter pointer entered certain preselected areas. They were instructed to pay close attention to the meter, while trying to meet the main experimental task of maintaining a steady heart rate. Neither the subject receiving correct feedback (II-E) nor the subject observing his yokemate's cardiac changes (II-C) was told that the display represented variations in cardiac rate.

Figure 2 shows time in the six beat target area for subjects receiving correct feedback, who were also instructed to use the meter to control their heart rate (I-E), and for subjects who were misdirected to a tracking task

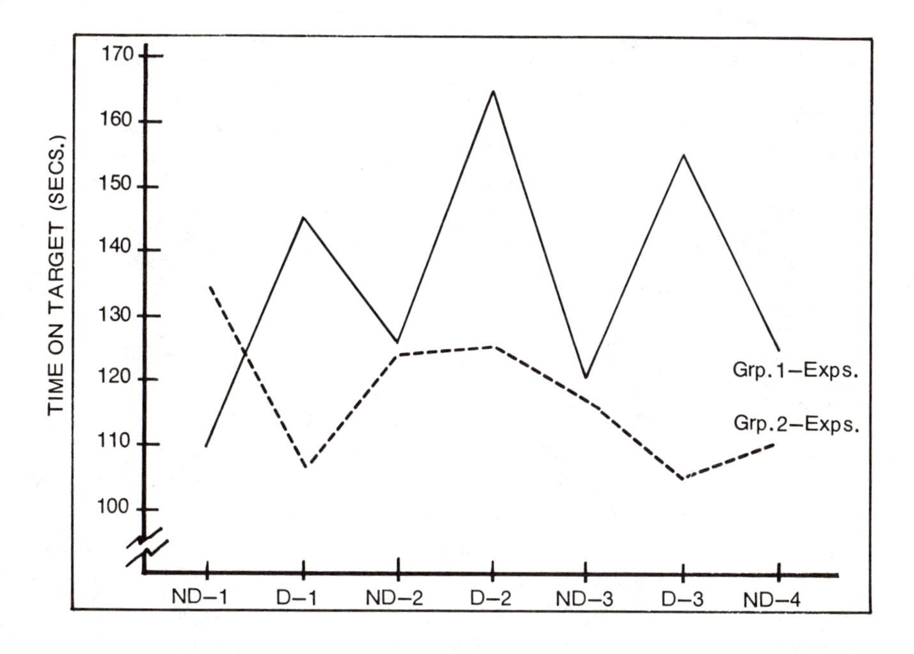

FIGURE 2. Changes in total time subjects' heart rate remained within the target range (6 bpm) for successive nondisplay (ND) and display (D) trials. (From P. J. Lang, L. A. Sroufe, and J. Hastings, "Effects of Feedback and Instructional Set on the Control of Cardiac Rate Variability, *Journal of Experimental Psychology, 75*, 1967, 425–431. Copyright 1967 by the American Psychological Association, and reproduced by permission.)

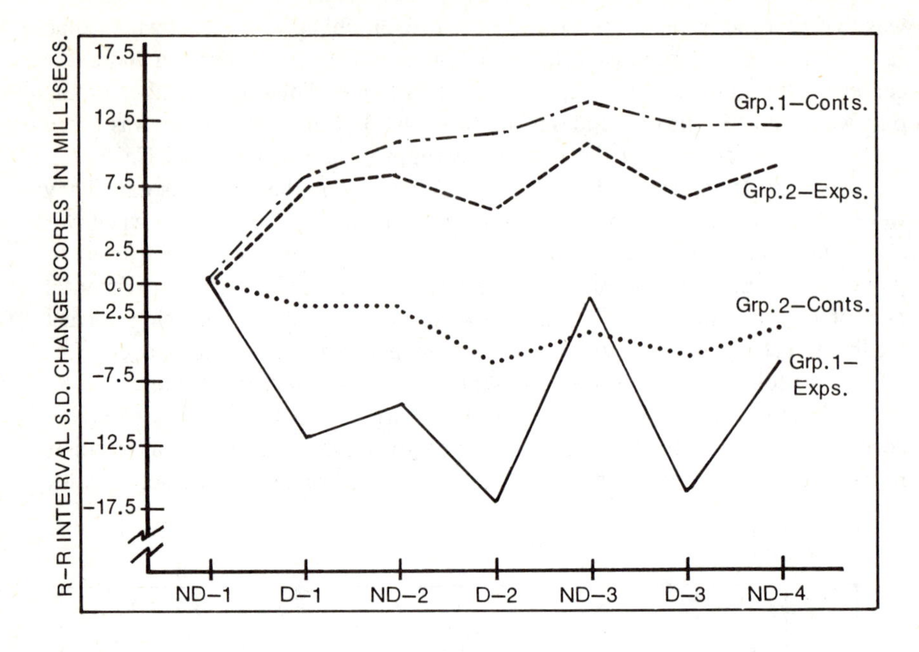

FIGURE 3. Average R-R interval standard deviations of experimental and control subjects for consecutive nondisplay (ND) and information display (D) trials. From P. J. Lang, L. A. Sroufe, and J. Hastings, "Effects of Feedback and Instructional Set on the Control of Cardiac Rate Variability, *Journal of Experimental Psychology, 75,* 1967, 425–431. Copyright 1967 by the American Psychological Association, and reproduced by permission.

(II-E). Relative increase in time-on-target is apparent for the subjects utilizing feedback to steady heart rate.

During the experiment the EKG of both members of a pair was continuously recorded on magnetic tape. Subsequently this information was replayed, through an appropriate interface, into a TMC computer of average transients. The R wave of each cardiac cycle initiated a time based scan of the 400 addresses of the computer; the next cardiac cycle stopped the scan, recorded a count at this address, and reinitiated a new scan within 50 microseconds. This was accomplished separately for both subjects, for each display and nondisplay period. The result is a series of frequency histograms of interpulse intervals, from which can be calculated the subject's period-by-period standard deviations and average heart rates.

Figure 3 shows the changes in standard deviation of R wave to R wave intervals for all four subgroups with the initial nondisplay period for each group taken as the reference point. It will be noted that the greatest reduction in standard deviation is found among the subjects instructed to stabilize rate utilizing the meter display. Differences between the feedback informed group and the other groups for the display periods were highly significant.

These results confirm our previous findings, that subjects can use cardiac rate feedback to control and stabilize heart rate. They further indicate that this is not an artifact of instructions or an unconditioned response to the task conditions. Similar evidence of rate control has been obtained by Engel and Hanson (1966), who are studying the ability of subjects to decelerate heart rate.

The studies of cardiovascular control are of particular interest, because a mechanism has been suggested by which changes in this system effect cortical activation and motor responses. Neurophysiological investigations indicate that the autonomic nervous system does not function exclusively as an effector system. Data are accumulating which show that "visceral afferent feedback loops" are present, which directly influence cortical and neuromuscular responses. One obvious example is the pressure sensitive baroceptors of the aortic arch and the cartotid sinus. Bonvallet, Dell, and Hiebel (1954) early demonstrated that distention of the carotid produced a decrease in cortical electrical activity. Lacey and Lacey (1958) and Lacey (1967) have reviewed this and other relevant work, and effectively argue that these feedback systems have profound effects on temperament and situational arousal. Similar arguments have been advanced by Gelhorn (1964), emphasizing the role of feedback from the muscular system in modulating emotional responses.

The direction and extent of interaction between autonomic responses and motor or verbal outputs is far from a settled theoretical or empirical issue. Schacter and Singer (1962) and Schacter and Wheeler (1962) have argued that autonomic responses are part of a generalized state of arousal—significant for emotion only to the extent that they are so interpreted and accompanied by the appropriate cognitions. However, others present data indicating significant differences in the autonomic substrata of different motivational conditions and emotional responses (Ax, 1953; Lacey & Lacey, 1958; Lacey, Kagan, & Moss, 1963). It is quite possible, as Gelhorn suggests (1964), that the specific feedback from peripheral muscular and autonomic systems may exert a subtle upward control over cognitive events and modulate emotional responses in important ways. We are likely to find the interactions complex, and clinical psychologists will need to attend closely to this research.

While neurophysiological and psychophysiological issues raised are many, the available evidence justifies an effort by clinical workers to instruct patients in the control of relevant physiological systems. When the central problem of the patient is fear or anxiety, the program of treatments should include efforts at reducing the somatic responses directly, and help the subject to gain positive control over the autonomic components of emotion. Muscle relaxation training appears to be an avenue to that end. However, as the findings reviewed above suggest, we may be able to achieve greater effects more efficiently, by working directly with the relevant autonomic systems.

PART IV

Self-Control in Clinical Practice

Extrapolations from Theory and Research

15

RATIONAL PSYCHOTHERAPY[1]

Albert Ellis

The central theme of this paper is that psychotherapists can help their clients to live the most self-fulfilling, creative, and emotionally satisfying lives by teaching these clients to organize and discipline their thinking. Does this mean that *all* human emotion and creativity can or should be controlled by reason and intellect? Not exactly.

The human being may be said to possess four basic processes—perception, movement, thinking, and emotion—all of which are integrally interrelated. Thus, thinking, aside from consisting of bioelectric changes in the brain cells, and in addition to comprising remembering, learning, problem-solving, and similar psychological processes, also is, and to some extent has to be, sensory, motor, and emotional behavior (Cobb, 1950; Ellis, 1956a). Instead, then, of saying, "Jones thinks about this puzzle," we should more accurately say, "Jones perceives-moves-feels-THINKS about this puzzle." Because, however, Jones' activity in relation to the puzzle may be *largely* focused upon solving it, and only *incidentally* on seeing, manipulating, and emoting about it, we may perhaps justifiably emphasize only his thinking.

Emotion, like thinking and the sensori-motor processes, we may define as exceptionally complex state of human reaction which is integrally related to all the other perception and response processes. It is not *one* thing,

Abridged with permission of the author and the Journal Press from *Journal of General Psychology*, 1958, *59*, 35–49.

[1] Paper presented at the session on "Recent Innovations in Psychotherapeutic Strategy" at the American Psychological Association Convention, August 31, 1956.

but a combination and holistic integration of several seemingly diverse, yet actually closely related, phenomena (Cobb, 1950).

Normally, emotion arises from direct stimulation of the cells in the hypothalamus and autonomic nervous system (e.g., by electrical or chemical stimulation) or from indirect excitation via sensori-motor, cognitive, and other conative processes. It may theoretically be controlled, therefore, in four major ways. If one is highly excitable and wishes to calm down, one may (*a*) take electroshock or drug treatments; (*b*) use soothing baths or relaxation techniques; (*c*) seek someone one loves and quiet down for his sake; or (*d*) reason oneself into a state of calmness by showing oneself how silly it is for one to remain excited.

Although biophysical, sensori-motor, and emotive techniques are all legitimate methods of controlling emotional disturbances, they will not be considered in this paper, and only the rational technique will be emphasized. Rational psychotherapy is based on the assumption that thought and emotion are not two entirely different processes, but that they significantly overlap in many respects and that therefore disordered emotions can often (though not always) be ameliorated by changing one's thinking.

A large part of what we call emotion, in other words, is nothing more or less than a certain kind—a biased, prejudiced, or strongly evaluative kind—of thinking. What we usually label as thinking is a relatively calm and dispassionate appraisal (or organized perception) of a given situation, an objective comparison of many of the elements in this situation, and a coming to some conclusion as a result of this comparing or discriminating process (Ellis, 1956a). Thus, a thinking person may observe a piece of bread, see that one part of it is mouldy, remember that eating this kind of mould previously made him ill, and therefore cut off the mouldy part and eat the non-mouldy section of the bread.

An emoting individual, on the other hand, will tend to observe the same piece of bread, and remember so violently or prejudicially his previous experience with the mouldy part, that he will quickly throw away the whole piece of bread and therefore go hungry. Because the thinking person is relatively calm, he uses the maximum information available to him—namely, the mouldy bread is bad but non-mouldy bread is good. Because the emotional person is relatively excited, he may use only part of the available information—namely, that mouldy bread is bad.

It is hypothesized, then, that thinking and emoting are closely interrelated and at times differ mainly in that thinking is a more tranquil, less somatically involved (or, at least, perceived), and less activity-directed mode of discrimination than is emotion. It is also hypothesized that among adult humans raised in a social culture thinking and emoting are so closely interrelated that they usually accompany each other, act in a circular cause-and-effect relationship, and in certain (though hardly all) respects are essentially the *same thing*, so that one's thinking *becomes* one's emotion and emoting *becomes* one's thought. It is finally hypothesized that since man is a uniquely sign-, symbol-, and language-creating animal, both thinking and emoting tend to take the form of self-talk or internalized sentences; and that, for all practical purposes, the sentences that human beings keep telling themselves *are* or *become* their thoughts and emotions.

This is not to say that emotion can under *no* circumstances exist without thought. It probably can; but it then tends to exist momentarily, and not to be sustained. An individual, for instance, steps on your toe, and you spontaneously, immediately become angry. Or you hear a piece of music and you instantly begin to feel warm and excited. Or you learn that a close friend has died and you quickly begin to feel sad. Under these circumstances, you may feel emotional without doing any concomitant thinking. Perhaps, however, you do, with split-second rapidity, start thinking "This person who stepped on my toe is a blackguard!" or "This music is wonderful!" or "Oh, how awful it is that my friend died!"

In any event, assuming that you don't, at the very beginning, have any conscious or unconscious thought accompanying your emotion, it appears to be difficult to *sustain* an emotional outburst without bolstering it by repeated ideas. For unless you keep telling yourself something on the order of "This person who stepped on my toe is a blackguard!" or "How could he do a horrible thing like that to me!" the pain of having your toe stepped on will soon die, and your immediate reaction will die with the pain. Of course, you can keep getting your toe stepped on, and the continuing pain may sustain your anger. But assuming that your physical sensation stops, your emotional feeling, in order to last, normally has to be bolstered by some kind of thinking.

We say "normally" because it is theoretically possible for your emotional circuits, once they have been made to reverberate by some physical or psychological stimulus, to keep reverberating under their own power. It is also theoretically possible for drugs or electrical impulses to keep acting directly on your hypothalamus and autonomic nervous system and thereby keep you emotionally aroused. Usually, however, these types of continued direct stimulation of the emotion-producing centers do not seem to be important and are limited largely to pathological conditions.

It would appear, then, that positive human emotions, such as feelings of love or elation, are often associated with or result from thoughts, or internalized sentences, stated in some form or variation of the phrase "This is good!" and that negative human emotions, such as feelings of anger or depression, are frequently associated with or result from thoughts or sentences which are stated in some form or variation of the phrase "This is bad!" Without an adult human being's employing, on some conscious or unconscious level, such thoughts and sentences, much of his emoting would simply not exist.

If the hypothesis that sustained human emotion often results from or is directly associated with human thinking and self-verbalization is true, then important corollaries about the origin and perpetuation of states of emotional disturbance, or neurosis, may be drawn. For neurosis would appear to be disordered, over- or under-intensified, uncontrollable emotion; and this would seem to be the result of (and, in a sense, the very same thing as) illogical, unrealistic, irrational, inflexible, and childish thinking.

That neurotic or emotionally disturbed behavior is illogical and irrational would seem to be almost definitional. For if we define it otherwise, and label as neurotic *all* incompetent and ineffectual behavior, we will be including actions of *truly* stupid and incompetent individuals—for example, those who are mentally deficient or brain injured. The concept of neurosis only becomes meaningful, therefore, when we assume that the disturbed individual is *not* efficient or impaired but that he is theoretically capable of behaving in a more mature, more controlled, more flexible manner than he actually behaves. If, however, a neurotic is essentially an individual who acts significantly below his own potential level of behaving, or who defeats his own ends though he is theoretically capable of achieving them, it would appear that he behaves in an illogical, irrational, unrealistic way. Neurosis, in other words, consists of stupid behavior by a non-stupid person.

Assuming that emotionally disturbed individuals act in irrational, illogical ways, the questions which are therapeutically relevant are: (*a*) How do they originally get to be illogical? (*b*) How do they keep perpetuating their irrational thinking? (*c*) How can they be helped to be less illogical, less neurotic?

Unfortunately, most of the good thinking that has been done in regard to therapy during the past 60 years, especially by Sigmund Freud and his chief followers (Fenichel, 1945; Freud, 1938; 1924–1950), has concerned itself with the first of these questions rather than the second and the third. The assumption has often been made that if psychotherapists discover and effectively communicate to their clients the main reasons why these clients originally became disturbed, they will thereby also discover how their neuroses are being perpetuated and how they can be helped to overcome them. This is a dubious assumption.

Knowing exactly how an indivdual originally learned to behave illogically by no means necessarily informs us precisely how he *maintains* his illogical behavior, nor what he should do to change it. This is particularly true because people are often, perhaps usually, afflicted with *secondary* as well as *primary* neuroses, and the two may significantly differ. Thus, an individual may originally become disturbed because he discovers that he has strong death wishes against his father and (quite illogically) thinks he should be blamed and punished for having these wishes. Consequently, he may develop some neurotic symptom, such as a phobia against dogs, because, let us say, dogs remind him of his father, who is an ardent hunter.

Later on, this individual may grow to love or be indifferent to his father; or his father may die and be no more of a problem to him. His fear of dogs, however, many remain: not because, as some theoritsts would insist, they still remind him of his old death wishes against his father, but because he now hates himself so violently for *having* the original neurotic symptom—for behaving, to his mind, so stupidly and illogically in relation to dogs—that every time he thinks of dogs his self-hatred and fear of failure so severely upset him that he cannot reason clearly and cannot combat his illogical fear.

In terms of self-verbalization, this neurotic individual is first saying to himself: "I hate my father—and this is awful!" But he ends up by saying: "I have an irrational fear of dogs—and this is awful!" Even though both sets of self-verbalizations are neuroticizing, and his secondary neurosis may be as bad as or worse than his primary one, the two can hardly be said to be the same. Consequently, exploring and explaining to this indivdual—or helping him gain insight into—the origins of his primary neurosis will not necessarily help him to understand and overcome his perpetuating or secondary neurotic reactions.

If the hypotheses so far stated have some validity, the psychotherapist's main goals should be those of demonstrating to clients that their self-verbalizations have been and still are the prime source of their emotional disturbances. Clients must be shown that their internalized sentences are illogical and unrealistic at certain critical points and that they now have the ability to control their emotions by telling themselves more rational and less self-defeating sentences.

More precisely: the effective therapist should continually keep unmasking his client's past and, especially, his present illogical thinking or self-defeating verbalizations by (*a*) bringing them to his attention or consciousness; (*b*) showing the client how they are causing and maintaining his disturbance and unhappiness; (*c*) demonstrating exactly what the illogical links in his internalized sentences are; and (*d*) teaching him how to re-think and re-verbalize these (and other similar) sentences in a more logical, self-helping way. Moreover, before the end of the therapeutic relationship, the therapist should not only deal concretely with the client's specific illogical thinking, but should demonstrate to this client what, *in general*, are the main irrational ideas that human beings are prone to follow and what more rational philosophies of living may usually be substituted for them. Otherwise, the client who is released from one specific set of illogical notions may well wind up by falling victim to another set.

It is hypothesized, in other words, that human beings are the kind of animals who, when raised in any society similar to our own, tend to fall victim to several major fallacious ideas; to keep reindoctrinating themselves over and over again with these ideas in an unthinking, autosuggestive manner; and consequently to keep actualizing them in overt behavior. Most of these irrational ideas are, as the freudians have very adequately pointed out, instilled by the indivdual's parents during his childhood, and are tenaciously clung to because of his attachment to these parents and because the ideas were ingrained, or imprinted, or conditioned before later and more rational modes of thinking were given a chance to gain a foothold. Most of them, however, as the freudians have not always been careful to note, are also instilled by the individual's general culture, and particularly by the media of mass communication in this culture.

What are some of the major illogical ideas or philosophies which, when originally held and later perpetuated by men and women in our civilization, inevitably lead to self-defeat and neurosis? Limitations of space preclude our examining all these major ideas, including their more significant corollaries; therefore, only a few of them will be listed. The illogicality of some of these ideas will also, for the present, have to be taken somewhat on faith, since there again is no space to outline the many reasons *why* they are irrational. Anyway, here, where angels fear to tread, goes the psychological theoretician!

1. The idea that it is a dire necessity for an adult to be loved or approved by everyone for everything he does—instead of his concentrating on his own self-respect, on winning approval for necessary purposes (such as job advancement), and on loving rather than being loved.
2. The idea that certain acts are wrong, or wicked, or villainous, and that people who perform such acts should be severely punished—instead of the idea that certain acts are inappropriate or antisocial, and that people who perform such acts are invariably stupid, ignorant, or emotionally disturbed.
3. The idea that it is terrible, horrible, and catastrophic when things are not the way one would like them to be—instead of the idea that it is too bad when things are not the way one would like them to be, and one should certainly try to change or control conditions so that they become more satisfactory, but that if changing or controlling uncomfortable situations is impossible, one had better become resigned to their existence and stop telling oneself how awful they are.
4. The idea that much human unhappiness is externally caused and is forced on one by outside people and events—instead of the idea that virtually all human unhappiness is caused or sustained by the view one takes of things rather than the things themselves.
5. The idea that if something is or may be dangerous or fearsome one should be terribly concerned about it—instead of the idea that if something is or may be dangerous or fearsome one should frankly face it and try to render it non-dangerous and, when that is impossible, think of other things and stop telling oneself what a terrible situation one is or may be in.
6. The idea that it is easier to avoid than to face life difficulties and

self-responsibilities—instead of the idea that the so-called easy way is invariably the much harder way in the long run and that the only way to solve difficult problems is to face them squarely.

7. The idea that one needs something other or stronger or greater than oneself on which to rely—instead of the idea that it is usually far better to stand on one's own feet and gain faith in oneself and one's ability to meet difficult circumstances of living.
8. The idea that one should be thoroughly competent, adequate, intelligent, and achieving in all possible respects—instead of the idea that one should *do* rather than always try to do *well* and that one should accept oneself as a quite imperfect creature, who has general human limitations and specific fallibilities.
9. The idea that because something once strongly affected one's life, it should indefinitely affect it—instead of the idea that one should learn from one's past experiences but not be overly-attached to or prejudiced by them.
10. The idea that it is vitally important to our existence what other people do, and that we should make great efforts to change them in the direction we would like them to be—instead of the idea that other people's deficiencies are largely *their* problems and that putting pressure on them to change is usually least likely to help them do so.
11. The idea that human happiness can be achieved by inertia and inaction—instead of the idea that humans tend to be happiest when they are actively and vitally absorbed in creative pursuits, or when they are devoting themselves to people or projects outside themselves.
12. The idea that one has virtually no control over one's emotions and that one cannot help feeling certain things—instead of the idea that one has enormous control over one's emotions if one chooses to work at controlling them and to practice saying the right kinds of sentences to oneself.

It is the central theme of this paper that it is the foregoing kinds of illogical ideas, and many corollaries which we have no space to delineate, which are the basic causes of most emotional disturbances or neuroses. For once one believes the kind of nonsense included in these notions, one will inevitably tend to become inhibited, hostile, defensive, guilty, anxious, ineffective, inert, uncontrolled, or unhappy. If, on the other hand, one could become thoroughly released from all these fundamental kinds of illogical thinking, it would be exceptionally difficult for one to become too emotionally upset, or at least to sustain one's disturbance for very long.

Does this mean that all the other so-called causes of neurosis, such as the Oedipus complex or severe maternal rejection in childhood, are invalid, and that the freudian and other psychodynamic thinkers of the last 60 years have been barking up the wrong tree? Not at all. It only means, if the main hypotheses of this paper are correct, that these psychodynamic thinkers have been emphasizing secondary causes or results of emotional disturbances rather than truly prime causes.

Let us take, for example, an individual who acquires, when he is young, a full-blown Oedipus complex: that is to say, he lusts after his mother, hates his father, is guilty about his sex desires for his mother, and is afraid that his father is going to castrate him. This person, when he is a child, will presumably be disturbed. But, if he is raised so that he acquires none of the basic illogical ideas we have been discussing, it will be virtually impossible for him to *remain* disturbed.

For, as an adult, this individual will not be too concerned if his parents or others do not approve all his actions, since he will be more interested in his *own* self-respect than in *their* approval. He will not believe that his lust for his mother is wicked or villainous, but will accept it as a normal part of being a limited human whose sex desires may easily be indiscriminate. He will realize that the actual danger of his father castrating him is exceptionally slight. He will not feel that because he was once afraid of his Oedipal feelings he should forever remain so. If he still feels it would be improper for him to have sex relations with his mother, instead of castigating himself for even thinking of having such relations he will merely resolve not to carry his desires into practice and will stick determinedly to his resolve. If, by any chance, he weakens and actually has incestuous relations, he will again refuse to castigate himself mercilessly for being weak but will keep showing himself how self-defeating his behavior is and will actively work and practice at changing it.

Under these circumstances, if this individual has a truly logical and rational approach to life in general, and to the problem of Oedipal feelings, in particular, how can he possibly *remain* disturbed about his Oedipal attachment?

Take, by way of further illustration, the case of an individual who, as a child, is continually criticized by his parents, who consequently feels himself loathesome and inadequate, who refuses to take chances at failing at difficult tasks, who avoids such tasks, and who therefore comes to hate himself more. Such a person will be, of course, seriously neurotic. But how would it be possible for him to *sustain* his neurosis if he began to think in a truly logical manner about himself and his behavior?

For, if this individual does use a consistent rational approach to his own behavior, he will stop caring particularly what others think of him and will start primarily caring what he thinks of himself. Consequently, he will stop avoiding difficult tasks and, instead of punishing himself for being incompetent when he makes a mistake, will say to himself something like: "Now this is not the right way to do things; let me stop and figure out a better way." Or: "There's no doubt that I made a mistake this time; now let me see how I can benefit from making it."

This individual, furthermore, will if he is thinking straight, not blame his defeats on external events, but will realize that he himself is causing them by his illogical or impractical behavior. He will not believe that it is easier to avoid facing difficult things, but will realize that the so-called easy way is always, actually, the harder and more idiotic one. He will not think that he needs something greater or stronger than himself to help him, but will independently buckle down to difficult tasks himself. He will not feel that because he once defeated himself by avoiding doing things the hard way that he must always do so.

How, with this kind of logical thinking, could an originally disturbed person possibly maintain and continually revivify his neurosis? He just couldn't. Similarly, the spoiled brat, the worry-wart, the ego-maniac, the autistic stay-at-home—all of these disturbed individuals would have the devil of a time indefinitely prolonging their neuroses if they did not continue to believe utter nonsense: namely, the kinds of basic irrational postulates previously listed.

Neurosis, then, usually seems to originate in and be perpetuated by some fundamentally unsound, irrational ideas. The individual comes to believe in some unrealistic, impossible, often perfectionistic goals—especially the goals that he should always be approved by everyone, should do everything perfectly well, and should never be frustrated in any of his desires—and then, in spite of considerable contradictory evidence, refuses to give up his original illogical beliefs.

Some of the neurotic's philosophies, such as the idea that he should be loved and approved by everyone, are not entirely inappropriate to his childhood state; but all of them are quite inappropriate to average adulthood. Most of his irrational ideas are specifically taught him by his parents and his culture; and most of them also seem to be held by the great majority of adults in our society—who theoretically should have been but actually never were weaned from them as they chronologically matured. It must consequently be admitted that the neurotic individual we are considering is often statistically normal; or that ours is a generally neuroticizing culture, in which most people are more or less emotionally disturbed because they are raised to believe, and then to internalize and to keep reinfecting themselves with, arrant nonsense which must inevitably lead them to become ineffective, self-defeating, and unhappy. Nonetheless: it is not absolutely *necessary* that human beings believe the irrational notions which, in point of fact, most of them seem to believe today; and the task of psychotherapy is to get them to disbelieve their illogical ideas, to change their self-sabotaging attitudes.

This, precisely, is the task which the rational psychotherapist sets himself. Like other therapists, he frequently resorts to the usual techniques of therapy which the present author has outlined elsewhere (Ellis, 1955a, 1955b), including the techniques of relationship, excessive-emotive, supportive, and insight-interpretive therapy. But he views these techniques, as they are commonly employed, as kinds of preliminary strategies whose main functions are to gain rapport with the client, to let him express himself fully, to show him that he is a worthwhile human being who has the ability to change, and to demonstrate how he originally became disturbed.

The rational therapist, in other words, believes that most of the usual therapeutic techniques wittingly or unwittingly show the client *that* he is illogical and how he *originally* became so. They often fail to show him, however, how he is presently *maintaining* his illogical thinking, and precisely what he must do to change it by building general rational philosophies of living and by applying these to practical problems of everyday life. Where most therapists directly or indirectly show the client that he is behaving illogically, the rational therapist goes beyond this point to make a forthright, unequivocal *attack* on the client's general and specific irrational ideas and to try to *induce* him to adopt more rational ones in their place.

Rational psychotherapy makes a concerted attack on the disturbed individual's irrational positions in two main ways: (*a*) the therapist serves as a frank counter-propagandist who directly contradicts and denies the self-defeating propaganda and superstitions which the client has originally learned and which he is now self-propagandistically perpetuating. (*b*) The therapist encourages, persuades, cajoles, and at times commands the clients to partake of some kind of activity which itself will act as a forceful counter-propagandist agency against the nonsense he believes. Both these main therapeutic activities are consciously performed with one main goal in mind: namely, that of finally getting the client to internalize a rational philosophy of living just as he originally learned and internalized the illogical propaganda and superstitions of his parents and his culture.

The rational therapist, then, assumes that the client somehow imbibed illogical ideas or irrational modes of thinking and that, without so doing, he could hardly be as disturbed as he is. It is the therapist's function not merely to show the client that he has these ideas or thinking processes but to persuade him to change and substitute for them more rational ideas and thought processes. If, because the client is exceptionally disturbed when he first comes to therapy, he must first be approached in a rather cautious, supportive, permissive, and warm manner, and must sometimes be allowed to ventilate his feeling in free association, abreaction, rôle playing, and other expressive techniques, that may be all to the good. But the therapist does not delude himself that these relationship-building and expressive-emotive techniques in most instances really get to the core of the client's illogical thinking and induce him to think in a more rational manner.

Occasionally, this is true: since the client may come to see, through relationship and emotive-expressive methods, that he *is* acting illogically, and he may therefore resolve to change and actually do so. More often than not, however, his illogical thinking will be so ingrained from constant self-repetitions, and will be so inculcated in motor pathways (or habit patterns) by the time he comes for therapy, that simply showing him, even by direct interpretation, *that* he is illogical will not greatly help. He will often say to the therapist: "All right, now I understand that I have castration fears and that they are illogical. But I *still* feel afraid of my father."

The therapist, therefore, must keep pounding away, time and again, at the illogical ideas which underlie the client's fears. He must show the client that he is afraid, really, not of his father, but of being blamed, of being disapproved, of being unloved, of being imperfect, of being a failure. And such fears are thoroughly irrational because (*a*) being disapproved is not half so terrible as one *thinks* it is; because (*b*) no one can be thoroughly blameless or perfect; because (*c*) people who worry about being blamed or disapproved essentially are putting themselves at the mercy of the opinion of *others*, over whom they have no real control; because (*d*) being blamed or disapproved has nothing essentially to do with one's *own* opinion of one-self; etc.

If the therapist, moreover, merely tackles the individual's castration fears, and shows how ridiculous *they* are, what is to prevent this individual's showing up, a year or two later, with some *other* illogical fear—such as the fear that he is sexually impotent? But if the therapist tackles the client's *basic* irrational thinking, which underlies *all* kinds of fear he may have, it is going to be most difficult for this client to turn up a new neurotic symptom some months or years hence. For once an individual truly surrenders ideas of perfectionism, of the horror of failing at something, of the dire need to be approved by others, of the notion that the world owes him a living, and so on, what else is there for him to be fearful of or disturbed about?

* * *

The rational therapist, then, is a frank propagandist who believes wholeheartedly in a most rigorous application of the rules of logic, of straight thinking, and of scientific method to everyday life, and who ruth-lessly uncovers every vestige of irrational thinking in the client's experience and energetically urges him into more rational channels. In so doing, the rational therapist does not ignore or eradicate the client's emotions; on the contrary, he considers them most seriously, and helps change them, when they are disordered and self-defeating, through the same means by which they commonly arise in the first place—that is, by thinking and acting. Through exerting consistent interpretive and philosophic pressures on the client to change his thinking or his self-verbalizations and to change his experiences or his actions, the rational therapist gives a specific impetus to the client's movement toward mental health without which it is not impossible, but quite unlikely, that he will move very far.

Can therapy be effectively done, then, with *all* clients mainly through logical analysis and reconstruction? Alas, no. For one thing, many clients are not bright enough to follow a rigorously rational analysis. For another thing, some individuals are so emotionally aberrated by the time they come for help that they are, at least temporarily, in no position to comprehend and follow logical procedures. Still other clients are too old and inflexible; too young and impressionable; too philosophically prejudiced against logic and reason; too organically or biophysically deficient; or too something else to accept, at least at the start of therapy, rational analysis.

In consequence, the therapist who *only* employs logical reconstruction in his therapeutic armamentarium is not likely to get too far with many of those who seek his help. It is vitally important, therefore, that any therapist who has a basically rational approach to the problem of helping his clients overcome their neuroses also be quite eclectic in his use of supplementary, less direct, and somewhat less rational techniques.

Admitting, then, that rational psychotherapy is not effective with all types of clients, and that it is most helpful when used in conjuncion with, or subsequent to, other widely employed therapeutic techniques, I would like to conclude with two challenging hypotheses: (*a*) that psychotherapy which includes a high dosage of rational analysis and reconstruction, as briefly outlined in this paper, will prove to be more effective with more types of clients than any of the non-rational or semi-rational therapies now being widely employed; and (*b*) that a considerable amount of—or, at least, proportion of—rational psychotherapy will prove to be virtually the only type of treatment that helps to undermine the basic neuroses (as distinguished from the superficial neurotic symptoms) of many clients, and particularly of many with whom other types of therapy have already been shown to be ineffective.

16

COGNITIVE PROCESSES, PROBLEM SOLVING, AND EFFECTIVE BEHAVIOR[1]

Thomas J. D'Zurilla
and Marvin R. Goldfried

As part of a research project on the identification, assessment, and facilitation of effective behavior in college freshmen, we have presented a conceptualization of effective behavior in terms of the individual's responses to certain critical problematic situations in the academic and social environment, and the likely consequences of those responses (Goldfried & D'Zurilla, 1969). An effective response is defined as a response, or pattern of responses, which alters the situation so that it is no longer problematic, and at the same time produces a maximum of other positive consequences and a minimum of negative ones.

In this paper we will describe a problem-solving approach to the facilitation of effective behavior which stresses the role of rational, cognitive processes. We will begin with a discussion of the nature of the "problematic situation" and "problem-solving behavior," and then present a possible cognitive strategy for effective problem solving in life situations, along with a discussion of how individuals may be trained in the use of this strategy so as to facilitate effectiveness.

[1] This paper is an extended version of a paper presented in M. R. Goldfried's (Chm.) "Cognitive Processes in Behavior Modification," symposium presented at the American Psychological Association, San Francisco, September 1968. The preparation of this paper was supported by research grant MH-15044 from the National Institute of Mental Health. For an extended version, the reader is referred to: D'Zurilla, T. J., and Goldfried, M. R. Problem solving and behavior modification. *Journal of Abnormal Psychology*, 1971, *78*, 107–126.

THE PROBLEMATIC SITUATION

Before turning to the question of problem-solving behavior, it would be helpful to define the "problem" in problem-solving situations. We find Skinner's (1953) definition to be useful here: "In the true 'problem situation' the organism has no behavior immediately available which will reduce the deprivation or provide escape from eversive stimulation" (p. 246). In such a situation, at least one effective response exists in the individual's behavioral repertoire, but cannot be emitted under present circumstances due to the absence of the necessary cues.

The problematic situation as defined above represents one type of "learning" dilemma which is described by Dollard and Miller (1950) as "a situation where the individual's old responses will not be rewarded." The importance of such situations in the learning history of the individual is emphasized by Dollard and Miller in their statement: "In the absence of a dilemma, no new learning of either the trial-and-error or the thoughtful problem-solving type occurs" (p. 45).

While it is obvious that problematic situations occur throughout an individual's lifetime, clinical experience as well as the literature in developmental psychology would suggest that they are most frequent and difficult during periods of transition from one environment to another (e.g., moving to a different location), or from one role to another (e.g., high-school student to college student, bachelor to husband, etc.). The following is an example of a situation which may be problematic for many individuals when they experience it for the first time:

> A college student, who rarely dated in high school, has been dating a particular girl steadily for several months when one day, after an argument, she announces that she is breaking up with him for good. Later in the evening, the student sits down at his desk to begin studying for an important exam coming up in a few days, but he finds himself constantly thinking about the girl, feeling depressed, and unable to concentrate on his studies.

In the above example, the situation is problematic to the student if responses which might correct the relationship with his girl and enable him to concentrate are actually in his behavioral repertoire, but the necessary cues for these responses are absent, thus precluding immediate effective action. The question of "finding a solution" in this situation brings us to the discussion of problem-solving behavior.

PROBLEM-SOLVING BEHAVIOR

For a general definition of problem-solving behavior, we once again refer to Skinner (1953), who makes a clear distinction between "emitting a response which is a solution" and "solving a problem." According to Skinner, problem solving is "behavior which, through the manipulation of variables, makes the appearance of a solution more probable" (p. 247). Problem solving, then, refers to the *process of finding a solution.* The solution, on the other hand, may be defined as the resulting response or pattern of responses which alters the situation in such a way as to eliminate or reduce its problematic nature. Skinner defines the "difficulty" of a problematic situation for an individual in terms of the availability in the repertoire of that individual of the response which constitutes a solution. He points out that as the similarity with earlier successful experiences increases, and with it the availability or likelihood of an effective response, a point is reached where it becomes idle or meaningless to speak of problem solving at all. By the same token, once a problematic situation is solved, that situation is not likely to require problem-solving behavior in the future, since it will no longer be novel and an effective response should be immediately available because it has been reinforced under similar circumstances.

It might be helpful at this point to clarify further the definition of problem-solving behavior by comparing it to trial-and-error—whether overt or covert—and the behavioral conception of "self-control." In trial-and-error learning, a number of high probability responses may be emitted because the problematic situation contains elements similar to those of previous situations in which these responses have been reinforced. By chance, one of these responses might be a solution. According to Skinner's (1953) definition, however, this is not problem solving. Behavior was not engaged in that made the solution more probable; it is simply "hitting upon a solution." As Skinner points out: "We can account for the emergence of each trial response in terms of the current occasion and the past history of the individual. There is a minimum of 'self-determination' " (p. 249). However, trial-and-error may often occur in connection with problem-solving behavior, as in the case of an individual who carries out procedures that make several possible responses available to him and he "tries out" each alternative (either overtly or symbolically) until he finds the "best" or most effective response. We will expand on this approach later in our discussion of the training strategy.

In behavioral terms, self-control may be said to occur when an individual deliberately controls his own behavior by manipulating the stimulus variables which influence it, including stimuli produced by his own overt and cognitive responses, as well as by external stimuli. From this point of view, effective problem-solving behavior is one form of self-controlling behavior and, therefore, possesses all of the likely long-term advantages of appropriate self-control, such as greater "independence" and "self-determination," greater flexibility of action, and feelings of competence and mastery. However, there is one important difference between problem solving and most other forms of self-control. In the usual self-control process, the response to be controlled is selected in advance, whereas in problem solving the controlling behavior is performed without prior awareness of the effective response. In fact, the primary objective of problem-solving behavior is to facilitate awareness of the effective response, after which other self-controlling operations may be employed to instigate action and maintain the effective behavior. Thus, problem solving may be viewed as the first phase of a more general self-control process, which may be described as "adjusting to new situations," or "coping independently with life's problems."

Thus far, our description of the problem-solving process has not differed significantly from the general approach of Skinner (1953). As we consider the process more specifically, however, we see that Skinner's orientation emphasizes *overt* behavior and the manipulation of *external* variables. In contrast, we would like to employ a broader definition of "behavior" and focus our attention on certain cognitive operations, or covert behavioral interactions if you will, which might be involved in effective "real-life" problem solving, but which may not necessarily be representative of any immediate overt behavior.

TRAINING IN PROBLEM-SOLVING SKILLS

Our conception of a *strategy* is similar to that of Breger and McGaugh (1965), who describe it as a central program or plan that mediates overt responses. According to our view, a strategy is basically an internal or mediational process involving both a particular *orientation* and a specific *set of cognitive operations*. The specific strategy which we will discuss here may be viewed as a conceptualization of "real-life" social and personal problem solving, which mediates effective behavior, as well as a set of procedures for training in problem solving with a clinical or counselling context.

As a first step, any attempt to facilitate problem solving must take into consideration those aspects of an individual's personality and environment which may be related to his problem-solving performance. To the extent that there are personality, emotional, or environmental factors which may seriously interefere with the learning process involved, other procedures or forms of treatment may be necessary to prepare the individual for problem-solving training. We will discuss this point further later.

Once it has been established that the individual is prepared to respond to problem-solving training, he may then progress through the following five training phases with respect to either real or hypothetical problematic situations: (1) orientation, (2) problem definition and formulation, (3) generation of alternatives, (4) decision making, and (5) verification. The specifics involved in each of these phases are derived from a variety of sources, including the research and theoretical literature on the process of problem solving and decision making (Kleinmuntz, 1966), research on training in productive thinking and creativity (Osborn, 1963; Parnes, 1967), and discussion of economic and administrative behavior (Gore & Dyson, 1964; Simon, 1957).

However, most of the procedures must be considered to be only at the hypothesis stage at this point. By and large, the research on problem solving and decision-making deals with problems designed to test various game-theoretical, mathematical, and computer-programming models, which tells us very little about how individuals are actually able to go about solving "real-life" social and personal problems (Simon, 1955, 1957). The literature on training in productive thinking and creative problem solving contains some relevant facts but the major research has been global in nature, designed to test the outcome of formal training courses in creativity and not the effects of specific, isolated procedures (Parnes, 1967). The literature on economic and administrative behavior is highly relevant but is primarily based on a kind of informal empiricism and, therefore, in need of experimental test. With these disclaimers out of the way, we may go on to discuss each phase of the proposed strategy.

Orientation

Becoming properly oriented to deal with problematic life situations is a matter of developing a set or attitude to (a) recognize and accept problematic situations when they occur, and (b) inhibit the tendency to either respond on the first "impulse" or to "do nothing".

To develop the set to recognize and accept problematic situations, the general nature of such situations, as well as the nature and objectives of the training program, are described and discussed. The fact is stressed that life is made up of an endless series of problematic situations, that this is the "normal" rather than "abnormal" state of affairs, and that one should anticipate more than the usual number of problematic situations when entering a new environment or social role. The client is instructed that when difficulties or uncertainties occur, he should immediately try to identify the external situation or situations that are producing these difficulties, rather than dwelling upon his own personal reactions or emotions. The client is also encouraged to accept the fact that he has the ability to solve problematic situations even though no solution is immediately apparent to him. The nature and objectives of problem-solving training are described and discussed at this point and the client learns that although some problematic situations are more complex, and consequently more difficult to solve than others, he usually has several potential courses of action available to him for dealing effectively with almost any problematic situation. According to research reported by Rotter (1966), there is reason to expect that if a belief in the control of one's destiny can be encouraged through the above procedures, independent problem-solving behavior will be facilitated. In turn, success in solving problems should help to strengthen the belief in self-control, resulting in a kind of self-reinforcing process.

The major function of the inhibitory set is to reduce the tendency to either react automatically to familiar stimuli in problematic situations (and perhaps inappropriately and even disastrously), or passively avoid the problem by "doing nothing."

Several authors have discussed this set as an important prerequisite for effective problem solving (Dollard & Miller, 1950; Osborn, 1963; Parnes, 1967; Shaftel & Shaftel, 1967; Thurstone, 1924). According to Dollard and Miller (1950), the first step in any but the simplest types of reasoning is to "stop and think." They point out that if a person makes an immediate, direct, instrumental response to a given problematic situation, there may not be sufficient time for the proper cue-producing (cognitive) responses to occur to ensure effective action.

In addition to the use of instructions and discussion to establish this inhibitory set, the entire strategy, if adequately practiced during training and reinforced by coping effectively with problematic situations, should strengthen the set and further weaken the tendency to respond automatically or not at all.

Problem Definition and Formulation

To begin the second phase, namely, problem definition and formulation, problematic situation *categories* are introduced for training (e.g., studying, dating, etc.). These may be prepared on the basis of the individual client's current life experiences, or a sample of common categories for particular types of environments (e.g., college life and work) might be prepared in advance for training purposes. These are placed in an hierarchical order based on their apparent difficulty level for the client. Training should begin with the least difficult and progress toward the more difficult categories.

Beginning with the first category, the client, with the help of the therapist or consultant, constructs a specific hypothetical or actual problematic situation. He is guided toward a *definition* of the problem in clear, specific terms. This is a very crucial step which is likely to have a highly significant effect upon the outcome of the entire strategy for that particular problem. By surveying the problematic situation very carefully, considering all the relevant facts, and then stating the facts in the clearest, most concrete terms, the client forces himself to make relevant what may have appeared at first to be irrelevant (Parnes, 1967). In pointing up the pertinent aspects of the problem in this way, the client increases the chances of a solution (Skinner, 1953). In addition, after describing the facts in specific terms, the client can more appropriately label or classify the situation, which in turn enables him to relate the problem to past situations in the same category and bring his past learning to bear upon it (Mowrer, 1960). This procedure also reduces the likelihood of inappropriate generalizations from past experience due to vague or ambiguous labeling (Dollard & Miller, 1950).

The next step for the client in this phase is to *formulate* the "target objectives" for problem solving, which refers to a clear statement as to what aspects of the problematic situation are to be changed and the exact nature of these changes. This step ensures the appropriate direction and setting of limits for the next phase of the strategy, namely, the generation of alternatives.

Generation of Alternatives

The search for alternatives is a creative, imaginative process as well as a process of remembering and recall. The recall of old solutions is good for solving problems similar to ones successfully handled in the past. However, in new problematic situations where old responses may be inappropriate, it is necessary to generate new solutions. That is, the client must think of ways of combining parts of different habitual responses into new actions (Osborn, 1963). Once again, it should be stressed that the production of a particular solution, whether creative or not, requires that the individual have in his repertoire the necessary responses or response elemnts that make up that solution.

The technique that we propose for facilitating the production of alternatives is based primarily on the procedures advocated by Osborn (1963) and Parnes (1967) for training in creative problem solving. Essentially, the client is instructed to produce associative responses, with respect to the particular problematic situation in question, in a way which helps to avoid "blocks" that may inhibit the associative process. The client is told that he is not to engage in "free association" but association with respect to the question: "What can a person possibly do *in this particular situation*?" Thus, the form and direction of the associations are governed by way in which the problem is stated and defined, and by the set to generate possible actions in the situation.

One way to facilitate associative responses and avoid "blocks" is through the "deferment-of-judgment" principle. According to this principle, the client tries to think of one alternative after another without concerning himself with the question as to their value, acceptability, or appropriateness. By avoiding thinking in terms of response consequences at this point, insofar as it is possible to do so, the client learns to avoid the following two pitfalls: (1) premature termination of the search with one of the first "good" alternatives to come to mind, and (2) discouragement and premature termination of the search due to an early series of "poor" ideas.

Related to the above is a procedure involving the principle that "quantity breeds quality." According to this principle, the more alternatives generated by the client, the more likely he is to arrive at the potentially best leads for a solution. Several studies on this point indicate that the best ideas for solutions in creative problem solving are unlikely to be among the first ideas that come to mind (cf. Osborn, 1963; Parnes, 1962, 1967). Thus, the client is instructed to continue generating possible alternatives until he is unable to come up with any more ideas. Obviously, this point will vary among clients, depending upon such factors as the content of their response repertoires, their ability for associative thinking (cf. Mednick, 1962), their success in deferring judgement, and other personal–social factors. When this point is reached, the phase of decision making is initiated.

Decision Making

Decision making involves the selection of the "best" alternative for action and is probably the most difficult phase in the strategy. This selection is based on the client's expectations as to the possible consequences of the various alternatives. The client is instructed to anticipate the possible consequences of each alternative, consider their value and likelihood of occurrence, and then select the alternative which appears to have the greatest chance of solving the problem satisfactorily while maximizing other positive consequences and minimizing negative ones.

It is in the area of decision making that the mathematical and computer-programming models place the most severe demands on the human problem-solver. These demands include the ability to specify the exact nature of outcomes, the ability to specify that one outcome is better than, as good as, or worse than any other, the ability to specify all possible outcomes, and the ability to attach definite probabilities to these outcomes (Simon, 1955). According to Simon (1955), "there is a complete lack of evidence that, in actual human choice situations of any complexity, these computations can be, or are in fact, performed." Thus, we might assume that because of the limitations of the human organism, his decision-making ability will represent, at best, an extremely crude and simplified approximation of the kind of process described by the mathematical and computer models (Wilson & Alexis, 1962; Simon, 1955).

Just as any one client would not be expected to think of *all* possible alternatives, he will also be unable to anticipate *all* possible consequences. There is no way that he actually can know all of the consequences of an action in advance, especially when considering a novel response or solution. However, based upon his knowledge of general empirical relationships from his own past experience, his knowledge of the experiences of others, and information about the existing problematic situation from a careful statement and definition of the problem, he can form expectations as to possible consequences (Simon, 1957).

Thus, the client is told to ask himself the question: "If I were to carry out *this* particular solution, what are the various things that could possibly happen as a result?" As an aid in this procedure, the client is instructed to consider consequences in four different categories: personal, social, short-term, and long-term.

In the personal category, the client attempts to valuate each alternative in terms of the personal needs it might satisfy, the personal goals it might attain—with particular reference to the "target objectives" in the problematic situation—and the effects it might have on his personal feelings and emotions. The social consequences refer to the effects that the alternative action might have on various "significant others" in the client's life and the reactions of others to him. The short-term consequences refer to the *immediate* personal and social effects in the problematic situation. In anticipating long-term consequences, the client considers the possible personal and social consequences that might occur in the future as a result of the immediate effects of each alternative, including the possibility of preventing similar problematic situations and the effects on long-range goals, plans, and personal–social functioning.

When the client has carefully examined the alternatives for their possible consequences in the four categories, he is then asked to consider the value and likelihood of occurrence of the various consequences. We might point out once again that at this stage the client is dealing with a limited number of possible alternatives and a limited number of possible consequences, and that clients will differ in the degree to which they are able to approach all possibilities—a factor which may be related to individual differences in effectiveness. The values assigned to consequences will also vary among clients, depending upon their particular reinforcement history and current life situation. Thus, an effective solution for one client may not necessarily be an equally effective solution for another client.

In assigning values to consequences, it is unlikely that individuals in life situations often consider more values than three: positive, negative, and neutral; or satisfactory, unsatisfactory, and neutral (Simon, 1955). Since there is no evidence at present to indicate that effectiveness would be increased by considering more categories, our strategy requires no further discrimination on the part of the client. The same approach is applied to the estimate of likelihood of occurrence of consequences. Clients are asked to consider a consequence as likely to occur, unlikely to occur, or as having a 50–50 chance of occurring. The client is then instructed to engage in a very rough approximation to an objective judgment process of weighing the various alternatives, one against the other, considering the various consequences of each with their values and likelihood of occurrence. He is then asked to select the one which seems to have the best chance of solving the problem satisfactorily (i.e., achieving the "target objectives") while maximizing the likelihood of other positive consequences and minimizing the likelihood of negative ones. This selection leads to the final phase of the strategy, namely, the verification phase.

Verification

Action in "real-life" problematic situations, following decision making, is not guaranteed. The client may fail to carry out the selected alternative after very efficient and effective problem solving up to that point for a variety of reasons, including motivational deficits, inhibitions due to emotional factors, and environmental obstacles. We will come back to this problem in a moment.

Assuming that the client does carry out the selected alternative, he is instructed to verify the solution by observing the various consequences of his action or actions in the life situation and testing or "matching" this outcome against the expected outcome on which he had based his decision. If the match is unsatisfactory to the client, he returns to the decision-making phase of the strategy once again and selects his "second-best" alternative for action, repeating this procedure until a satisfactory match is achieved, at which point the solution is considered verified and the strategy is terminated. Obviously, the requirements for a satisfactory match will differ among clients. Throughout the training program, the therapist–consultant must use his knowledge of the client's relevant characteristics—i.e., his particular assets, liabilities, needs, goals, values, etc.—and his understanding of the client's current life situation, to help him guide and direct the client through the various steps in the program.

DISCUSSION

The training procedures described above may be carried out in either a group or individual setting. In a group program, the therapist–consultant structures the group sessions and serves as the group discussion leader. The major advantage of the group is that a greater sum total of knowledge and information is made available regarding alternatives and consequences, thus providing a more adequate "model" for problem solving. In addition, group discussion may encourage a more adequate critical appraisal of alternatives and, as a result, increase the effectiveness of decision-making training. The interpersonal interaction and social reinforcement made possible by a group setting may also help to facilitate generalization of problem solving to "real-life" social situations (cf. D'Zurilla, 1966).

Training in problem solving should be continued, working on one problematic situation after another in the session and during home practice sessions, until sufficient evidence is obtained that the client is dealing effectively with new problematic situations in the first category (e.g., dating, employer–employee interactions). Problematic situations in the next category are then constructed and worked on, and so on until further treatment is no longer required. An important point to be stressed is that the goal of such training is not to teach specific responses or solutions to specific problematic situations; but, instead, to teach a *general strategy* or approach to problem solving that could be applied to *any* soluble personal or social problem.

A question may be raised as to when problem-solving training might be an appropriate behavior modification technique in the clinical setting. The answer to this question in a particular case clearly requires a careful assessment of the client's ineffective behavior (cf. Goldfried & Pomeranz, 1968). Ineffectiveness in problematic situations could result from any one or a combination of at least four different antecedent conditions:

1. An inhibition of effective responses for specific problematic situations due to anxiety or some other aversive stimulation.
2. An actual deficit in potential effective responses for specific problematic situations.
3. An inhibition of existing cognitive problem-solving operations.
4. A deficit in the problem-solving operations themselves.

In the first two cases, where there is either an inhibition of, or deficit in effective responses, it is obvious that special behavior modification procedures are required to either train the client to respond effectively to specific situations, or remove inhibitions associated with those responses, as the case may be. In the third or fourth case, namely, an inhibition of or deficit in general problem-solving operations, training in effective responses or desensitization with respect to those responses might constitute *incomplete* treatment, and perhaps even *inappropriate* treatment.

Where a strong inhibition of general problem-solving operations exists, such as in a case where the client cannot tolerate even a short period of indecision or where anxiety interferes with the production of alternatives, desensitization may be required as a first step in treatment. Depending on the duration and intensity of the inhibition, training in problem solving may or may not be required to complete treatment. In cases where a defecit in general problem-solving operations exist, training in problem solving is clearly required; that is, if the goal is to facilitate independence and self-control, and not simply the learning of specific responses to each new problematic situation.

The authors are currently involved in research to evaluate the outcome of a training program based upon the problem-solving strategy described above. Hopefully, we may also be able to test the effects of certain specific steps in the strategy. We hope that other investigators will join in the study and development of behavior modification techniques that stress the role of rational, cognitive processes and mechanisms. We believe that such complex cognitive processes as the problem-solving and decision-making strategies, can and should be reconciled with learning principles, and some promising steps have already been taken in that direction (e.g., Kendler & Kendler, 1962; Mowrer, 1960; Staats, 1966).

We would like to close with a quote from Jerome Bruner (Bruner, Goodnow, & Austin, 1956) on the state of affairs regarding theories of problem-solving in concept attainment before 1956, since it seems to apply to the dissatisfaction that we have with current theories of behavior modification:

> To account for the exquisite forms of problem-solving that we see in everyday life, and may see in our laboratories any time we choose to give our subjects something more challenging than key-pressing to perform, highly simplified theories of learning have been invoked. . . . If we have at times portrayed conceptual behavior as perhaps overly logical, we will perhaps be excused on the ground that one excess often breeds its opposite. Man is not a logic machine, but he is certainly capable of making decisions and gathering information in a manner that reflects better on his learning capacity that we have been as yet ready to grant (p. 79).

17

THE CONTROL OF EATING

Charles B. Ferster,
John I. Nurnberger
and Eugene E. Levitt

Although many investigators have described patterns of eating behavior and reported a wide range of factors related to obesity (Bruch, 1957; Cappon, 1958; Galvin & McGavack, 1957; Stunkard, 1959a, 1959b, 1959c), specific techniques for changing an individual's eating behavior are given little or no attention in published reports, and programs of weight control based on behavioral principles are virtually non-existant. This report is an account of the application of some elementary general principles of reinforcement theory (Skinner, 1958), to the analysis of the behavior of the human eater. This theoretical framework of reinforcement was used to analyze actual performances in eating, and particularly self-control of eating. Supplementing the account of this system are descriptions of experimentally developed techniques which should illustrate practical applications of the theoretical principles of self control.[1]

The theoretical analysis begins with the simple observation that the act of putting food in one's mouth is reinforced and strongly maintained by its immediate consequences: the local effects in the gastrointestinal system. But excessive eating results in increased body-fat and this is aversive to the individual. The problem is therefore to gain control of the factors which determine how often and how much one eats. An individual will manipulate

Reprinted by permission of the authors from *Journal of Mathetics,* 1962, *1,* 87–109.

[1] The experiments are still underway and will be reported separately by the second and third authors.

these variables if the control of eating is reinforcing to him—if he escapes from or avoids the *ultimate aversive consequences of eating* (UAC). Unfortunately for the overeater, the long-term or ultimate aversive consequences of obesity are so postponed as to be ineffective compared with the immediate reinforcement of food in the mouth. Alcoholism is a similar example in which hangover symptoms and the full impact of asocial activity are not suffered until considerable time has elapsed. Realization of self-control, then, demands an arrangement that will bring the influencing conditions into closer association with the reduction of eating behavior.

The analysis and development of self-control in eating involves four steps:

1. *Determining what variables influence eating.* Almost every known behavioral process is relevant to this. Among these are control of eating by stimuli, effect of food deprivation, chaining, avoidance and escape, prepotent and competing behaviors, conditioned alimentary reflexes, and positive reinforcement (Cappon, 1958).
2. *Determining how these variables can be manipulated.* Specification of performances within the repertoire by which the individual can manipulate these variables. One example would be the choice of foods which are weak reinforcers, yet rewarding enough to maintain the behavior of eating them at some low level.
3. *Identifying the unwanted effects (UAC) of over-eating.* Avoidance of these is the basic motive for developing the required self-control.
4. *Arranging a method of developing required self-control.* Some of the required performances may call for so drastic a change of behavior that it may be necessary to produce the required repertory in stages by reinforcing successive approximations.

Self-control requires for our purposes a more precise definition than is conveyed by the term "will-power." It refers to some specific performances which will lower the disposition to emit the behavior to be controlled. These performances involve the manipulation of conditions influencing this behavior. A convenient datum for our analysis is the *frequency* of the behavior's occurrence. The strength, durability, or persistence of the behavior is measured by its frequency. Frequency has the measurement advantage of being a continuous variable. Similarly, the disposition to eat can vary from small to large. The various conditions which the individual himself can manipulate to lessen the frequency of the controlled behavior will be presented in detail in the next section, *Avenues of Self-Control.* The technical problem of generating the self-control performance and maintaining it in strength will be dealt with in the section *Shaping and Maintaining the Self-Control Performance.*

AVENUES OF SELF-CONTROL

THE ULTIMATE AVERSIVE CONSEQUENCES

Avoidance of the ultimate aversive consequences (UAC) of uncontrolled eating is essential in developing performances with which a person may regulate his eating behavior. Self-control is needed because of the time lapse between the act of eating and its UAC. To overcome this time lapse, techniques were sought which would derive a conditioned stimulus from the UAC and apply it at the time the disposition to eat was strong. This is based on the principle that almost any event may become aversive when paired with a known aversive event. Such a conditioned stimulus may be the person's own verbal behavior, if specific training procedures are applied. It is not enough for the subject to *know* what the aversive effect of overeating is, for such knowledge by itself leads only to verbal responses weaker than the food-maintained behavior and may not lessen the strong disposition to eat. Therefore an extensive repertoire must be established so that the subject has under his control large amounts of verbal behavior dealing with the consequences of eating. The continued intensive pairing of facts about the UAC with various kinds of eating performance will make the performances themselves conditioned aversive stimuli. Once a given performance such as eating a piece of pie acquires conditioned aversive properties, any approach to it will produce aversive stimuli. These stimuli will reinforce any self-control because the self-control terminates the averisve stimulus and prevents the uncontrolled act. By such a process, certain foods like pies, cakes, cokes, doughnuts, or candy may become conditioned aversive stimuli, at least until other avenues of control become available.

Before the unwelcome consequences of overeating can be used in developing self-control, they must be identified and developed for the individual. It cannot be assumed that an obese person already has a repertoire about the UAC of eating. In the application of the principles to human subjects being studied, the development of the UAC was one of the major parts of the practical program. However, developing a repertoire by which the subjects could create an aversive state of affairs for themselves presents serious technical problems. First, to establish this repertoire, the actual aversive events must be identified for the subject in terms that are meaningful for his daily life. Second, the subject must learn an active verbal repertoire with which he can translate caloric intake into ultimate body fat.

We first disclosed, in great detail, the consequences of uncontrolled eating for each individual. After each subject described anecdotes about UAC in group sessions, we helped each one to develop a fluent verbal repertoire about the relevant aversive consequences. We found that simply *recognizing* the various aversive consequences did not give these subjects an active verbal repertoire which could be invoked immediately and whenever needed. To develop an active repertoire about the UAC, we arranged rehearsals, frequent repetitions, and written examinations. In general, the subjects were unaware of their inability to verbalize the relevant aversive consequences, and were surprised by the poor results of the early written and oral examinations. Verbal descriptions of aversive consequences the subjects had actually experienced were far more compelling than reports of future and statistically probable consequences, such as diabetes, heart disease, high blood pressure, or gall bladder disorder. In other words, descriptions of actual or imagined social rejection, sarcastic treatment, extreme personal sensitivity over excess weight, demeaning inferences concerning professional incompetence or carelessness, or critical references to bodily contours or proportions were much more potent. All of our subjects found their constant and unsuccessful preoccupation with dieting aversive, and any ability to control their own habits highly rewarding.

All of the exercises in this area were designed to develop a strong and vivid repertoire that could be introduced promptly in a wide variety of situations intimately associated with eating and despite a strong inclination to eat. The actual aversive effects of being overweight are largely individual matters which differ widely from person to person. We therefore used group discussions as an aid for each person to discover how her body weight affected her life. The discussion was guided toward explicit consequences and anecdotes rather than general statements such as "I want to lose weight because I will feel better." We found that after only four or more group sessions, subjects shifted from vague statements such as "I'll look better in clothes" to specific ones such as "My husband made a sarcastic remark about an obese woman who crossed the street as we were driving by." Perhaps, the verbalization of the UAC was too aversive before we had demonstrated that self-control was possible.

AMPLIFYING THE AVERSIVE CONSEQUENCES OF OVEREATING. To establish the bad effects of eating more than one's daily requirements, it is necessary that the individual know the metabolic relationships between different kinds of food, general level of activity, and gain or loss of weight. Phrases like "Evertyhing I eat turns to fat" illustrate that the required repertoire is frequently absent. Thorough training should be given in the caloric properties of all of the kinds of foods which the individual will encounter. The aversive effects of eating certain undesirable foodstuffs can be amplified by generating verbal repertories which describe the full consequences of eating them. For example, the subject should be made to recognize that a 400-calorie piece of pie is the caloric equivalent of a large baked potato with butter plus a medium-size steak. The pie is equivalent to one-tenth of a pound of weight gained, and so forth. Again, *knowing* these facts is not at issue. The issue is that a strong-enough repertoire be established, and with enough intraverbal connections, that the UAC behavior will occur with a high probability in a wide enough variety of situations.

An important exercise early in the weight-control program is the identification of the individual's actual food intake. The subject's casual summaries of his daily food intake are likely to be grossly inaccurate. His ability to recognize his actual food intake is improved by an interview technique in which the interviewer probes and prompts him: "What did you have for breakfast?" "How many pieces of toast?" "How many pieces of bread?" "What did you do between ten and eleven in the morning?" "Were you at a snack bar or a restaurant at any point during the day?" "Were you offered any candy at any point?" and so forth.

With the pilot subjects, we leaned most heavily on a written protocol which we used as a basis for individual interviews about their diets. Each subject kept a complete written account of everything she had eaten, along with calculations of fat, carbohydrate, protein, and numbers of calories. A large part of the early sessions was devoted to problems in recording food intake, such as difficulties in estimating mixed foods like gravies, stews, or sauces.

For the first four weeks of the program, when some simpler kinds of self-control were developed, the subjects' caloric intake was set to maintain a constant weight. We over-estimated the maintenance levels, and all subjects gained weight during this month. However, the weight increase proved the relationship between caloric intake and weight change in a situation where the caloric intake was carefully defined. In spite of the weight gain, however, some measure of self-control emerged, particularly in changes in the temporal pattern and regularity of eating.

DEPRIVATION

The effect of food deprivation may be observed in a pigeon experiment in which the frequency of a pigeon's key pecking, maintained by producing food, is measured as a function of changes in the level of food deprivation. Changes in the level of food deprivation produce continuous changes in the bird's performance over an extremely wide range if we can measure the frequency of the bird's pecking. This frequency of pecking is intuitively close to notions like the bird's disposition to eat, probability of action, or motivation. When a wide range of frequency response can be measured sensitively, the level of deprivation affects the bird's performance continuously, from free-feeding body weight to as low as 65 to 70 per cent of normal body weight. Food deprivation of the order of six to twenty four hours constitutes a very small part of the effective range. The magnitude of food deprivation therefore continues to increase the organism's disposition to emit responses, reinforced by food, long after no further changes occur in gastrointestinal reactions (e.g., hunger pangs) and other conditioned effects of food in the mouth. The hunger pangs, which are ordinarily taken as symptoms of hunger (from which the effect of food deprivation is inferred), are more closely related to the conditioned stimuli accompanying past reinforcements of eating than to the level of food deprivation. The conditioned reflexes involving the gastrointestinal system occur at relatively low levels of deprivation compared with the effective range of food deprivation in respect to the changes in frequency of operant behavior. There may be a similar lack of correspondence between the tendency to verbalize, introspectively, reports of hunger and the actual disposition to eat. For purposes of developing self-control, the actual performances resulting in food in the mouth are more relevant than the introspective reports of "hunger."

Controlling the rate at which the subject loses weight proves to be a major technique of self-control. For any degree of establishment of a self-control repertoire, there is probably some level of food deprivation which will cause the subject to eat in spite of the self-control behavior. Therefore, a major principle of self-control would be to pace the rate of the subject's weight loss so that the effect of the weight loss on the disposition to eat would be less than the given stage of development of self-control. Many avenues of self-control may be learned without causing any weight loss. Placing the eating behavior under the control of specific stimuli or breaking up the chain of responses usually present in the compulsive eater are examples of this. The former will be discussed below. Breaking up a chain causes the eating performance to become a series of discrete acts which are more easily interrupted than a continuous performance in which each chewing response or each swallow occasions placing the next bit of food on the fork.

If the self-control performances which may be developed are to be useful, they must be maintained by conditions which will be present continuously, even after the weight-control therapy procedures are discontinued. Many unsuccessful crash diet programs illustrate the way in which too rapid a loss of weight produces a level of deprivation and a disposition to eat exceeding the existing self-control. The usual diet involves some program which taps the motivation of the dieter temporarily. For example, slight aversive pressure from the husband or family doctor may produce a rapid loss in weight, perhaps on the order of three to five pounds a week. The effect of the rapid weight loss is a large increase in the disposition to eat which then overcomes the subject's temporary motive.

Limiting the diet to one specific food, such as protein, probably will produce a heightened disposition to eat other food stuffs regardless of the general weight level. These are the traditional specific hungers. An all-protein diet, for example, even if taken without limit of calories, would probably generate an enormous disposition to eat carbohydrates, sugars, and fats. Therefore, a balanced diet should be maintained and a weight loss brought about by a uniform reduction in amount rather than kind of food.

Although the major effects of food deprivation appear when weight losses are of the order of pounds, the time elapsed since eating would have local effects on the disposition to eat. Local satiation effects may best be used as a limited avenue of self-control by arranging the eating schedules so that the subject ingests a meal or a significant amount of food just before a situation in which the disposition to eat might be unusually strong. An example is a social situation in which eating has frequently occurred in the past or when preferred foods are present. The housewife who eats continuously while preparing dinner can control the disposition to nibble the foods being prepared by shifting the preparation of the dinner meal to the period of time immediately following lunch, when her disposition to eat is lower because she has just eaten.

In the application of the self-control principles to actual exercises, we specified a weight loss of one pound per week and insisted that our subjects adhere to this rate of weight loss even though each of them wanted to cut her diet more stringently in order to lose weight at a greater rate. Different rates of weight loss might possibly be arranged at different stages of development of self-control after more is known about the effectiveness of different avenues of self-control and about the relative effects of weight loss depending upon the initial level.

The continued ingestion of food during a meal provided another variation in level of food deprivation which was used to provide a gradual transition to the final self-control performances. Exercises, such as brief interruptions in eating, were first carried out toward the end of the meal when some satiation had occurred. After the subjects began to learn how to use auxiliary techniques to stop eating and their existing eating patterns began to break down, the exercises were moved progressively toward the early part of the meal, when their levels of deprivation were higher so that the exercises had to be more difficult.

Self-control by Manipulating Stimuli

The characteristic circumstances when an individual eats will subsequently control his disposition to eat. The process is illustrated by the pigeon whose key pecking produces food only when the key is green and not when it is red. The frequency with which the pigeon pecks the key (reinforced by food) will later depend upon which color is present. Thus, changing the color of the key can arbitrarily increase or decrease the frequency of pecking independently of the level of food deprivation. A frequent factor in the lack of self-control in the obese person may be the large variety of circumstances in which eating occurs. In contrast, a much narrower range of stimuli is present during the more infrequent eating periods of the controlled person. Therefore, the disposition to eat possibly could be decreased by narrowing the range of stimuli which are the occasions for the reinforcement by food. By proper choice of the actual stimuli controlling the eating behavior, it should also be possible to increase the individual's control over these stimuli. There are circumstances when even the pathologically compulsive eater will have a considerably lower disposition to eat for periods of time simply because the environment is novel enough so that eating has never occurred then. Consider, for example, walking in an isolated forest area.

The first step in the development of self-control in this category is to narrow the range of existing stimuli which control eating. The overweight individual eats under a large variety of circumstances. Thus, the problem of self-control is made difficult by the large number of daily occasions which bring the tendency to eat to maximal levels because in the past they have been the occasions when eating has occurred. Two kinds of behavior need to be brought under stimulus control. The first is the elicited reflex effects of food, such as salivation, gastric secretion, and other responses of the gastrointestinal tract. The other involves operant behavior, or the behavior involving the striated musculature of the organism—walking, talking, reaching, cooking, and so forth. In the so-called voluntary behaviors, the major datum is the frequency of the behavior rather than the magnitude of an elicited reflex, as with the smooth-muscle response of the digestive system. Although these two types of behavioral control are inevitably tied together, their properties are different and they must be distinguished both dynamically and statically. In order to break down the control of eating by the stimuli which have been the characteristic occasions on which eating has been reinforced in the past, the stimuli must occur without the subsequent reinforcement by the food. The process is a direct extrapolation from the extinction of a Pavlovian conditioned response. If the dog is to discontinue salivation on the occasion of the bell, the bell must be presented repeatedly in the situation in which the food no longer follows. The amount of saliva the bell elicits then declines continuously until it reaches near-zero. Similarly, the stimuli characteristic of the preparation of a meal will cease to control large amounts of gastric activity if these stimuli can be made to occur without being followed by food in the mouth. Initially, the stimuli will elicit large amounts of gastric activity; but with continued exposure to these stimuli, the amount of activity will decline continuously until low levels are reached.

Delimiting existing stimulus control of eating may take considerable time because (1) the loss of control by a stimulus is a gradual process, requiring repeated exposure to the relevant stimuli; and (2) it may be a long time before the individual encounters all of the situations in which he has eaten in the past. The sudden temptation of the ex-smoker to light a cigarette when he meets an old friend is an example of the latter kind of control.

Self-control developed under procedures involving very special situations and foods (for example, liquid diets, all-protein diets, or hard-boiled eggs and celery) will be difficult to maintain when the diet circumstances return to normal. The very abrupt shift in eating patterns, kinds of food eaten, and characteristic circumstances surrounding eating will weaken the self-control performances as well as strengthen eating behaviors which were previously in the person's repertoire under the control of the more normal environment. Hence, self-control performances must be developed under circumstances and with foods which are to be the individual's final eating pattern.

Temporal Control of Eating

The time of day is an important event controlling eating. With the individual who characteristically eats at regular intervals, gastric activity comes to precede these occasions very closely, and is at low levels elsewhere regardless of levels of deprivation. The same can be said for operant behavior associated with eating, although the order of magnitude of some of the parameters may be different. After the conditioned responses associated with eating are brought closely under the control of a strict temporal pattern, feelings of hunger should disappear except just before meal-time. However, many individuals have no such routine patterns of eating, so that the temporal pattern of eating does not limit the amount of gastrointestinal activity. The obese person frequently eats in the absence of any gastric activity. A technique of self-control in this category would rigidly specify a temporal pattern of eating and find conditions for adhering to it. As with the gastrointestinal reflexes, this general disposition to engage in operant behaviors reinforced by the ingestion of food can be brought under the control of a temporal pattern of eating, with a resulting lower disposition to eat during the intervals between regular meals. In the early stages of learning self-control, the development of a rigid temporal pattern perhaps should be carried out under conditions in which no weight loss is to be expected and the amount of food, ingested at specified meals, is large enough to minimize the disposition to eat on other occasions. The subsequent maintenance of this temporal pattern of eating when the subject begins to lose weight will depend upon the concurrent action of other categories of self-control performances. The control of eating by temporal factors can also be developed for situations other than the normal routine meals, as, for example, at social gatherings and parties. Because the availability of food is predictable here, early stages of self-control can include arranging a specific time when the eating will occur rather than indeterminate consumption of whatever foods happen to be available.

The Eating Situation

As with the temporal properties of eating, the actual characteristics of the eating situation may be used to control the disposition to eat. However, the stimuli here are clearer and probably exert control of an even larger order of magnitude than that of the temporal pattern. This application of the principal of stimulus control is the same as in the temporal contingency: to arrange that eating occur on limited and narrowly circumscribed occasions and never otherwise. To simplify the development of the stimulus control, eating situations should be associated with stimuli which occur infrequently in the individual's normal activities. For example, an eating place in the home should be chosen so that it is maximally removed from the routine activities of the day. Nor should eating occur together with any other kind of activity such as reading. If reading occurs frequently enough while the subject is eating, then reading will increase the disposition to eat because it has been an occasion on which eating has been reinforced.

Emphasizing the Stimulus Control

The occasions characterizing eating can be emphasized by deliberately arranging very obvious stimuli. For example, the subject always eats sitting down at a table which has a napkin, a place setting, and a purple table cloth. The latter makes the situation even more distinctive. In the exetreme case, a specific item of clohing might be worn whenever the subject eats. Narrowing the range provides another form of stimulus control. By eating only specific foods in specific places, the disposition to eat when other foods are available will be minimized. This factor will also be discussed under chaining; but the aspect emphasized here is the effect of the foods eaten as one of the elements in the occasion associated with eating. If a subject has eliminated ice cream, candy, and cake from his diet, the sweet shop will have little control over his behavior.

In the actual procedures with subjects, stimulus control was the first avenue of self-control developed. The subjects learned to keep daily diet protocols during the first few meetings and to determine the number of calories necessary to maintain their weight. We restricted eating to three meals a day, eliminated concentrated fats and sugars from the diet, and attempted to bring about an increase in the amount of food taken in at meals, particularly at breakfast, to bring about a normal pattern of eating without any expected weight loss. For individuals having difficulty in restricting their eating to meals, we arranged a specific and routine extra feeding, as, for example, a glass of milk and a few crackers at bedtime. The extra feeding was to be taken routinely, however, so it did not become a reinforcer for increasing the probability of eating on a wide variety of occasions. No weight loss was attempted until the subjects were successful in eating a normal range of food at meals without any eating at other times. We attempted to create an eating pattern which could be carried out without interruption after the weight-control program was terminated. Our major problems were insufficient protein or excess fat in the diet. None of the subjects ate excessive amounts of carbohydrate except perhaps as candy. However, all subjects had trouble eating a full meal. It was paradoxical that women who joined the program because they could not limit their eating had difficulty in ingesting a maintenance diet at mealtimes. One complained of nausea, another of chest pains, and a third of discomfort from overeating. All of the complaints disappeared in a week, however.

Chaining

Eating is a rough designation for a chain of behavioral sequences culminating in swallowing and the subsequent gastrointestinal reflexes. An illustrative sequence might be as follows: Dressing makes possible leaving the house; leaving the house leads to walking to the store; entering the store is followed by the selection of foods; a basket of food is the occasion for paying the clerk and leaving the store; a bag of groceries at home leads to storing the food; stored food is the occasion for cooking or otherwise preparing the food; the prepared food is the occasion for setting the table and sitting down; the sight of food is the occasion for cutting it with a fork or knife; the dissected food leads to placing food in the mouth; food in the mouth is followed by chewing; and chewing is followed by swallowing. The sequence differs from individual to individual and from time to time, but any selected elements illustrate the process.

Because the frequency of occurrence of the final member of the chain depends on the nature of the earlier members of the eating sequence, some degree of self-control can be arranged by dealing with the dynamic properties of the eating sequence. The length of the chain of responses leading to swallowing will markedly influence the frequency with which the eating sequence is carried out. The longer the sequence of behaviors in the chain and the more behavior sequences in each member of the chain, the weaker will be the disposition to start the chain. This property of chaining suggests a technique of control which could be useful if used in conjunction with the other avenues of control. By arranging that all of the foods available or accessible require a certain amount of preparation or locomotion, the tendency to eat can be reduced simply because the chain of responses leading to swallowing was lengthened. Keeping food out of areas normally entered, shopping on a day-to-day basis (at a time when the disposition to eat is low), buying foods which are not edible without cooking or other preparation, and placing food in less accessible places are some techniques for weakening the disposition to eat by lengthening a chain. As in some of the avenues of control, this technique would be inadequate under extreme levels of deprivation without additional support from other types of control. The chain must not be lengthened too much, or it might become so weakened that prepotent eating behaviors would occur or the chain shortcircuited.

The actual form of the eating chain in the latter members just before swallowing may be rearranged to reduce the rate of eating. The behavior of swallowing is so strongly reinforced that it could occur very soon after food enters the mouth, without very much chewing. Similarly, the behavior of placing food in the mouth (reinforced by the taste of food) has high strength and occurs as soon as the mouth empties. Many eaters carry out this sequence at a very high rate by reaching for additional food just as soon as food is placed in the mouth and by swallowing while the fork is in transit to the mouth. This analysis is confirmed by the high rate with which many obese people eat compared with that of non-obese eaters.

To reduce the rate of eating and to make it possible for the subject to stop eating at any point, we designed simple exercises to break the chain, particularly the near-final members, so that the occasion for placing food on the fork is swallowing rather than chewing. The new sequence was: food on the fork only after other food is swallowed and the mouth is empty. These exercises depended on ancillary techniques of control already developed by other techniques of self-control. At the start, the interruptions were only a few seconds; then, they were gradually increased to several minutes. The ability to stop eating at *any* point represents the final effect of nearly all of the other avenues of control; nevertheless, it constitutes a separate technique of control demanding special exercises. In later, more difficult exercises, the subject holds food on a fork for various periods of time without eating. Similarly, chewing is prolonged before swallowing for increasing periods. These exercises are carried out initially at the end of a meal, when the deprivation level is low.

The type of food eaten is of major importance in how reinforcing it would be, and hence how long a chain of responses can be maintained by the food reinforcement. The disposition to eat could be somewhat regulated by a selection of foods in the individual's diet that are sufficiently reinforcing (appetizing, caloric, etc.) to be eaten, but minimally reinforcing so as to minimize the resulting disposition to eat. A certain balance must be achieved; if the foods chosen are so unappetizing or unappealing that their reinforcing effect is negligible, the subject will simply switch to other foods. Also relevant here are the dynamic effects of food deprivation. Foods which are maximally reinforcing should be eaten when the individual is less deprived, and minimally reinforcing foods should be eaten under stronger conditions of deprivation. In other words, the effect of the highly reinforcing food stuffs on the disposition to eat would be minimized by a lower level of deprivation so that the subject can stop eating more easily. In special cases, the food intake could be increased temporarily in order to minimize the highly reinforcing effect of certain foods. For example, if an individual who is highly reinforced by caloric pastries knows she will be in a situation where such pastries are being served, she could lessen the probability of eating them by increasing her food intake during the preceding meal or by a glass of milk before entering the situation.

Prepotent Repertoires

One way to lessen the disposition to eat is to supplant it by establishing other activities incompatible with eating. In an extreme case, an apparently large disposition to eat is often due to a behavioral repertoire in which eating appears strong because the rest of the repertoire is weak. Some degree of self-control should be possible if some activity could be maintained at a potentially high strength and circumstances arranged so that the subject could engage in this activity whenever the disposition to eat was strong. An example of such an activity might be telephoning a friend just after breakfast instead of indulging in the customary between-meal nibbling. The use of prepotent repertoires as a technique of control implies a certain amount of control over the prepotent repertoire. In order for these substitutive repertoires to be effective, special attention must be given to methods for strengthening them, particularly when they are needed. For example, instead of reading the newspaper as soon as it arrives, it could be put aside until some time when the peak tendency to eat occurs. Similarly, the telephoning of friends could be postponed in order to keep this behavior at high strength. Such activities occur initially because of independent reinforcement. Another kind of prepotent repertoire may be established by starting some strongly reinforced activity whose reinforcement occurs only if the behavior occurs uninterrupted for a period of time. Examples are washing a floor, going to a movie, taking a bus ride, reading a short story, or going for a walk. Such performances will be prepotent over eating because of the temporary aversive consequences resulting from their interruption. In many cases, the prepotent repertoires physically remove the individual from the place where eating can occur.

The effective use of prepotent repertoires depends upon the development of other avenues of control. Probably no one of these "prepotent" performances would be effective by itself if the disposition to eat were strong. For example, the individual going for a walk could simply stop at a restaurant to eat. Nevertheless, there is still a net advantage, because the supplementary types of self-control needed are relatively easy. For example, compare the disposition to stop at a restuarant during a walk with the disposition to eat in the normal situations when eating usually occurs. If the individual usually eats at home, the tendency to stop at a resturant and eat will be considerably less than the tendency to eat at home. No explicit training was required in the pilot experiment to establish self-control by the use of prepotent repertoires; but all of the subjects used them during several phases of the experiment.

Prepotent repertoires may be affected by emotional factors. For example, many persons eat when depressed, affronted, thwarted, or frustrated. In terms of the functional analysis of eating used here, emotional factors may weaken behaviors other than eating so that eating becomes relatively stronger. Putting food in one's mouth remains a highly reinforcing activity even if the remainder of the individual's repertoire is severely depressed. Eating then occurs because it is less disrupted by the emotional variables depressing the rest of the individual's repertoire.

Eating may interact with emotional factors in more subtle, but nonetheless important, ways, as a mechanism by which a person might escape or avoid emitting verbal behavior which is highly aversive, *e.g.*, thinking about impending circumstances which are highly aversive. Because of its very strong and immediate reinforcement, eating will be prepotent over thinking about anxiety-evoking occurrences. Thus, eating comes to acquire two sources of strength: The immediate reinforcement from food in the mouth, and the reinforcement from postponing or avoiding the aversive consequences of emitting the verbal behavior which the eating supplants. Emotional disturbances will also disrupt the performances by which the individual controls himself, as will any general depression or disturbance of the individual's over-all repertoire. Self-control performances will be especially liable to disruption early in their development, before they become strong and maintained.

The manipulation of factors to minimize the effects of emotional disturbances is a separate topic, involving self-control of variables different from those in eating and thus requiring a separate analysis. The main avenue of control in eating lies in increasing the strength and durability of the self-control performances so that they will remain intact during emotional disturbances. For example, a person who has acquired an active and extensive verbal repertoire about all of the personal aversive consequences of being overweight will be able to emit these behaviors even during some general depression of his behavioral repertoire. The behavior about the ultimate aversive consequences of eating will be even more durable during possibly disrupting situations if it has already been affective in producing self-control, that is, if the behavior about the UAC has been reinforced effectively by suppression of the disposition to eat.

If existing levels of self-control are certain to break down because of an emotional disturbance, the individual should be trained to plan a controlled increase in food intake. The advantage of explicitly increasing the level of food intake would be that the food would be eaten under controlled conditions, so that stimulus control and other factors of self-control already developed would be maintained, and the effects of absence of progress in self-control would be minimized. Overeating under planned conditions would probably weaken the already developed self-control repertoires less than unplanned or uncontrolled eating.

In many situations, the general depression of an individual's repertoire occurs only for a limited time. Here, the necessary self-control performances would be a manipulation of the physical environment so that food is not available then, or would be the creation of a prepotent environment. The depressed individual who wishes to control his eating goes to a movie, takes a ride on a bus, or goes for a long walk. These activities give time for the emotional states to disappear and simultaneously provide an environment in which eating has not been reinforced very frequently in the individual's past experience. Of course, applications of these techniques of control depend upon the prior achievement of a certain amount of self-control, and probably are some of the most difficult areas of self-control to acquire. Such items would not be attempted at an early stage of the self-control program.

SHAPING AND MAINTAINING THE SELF-CONTROL PERFORMANCE

Self-control is a very complex repertoire of performance which cannot be developed all at once. If self-control consists of items of behavior with the same dynamic properties as those of the rest of human behavior, the self-control performance, as a complicated repertoire, must be developed in slow steps. These would begin with some performance already in the individual's repertoire and proceed in successive stages to more complicated performances. With each gain in self-control, the individual has a repertoire from which a new degree of complex behavior may emerge. Simply "telling" the subject the nature of the performances required for the development of self-control is not a sufficient condition for their development. The situation is analogous to that of a complicated motor or intellectual activity. One cannot explain to the novice how to differentiate an equation in calculus without first establishing a repertoire in algebra. Similarly, as most golfers have learned, no amount of verbal instruction will take the place of slow development of behavior reinforced by its effect on the golf ball. The actual disposition to emit the self-control behavior builds up because it was emitted successfully to reduce the long-term aversive affects of the behavior to be controlled. What is required here is to begin with some performance very close to one in the individual's repertoire, and to arrange circumstances so that those performances have at least some effect on the disposition to eat. The early reinforcement of this initial repertoire by a discernible movement in self-control provides the basis for the subject's continued attendance to the self-control program.

In the development of self-control, the concern is not simply the presence or absence of a self-control performance. A group of behaviors must be built constituting a repertoire that will occur with a sufficient degree of certainty to be maximally effective.

Just as the disposition to eat can vary from near-zero to very large values, the behaviors involved in self-control can also be weak or strong. Whether the individual "knows" what the potential techniques of self-control are, or even can emit them, is not so important as the durability of the self-control repertoire. A set of performances is needed which will occur with high-enough probability despite competition from the individual's other repertoires. The maintaining event for the self-control performance is the reduction in the disposition to eat. The effect of the reinforcement is not an all-or-none matter, and the reinforcing effect of gains in self-control repertoires can be variously small, large, or even intermittent. Uncontrolled eating should not be viewed as a failure in control, but simply as the absence of progress. If the positive aspects of the program are emphasized, as well as the development of specific performances to control the disposition to eat, each small increment in the ability of the subject to control himself will reinforce further participation in the self-control program. A failure of a self-control performance to prevent eating defines an intermittent schedule of reinforcement of the self-control behavior. It may still continue to maintain the performances, just as any other act that is intermittently reinforced.

Some types of self-control require that old performances disappear rather than a specific repertoire, as, for example, the development of stimulus control, be built. The development of this kind of self-control is largely a function of the number of exposures, without eating, in situations when the individual has eaten in the past. Verbal behavior has only limited relevance here, since it can be little more than a report of what is taking place. Recognizing that the preparations for dinner are increasing the disposition to salivate and eat is of little use in controlling these effects. Extinguishing the effects of these stimuli is an orderly process requiring only exposure to the stimuli and passage of time. However, knowledge of the process might be of use in conjunction with the various avenues of self-control, particularly in repect to emphasizing the stimuli involved. Once the subject recognizes that the extinction of the stimulus control is a slow process, even minor decrements in the extent of the control by the stimuli will provide reinforcements for maintaining the self-control, as, for example, when several days are required for extinction. In the absence of knowledge of the order of magnitude of the course of the process, weakly maintained self-control behaviors might extinguish. In the actual self-control program, noting reductions in the strength of eating behavior during its extinction provides interim reinforcement for the self-control performances.

DISCUSSION

Traditionally, the development of self-control has been in a framework of classical psychoanalytic and dynamic psychotherapeutic approaches to human behavior. These approaches view self-control in terms of its developmental and dynamic origins and the inner-directed, private forces which sustain, direct or distort its external manifestations. Prior life experiences are considered in detail through interviewing and related techniques including analyses of current actions and attitudes (transference and counter-transference). The focus is on the past to assist the individual in discovering those formative experiences and relationships which have functioned to establish current attitudes and current modes of alleviating anxiety and guilt. A major structural goal of this system is the development of effective insight with increased intellectual freedom and more realistic self-appraisal. A major symptomatic goal is the ultimate reduction of anxiety and guilt, with a resultant diminished need to exploit heroic or uneconomic measures in the control of either or both. A fundamental assumption here is that the human being who becomes sufficiently aware of his personal developmental behavioral determinants and who is sufficiently relieved of neurotic anxiety of guilt, will, by virtue of this achievement, progressively lose his dependence on irrational and restrictive defenses. A corollary is that a healthy behavioral repertoire is potentially available at any time the individul gains relief from the guilt and anxiety of his deviant developmental history. These assumptions are not at all unreasonable for many problems encountered by the clinician, and sometimes appear to be convincingly supported by satisfactory therapeutic outcome. However, there are outstanding exceptions, characterized by certain common behavioral elements. Among these are (1) elaborately ritualized performances; (2) long-standing maintenance of such patterns; and (3) large amounts of strongly maintained and sustained activity. These are the symptoms present in many alcoholic individuals, in all obsessive-compulsive neurotics, in many patients with neurotic depressive reactions, in drug addicts, in a variety of schizophrenic patients, and in many individuals with eating disturbances (obese as well as anorexic). Successful and sustained therapeutic improvement is exceptional for all, including the obese (Stunkard, 1959c), however prolonged and insightful the therapeutic experience may be. The kind of functional analysis of behavior proposed here may provide a conception of human behavior as an alternative to the classical psychoanalytically oriented systems.

The terms in such an analysis are the actual performances of the patient and their exact effects on his environment. The frequency of occurrence of the performance is studied as a function of its effect on the environment, and every attempt is made to observe and deal with the relevant performances rather than with inferred processes. The specificity of the analysis does not mean that the patient must have an intact repertoire by which he deals with the world, and attention can be focused on creating whatever repertoire is necessary. Most of the present report is a presentation of certain practical techniques which can be applied to the problem of uncontrolled eating. The preliminary results of this pilot program are not included as a record of even mediocre success, but rather as a description of the medium within which the specific techniques of control were imparted. A much longer follow-up period and a larger number of cases are necessary to develop a successful program as well as test it. Nor can we now designate these aspects of the program which were effective or ineffective. This report is intended to provide a theoretical and practical model for more structured programs of self-control in eating. We have shown eating habits can be changed in a short-term, small-group-therapy program by the use of the basic principles outlined here. Whether or not the weight losses reported during the first 15 sessions are primarily due to the application of the principles outlined can be determined only by appropriately controlled study experiments. We are not concerned whether one or another program can effect weight loss, since many pharmacologic individual- and group-therapy programs lead to temporary loss of weight, as is generally known. The central issue is the development of self-control in eating which will endure and become an available part of the individual's future repertoire. Most conventional programs do not focus on the eating patterns available to the subject after he has lost weight, nor do they present recognizable techniques for developing such future control. Possible exceptions are in individual programs of psychotherapy which are directed toward an exploration and resolution of the unconscious determinants of eating behavior, and in certain of the conditioned-reflex techniques. Yet, even in these programs, this question remains: Do proper eating habits exist after the individual is free of the relevant disability? The program outlined here has the special advantage of focusing directly and specifically on future eating behavior, and of presenting even more specific techniques for bringing this behavior under control. Application of the basic principles requires no special instrumental or technical training and is relatively economical. Slow and controlled weight loss under relatively high-caloric intake levels minimizes medical and psychological problems.

We cannot state whether the program we carried out is suitable for severely obese individuals (particularly those who have medical or psychiatric complications). Nor can we specify how the technical principles and procedures can be applied to subjects of low educational level or of limited intelligence. A major problem here would undoubtedly be the difficulty of daily and accurate caloric-intake records. Some of these fundamental questions are subjects for future study.

18

CONTROL OF COVERANTS: THE OPERANTS OF THE MIND[1]

Lloyd E. Homme

The phrase, operants of the mind, is used only in part because it is ridiculous. It is used also to emphasize the conviction that it is time operant conditioners come to grips with private events. The layman calls them mental and knows they are important, but behaviorists are of very little help in elucidating them. Usually, the best a psychologist can do is mention that, when the man on the street speaks of mental events, he is really talking about behavior. Important exceptions here, as in other areas, are Kantor (1924; 1926) and Skinner (1953; 1957). They discuss the general topic of private events at some length, but one statement of Skinner typifies the viewpoint of both and is of particular relevance to developments in this paper: "We need not suppose that events which take place within an organism's skin have special properties for that reason." The assumption that private behavioral events obey the same laws as nonprivate ones underlies the present discussion.

It is not that private events have been entirely ignored by other psychological writers. On the contrary, every self-respecting elementary textbook discusses thinking, often with a strong emphasis on elecromyographical data. But that is just it. Modern behaviorism has gotten so bogged down in examin-

Reprinted by permission of the author and publisher from the *Psychological Record*, 1965, *15*, 501–511.

[1] Thanks are due to all of the author's Westinghouse colleagues, especially D. T. Tosti, C. B. Chadwick, J. A. Colosimo, P. C. deBaca, and K. M. Kamerman, for their more or less successful attempts at withholding aversive stimulation during the development of the notions which appear in this paper, and for occasionally generating old shopworn ideas which could be refurbished into the sparkling new ones found here.

ing the topography of these responses that no attention has been paid to the problem of controlling the frequency of their occurrence. This paper will discuss some of the reasons for behaviorists' neglect of the control of private events and why these reasons are no longer valid.

What Are Coverants?

The word *coverant* is simply a contraction of *covert operant.* Since the word *operant* comes from the fact that it refers to a response which operates on the environment (Skinner, 1938), it may seem strange that any covert behavior should be called an operant. Yet, as will be clear later, if contingencies are properly managed, coverants do indeed have environmental consequences. But the main reason for emphasizing that the topic under discussion is some kind of operant is that the responses discussed here are not parts of reflexes, nor are they states of the organism. Instead, it is assumed that, since coverants have the properties of responses, they are responses.

Coverants are events the layman calls mental. These include thinking, imagining, ruminating, reflecting, relaxing, daydreaming, fantasying, and so forth. Difficulties in the control of one or the other of the coverant class undoubtedly underlie a good many behavior or personality disorders.[2] Even if this is only partially true, agreement can probably be reached that these coverants are important. If this is so, why have not operant conditioners paid more attention to them?

It is the thesis of this paper that the development of a technology for controlling the occurrence of private events such as these has been held back by two problems which are no longer problems:

1. The difficulties in the detection of the occurrence or nonoccurrence of the response because of difficulties in the description of the response's topography; and
2. The availability and control of reinforcers contingent upon the response.

The Pseudoproblem of Coverant Response Definition and Detection

At least part of the responsibility for the neglect of these interesting private events has to be laid to their labels. The labels referred to are those which designate private events as states of the organism. Relaxation, for example, is typically spoken of as a state of the organism. Since there is no

[2] Because emotional disorders more than likely involve behaviors with both respondent and operant components, let us avoid complications by restricting the discussion, for the time being, to those responses relatively free of respondent components.

body of behavioral technology for controlling the frequency or extent of states, this formulation leads nowhere. If, however, relaxation is treated as a coverant, the whole body of operant conditioning techniques can be brought to bear (Homme, 1965a).

But the faulty labeling presents only a trivial problem in comparison to the main one. If coverants are private events, how is the experimenter to know when one occurs? The whole problem of response definition, of course, is the main reason for the neglect of the study of coverant control. In principle, there is no real difficulty in detecting the occurrence of a coverant. With sufficient instrumentation it is, in principle, possible to make public when *S* is thinking about a chair, say, rather than a table. However, the instrumentation, which presumably would have to include highly sophisticated computers, is enough to persuade any one that the venture would be one of staggering magnitude. In practice, no one is going to make the investment required to make discriminations between coverants of the sort mentioned. Fortunately, this sort of investment is entirely unnecessary. Each *S* is a highly sophisticated computer when it comes to discriminating the occurrence or nonoccurrence of behavior in himself. Whether he is thinking about a chair or thinking about a table is a simple discrimination which he can make with great reliability. The same discrimination would not be impossible for a computer, but it would be difficult and expensive.

Interwoven with the detection problem is the tremendous difficulty involved in the description of coverants' topography. None of these difficulties, it is here argued, need stand in the way of the development of a technology for the control of coverants.

The Reinforcement of Coverants

The key to the control of any operant, coverant or otherwise, lies in the control of reinforcing events. Here is another important reason for the neglect of the technology of the control of coverants—the control of the reinforcer. Skinner's comment, "The place of operant reinforcement in self-control is not clear," (1953) is an indication that the technology of self-reinforcement has lagged markedly behind the rest of operant conditioning's technology. The lack of easily available self-reinforcers, plus the pseudo-problems of response definition and response detection, probably accounts for the behaviorist's lack of power in the area of coverants. Now, however, due to the work of Premack (1965), this situation no longer obtains.

Premack's Differential Probability Hypothesis

The sine qua non of a technology for the self-control of coverants is the easy availability of a large number of self-reinforcers. If Premack's differential probability hypothesis (which can be conveniently abbreviated

P-hypothesis where P stands for either probability or Premack) is correct, a reinforcer is *always* available (Premack, 1959).

Premack's statement of the P-hypothesis is elegantly simple: "For any pair of responses, the more probable one will reinforce the less probable one" (Premack, 1965). Another property of operants not often verbalized is a part of Premack's Indifference Principle (Premack, 1965). Paraphrased, it is that the same rules hold regardless of the response's topography. This is particularly important in the case of coverants since often one has only the faintest notion of their topography. Yet their occurrence can be detected easily by the person to whom they are private. For example, it would be a formidable task indeed to describe the topography of the response which occurs when *S* thinks about the paper he is to write, but the occurrence or nonoccurrence of this event is easily detected by the one doing the thinking. If there should be any reason for strengthening this coverant, it can easily be done. All that is required is that *S*, to whom it is private, demand that it occur immediately prior to the execution of some momentarily high probability behavior.[3]

For example, he can say to himself (if getting a cup of coffee is a high probability behavior), "As soon as I think about that paper I am to write, I will get some coffee." In this example, *S* has self-managed his contingencies so that the execution of a high probability behavior (getting coffee) was contingent upon the execution of some lower probability behavior (thinking about the paper). If Premack is correct, the tendency to think about the paper ought to increase in frequency. It is interesting to note that contingencies do not automatically get thus managed. Without keeping the P-hypothesis in mind, it seems just as reasonable for *S* to say to himself, "As soon as I get my coffee, I'll think about the paper."

Take another example. Suppose lighting a cigar is a high probability behavior at a given instant. Further suppose that the lower probability behavior one wishes to strengthen is the relaxation coverant. Does one light the cigar and then relax? Not if one's intent is to strengthen the relaxation coverant. Instead, one will say to oneself, "As soon as I relax, I may light this cigar."

Both of these coverants have the standard properties. Their occurrence or nonoccurrence is easily detected by *S*, yet nothing need be known by *S* about their topography, and control of their frequency can be manipulated by making the occurrence of a higher probability behavior contingent on their emission.

The reader will recognize that underlying this whole discussion is the assumption that, as Slack (1965) puts it, nature doesn't really care who manipulates the independent variables of which behavior is a function. And this includes the person doing the behaving.

[3] The probability referred to here, of course, is not based on formal frequency or duration data; it is a kind of phenomenological probability estimate. The assumption is that *S* can predict what he is likely to do next.

Difficulties in Coverant Control

To keep things from getting complicated, the problem of reinforcement for the self-contingency manager (self CM) has been ignored until now. But it is a central problem. If the self CM does not get reinforced for self-management, extinction will occur. This means, in practice, that the self CM must discriminate some consequences of his own self-management. Skinner (1953) and Holland and Skinner (1961) speak of the controlling response and the controlled response in self-control. In their terms, then, under discussion is the question of maintaining the controlling response. As it should, all evidence indicates that the *S* must observe something—a weight loss, a decline in the number of cigarettes smoked, or he must "feel better"—something discriminable must happen for self CM to be maintained. Exactly what properties this something should have is at present a matter of speculation.

There is another problem possibly even more basic. This is the engineering problem of getting self CM going in the first place. Awaiting development is a technology for getting the *S* to isolate one feature of his own behavior and say, in effect, "I'm going to increase the frequency of that response class." *S* is much more likely to say, "I wish I could refrain from making a certain response." This is much more in line with the traditional view of self-control which emphasizes refraining from doing something which is automatically reinforcing.

Although the point has been made implicitly, it should be emphasized that the contingency management in general has no technology for "getting rid" of a response. CM has only a technology for strengthening a behavior which is incompatible with the response to be eliminated. This can be further illustrated by considering some applications of self contingency management.

SOME APPLICATIONS OF COVERANT CONTROL

It goes without saying that techniques for the control of operants such as those spelled out by the superb analysis of Ferster, Nurnberger, and Levitt (1962) and Goldiamond (1965b) can and should be used concurrently with the techniques of coverant control mentioned here.

Encountering coverant control for the first time, some students of behavior ask, "Isn't this the same as positive thinking?" The answer to a question like this has to be the same as to a question like "Isn't fruit the same as oranges?" Or "Isn't fluid the same as water?" The answer, of course, is that oranges are not identical with fruit, nor is water identical with fluid. Oranges are members of the fruit class, and water is a member of the class, fluids. In the same way, positive thinking can be a special case of coverant control, not the other way around. As we shall see, self CM often involves increasing the frequency of negative thinking, as well as positive.

Smoking

A science is often judged by the technology which it produces. On these grounds, psychology, specifically operant conditioning, has come a long way, but still has a way to go. This is nowhere better illustrated than in the case of cigarette smoking. Considerable data are now available to show the relationship between smoking and ill health. Yet many scientists, psychologists included, in full knowledge of the facts, continue to smoke cigarettes. When questioned about this, they will reply something like, "I know I should give it up. I quit once, but found I couldn't get any work done. All I could think about was a cigarette. I concluded that my work was more important than my giving up smoking."

This example furnishes a beautiful illustration of the futility of invoking such concepts as willpower to implement self-control of behavior. When willpower works, it works because of the aversive consequences of not controlling. That is, one tells oneself (or one's peers tell one) it is shameful not to have sufficient willpower. We cannot conclude that we have a technology of self-control until we can dispense with terms such as willpower. There is a good chance that coverant control points the way to such a technology.

In teaching *S* the application of coverant control to the problem of quitting smoking, one proceeds as in the control of any other behavior. One searches for and inventories behaviors which are incompatible with the response to be eliminated. Once these behaviors are discovered, they can be strengthened through appropriate contingency management, that is, by making high probability behaviors contingent on their occurrence.

In the case of smoking, finding incompatible coverants presents some difficulties. One can think about almost anything while smoking. Almost, but not quite. An interesting clue in the identification of coverants incompatible with smoking may be found in the verbal behavior of scientists and others. After reading an accumulation of data on the subject such as that presented by Hammond (1962), they will say such things as "That article almost got to me. For about ten seconds, I considered giving up smoking again." Or, "While reading the article, I really did feel silly smoking. All the while the data continue to pile up." The *S* is revealing that thinking about events such as cancer, early death, increased susceptibility to heart disease, and so on, are, to some degree at least, incompatible with the smoking response.

Once incompatible coverants have been determined, the problem becomes very straightforward. The problem becomes simply one of increasing the frequency of these incompatible coverants. In turn, this is accomplished by making high probability behaviors contingent on the execution of these coverants.

In practice, one proceeds as follows: The *S* is instructed to make a list of verbal events *he* finds particularly aversive in relation to smoking. These may be of the sort mentioned above, the shortened lifespan, increased tendency to cardiovascular disorders, and so on. Or they may be a sort which seem trivial to an outsider, such as bad breath, discolored teeth, and so on. The important point is that the list should be comprised of verbal events the *S* finds highly aversive.

The next step is to select one activity which is a high probability many times a day for this *S*. The one activity which must be excluded in the selection of this behavior is, of course, smoking. To select smoking as the high probability behavior to reinforce the anti-smoking coverant is to invite adaptation to the aversiveness of the coverant.

A helpful and quite possibly important device in coverant control is a hand counter. Each occurrence of the desired coverant should be followed immediately by the operation of the counter. Once conditioned, the operation of a counter appears to act as a reinforcer in its own right.

Pitfalls in Conditioning Anti-smoking Coverants

I have already mentioned the most treacherous and also the most common error in managing anti-smoking coverants. That is, using smoking as a high probability behavior (HPB) to reinforce occurrence of anti-smoking coverants. According to our experience, adaptation will certainly occur. *S* will typically report,[4] "This conclusion (or this piece of data) which seemed so horrifying to me at first, doesn't bother me any more." Sooner or later it will happen that the anti-smoking coverant will occur just as a cigarette is about to be lighted. When this does happen, it is best to wait several minutes before smoking. Considering the generality of the Premack principle, there are available literally hundreds of other high probability behaviors from which to choose for reinforcers. There is no point in using smoking.

Even when a non-smoking behavior is used as a HPB to reinforce anti-smoking coverants, there is a danger that adaptation to their aversive properties will occur. It appears that this adaptation can be mitigated by:

1. Using as many different anti-smoking coverants as possible. That is, *S* should have a list (which he will soon memorize) of anti-smoking items, using a different item for each successive time an anti-smoking coverant is to get reinforced.
2. Following an anti-smoking coverant with a pro-non-smoking one and *then* permitting the HPB to occur. The pro-non-smoking coverant class contains those thoughts about all the advantages there are to non-smoking. "I will feel better." "I will taste my food," etc.

[4] *S*s referred to here are the author's students and colleagues whose cooperation is gratefully acknowledged.

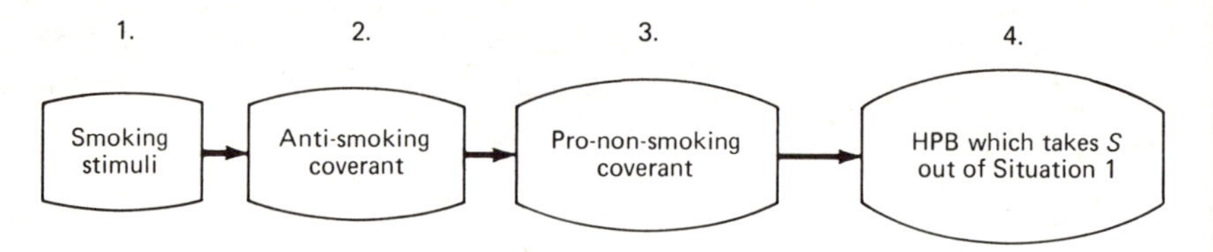

FIGURE 1. Sequence of self-managed behavioral events recommended when smoking stimuli are encountered.

In spite of a general attitude change which the *S* will notice almost immediately, there will be times when he will be in the presence of stimuli so strongly conditioned to smoking that the tendency to smoke is quite compelling. (*S*s under these circumstances give reports like, "I really didn't want to smoke, but I had to.") Under these circumstances, *S* can be instructed to think of a coverant pair such as described above, that is, an anti-smoking coverant followed by a pro-non-smoking coverant, which in turn is followed by a HPB *which takes S out of the situation.* This sequence is diagrammed in Figure 1.

Although *any* HPB will reinforce anti-smoking coverants, it is advisable to select a single activity to be contingent on the occurrence of the anti-smoking coverant. The reason for selecting only one class of HPBs for use as a reinforcer of these coverants is that to do otherwise risks the circumstance that the low probability coverant will not get made. Reasons for this are not entirely clear, but it is a fact that distressingly often *S* will report he forgot about it. Making one class of behaviors contingent on having emitted the anti-smoking coverant appears to make it more discriminable—easier to remember. For example, *S* may select coffee-drinking as a class of activities which are contingent on having made the coverant. He will then think about some aversive property of smoking before he goes to get the coffee in the first place and before he takes a sip in the second place, and so on. Or the *S* may select getting up and sitting down in his office chair as HPBs. He will think one aversive thought about smoking before he gets up, say, and later, before he permits himself to sit down. But, of course, any HPB will do, so long as it is a highly discriminable behavior.

If the coverant control is well done, *S* will report that he "just doesn't feel like smoking any more." When things work well, *S*s report that there was absolutely no "willpower" or "self-discipline" involved. They "just did not want to smoke any more." The encouraging thing is that, when coverant control works in this case, results are typically dramatic in their suddenness. An observable decline in smoking rate is typically observed in a few hours, and the termination of smoking altogether can occur in a single day.

WEIGHT CONTROL

There are those people (many consider them fortunate) who find it nearly impossible to gain weight. Typically in their twenties, these people report a series of failures in attempts to gain weight. They report ingesting many, many milkshakes with egg in them, hundreds of rich deserts, and so on, with the same result. No weight gain. Without passing on the desirability or undesirability of weight gain (there is some evidence that those who are underweight should be happy about it), contingency management can be applied here in a straightforward manner. Since coverants are not the main behaviors involved, suffice it to say that weight gain may be brought about simply by treating eating as a low probability behavior and reinforcing it with high probability behaviors. Although coverant control is not necessarily involved in a direct way, there is no reason why it could not be. (Indeed, *S*s sometimes report that they end up thinking of nothing but food.) Interesting as the weight-gain problem is, it is generally thought (correctly or not) that weight loss is more difficult.

Going on a diet shares many of the aversive properties of giving up smoking. The dieter who diets by conventional means, that is, by exercising "self-discipline" or "willpower," grits his teeth and suffers untold agonies. He is likely to think of nothing but food all day long, and refraining from eating becomes an exercise in heroism.

Coverant control offers an alternative to this excruciating process. In much the same way that smoking frequency is displaced by making thinking of the aversive properties of smoking a high frequency event, so the dieter should be advised to make executing higher probability behaviors contingent upon having thought of some of the aversive consequences of overeating. Here again, it is probably safest not to use eating as a high probability behavior with which to reinforce thinking of the aversive consequences of eating, even though for reasons unknown it does appear to be less dangerous than in the case of smoking. This is as good a place as any to mention that the aversive thought about overeating may be purely imaginary. All that is required is that it be aversive. For example, some female dieters use the coverant of imagining themselves bulging out of the bathing suit they wish to purchase for the summer. Others imagine themselves in other situations in which they are horribly fat and ugly. One *S*, a nurse, imagined a scene she had witnessed in the operating room in which a very obese person was being operated upon. She imagined herself with the rolls and layers of the ugly yellow fat she saw on the patient.

With skillful coverant control the *S*'s whole attitude toward eating is altered, and he refrains from doing much of it without any painful self-control whatsoever.

Coverants as Approximations

It is easy to overlook the fact that thinking about making a response is an approximation to it. This is most clearly seen, perhaps, in the case of sexual behavior. If one thinks about sex, the probability that one will engage in sexual behavior is proportionately increased. This phenomenon is less apparent in the case of other behaviors, but there is no reason to doubt its generality.

The implication is clear that, if *S* has a task to perform which is a low probability one, he could approximate that task by making thinking about it a HPB. He should establish the coverant of thinking about some feature of this task as a prerequisite for the performance of some class of HPBs.

An interesting special case of the use of coverants as an approximation to more overt behavior appears in the case of stutterers. In these *S*s, fluent speech is, of course, the low probability behavior which requires strengthening. This may be approximated by having the stutterer imagine himself to be in a social situation, speaking fluently. Immediately after this coverant, a previously selected HPB is permitted to occur.

It appears to be important to instruct the *S* to think of himself as uttering particular words or phrases, rather than just being "in a fluent situation."

Self-Confidence and Happiness

The whole gamut of positive thinking phenomena appears conditionable by the technology outlined here. Furthermore, it appears to be worthwhile doing. The procedure, which is simple and straightforward, is no different from that used in strengthening other coverants. In dealing with self-confidence, for example, *S* is first asked to inventory and list reasons why he should be confident. (This is astonishingly difficult for most *S*s to do; they may need a good deal of prompting.) After the inventory has been taken, thinking about one of these list items is required before HPB occurs. The increase in frequency of thinking self-confident thoughts displaces the thoughts about defeat because the confidence thoughts are incompatible with them.

Similarly with conditioning the happiness coverants. First, an inventory is made listing the reasons why the *S* should be content. In *S*s with strong tendencies in the opposite direction, again a good deal of prompting may be required. They may need to be reminded, for example, that they are adequately housed and fed, that their wives love them, that they have good friends, and so on. Once the inventory is four or five items long, coverant management can begin. As before, the *S* requires thinking about one of the items on the list before permitting high probability behaviors to occur.

An interesting exercise in self-management is to make two inventories: one of the sort mentioned and the other an unhappiness list. *S* can be instructed to reinforce happiness coverants for a given period of time, say, fifteen minutes. Then for the next hour, reinforce unhappiness thoughts. Then for the next quarter hour switch himself back again to the happiness coverants. The rapidity with which moods can thus be changed is impressive to most *S*s.

SUMMARY AND CONCLUSIONS

The likelihood that techniques of operant conditioning will be effective in the control of frequency of private events such as thinking and imaging is discussed. The possibility of control of coverants (covert operants) rests on three assumptions:

First, everybody is an organism and obeys the same laws of nature including the laws of reinforcement.

Second, the occurrence or nonoccurrence of coverants can reliably be discriminated by at least one organism, the one to whom they are private.

Third, the organism to whom the events are private can control the presentation of reinforcement in the form of permitting the occurrence of high probability behaviors.

Examples of the use of coverant control in quitting smoking, dieting, and other areas of self-control are cited.

It is concluded that the requirements for coverant control can reasonably be met and that, although only a bare beginning has thus far been made, a technology for the control of frequency of coverants is indeed feasible.

19

COVERT SENSITIZATION[1]

Joseph R. Cautela

From a behavioral standpoint, maladaptive behavior can be divided into maladaptive avoidance responses and maladaptive approach responses. Maladaptive avoidance responses, such as phobias, fear of failure, fear of criticism, have been treated effectively by reciprocal inhibition procedures developed by Joseph Wolpe (1958). These procedures include desensitization, assertive training, and the use of sexual responses. Other methods of dealing with the anxiety components of this type of response involve thought stopping and aversion-relief therapy.

The treatment of such maladaptive approach responses as obsession, compulsion, homosexuality, drinking, and stealing has employed aversive stimulation in the reduction and/or elimination of the frequency of the faulty approach behavior. In the usual technique of aversive stimulation, shock is presented contiguously with a socially undesirable stimulus (e.g., a picture of a homosexual is flashed on a screen at the same time a shock is delivered to the feet [Thorpe, Schmidt, & Castell, 1963] or shock is administered in the presence of a fetish object [Marks, Rachman, & Gelder, 1965]).

Recently, I have developed a new procedure for treating maladaptive approach behavior (Cautela, 1966_b). This procedure is labeled "covert sensitization." It is called "covert" because neither the undesirable stimulus

Reprinted by permission of the author and Southern Universities Press from *Psychological Reports*, 1967, *20*, 459–468.

[1] Paper presented to DeJarnette State Sanitorium and Blue Ridge Psychology Club on October 7, 1966.

nor the aversive stimulus is actually presented. These stimuli are presented in imagination only. The word "sensitization" is used because the purpose of the procedure is to build up an avoidance response to the undesirable stimulus.

Description of Procedure

The patient is taught to relax in the same manner as used in the desensitization procedure (Wolpe, 1958, pp. 139–155). He is asked to raise his index finger when he can relax completely without any tension. This usually takes no more than three or four sessions. When the patient is able to relax completely, he is told that he is unable to stop drinking in excess (or eating, or whatever is the problem to be treated) because it is a strong learned habit which now gives him a great amount of pleasure. He is also told that the way to eliminate his problem is to associate the pleasurable object with an unpleasant stimulus. The patient is then asked (while relaxed with his eyes closed) to visualize very clearly the pleasurable object (e.g., food, liquor, homosexual). When he can do this, he is told to raise his index finger. After he signals, he is told to next visualize that he is about to take the object (commit the compulsive act). If the object is liquor, for instance, he is asked to visualize himself looking at the glass with the alcoholic beverage in it. Then he is to visualize a sequence of events: holding the glass in his hand, bringing it up to his lips, having the glass touch his lips. When he imagines this latter scene, he is told to imagine that he begins to feel sick to his stomach. In imagination, he begins to vomit. The vomit goes all over the floor, the drink, his companions and himself. He is then asked to visualize the whole scene by himself and to raise his finger when he can picture it and actually feel nauseous when he had the intention of drinking, gradually getting sicker as he touches the glass, raises it, etc.

A feeling of relief is provided in scenes when he turns away from the pleasurable object. He is told to imagine that as he rushes outside into the fresh clean air, or home to a clean, invigorating shower, or whenever he is tempted to drink and refuses to do it, the feeling of nausea goes away and he no longer feels ill.

After several practice trials in the therapist's office, the patient is instructed to continue treatment on his own twice a day by means of "homework" assignments which are 10 to 20 repetitions of the trials experienced in the office. He is also carefully instructed to imagine immediately that he has just vomited on his drink whenever he is tempted to drink, or about to order one, or about to ingest it. Patients report that treatment is quite effective whenever it is followed conscientiously. As therapy progresses, the use of this procedure as a self-control technique usually continues, and the patients are able to monitor their behavior very well. It is important to note that, when anxiety is an essential part of the maladaptive response, desensitization is also utilized.

Theoretical Basis

Since the individual is asked to imagine an aversive situation as soon as he has thought of drinking or is about to drink, this is a punishment procedure. An aversive stimulus is made to follow the response to be reduced. Evidence indicates that punishment is quite effective in reducing the frequency of responses and that this reduction can be long lasting or permanent (Kushner & Sandler, 1966). Certain conditions should be carefully arranged to produce a decrease in response frequency. The noxious stimulus should be contiguous with that response. The response should have a history of positive reinforcement (e.g., drinking). The aversive stimulus should be presented on a continuous basis, at least initially, after which a partial schedule can be presented. The level of punishment should be clearly noxious but not so intense as to immobilize the organism.

Since the patient is usually told that the nausea and vomiting behavior decreases and he feels better as soon as he turns away from the undesirable object (e.g., beer, food, homosexual), this is analogous to an escape procedure which occurs when a particular behavior terminates the presentation of a noxious stimulus. Eventually, avoidance behavior occurs, as evidenced by the fact that the patients report they no longer have the urge or the temptation for the particular stimulus. The cues which have been previously associated with the noxious stimulation of nausea and vomiting now have become discriminatory stimuli for avoidance behavior (Hall, 1966, p. 212).

TREATMENT OF SPECIFIC MALADAPTIVE APPROACH RESPONSES

Treatment of Alcoholic Problems

Besides the usual brief history taken in all behavior therapy cases, special attention is paid to certain characteristics of the client's drinking behavior. With the use of a specially constructed questionnaire and interviews, the following factors are determined: (1) history of the drinking problem, (2) frequency of present drinking behavior, (3) where *S* usually does his drinking, (4) what *S* drinks, and (5) antecedent conditions that are followed by drinking behavior.

A client may, for example, do most of his drinking in a bar room and may usually drink straight whiskey and sometimes beer. The covert sensitization sessions will then consist of scenes in which the client is about to drink whiskey in a bar room. If he drinks alone at home, scenes concerning the home will also have to be included. Essentially we try to cover all the applicable kinds of drinking and all the places where the particular drinking behavior occurs.

A practical problem still exists concerning whether to proceed first with the kind of drinking he does most often in the most usual situations or to begin covert sensitization with the type of drinking and its situations which occur the least often. For the most part, I have used the first method. The primary advantage of the second method, however, is the provision of some measure of success since it involves the least amount of habit strength and will make the client more eager to continue treatment. A description of the procedure is as follows:

> You are walking into a bar. You decide to have a glass of beer. You are now walking toward the bar. As you are approaching the bar you have a funny feeling in the pit of your stomach. Your stomach feels all queasy and nauseous. Some liquid comes up your throat and it is very sour. You try to swallow it back down, but as you do this, food particles start coming up your throat to your mouth. You are now reaching the bar and you order a beer. As the bartender is pouring the beer, puke comes up into your mouth. You try to keep your mouth closed and swallow it down. You reach for the glass of beer to wash it down. As soon as your hand touches the glass, you can't hold it down any longer. You have to open your mouth and you puke. It goes all over your hand, all over the glass and the beer. You can see it floating around in the beer. Snots and mucus come out of your nose. Your shirt and pants are all full of vomit. The bartender has some on his shirt. You notice people looking at you. You get sick again and you vomit some more and more. You turn away from the beer and immediately you start to feel better. As you run out of the bar room, you start to feel better and better. When you get out into clean fresh air you feel wonderful. You go home and clean yourself up.

An important characteristic of the covert sensitization procedure is that its effects are very specific. If one treats for aversion to beer, there will be very little generalization to wine and whiskey. Avoidance to wine and whiskey must be treated separately. Sometimes I combine a covert sensitization trial for wine, beer and whiskey by having the client see a glass of wine, a glass of beer, and a glass of whiskey on a table. As in the manner described above, he is told that he is sick and he vomits over all three beverages.

Treatment of Obesity

APPROACH. The client is requested to write down everything he eats or drinks from session to session. Other details of his eating behavior are determined in a manner similar to that used in treating an alcoholic patient. A questionnaire has also been constructed for this purpose. Covert sensitization sessions are not begun until two or three weeks have passed, in order to obtain some kind of baseline in terms of the eating habits. The therapist is especially concerned with four factors when he reads over the client's eating behavior of the previous week: (1) nature of the food, (2) when he eats (with special concern for eating between meals), (3) how much he eats, and (4) where he eats.

At first covert sensitization is applied to sweets of all types, especially to foods with heavy carbohydrate content, and then to between-meal eating. The amount of food is usually the prime concern after the kinds of food and the time of eating has been considered. If the therapist finds that the patient is eating too much apple pie or pastry for dessert, for instance, he can proceed in the following manner:

> I want you to imagine you've just had your main meal and you are about to eat your dessert, which is apple pie. As you are about to reach for the fork, you get a funny feeling in the pit of your stomach. You start to feel queasy, nauseous and sick all over. As you touch the fork, you can feel food particles inching up your throat. You're just about to vomit. As you put the fork into the pie, the food comes up into your mouth. You try to keep your mouth closed because you are afraid that you'll spit the food out all over the place. You bring the piece of pie to your mouth. As you're about to open your mouth, you puke; you vomit all over your hands, the fork, over the pie. It goes all over the table, over the other peoples' food. Your eyes are watering. Snot and mucus are all over your mouth and nose. Your hands feel sticky. There is an awful smell. As you look at this mess you just can't help but vomit again and again until just watery stuff is coming out. Everybody is looking at you with shocked expressions. You turn away from the food and immediately start to feel better. You run out of the room, and as you run out, you feel better and better. You wash and clean yourself up, and it feels wonderful.

In addition to the scenes (about ten per session) in which the patient gives in to the temptation and vomits, scenes in which the patient is initially tempted and then decides not to eat the food are also included in equal number. An example of such a scene is a follows:

> You've just finished your meal and you decide to have dessert. As soon as you make that decision, you start to get that funny feeling in the pit of your stomach. You say, "Oh, oh; oh no; I won't eat the dessert." Then you immediately feel calm and comfortable.

HOMEWORK. The patient is asked to repeat the scenes presented during the therapy session twice a day until the next therapeutic session. He is also asked to imagine he is vomiting on a particular food whenever he is tempted to eat it. For instance, if he is tempted to eat potato salad, he is told immediately to imagine that the potato salad has vomit all over it.

SOME GENERAL COMMENTS ON THE TREATMENT OF OBESITY. A physical examination, including an investigation of thyroid activity and metabolic rate, is required of all patients prior to treatment. Each week they are asked about their general health and well-being in order to ensure that no physical harm is being done.

The patients are weighed at the beginning of each session. If there is indication that eating food is a mechanism of anxiety reduction, the patient is also treated to reduce the sources of anxiety.

After they have lost 15 pounds, the patients are often asked to perform simple neck and arm exercises to avoid loose skin in these regions. They are also encouraged to walk as much as possible. After the patient has reached the weight desired, as determined by height-weight charts taking the body frame into consideration, the same eating habits which have occurred during the past two or three weeks are encouraged. *S* continues to be monitored in therapeutic sessions for another month. He is then asked to keep track of his own eating habits, and he is taught when and how to apply covert sensitization to himself whenever he finds he is nearing the maximum weight assigned to him. If he finds that he can't do this on his own, he can call the therapist for a "booster" session. This happens rarely, however. Most of the patients are able to control their weight very well. The patients report that they still enjoy the food they eat.

Of all the syndromes treated, covert sensitization seems to be most effective in dealing with the problems of obesity. This treatment is also very specific in its effects.

TREATMENT OF HOMOSEXUALITY

In the treatment of the behavior disorders indicated above, the task of the therapist is to somehow break the relationship between the stimulus (alcohol or food) and the response (drinking or eating). In the case of homosexuality, the stimulus is an individual of the same sex who elicits a response of sexual approach behavior. The therapist then attempts to identify individual characteristics which are sexually attractive and under what conditions. For example, some individuals prefer obese sexual objects, some prefer short, young, or intellectual ones.

DESCRIPTION OF PROCEDURE. The following instructions may be given:

> I want you to imagine that you are in a room with X. He is completely naked. As you approach him you notice he has sores and scabs all over his body, with some kind of fluid oozing from them. A terrible foul stench comes from his body. The odor is so strong it makes you sick. You can feel food particles coming up your throat. You can't help yourself and you vomit all over the place, all over the floor, on your hands and clothes. And now that even makes you sicker and you vomit again and again

> all over everything. You turn away and then you start to feel better. You try to get out of the room, but the door seems to be locked. The smell is still strong, but you try desperately to get out. You kick at the door frantically until it finally opens and you run out into the nice clean air. It smells wonderful. You go home and shower and you feel so clean.

One essentially builds up a hierarchy of the desirable sexual objects and the available contacts of likely sexual stimulation. Covert sensitization is applied to all items in the hierarchy, with the most desirable sexual object usually being treated first.

Scenes are also presented in which the patient sees pictures of homosexuals and vomits on them. Homework similar to that given in the treatment of the other disorders is given in this case as well. The homosexual patient is also told that if he sees someone and becomes sexually attracted to him or whenever he starts to have a sexual fantasy about an undesirable sexual object, he is immediately to imagine that the object is full of sores and scabs and he vomits on the object.

EXAMPLES. This method has been only recently applied to homosexuals. I have treated two cases; one case has been treated at Temple Medical School.

One of my cases was a delinquent in a training school. According to his reports and those of the staff and of other boys in the training school, he has not engaged in homosexual behavior since the termination of covert sensitization treatment and has now been released from the training school.

My second case was a member of the Armed Forces. This individual's behavior was primarily vicarious. All his sexual fantasies, with and without masturbation, were homosexual in nature. This behavior has been reduced to about four temptations a week which last about a second. This case is still in the process of treatment.

In the Temple Medical School case, it has been four months since the last therapeutic session, and the patient has not engaged in any homosexual behavior to date, according to his own reports and those of his wife. He is continuing with the homework.

All in all, the preliminary results are promising, although much work still remains to be done in this area.

Treatment of Juvenile Offenders

Since March 1966, I have been using behavior therapy procedures in individual and group settings with juvenile offenders at the Rhode Island Medical Center. My preliminary guess, based on this experience, is that the usual behavior therapy procedures, such as relaxation, desensitization, and Thought Stopping, can be effective in the treatment of juvenile offenders. I have also used covert sensitization where applicable. In one case, it was used in the treatment of homosexuality as I reported above. Currently under treatment is a boy with a severe alcoholic problem. His juvenile offenses have always occurred while he was drinking. Covert sensitization seems to be quite effective with this boy. He is allowed to go home on weekends. Reports from him and his mother indicate that his drinking has been drastically reduced on these weekends at home when previously he used to drink himself into a two-day stupor.

I have also treated stealing behavior (car stealing and breaking and entering offenses). Car stealing is one of the most frequent offenses of juvenile offenders. In the treatment of this type of behavior, the boy is asked what cars he prefers to steal and under what conditions. A hierarchy is then constructed from that information. A typical scene is as follows:

> You are walking down a street. You notice a real sharp sports car. You walk toward it with the idea of stealing it. As you're walking toward it you start to get a funny feeling in your stomach. You feel sick to your stomach and you have a slight pain in your gut. As you keep walking, you really start to feel sick, and food starts coming up in your mouth. You're just about to reach for the handle of the door and you can't hold it any longer. You vomit all over your hand, the car door, the upholstery inside, all over your clothes. The smell starts to get to you and you keep puking from it. It's all over the place. It's dripping from your mouth. You turn around and run away and then you start to feel better.

I've also treated some cases of glue sniffing in a similar manner. My main surprise in working with juvenile offenders is that most of them will cooperate well with the behavior therapy procedures. Group relaxation also seems usable without too much difficulty.

EXPERIMENTAL DATA

In behavior therapy our procedures are usually derived from the results of controlled laboratory studies. We also try to test the validity of our techniques by appropriate experimentation.

Donner and Ashem,[2] at the New Jersey Neuro-psychiatric Institute in Princeton, attempted an experimental test of the efficacy of covert sensitization in the treatment of institutionalized alcoholics. Preliminary data indicate that 3 out of 4 of the non-treated controls resumed drinking after a 6-month follow-up. Only 2 out of 7 of the covert sensitization group resumed drinking

[2] L. Donner, and B. Ashem. Unpublished research data from a study at the Neuro-psychiatric Institute in Princeton, New Jersey, 1966.

after a 6-month follow-up. All treated *S*s received 9 sessions. These data are only preliminary, since more *S*s remain to be followed-up. Investigators are waiting for the 6-month period to be completed.

In this study, one *S* had to be eliminated after some training sessions because the mere mention of alcohol made him actually vomit. This is important to note because the treatment of covert sensitization should explicitly applied to the individual's *desire* to drink alcohol, not just to the alcohol itself. All of the covert sensitization *S*s were also given relaxation training. Study is needed to determine whether relaxation is necessary for effective treatment; I have used it to help develop clear imagery.

Forward and backward covert sensitization groups were included in the study. In the backward covert sensitization group, individuals were asked to imagine vomiting before they took the alcohol. No differences were found between the backward and forward conditioning covert sensitization groups. One can easily hypothesize that the backward conditioning group was not truly backward conditioned, since the nausea could still be present from a previous trial.

Another study, using aversive electric stimulation (MacCulloch, *et al.*, 1966), has reported no success in the treatment of four cases of alcoholism. These results are somewhat puzzling since, using the same procedure, they were able to successfully treat homosexuals (MacCulloch, *et al.*, 1965). There are a number of possible procedural differences that either individually or collectively might account for the efficacy of covert sensitization as compared to the use of electrical stimulation as an aversive stimulus in the treatment of alcoholism. One of the crucial procedural differences is that in covert sensitization the patients are taught to apply the procedure to themselves outside of the office situation in a prescribed manner. Patients are usually told to practice the procedure 10 to 20 times a day. Also, they are told to apply the procedure any time they have a temptation to drink. This assigned "homework" accomplishes three important behavioral effects. In the first place, more conditioning trials are used (there are more reinforcements). Secondly, the patient now has a procedure under *his* control that can be applied whenever the temptation actually occurs. So a lot of *in vivo* conditioning occurs when an individual is tempted in particular situations. Thirdly, according to reports by patients, just knowing they have a procedure they can use whenever they need it, reduces the over-all anxiety level. Another difference between the procedures is that the aversive stimulus used in covert sensitization (vomiting) has stimulus and response properties that have probably been presented quite often when the patient has been drinking. With the covert sensitization procedure, we are using a behavior that has already accompanied the stimulus to drink and the response of drinking. We have some conditioning trials even before we start our formal treatment procedure.

A major difference between procedures that has yet to be explored systematically is the difference in effect of presenting the aversive stimulus in imagination or in actuality. In *a priori* speculation, one would assume that the actual presentation of the aversive stimulus would be more effective than the imaginary presentation of the stimulus, since in the actual presentation of the stimulus there is more control over the intensity and occurrence of the aversive stimulus. Also, the actual presentation of the stimulus probably results in greater perceived pain.

Perhaps none of the above differences in procedure is responsible for the apparent difference in results when using covert sensitization as compared to electrical stimulation. Perhaps MacCulloch, *et al.*'s (1966) procedure simply needs modification for effective results. For example, the interval between the CS and the US can be varied; or the number of conditioning trials per session can be an important factor; also the intensity of the electrical stimulation used may not be the most appropriate.

Covert sensitization, as I have used it, is a relatively new procedure. But, of course, the use of aversive stimulation to overcome faulty approach behavior is not new. I have applied my procedure to a wide variety of behaviors and the technique looks quite promising. One of the reasons for its effectiveness is probably the sense of control the individual feels over his own behavior. So far, the treatment of obesity appears to show the greatest promise in terms of probability of remission and number of sessions required for change. Treatment of alcoholic problems appears the most difficult in terms of prognosis and number of treatment sessions necessary. There are two factors that could account for this. (1) The habit strength for the alcoholic responding is much higher because of the large number of reinforcements possible within a given day. The number of homosexual contacts one can make, or the number of times a car can be stolen are relatively small by comparison. (2) The drive-reducing properties of alcohol are quite strong because of the physiological effect alcohol has on the nervous system. So even though one could argue that, if you count every mouthful of food as a reinforcement, it is possible to have as many reinforcers in a given day as are possible with drinking, it is unlikely that food as a rule has the strong reducing properties of alcohol.

More controlled studies are needed in this area, such as the one carried out by the Neuro-psychiatric Institute.

SUMMARY

A new treatment for maladaptive approach behavior ("covert sensitization") is described. The term "covert" is used because neither the undesirable stimulus nor the aversive stimulus is actually presented. These stimuli are presented in imagination only. The word "sensitization" is used because the purpose of the procedure is to build up an avoidance response to the undesirable stimulus. A description and rationale for covert sensitization is presented. Treatment of alcoholism, obesity, homosexuality, and delinquent behavior by covert sensitization is also described.

20

THREE TECHNIQUES OF AUTOHYPNOSIS

Andrew Salter

There remains one aspect of hypnosis which, so far, has been untouched by modern experimental techniques. That uninvestigated area is autohypnosis.[1]

By autohypnosis is meant the ability to induce, *upon oneself*, the trance of sleeping hypnosis together with such of its phenomena as may be desired. Included are catalepsies, anaesthesias, and amnesias (both in the trance and post-hypnotically) and the varied post-hypnotic suggestions, including positive and negative hallucinations—in short, all the classic phenomena. In autohypnosis not only does the "subject" hypnotize himself and administer the suggestions to himself, but he also has complete control of the trance state at all times. To use a word that should be obsolete, the only person with *rapport* is the subject, and that *rapport* is with himself.

So much for what autohypnosis is. Now let us see what it is not.

It is not the same as the self-hypnosis often mentioned in considering the persistence of symptoms in hysteria; nor is this definition of autohypnosis quite identical with autosuggestion, for the latter is a waking phenomenon

Reprinted by permission of the author and the Journal Press from *Journal of General Psychology*, 1941, *24*, 423–438.

[1] Wells' work on "waking hypnosis" did not deal with "the production of a sleeping or even a drowsy state" (1924, p. 396). His concept of autohypnosis is made clearer when he says, "The step to effective autosuggestion, or autohypnosis, is shorter from waking than from sleeping hypnosis." We can identify his "waking hypnosis" with what we might term *advanced waking suggestion.*

I should like here to record my debt to the work of Clark L. Hull, W. R. Wells, and Paul Campbell Young, and in particular to the first mentioned.

and the former involves a trance state. As for the possible identity of autohypnosis with the "samadhic (trance) state of yoga," Behanan (1937, p. 237) says of hypnosis that "It would be mere speculation of doubtful value either to affirm or deny that the two are essentially similar." This possibility will receive consideration later. Autohypnosis, then, as used herein, is the same as the customary sleeping hypnosis, except that the trance is induced by the "subject" upon himself, and only the "subject" retains complete control of the trance.

Such a condition is of the greatest psychological interest. It is the basic purpose of this paper to present three techniques of autohypnosis in such detail as to make them available to those wishing to do research in this field, and only incidentally to touch upon some of the uses and possible theoretical implications of the techniques.

The first method of autohypnosis may seem obvious, yet I have not encountered its equivalent in the literature. Briefly, we may term it autohypnosis by post-hypnotic suggestion.

In using this technique I find out if the person who wishes to learn autohypnosis is a good hypnotic subject in the first place. I try the usual sleeping hypnosis on the potential subject. If I can produce any limb catalepsies or a glove anaesthesia, or better—and by better I mean a "depth score" of 13 or higher on the scale of Davis and Husband (1931, p. 176)—I find that it is possible to teach autohypnosis with distinct value to the subject. I consider a limb catalepsy of some sort, or inability to get out of the chair, as a *sine qua non* of the trance before I make any endeavor to teach autohypnosis.

I tell the subject, *who is wide-awake*, and has previously been developed into as good a hypnotic subject as possible, that if he wishes, he can be taught to put himself into a trance wherein he can give himself suggestions exactly as I would give them, and with the same effect, if not better. "We might say," I declare jokingly, "that you can be your own Svengali and Trilby simultaneously." (This expression always appeals to subjects.)

After a discussion of the uses that the subject can make of self-induced post-hypnotic suggestion (else why autohypnosis?) I proceed to emphasize that post-hypnotic suggestions are very effective. I cite instances involving the subject, and tell him that in a few minutes I will hypnotize him and while in the trance I will give him a post-hypnotic suggestion dealing with hypnosis.

> I will tell you that whenever you wish to hypnotize yourself, you have merely to sit or lie down as comfortably as you can at the moment, and let the thought flash through your mind that you wish to hypnotize yourself. You will take five deep breaths, and on the fifth breath you will be in the deepest possible trance[2] and then you will give yourself whatever

[2] This may be varied by telling the subject, instead, that it will be necessary only to tell himself "*Fast asleep*" five times to "be in the deepest possible trance." Other variations are, of course, possible. The point is that a convenient post-hypnotic suggestion of autohypnosis is given.

> suggestions you wish, and wake up whenever you want to. Every time you awaken from a trance you will feel fine—splendid.
>
> Don't worry about waking up. It won't be a problem. You know that a mother can sleep through a thunder storm, but the moment her baby stirs in its crib, or utters the slightest cry, the mother is wide-awake. Let us simply say that the mother's subconscious mind, and yours, are never asleep. The "subconscious" is a debatable matter, but it's a handy concept here. So you see, if you're in a trance, and anybody shouts *"Fire!"* or calls you for any reason, or you *have* to awaken for any reason —you will awaken. You will have no trouble at all, as you shall see.

A good part of the pre-trance instruction is given to mold the subject's future autohypnotic behavior. Young (1927) has a splendid discussion of the effect of pre-trance instruction on trance behavior. I have been guided by his results, and I agree with him that "a genuine hypnosis can exist without the semblance of rapport" (1927, p. 139). I shall prove this of autohypnosis later.

After these "pre-trance" instructions I have the subject stand up and I demonstrate the "you're falling forward" waking suggestion technique. It works quickly. I then tell the subject to repeat the "falling forward" suggestions to himself, without speaking. *"Just say them mentally, and I'll catch you as you fall forward."* The subject gives himself the "falling forward" autosuggestions, and I catch him as he falls forward.

> "You see," I explain. "It doesn't make any difference *who* gives you the suggestions. They work, if you want them to work, and such will be the case when you hypnotize yourself. The source of the suggestions doesn't matter. They may come from within or without. As long as you coöperate, with me or with yourself, the suggestions work. And that's the way it will be when you hypnotize yourself. Is everything clear?"

Here the subject often asks one or more of three questions: (*a*) Will I be able to wake myself easily? (*b*) Should I talk to myself in the trance to give myself the suggestions, or should I just think them? (*c*) Will the suggestions I give myself be as effective as the ones you gave me?

To show how easy it is to wake up oneself I re-explain the analogy of the sleeping mother and child, and conclude therefrom that anything that *should* awaken the subject, *will* awaken him.[3] I emphasize, in addition, that the only one in "rapport" with the subject will be the subject himself. Consequently, whenever he wants to awaken it will be no problem at all because of his "self-rapport."

[3] One of my subjects, the top-ranking student in the art school of a large Eastern college, hypnotizes herself as she rides to school from the suburbs in a trolley car each morning. When somebody calls her by name she awakens instantly and usually hears, "*Oh, you're sleeping. Where were you last night?*" She never misses her corner.

It cannot be emphasized too much that there is no difficulty or shock of any sort when an autohypnotized person "must" awaken.

"Should I talk to myself in the trance to give myself the suggestions, or should I just think them?"

I tell the subject to "think them," that is, to repeat the suggestions mentally. I always tell the subject that parrot-like mimicry of my suggestions is not essential, but that following the general basis and outline of the post-hypnotic suggestions is what matters. I usually give the subject written post-hypnotic suggestions, which he inspects in his waking state whenever he later wishes to practice autohypnosis.

As for whether autohypnotic suggestions are as effective as what we might call "heterohypnotic" suggestion, I tell the subject that autohypnotic suggestion is at least as good as, or better than, the usual hypnotic suggestion. In the latter, I explain, suggestion comes from the outside, and works on the subject because of his desire to coöperate. In autohypnosis the immediate source of the ideas is "within" the subject, and surely a person will coöperate with himself. The subject's attention is called to his behavior in the "falling forward" demonstration, and I reiterate that the source of the ideas is immaterial, as long as the subject wishes to follow them. The subject is told that, if anything, a well-organized autohypnotic suggestion should work on him more than a "heterohypnotic" one, for the *rapport* of autohypnosis is as complete as can ever be possible. (Remember that up to this point the subject is in a full normal waking state.)

After answering the subject's questions, and making sure that he is at ease, I hypnotize him and tell him all that I have just told him, save in more detail should I consider it necessary. In addition I tell the subject that he will be able to talk to me when he later enters his self-induced trance. I particularly emphasize this suggestion about being able to talk to me while he is in his autohypnotic trance, because I wish to guide the subject and to preclude the faint possibility of my not having *rapport* if the subject were to misunderstand my instructions.

The entire procedure thus far described takes much less time to go through than might at first seem necessary. Twenty minutes is ample. This includes everything so far described, starting with my statement to the subject *that in a few minutes I will hypnotize him and while in the trance I will give him a post-hypnotic suggestion dealing with hypnosis.*

I awaken the subject and inquire whether there is an amnesia for the trance. This is desirable, but not essential. The subject's answer may usually be guessed by the extent of the amnesia in previous trances. Even with a somewhat poor subject, I find that appropriate training can teach a fairly surprising amount of amnesia, superficially at least. In any event, if the subject seems to remember something, I give some indirect waking suggestion along the lines:

> "Yes, of course. You'll forget it. You know how it is with a dream. We forget it a few moments after we awaken," etc.

"Let's take a rest," I then tell the subject. I engage him in conversation about some news item, or any other matter that seems apart from psychology. After no more than five minutes of such discussion, I say something like, "Well. I gave you some instructions about how to hypnotize yourself. Let's see you practice them. You don't even have to try. It will just happen. Five deep breaths, and then you're in a real trance. Come on."

The subject usually smiles and says, "I'll try," or "Here's hoping."

"Go ahead," I say.

The subject takes five breaths (they are often not very deep), his eyes close and he remains quiet.[4] I let him sit quietly for about a half minute.

"You are fast asleep, aren't you?" I say.

"Yes," is the answer in the usual low voice.

From here on the procedure varies. I usually ask the subject to make a glove or wholearm anaesthesia. *"Let me see you make your right arm anaesthetic,"* I say, *"and tell me when you're ready."*

When careful investigation shows an anaesthesia, at least overtly to me and covertly by the subject's report, it may be taken for granted that all will be well. I have the subject restore sensation to his arm, and tell him to give himself suggestions about his studying (or fingernails, or piano-playing, or whatever the problem is).

"Use as much of my general language as you can recall. Just think those suggestions with all your might for about (say) five minutes, and tell me when you're ready."

In about that time, more or less (there are never any miracles of accentuated perception of time intervals in hypnosis), the subject says he is ready. *"Very well,"* I say. *"Wake up when you decide to—say in a few minutes."* I give some suggestions about permanent waking amnesias for the trance states and that the subject will always feel splendid on awakening.

Soon the subject opens his eyes and looks around. He is wide awake, and feels fine.

A subject with whom anaesthesias could not be "heterohypnotically" produced, would be told in his first autohypnotic trance to produce other effects upon himself which previous experience had shown could be produced by the experimenter. Simple kinaesthetic suggestions will do. The more impressive the effect, the better.

In any case, whether or not anaesthesias can be produced in the trance, if the subject seems to have a slight difficulty in awakening, I say, *"Come on. You can wake up. You're the boss. You're in control. Wake up."* These directions, self-contradictory as they are, will suffice. It will be noted how even these directions stress the subject's autohypnotic control.

[4] If the subject does not fall asleep very easily, as he breathes I say *"Fast asleep,"* several times. This suffices but is seldom necessary.

We shall consider two other methods of autohypnosis before entering upon a general discussion of all three methods. This procedure will be most conducive to clarity and brevity.

In the autohypnotic method just described it will be recalled that there was frequent mention of the fact that to the subject it does not matter whether the suggestions he gets come from "within" as autosuggestion, or from "without" as heterosuggestion. (I am using the terms auto- and heterosuggestion in the broadest possible sense, to include all ramifications of waking and trance phenomenon.)

If such is the case, what would happen if a good hypnotic subject were given the pre-trance preparation described before, with the exception that he would not receive instructions regarding the acquisition of autohypnotic control through post-hypnotic suggestion, nor would he be given such related suggestions hypnotically? I think that it may be agreed that the result would be the same originally good hypnotic subject, who would now be fairly well informed (and *convinced*) about the theory and operational truths of hypnosis.

It is such a "well informed (and *convinced*)" subject that we need for the second technique of autohypnosis. Remember that the first or post-hypnotic, method will not be used with this subject.

I give such a subject some typed autohypnotic material which parallels the "heterohypnotic" suggestions I have previously found effective with him. There is no point in giving a complete verbatim example, for the directions vary from case to case. The illustrative material that follows is composed of a few typical cross-sections of what the subject is instructed to memorize at home, at leisure, and while wide-awake. It reads, in part, something like this:

> I feel very comfortable. My arms are so relaxed. My feet feel very relaxed and heavy. I feel so very comfortable and relaxed. My whole body feels comfortable and relaxed. I just want to sleep. I feel so comfortable.
>
> My eyes are getting heavy, so very heavy. They're closing bit by bit, they feel so heavy and relaxed. I feel them closing more and more. I want to sleep, and I want my eyes to close.

These instructions continue and should be adjusted to the subject. It will be noted that the instructions to be memorized are tantamount to the usual hypnotic directions. Toward the end the instructions read:

> Now I am fast asleep, in the deepest possible hypnotic sleep. I am in a deep sleep, as deep as the deepest hypnotic sleep I have ever been in. I have complete autohypnotic control of myself. I can give myself autohypnotic suggestions and awaken whenever I wish. I can talk to the person who gave me these autohypnotic instructions, yet I will still remain fast asleep. I will follow such instructions as he gives me, yet I shall still have autohypnotic control.

The subject is told to memorize these instructions, and not to concentrate too much on their meaning. He is told that he may paraphrase them if he wishes. The subject is told not to try to hypnotize himself with these instructions until we have gone over them together, and I have shown him how to use them.

When the subject tells me that he has memorized the instructions, or their essence, I sit him down in a comfortable chair, and tell him that now he can hypnotize himself.

> There is no such thing as *A* hypnotizing *B*. All that *A* does is to tell *B* which roads to follow to get to his destination—hypnosis. It doesn't matter who tells you what roads to follow—whether I tell you these roads (or directions), or whether you tell yourself those roads. In any case, if you *follow* those roads, you will hypnotize yourself.

I then repeat most of the pre-trance instructions and demonstrations mentioned in connection with the first method, with the exceptions as previously noted. I explain the concept of an ideomotor act, and I tell him that he has memorized a series of ideomotor acts in his autohypnotic series of directions. This is further explained, and then the subject is told that as he repeats the autohypnotic directions, and puts his entire heart into them, he will find them having effect on him—just as I previously hypnotized him with similar ideomotor suggestions. I answer such suggestions as the subject may have.

The memorized instructions may be said slowly by the subject in a low voice, or repeated mentally. The former is desirable at first (for the experimenter's sake) if the subject so prefers it, but either will do. It may be necessary to have the subject go through the memorized suggestions three or four times, or more, in order to show the subject the most efficacious way to give himself the suggestions. The experimenter may even help the subject along with some heterosuggestion when the subject seems to need an extra push, but this can be kept to a minimum.

In a short while it will be found that the subject can put himself in an autohypnotic trance. Once he is in the trance, the method proceeds essentially as Method 1, with such differences as are obvious. With practice, the subject can quickly put himself into a trance whenever he wishes. As time goes on the autohypnotic material he thinks (or mumbles) may become more abbreviated, and after a half dozen or more spaced trances the subject finds that he has to spend very little time to get into a trance. A few cursory thoughts about hypnotizing himself will suffice to produce a deep trance, for practice effects are very marked. This will all be considered in my discussion.

We come now to the third and last method of autohypnosis, which method is probably the most fundamental of the three. This might be termed "fractional autohypnosis." Hull in discussing "susceptibility to prestige suggestion" (1933, p. 392) says:

> The essence [of hypnosis] lies in the experimental fact of a quantitative *shift* in the upward direction which may result from the hypnotic procedure. So far as the writer can see, this quantitative phenomenon alone remains of the once imposing aggregate known by the name of hypnosis. But this undoubted fact is quite sufficient to give significance and value to the term.

I should like now to present a method of autohypnosis whereby this "quantitative *shift*" of suggestibility in an upward direction may be induced without the usual hypnotic procedure. It may be compared, in a sense, to the part method in learning, that is, the trance state will be assumed as being composed of discrete parts, each of which will be taught to the potential subject. This analogy will not be followed implicitly, but it gives a good idea of the method.

For this method we need a person with whom it has been found possible to produce, by waking suggestion, some limb catalepsy or an inability to get out of the chair. These qualifications are not at all stringent, and surely not for experimentation. (I shall have more to say later in regard to the selection and percentage of subjects in any of the methods of autohypnosis.)

Once such a potential subject has been selected, the "you're falling forward" waking suggestion technique is demonstrated with him. The subject is then taught to "autosuggest" the falling forward. Some time is spent on this, and in emphasizing that "it doesn't matter *who* gives you the suggestions," as has been described in Method 1.

After the subject has been taught to produce quickly the falling forward postural technique upon himself, and the implications of it have been *hammered* home upon him, a similar demonstration is given of Chevreul's pendulum. No "magnetic" bar is used, and the subject is given waking suggestion that "it's going back and forth, back and forth, like a pendulum," etc. The pendulum is then made to go "round and round." All this, of course, works. The subject then produces the same results upon himself through autosuggestion. This is practiced until the subject, through auto-suggestion, can *quickly* produce substantial swinging of the pendulum—both "back and forth" and "round and round."

The subject, in working with Chevreul's pendulum, has been seated in a comfortable armchair. Waking suggestion is now given that the subject's "right arm feels very heavy," etc. This is kept up for some minutes—say five —and the subject will report that his right hand feels very heavy. Some subjects will be unable to move their right hand. (Such subjects will prove to be splendid for other more advanced phenomena.) In any case, the subject is then taught to autosuggest the heaviness of the right hand. In a short while the subject can do this quickly. A similar procedure is followed, separately, with the left hand, the right leg and then the left leg, that is, heterosuggestion in the waking state is followed by intensive autosuggestion. Then the subject is drilled until, by autosuggestion, he can make either hand or foot very heavy in a short while. This may be done by calling out one extremity after another at random.

A similar procedure is used now to produce heaviness of the entire body, first by heterosuggestion and then by autosuggestion. The latter is drilled thoroughly. A similar procedure is followed in producing catalepsy of the eyes.

After this effort the subject may often complain of fatigue. Whether the subject does so or not, he is told to autosuggest a comfortable and rested body, and he usually does. If he doesn't, a slight "heterosuggestive" push will. This is enough for a beginning, and the subject is told to go home and practice autosuggesting the different phenomena in different combinations. First both arms simultaneously and then both legs simultaneously. Then the entire body is to feel heavy. After this, the eyes are to be shut tight, and he will be able to open them when he decides to do so. He is told that the purpose of this practice is to teach him to make his entire body feel heavy (or relaxed) in a few moments whenever he decides to do so, and at the same time he is to get a catalepsy of the eyes. Should he feel tired after this practice, he will be able to autosuggest it away.

When I next see the subject I have him demonstrate how quickly he can make his entire body feel heavy (or relaxed) coincident with a self-induced catalepsy of the eyes. The subject can produce this quickly if he has given himself a modicum of practice at home.

When I see that the subject can turn this state on and off, almost like an electric light, I give him some more pre-trance preparation. This time it runs along the following lines:

> You see that you are learning autohypnosis. It might be clearer if we called it "auto-concentration," for in a sense that's what autohypnosis is. Your entire mind and body are *concentrated* upon whatever effect you wish to produce, and when your entire organism is focused upon one thing, the results may seem remarkable.[5] We have utter concentration and no divergence of attention, and that's very important. You know, sometimes you find a scratch or bruise on yourself, and have no recollection of having acquired it. You must have had your attention focused on something else, so to all intents and purposes you had an anesthesia. Well, by appropiate use of autohypnosis you can produce an anaesthesia on yourself, as you shall see.

[5] I grant that this language is in the worst tradition of the inspirational psychologists (?) but it is nevertheless clearer to subjects than would be an explanation in terms of "sensory focalization" and "mental set."

Following Wells' analogies (1924, p. 397) I then compare the illusions and hallucinations of hypnosis to normal dreams, and explain that the amnesia that follows hypnotic sleep is much like the amnesia for one's dreams that usually follows on waking from natural sleep.

After this, I describe a typical heterohypnotic somnambulistic trance and I endeavor to act it out very realistically. If it is possible to demonstrate a good subject, that, of course, is to be preferred. The purpose of all this is to convince the subject that there is nothing extraordinary about hypnosis (or autohypnosis) and by pretrance learning, direct and indirect, to mold his future trance behavior.

Then heterohypnosis is mixed with autohypnosis, i.e., the subject brings himself into as deep a trance as he can, and the experimenter (having shown the subject that the point of origin of the suggestions is immaterial) produces the different trance effects. After this, the experimenter shows the subject how to produce those effects himself.

Some subjects, from the start, need very little heterohypnotic aid before they can produce deep trance phenomena autohpynotically. I advise the experimenter to be careful in his efforts to induce anaesthesias, for when such attempts fail, the subject's confidence is particularly weakened. For that matter, of course, a subject's confidence is weakened by an suggestion that fails.

I remind all of my subjects that aches and pains are warning signals of something wrong with the body. Consequently, they should be careful not to misuse their autohypnotic ability so as to mask physical ailments, and since they probably cannot diagnose their ailments—aside from temporary fatigue and "nervous headaches"—they should let alone that aspect of autohypnosis, as a general rule.

Usually a five-minute trance is enough time for a subject to give himself autohypnotic post-hypnotic suggestions. A longer period can only help, and is often desirable. Most subjects find that the best time for such suggestions is the morning, a short while after awakening, but this has its exceptions.

We have seen three techniques of autohypnosis. The first and second methods begin by choosing desirable subjects through heterohypnosis, and the third method begins by finding appropriate subjects through simple waking suggestion. Thereafter autohypnosis is taught by: (*a*) Method 1—post-hypnotic suggestion; (*b*) Method 2—memorized trance instructions; (*c*) Method 3—fractional autohypnosis, i.e., the elements of the trance are taught part by part. In each method the character of the pre-trance instructions and demonstrations is important.

These techniques were developed through heterohypnotic work, spaced over two years, with approximately 150 subjects, and through autohypnotic work from an essentially clinical point of view with close to 40 selected cases. At least 20 more subjects, who varied in age from 18 to 30, were used in non-therapeutic autohypnotic experimentation.

May I present a caution. There is no reason, save for experimental purposes, to teach autohypnosis so thoroughly to a good subject that he can produce positive or negative visual and auditory hallucinations. If autohypnosis is taught so thoroughly, it is good policy to give the subject heterohypnotic suggestions that block such autohypnotic hallucinations completely, otherwise you may have a worried subject on your hands.

There are some definite advantages attached to autohypnosis. Hull (1933, p. 156) says:

> The general nature and proportions of the curve diminution of [the durability of post-hypnotic suggestion] with the passage of time have become of special significance in [clinical practice] because it has been found that striking improvements in symptoms observable during the trance too often disappear disappointingly soon after its termination, and in spite of the use of vigorous post-hypnotic suggestion.

Autohypnosis completely surmounts this diminution of posthypnotic suggestion. The subject administers the post-hypnotic suggestions to himself whenever he so desires and what in heterohypnosis would be a remission of symptoms, becomes a self-controlled and periodically reinforced remission.

The important advantage of autohypnosis lies in its ability to overcome the diminution of the effects of post-hypnotic suggestion. For example—one of my cases, a stutterer, treated heterohypnotically, would speak impeccably for about two days, and then relapse to her old level. With autohypnosis she has no occasion to revisit me. The fundamental reasons for her stuttering were fairly clear, and were fixed, and not variable factors at the time.

There is another advantage to autohypnosis. It means a good deal to a subject not to have to revisit persistently the psychologist for frequent hypnotic aid, whether it be for the problem under treatment or in another connection.

The most impressive thing about the therapeutic use of autohypnosis is the rapidity with which it weakens the feeling of dependency upon the psychologist held by most cases under treatment. True enough, the psychologist temporarily remains the subject's guide, but what is important is that the subject soon realizes that it is only he himself who will do the real work of the cure. In some instances, what the subject is instructed to do with his autohypnotic ability is expected to help him only slightly, but the concepts that he absorbs serve to gain his whole-hearted coöperation in following out the (non-hypnotic) courses of action which may be the real crux of the therapy.

I have used autohypnosis with success in cases of stuttering, nailbiting, anaesthesia for dental use, insomnia, smoking, and the "will to diet." I have been especially interested in teaching it to people who wish to inculcate the "work urge" in themselves. Acting, music, and the "will to write" have been the customary fields here. The results in acting have been quite gratifying, because it seems possible to break completely any trace of self-consciousness.

Practice effects occur, no matter by which method autohypnosis is taught. After a few autohypnotic trances, induced by the subject without any heterohypnotic aid, a minute becomes ample time for the self-induction of the trance, and often a half-minute suffices. Practice effects always occur in heterohypnotic work, so this is no excaption, save that the effects seem more marked.

As far as the question of *rapport* is concerned, it seems fair to conclude that there is no *rapport* in autohypnosis, unless it is grafted on the subject in the early stages of teaching autohypnosis. It is true, however, that the subject can voluntarily grant this *rapport* or withhold it in his latter trances. The use of the word *rapport* in this connection is convenient, and for that reason I am using it.

I have not found anything in my work with autohypnosis that conflicts with the "Interpretations" of Hull (1933, p. 387) in regard to heterohypnosis. Particularly would I like to emphasize his point that it really makes no difference to the subject if the suggestions come from within or without. (See especially Hull's section "Ideomotor Action and Monoideism Conceived as Habit Phenomena," 1933, pp. 398–399.)

It is my impression, subjective of course, that the distributions of subjects who go to various depths in autohypnosis would not differ significantly from those usually found in heterohypnotic work. Davis and Husband present a fine scale and typical results (1931). Since my techniques were constantly changing until I developed the present methods, distributions that I could present would be fallacious. I have found, however, that at least one of five, and no more than two out of five adults can be taught autohypnosis so thoroughly that they will be able to produce upon themselves the whole gamut of hypnotic phenomena as enumerated in the scoring system of Davis and Husband (1931, p. 176). The figure is probably closer to one out of five.

This means that it is possible to teach at least one out of five people to produce, autohypnotically, extensive anaesthesias and catalepsies, and positive and negative visual and auditory hallucinations—particularly positive ones. This can all be done heterohypnotically, but when it is done autohypnotically it brings to mind a question. What about the possible identity of autohypnosis with the trance state of yoga? I cannot answer this except to say that the autohypnotic techniques here presented can probably provide an answer to this question.

This may be relevant. A subject of mine was seated in an ice cream parlor, and spoke of his ability to induce anaesthesia upon himself. (I had been doing some experimental work with him.) To convince his skeptical listeners and to win a bet, he put himself into a trance, gave himself a posthypnotic anaesthesia of his left hand, and told himself that he would not feel the residual pain when he later told himself, in a waking state, to "shut off" the post-hypnotic anaesthetic suggestion. Everything worked perfectly. I might add that the pain stimulus was a lighted cigarette. The burn healed without any trouble, except some pain a few days later, which some autohypnotic suggestion blocked.

It is true that autohypnotic anaesthesias and catalepsies do not equal the *samadhic* (trance) state of yoga, except, perhaps, on the vaudeville stage. "Sensory withdrawal" is a rather important element (Behanan, 1937). A good autohypnotic subject who tells himself, in a trance, that *nothing whatever* will disturb his trance for the next five minutes seems to have a startlingly complete "sensory withdrawal." It is essential that the subject clearly understand the condition he is to produce upon himself.

In closing, I should like to point out some additional problems that could be investigated with fruitful results.

1. A large group, naïve and untested to waking suggestion and hypnosis, should be given trance instructions to memorize. How many would learn autohypnosis? How deep would different subjects go?
2. A large group should be given trance instructions to memorize *after* elaborate explanation and demonstration of waking suggestion and hetero- and autohypnosis. How many would learn autohypnosis? How deep would they go?
3. An effort should be made to teach a large group "fractional hypnosis," i.e., teaching the elements of the trance part by part without first picking the better subjects through preliminary waking suggestion. What would the results be?
4. What are the minimum elements that need be explained and demonstrated to prepare a subject for autohypnosis?
5. What connection, if any, is there between autohypnosis and progressive relaxation?
6. To what extent can autohypnotic subjects be trained to get their results in a waking state by their own post-hypnotic suggestion, and thus obviate the necessity for their trances?
7. A careful investigation of positive and negative visual and auditory hallucinations (autohypnotically produced) might throw some light on aspects of imagination. The positive hallucinations, rather than the negative ones, might yield the more significant data.

21

SYSTEMATIC DESENSITIZATION AS TRAINING IN SELF-CONTROL[1]

Marvin R. Goldfried

On the basis of an ever-growing body of experimental evidence (e.g., Cooke, 1968; Davison, 1968b; Lang, 1969; Lang & Lazovik, 1963; Lang, Lazovik, & Reynolds, 1965; Paul, 1966, 1969b), it is becoming strikingly clear that systematic desensitization is a highly effective procedure for the reduction of fears and phobias. Indeed, desensitization probably represents the most frequently used and empirically well-founded technique currently available to the behaviorally oriented clinician.

The specific procedures typically employed in systematic desensitization follow logically from the theoretical description of the treatment process as outlined by Wolpe (1958). According to the principle of reciprocal inhibition, Wolpe maintains:

> If a response antagonistic to anxiety can be made to occur in the presence of anxiety-evoking stimuli so that it is accompanied by a complete or partial suppression of the anxiety responses, the bond between these stimuli and the anxiety responses will be weakened [p. 71].

Although research evidence clearly indicates that systematic desensitization does indeed work, one can nonetheless call into question the ade-

Marvin R. Goldfried, "Systematic Desensitization as Training in Self-Control," *Journal of Consulting and Clinical Psychology, 37*, 1971, 228–234.

[1] The preparation of this paper was supported by Research Grant MH-15044 from the National Institute of Mental Health. The author is grateful to Thomas J. D'Zurilla, Gerald C. Davison, and Stuart Valins for their many helpful comments on an earlier version of this paper.

quacy of Wolpe's theoretical explanation for the underlying process. For example, it has yet to be demonstrated that relaxation functions in the way in which Wolpe suggests, namely, as a response which is inherently antagonistic to anxiety (Lang, 1969). An even more basic assumption underlying Wolpe's theory—and one toward which the present paper addresses itself—is that the relearning which occurs during the treatment sessions represents a relatively passive process of deconditioning. As indicated below, it would seem more appropriate to construe systematic desensitization as more of an active process, directed toward learning of a general anxiety-reducing skill, rather than the passive desensitization to specific aversive stimuli.

Following the description of a mediational model to explain the effectiveness of desensitization, and a discussion of the available corroborative research findings for this alternative explanation, specific procedural modifications for systematic desensitization are suggested.

A MEDIATIONAL INTERPRETATION

Rather than viewing relaxation as "reciprocally inhibiting" the anxiety reaction, a mediational conceptualization of desensitization would instead describe the situation as follows: Because of the individual's previous life experiences, he has learned to react to certain environmental situations with an avoidance response. Further, this overt response may be conceptualized as being the end product of a series of mediational responses and stimuli. According to this view, one can maintain that systematic desensitization involves not so much a passive "reciprocal inhibition" as it does the *active building in of the muscular relaxation response and cognitive relabeling into the r–s mediational sequence.*

During the process of systematic desensitization, the client is taught to become sensitive to his proprioceptive cues for tension, and to react to these cues with his newly acquired skill in muscular relaxation. He is also taught to differentiate the proprioceptive feedback associated with tension from that associated with relaxation, and to identify this feeling of "calm" with the state of muscular relaxation. Once the client has been successful in reducing muscular tension and experiencing the feeling of "calm" in the aversive situation, he is in a better position to approach, rather than avoid, the heretofore fearful object. According to this view, then, what the client learns is a means of actively coping with the anxiety, rather than an immediate replacement for it.

With further practice—both in the consultation session and in vivo—the client becomes better able to identify his proprioceptive cues for muscular tension, to respond by voluntarily relaxing it away, and to relabel his emotional state accordingly (cf. Schachter & Singer, 1962). As this learning proceeds still further, relaxation responses may become anticipatory, thereby completely or partially "short circuiting" the anxiety reaction. In line with Osgood's

(1953) discussion of mediation, one might also expect that with repeated practice of the mediational sequence, the responses and cues which initially have been proprioceptive would continue, but at a cortical level.

Supporting Evidence

Although there have been no studies carried out as yet to test directly the appropriateness of this mediational explanation of systematic desensitization, there are a number of findings which can more readily be explained by the mediational model than by the counterconditioning hypothesis.

In an attempt to look for possible symptom substitution accompanying successful desensitization, a number of studies (Cooke, 1966; Lang & Lazovik, 1963; Lang et al., 1965; Paul, 1966, 1967; Paul & Shannon, 1966) report that in marked contrast to the possible emergence of new fears, *S*s tend to report a general decrement in fearfulness. Of particular importance is the fact that this generalized anxiety reduction occurs with respect to objects or situations which differ widely as to their stimulus properties—a finding that is not easily explained by the stimulus generalization which is likely to follow from the counter-conditioning of specific fears. On the other hand, these findings are quite consistent with the hypothesis that successful desensitization results in the learning of a more generalized anxiety-reducing skill, which the individual learns to apply at times he experiences tension.

Some studies have noted that although anxiety reduction does indeed occur during the desensitization sessions themselves, the amount of transfer to real-life situations is not complete (Agras, 1967; Davison, 1968b; Lang & Lazovik, 1963; Lang et al., 1965). Thus, although they are better able to approach the previously feared objects, successfully desensitized *S*s nonetheless do report experiencing tension. Although it may be possible to explain this lack of perfect transfer by referring to the discrepancies between the situations presented in imagination and those occurring in real life (Davison, 1968b), the present writer would agree more with Agras' (1967) interpretation of these findings. Agras suggests that there may be two phases which account for the successful results achieved with systematic desenitization: the learning which occurs during the desensitization sessions themselves and the changes which occur in vivo. This view of desensitization is very much in accord with the mediational paradigm described above, where the treatment procedure provides the client with a technique for coping with anxiety which may be expected to prevent (i.e., short circuit) anxiety only after it is fully learned by repeated trials in the real-life situation.

In an attempt to determine the necessary and sufficient procedural conditions for anxiety reduction through systematic desensitization, researchers have consistently found that relaxation training per se appears to have little effect on *S*s (Cooke, 1968; Davison, 1968b; Lang et al., 1965; Rachman, 1965). At first blush, these findings appear to contradict the mediational interpretation of desensitization. Inasmuch as the *S*s in these investigations were simply trained in relaxation and never really instructed in how or when to use this response, however, the role of relaxation in systematic desensitization was studied only in a limited sense. In addition to clinical reports (e.g., Davison, 1965; D'Zurilla, 1969; Gray, England, & Mohoney, 1965) attesting to the effectiveness of relaxation used in vivo, Zeisset (1968) has recently presented some empirical findings consistent with these clinical observations. After training *S*s in relaxation, Zeisset instructed them to "use" this newly acquired skill in everyday life whenever they began to experience tension. In contrast to previous studies indicating that relaxation alone was not effective in reducing anxiety, it was found that relaxation training plus the instruction to apply this technique when anxious was more successful in reducing anxiety in the criterion situation (i.e., "interview anxiety") than placebo and no-contact controls, and just as effective as systematic desensitization which utilized a criterion-relevant hierarchy.

The work on the use of drug-induced (methohexitone sodium or Brevital) relaxation in systematic desensitization provides some findings which appear to be consistent with a mediational, self-control model. Commenting on the variable results others have had in utilizing Brevital to induce states of relaxation, Brady (1967) has suggested that an important procedural detail for the successful use of the drug involves instructions that the client "work along with it" and allow himself to relax. Davison and Valins (1968) have similarly noted the importance of having the client "let go" even when drugs are being used to aid in the induction of muscular relaxation, so that the success in relaxation can be attributed, at least in part, to his own efforts. From this point of view, effective fear reduction follows from an active attempt on the part of the client to relax himself, rather than simply presenting aversive stimuli when the individual happens to be in a state of relaxation.

A number of recent desensitization studies have had as their primary focus the importance of cognitive factors in bringing about anxiety reduction (Leitenberg, Agras, Barlow, & Oliveau, 1969; Marcia, Rubin, & Efran, 1969; Valins & Ray, 1967). By experimentally manipulating the individual's expectancy for improvement, Leitenberg et al. (1969) were able to enhance the effectiveness of systematic desensitization. Similarly, Marcia et al. (1969) found a placebo-type therapeutic manipulation—which led *S*s to believe that their fears would be reduced—to be just as effective as desensitization. Using false heart-rate feedback to manipulate *S*'s cognitions regarding his state of emotional arousal in the presence of fear stimuli, Valins and Ray (1967) were able to "desensitize" *S*s to the point where they were able to approach the heretofore feared object. These several studies clearly indicate that the individual's cognitions, particularly as they relate to expectancy for improvement and control over their own internal state, may play a significant role in the effectiveness of systematic desensitization.

In discussing the possible role of cognitive variables in desensitization,

Lang (1969) has hypothesized that the client may be learning a "cognitive set" regarding his emotional arousal, whereby

> desensitization is an operant training schedule, designed to shape the response "I am not afraid" (or a potentially competing response such as "I am relaxed" or "I am angry") in the presence of a graded set of discriminative stimuli. When well learned, the response could have the status of a "set" or self-instruction, which can then determine other related behaviors . . . [p. 187].

Lang's suggestion that such learning may be inadvertently reinforced by the therapist (and the client himself), as well as the recent finding by Leitenberg et al. (1969) that the systematic reinforcement of the individual's progress during systematic desensitization facilitates improvement, further supports the hypothesis that desensitization is actually providing the client with an active coping skill.

It is of considerable interest to note that even with the therapist viewing systematic desensitization as a counterconditioning of specific fears, the client often perceives the beneficial effects of treatment as his having learned a strategy for coping with stress in general. For example, in their study on the effects of group desensitization, Paul and Shannon (1966) report that

> subjects in the group seemed to perceive the desensitization method as an active mastery technique which they could acquire and use themselves, more than in the individual application. Clients' descriptions of utilizing desensitization training to master anticipated areas of stress themselves suggest the development of a confidence-building "how to cope" orientation [pp. 133–134].

The frequently noted generalized improvement resulting from systematic desensitization, which can be more readily explained with a self-control model, would certainly attest to the possibility that desensitization results in the learning of a generally applicable stress-reducing strategy.

Although a mediational, self-control view of systematic desensitization may be used to explain what goes on during the treatment process, the intent of this paper is not simply to provide an alternative theoretical paradigm. The author agrees with Bandura (1961) that behavioral principles should not be used solely to explain currently available treatment methods, but rather to generate innovative, more effective procedures. It is toward a description of certain suggested procedural modifications that the next section is directed.

SUGGESTED PROCEDURAL MODIFICATIONS

Based on a mediational model of desensitization, as well as the supporting evidence for this general self-control orientation, several modifications in technique would appear to be indicated. These suggested procedural changes, the effectiveness of which is amenable to empirical test, include (*a*) a different rationale for systematic desensitization given to the client, (*b*) a different focus placed on the purpose of relaxation training, (*c*) different guidelines used in the construction of the hierarchy, (*d*) a modified manner in which the scenes are presented in imagination, and (*e*) a greater emphasis on instruction in the use of relaxation responses in vivo.

Rationale Presented to the Client

In "structuring" the therapeutic procedures for the client by describing the underlying rationale for desensitization, the following can be explained:

> There are various situations where, on the basis of your past experience, you have learned to react by becoming tense (anxious, nervous, fearful). What I plan to do is help you to learn how to cope with these situations more successfully, so that they do not make you as upset. This will be done by taking note of a number of those situations which upset you to varying degrees, and then having you learn to cope with the less stressful situations before moving on to the more difficult ones. Part of the treatment involves learning how to relax, so that in situations where you feel yourself getting nervous you will be better able to eliminate this tenseness. Learning to relax is much like learning any other skill. When a person learns to drive, he initially has difficulty in coordinating everything, and often finds himself very much aware of what he is doing. With more and more practice, however, the procedures involved in driving become easier and more automatic. You may find the same thing occurring to you when you try to relax in those situations where you feel yourself starting to become tense. You will find that as you persist, however, it will become easier and easier.

The general procedures of relaxation training, hierarchy construction, and successive presentation of items for imagination are then described to the client, with the additional indication that the purpose of the desensitization sessions is (*a*) to provide practice in learning to "relax away" tensions as they start to build up, and (*b*) to provide rehearsal for certain specific situations where the client may actually try out his relaxation skills in vivo.

Focus Placed on Relaxation Training

As a fairly representative method of relaxation training typically used in desensitization, we may note the procedure outlined by Paul (1966). This technique simply involves having the client tense separate muscle groups for approximately 5–7 seconds, taking note of the muscles that are tense, relaxing them for 20–30 seconds, and focusing on the sensations which are associated with relaxation.

The suggested modification of this procedure is slight and involves informing the clients that (*a*) the tension phase is provided so that they can be aware of those sensations that are involved in being tense, and (*b*) these sensations will serve as a signal or cue for them to relax away the tension—as they will be doing during the training sessions and in vivo. As they become better able to relax themselves using the tension–relaxation procedure, they are given training in identifying the already-present tensions of which they may be aware, and then relaxing these away. Hence, in addition to learning a relaxation response, this phase of the desensitization procedure also provides the client with practice in recognizing the proprioceptive feedback associated with tension so it can serve as a cue for the appropriate use of relaxation.

Guidelines for Hierarchy Construction

In the construction of the hierarchy, the typical approach used in desensitization involves a selection of graded variations of anxiety-provoking situations which reflect a given theme. Wolpe and Lazarus (1966) have also noted that there may be times when systematic desensitization would involve several themes, but that separate hierarchies should be compiled for each.

In using a mediational interpretation of desensitization, the nature of the specific environmental situation eliciting the anxiety becomes less important than the tension response itself. According to the mediational paradigm, *the client is being taught to cope with his proprioceptive anxiety responses and cues rather than with situations which elicit the tension.* What is being suggested here, then, is that the typical practice of establishing hierarchies which reflect carefully selected themes may not be essential to the successful application of systematic desensitization. Inasmuch as the client is being trained to relax away anxiety as it begins to build up, one need only construct a single hierarchy composed of situations eliciting increasing amounts of anxiety, irrespective of whether or not the items appear to reflect any given theme. In fact, the therapist might choose to select items which reflect a variety of different anxiety-producing situations in the individual's current life in order to facilitate generalization of the effect of desensitization. This would be particularly indicated in cases where the client responds with anxiety in a variety of different situations.[2]

Presentation of Scenes in Imagination

During the course of the systematic desensitization itself, the therapist typically asks the client to visualize the scene for approximately 10–15 seconds, provided there is no anxiety response. Should the client indicate that

[2] Although the hierarchy may be comprised of diverse situations which elicit anxiety in the client, only those which reflect unrealistic fears would be included.

he is beginning to feel tense, he is usually instructed to stop imagining the scene and concentrate only on trying to relax. This procedure is based on the assumption that in order to effect a successful counterconditioning, the relaxation response must be stronger than the anxiety response. Based on a mediational interpretation, however, the client would *not* be told to eliminate the scene once he begins to feel tense. In real life, the client cannot always remove himself from a situation once he starts becoming anxious. By viewing the desensitization session as a rehearsal for anxiety reduction in specific real-life situations, as well as practice in successfully coping with anxiety in general, it would follow logically that the client should *maintain the image even though he is experiencing anxiety, and additionally to relax away this tension.* By using this approach, one more realistically parallels potentially stressful life situations, thereby providing the client with practice in modifying the mediational sequence. On the basis of the clinical experience of the author and several of his colleagues in the routine utilization of this procedure (e.g., D'Zurilla, 1969), this modification of desensitization has proven to be quite successful.

Use of Relaxation In Vivo

In accordance with the view of systematic desensitization as self-control training for the reduction of anxiety, the client should be encouraged to practice this skill in vivo. Thus, the client is told to identify his feelings of tension, to instruct himself to "relax" (cf. Bond & Hutchison, 1960; Cautela, 1966a; D'Zurilla, 1969), and then actually to "let go" of his muscles. Although the utilization of relaxation in vivo may parallel some of the items in the desensitization hierarchy, it may also involve situations which were not incorporated into the hierarchy. Indeed, the present author has been struck with the success that some clients report in relaxing away tension in situations never discussed during therapy (e.g., one client who was being desensitized for speech anxiety found that the use of relaxation in vivo was instrumental in improving his golf game!). In encouraging the client to practice anxiety reduction in vivo, the client should be forewarned that at times he may experience some difficulty in being completely successful at relaxing away tension. This would be particularly the case in those instances where the anxiety reaction is strong.

GENERAL CONCLUSIONS

The concept of self-control appears to be playing an increasingly significant role in the understanding and modification of a variety of different forms of maladaptive behavior (Cautela, 1969; D'Zurilla & Goldfried, 1971; Goldfried & D'Zurilla, 1969; Goldfried & Merbaum, 1973; Goldiamond, 1965c; Homme, 1966; Kanfer, 1970). In accordance with a self-control orientation, the present paper has presented a mediational model of systematic desensitization, together with some of the procedural implications which follow this view. Thus, rather than construing desensitization as involving a more or less passive elimination of specific fears, the therapeutic procedure is seen as being directed toward providing the client with a more general skill for reducing anxiety, thereby enabling him to exercise greater self-control in a variety of anxiety-provoking life situations. Although clinical experience and indirect empirical evidence would suggest that this alternative view is potentially quite fruitful, the eventual utility of the mediational explanation awaits more direct experimental confirmation.

SUMMARY

As an alternative to conceptualizing systematic desensitization as a passive elimination of specific fears, the therapeutic procedure is interpreted within a mediational framework and is viewed as offering the client a more general skill by which he may actively reduce anxiety. Research findings supporting the contention that desensitization may provide the individual with a greater ability for self-control in a variety of anxiety-provoking situations are discussed, and specific procedural modifications stemming from this self-control orientation are outlined.

PART V

Case Studies in the Clinical Application of Self-Control

22

A HOMOSEXUAL TREATED WITH RATIONAL PSYCHOTHERAPY

Albert Ellis

PRESENTING PROBLEMS

The client came for psychotherapy primarily because he had been exclusively homosexual all his life and thought that it was about time he settled down and married. He had read about the therapist's work with homosexuals in a magazine and was self-referred. In addition to his homosexual problem, he suffered from heart palpitations which had been consistently diagnosed as being of purely psychogenic origin, and he wondered whether something could be done about them, too. He vaguely thought that he might have other problems, but was not certain what they were.

BACKGROUND DATA

The client was a thirty-five-year-old male, living in Brooklyn with his parents, and operating his disabled father's toy factory. He had been raised as a Catholic, but no longer considered himself a believer. He was the only son of what he described as a "very religious and very neurotic" mother and an "exceptionally weak, dominated father" who had been disabled by a serious stroke two years before the client came for treatment. He had always been quite close to his mother, and usually did her bidding, even though he

Reprinted by permission of the author and Clinical Psychology Publishing Co., Inc. from *Journal of Clinical Psychology*, 1959, *15*, 338–343.

bitterly resented her persistent attempts to control himself and his father. He liked but did not respect his father.

The client, whom we shall call Caleb Frosche, was born and raised in Brooklyn; had a shy, uneventful childhood; spent three unhappy years in the Navy; always did well in school; did some college teaching for a short time after obtaining his doctorate in zoology; and reluctantly took over his father's business, and was carrying it on successfully, after the father had had a serious stroke. Caleb had a few dates with girls when he went to high school, but was afraid to make any sexual overtures, for fear of being rejected, and consequently had not even ever kissed a girl. While in the Navy he was plied with liquor by two other sailors and induced to have his first homosexual experience at the age of nineteen. Since that time he had engaged in homosexual acts every two or three weeks, always making his contacts at public urinals and never having any deep relationships with his partners. He occasionally dated girls, mainly to show others that he was heterosexual, but he was not particularly attracted to any of them and never made any advances or got seriously involved.

Shortly after his father began to have difficulties with his heart (10 years ago) Caleb began to experience sudden attacks of heart palpitations and chest pain. These would spontaneously subside a few minutes after they began, but he would be left in a shaken condition for several hours or days afterward. Continual medical examination had revealed no heart pathology, and he referred to himself as a "cardiac neurotic".

THERAPEUTIC APPROACH

Caleb was one of the first clients treated with a special therapeutic approach which the therapist developed after many years of practicing orthodox psychoanalysis and psychoanalytically-oriented psychotherapy. *Rational psychotherapy*, (Ellis, 1956b, 1957a, 1957b, 1958) as the technique is called, stems from the hypothesis that most significant human emotions and actions, including neurotic feelings and behavior, stem from basic assumptions, beliefs, or philosophies which the individual consciously or unconsciously holds. Neurotic symptoms, it is held, are caused and maintained by illogical or irrational ideas and attitudes, and tend to reinforce these illogical beliefs. To accomplish effective psychotherapy, the basic irrational philosophies or value systems of the disturbed individual not only have to be brought to conscious attention, and their origins interpreted (as is done in all analytically-oriented therapies) but, even more importantly, the client must be shown how he is now, in the present, wittingly or unwittingly *maintaining* his irrational beliefs by continually re-indoctrinating himself, through self-verbalization or autosuggestion, with the nonsensical philosophies he originally acquired. The client must also be shown, most specifically and concretely, how to depropagandize or de-indoctrinate himself from his self-defeating philosophies and how to substitute more rational value judgments in their place. Depropagandization is taught the client by the therapist inducing him (a) to assume that all his exaggerated fears, anxieties, hostilities, guilts, and depressions must be grounded in illogical beliefs and attitudes; (b) to trace these illogical beliefs to their basic assumptions; (c) to question these assumptions; (d) to attack them in the light of logical and rational methodologies; (e) to counter them, in action, with behavior that directly contradicts them; and (f) to replace them, ultimately, with rational, non-defeating values and beliefs which, when they are ultimately accepted, will automatically encourage non-neurotic behavior.

ATTACKING THE CLIENT'S FIXED HOMOSEXUALITY

The first major symptom of the client which was attacked by the therapist was his pattern of exclusive homosexuality, as this was the aspect of his behavior with which he was most concerned when he came to therapy. In tackling the client's homosexual pattern, the therapist first carefully explained why this mode of behavior was neurotic. He showed the client that although homosexual activity is not in itself a product of emotional disturbance, its *fixed* or *exclusive* form is invariably a neurotic symptom because it rigidly, prejudicedly, and fetishistically eliminates *other* modes of sexual fulfillment, notably heterosexuality. This means that the homosexual arbitrarily, out of some illogical fear or hostility, forfeits sexual desire and satisfaction in connection with half the population of the world; and, to make his behavior still more illogical in our culture, confines himself to sex acts with those partners with whom he is most likely to get into serious legal and social difficulties, including arrest and blackmail.

Caleb was shown, at the start of therapy, that there would be no attempt on the therapist's part to induce him to surrender his homosexual desires or activities—since there was no logical reason why he should not, at least, maintain inverted *desires*—but that the goal of therapy would be to help him overcome his irrational blocks against heterosexuality. Once he overcame those, and actively desired and enjoyed sex relations with females, it would be relatively unimportant, from a mental health standpoint, whether he still had homosexual leanings as well.

The basic assumptions behind Caleb's homosexual pattern of behavior were then quickly brought to light. From questioning him about his specific homosexual participation, it was revealed that he invariably would enter a public urinal or a gay bar, would wait around until some male approached him, and then, whether this male appealed to him or not, would go off to have sex relations. On never a single occasion, in sixteen years of homosexual activity, had he ever actively approached a male himself.

On the basis of this and allied information, it was made clear to Caleb that his outstanding motive for remaining homosexual was his strong fear of rejection by (a) all women and (b) most males. He was so convinced that he might be rejected if he made sexual approaches to either women or men, that he had arranged his entire sex life so that no active approach, and consequently no possibility of rejection, was necessary. He had obviously acquired his fear of rejection, as further questioning soon brought out, at an early age, and it was probably related to the fact that he had been a rather chubby and unattractive boy, and that even his own mother had kept remarking that he would have trouble finding and winning an attractive girl.

Rather than spend much time belaboring the point that Caleb's fear of rejection probably stemmed from his childhood, the therapist convinced him, on purely logical grounds, that this was so since he had apparently feared being rejected by girls when he was in his early teens, and his fear must have originated sometime prior to that time. The therapist, instead, tried to get, as quickly as possible to the source of his fear of rejection: namely, his illogical *belief* that being rejected by a girl (or a fellow) was a terrible thing. Said the therapist:

T: Suppose, for the sake of discussion, you had, back in your high school days, tried, really tried, to make some sexual passes at a girl, and suppose you had been unequivocally rejected by her. Why would that be terrible?

C: Well—uh—it just would be.

T: But *why* would it be?

C: Because—uh-I—I just thought the world would come to an end if that would have happened.

T: But *why?* Would the world *really* have come to an end?

C: No, of course not.

T: Would the girl have slapped your face, or called a cop, or induced all the other girls to ostracize you?

C: No, I guess she wouldn't.

T: Then what *would* she have done? How would you—*really*—have been hurt?

C. Well, I guess, in the way you mean, I wouldn't.

T: Then why did you think that you would?

C: That's a good question. Why did I?

T: The answer, alas, is so obvious that you probably won't believe it.

C: What is it?

T: Simply that you thought you would be terribly hurt by a girl's rejecting you merely because you were *taught* that you would be. You were raised, literally raised, to believe that if anyone, especially a girl, rejects you, tells you she doesn't like you, that this is terrible, awful, frightful. It isn't, of course: it isn't in any manner, shape, or form awful if someone rejects you, refuses to accede to your wishes. But you *think* it is, because you were *told* it is.

C: Told?

T: Yes—literally and figuratively told. Told literally by your parents, who warned you, time and again, did they not, that if you did wrong, made the wrong approaches to people, they wouldn't love you, wouldn't accept you—*and that would be awful, that would be terrible.*

C: Yes, you're right about that. That's just what they told me.

T: Yes—and not only they. Indirectly, figuratively, symbolically, in the books you read, the plays you saw, the films you went to—weren't you told the same thing there, time and again, over and over—that if anyone, the hero of the book, you, or anyone else, got rejected, got rebuffed, got turned down, they *should* think it terrible, should be hurt?

C: I guess I was. Yes, that's what the books and films really say, isn't it?

T: It sure is. All right, then, so you *were* taught that being rejected is awful, frightful. Now let's go back to my original question. Suppose you actually did ask a girl for a kiss, or something else; and suppose she did reject you. What would you *really* lose thereby, by being so rejected?

C: Really lose? Actually, I gucss, very little.

T: Right: damned little. In fact, you'd actually gain a great deal.

C: How so?

T: Very simply: you'd gain experience. For if you tried and were rejected, you'd know not to try it with that girl, or in that way, again. Then you could go on to try again with some other girl, or with the same girl in a different way, and so on.

C: Maybe you've got something there.

T: Maybe I have. Whenever you get rejected—as you do, incidentally, every time you put a coin in a slot machine and no gum or candy comes out—you are merely learning that this girl or that technique or this gum machine doesn't work; but a trial with some other girl, technique, or machine may well lead to success. Indeed, in the long run, it's almost certain to.

C: You're probably right.

T: O.K. then. So it isn't the rejection by girls that *really* hurts, is it? It's your *idea*, your *belief*, your *assumption* that rejection is hurtful, is awful. *That's* what's really doing you in; and that's what we're going to have to change to get you over this silly homosexual neurosis.

Thus, the therapist kept pointing out, in session after session, the illogical fears behind the client's fixed homosexual pattern of behavior—and *why* these fears were illogical, *how* they were merely learned and absorbed from Caleb's early associates, and, especially how *he* now kept re-indoctrinating himself with these fears by parroting them unthinkingly, telling himself over and over that they were based on proven evidence, when obviously they were completely arbitrary and ungrounded in fact. His fear of rejection, of losing approval, or having others laugh at him or criticize him, was examined in scores of its aspects, and revealed to him again and again. It was not only revealed, but scornfully, forcefully *attacked* by the therapist, who kept showing

Caleb that it is necessarily silly and self-defeating for anyone to care too much about what *others* think, since then one is regulating one's life by and for these others, rather than for oneself; and, moreover, one is setting up a set of conditions for one's own happiness which make it virtually impossible that one ever will be happy.

Caleb's homosexual pattern of behavior, then, was consistently, forthrightly assailed not on the grounds of its being immoral or wrong, but solely on the grounds of its being self-defeating and limiting—and of its stemming from basic, largely nonsexual assumptions which had ramifications in all the rest of his life, and kept him from enjoying himself in many other ways as well.

ACTIVITY HOMEWORK ASSIGNMENTS

At the same time that the philosophic assumptions underlying Caleb's fear of rejection, and his consequent homosexual behavior, were being directly questioned and attacked, he was encouraged by the therapist to date girls, so that he could, in actual practice, overcome his fears concerning them. He was warned that his first attempts at dating might well result in embarrassment, awkwardness, and failure; but was told that only by working through such situations, with the help of the therapist, was he likely to overcome his irrational fears in these connections.

On his first date, which he made the week following his first therapy session, Caleb saw a girl who was very nice and refined, but who was quite cold, and who obviously had severe problems of her own. On his second attempt, he met a librarian, a year younger than he, who was warm and accepting, and with whom he immediately began to pet heavily, but who also turned out to be severely disturbed. While still going with her, he went to a party with a girl whom he had known in a friendly way for some time, but whom he had never actually dated; and he wound up by having intercourse with her, which he thoroughly enjoyed. The girl, however, moved to another town shortly thereafter, and he did not see her again.

While Caleb was seeing these girls, the therapist went over with him in detail his behavior with and his reactions to them. He was given specific information and instruction in regard to how to make dates; what to expect from the girls; how to understand them and their problems; how to avoid being discouraged when he was rebuffed; what kinds of sexual overtures to make and when to make them, etc. His mistakes and blunders were gone over in an objective, constructed manner; and he was shown how, instead of blaming himself for these mistakes, he could put them to good self-teaching uses.

After he had seen the therapist seven times, on a once a week basis, Caleb met a girl whom he thought was most desirable, and was at first sure that he would not be able to get anywhere with her. The therapist consistently encouraged him to keep seeing her, even when things looked rather black in their relationship, and insisted that he not give up too easily. Largely because of the therapist's encouragement, Caleb did persist, and soon began to make headway with this girl. He not only managed to win her emotional allegiance; but in spite of the fact that she had a history of sexual indifference, he gradually awakened her desires and, through heavy petting, was able to give her, much to her surprise, tremendous orgasmic release. She was the one who finally insisted that they have intercourse: and this, too, proved to be supremely enjoyable for her and Caleb. The thing that most impressed Caleb, however, was not his sexual prowess with the girl but his ability to win her emotional responsiveness against initial great odds, after he had first convinced himself that he could never succeed. His basic philosophy of his own worthlessness, or the necessity of his failing at anything he really wanted very badly, was rudely shaken by this practical lesson in the value of continuing to fight against odds.

Although Caleb's homosexual proclivities were barely mentioned after the first two sessions, and no direct attempt was made to get him to forego them, he completely and voluntarily renounced homosexuality as soon as he began to be sexually and emotionally successful with females. By the time the twelfth week of therapy had arrived, he had changed from a hundred per cent fixed homosexual to virtually a hundred per cent heterosexual. All his waking and sleeping fantasies became heterosexually oriented, and he was almost never interested in homosexual outlets.

ATTACKING THE CLIENT'S PSYCHOSOMATIC SYMPTOMS AND VOCATIONAL PROBLEMS

Since this paper largely focusses on the treatment of homosexual symtomatology, only a short summary will be given of how this client's nonsexual problems, particularly his psychosomatic and vocational symptoms, were attacked and overcome by the application of principles of rational psychotherapy. He was shown how he had originally begun to tell himself fear and hostility-creating nonsense, bringing on his cardiac neurosis and then, once his symptoms arose, reinforcing them with more illogical ideas. Thus, he kept propagandizing himself with two basic irrational philosophies of living: first, the idea that he must be perfectly competent, achieving, and successful in everything he did; and second, the idea that when he failed or made a mistake at any task, he should blame himself severely. These philosophies, of arrant perfectionism and self-blame, the therapist clearly showed Caleb, necessarily *had* to lead him to acquire some kind of symptoms, such as his heart palpitations, in the first place, and induce him to aggravate and perpetuate them in the second place.

When Caleb, in the course of the ninth session, finally began to see that his having his heart palpitations were originally related to intense dislike for having to take over his father's factory, instead of pursuing his own chosen career, and that they were enormously exaggerated by his fear that he would not be strong and competent enough to control them, his heart symptoms quickly began to abate and within a few more weeks he was entirely free of them. As he lost his hostility to his parents and himself, his strong desire to be a professor of zoology came to the fore, and he began to prepare himself for that vocation.

THE CLOSE OF THERAPY

Caleb unexpectedly said he thought he would discontinue therapy and try to go it on his own at the end of the nineteenth session; and, although the therapist thought this was a rather premature closing, he went along with the client's wish, on the assumption that Caleb would soon get into difficulty and return for further therapy later. As it happens, however, almost three years have now passed and Caleb has not returned. He has written two long letters, and it appears that he has married the fourth girl he dated and is getting along nicely in this marriage. He is teaching zoology in a midwestern university and is getting along well, if not perfectly, in most respects. He is completely disinterested in homosexual relations at present and is free from the psychosomatic heart symptoms with which he came to therapy.

One of the most interesting aspects of this case is that some basic issues in Caleb's life were virtually never discussed during the entire therapeutic procedure—partly becaue the therapist thought that some of them would be analyzed in more detail later, and partly because he thought that some of the issues were largely irrelevant to Caleb's basic problems. Thus, the therapist felt that Caleb's homosexual pattern of behavior was, at least in part, caused by his over-attachment to his mother, and by his unconsciously feeling incest guilt. In the entire course of therapy, however, relatively little reference was made to Caleb's relations with his mother, and no detailed analysis of this relationship was affected. Nonetheless, Caleb's deviated pattern of homosexuality completely changed in the course of therapy—largely, in all probability, because the *main* cause of this homosexuality was *not* his Oedipal attachment to his mother but his severe feelings of inadequacy and fear of rejection—which *were* thoroughly analyzed and attacked in the course of therapy.

By the same token, although Caleb's hostility to his father, and his probable jealousy of the father's hold over his mother, was never, largely because of lack of time, thoroughly interpreted to him, he wound up by being, on the one hand, much less hostile toward and, on the other hand, more able to break with his father. This was because his basic philosophies of blaming both himself and others were steadily and powerfully attacked in the course of therapy; and, once these philosophies started to change, he had no need of being jealous of and hostile toward his father.

SUMMARY

In this case of a thirty-five-year-old male who entered therapy because he was severely troubled by a fixed pattern of homosexuality, a swift frontal attack was made by the therapist on the basic assumptions or philosophies illogically underlying the client's symptoms. In the course of this attack the client was shown, by the therapist's rigorously unmasking and then inducing the client himself to contradict and act against his irrational beliefs, that his homosexual pattern of behavior and his other neurotic symptoms were not hopelessly ingrained and that he himself could control his own destiny by changing his assumptions. Specifically, the client was helped to see that it was not overly important if others did not love or approve him; that failing at a task was not a crime; and that perfect achievement is a silly goal for a human being to strive for. As he began to change the fundamental irrational beliefs that motivated his homosexual and neurotic behavior, the client's symptoms almost automatically began to disappear and he was able to change from a fixed, exclusive homosexual to a virtually hundred per cent heterosexually oriented individual.

23

SELF-CONTROL PROCEDURES IN PERSONAL BEHAVIOR PROBLEMS[1]

Israel Goldiamond

The present discussion is concerned with the application of self-control procedures to the solution of certain limited behavioral problems.

Often one person comes for help from another because he cannot cope with problems that face him. The appropriate behaviors are not available. The means by which the behavioral deficit can be overcome are varied. Simple instructions often suffice, as when *S* cannot study because he does not have the assignment. On the other hand, *S* may not be able to study because he cannot allocate his time appropriately, because he daydreams at his desk, or because he engages in other behaviors which come under the general heading of lack of self-control. In these cases, simple instructions will not remedy the deficit since *S* himself knows what it is. He has often tried to instruct himself to behave appropriately but with little success. Indeed, the numerous jokes surrounding New Year's resolutions indicate both the prevalence of the problem and the ineffectiveness of its instructional solution, whether imposed by others or by one's self in self-instruction.

The specific behavioral deficit, or presenting problem, is often part of

Reprinted by permission of the author and Southern Universities Press from *Psychological Reports*, 1965, *17*, 851–868. Monograph Supplement 3-V17 ($1.00 per copy available as a separate from the journal).

[1] Paper presented at Eastern Psychological Association, April 23, 1965. Written under contract between the Office of the Surgeon General and the Washington School of Psychiatry, DA-49-193-MD-2448. The views expressed herein are those of the author and do not necessarily reflect the views of either contracting agency.

a larger context of deficits. Rather than trying to overcome the presenting deficit directly, the therapist may turn his attention to other, "deeper" behaviors or behavioral deficits. In this case, the presenting problem is considered a symptom, by exactly the same defining operations that make a skin rash a symptom. Here, the dermatologist states that to get rid of the rash he will treat in addition something else, possibly a blood imbalance, rather than only treating the rash itself (Goldiamond, Dyrud, & Miller, 1965). For example, we know of a woman who assumed a fetal posture for three days after an argument with her husband. She was restored to mobility by direct modification of this behavior. It can be argued that a woman who maintains control over her husband by such extreme behaviors is so lacking in more appropriate behaviors that her treatment will require considerably more than the two hours which restored her mobility. This case may be an example of treating a symptom, since behaviors other than the presenting complaint may also require modification. However, the "underlying" problem can still be considered as a behavioral one: in this case, the absence of those behaviors whereby wives normally control their husbands. Yet this general deficit also may be treated directly, as in our research on stuttering where we have, within the laboratory, replaced stuttering by fluent and rapid speech in 30 of 30 cases run thus far (Goldiamond, 1965b). Indeed, one of our stuttering patients, who had been suicidal, became able to read bedtime stories to her children at home, and certain other personal problems at home cleared up because her stuttering cleared up. Some of her other behaviors were accordingly symptomatic of stuttering (Goldiamond, 1965a), as we have defined "symptom."

If there is a danger in premature assignment of behavioral deficits as symptomatic, there is also a danger in premature assumption that the alteration of the presenting problem is the final solution. Further analysis in light of current knowledge will undoubtedly both modify and confirm practice in this area.

Classification of behavior as a problem for treatment or as a symptom may also be an economic or contractual matter. For example, in a marital problem, the presenting complaint may be cleared up in a short period of time, but other problems are sometimes uncovered which may require extensive treatment. At what point is the implicit contract between patient and therapist (cf. Sulzer, 1962) to treat the marital behaviors extended to behaviors in other areas? The answer to this question must depend on the extent to which *S* can afford the treatment or can afford not to get it, that is, can do without it. It would be nice to have a new car when the present one seems to require extensive repairs, but there may be other considerations such as a piano or a child's education. For going to and from work, minor adjustment may be sufficient. The economy may also be behavioral: is it worth the upset?

The present discussion will be limited to cases where the concern was with a specified behavioral problem. These cases should be interpreted in the context of the foregoing discussion: namely, that the procedures used are not intended to question other more extensive procedures, which may be necessary for other kinds of behavioral deficits.

The discussion will be concerned with self-control (Skinner, 1953) and procedure for its establishment. The procedures to be discussed center around the position that behavior is not an emergent property of an organism or a property solely of its environment but is described by a functional relation between the two. More technically, given a specified behavior B and a specified environmental variable x, a lawful relation can be found, such that $B = f(x)$, under certain empirical constraining conditions c. This implies that when the constraints c are set up, and x is set at a stipulated value, then B will have a stipulated value, given by the value of $B = f(x)$. When E sets x at that value, *he* will get the B stipulated. This defines the experimental control of behavior which has been demonstrated repeatedly in operant and other laboratories. When S himself sets x at that value, *he* will get his own B, as stipulated. This defines self-control.

If you want a specified behavior from yourself, set up the conditions which you know will control it. For example, if you cannot get up in the morning by firmly resolving to do so and telling yourself that you must, buy and set an alarm clock. Within this context, the Greek maxim, "Know thyself," translates into "Know thy behaviors, know thy environment, and know the functional relation between the two." Although the relation between an alarm clock and waking up is a simple and familiar one, other relations are neither this simple nor this familiar. There have, however, been developed in laboratories of operant behavior a body of known functional relations between behavior, and programs and other procedures which can alter even more complex behavior systematically. Self-control derived from such research can take at least two forms. One is to instruct S to set up the procedures which change his environment and which thereby bring his behavior under different control. I shall present some cases to this effect. Another form is to train him in the functional analysis of behavior and have him try to determine for himself the procedures which he should apply. This approach will also appear in the following cases.

Inherent in both types of self-control is the problem posed by the tremendous gap between theory and practice. The same theory may dictate numerous alternative methods or solutions, but all may not be equally available, practical, or applicable. The operant paradigm suggests that there are at least 12 different ways to maintain or attenuate behavior (cf. Holz & Azrin, 1963). Which are appropriate to the problem?

One way for selecting effective practical measures is to have S report back to E every week with his results. This hour becomes a session for analysis of data and discussion of changes in procedure. In the laboratory, operant procedures are so arranged that relations between ongoing behavior and its conditions are continuously observed and recorded. Through successes and failures, *E*s may learn to analyze behavior and conditions and may develop a "feel" for their data, as do other behavioral practitioners in interaction with their subject matter, for example, skilled psychiatrists. Hopefully, such a program of systematic trial and analysis will sensitize *S* to his own behavior and his own conditions. By training *S* in control procedures to the extent that these exist and are applicable, we are providing for self-enhancement and self-actualization (Rogers, 1951). Of the individuals who can apply control procedures, *S* is the one most concerned with his behavior and is most in contact with it, its conditions, and its consequences. Initially *E* is the consultant, and eventually *S* becomes his own *E*. The procedures may be limited to *S*s who are intellectually capable of such analysis or who are not otherwise incapacitated. Our *S*s were mainly college students. Where systematic training in behavior analysis was used, the sessions started with individual tutorials in behavior analysis, homework assignments from standard texts (Holland & Skinner, 1961), and readings. Given this intellectual base, we could move on to discussions of the problem in question.

Our first cases were referrals from clinical psychologists who felt that we should work on some of the simpler overt problems, while they tackled their deeper meanings. One of these was a young man who was overweight, and another was a girl who had difficulty studying.

These two problems yielded, for these *S*s, to procedures involving *stimulus control.* The program with the young lady started with human engineering of her desk. Since she felt sleepy when she studied, she was told to replace a 40-w lamp with a good one and to turn her desk away from her bed. It was also decided that her desk was to control study behavior. If she wished to write a letter, she should do so but in the dining room; if she wished to read comic books, she should do so but in the kitchen; if she wished to daydream, she should do so but was to go to another room; at her desk she was to engage in her school work and her school work only.

This girl had previously had a course in behavioral analysis and said, "I know what you're up to. You want that desk to assume stimulus control over me. I'm not going to let any piece of wood run my life for me."

"On the contrary," I said, "you *want* that desk to run you. It is you who decides when to put yourself under the control of your desk. It is like having a sharpened knife in a drawer. You decide when to use it; but when you want it, it is ready."

After the first week of the regimen, she came to me and gleefully said, "I spent only ten minutes at my desk last week."

"Did you study there," I asked.

"Yes, I did," she said.

"Good," I said, "let's try to double that next week."

For the next few weeks we did not meet, but she subsequently reported that during the last month of the semester she was able to spend three hours a day at her desk for four weeks in a row, something she had been unable to do previously. When she sat at her desk she studied, and when she did other things she left her desk. The variable maintaining this increase in behavior as the semester drew to an end was apparently the forthcoming final examinations.

With regard to the young man who overate, stimulus control, chaining, and withdrawal of reinforcement were used. The stimulus for overeating is normally not food (Ferster, Levitt, & Nurnberger, 1962). In our culture, food is normally hidden; it is kept in a refrigerator or cupboard. In the cafeteria, where it is in the interests of the management to get people to eat, food is exposed.

The initial strategy for slimming the young man was to bring his eating behavior under the control of food alone, since food is normally not available as a stimulus. He was instructed to eat to his heart's content and not to repress the desire. He was, however, to treat food with the dignity it deserved. Rather than eating while he watched television or while he studied, he was to devote himself to eating when he ate. If he wished to eat a sandwich, he was to put it on a plate and sit down and devote himself exclusively to it. Thus, reinforcing consequences such as watching television or reading would be withdrawn when he engaged in the behaviors of preparing the food, eating, and cleaning up. Responding to the refrigerator in between meals resulted in withdrawal of such consequences, as did going to the refrigerator while watching television. Television, studying, and other stimuli would lose their control of initiating the chain of behaviors and conditions that terminated in eating. Within one week, the young man cut out all eating between meals. "You've taken the fun out of it," he said to me. We then worked on the contents of the meals as well, and he stopped attending sessions. I met him about three months later; he was considerably slimmer and remarked that he needed neither me nor the clinical psychologist to solve his problems. He could handle them himself.

No claim is made that all problems should be treated in this manner, or that the *S*s had no other problems. The aim was to alter the specified behavior. We started out with the simplest procedures. Had these not been effective, we would have tried others. Some more complex cases will be presented next.

An interesting aspect of these and other cases as well was the fact that in a very short time *S*s ran off by themselves to apply the procedures they had learned. In some cases, I would have preferred more extensive interchange and wondered how clinical psychologists were able to keep *S*s coming week after week. Finally, I attributed the tenure of the relationship to what might be called the Scheherazade effect. Scheherazade, as you will recall, became the consort of a king who killed each bedmate after one night, having generalized the infidelity of a previous wife to all women. Scheherazade told him a story on the first night, which was not completed by dawn. The king paroled her for the second night to hear the rest of the story, and having been reinforced, she repeated her behavior. The schedule maintained such behavior for 1001 nights, and the result is known as the *Arabian Nights*.

Few things are more interesting and will sustain behavior better than support for talking about one's self; one is never finished in 50 minutes. Hence, such discussions may maintain therapy sessions and allow the therapist to interact with the patient over an extended period of time. An individual tutorial may serve the same function.

MARITAL CASE

The husband in this case was a young man, 29, who was working on his master's degree. His wife was taking my course in behavioral analysis, and they both decided that he should come to see me about their marriage, which both wanted to maintain. The issue, as *S* told me, was that his wife had committed the "ultimate betrayal" two years ago with *S*'s best friend. Even worse, it was *S* who had suggested that the friend keep his wife company while he was in the library at night. Since that time, whenever he saw his wife, *S* screamed at her for hours on end or else was ashamed of himself for having done so and spent hours sulking and brooding. Since the events that led to the "betrayal" were an occasion for bringing home the first lesson on the consequences of behavior, we started from there.

Relation of Behavior to Its Consequences

Early discussions concerned the analysis of behavior in terms of its consequences. *S*'s behavior provided stimuli for his wife's behavior. If he wished his wife to behave differently to him, then he should provide other stimuli than the ones which produced the behaviors he did not like. There was considerable analysis of such interactions. This conceptualization of behavior was apparently new to *S*, who took detailed notes; I have discovered it to be new to many other *S*s as well.

Stimulus Change

Altering the consequences of operant behavior will alter the behavior itself. However, this process may take a considerable amount of time. One of the most rapid ways to change behavior is by altering the conditions under which it usually occurs. This is called *stimulus change* or the effects of novel stimuli. If the novel stimuli are then combined with new behavioral contingencies designed to produce different behavior, these contingencies are apt to generate the new behavior much more rapidly than they would in the presence of the old stimuli.

As part of the program of establishing new stimuli, *S* was instructed to rearrange the use of rooms and furniture in his house to make it appear considerably different. His wife went one step further and took the occasion to buy herself a new outfit.

Establishment of New Behavior

Since it was impossible for *S* to converse in a civilized manner with his wife, we discussed a program of going to one evening spot on Monday, another on Tuesday, and another on Wednesday.

"Oh," he said, "you want us to be together. We'll go bowling on Thursday."

"On the contrary," I said, "I am interested in your subjecting yourself to an environment where civilized chit-chat is maintained. Such is not the case at a bowling alley."

I also asked if there were any topic of conversation which once started would maintain itself. He commented on his mother-in-law's crazy ideas about farming. He was then given an index card and instructed to write "farm" on it and to attach a $20 bill to that card. The $20 was to be used to pay the waitress on Thursday, at which point he was to start the "farm" discussion which hopefully would continue into the taxi and home.

Stimulus Control

Since in the absence of yelling at his wife *S* sulked and since the program was designed to reduce yelling, *S*'s sulking was in danger of increasing. *S* was instructed to sulk to his heart's content but to do so in a specified place. Whenever he felt like sulking, he was to go into the garage, sit on a special sulking stool, and sulk and mutter over the indignities of life for as long as he wished. When he was through with his sulking, he could leave the garage and join his wife. He was instructed to keep a daily record of such behavior and bring it to each session. The graph is presented in Figure 1. Sulking time had been reported as 7 hours on the preceding day, and, with occasional lapses, it was reported as dropping to less than 30 minutes before disappearing entirely. The reported reversals and drops were occasions for discussions.

Since the bedroom had been the scene of both bickering and occasional lapses, the problem was presented of changing its stimulus value when conjugality was involved. If this could be done consistently, eventually the special stimuli might come to control such behavior. The problem was to find a stimulus which could alter the room entirely and would be easy to apply and withdraw. Finally, a yellow night light was put in, was turned on when both felt amorous, and was kept turned off otherwise. This light markedly altered the perceptual configuration of the room.

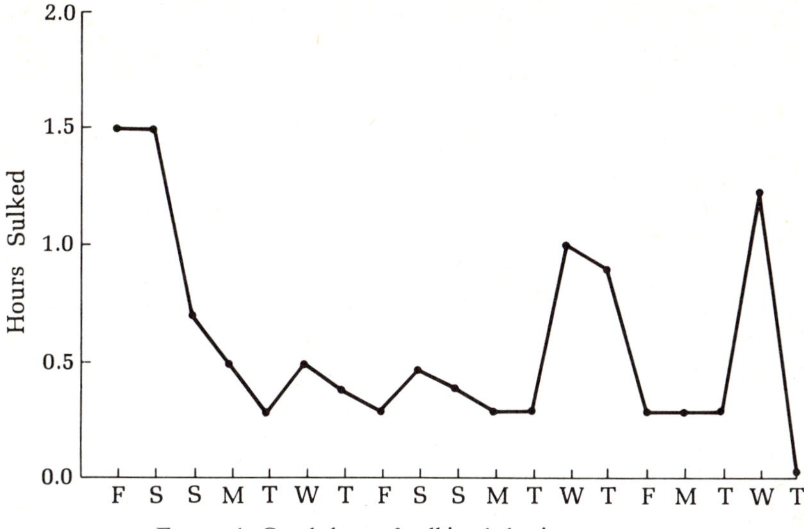

FIGURE 1. Graph kept of sulking behavior

RECORDS

Daily notes of events were kept in a notebook, as was the graph. *S* took notes of the discussions with *E*. These notes were discussed at each weekly session.

One of the notions which *S* held very strongly was that his wife's behavior stemmed from some inaccessible source within her, and that many of his own behaviors likewise poured out from himself. In this context, the final sharp rise in the sulking curve was discussed. "The whole procedure won't work," he said, "my wife doesn't need me as much as I need her." The psychiatric message was that he had no control over his wife, but I chose to ignore this message in favor of a didactic one on the behavioral definition of needs. He was asked how he knew what his wife's needs were. Was he an amoeba slithering into her tissues and observing tissue needs? Was he a mind reader? After my repeated rejection of subjective definitions of needs, he redefined the problem behaviorally, namely, that his wife behaved a certain way less than he did. He said that stated this way it sounded silly, but I said, "No, it's a problem to you and not silly."

What were these behaviors? They apparently included such dependency behaviors as asking him to do things for her. "When was the last time she asked you to do something for her?" I asked. He replied that the previous day she had asked him to replace a light bulb in the kitchen. Had he done so, I asked. "No," he said. He was then asked to consider the extinction of pigeon behavior and took notes to the effect that, if he wished his wife to act helpless, he should reinforce dependency by doing what she asked.

A discussion on needs and personality ensued. "If by personality all that is meant is my behavior," he said, "then my personality changes from one moment to the next, because my behavior changes," he stated.

"I should hope so," I said.

"Well, what is my true personality, what is the true me?" he asked.

"Do you have a true behavior?" I asked.

He reported this as a viewpoint he had never considered; his previous training had been in terms of being consistent to his self, and of searching for "thine own self (to which he could) be true." He took extensive notes.

The next week he came in and stated: "I did something last week that I have never done before in my life. When I teach in classrooms I am able to manage my students, but when I talk to tradespeople I find I am very timid and allow myself to be cheated. Well, last week my carburetor gave out. I knew if I went to the garage they would make me buy a new one even though I have a one-year's guarantee. I sent my wife down to the garage instead. She is a real scrapper. She came back with a new carburetor. It didn't cost us a cent. Why should I have to be all things to all men? In school I control things, but with tradespeople I don't. So what?"

These weekly sessions continued during ten weeks of the summer term. After the initial training, *S* was assigned homework along with his wife who was taking the course in behavioral analysis. The weekly discussions were centered around behavioral analysis and how it might apply to his problems.

During the course of one of the sessions, *S* started to talk about his childhood and was summarily cut off.

"Shouldn't I talk about this with a psychologist?" he asked. "Isn't this one of the things that interests you? Doesn't it affect me now?"

"Look," I said, "a bridge with a load limit of three tons opens in 1903. The next day, a farmer drives eighteen tons over it; it cracks. The bridge collapses in 1963. What caused the collapse?"

"The farmer in 1903," he said.

"Wrong," I said. "The bridge collapses in 1963 because of the cracks that day. Had they been filled in the preceding day, it would not have collapsed. Let's discuss the cracks in your marriage."

At the end of the period, there was no sulking in the garage and the partners were able to commune.

MARITAL CASE 2

This case concerned a younger couple who had been married almost 10 years; their sexual relations throughout marriage had been limited to about two contacts a year. Both husband and wife ascribed the difficulty to the husband. Both *S*s were professionals, intelligent, were socially well at ease, and highly regarded by their friends and the community. They were Roman Catholic and determined to maintain the marriage, but the wife thought she might be driven into extramarital relations. Both felt that, if only they could get started, the behavior might carry itself.

Husband and wife were seen separately every week, for one hour each. Both were instructed to discuss with me only that which they could discuss with each other, since I would make constant cross reference between the two sessions.

Various procedures were assayed by *S*s, but proved ineffective. Fondling was repulsed. *Playboy* was recommended to initiate amorous activity, but the husband fell asleep reading it. During the lesson on deprivation, the wife stated: "I am at my wit's end as to how to shape his behavior. I don't know what reinforcements I have. The characteristic of good reinforcement is that it can be applied immediately and is immediately consumed. I could withhold supper, but that is not a good reinforcer because I can't turn it off and on. I can't apply deprivation, because that's my problem. I don't know what to do."

The husband was a rising business executive who took evening courses and whose time was so tight that he had to schedule almost every minute of his day. We discussed the possibility of his scheduling his wife in the appointment book for two evenings a week. He thought this might work, but his wife was a bit more dubious. These appointments were kept two weeks in a row, but then lost their control. We then discussed the nature of the control over behavior exerted by discriminative stimuli, of which instructions are one example (Goldiamond, in press). There were differential consequences attached to keeping and not keeping the business appointments, but no differential consequences had been attached to meeting or not meeting appointments with his wife. Hence, the instructions lost their control (Ayllon & Azrin, 1964).

Both *S*s were extremely well-groomed. Their clothing was always in best array. The wife visited the beautician once a week and the husband went to the barber every other week. In the session following the failure of control by the appointment book, the husband suggested that they might attach the opportunity to visit the beautician or barber as consequences to keeping the appointments. In the event that the appointments were not kept, the visits would not be allowed and could be resumed only when the appointments had been kept. His wife also felt that this would be extremely effective.

The next week, both showed up somewhat bedraggled. Thereafter, they were not bedraggled and the appointments were kept for the rest of that semester, at least.

As an incidental effect of the sessions, *S*s attempted to apply behavioral analysis to other problems as well. They mentioned a staff party which had been held at their home. The behavior of an inefficient secretary was being discussed.

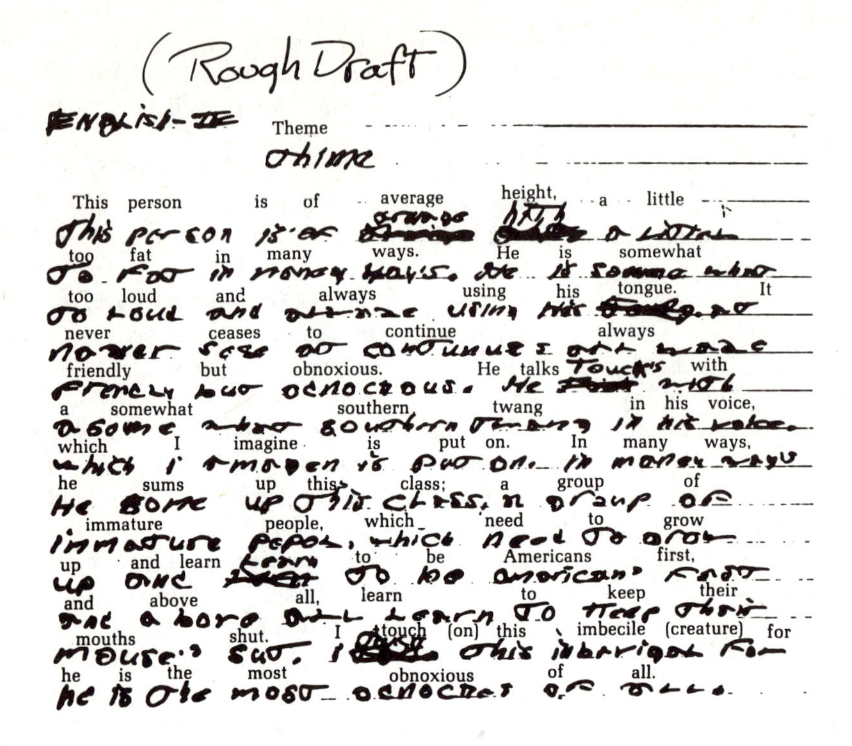

FIGURE 2. Sample of initial handwriting; translation appears above line

"But you're using aversive control," one of the participants said.

"Well, she has no behaviors that I can reinforce her for," was the answer.

STUDY CASE 1: HANDWRITING

S was a seventeen-year-old high school senior of normal intelligence, who was 28th in a class of 28 and whose handwriting was illegible. He was a referral from a school psychologist.

An example of his early handwriting is given in Figure 2. Lettered lines of translation alternate with cursive lines of handwriting. During the first session, I asked *S* to sit at my desk and write from dictation. He leaned forward to write but no part of his hand or arm touched paper or desk; the entire force of his shoulder and arm was transmitted to the pencil point, making fine control impossible. Since the primary grades, no one had ever observed his writing behavior; they had, however, criticized its product. I instructed him to keep his arm on the table and to manipulate his pencil from the wrist and fingers. Some simple physics were explained to him. Sheets of onion skin were interlaced with carbon paper, and he was given exercises requiring modula-

now is The Time ALL
good men To come To
The ade of Thair party.

FIGURE 3. Stimulus control of ensuing letter size by writing T as capital of same size as preceding letter

tion of force so that he would go through five sheets, four sheets, three sheets, and two sheets. He was instructed to print.

At a later session, his letter size being erratic, he was asked to letter the familiar, "Now is the time . . ." phrase. Figure 3 presents that initial attempt. The paper is lined, and the writing starts out filling up the space between the lines. The writing becomes smaller and smaller. This tendency can be traced to the letter T. In all cases, T is the same size as the preceding letters, and is also a capital. Since capital letters are followed by small letters, these Ts control the size of the small letters that follow them. The first T in the the second line produces a row of small letters following it, and the first T in the third line takes off from this size and again cuts down the size of the following letters until the final T produces a tinier Y. *S* was instructed to write his Ts so that they were larger than the preceding letters. Figure 4 reiterates the control this letter had over the following letters. The letters which follow T are smaller than T, but since T is above the line they stay within the line. The effect has been reversed, demonstrating a causal relation. Incidentally, since T is the second most frequently used letter in English, it is a powerful source of control. In the later sessions, *S* was instructed to differentiate between capital and small T.

The passage presented is the same as that in Figure 2. The change in legibility is evident. The numerous spelling errors are of interest. As long as the writing is undecipherable, spelling errors cannot be noted and corrected.

Many letters contain similar forms. For example, the letters a, b, d, o, p, and q all contain a complete circle of the same size. These circles are modified in letters such as c and e. *S* was instructed to bring an assortment of buttons to the session and a suitable button was found for him to use for these letters, with other buttons for other letters. He was also instructed in other principles of writing. He practiced at home and brought his material in weekly. After a period of lettering, *S* was instructed to link his letters in an effort to produce cursive writing.

His handwriting improved markedly during this period, and he rose from 28th in his class to 13th. The undergraduate assistant[2] who worked with

[2] I wish to express my appreciation to Mr. Richard David, then an undergraduate psychology major, who brought *S* to and from sessions and assisted in them.

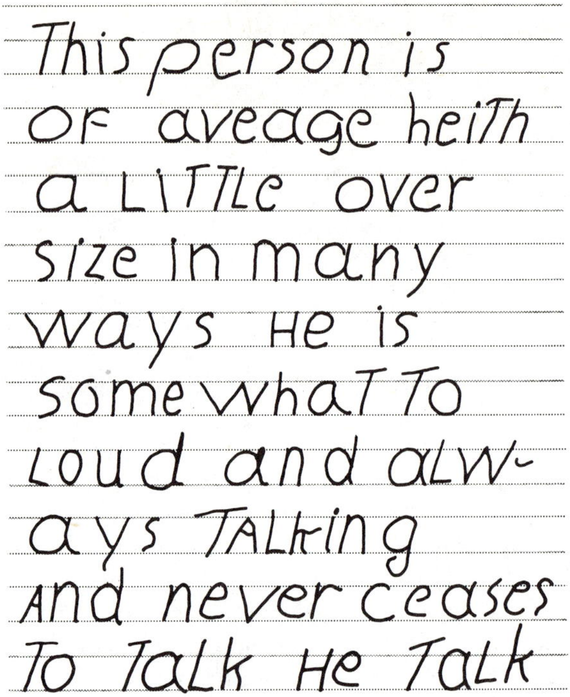

This person is
OF aveage heiTh
a LITTLe over
size in many
ways He is
somewhaT To
Loud and aLw-
ays TALking
And never ceases
To TaLk He TaLk

FIGURE 4. Reversal of effect by writing T above line

him at home paid him money for lines completed and, as long as this procedure was used, *S*'s handwriting was legible and showed evidence of training. When this pay was dropped, the handwriting deteriorated. Although legible handwriting was now contingent upon reinforcement, differential reinforcement alone would not have produced the new behavior. Indeed, without making them contingent upon a program to alter behavior, differential consequences may be ineffective and may result in aversive control, as did the nagging and poor grades he consistently obtained. Now that *S* has the new behavior, differential consequences can be applied to maintain it; hopefully, these will be provided by society. The requirement of extrinsic consequences was probably related to difficult conditions at home. He had no desk or work place, and he lived alone with his mother.

Several conclusions can be drawn from this case. One is that observation of the behavior itself may on occasion be far more useful than observation of its end product. Another is that behavior may be controlled by the very stimuli that the behavior itself produces, as in the size of the letters following T. A third is that merely establishing a behavior will not necessarily maintain it. The consequences which maintain it must be considered, but as a fourth conclusion, these consequences should often be related to a program of behavioral modification. Penalizing his poor writing behavior, as his teachers had done, did not eliminate that behavior. It did, however, bring him in for treatment.

STUDY CASE 2: STUDY PROBLEM

This case involved a junior in college who was being expelled because of his academic record. Inasmuch as I had given him one of his Ds, he came to me for advice. I told him that I would try to get him reinstated, providing he put himself under my control. He agreed and was given a conditional year. *S*'s parents were professionals. Two siblings were at prominent Eastern universities. *S* was alert, and his IQ tests were within the range of college populations.

S had never actually studied. Accordingly, a self-control regimen for studying was introduced following some of the procedures which were discussed earlier. A daily record was kept of the total number of hours spent in study, for each course and for the total day.

At that time, *S* studied for an average of six hours a day, but his study hours were not evenly distributed among the various classes. Figure 5 presents the study curves for two different courses. The upper curve depicts minimal studying, except for one peak. [Guess when the test was given!] This fixed interval curve characterizes the behavior of pigeons as well. The lower part of the curve represents the studying pattern for a language class which involved a daily recitation. *S* studied at regular intervals. These curves so impressed me that I institute daily quizzes in my classes and was gratified to see the averages rise.

Every week *S* brought his notebooks, his examinations, and his weekly records for inspection and discussion. Different procedures for keeping notes were developed for each course. In the foreign language, for example, a separate sheet was kept for masculine and feminine nouns and for each verb class. Grammatical classes represent similar ways of treating a word. By putting words of the same grammatical class together, there may be generalization from the changes learned for one word to the changes learned for another. Flash cards which are uniform may not lend themselves to such generalization.

S was taught to outline social science texts. He was asked to be a detective and resurrect the author's outline (where he had one). Red and black ink were used for headings and entries. The outlines were topical rather than sentence outlines. This required restating the sentences in his words, rather than copying them from the book.

In English, we were both at a loss. Several novels were required, and neither one of us knew what should be considered. We used the conventional procedure to find out, namely, the first exam. This told us what the instructor considered to be the terminal behaviors.

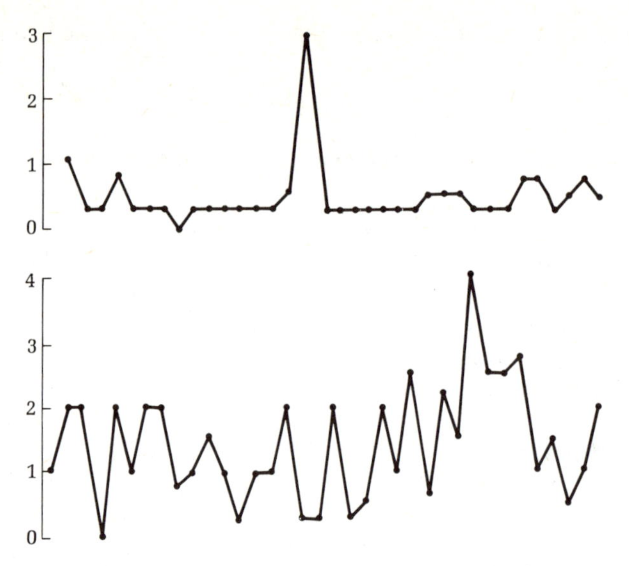

FIGURE 5. Daily study charts for class with one examination (upper), and class with daily recitations (lower)

At the end of the first semester, *S*'s grades changed from the two Ds and three Es of the preceding semester to two Cs and two Ds. Although this was an improvement, one class was dropped. I was disturbed since I felt that, with this much study and careful outlining, *S* should have obtained As. A more detailed analysis was then undertaken.

S was taking a course in international trade, for which a knowledge of geography is requisite. He said that he knew his geography quite well and was asked to draw a map of South America. Figure 6 represents the map he drew. Brazil extends from sea to shining sea. The body of water above Venezuela is designated Lake Maracaibo, and Bolivia is north of Peru and abuts on Venezuela.

I asked *S* what grade he would assign himself for this map, and he looked at it confidently and said, "Oh, 75 per cent or a C." I said that I would give him 20 per cent. Incidentally, in work with other *S*s since then who have trouble with history, I have often found that they lack knowledge of geography, and even of map-reading. Accordingly, historical movements become disconnected facts which have to be learned for each case.

This map may be used to exemplify a behavioral definition of stupidity. Many behaviors require other behaviors as prerequisites for their acquisition and maintenance. It is possible that, in one form of stupidity, the prerequisites to the attempted behavior are absent, as well as those disciriminative behaviors which differentiate the presence of adequate behaviors from their absence. Stated otherwise, the person we call stupid is lacking certain behaviors but

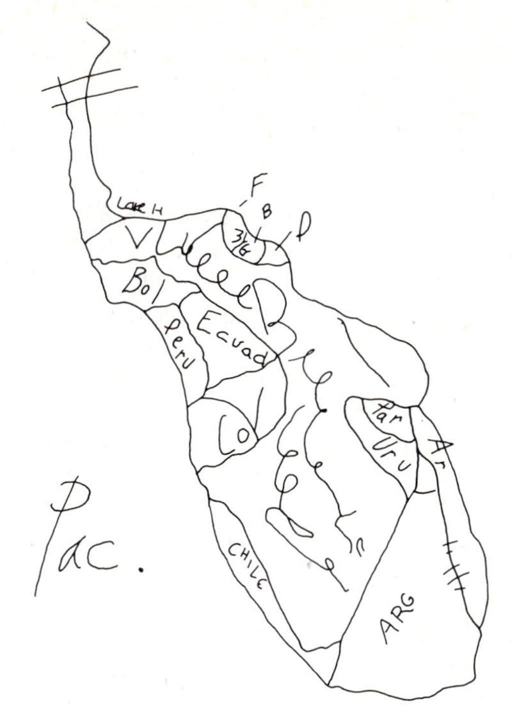

FIGURE 6. Map of South America drawn from memory by college junior taking a course in international trade

behaves as if he is not so lacking. He does not know to ask. He confidently undertakes assignments and often starts out successfully. However, where the new behaviors require older ones and these are missing, we may obtain the egregious blunders we call stupid. The blunders may be unpredictable to us simply because, in a long sequence, there are too many places in which deficits can occur for us to have come across every one.

These behavioral deficiencies were found in one area after another. Since *S* was taking courses which had as prerequisites other courses, which he had passed with Ds, he was being required to acquire new behaviors when the prerequisite foundation for them was rather shaky. Accordingly, we "regressed" to the freshman texts in those courses in which he had obtained a D.

But there were deficiencies here, as well. In the economics texts, Humpty-Dumpty was quoted to the the effect that words meant what *he* intended them to mean. The point here was that the economist's use of words might differ from their common usage. Humpty-Dumpty appeared in red in *S*'s notes. *S* knew that Humpty-Dumpty was an egg who fell. I asked why the egg led his paragraph and could obtain no answer. It turned out that *S* had not read *Alice in Wonderland*, nor any of the childhood classics, nor for that matter *Tom Swift*, nor even comic books. He simply did no home reading as a child.

I had obtained excellent control over *S*'s behavior, but this was like successfully getting someone to work six hours a day copying Chinese letters with a brush, without his ever having learned how to hold a brush or what the significant calligraphic nuances were. I suggested a program of visiting the art galleries, listening to concerts, reading the classics, and otherwise acquiring the behaviors relevant to our cultural heritage.

There are two types of behavioral sequences. In one type of sequence, called the *chaining* sequence, a chain of behavior is maintained by the consequences attached to the last element in the chain. Thus, Lundin (1961) reports a rat who went through various behavioral gyrations, then up five stories and down an elevator. All of these behaviors were maintained by the food he received at the end. In this type of sequence, the order of training is the *reverse* of the chronological order in which the sequence of behavior is performed. The pressing of the lever for food was established first. This was made contingent upon manipulation of the elevator. Then the ride in the elevator was made contingent upon the preceding step and so on. The entire chain was maintained by the food. Thus, if the product of education is not reinforcing, the behaviors which lead to it may not be maintained. Chaining was also exemplified in the weight reduction case, when watching television no longer served as a consequence of going to open the refrigerator.

Another type of sequence, which we shall call the *systematic* sequence, is exemplified in the case of this student. A systematic sequence can be compared to a course or an educational curriculum; the acquisition of one behavior depends upon the *prior* existence of another, just as the acquisition of new knowledge depends upon a grasp of other presupposed knowledge. Thus, in order to learn algebra, we must know how to read. In order to learn to read, a certain degree of socialization must first occur. Such curricula exist not only in academic subjects but are implicit in other types of behavior as well. It is entirely possible, for example, that certain behaviors necessary for marital success presuppose the existence of other interpersonal behaviors, whose acquisition depends upon the existence of yet other behaviors.

Stated otherwise, there are behavioral curricula involved in almost all behaviors. Where the present behavioral deficit exists because an earlier behavior was not acquired, a procedure which attempts to correct the ongoing deficit must consider some of the earlier deficits of which the present one may be an outgrowth. When this is true, in contrast to the first marital case presented, discussion of childhood may be necessary.

The cases presented here have involved different behavioral deficits. Although the content or the topography of these and other behaviors differs, the functional relations of such differing behaviors to their environment may be similar. This may be true not only when the differences are in such categories as marital or academic, both of which involve human behavior, but also where the differences categorize species. Pigeons peck and people talk. Topographically these are different behaviors. However, if the consequences which maintain pecking are scheduled in a certain manner and the (quite different) consequences which maintain speech are scheduled in the same manner, then the differing behaviors of pecking and speech will undergo similar changes in rate. It is upon this functional, or dynamic, similarity in the relation of behavior to its environment that the possibility of the extension of procedures from the laboratory to the clinic rests. It also suggests that problems in the clinic may be used for research in the laboratory.

The cases presented here demonstrate a simple application of certain self-control procedures derived from the laboratory. As was explicitly indicated earlier, they are not intended to supplant or question other more complex procedures (for a more extended analysis see Goldiamond, *et al.*, 1965). However, we are currently examining some of these complex procedures and are discovering that the explicit language of the laboratory may be very useful in analyzing and describing some of the behavioral transactions and changes that go on in other forms of psychotherapy (Goldiamond, Dyrud, & Miller, 1965).[3] Developments in other areas where explicit analysis is utilized may be considered for their relevance to psychotherapy, and psychotherapy, by a reverse lend-lease, may suggest areas for study under more controlled procedures (Goldiamond, 1966).

Laboratory research has necessarily been characterized by a simplicity of procedures and concepts, and their extension to the solution of complex human problems requires considerable precaution and careful examination. Nevertheless, these procedures and concepts may provide methods for the analysis and restatement of complex problems in observable and manipulable terms and may thereby assist in the explicit assessment of behavioral change and effectiveness.

The cases presented here involve behavioral problems which could be analyzed by *S*s themselves. This training of *S* to become his own therapist is one of the goals of most branches of psychotherapy. The method used to accomplish this will depend on the state of the art, the nature of the problem, *S*'s past history, and social and other constraints upon *S*'s behavior. In some cases, these factors may dictate a strategy of not instructing *S*, or not having him define the problem or discover its solution immediately, since such a procedure may disrupt other behaviors and the consequences currently maintaining them.[4] The course of treatment might then be considerably different from

[3] Research being performed under Contracts DA-49-193-MD-2628 and DA-49-193-MD-2448 between the Office of the Surgeon General and the Institute for Behavioral Research and the Washington School of Psychiatry, respectively. These projects involve collaboration between Jarl Dyrud, M.D., Miles Miller, M.D., and the author.

[4] I am indebted to Jarl Dyrud for this observation.

any of those discussed here. Other problems and possible procedures could be cited as well. But the cases presented here suggest that, in some areas at least, simple procedures can lead to complex changes.

SUMMARY

A rationale for the use of self-control procedures in counseling is presented, along with illustrative material from several case studies. Self-control, as used here, involves specification of the behavioral deficit or desired behaviors which are lacking, and having *S* himself set up or progarm the conditions which may produce the desired behavioral modification. The procedures selected are extensions from laboratory research in operant modification of behavior, and the counseling sessions may include training *S* in behavior analysis, with his own behaviors as the experimental data.

24

TREATMENT OF COMPULSIVE BEHAVIOR BY COVERT SENSITIZATION

Joseph R. Cautela

Two prominent kinds of problems of neurotic individuals involve the avoidance of objectively harmless objects due to fear, and the approach to undesirable but pleasurable activities (obsessions and compulsions). Wolpe's (1958) desensitization procedure has proven very effective in reducing and eliminating fear to objectively neutral or positive stimuli. Aversion therapy has been shown to be effective in the treatment of obsessive and compulsive behavior. The purpose of aversion therapy is, of course, to sensitize individuals to particular objects.

As far back as 1920 Watson and Reyner demonstrated how aversive stimulation could elicit a withdrawal response to a previously neutral stimulus. The use of aversion therapy first received widespread use in the treatment of alcoholism. Treatment of alcoholics by aversion therapy where drugs have been used as the aversive stimuli has not led to the desirable results predicted by learning theory. Franks (1958) points out that the lack of success of aversion therapy with alcoholics is due to lack of rigorous experimental procedure. The use of drugs makes it difficult to control the pairing of the conditioned and unconditioned stimulus. Often the US (aversive stimulus) appears before the CS (alcohol). This results in a backward conditioning procedure which many investigators (Brogden, 1951, pp. 158–159; Deese, 1958, pp. 43–44; Kimble, 1961, pp. 579–580; Woodworth & Scholsberg, 1958, pp. 567–568), feel is not true conditioning. The use of electric shock as the US aversive

Reprinted by permission of the author and publisher from the *Psychological Record*, 1966, *16*, 33–41.

stimulus in the treatment of alcoholism appears more promising because of the greater control of the time interval involved in the CS-US pairing. McGuire and Vallance (1964) successfully treated a case of alcoholism using shock as the US. The subject was given a shock as soon as he sniffed a tube containing whiskey.

Because other methods have not shown much promise in the treatment of obesity, aversion therapy has been recently employed in this regard. Meyer and Crisp (1964) treated two cases of obesity with aversion therapy (shock). Tempting food was presented to the *S* in an isloated room. When the *S* attempted to go toward the food he received an electric shock. The treatment appeared to be successful in one case and not the other. This was probably due to the lack of precise and absolute pairing of the CS and the US.

While aversion therapy shows some promise in the treatment of alcoholism and obesity because of the greater control of the CS and US pairing, the use of electric shock as the US has certain disadvantages:

1. Some patients avoid the therapeutic session because they are too painful or uncomfortable.
2. There is the problem of adjusting the apparatus so that it can be effective as an aversive stimulus and yet not be harmful.
3. Since apparatus is involved, the treatment has to be carried out only in the therapist's office or clinic; the patient is not able to carry on treatment at home by himself (an advantage of the method to be presented in this paper).

In this paper a method is presented whereby aversive therapy is used in the treatment of two compulsions; a maladaptive alcoholic drinking problem, and excessive eating (obesity). This method does not employ either drugs or electric shock. In fact, no aversive stimulus is presented externally. Before the method is presented in detail it would be well to examine the development of aversion therapy in the treatment of homosexuality.

Blakemore, Thorpe, Barker, Conway and Levin (1963) used faradic aversion to successfully treat a male transvestite who was shocked while undressing and dressing in female clothing. Thorpe, Schmidt and Castell (1963) presented photographs of male nudes to a male homosexual while delivering a strong electric shock to the patient's bare feet. Of the three treatment procedures used with this patient, the electric shock seemed to be the effective treatment in achieving heterosexuality.

Thorpe et al., (1963) successfully treated six homosexual *S*s (who later engaged in heterosexual behavior almost exclusively) by presenting homosexual words on an illuminated disc. The *S* was required to read the list (which included such words as "gay pub," and "in bed with a male") and after each word was read aloud he was given a shock as soon as possible. The shock was usually not administered any longer than 0.05 sec, after the word was read. The last word in the list which signaled the end of the list was a non-homosexual word (e.g. girl).

Gold and Neufield (1965) as part of their treatment of a homosexual asked him to visualize himself in a homosexual situation that was associated with a noxious stimulus. The patient was asked to imagine himself in a toilet along side a most unprepossessing old man, or in a toilet with an attractive homosexual with a policeman nearby. Until such studies as those of Thorpe et al. (1963) and Gold and Neufeld (1965) it had been assumed that actual presentation of the attractive stimulus (but in some respects undesirable) or its photograph was necessary to pair with the US (aversive stimulus). It now seems reasonable that symbols (words) or visualizations can successfully be used as the CS when paired with the US. Also it appears that the noxious stimulus itself does not need to be applied externally (Gold & Neufield's study) but can be visualized or imagined by the *S*. In other words, both the CS and US can be convert stimuli. In an excellent paper, concerning private behavioral events, Homme (1965b) maintains that private behavioral events obey the same laws as nonprivate ones.

It is the purpose of this paper to present a method for treating compulsions such as alcoholism and obesity where a covert CS and US are used. The method will be illustrated by presenting the treatment of a case of strong alcohol craving and a case of obesity.

Treatment Procedure

The patient is taught to relax in the same manner as used in the desensitization procedure. He is asked to raise his index finger when he can relax completely without any tension. Usually this doesn't take more than three or four sessions. The patient is asked to practice relaxing at least once a day between therapy sessions. When the patient is able to relax completely he is told that he is unable to stop drinking (or eating) in excess because it is a strong learned habit which now gives him a great amount of pleasure. He is also told that the way to help eliminate his compulsion is to associate the pleasurable objcct with an unpleasant stimulus. The patient is then asked (while relaxed with his eyes closed) to visualize very clearly the pleasurable object; e.g., a highball. When he can visualize the object very clearly he is to raise his index finger. After he signals he is told to now visualize that he is about to take the object (commit the compulsive act). If the object is liquor he is asked to visualize himself looking at the glass with the alcoholic beverage in it. Then he is to visualize holding the glass in his hand. He is then instructed to imagine he is just about to bring the glass to his lips. The glass is just about to touch his lips and then he begins to feel sick to his stomach. He is starting to vomit. The vomit goes up to his mouth and then he can't stop it. He vomits all over the floor of the bar or restaurant or home, wherever he does his drinking. He is asked to visualize the whole scene again by himself and to raise his finger when he can visualize the scene and actually feel nauseous as the drink is about to go to his lips.

If he is not able to do this right away, more instructions are again presented such as: "As soon as you touch the glass to your lips, you really start to feel sick and you vomit all over your girl friend (or companion). It goes all over the floor." In the author's experience it only takes a few trials before the patient actually feels nauseous. When the patient signals he feels nauseous he is then told to visualize the same scene; only this time as he is about to take the drink he starts to feel nauseous and he puts the glass down immediately. The sick feeling then goes away and he feels calm and relaxed. After the patient signals that he is experiencing as directed, he is given five more trials of vomiting and feeling ill, and five trials of not taking the drink and feeling calm and relaxed. In my procedure I have alternated vomiting trials and calm trials. After the session he is told to practice this procedure at least once a day at home. He is to be very careful that the vomiting or sickness occurs as he is just about to drink, or when he has the first taste.

The aversion procedure presented in this paper grew out of the following two cases. The procedure was tried more or less concomitantly in the two cases.

ILLUSTRATION OF THE METHOD

Case 1. Alcohol problem

Background–A twenty-nine-year-old nurse was treated for pervasive anxiety by reassurance, desensitization, assertive training, and anxiety relief through relaxation. Before the treatment the patient had great anxiety in almost any social situation. She often trembled if she was eating out with anyone. She had insomnia and anxiety at night because she worried about the social situations of the next day. She started drinking in social situations about eight years ago. She said it helped her get through a date or a party or being home in her apartment. She discovered that lately the liquor did not help much, though she was now drinking a great deal, especially on dates. She used to wake up with a "hangover" and then have to have a few drinks to calm herself down. After the above treatment she was quite at ease at work and did not drink as often as before. She usually went days without a drink. She still had to drink if she was going out for the evening at a dance or on a date. She used to have eight or nine drinks and get sick. She was taught to relax herself before a date or dance. When she was on a date or at a dance she was to say: "I am calm." She said that this procedure helped a little but that she still did not have confidence enough to herself to get through the evening. The patient was well adjusted at work. She had at this time little or no anxiety during the day. She slept very well. Her problem was still drinking when she went out on a date, party or at a dance. If she did not engage in these social situations she felt no anxiety and did not drink. Desensitization was attempted toward these social situations. Though she could visualize the social events with no anxiety, there was no transfer to the real life situation to give her confidence not to drink. She was told that she was perfectly capable of getting through the evening without drinking. She was fooling herself into thinking the liquor got her through the evening. She said maybe that was so, but she still couldn't help it if she was too unsure of herself in these situations.

Something the patient said about her drinking provided a clue to the hypothesis that she was anxious because she was drinking, and not drinking because she was anxious. She remarked that she felt well adjusted in all areas of her life, but in the drinking area. She would not feel completely adjusted until she could give up her drinking at parties, dances, and dates. This statement led the author to posit a learning theory interpretation of her "need" to drink. In the past there was high drive (anxiety) in social situations. The drive was reduced by alcohol which served as a primary reinforcement. The situation can be depicted in the following manner—stimuli (dance hall, band, waiter, restaurants, etc.) plus anxiety—drinking response—reinforcement. Even with the anxiety gone part of the stimulus compound is present. Now we have stimuli—drinking response at a high habit strength level. The habit is so strong that it is difficult to overcome. In the patient's case most of the original anxiety was gone, but when during the evening she found she "had" to drink, this would lead to anxiety and this now presented the whole stimulus compound of S plus anxiety and of course this was further reinforced by drinking. Under this analysis it is quite possible for the original source of anxiety to be gone, but the drinking to be continued under sheer habit (little or no anxiety present). If the above analysis is valid then it is not enough to remove the anxiety in the situation. The other part of the stimulus compound of S-R (drinking) also has to be broken.

Treatment–The learning theory approach was explained to the patient. She was also told the treatment was a new approach, but theoretically it should work. She was asked to relax and indicate by raising her index finger when she felt completely relaxed. She was asked to signal when she could do this vividly. After she gave the signal the patient was told: "Now I want you to imagine that you ask the waitress to give you your favorite drink." She brings the drink. Just as you reach for the drink you start to feel sick to your stomach. As you hold the glass in your hand you feel yourself about to vomit. As you are just about to put the glass to your lips you vomit. It comes out of your mouth all over the table and the floor. It is real mess. When you can visualize the whole scene clearly and feel a little sick to your stomach, raise your finger." The patient raised her finger about 10 sec. after the instructions. She was then given similar instructions about being at a party, but this time she vomited all over the hostess' dress. When she signaled this time she was asked to relax and try to erase the scene from her mind. She was then asked to imagine she was about to take a drink at a dance; when she did she started to feel ill, but this time she would not try to drink it and then she would immediately feel calm. She was given 10 more trials in this manner in the first session. On every other trial she was told that she refused to take the drink and she immediately felt calm.

After the trials were over she was told to do the same thing at home. She was cautioned to visualize the scene very clearly and visualize herself starting to feel ill as soon as she saw the glass. She would then vomit as soon as the glass touch her lips. The patient was seen two days later. She was all excited. She said the previous night she went to a dine and dance place and for the first time in five years didn't even take one drink. She felt so proud of herself she told all her roommates. She also admitted that she did not give herself any trials at home because the visualization actually made her feel nauseous. She was praised for her lack of drinking, but she was also told that it was doubtful that the treatment could be long lasting and effective if she did not have more sessions in the office and at home. She agreed to this. In the next session she said that she didn't drink hard liquor any more, but she was drinking a lot of beer. In this session half of her trial included drinking beer and feeling sick and vomiting. In the next session one week later she reported she was now drinking wine coolers once in a while (two drinks since the last session). In this session she was also sensitized against wine. One scene was presented in the following manner: "You walk into your kitchen. You see a highball, a glass of beer, and a bottle of wine on the table. You start to feel sick to your stomach as you reach for one of the beverages. You vomit all over the beverages. You vomit all over the beverages and all over the floor."

She was given 7 more session at the office once each week. She also went through the procedure every day. She reported that she did not take one drink in all this time. She was asked if she felt sick at all when she went out even if she didn't drink. She replied that she felt fine as long as she did not think of getting a drink. She expressed great satisfaction in stating that she didn't have to drink to have a good time. Since with this treatment all her symptoms were gone, therapy was terminated. She was told she did not have to continue her sessions at home unless she was beginning to feel tempted. A follow-up interview eight months later revealed that she has not taken a drink since she left therapy. She did have to have self-relaxation aversion sessions three times when she felt she was weakening.

Case 2. Obesity

Background–The patient was a forty-nine-year-old school teacher. When she first came to treatment her alcoholic husband and disturbed children exhibited a classic example of the "sick family." After years of psychotherapy (not based on learning theory) the family was very much improved and the patient herself seemed well adjusted in all but one respect. She was quite obese. She was 5′ 4½″ tall and weighed 200 pounds. The treatment of the excessive eating was the only remaining maladaptive behavior to be eliminated.

Treatment–The patient was asked to keep a strict account of everything she ate during the week. She was instructed to include everything she ate no matter how minute. This procedure was to provide a guide to her eating habits. An interesting feature was that this procedure (as well as the other information-getting interviews) resulted in a loss of five pounds in two weeks. Since this procedure seemed to influence the patient's eating habits, it was continued for four more weeks without any other course of treatment except the discussion of the foods she had eaten. During its first week period the patient reported that there was no further weight loss. A study of her eating habits revealed that her main meals were actually light meals. (Ferster, Nurnberger, and Levitt (1962) report that, in general, obese women eat light meals.) If she could only stop eating between meals she would certainly lose weight. Her period of greatest eating was as she was preparing meals. She said she ate as much as eight or nine peanut butter and jelly sandwiches while she was preparing meals. Sometimes she ate a whole cake. She ate any sweets available until she had practically eaten them all. She was asked if she could have someone else prepare the supper meal. She replied that everyone's schedule was such that she was the only possible one to prepare the meals.

At this point she was taught how to relax. She was told to say: "I am calm." When she felt completely relaxed, this was repeated 10 times. She was asked to do this at home every day for the next week. At the next session she was told to say "I am calm and relaxed," when she was preparing the meals and was tempted to eat. It was assumed that eating was tension reducing and that reducing the tension at the time of temptation would increase the probability of not eating. The next week she reported she was still eating while preparing the supper meal. In fact she gained two pounds. Preparing the supper meal was one of the times she could eat without being observed by members of her family. She was now told that perhaps the habit could be broken if she associated something unpleasant with eating while she prepared supper for the family. She agreed that this might work.

She was relaxed and asked to visualize that she was preparing supper. While she was preparing the supper she started to reach for a piece of bread to make a peanut butter sandwich. Just as she reached the bread she would begin to feel sick to her stomach. She could feel the vomit come up to her mouth and then she would vomit all over the supper she was preparing. She then would have to clean it all up. When she could visualize the complete scene and feel a little sick to her stomach she was to signal with her finger. This was repeated three more times using cake, cookies, and pie as the tempting foods. On the next trial she was asked to visualize that when she was tempted to eat a piece of cake she felt a little sick but that this time she would say to herself "Oh, I don't want that food." She then would feel immediately calm and relaxed. Ten additional trials (scenes) were presented. On every other trial she would resist the temptation and feel calm and relaxed. She was asked to repeat this procedure at home, every day until the next therapy session. Two weeks later, at the next session she reported that the eating while preparing food was completely eliminated. She lost six pounds the first week, but after the first week she ate some snacks after meals. Her weight stayed the same for the second week. Her overall loss was still six pounds.

It was determined that she only ate snacks if she was alone so in this session scenes of being alone and tempted by food were presented. In some cases she was tempted, gave in to the temptation, and vomited. In other scenes she resisted the temptation and felt relaxed. In the next session two weeks later she said she had lost 10 pounds and was doing very well. She wasn't picking between meals and she did not eat any extra food at her regular meals. Whenever she thought of eating a snack she felt sick to her stomach. In the next four sessions the procedure was repeated. She lost weight steadily at the rate of three pounds a week. At the next session she said she was still losing gradually, but the interesting feature was that she still enjoyed her regular meals. This procedure was continued for the next three months until it appeared that she had leveled off to 134 pounds. She felt fine and happy. She was told to continue the session for herself only once a week now for another month. After that she was to sensitize herself only if she noticed she was slipping. A follow-up appointment seven months later revealed that she was still at 134 pounds. She had eaten snacks one or two times, but then she immediately sensitized herself and stopped eating snacks for a couple of weeks.

DISCUSSION

The cases presented above indicate promise in the treatment of alcoholic craving, obesity, and other compulsions by the method of covert sensitization. It appears from the two cases presented and from some results with other patients that the treatment is very specific. If someone has a compulsion toward drinking a particular kind of beverage or food, covert sensitization of the particular food-stuff does not seem to generalize toward other foods or drinks. It is also evident from some of my investigations that after the subject has been sensitized toward one object it is easier to sensitize toward other objects. This statement seems to contradict the observation of lack of generalization from one object to another. Perhaps in the cases investigated, some generalization did occur; but the habit strength was not great enough to raise the reaction potential above the excitatory threshold. This would account for the lack of obvious transfer from one object to another until sensitization toward the similar object is attempted.

Another point: it is not clear at the moment whether the *S* has to experience the sick feeling or nausea during the sensitization session for treatment to be effective. In both cases *S*s did feel nauseous after a few scene presentations. As long as it seems quite likely that almost all patients will experience some ill feeling during the sensitization the point is not important for the moment. If the scenes are presented vividly enough the sick feeling is quite likely to occur.

The effectiveness of the method for the treatment of alcoholism has yet to be demonstrated. The case presented above, though one of strong alcohol craving in particular situations, was not strictly speaking the treatment of alcoholism. In the above cases the *S*s were highly motivated and were convinced the behavior therapy was effective. This alone could not account for the remission of the compulsions since other behavior therapy approaches were tried and were ineffective.

A very interesting feature of covert sensitization is the possibility that alcoholics or individuals with strong alcoholic craving can be trained to take only one drink. They could be instructed as follows: "After you take your first drink you start to reach for a second one. As soon as you do you start to feel sick and nauseous. You can feel the vomit going up to your mouth. You vomit all over the floor. You realize that you can only take one drink. Any more than one drink will make you feel ill." The present treatment of a patient indicates that the above method could be effective in limiting a compulsive drinker to one drink (or even two).

It seems quite likely that covert sensitization can be effective in other compulsions such as smoking, gambling, and even handwashing. Obsessions could also be treated by this method. The individual could be trained to feel nauseous as soon as the undesirable thought starts.

Although much work remains to be done in the investigation of covert sensitization, the author felt it important to present the method as soon as possible for further investigation by other researchers and therapists. Controlled studies in this area will be attempted by the author.

SUMMARY

Behavior therapy has achieved some success in the treatment of homosexuality, obesity, alcoholism, and other compulsions. Heretofore the aversive stimulus has been externally applied in the presence of the pleasurable but undesirable stimulus (or its substitute; e.g., words and pictures). In the method of covert sensitization the subject is asked to visualize the pleasurable stimulus while at the same time he is given instructions to imagine an unpleasant sensation such as vomiting. The method of covert sensitization is described, and two cases are presented illustrating its use.

25

REDUCTION OF GENERALIZED ANXIETY THROUGH A VARIANT OF SYSTEMATIC DESENSITIZATION[1]

Marvin R. Goldfried

Although systematic desensitization was originally introduced by Wolpe (1958) as a procedure for eliminating specific fears and phobias, research findings and case studies have indicated that the positive effects of desensitization typically extend well beyond those problem behaviors which were the target of therapy (Lang, 1969). Some of these findings may be explained in terms of stimulus generalization. What has also been found, however, is that anxiety reduction occurs in areas completely *unrelated* to the fear dimension on which the therapy had focused (e.g., Paul & Shannon, 1966). On the basis of this latter finding, as well as other corroborative evidence (e.g., Zeisset, 1968), systematic desensitization has been construed as a method by which clients may actually be learning a general skill in anxiety reduction, which they then apply in the presence of a variety of aversive stimuli (Goldfried, 1971).

Toward the goal of more effectively training clients in this generalized anxiety-reduction skill, certain procedural modifications in the usual desensitization procedures have been suggested (Goldfried, 1971). The modifications associated with this variant of systematic desensitization deal with: (a) the rationale for the treatment procedure which is presented to the client, (b) the emphasis placed on the purpose and use of relaxation training, (c) the guideline for constructing the hierarchy, and (d) the manner of exposing the client to the anxiety-provoking scenes during desensitization proper. The purpose

[1] This case report was prepared especially for this volume. The author would like to thank Anita P. Goldfried for her helpful comments.

of the present report is to illustrate the use of each of these procedural modifications in the treatment of a client for whom the primary problem consisted of generalized anxiety.

DESCRIPTION OF PROBLEM

The client, Lynne, a seventeen-year-old high school student, was the second of three girls born to an upper-middle-class, professional family. She was referred to therapy by her father, who had previously been seen in treatment by the writer.

On the basis of an intake interview, personal data questionnaire, and a slightly expanded 86-item version of Wolpe and Lang's (1964) Fear Survey Schedule, it was evident that Lynne's fear reactions were pervasive. Included among the long list of objects and situations which elicited anxiety were insects, elevators, high places, being alone at night, traveling by herself, criticism by others, people, situations, or activities with which she was unfamiliar, speaking in public, examinations, and listening to her sister and parents argue. In addition to experiencing subjective discomfort when placed in these situations, Lynne would often respond with uncontrollable crying. As far as could be determined, her anxiety reactions to these various situations were of long-standing duration.

THERAPEUTIC PROCEDURE

The first two sessions were used for gathering information relevant to the client's presenting difficulties. When it became reasonably evident that desensitization was the appropriate treatment procedure to attempt with Lynne (e.g., there did not appear to be any striking deficiencies in interpersonal skills which might account for her anxiety reactions), the treatment rationale was described. Toward the end of the second session, she was told that she would be trained in relaxation, and also would be taught how to apply this anxiety-reduction skill in those various life situations which typically upset her. A description was given of relaxation training, hierarchy construction, and desensitization proper, and the consultation sessions were described as a means for providing her with practice in "relaxing away" her upset, which eventually was to be carried out in the actual life situation.

Relaxation training began with the third session and used the abbreviated version of Jacobson's method, as described by Paul (1966). Lynne responded quite favorably to the first training session (i.e., achieving a relaxation level of 30 SUDS—Wolpe & Lazarus, 1966). She was provided with a tape recording of the instructions for relaxation, with which she practiced at home between weekly therapy sessions. It was emphasized that, in addition to providing her with the ability to relax voluntarily, relaxation training (particularly the tension phase) would also sensitize her to those proprioceptive cues for tension, which would serve as a signal for her to "relax." By the fifth session, Lynne was capable of sitting quietly in an easy chair and—utilizing only her own covert instructions for relaxation—relaxing herself to a level of 25 SUDS within five minutes.

As it became evident that Lynne was able to relax with little difficulty—at least during the consultation sessions or when practicing at home—she was encouraged to use this newly-acquired skill *in vivo* when she felt herself just starting to become upset. Lynne initiated attempts to relax herself *in vivo* just prior to the beginning of desensitization proper, and continue to do so throughout the period of treatment. The instructions to utilize relaxation *in vivo* constituted an on-going homework assignment, where the beginning portion of each session involved a discussion and reinforcement of her attempts at relaxing away anxiety. The results and follow-up section note Lynne's success at relaxation *in vivo*.

As mentioned earlier, the number and variety of situations to which Lynne reacted with anxiety were numerous. Although the usual desensitization procedure would involve the construction of several hierarchies (Wolpe & Lazarus, 1966), each reflecting a different theme (e.g., fear of criticism, new activities, examination-anxiety, insects, etc.), a *single hierarchy* was used with Lynne. Since she was being trained to use her own *internal cues for tension*—and not the external situations themselves—as a signal to relax, the usual requirement of carefully delineated themes was not seen as being necessary. In fact, toward the goal of providing Lynne with practice in anxiety reduction which was likely to generalize to the diverse anxiety-provoking situation in her current life, the hierarchy employed contained a sampling of the various situations which Lynne found to be problematic. In order of increasing anxiety, the multithematic hierarchy was as follows:

1. With your boyfriend, sitting near a pond (pleasant scene).
2. Taking an English test, and not knowing exactly how to answer the question.
3. Sitting next to father, who is driving the car.
4. Sitting next to boy friend, who is driving the car.
5. Driving car at night on highway, with boy friend sitting in front seat.
6. Driving car alone at night on highway.
7. Standing on top of beginner's hill, about to ski down.
8. Walking into a girl friend's house for the first time.
9. Sitting in bar with boy friend, and wondering if they will check proof of age.

10. Teacher is about to distribute questions for history test.
11. Baby sitting at night by yourself, watching T.V.
12. Helping father at work, and don't know where to find something he asks for.
13. Standing in a lobby, waiting for the elevator.
14. Walking into an elevator alone and pressing the button.
15. Girl friend tells you she doesn't like your hairstyle.
16. Standing in front of class, about to read a paper.
17. At home alone during the day, sitting in your room.
18. With boy friend at train station, and he leans over to see if train is coming.
19. At beach during vacation, and walk over to a group of strangers your age to say hello.
20. Boy friend on top of hill, calling for you to climb up.
21. Holding rail at skating rink, about to skate away from it.
22. Sitting in large auditorium, taking state-wide exams.
23. At home alone at night, sitting in room, and thinking you hear noises.
24. Sitting in room, and hearing your parents and sister having a loud argument.
25. Sitting in living room with your father and sister, who are arguing.

The essential guidelines used in constructing this heterogeneous hierarchy were (a) that the situations represent events in Lynne's current life situation—that is, she was likely to encounter such situations in the relatively near future—and (b) that the interval between items represent a minimal increase in subjective anxiety (e.g., 5 SUDS).

Desensitization proper began during the seventh meeting, and lasted for a total of six sessions. Inasmuch as the desensitization conducted during the consultation sessions was construed as providing the client with practice in anxiety reduction in general, as well as a rehearsal for actively coping with anxiety in specific situations, Lynne was asked to *maintain the image* even if she signaled that she was experiencing tension, and then to relax away this anxiety. This procedure differs markedly from the usual way in which desensitization is conducted, where the client is asked to stop visualizing the situation if he feels anxious, and concentrate only on the feelings of relaxation. Contrary to Wolpe and Lazarus' (1966) contention that failure to shut off the anxiety-provoking stimuli will result in a resensitization, Lynne was *always* successful in her attempts to relax away the tension. Although Lynne initially reported some difficulty in concentration on both the scene and her attempts at relaxation, the suggestion to imagine herself relaxing in the situation itself eliminated this problem. With the exception of items 1, 2, 17, and 23, Lynne signaled anxiety for each of the items. In most of these instances, she was able to eliminate these feelings of anxiety within 30 to 40 seconds. For example, her response to item 14 was as follows:

Trial 1: Scene presented (1 sec.) Anxiety signal (40 sec.) No anxiety (20 sec.) Scene terminated.
Trial 2: Scene presented (1 sec.) Anxiety signal (30 sec.) No anxiety (20 sec.) Scene terminated.
Trial 3: Scene presented (2 sec.) Anxiety signal (15 sec.) No anxiety (20 sec.) Scene terminated.
Trial 4: Scene presented. No anxiety (20 sec.) Scene terminated.

As can be seen by the time intervals indicated in parentheses, there was a progressive reduction from trial to trial in the amount of time required for successful anxiety reduction. The criterion used for moving on to the next item in the hierarchy consisted of two presentations with no report of anxiety for a period of 20 seconds. Most of the items in the hierarchy required either three or four presentations to meet this criterion.

In the case of a few items (9, 15, 22, 24, and 25), Lynne re-experienced anxiety within a particular trial after having initially relaxed away the tension. For example, the trials associated with item 22 were as follows:

Trial 1: Scene presented (1 sec.) Anxiety signal (25 sec.) No anxiety (10 sec.) Anxiety signal (5 sec.) No anxiety (20 sec.) Scene terminated.
Trial 2: Scene presented (1 sec.) Anxiety signal (5 sec.) No anxiety (10 sec.) Anxiety signal (10 sec.) No anxiety (20 sec.) Scene terminated.
Trial 3: Scene presented (2 sec.) Anxiety signal (5 sec.) No anxiety (20 sec.) Scene terminated.
Trial 4: Scene presented. No anxiety (20 sec.) Scene terminated.
Trial 5: Scene presented. No anxiety (20 sec.) Scene terminated.

The progressive changes which occurred from trial to trial for this item is typical of her response to items 9, 15, 24, and 25 as well, indicating what appears to be a gradual strengthening of the relaxation response. For those items where anxiety reoccurred during a trial, the criterial adopted for completion of the item was slightly more stringent, and consisted of three successive presentations with a 20 second anxiety-free interval.

RESULTS AND FOLLOW-UP

As noted above, Lynne was encouraged to apply her relaxation skills *in vivo* whenever she felt herself becoming anxious. So as to prevent her from becoming discouraged after any unsuccessful attempts at relaxation, she had been forewarned that she might experience difficulty in certain highly anxiety-provoking situations. As things turned out, however, Lynne was typically able to calm herself in a wide variety of situations. Between the seventh and twelfth sessions, when desensitization proper was being conducted, Lynne reported only one unsuccessful attempt (involving an argument with her younger sister), where she "forgot" to relax. In addition to situations which had been covered during our consultation sessions, she was able to relax herself in situations where she had *not yet* been "desensitized" during the session, as well as situations completely unrelated to any of the items on the hierarchy (e.g., swimming in the ocean). All this occurred prior to the completion of desensitization proper.

The final item on the hierarchy was completed during the twelfth session. The following session, held some three weeks later, began with Lynne stating: "I think I'm cured." She elaborated by indicating that she had experienced little anxiety during the past few weeks, and found herself "automatically" relaxing whenever she sensed herself becoming upset. Lynne was able to relate specific instances when this was the case. In contrast to her behavior pattern prior to therapy, she no longer cried over the minor events that she previously had found unsetting. A review of the items on the hierarchy revealed that, with the exception of one item in which it may have been realistic to be anxious (i.e. item 4, where her boy friend usually drove recklessly), Lynne had either been in the situation without feeling anxiety, or else did not anticipate experiencing any upset. The Fear Survey Schedule was readministered during the thirteenth session, and the results were compared with those obtained at the outset of treatment. With a 5-point rating scale to indicate increasing levels of anxiety for each item, the posttherapy score was 1.58, in contrast to the pretherapy score of 2.43. On the basis of a sign test, the anxiety decrement, as measured by the Fear Survey Schedule, is highly significant ($z = 4.86$; $p < .001$). It is of interest to note that many of the objects and situations which were reported as being less anxiety-provoking had little in common with the items included in the hierarchy (e.g., crawling insects, sick people, dogs), a finding which is consistent with the interpretation that Lynne had learned the generalized skill of anxiety reduction.

In addition to Lynne's own observation of change, she reported that other people had commented on her more relaxed appearance. For example, her father mentioned to her that she seemed to be less upset when he was critical of her on some matter. A secretary at the office where Lynne worked commented that she appeared to be more sure of herself. According to this secretary's observation, Lynne had previously been reluctant to carry out various routine tasks at work unless someone explicitly told her to do so; by contrast, she now showed greater independence and initiative.

Lynne was seen for a follow-up session some five months later. A review of the items in the hierarchy revealed that Lynne had encountered virtually all of the situations in real life without feeling anxious. In one situation, where she was reluctant to climb to the top of a hill (item 20), a simple reminder from her boy friend about what she had learned in therapy was sufficient in help her overcome the difficulty. The Fear Survey Schedule was re-administered during the follow-up, and the score of 1.78 continued to reflect a significant decrement in anxiety from her pretherapy level ($z = 3.63$; $p < .001$).

CONCLUSION

This case has illustrated the use of a variant of systematic desensitization to provide a pervasively anxious client with the use of relaxation as an active coping skill. The procedural modifications involved the use of a multidimensional hierarchy in which the client was provided with practice in "relaxing away" anxiety during the consultation session, as well as the direction to employ this same procedure whenever she felt tense *in vivo*.

Some comment might be made regarding the use of a single, multithematic hierarchy, as opposed to the usual procedure of employing several different thematic hierarchies. The purpose of the desensitization with Lynne was to facilitate the learning of a generalized skill for anxiety reduction, which could be utilized in situations varying widely as to their overt or underlying thematic dimensions. Consequently, the stimuli which Lynne was taught to utilize as a signal for relaxation consisted of her own proprioceptive cues for anxiety, rather than the multitude of external stimuli provoking the reaction. Whereas the proprioceptive cues associated with anxiety previously provided a signal for concern, uncontrollable crying, escape from the situation, and other maladaptive responses, the training procedures were directed at teaching her to utilize her relaxation skills to provide an alternate response to these same proprioceptive cues. With practice—during the consultation sessions and *in vivo*—the relaxation response gradually became anticipatory, until little or no upset was experienced in the multitude of situations which previously elicited anxiety.

The practice of having the client maintain the image in the presence of experienced anxiety represents a somewhat radical departure from the usual desensitization procedure of removing the individual from the situation at the first sign of anxiety. In a sense, this variant of systematic desensitization bears some similarities to flooding, or the technique of implosive therapy as described by Stampfl and Levis (1967). These latter procedures are based on the assumption that anxiety responses will eventually extinguish if their prolonged occurrence in the presence of aversive stimuli is not followed by any objectively noxious consequences. However, if one views extinction as involving the weakening of a given response in relation to other competing responses to the same situation (e.g., Guthrie, 1935; Estes, 1959), then the practice of having the client maintain the anxiety-provoking image while deliberately attempting to relax may be seen as a more effective method for facilitating the extinction process.

One final point regarding the role of relaxation training in this variant of systematic desensitization: Although several studies on desensitization (e.g., Cooke, 1968; Davison, 1968) have found that training in relaxation alone had little effect in the reduction of fear reactions, research evidence (Zeisset, 1968) as well as clinical reports (Davison, 1965; D'Zurilla, 1969; Gray, England, & Mahoney, 1965) have demonstrated that, under certain circumstances, relaxation training itself *can* be effective. Specifically, it has been noted that when clients are specifically instructed *to utilize* their relaxation skills outside of the consultation sessions—as opposed to simply providing them with relaxation training without any direction as to the relevance of the training to anxiety reduction *in vivo*—they are typically successful in minimizing their anxiety reactions. In terms of Kanfer and Phillips' (1965) classification of behavior therapy techniques, the procedure illustrated in this case study could be categorized as reflecting a combination of both *replication* and *instigation* therapy. That is, the treatment procedure may be construed as a replication of the real-life situation, in which the client engaged in behavioral rehearsal for coping with anxiety, as well as a means for instigating the client to utilize this relaxation skill outside of therapy for the purpose of achieving greater self-control in anxiety-provoking situations.

SUMMARY

A variant of systematic desensitization is described in the treatment of a case of generalized anxiety. The procedural modifications employed focus on changes in the treatment rationale presented to the client, the purpose and use of relaxation training, the guideline for constructing the hierarchy, and the method of exposing the client to anxiety-provoking scenes during the desensitization itself. By focusing on the training of an anxiety-reduction coping skill, this variant of desensitization is presented as a method for providing generally anxious clients with greater self-control in dealing with a wide variety of anxiety-provoking situations.

26

REDUCING HETEROSEXUAL ANXIETY[1]

Thomas J. D'Zurilla

Behavioral counseling techniques may be extended well beyond the traditional interview sessions to include *in vivo* or in-real-life procedures if those experiences are appropriately used to facilitate desired changes in behavior. One possible method in this regard is instructing the client to manipulate and control certain aspects of his own behavior and experiences, over which he currently has good control, to produce favorable changes in other, poorly controlled aspects of his behavior. The deliberate and systematic use of this procedure should lead to the self-control of the problem behavior; that is, control of the problem behavior primarily by stimuli produced by other responses of the same individual (Bijou & Baer, 1961; Goldiamond, 1965c; Skinner, 1953). This self-control procedure should facilitate independent problem-solving ability and add considerably to the effects produced by other techniques in the interview setting. In some cases, it may be an effective treatment in its own right.

Using *in vivo* "homework assignments" with clients is a practice of long standing. Too often, however, very little planning goes into these *in vivo* assignments for clients, along with scant regard for factors governing behavior change and self-control. For example, a client may be asked to perform a pattern of behavior over which he has little control at the time, or he may

Reprinted by permission of the author and Holt, Rinehart and Winston from J.D. Krumboltz and C.E. Thoresen (Eds.) *Behavioral Counseling: Cases and techniques*. New York: Holt, Rinehart and Winston, © 1969, pp. 442–454.

[1] The author wishes to express his appreciation to Marvin R. Goldfried and Gerald C. Davison for their suggestions and criticisms.

be asked to perform a response in a situation where an incompatible response tendency is much stronger. As a result, the client often fails to respond and the counselor simply concludes that he is not yet "ready" or "motivated" to carry out *in vivo* assignments. Rarely have comprehensive, systematic programs been planned and prescribed, as the primary treatment method, for progressive self-control and elimination of problem behaviors.[2]

Recently, however, the concept of self-control has been receiving more attention in the research and theoretical literature (Aronfreed, 1964; Aronfreed & Reber, 1965; Bandura & Walters, 1963; Goldiamond, 1965c; Homme, 1966; Kanfer & Goldfoot, 1966), and there have been promising results in counseling settings.[3]

COUNSELING FOR SELF-CONTROL

These two case reports illustrate the self-manipulation of certain behaviors and experiences, notably differential relaxation, by male clients to help control and overcome chronic anxiety and gastric distress related to females. The first case, that of Frank, describes the use of *in vivo* self-controlled procedures to supplement the primary treatment of systematic desensitization. Although similar procedures have been encouraged in most systematic desensitization cases, counselors rarely have attempted to maximize their effects by explicitly training the client in their use and checking on their application during the course of counseling. Most counselors assume that the major effects of counseling will result directly from what goes on in the interview setting.

The second case, Steve, is unique in that after several initial assessment and training sessions the entire treatment program was carried out by the client himself without any contact with the counselor.

FRANK'S ANXIETY AND NAUSEA WITH GIRLS

Frank was a 21-year-old student in his senior year at the State University of New York at Stony Brook. He came to Psychological Services complaining of disturbing anxiety and nausea (with occasional vomiting) in social situations with girls, especially when the contact was close and personal, such as on a date. Anxiety and nausea occurred on every date

[2] Notable exceptions to this have been the work of Salter (1949), Wolpe (1958), and Wolpe and Lazarus (1966), using *in vivo* assertive and sexual responses by clients to gradually eliminate certain fears.

[3] For examples, see Cautela (1966a, 1966b); Davison (1969); Ferster, Nurnberger, and Levitt (1962); Goldiamond (1965c); and Gray, England, and Mahoney (1965).

with varying severity depending upon time since the last meal, type of food eaten, and the nature of the activity. The reaction was usually the strongest when the client arrived at the residence of his date and continued at a high level of intensity on the way to the planned activity. In most instances, the reaction gradually became less disturbing during the date and occasionally disappeared, especially if considerable activity was involved, such as playing tennis or going swimming. Because of this problem, Frank had avoided frequent dating. For approximately three months prior to counseling he had been dating only one girl, Alice, a student at Smith College.

Frank's anxiety-nausea on dates had been a problem for approximately six years. Before the problem developed, he had dated girls without special difficulty, although he reported that he had always felt somewhat uncomfortable with girls. The client also reported that the problem had been getting worse in the past few years. He first sought help from his family doctor soon after the reaction became a problem. He was told that he was merely experiencing "growing pains" and that the reaction would soon disappear. About six months prior to seeing me, Frank consulted a private psychiatrist. He received psychoanalytically-oriented psychotherapy for about three months but terminated because he could see no evidence of progress.

Other difficulties reported by Frank included frequent mood swings, irritability, chronic dissatisfaction, feelings of inferiority, and lack of self-confidence. He recalled that these difficulties seem to have developed during the six years in which the anxiety-nausea problem had been in existence.

Starting Systematic Desensitization

After several assessment sessions the decision was made to use systematic desensitization along with *in vivo* "assignments." The first four treatment sessions were used for training in deep muscle relaxation, construction of the initial anxiety-hierarchy, and instructions for *in vivo* self-control. During relaxation training, the client was also instructed to practice the method at home at least once per day. In the initial hierarchy, it was decided to focus upon Frank's girlfriend, Alice, since she was the only girl with whom he had been having regular personal contacts. The casual contacts which he had been having with girls on campus presented no disturbing problems. At first, several themes involving mediating or internal variables (for example, anticipation of rejection and disapproval and sexual feelings) were considered but were discarded as being less appropriate, at least initially, than the simple dimension of proximity to Alice in terms of time and space. Frank reported that his next personal contact with Alice would be at the time of the Thanksgiving vacation when he planned to drive to Smith College and bring her home for the vacation. Before this time, only contacts by telephone and letter were anticipated, which also tended to elicit the anxiety-nausea responses.

Preparing for Contact with Alice at Smith

The following anxiety hierarchy was constructed:

1. Relaxing in comfortable chair in room at home, thinking only of relaxing
2. Talking with friends on campus, someone mentions the name "Alice"
3. Relaxing in comfortable chair in room at home, thinking of Alice
4. Writing a letter to Alice in room at home
5. Eating dinner at home with parents, talking about going to pick up Alice
6. Driving in car on the way to Smith College
7. Reading a letter from Alice in room at home
8. Talking with Alice on the telephone
9. Driving in car at Smith College, seeing Alice standing in the distance
10. Driving in car with Alice on the way to go sailing
11. Driving up to Alice's dormitory, seeing her coming out and walking toward you
12. Walking around the campus with Alice
13. Talking to Alice in her dormitory room

When Frank became efficient in being able to relax himself, he was given specific instructions to begin anticipating tension-provoking situations in his daily activities, recognizing tension at the first sign of its appearance, and relaxing it away using covert verbal cues such as saying "relax, let go completely" to himself and tension-release exercises. The situations discussed corresponded to the items of the anxiety-hierarchy.

Frank was also instructed to manipulate his eating behavior and activities relating to the items of the hierarchy. To begin with, he was to avoid food-intake for several hours prior to initiating any phone, letter, or personal contact with Alice with the exception of certain liquids, such as water and coffee. Moreover, the last meal before a contact was to include only easily digestible foods. A typical "ulcer diet" was referred to for this program.

Frank was also instructed to expose himself to situations and experiences of low anxiety-provoking potential, such as talking to a friend and mentioning Alice's name (see hierarchy), and to avoid experiences of medium and high anxiety potential. The above factors were to be manipulated by the client according to a "graded tasks" procedure where steps toward experiences with a higher potential for disturbance are taken only when the lower step is accomplished without disturbance. Thus, he was instructed *gradually* to bring the time of food-intake closer to the time of contacts with Alice, to eat a greater variety of foods, and to initiate contacts higher up in the anxiety-hierarchy.

Counseling sessions involved working up the hierarchy according to the usual systematic-desensitization procedures and checking on progress regarding the self-control procedures. One modification was made to facilitate *in vivo* self-control. For the first six items, Frank was instructed to signal when he experienced tension, stop imagining the scene, and to relax away the tension. No further relaxation suggestions were given by the counselor during this procedure unless the client was unable to relax away the tension using self-produced cues, such as "relax, let go completely," in about 30 seconds. The next item was presented only when the client signaled a return to his previous, relaxed state. For the remaining items, the client was asked to relax away the tension *while maintaining the image.* He was instructed to stop imagining the item only if it appeared that anxiety was increasing or if he was unable to relax away the tension in about 30 seconds.

In the fifteenth session the first anxiety-hierarchy was completed in systematic desensitization. According to Frank, it appeared that the combination of systematic desensitization and the *in vivo* procedures had enabled him to overcome all disturbance associated with life experiences up to and including item 8 on the anxiety-hierarchy.[4] The remaining situations were not experienced in real life since Alice had changed her Thanksgiving vacation plans and decided to spend the time with relatives who lived near Smith College. However, Frank reported that he was planning to drive to Smith the following week to bring Alice home for the Christmas holidays.

At this time Frank reported a successful experience with another girl at Stony Brook the week before the fifteenth session. The girl had invited him to visit her in her off-campus apartment and he accepted. He experienced no nausea during the entire visit. Some anxiety and tension were felt, however, which he successfully controlled and eliminated by employing self-induced differential relaxation. It is interesting to note that this successful experience occurred before the personal contact items of the anxiety-hierarchy were worked through in systematic desensitization.

[4] Progress in systematic desensitization did not proceed without difficulty, although smooth progress has often been suggested in case reports. Difficulties occurred in relaxation. On several occasions the client was faced with conflicts and difficult decisions in the life situation which tended to disrupt desensitization treatment temporarily. However, space limitations prevent a more detailed description of these difficulties here. The main objective at this time is to focus upon those procedures and experiences which are directly related to the self-control aspect of treatment.

Successfully Dating Alice and Giving a Speech

In the fifteenth session, the following short hierarchy was constructed to help Frank handle any disturbance that might be associated with activities leading up to a date with Alice during the Christmas vacation:

1. Dressing in room before leaving for a date with Alice
2. Driving in car on the way to Alice's home for a date
3. Walking up to the front door of Alice's home
4. Standing in the doorway as Alice opens the door and invites you in
5. Sitting in the living room talking to Alice and her mother

This hierarchy was completed in the seventeenth session. At this point, Frank reported that he had become more generally relaxed and confident in all interpersonal situations.

He reported success in controlling and significantly reducing anxiety in a speech-making situation using the self-control method. The experience involved delivering a talk before the class in a psychology course. In the past he had always experienced considerable anxiety and distress prior to and throughout such an experience. This time he employed differential relaxation at the first appearance of tension and successfully completed the talk without any disturbing anxiety.

The seventeenth session was the last before the Christmas vacation, when the client would be driving to Smith College to bring Alice home. He was instructed to employ differential relaxation on the trip as he did in connection with the speech-making experience.

Reducing Nausea

In the eighteenth session, the first following the Christmas holidays, he reported that he had experienced anxiety on the way to Smith but had successfully controlled and relaxed it away. At one point he was unable to reduce anxiety through differential relaxation while driving so he pulled over to the side of the road and relaxed more deeply. Frank also reported that there was no vomiting and no significant anxiety during several dates with Alice during the vacation period. However, on one occasion he experienced nausea. This occurred during a Christmas party when he ate and drank much more than was appropriate. This was the first time since the beginning of counseling that the taking of any kind of food or drink had been attempted in a dating situation.

At this point the possibility was considered that a nausea response might have been developed in this client as an independent condition response to a stimulus complex involving the presence and comsumption of food and drink within the context of a date with a girl. An attempt was made to deal directly with this possibility through the use of a modified desensitization approach. First, the following dinner-date hierarchy was prepared:

1. Lying in bed the morning of the dinner date
2. Eating breakfast the same day
3. Eating lunch the same day
4. Dressing just before leaving for the date
5. Driving in car on the way to the date
6. Walking up to the door of Alice's home
7. Sitting in the living room, talking to Alice and her mother
8. Sitting in the living room, seeing plates, glasses, and so forth on the dining table
9. Sitting in the living room, seeing Alice and her mother putting food on the table—vegetables, turkey, and so forth
10. Getting up and walking to the dining room, looking at the food
11. Sitting at the table next to Alice, looking at the food
12. Putting food on your plate
13. Putting food in your mouth
14. Drinking milk and eating cake following the meal

The modification in usual desensitization procedures involved the placing of one of the client's favorite peppermint candies on his tongue following relaxation and just prior to imagining the items from the hierarchy. The client was instructed to let the candy dissolve in his mouth during the desensitization procedure. He was asked to signal whenever he felt either nausea or anxiety. It was hypothesized that the candies might help to counteract and eliminate the nausea response to the hierarchy situations. The client was also instructed to use the same peppermint candy in the life situation prior to any eating situation with a girl.

After two more sessions the dinner-date hierarchy was completed. During this time Frank reported that he had dated two girls from Stony Brook. On one of the dates he ate food with no disturbing reactions. He used peppermint candies with apparent success. Two weeks later he reported that he had again dated the same two girls. This time food was eaten on both dates with no anxiety or nausea. He indicated that the dates were quite pleasant and satisfying. On neither of these dates was it necessary to use the candies.

Some Results

In the twenty-eighth and final session, Frank reported greater self-confidence, more satisfaction with life in general, greater stability in mood, and less general anxiety. There was no longer any disturbing anxiety or nausea during heterosexual contacts. A very important step forward was the fact that he had just accepted an invitation to go to a "Sadie Hawkins" dance with a girl with whom he was only slightly acquainted. He said that he definitely would have refused only a few months ago.

A follow-up interview three months later revealed that there had been no setbacks and no substitute "symptoms" or additional problems. In fact, he had continued to improve in most areas, especially frequency of and satisfaction with dating, self-confidence, and feelings of adequacy.

STEVE'S FEAR OF GIRLS

Steve was a 21-year-old student in his junior year at Stony Brook. He came in complaining of anxiety and nausea associated with personal contacts with girls. Again, the problem was especially disturbing on dates. Steve was not dating at all at the time of treatment because of this reaction.

This problem dated back about ten years. When he was about 11 years old he began to feel anxious and nauseous when he talked to or thought about a pretty girl that he liked. If he had recently eaten, the reaction would be particularly intense and vomiting would usually occur. The client soon learned to avoid eating for several hours prior to any expected social contacts with attractive girls to prevent vomiting. However, anxiety and nausea continued. In the case of any unexpected contacts soon after food intake, the reaction again occurred to the degree that the client was forced to remove himself from the situation to avoid vomiting.

Because of this disturbing problem the client had done very little dating until about two years before he came in for counseling when he had tried "going steady." He had attempted to cope with the situation by controlling eating and using "self-hypnosis." The latter involved lying down on a bed, trying to relax, and giving himself hypnotic suggestions taken from a book on hypnotic induction. He had also given himself suggestions to the effect that the anxiety-nausea reaction would not occur. The client employed this procedure before each date for about one month. When this method failed to produce significant improvement, the client gave it up and relied primarily on the procedure of controlling eating.

After about six months of going steady, Steve finally had ended the relationship because of the difficulties involved, even though the steady dating resulted in some reduction in the frequency and intensity of the reaction. During the year and a half before treatment the client never dated the same girl more than three times. He felt that the reaction had greatly interfered with his heterosexual development during adolescence and had resulted in a lack of self-confidence in social relationships and feelings of inadequacy. Other problems reported by the client were anxiety associated with taking examinations and disturbing thoughts about possible illness and disease.

Starting Desensitization

After Steve and I explored details of his problem, three problem categories were identified: formal date, telephone conversation, and informal meetings, such as meeting a girl in a bar and "picking her up." As in the case of Frank, the presence and consumption of food and drink tended to aggravate the anxiety-nausea reaction in these situations. Since Steve was interested in a particular girl, Ellen, she was used in the anxiety hierarchies. The one concerning a date was as follows:

1. Lying in bed in the morning on the day of a date with Ellen
2. Getting out of bed in the morning on the day of the date
3. Eating breakfast on the day of the date
4. Driving home from school for dinner on the day of the date
5. Eating dinner with parents on the day of the date
6. Getting out of the car at Ellen's home
7. Walking up to the door of Ellen's home
8. Meeting Ellen at the door
9. Driving in car with Ellen on the way to a restaurant
10. Sitting at a table with Ellen in the restaurant waiting to be served
11. Eating with Ellen in the restaurant
12. Sitting in the car with Ellen—you attempt to kiss her
13. You attempt to kiss Ellen, she turns away without saying anything
14. You attempt to kiss Ellen, she verbally rejects your advances

Self-administered Counseling

At this point the academic semester ended after eight counseling sessions. It was not possible to continue counseling through the summer as planned since Steve had decided to take a job in his home town. It was agreed that he would attempt to apply desensitization principles on his own during the summer and return in the fall to begin formal desensitization treatment.

He was enthusiastic about desensitization treatment and well-motivated to try out a self-control program. First, the client decided that he must try to arrange as many "treatment trials" as possible during the summer. He contacted a girl, Carol, who lived in his neighborhood, and began to see her regularly, nearly every day. His "procedure" was based upon the self-manipulation of three behavioral variables: (1) eating, (2) relaxation, and (3) activities associated with the anxiety hierarchies.

Eating Treatment–With regard to eating behavior, he started by setting up a three-hour minimum time period between eating a meal and contacts (both phone and personal) with Carol. Gradually, with each success experience, that is, contacts without disturbing anxiety or nausea, he moved the mealtime closer to the time of the contract until he was able to eat a meal with Carol on a date without disturbance. In addition to manipulating time of eating, he also manipulated the amount of food. He began by eating very small portions and gradually increased the amount until he was eating an average portion before and during a date.

Relaxation Treatment–In regard to the use of relaxation, Steve started by practicing deep muscle relaxation, following the procedures used during relaxation training in counseling, in his home before each date with Carol. He initiated the procedure each time at the first sign of anxiety. In employing this procedure, Steve patterned his self-produced cues after the verbalizations of the counselor during relaxation training; that is, he talked to himself in such terms as "Tense the muscles of your arms," "Relax," "Let go completely," "Notice the contrast," and so forth. In addition to employing complete deep relaxation in this manner, the client used differential relaxation to relax away any tension he experienced during activities just prior to and on the date. After a few weeks of successful dating without a major reaction, the client began to rely entirely upon the latter procedure to maintain control over anxiety.

Confronting Actual Situations

With the regular and systematic use of these procedures, Steve reported that he had completely eliminated the problem with telephone contacts in about two or three weeks. In regard to personal contacts with Carol, progress occurred more slowly but steadily. After about six weeks, he felt that he had the reaction completely under control.

Then a setback occurred. On several occasions he became anxious and experienced nausea at Carol's home. He relaxed himself somewhat in the situation by using differential relaxation with tension-release exercises. Then he removed his mealtime before a date back about 20 minutes, gradually decreasing the time period again on future dates. The client reported being surprised about the effectiveness of a 20-minute change in mealtime. At this point he also returned to practicing complete deep relaxation before a date. He reported that this procedure eliminated the reaction again in a few days. There were a few subsequent relapses following periods of several days when Steve was unable to see Carol for various reasons. In each case he coped successfully with the problem in the same manner as reported above.

After three months the client was able to eat a meal immediately before a date without experiencing disturbing anxiety or nausea and without subsequent relapse. After five months he was eating meals with Carol on a date without any anxiety or nausea.

Dealing with a Failure–The first setback reported above appeared to be related, at least in part, to considerable anxiety associated with the client's sexual experiences with Carol. At the time of this setback, the client had attempted sexual intercourse with Carol for the first time. This was his first attempt at sexual relations with any girl. Although Carol was co-operative, he became highly anxious and could not maintain an erection. In co-operation with Carol, the client postponed intercourse at this time and began systematically to employ Wolpe's (Wolpe & Lazarus, 1966) self-control procedure for using sexual responses to overcome anxiety and inhibition associated with sexual behavior. (He had become acquainted with this procedure in his abnormal psychology course.) He also used differential relaxation as an aid in the procedure. For one week, sexual intercourse was not attempted. Instead, he and Carol engaged in various kinds of precoital sexual behavior which had lower anxiety-provoking potential until he was getting aroused with a strong erection and anxiety was virtually eliminated. Then intercourse was again attempted with much greater success this time. The procedure was repeated until the problem was completely overcome.

Effects of Counseling

When the client returned in the fall, he described the above procedures and results and expressed confidence in his ability to continue on his own. Therefore, no formal counseling was initiated at that time. In a follow-up interview in January, Steve reported that the problem had been completely eliminated since October and that there had been no further relapses. At the time of the interview he was still going steady with Carol. There was no evidence of substitute "symptoms" or new problems. The client reported feeling much happier in general, more satisfied with life, and more adequate as a person. However, the client's other two problems—that is, test anxiety and disturbing thoughts about illness—remained essentially unchanged even though he made some attempt to deal with these situations on his own as well. This failure could be interpreted as reflecting the need for a careful and thorough assessment of the major determinants of the problem behavior before a self-control program is planned and prescribed.

OBSERVATIONS ON THE CASES OF FRANK AND STEVE

These case illustrations suggest what a client is capable of doing, independently, in the life situation to control and overcome his own disturbing "neurotic" reactions, provided that he receives the necessary training and instructions. As far as providing evidence for the effectiveness of the specific procedures described here, however, it must be stressed that such case illustrations are grossly inadequate. Case reports are necessarily incomplete. However, the present reports have value in that they illustrate one possible set of procedures that may account for success with this type of problem. Controlled research must then take over to isolate all of the active ingredients.

The major advantages of a self-controlled approach appear to be the following: (a) reduction in the frequency of counseling sessions, enabling counselors to handle more clients and provide more services, (b) extension of counseling beyond the interview setting, which should significantly reduce the time required for treatment, and (c) reinforcement of active self-control of emotions and overt behavior and of independent problem-solving, which should strengthen a sense of personal responsibility and increase feelings of competence and mastery (Cautela, 1966a, 1966b; Homme, 1966). It is important to point out, however, that it is presumptuous to expect that any single therapeutic approach would be equally effective in all cases, even in all cases where the "target problem" is the same, as in the two cases reported here. Studies must be done to investigate not only the effects of self-controlled procedures with a large number of clients, but also the possible differential effects depending upon such factors as type of client (for example, anxiety level, general self-control ability, and other personal-social characteristics) and type of anxiety problem (for example, pervasive interpersonal, and inanimate).

Three observations about the present case studies might be mentioned in closing which tend to point up the potential value of *in vivo* self-manipulations in desensitization programs. The first is that in the case of Steve a chronic anxiety problem was apparently overcome through the client's own efforts without the help of imaginal desensitization in the counseling room. Secondly, in the case of Frank, anxiety was controlled and overcome in several real-life situations *before* those situations were "desensitized" in counseling. Finally, again in the case of Frank, anxiety was sometimes experienced in life situations *following* "desensitization" of those situations in imagination, which was then controlled and eliminated by self-control.

27

THE CONDITIONED INHIBITION OF UNCINATE FITS[1]

Robert Efron

HISTORICAL BACKGROUND

It has been repeatedly observed, since ancient times, that a specific sensory stimulus could arrest epileptic fits, but the physiological explanation of this phenomenon is still unknown.

Similarly, seizures spontaneously arrested during the aura (aborted for reasons which cannot be ascertained, but not *apparently* by sensory stimulation) are reported by almost every epileptic from time to time. In one of the rare references to this phenomenon in the last twenty years, S. A. K. Wilson (1935) noted that the *grand mal* fit sometimes "fails to evolve according to rule . . . the process becomes arrested at some point, for reasons difficult to fathom." He called these abortive fits "fragments."

It has also been observed that spontaneous arrests during different stages of the aura are more frequently noted after treatment with anticonvulsant drugs, especially phenytoin. (The suggestion so often made when a spontaneous arrest of "fragmentary" fit occurs—that the "threshold for the spread of the fit was not achieved at that moment" is mere tautology.)

This phenomenon of seizure-arrest, known for so long, has not been seriously investigated in the laboratory or clinic although hundreds of papers

Reprinted by permission of the author and publisher from *Brain*, 1957, *80*, 251–262.

[1] The opinions expressed in this article are those of the author and are not necessarily to be construed as representing those of the Navy Department or the Naval service at large.

have recently been published on methods of precipitating fits. This neglect is surprising since a study of naturally arrested seizures is both of theoretical interest and pertinent to therapy.

In the last and most exhaustive study of the phenomenon of sensory arrest of seizures, Gowers (1881) pointed out that the repeated arrest of Jacksonian fits by ligatures could permanently alter the subsequent development of the fit. He reported the case of a "patient whose fits always commence in the hand by a sensation which passes up the arm, and could be arrested by the ligature applied just above the elbow. After employing the ligature in this manner for some months, he found that the fits, commencing in the same way, stopped of their own accord at the spot at which they had been repeatedly arrested by the ligature. They never stopped thus before the patient commenced the use of the ligature, which appeared to have produced a permanent increase of resistance at a certain part of the unstable nerve tissue."

Another case of permanent cure by application of the ligature, reported originally by Lysons (1772) was mentioned by Gowers. In Lysons' patient, the fits began in the foot and were arrested by repeated applications of a tight garter at the knee at the onset of each fit. "The fits afterwards became weaker, and the same means being used, whenever notice was given of their approach, they were at last entirely cured without medicine."

Lysons did not indicate, however, whether or not his patient continued to experience the early phases of the fit. Gowers' patient continued to have fits which were spontaneously arrested without any *apparent* sensory stimulus from a ligature.

PRESENT INVESTIGATION

In reading these case reports one is forcibly struck by the resemblance of this phenomenon to the establishment of conditioned reflexes in animals and man by the repeated temporal association of a non-specific (conditioned) stimulus with a specific (unconditioned) stimulus. Indeed, Gowers' own language—"permanent increase of resistance . . . of the unstable nerve tissue" —is almost identical to that used by I. Pavlov (1928) in explaining the behaviour of his dogs. To use this analogy: we may say that the ligatures (specific unconditioned stimuli) became linked, as a result of repeated temporal association, with a non-specific stimulus—which in turn became as effective in arresting the fit as was the original "specific" ligature itself. We cannot determine, from the reports of Gowers and Lysons, what the non-specific stimulus might have been in their patients.

In a previous paper by the author (Efron, 1956) a case of temporal lobe epilepsy was reported which was characterized by depersonalization, forced thinking, olfactory hallucination, auditory hallucination and adversive head movement preceding the *grand mal* climax. These attacks had persisted for twenty-six years and the sequence had been identical for each fit. No arrested seizures had ever occurred: once the first part of the aura had begun, a stereotyped fit was inevitable. Application of a specific sensory stimulus (an unpleasant odour) prior to the stage of forced thinking, invariably arrested further development of the aura and prevented the occurrence of the tonic and clonic seizure. Application of the unpleasant odour at the appearance of the stage of forced thinking resulted in bizarre fragments of adversive seizures, gyratory epilepsy and epilepsia cursiva. Further delay in administration of the stimulus failed to alter the pattern of the seizure in any way.

The patient has since been able to arrest every seizure by inhaling from a vial the odours of various aromatic chemicals or essential perfume oils. The frequency of her attacks has remained unchanged. The only failures to arrest seizures have been at night when she slept throughout the early phases of the aura (which on other occasions had awakened her) and had no opportunity to inhale the essence. For details concerning the lysis of the aura as a result of these stimuli, the reader is referred to the original report.

In attempting to explain, in physiological terms, the effectiveness of the olfactory stimulus in our patient, the activation of a widespread inhibitory system by the unpleasant (nociceptive) olfactory stimulus was predicated. It was assumed that the nociceptive stimulus activated this inhibitory system in a "reflex" or automatic fashion. Yet, Gowers' patient was eventually able to inhibit his fit *without* the application of a nociceptive stimulus. It thus seemed possible to produce an activation of this reflex fit inhibition (originally produced by a nociceptive stimulus) by a conditioned, non-specific stimulus, in the same way that a dog may eventually be led to salivate by hearing a tuning fork.

It is the object of this paper to report the arrest of seizures not only by a conditioned, non-specific visual stimulus but also by a second order conditioned reflex (2° C.R.) which was concurrently, but inadvertently, established.

METHODS

Every fifteen minutes (approximately) for a period of eight days, two stimuli were simultaneously presented to the subject. The first was a concentrated odour of jasmine which had previously been found effective in arresting the uncinate seizures. The second was an inexpensive silvered bracelet. She was instructed to stare intently for 15–30 seconds at the bracelet while sniffing a vial of essence of jasmine.

The patient was permitted seven hours sleep at night and the conditioning was begun anew each morning lasting until bedtime. Five different persons[2] exposed her to the sight of the bracelet and to the jasmine odour

[2] T/Sgt. R. Koran, U.S. Air Force; T/Sgt. C. Martin, U.S. Army; HM2 M. Cassidy, U.S. Navy; HM3 M. Shepherd, U.S. Navy; HN J. Cohill, U.S. Navy.

during the eight-day period, so that the response would not depend on the presence of any particular person. Similarly, the double stimulation was performed in the patient's hospital room, the day room, during walks in the hospital grounds, and while reading, etc., to avoid unrelated conditioning by specific aspects of her environment. Except for the 15–30 second interval during which the stimuli were simultaneously applied, the subject was not exposed to either of them.

Twice during the eight-day conditioning period the patient developed spontaneous seizures, each of which was arrested by the use of the odour alone. This unintentional failure to reinforce the conditioning process occurred because the attacks developed at night after the bracelet had been removed from her room.

INTERPRETATION OF RESULTS

At the end of eight days of conditioning the bracelet alone was presented to the patient and she experienced the odour of the concentrated jasmine in a vivid fashion. The olfactory hallucination persisted while the bracelet was exposed and receded in a few seconds when it was removed from her sight.[3]

For the next week the patient was exposed only twice a day . . . to the bracelet and the jasmine, a programme instituted to maintain reinforcement. During the second week *a spontaneous seizure occurred which was arrested by the patient's merely staring at the bracelet for a few seconds.*

This seizure began in its stereotyped form and the patient reported its arrest as a gradual lessening of the intensity of the depersonalization, remoteness and dreamy state. There were two significant subjective differences, however, in the response to the specific stimulus (essence of jasmine) and the one to the non-specific conditioned stimulus (bracelet). The patient reported that the "dissolving" of the seizure began later after exposure to the bracelet, than it usually did after exposure to the essence of jasmine. This increased latency of response is a finding usually noted in conditioned reflexes as compared to unconditioned reflexes. In addition, she described the lysis itself as more "abrupt" when terminated by the essence of jasmine. When the bracelet was used, the fit "faded away" more slowly, and this appeared to be a consistent finding in further arrests with the bracelet. As the lysis of the depersonalization was gradual in both cases and persisted for about "half a minute," it was difficult to be certain of the precise moment

[3] This type of response to conditioning is not unusual. The work of C. and N. A. Popov of Paris (1953, 1954, 1955) showed that visual hallucinations (after-images) can be easily induced by Pavlovian techniques. Further reference will be made to their work in the discussion.

the lysis began and the exact moment normality was achieved. For this reason, measurements of the latency and the duration of the lysis were impossible to obtain with any accuracy.

Following this success, the patient was permitted to go home with only the bracelet to control her seizures. (Anticonvulsant medication had been discontinued after the initial success with aromatic chemicals some months previously.) The patient entirely discontinued the use of the vials of aromatic chemicals, and successfully used the bracelet to arrest seizures for a period of eight months. Further formal reinforcing conditioning has not proved necessary, as each arrested seizure appears to serve as a reinforcement.

On three occasions, shortly after the initial success with the bracelet, the patient was instructed to delay the exposure of the bracelet until later in the aura (just prior to the olfactory hallucination) to see if any forms of larval epilepsia cursiva or gyratory epilepsy would develop—as they had when applications of the primary olfactory stimulus was delayed. In the first two of these attempts, the patient experienced such passivity and inertia at this late stage of the seizure, that she was unable to get up to take the bracelet out of her purse. She experienced a complete *grand mal* seizure both times.

On the third occasion, at the earliest stage of the aura, she removed the bracelet from her purse (without looking at it), and placed it on a table in front of a chair. Then, with head averted, and eyes open, she sat in front of it, having only to turn her head to bring the bracelet into view. The patient reported that in performing these activities she was extremely conscious of the existence of the bracelet at all times, and was puzzled as to the slowness with which the aura developed in this particular fit. However, she finally reached the stage of forced thinking, impending olfactory hallucination, and passivity, when she turned her head and looked at the bracelet. She experienced the smell of jasmine and the fit rapidly subsided without the development of the *grand mal* component. This was the first time that success had been achieved at such a late phase in the fit.

Following this, no further delays were suggested and the patient continued, *without fail,* to arrest seizures by staring at the bracelet in the early phase of her attacks. She had attacks at about the same frequency as before. With continued practice, she became more socially adept at controlling her fits in varying situations. On one occasion, while performing at a theatrical benefit, she was forced to leave her purse in a distant room. Fearing the possibility of a seizure while performing before a large audience, she put the bracelet on her wrist, and covered it with a kerchief. During her song, she began to experience the characteristic depersonalization of her attacks. She also noted that the conductor was signalling for her to slow down. (Her disturbed time sense in an early stage of the aura has been previously reported.) She uncovered her bracelet while singing. The hallucination of jasmine and the lysis of the aura occurred, and she finished her performance uneventfully. Only the conductor knew that "something had gone wrong."

ELECTROENCEPHALOGRAPHIC STUDIES

In the previous investigations of this patient, EEG confirmation of an arrested seizure (aborted by B.A.L.) was obtained with the aid of metrazol activation. On one occasion 75 mg. metrazol induced a self-sustained seizure and on another 50 mg. did so. A third attempt was made to perform the experiment using the bracelet as the arresting stimulus. Sphenoidal electrodes were placed by a modification of the techniques of Arellano and MacLean (1949) and adequate control tracings were secured. Metrazol was administered intravenously in the dosage of 30 mg. over a two-second period every thirty seconds. Once the aura was precipitated the metrazol infusion was discontinued. The whole procedure was similar to prior procedures, including the placing of the sphenoidal electrodes with local cocaine anæsthesia. The single difference was that where, in the earlier experiments, the patient was told that the vial of aromatic chemical would be placed beneath her nostrils at the critical moment—on this occasion she was instructed to open her eyes at the critical moment in order to see the bracelet about two feet away.

Two very surprising things happened. In the first place, injection of 60–90 mg. metrazol failed to precipitate even the earliest stages of the patient's specific aura. It was found that rapid injection of 150 mg. was necessary to "switch" from the fright and lightheadedness that normally follows a metrazol injection, to the patient's own characteristic type of depersonalization, dreamy state, etc. . . . the hallmarks of her fit. Secondly, the fit did not progress as it had on previous occasions. Even though the bracelet had not yet been viewed, the patient reported that the aura was "hung up," meaning by this that the subjective intensity was not worsening, that the depersonalization and dreamy state were static. After being "hung up" in such a fashion for about two to three minutes she reported that the fit was subsiding. After she experienced, for the first time in her life, four such *spontaneously* abortive attacks, it was realized that the threshold for metrazol had changed in two respects. Firstly, more was required to precipitate an attack. Secondly, the aura, once precipitated, did not sustain itself and progress into a full-blown fit. Because of this resistance to metrazol, an attempt was made to sustain the aura, and cause it to progress by continuous infusion of metrazol.

After a five-minute rest period, the patient was given 150 mg. metrazol over a one-minute period and 50 mg. every 30 seconds thereafter. She reported the onset of a fit, in the usual fashion, and even at this rate of continued metrazol infusion the aura remained almost motionless, with perhaps the slightest progression, for ten minutes. She received a total of 1,150 mg. over this eleven-minute period. Opening her eyes and viewing the bracelet resulted in a rapid lysis of the subjective sensations of the fit *despite* the fact that metrazol was still being slowly infused. The patient was made extremely anxious by this procedure, and in view of the large quantities of metrazol administered (1,350 mg. in thirteen minutes), the procedure was discontinued.

Although five different fits were induced, only the earliest psychic stages could be precipitated, there being an obvious resistance offered by some mechanism to the development of a self-sustaining fit. The EEGs showed no localized or generalized abnormality during the stage of the aura. When the patient was reporting the lysis of a seizure, either by use of the bracelet or spontaneously, some bursts of high voltage 30 cps activity were recorded from the bisphenoidal electrodes.

DEVELOPMENT OF A SECOND ORDER (2° C.R.) CONDITIONED REFLEX

On questioning the patient subsequently about her reactions during the metrazol infusions, it emerged that she was thinking almost continuously about the bracelet, whether it would really be presented to her in "time," and whether it would "work," etc.

It seemed plausible that the alteration in the patient's sensitivity to metrazol was caused by a *premature activation* of the "inhibitory" mechanism—precipitated by *thinking* about the bracelet. This might serve not only as an explanation for the results of the experiment with metrazol but for the earlier success of the bracelet in the late stage of the aura just prior to the olfactory hallucination.

It thus became essential to prove that the patient's seizures could be arrested by having her think of the bracelet when a spontaneous fit developed. The test was made and *the act of thinking intently about the bracelet proved sufficient to inhibit the seizure*. When the patient merely thought of the bracelet she also developed the olfactory hallucination of jasmine.

The patient reported that it took even longer for the fit to begin to subside when she was thinking of the bracelet than it did when she actually looked at it. She was not certain that there was any change in the time taken to return to normality.

For a period of six weeks the patient continued to arrest her seizures by thinking of the bracelet as the seizure developed. During this period, she observed that on several occasions, when she did *not* think of the bracelet, a spontaneous odour of jasmine suddenly enveloped her. This occurred once at night during this early period and awoke her from sleep. However, at these times she had no subjective manifestations of her seizure.

The spontaneous hallucinations of jasmine, lasting for one to one and a half minutes became increasingly frequent over the next three weeks, during which time she experienced fewer seizures. Those seizures which did develop were arrested by thinking of the bracelet. For *fourteen* full months, the patient has had no seizures at all. She developed no episodes of depersonalization and did not need to rely upon any external method of arresting attacks: she experienced only spontaneous, abrupt (one minute) hallucinations of smell. At these times, she did not "smell" the original odour which was associated with her uncinate discharges, but, instead, was "overwhelmed" by the odour of jasmine.

For the first four to six months these hallucinations occurred at the same frequency (seven to fifteen a month) as did her original uncinate seizures. This six-month period of frequent olfactory hallucinations (but no seizures of any type) was followed by another eight-month period during which she was still free of seizures, but had only three episodes of hallucination. Two of these were at night and awakened her, the third occurred while she was singing.

Although she was at first extremely anxious and preoccupied about her experiences, she soon adjusted to her hallucinations of jasmine, and now that she has no seizures or hallucinations she has returned to a full-time singing career. She considers herself "cured" as she had not, in the previous twenty-six years, been free of seizures for more than a fortnight.

DISCUSSION

In our attempt to "explain" the case reports of Gowers and Lysons, it had been assumed that conditioned reflex had been established in their patients which then served to arrest the focal seizures as the ligatures had done previously. In this patient, a conditioned stimulus (bracelet) arrested uncinate seizures just as successfully as did the primary unpleasant olfactory stimulus. Furthermore, the thought of the bracelet was later sufficient to arrest a seizure.

Hudgins (1933) has shown that the pupillary reflex in man could be conditioned to the sound of a bell, and that a second order conditioned response could then be established between the bell and the spoken verbal command, "constrict." Finally, the spoken command was conditioned, by frequent repetition to the thought "constrict." Upon completion of this complex series of conditioning experiments. Hudgins' subjects could constrict their pupils by merely thinking the word "constrict." The latency of the response was about seven to ten times longer than the latency of the direct pupillary response to light.

Similarly, Jasper and Shagass (1941*a* and *b*), Shagass (1942, 1943) Laufberger (1950), as well as Travis and Egan (1938) conditioned the alpha blocking reaction in the human EEG to a sound. Following Hudgins, they then conditioned the blocking response to the verbal command "block" and finally to the thought "block." Laufberger (1950) conditioned the alpha blocking response to a phoneme and showed that the thought of the phoneme would similarly block the alpha rhythm. In these experiments the investigators were conditioning an electrical response of the cortex to stimuli which were ineffective in altering the EEG pattern prior to the conditioning procedure. Jasper and Shagass (1941*b*) described in detail how every type of conditioned reflex in dogs, as described by Pavlov, could be similarly established in the human EEG by using the alpha blocking response as the test indicator. They were able to produce simple conditioned reflexes, delayed, differential, differential delayed, and cyclical conditioned reflexes. They also showed tracings which clearly depicted "anticipation" of the conditioned blocking response in cyclical conditioning. There seems to be little difference between "anticipation" as seen in Jasper and Shagass' records and the "premature activation of the inhibitory mechanism" which we have just postulated.

Morrell and Jasper (1956) have gone even farther and have convincingly demonstrated in monkeys that not only alpha-blocking responses could be conditioned, but that certain occipital augmentation rhythms (photically activated) could be conditioned in identical fashion. They found that a photic flicker rate of eight cycles per second produced a frequency-specific occipital response, and that this cortical response could be produced by the conditioned stimulus after a suitable number of paired stimuli. Similarly, a cortical response to a twelve cycle per second flash could be conditioned to a 500 cycle per second tone and the frequency of the cortical response to that tone was at 12 cycles per second. Sounding a 1,000 cycle per second tone would not evoke any occipital augmentation pattern.

The work of the Popovs is also most interesting. They, too, have conditioned the alpha-blocking response to a sound stimulus, but they have been primarily studying after-images. They have found that at the time when the alpha rhythm blocks to the specific conditioning sound stimulus, the subject reports seeing after-images—identical to those after-images experienced following the original light flash. They have thus claimed that the after-image is not primarily a retinal reaction, such as might be due to regeneration of visual purple, but, rather a purely cerebral response as it can be produced without light by a conditioned reflex.

These experiments in human beings (Hudgins, Shagass, Jasper, the Popovs, Travis and Egan, Laufberger, etc.) and in lower animals (Jasper, Morrell and Jasper, Morrell and Ross, the Popovs) in which *normal* neurophysiological responses have been conditioned to an indifferent stimulus, and finally (in man) to the thought of the indifferent stimulus, closely parallel our attempt similarly to condition a *pathological* response of neural tissue—a fit.

That pathological neural responses (fits) *can* be conditioned has been known for many years. James Dunsmure (1874) presented a case of a boy whose fits could be readily elicited by patting him on the head. However, if he was prepared for the stimulus, a fit did not occur. Jackson (1887) similarly described a patient whose fits were always precipitated if his face were touched, especially if there was an element of surprise in the touch. If he thought that his face would be touched, the stimulus would not evoke the fit. In this case, the reflex epilepsy could be inhibited. Wilson (1930) described another such case.

In recent years, Mitchell, Falconer and Hill (1954) reported the case of a fetishist with temporal lobe epilepsy who would precipitate fits (autoerotically) by staring at a safety-pin. He found that scissors and paper clips were also effective, but less satisfying methods of producing his fits. Following temporal lobectomy which cured him of both fits and fetish, he told how, previous to surgery, merely "phantasizing" a safety-pin in his mind was an adequate stimulus to produce an attack. In this case, the displacement from the specific stimulus to the intellectual or symbolic conception of it, was still sufficient to "trigger" the mechanism.

We now find an analogy in our patient who was eventually "cured" of her seizures by repeated arrests by sensory stimuli or by their conditioned equivalents. Review of the literature does not reveal a similar case although it is strongly suspected that Gowers' (1881) case may have been due to an identical mechanism. Similarly, the "cure" of focal seizures by repeated application of the ligature which Lysons (1772) described is probably explicable on this basis.

In the case of our patient, the spontaneous hallucinations of jasmine which occurred for six months at the same frequency as did the original seizures, and then disappeared, probably represents an extreme degree of "anticipation" . . . that is, the inhibitory mechanism, once conditioned, is now being activated almost immediately after the initial epileptic discharge commences. With the activation of the reflex fit inhibitory mechanism occurring prior to the development of any *subjective manifestations* of the fit, the patient experiences only the manifestations of the inhibitory reflex (hallucination of jasmine). She would most likely be unaware that a fit had started and might have matured, had this hallucination not occurred. It is not clear, at the present time, why even the hallucinations of jasmine have disappeared. It may represent even a further degree of anticipation, or may possibly reflect a decay in the conditioned reflex as a result of lack of reinforcement.

Recalling S. A. K. Wilson's (1935) remarks about the high frequency of fragmentary seizures in all epileptics, we may wonder if these, too, are not examples of fit inhibition, either by an undetected sensory stimulus, or perhaps by an intellectual event. It is not infrequent to hear a patient describe twice as many auræ as fits and to have him claim that he "fights off" half of his attacks. Such methods of arresting seizures in other of our patients currently under treatment are: "intense concentration on the conversation or on the radio," "rapidly putting my head between my knees," "getting up to walk it off," and "eating a piece of chocolate" (sugar is not effective). In a child of 6 years, his mother has found that his focal, adversive attacks which are followed by complete immobility can be arrested by tickling him at the onset of the adversive movement. Sometimes his fits stop when he sees his mother approach to tickle him. The family of a 19-year-old boy has discovered that a quick jerk of his head in a direction opposite to the first adversive movement will abort a *grand mal* seizure.

Reflex fit precipitation (musicogenic, photogenic, etc.) has been studied extensively, as it has been thought by some to be frequent if specifically looked for, whereas reflex fit inhibition has been almost totally neglected in recent times as it is considered to be extremely rare. Yet we may be fairly certain that the mechanism of one is closely related to the other. They must both represent converse aspects of the process of excitability of neural tissue. This would seem to be a fruitful area for therapeutically oriented research.

SUMMARY

1. A patient who had been able to arrest uncinate seizures by a properly timed, unpleasant olfactory stimulus was conditioned (Pavlov) to a non-specific visual stimulus. After conditioning, seizures were as successfully arrested by the visual stimulus as they had previously been by the olfactory stimulus.
2. It was discovered that the "intellectual" act of thinking about the visual stimulus was equally effective in arresting seizures.
3. Metrazol activation studies following conditioning showed a marked decrease in sensitivity to this drug.
4. The clinical literature referable to conditioned inhibition and conditioned precipitation of seizures is reviewed and the physiological studies of electroencephalographic conditioning are described.
5. An analysis of the physiological mechanisms is attempted.

PART VI

Outcome Studies on the Clinical Application of Self-Control

28

GROUP INSIGHT VERSUS GROUP DESENSITIZATION IN TREATING SPEECH ANXIETY[1]

Donald H. Meichenbaum, J. Barnard Gilmore, and Al Fedoravicius

In two large reviews of the psychotherapy literature, Eysenck (1952, 1961) concluded that only three studies offered even meager evidence for the existence of psychotherapeutic effectiveness. Two of these three studies used the "semantic" psychotherapies of Phillips (1956) and Ellis (1957, 1962); the third approach to yield evidence of effectiveness was the desensitization therapy of Wolpe (1958). Since Eysenck's review, much recent work has seemed to confirm the efficacy of desensitization treatment (Lang, 1969; Paul, 1969b). Yet little research has been conducted to discover what might determine the effectiveness of semantic psychotherapies.

The more traditional insight-oriented psychotherapies do not lend themselves to ready testing if only because their methods are typically too subtle and too difficult to explicate or control experimentally. In addition, in cases where researchers have been brave enough to press on anyway, experimental results have often appeared to show that such therapies are no more effective than are control group procedures. It is argued that this apparent result is quite possibly appropriate to some insight-oriented therapies, but that there are also many distinguishable insight therapies of great efficacy. The authors caution against the effects of what Kiesler (1966) has called the "therapist uniformity myth." When applied to psychotherapy research, the uniformity myth assumes

Donald H. Meichenbaum, J. Barnard Gilmore, and Al Fedoravicius, "Group Insight Versus Group Desensitization in Treating Speech Anxiety," *Journal of Consulting and Clinical Psychology, 36,* 1971, 410–421.

[1] Portions of this paper were presented at the Midwest Psychological Association, May 1969. This study was assisted under Grant 120 of the Ontario Mental Health Foundation.

that findings from most procedures labeled "insight-oriented therapy" will be equivalent since the treatment methods are assumed to be equivalent.

A recent example of the uniformity assumption is illustrated in a comprehensive study by Paul (1966) which compared insight and desensitization treatments of speech anxiety. In describing the treatments in his study, Paul presented an explicit therapist manual of the desensitization treatment; but in describing the insight-oriented psychotherapy he said only, "this treatment consisted of the traditional interview procedures used by the respective therapists in their daily work." The only hint concerning therapist's techniques was given by their scores on a Therapist Orientation Sheet. The explicit treatment techniques used by the therapists to effect insight, and their respective definitions of insight, were not indicated by Paul. Paul found the insight procedures to be ineffective relative to the desensitization treatment in reducing speech anxiety. But just what it was that may not have been effective is not at all clear. It seems too easy to conclude from Paul's data and his discussion that all "insight" procedures are ineffective in treating speech anxiety.

In this study, one particular form of "insight" therapy is used, and some data are presented suggesting when and how this approach can be shown to be effective in the treatment of speech anxiety. The insight approach selected for this study has been derived principally from Ellis's rational–emotive therapy. This treatment technique attempts to make the client aware of those self-verbalizations that can contribute to his maladaptive behavior, and it encourages the client to examine possible incompatible self-instructions and behavior. That cognitive factors such as self-verbalizations may play a large role in mediating emotional responses has been demonstrated in the recent work on emotional labeling carried out by Schachter (1966) and Schachter and Singer (1962). Further, the assumption that maladaptive self-verbalizations mediate the production of anxiety is basic to the treatment approaches of Coué (1922), Korzybski (1933), Johnson (1946), Dollard and Miller (1950), Kelly (1955), Phillips (1956), as well as that of Ellis (1962). It could be very useful to *specify* one form of insight therapy, based on the possible role of self-verbalization in producing either anxiety or calm, and to put it to a well-controlled test.

Thus, this study compared the proven therapeutic technique of desensitization to that of a specific insight-oriented therapy which centered on promoting an awareness of anxiety-producing self-verbalizations. The *S*s suffered from speech anxiety and were treated for that specific problem. "Improvement" was measured on this specific problem, both objectively and subjectively. In order to determine if the relaxation skills taught in desensitization therapy might also prove unusually effective in the hands of *S*s trained for insight into the self-instructions which typically make them tense and anxious, an experimental treatment group given combined desensitization and insight therapy was also included. Two kinds of control groups were included. One kind met their therapists (and held discussions on neutral topics) with the same regularity as did *S*s in experimental groups. This afforded an index of improvement due to factors of attention, "treatment," and any demand characteristics inherent in the measures of improvement. This group was called the speech-discussion placebo control. In addition, a waiting-list control group of *S*s was measured for improvement over the period of the study while awaiting their treatment to be made available.

METHOD

Subjects

Fifty-three volunteer *S*s (35 males, 18 females), ranging in age from 18 to 26 years, all of whom had responded to an advertisement in the university newspaper for "treatment of speech anxiety," participated in the present study. Most of the *S*s were undergraduates, but a few secretaries ($N = 2$) and nonstudents ($N = 3$) from the community also participated. Manifest and subjectively experienced fear in a stressful speech-giving situation were measured before and after treatment, as dscribed below. Following the pretreatment assessment, *S*s were assigned to one of nine groups. One group comprised the waiting-list control group ($N = 9$). The remaining eight groups were of four treatment types, and both psychotherapists in the study treated one of each of these four types. These four types of groups included an insight treatment ($N = 5$ and 6), a desensitization treatment ($N = 6$ and 5), and a combined insight and desensitization treatment ($N = 6$ and 6). Assignment to these nine groups was done randomly, subject to the two constraints of (*a*) matching the groups on sex composition (each group had two females) and (*b*) matching the groups on their speech anxiety as shown by a timed behavioral checklist measure taken in a speech situation prior to treatment. After eight sessions of group treatment, a posttreatment assessment in a test speech situation and a three-month follow-up battery of anxiety self-report scales were administered to all *S*s.

During the school year a Fear Survey Schedule, which assessed the degree of fear toward a range of situations and objects, was administered to several different undergraduate classes. This Fear Survey Schedule was similar to that of Geer (1965), and it measured fears along a 7-point scale. From a sample of 345 *S*s completing this schedule, 15 additional low-speech-anxious *S*s (8 males, 7 females) were selected who indicated no fear (circled "none") both to "speaking before a group" and to "feeling rejected by others." These low-speech-anxious *S*s, who were paid $1.50 to receive the same pretreatment stress condition measures as the speech-anxious *S*s, were interspersed with the high-anxious *S*s during pretesting. Raters of pretreatment anxiety were unaware that such *S*s were included in the study.

These low-speech-anxious *S*s afforded a base-line measurement for each measure of anxiety as elicited in the test speech situation and a comparison group for the high-speech-anxious *S*s before and after treatment.

Instruments

Two general classes of dependent measures were used to assess the relative effectiveness of the different treatment approaches. The first class of measures included behavioral manifestations of anxiety in a test speech situation. The second class of measures included behavioral manifestations of anxiety in a test speech situation. The second class of measures involved self-report indexes which were designed to assess (*a*) the degree to which speech anxiety was a problem for *S* and (*b*) *S*'s emotional state during the speech situation.

Behavioral Speech-Anxiety Measures–During presentation of test speeches, each *S* was scored on the timed behavioral checklist for performance anxiety as developed by Paul (1966). This instrument lists 20 observable manifestations of anxiety, the presence or absence of which are recorded by two pairs of trained observers during successive 30-second time periods of the first four minutes of a speech presentation.

Further behavioral indexes of anxiety were taken from each *S*'s speech. A tape recorder was placed on a table in the assessment room, and all *S*'s speeches were recorded. Several investigators (Boomer & Goodrich, 1961; Davids & Erikson, 1966; Geer, 1966; Mahl, 1956; Pope, Siegman, Blass, & Raher, 1968) have related anxiety to aspects of speech characteristics such as word count, duration of silences, and number of "ah" statements. The present study used these three indexes as additional dependent measures of anxiety.

Self-Report Speech-Anxiety Measures–The four self-report measures used to assess speech anxiety were (*a*) the Personal Report of Confidence of a Speaker (Paul, 1966); (*b*) the Social Anxiety Scale (Watson & Friend, 1969); (*c*) the anxiety differential (Husek & Alexander, 1963); and (*d*) the Adjective Checklist for Anxiety (Zuckerman, 1960). The authors' Confidence of Speaking Scale was Paul's short form (30 true–false items) of the original scale by Gilkinson (1942). The Personal Report of Confidence of a Speaker Scale gave a measure of each *S*'s confidence and ability in making a speech before an audience. The second self-report measure was the 58-item true–false Social Anxiety Scale. This scale consists of two subscales measuring social avoidance and distress and fear of negative evaluation. The Social Avoidance and Distress Scale (28 items) questions the degree of interpersonal anxiety experienced in many social situations. It was used to assess the degree to which the *S*'s speech anxiety is a characteristic reponse style that is elicited in a variety of interpersonal situations versus the degree to which such anxiety is circumscribed to making speeches before an audience. The Fear of Negative Evaluation Scale (30 items) reflects the degree to which *S* worries about people's evaluations of him. The Confidence of Speaking, Social Avoidance and Distress, and Fear of Negative Evaluation scales were administered as pre, post, and follow-up measures to all groups.

Two self-report measures were administered immediately prior to each test speech. One of these was the anxiety differential which uses the semantic differential format for rating a series of words in terms of polar adjectives. It yields a cognitive measure of anxiety. The Adjective Checklist for Anxiety reflects the subjectively experienced emotional state of the *S* during an assessment situation.

Procedure

The *S*s who answered the newspaper advertisement were assessed on two occasions prior to the beginning of treatment. In his first session, *S* was seen individually by a secretary and asked to fill out several self-report measures (the Confidence of Speaking, Social Avoidance and Distress, and Fear of Negative Evaluation scales) together with an open-ended questtionnaire concerning his speech anxiety. In the second session, *S*s were seen by a male graduate student who informed them that they would be required to give a pretreatment test speech before "a group of clinical psychologists, students, and speech people who will help us evaluate your reactions." The *S* was told that the topic of his speech would be "What I expect to get out of college life."[2] The *E* then indicated that he would check to see if the judges were ready, and he had *S* fill out the anxiety differential in the interim. Four minutes later, *E* returned and directed *S* to the speech room (a laboratory room which could seat about eight people). The audience consisted of six judges (three males and three females) who did not give any feedback to *S* (such as eye contact or smiling), thus increasing the stressfulness and standardization of the speech assessment. Prior to beginning his speech, *S* filled out the adjective checklist describing how he felt. During *S*'s four-minute speech, timed checklist frequency counts were taken by four observers, and the speech was tape recorded. This assessment procedure was the same for the 15 low-speech-anxious *S*s.

Following the pretreatment assessment, *S*s were rank ordered on the basis of their behavioral checklist scores, and then they were distributed to the treatment and control groups. The *S*s in the waiting-list group were told

[2] In Paul's (1966) study, *S*s were permitted to select their own topics, usually one they previously gave in speech class. They also served as members of the audience prior to their own speech presentation permitting possible modeling effects. Preliminary pilot work indicated that topic selection and listening to others present speeches significantly affects the degree of speech anxiety manifested.

that "more *S*s applied than was possible to treat and their names were selected by chance not to receive therapy at this time." They were told that a post assessment was necessary and that therapy would be provided in the future if they so desired at that time. No waiting-list *S* later requested such therapy.

The *S*s in the treatment groups were given eight group therapy sessions, following which a postassessment was administered to all high-speech-anxious *S*s. The postassessment differed in only three minor ways from the preassessment, namely, (*a*) all measures were collected in one session rather than two, (*b*) the topic of the posttreatment speech was "What I expect to be doing in the future," and (*c*) the stressfulness of the postassessment was increased somewhat by changing the testing room and by increasing the size of the audience with five additional members. A posttreatment questionnaire designed to assess *S*s' perception of treatment and resulting change in behavior was also administered.

A three-month follow-up assessment of the self-report measures (Personal Report of Confidence of Speaking, Social Avoidance and Distress, and Fear of Negative Evaluation scales) was mailed to each *S*. All but one *S* (who was in the waiting-list group) returned his questionnaire.

Therapists

The two senior authors, both clinical psychologists, with three and five years' clinical experience, respectively, administered the group treatments. The two therapists differed in that one had experience with individual and group desensitization, whereas the other therapist had no prior experience with desensitization. The orientation of the therapists also differed as assessed by the Therapist Orientation Sheet (Paul, 1966), with one indicating primary affiliation to behavioral therapy approaches and the educative approaches of Kelly and Ellis. The other therapist specified primary affiliation to the psychoanalytic orientations of Freud and Dollard. All treatment sessions were tape recorded and discussed regularly by the therapist in order to insure comparability of treatments. An attempt was made in such discussions to insure that both therapists followed the prescribed treatment manuals exactly.

Treatments

Each of the two therapists administered each of the four treatment groups for eight weekly sessions of 60 minutes each. The therapists were instructed that the criterion of improvement was to be a reduction in speech anxiety, and an attempt was made to relate each of the therapies to this goal.

Group Desensitization–This treatment followed the general procedures described by Wolpe (1958), Lazarus and Rachman (1960), and, in detail, that of Paul and Shannon (1966). The basic procedures included progressive relaxation training, group hierarchy construction, imagery training, and group desensitization as described by Paul and Shannon (1966). A 16-item anxiety hierarchy was used which contained items related to public speech situations and to other social anxiety-producing situations. The *S*s were encouraged to practice relaxation at home and, once mastered, to use relaxation procedures in any potentially stressful situations.

Group Insight-Oriented Psychotherapy–The insight treatment approach emphasized the rationale that speech anxiety is the result of self-verbalizations and internalized sentences which are emitted while thinking about the speech situation. The *S*s were informed that the goals of therapy were for each *S* to become aware of (gain insight into) the self-verbalizations and self-instructions which he emitted in anxiety-producing interpersonal situations and, in addition, to produce both incompatible self-instructions and incompatible behavior. These groups discussed the following points: (*a*) the specific self-verbalizations group members had emitted in the pretreatment speech situation; (*b*) the range and commonality of interpersonal situations in which they made the same or comparable self-verbalizations; and (*c*) the irrational self-defeating and self-fulfilling aspects of such statements. No behavioral rehearsal or assertive training (Wolpe & Lazarus, 1966) was conducted in therapy, but toward the end of therapy, *S*s were encouraged by both the therapist and other group members to emit incompatible self-verbalizations and to behave in accord with the new self-instructions.

Combined Group Desensitization and Insight–This treatment group followed the same procedure as for the desensitization group, but in Sessions 4 through 8 the insight procedure was also followed. These last four sessions were divided, with the first half-hour used for the insight procedure and the second half-hour for group desensitization.

Speech-Discussion Placebo Group–This group was included to assess the extent of improvement resulting from nonspecific group treatment factors such as expectation of relief, suggestion, therapist-patient relationships, and group spirit. The group also provided a control for the therapeutic effects on speech-anxious *S*s of weekly group discussions. An effort was made to involve these *S*s in a treatment procedure which was therapeutically neutral except for the therapist–client, and client–client relationship. The rationale presented to this group was as follows:

> Your speech anxiety is learned and can be unlearned by speaking in this group. By participating in discussions with others you will come to realize that you can do so without experiencing anxiety and tenseness. This ability will in turn transfer to other groups and other situations.

In order to keep the affect as neutral as possible, only bland, neutral, intellectual topics were discussed, for example, legalized gambling, Canadian-United States relationships. Any reference topics which could elicit strong affect were redirected or terminated by the therapist, for example, speech anxiety and Vietnam. An attempt was made to have each *S* contribute to the discussion. In the first two sessions, *S*s questioned whether such a procedure could aid them, but they were willing to try it. By the third session, the majority of *S*s thought it was helping, and this question did not arise again. Even though the project was conducted toward the end of the school year when academic pressures were increased, attendance in this group (as well as all other treatment groups) was excellent, namely, an average of over 90% attendance in all groups.

Waiting-list Control Group–This untreated control group received the same pre–post follow-up assessments as the treatment groups. This group was included to assess the extent of improvement from (*a*) nonspecific therapeutic factors accruing from the environment, (*b*) "spontaneous remissions" (Goldstein, 1960, 1962), (*c*) assessment procedures, and (*d*) the promise of treatment sometime in the future.

RESULTS

Reliability of Dependent Measures

Before proceeding to the analyses of treatment effectiveness, the reliability of total scores over pairs of observers on the timed behavioral checklist for pretreatment and posttreatment speeches was determined. The range of correlations between pairs of observers for the speech assessments was .78 to .90 ($N = 65$), with a median correlation of .85, which is consistent with Paul's (1966) finding of high reliability and objectivity of such a measure in assessing behavioral manifestations of anxiety. The reliability of the tape-recorded speeches for the behavioral speech measures of word count, duration of silences, and the number of "ah" statements ranged between .85 and .93 ($N = 30$), with a median correlation of .88. The analyses of the behavioral indexes of anxiety dependent variables are restricted only to the pretreatment and posttreatment assessments, leaving only the self-report measures to be included in the additional follow-up assessment.

The initial equivalence prior to treatment of the three treatment groups and the two control groups on the behavioral and self-report measures was ascertained by simple analyses of variance ($F < 1.0$). (See Table 1 prescores for the comparability of groups prior to treatment.)

In analyzing *S*'s change level of speech anxiety from the pretreatment to posttreatment assessments, the first major factor examined was possible therapist differences. Even though the therapists differed in their experience with the desensitization treatment and therapy orientation, no significant or suggestive therapist effect or Therapist $\times$ Treatment interaction ($F < 1.0$) was found on any of the dependent measures. The therapist variable was not considered further in the analyses.

Primary Measures of Improvement

The amount of anxiety *S*s manifest in the pretreatment–posttreatment test speech situations was assessed by (*a*) the timed behavioral checklist, (*b*) recorded speech behavior, (*c*) self-report of anxiety on the adjective checklist, and (*d*) a cognitive measure of anxiety, the anxiety differential. Each of these dependent measures was subjected to a Lindquist Type I analysis of variance testing for effects of treatment, trials (pre–post), and Treatment × Pre–Post interaction. Group means and standard deviations for both pretreatment and posttreatment conditions are presented in Table 1. These data do not include results from two speech-discussion placebo *S*s and two waiting-list *S*s who refused to complete the posttreatment test speech because they found it too upsetting. Strong persuasion and financial inducements could not alter their decisions. It is assumed that these *S*s remained at the same or increased level of speech anxiety, and thus the differences reported here between treatment and control groups are likely to be *underestimates.*

The analyses of the test speech dependent measures revealed only a highly consistent and significant Treatment × Pre–Post interaction, indicating different improvements among treatment groups. The Treatment × Pre–Post interactions for all dependent measures were significant ($p < .05$, two-tailed). Multiple comparisons of the improvement scores (Duncan's test, Edwards, 1960) were performed on each of the dependent measures. Figure 1 graphically presents the mean reduction in anxiety from pretreatment to posttreatment.

It can be seen in Figure 1 that the improvement of *S*s in the various treatment groups was similarly reflected by each dependent measure. Results on the behavior checklist measure (rated objective manifestations of anxiety while giving a speech) closely matched the results from the adjective checklist measure (a self-report measure of subjective state). There were significant group differences in improvement seen with the two checklist measures, as indicated by the Treatment × Pre–Post interactions ($F = 4.04$ and 4.23, respectively, $df = 4/43$, $p < .01$). Comparisons among groups on the behavioral and adjective checklist measures revealed that (*a*) waiting-list control *S*s showed significantly less improvement than did all other groups ($p < .05$), (*b*) speech-discussion controls and combined desensitization plus insight group *S*s did not improve differentially, (*c*) both these speech-discussion and desensitization plus insight groups showed significantly less improvement than did the desensitization group and the insight-treatment group ($p < .05$), and (*d*) the desensitization group and the insight-treatment group produced roughly equal, and marked, improvement over control conditions. Figure 1 further shows that with the cognitive measure of anxiety (the anxiety differential), the three treatment conditions (desensitization, insight, and desensitization plus insight) did not significantly differ from each other,

Table 1: Mean Pre–Post Anxiety Scores on Test Speech Measures

Treatment	N	Behavior Checklist		Anxiety Checklist		Anxiety Differential		Word Count		Duration Silences in Four Minutes		No. "ah" Statements	
		X	SD	$\bar{X}$	SD	X	SD	$\bar{X}$	SD	$\bar{X}$	SD	$\bar{X}$	SD
Desensitization	11												
Pre		143.9	10.3	14.6	3.1	72.8	16.8	397.4	192.3	69.7	47.8	19.1	6.3
Post		130.0	6.7	8.1	2.7	60.7	12.6	457.6	160.1	58.5	39.2	18.4	9.2
Insight	11												
Pre		148.9	5.8	17.1	2.9	76.8	14.9	336.2	155.3	64.6	22.9	25.7	17.9
Post		134.1	5.4	11.8	3.1	66.5	11.9	416.1	105.1	53.5	43.1	24.1	14.9
Combined desensitization and insight	10												
Pre		147.0	8.1	15.8	2.1	77.9	13.8	345.1	131.9	51.8	40.6	24.4	13.1
Post		139.4	4.7	12.7	2.8	68.4	12.7	422.1	126.4	40.0	28.1	27.1	16.2
Speech discussion	10												
Pre		145.3	7.2	16.4	3.1	79.6	10.7	323.5	149.4	72.4	47.5	18.6	14.7
Post		137.7	3.9	14.1	2.5	74.9	7.1	353.9	147.1	146.1	74.9	28.5	9.3
Waiting list	7												
Pre		143.5	7.6	13.6	4.9	68.1	13.6	334.3	101.8	71.0	51.6	18.4	10.3
Post		144.9	14.1	12.7	4.2	70.7	18.4	333.6	159.9	174.1	71.7	26.7	19.9
Individual insight[a]	6												
Pre		143.2	12.8	16.8	1.6	77.3	13.9	302.0	109.5	96.6	48.3	11.7	7.2
Post		133.9	7.8	10.7	3.5	70.2	20.3	425.6	156.1	45.5	40.2	13.6	9.9
Low speech anxious	15												
Pre		128.1	8.5	9.8	2.3	54.6	6.5	588.0	120.6	113.4	28.5	19.3	3.8

[a] See Footnote [3].

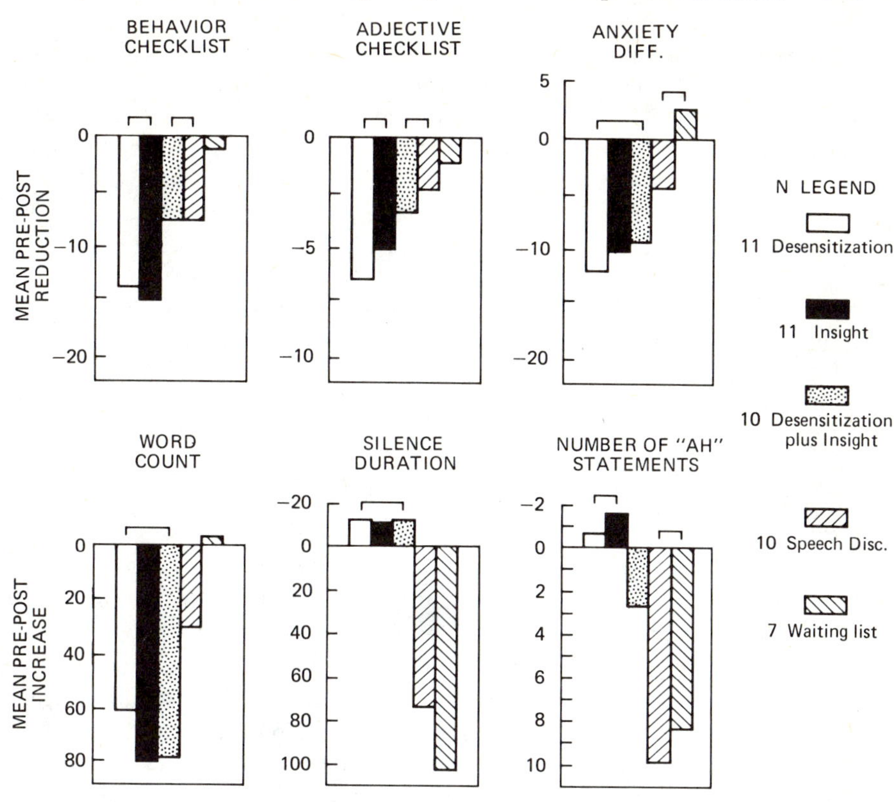

FIGURE 1. Mean reduction and increase in manifestations of anxiety from pretreatment to posttreatment on test speech measures (groups not connected by solid line are significantly different at .05 level).

but they did show significantly greater improvement than did the speech-discussion and waiting-list control groups ($p < .01$). Finally, it can be seen in Figure 1 that on the three measures of speech disruption, there was similar evidence that the desensitization and the insight-treatment groups experienced the greatest improvement ($p < .01$) compared to control conditions, while the combined desensitization plus insight-treatment group experienced a similar degree of improvement on increased number of words, and on decreased silence time, while showing less (but significant, $p < .05$) improvement on decreased number of "ah" statements, as compared to control conditions.

Thus, all measures of improvement shown in Figure 1, objective and subjective, overt and covert, showed generally similar results. To recapitulate, greatest (and approximately equal) improvement was seen with the desensitization and the insight-treatment conditions. Less consistent but general improvement was evidenced by the combined desensitization plus insight group and the speech-discussion (placebo control) condition. The latter conditions appeared significantly more improved than did the waiting-list control condition. Waiting-list control *S*s showed relatively unchanged levels of anxiety over the period of the study, and in measures of speech disruption they showed a slight worsening in performance. This worsening may have reflected the increased stressfulness of the post-treatment speech test. It should be kept in mind that the above results do not include postassessment scores from two speech-discussion and two waiting-list control *S*s, who were too anxious to be willing to participate in a second speech test. Assigning these *S*s zero improvement scores, and reanalyzing the data, further increases the significances and trends noted above.

Additional Self-Report Measures of Improvement

Three additional self-report indexes were used in this study. Two of them, the Social Avoidance and Distress Scale and the Fear of Negative Evaluation Scale, presumably reflect a more general index of chronic *social* anxiety as compared to the measures discussed above which reflect aspects of social anxiety in an acute stress situation, that is, while giving a test speech. The third self-report measure considered here, the Confidence of Speaking Scale, presumably reflects chronic *speech* anxiety, again as compared to acute speech anxiety experienced in this test. Analyses of variance yielded only significant Group $\times$ Trial interactions ($p < .05$) for each of these three general measures. Figure 2 presents the scores on each of the measures for pre, post, and follow-up periods. Here too we find a consistent pattern across measures. The three treatment groups (desensitization, insight, desensitization plus insight) were significantly improved at post-treatment and follow-up assessments over the speech-discussion and waiting-list control groups ($p < .05$), but they did not significantly differ among each other. The improvement which was reported at the posttest for the treatment groups continued in evidence at the three-month follow-up. The speech-discussion and waiting-list groups did not significantly differ from each other on the posttest, but they did significantly differ at the follow-up assessment on the Confidence of Speaking and Fear of Negative Evaluation measures ($p < .05$). On both these measures, the speech-discussion group was significantly worse than its pretreatment performance ($p < .05$). In summary, the conclusions drawn from the analyses of the test speech measures are further supported by the analyses of these general self-report measures.

Comparison with Low-Speech-Anxious Subjects

The performance of low-speech-anxious *S*s provides a base-line index of measured "anxiety" for each measure used, as gathered in the pretreatment speech situation. Table 1 also presents the means and standard deviations for low-speech-anxious *S*s on the dependent measures. A comparison of pretreatment performance of low-speech-anxious *S*s ($N = 15$) with high-speech-

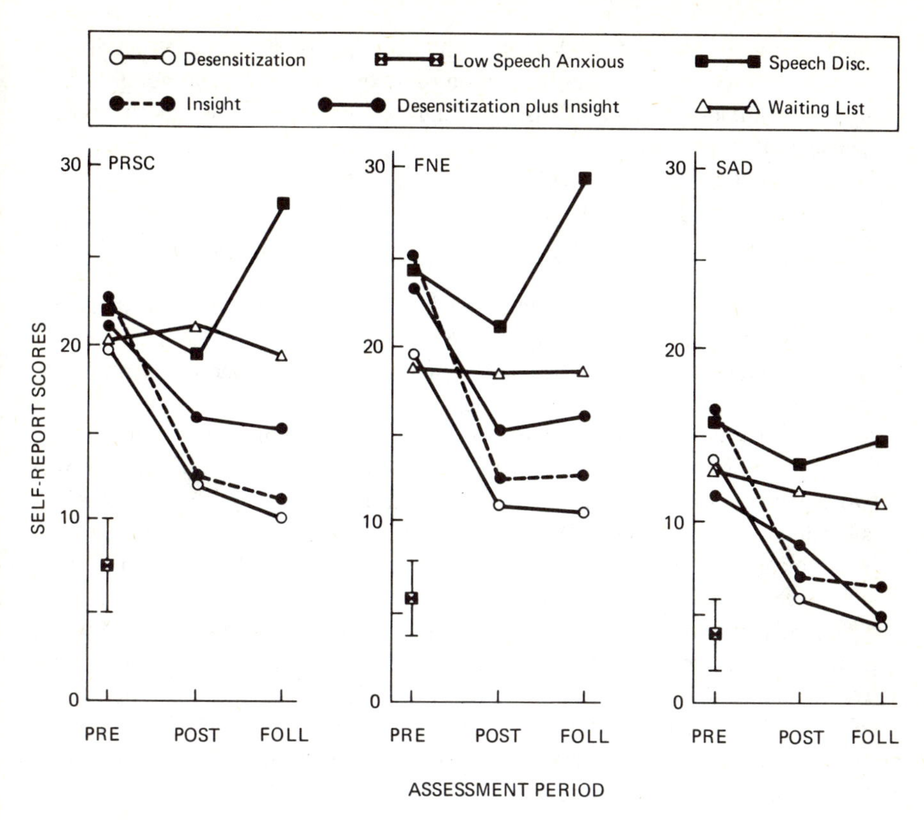

FIGURE 2. Mean self-report of anxiety on Personal Report of Confidence of a Speaker (PRCS), Fear of Negative Evaluation (FNE), and Social Avoidance and Distress (SAD) scales at pretreatment and posttreatment and at three-month follow-up. (Note that "improvement" is reflected here by lowered scores.)

anxious *S*s ($N = 53$) indicated that on all dependent measures except number of "ah" statements there was a significant difference ($p < .05$) prior to treatment.

The posttreatment performance of high-speech-anxious *S*s in the two most effective treatment groups (desensitization and insight) on behavioral, cognitive, and self-report measures approximated, and did not significantly differ, from low-speech-anxious *S*s. This finding provides further evidence that the treatments were highly effective in removing speech anxiety.

An interesting paradox is apparent in comparing the silence behavior of low-speech-anxious *S*s who were in the three treatment groups (desensitization, insight, and desensitization plus insight). The effect of treatment was to reduce silences to an extremely low level ($\bar{X} = 46.1$ seconds) from an initial moderate level ($\bar{X} = 67.28$ seconds). This reduction is in the opposite direction from the behavior of low-speech-anxious *S*s ($\bar{X} = 113.4$ seconds). It is suspected that the low-speech-anxious *S*s were using silences constructively to think about the content of their speech; whereas for high-speech-anxious *S*s, silences allowed time for the production of anxiety-engendering thoughts which increased anxiety further. Thus, the high-speech-anxious *S*s on the posttest speech may have produced less silences than they did on the pretest speech in order to control their potential anxiety.

Post Hoc Treatment × Patient Interaction

Listening to *S*s who volunteered for treatment suggested that they were of two general types. For one type of *S*, speech anxiety appeared to be a part of a characteristic shy response style that was manifested across a number of interpersonal situations; whereas the other type of *S* gave indications that speech anxiety was only a problem in public speaking situations. The *S*s within each treatment group were classified into one or another of these two client types on the basis of their pretreatment scores on the Social Avoidance and Distress Scale. This scale assesses the generality of the *S*'s interpersonal anxiety. A median split (14 and above) was used for identifying *S*s who were generally shy versus those *S*s (scoring below 13) who appeared to suffer only circumscribed public speaking anxiety. The median split for each treatment and control group of *S*s was as follows: (*a*) desensitization group—five *S*s above median, six below median; (*b*) insight group—six above, five below; (*c*) desensitization plus insight group—four above, seven below; (*d*) speech-discussion placebo group—seven above, five below; and (*e*) waiting-list control—four above, five below.

A significant Treatment × Type of Client interaction was found in the desensitization, insight, and desensitization plus insight groups, but not in the speech-discussion and waiting-list control groups. In the desensitization group, those *S*s ($N = 6$) below the median on the Social Avoidance and Distress Scale (i.e., *S*s truly speech anxious) in comparison with those ($N = 5$) above the median (i.e., *S*s socially anxious) benefited significantly *more* from the desensitization treatment ($p < .05$) as assessed on the behavior checklist and cognitive measure of anxiety (anxiety differential). The mean change scores for *S*s below and above the median on the Social Avoidance and Distress Scale, respectively, were 12.5 and 2.5 on the behavior checklist and 19.5 and 3.5 on the anxiety differential. The two types of *S*s in the desensitization group did not significantly differ on any of the other dependent measures.

Thus, for two dependent measures, there was clear evidence to suggest that desensitization treatment was effective primarily with those *S*s having anxiety specific to speech situations. Further, a consistent pattern of complementary results was found for the insight and desensitization plus insight groups. The *S*s above the median on the Social Avoidance and Distress Scale (socially anxious), manifested significant improvement from insight procedures ($p < .05$) as measured by the behavior checklist, anxiety differential, word count, and number of "ah" statements. The mean change scores for the insight group *S*s below ($N = 5$) and above ($N = 6$) the median on the Social Avoidance and Distress Scale, respectively, were 3.7 and 18.5 on the behavior checklist and 5.5 and 12.5 on the anxiety differential. Thus, for four dependent measures, there was clear evidence to suggest that insight therapy (as defined in this study) was effective primarily with those rather generally anxious *S*s for whom desensitization procedures seemed ineffective.

In summary, *S*s for whom speech anxiety was a generalized response style significantly benefited from the group insight treatment and the combined desensitization and insight treatment, whereas *S*s for whom speech anxiety was a circumscribed problem confined mainly to the public speaking situation significantly benefited from the group desensitization treatment. That such findings should reach significance with the small *N*s of this study make this result interesting and highly suggestive.

DISCUSSION

The results of this study indicate that a group insight treatment emphasizing self-instructional training was as effective as was a group desensitization in reducing speech anxiety.[3] Insight-oriented psychotherapy and desensitization therapy produced a consistently greater measurable reduction in anxiety as reflected on behavioral, cognitive, and self-report measures than did all control conditions and other forms of therapy. Further, the superiority of desensitization and of insight treatment was maintained at a three-month follow-up period. The combination therapy of insight with desensitization resulted in less consistent reduction of anxiety, and on the behavior and adjective checklists it did not lead to significant improvement over the speech-discussion (attention placebo) group. The combined group (desensitization plus insight) received insight training only in the last four treatment sessions. In retrospect, it was felt that this treatment sequence did not leave sufficient time to explore incompatible self-instructions and behaviors. The research on emotion (Schachter, 1966; Schachter & Singer, 1962) and on cognitive appraisal under stress (Lazarus, 1966, 1967) suggests that modifying both the autonomic arousal as well as the accompanying cognitive determiners or self-verbalizations should provide maximal change. Variations of the present combination

[3] Further evidence for the effectiveness of the present insight treatment was found. The senior author treated six additional speech-anxious *S*s in individual insight treatment over five sessions because their schedules did not permit them to participate in group treatment. These *S*s were assessed in the same manner and at the same time as the other *S*s. The analyses of the test speech measures and self-report measures indicated that individual insight treatment was as effective as group insight desensitization in reducing speech anxiety. See Table 1 for performance on anxiety measures in pre–post speech assessments. Also, the significant Client × Treatment interaction found with the group insight *S*'s was evident with the individual insight *S*s.

of desensitization and self-instructional insight therapy, which attempt to deal with both components of the emotional response, may still prove to be the most effective treatment for reducing speech anxiety.

The speech-discussion (attention placebo) group showed reduced anxiety in the posttreatment assessment, although the amount of reduction was significantly less than the desensitization and insight groups. The speech-discussion group data suggest that there is a therapeutic benefit accruing just from weekly group discussion and the non specific aspects of therapy. However, at the three-month follow-up, the speech-discussion group reported significantly greater interpersonal anxiety than they had in their original pre-treatment assessment. These increased follow-up anxiety self-report scores for the speech-discussion group may reflect *S*s' communication to *E*s that treatment was ineffective and/or a veridical report of felt anxiety. The waiting-list control group remained stable in their level of speech anxiety across assessments.

That findings emerged which were consistent across dependent measures and were significant with modest *N*s should serve to indicate the reliability of these data. It would appear that there may be a number of insight therapies which, when explicated and put to a controlled test, would prove of equal or greater efficacy in treating different forms of anxiety. Perhaps we will be ready soon to see many studies begun that are concerned with determining which specific aspects of therapies are curative aspects.

Perhaps most intriguing in this study was the post hoc finding that different types of clients received differential benefit from desensitization and insight treatments. Clinicians have long dreamed of matching clients with therapies to best effect. The present data suggest that an insight therapy based on attending to, and modifying, self-verbalizations in an anxiety-producing situation differentially benefits clients with high, but not low, social distress. Conversely (at least with respect to removing speech anxiety), desensitization works well with clients low, but not high, in general social distress. This latter finding is consistent with an increasing literature (Clark 1963; Gelder, Marks, Wolff, & Clarke, 1967; Lang & Lazovik 1963; Lazarus 1963; Marks & Gelder 1965; Wolpe 1964) which suggests that systematic desensitization works well with monosymptomatic phobias and poorly with so-called free-floating anxiety states. The Social Avoidance and Distress Scale (Watson & Friend 1969) may prove to be very useful in determining probable success with desensitization therapy and with the insight-type approach followed in this study. Additional studies, treating different symptoms and complaints, can suggest how general our findings may be.

Finally, the present study is one of a series designed to assess the role of cognitive factors in behavior modification. The insight approach used in this study emphasized making the client aware of his self-verbalizations and then modifying them. We have explored the usefulness of other treatment techniques such as modeling, operant conditioning, and anxiety relief to modify such self-verbalizations (Meichenbaum, 1970). In each case, therapeutically attending to the patient's self-verbalizations as well as his overt maladaptive behavior has led to significant behavioral change, greater generalization, and persistence of treatment effects.

SUMMARY

Three forms of group treatment were compared for their relative therapeutic effectiveness in reducing speech anxiety. Treatments included desensitization, "insight," which emphasized making *S*s aware of both their anxiety-producing self-verbalizations and ways they might counter such verbalizations, plus a combined desensitization and insight treatment condition. Both a "discussion group" (attention placebo) and a waiting-list control group were also included. Results indicated that the insight group was as effective as the desensitization group in significantly reducing speech anxiety over control group levels as assessed by behavioral, cognitive, and self-report measures given immediately after posttreatment and later at a three-month follow-up. The desensitization group treatment appeared to be significantly more effective than insight treatment with *S*s for whom speech anxiety was confined to formal speech situations; conversely, insight group treatment appeared to be significantly more effective with *S*s who suffer anxiety in many varied social situations.

29

REDUCTION OF SOCIAL ANXIETY THROUGH MODIFICATION OF SELF-REINFORCEMENT

AN INSTIGATION THERAPY TECHNIQUE[1]

Lynn P. Rehm and Albert R. Marston

Skinner (1953) suggests that one of the ways in which individuals control their own behavior is by the administration of rewards to themselves without environmental restrictions and contingent upon certain behaviors. A series of studies (Bandura & Kupers, 1964; Kanfer, Bradley, & Marston, 1962; Kanfer & Marston, 1963a, 1963b; Marston, 1964, 1965a; Marston & Kanfer, 1963) have investigated variables which influence this phenomenon of self-reinforcement in experimental analogues. In discussing the relevance of self-reinforcement for psychotherapy, Marston (1965b) asserted that certain clinical problems can best be conceptualized and treated in psychotherapy in self-reinforcement terms. Behavioral problems which are described as involving a low self-concept can be seen as a malfunction of the client's self-reinforcement. In particular, a desired behavior may occur but is negatively evaluated, leading to discomfort; or the client is capable of the desired behavior, but emits it infrequently because of lack of positive self-reinforcement.

The present experiment was an attempt to demonstrate the therapeutic

Lynn P. Rehm and Albert R. Marston, "Reduction of Social Anxiety through Modification of Self-Reinforcement," *Journal of Consulting and Clinical Psychology, 32,* 1968, 565–574.

[1] This paper is based on portions of a thesis submitted by the first author in partial fulfillment of the requirements for the degree of Master of Arts at the University of Wisconsin, 1966. This investigation was supported, in part, by a United States Public Health Service Research Fellowship Award 5-F1-MH-29, 410-02 (MTLH) from the National Institutes of Health to the first author, and in part by Research Grant MH-12235 awarded by National Institutes of Mental Health to the second author.

utility of a technique for handling a clinical problem involving faulty self-reinforcement. The procedure combines elements from a number of sources, but essentially uses manipulation of overt self-reinforcement to effect a positive change in self-concept with associated reduction in anxiety and increased approach to feared situations. The experimental effort was exploratory in the sense that it was aimed at demonstrating the viability of the technique as a whole, compared to other procedures, rather than at assessing the separate contribution of the several elements independently. The general strategy was to compare a group receiving the total experimental therapy with two control therapies (*a*) nonspecific counseling; (*b*) minimal urging toward self-help.

The study investigated college males who reported a problem in meeting and dating girls; that is, the problem involved feeling uncomfortable in social situations with girls and avoiding such situations. It was assumed that *S*s were otherwise adequately functioning males with at least a minimum repertoire of social skills, but that they evaluated themselves negatively when they did contact girls or they avoided heterosexual contact because of negative self-evaluation. The experimental therapy was a behavior therapy of the instigation type (Kanfer & Phillips, 1965) in that major emphasis was on the training of *S* in systematic self-help procedures. The major elements of the treatment involved gradual approach to feared situations via a hierarchy of stimuli, objective restructuring by *S* of his behavioral goals, and encouragement of increased positive self-reinforcement.

METHOD

Subjects

The *S*s for the experiment were 24 college males who responded to either a verbal announcement made in psychology classes or a mimeographed notice sent to men's residence halls. The announcement described the type of problem to be considered and requested anyone who felt he had such a problem and wanted help in working on it to contact the Psychology Department Research and Training Clinic for an interview. Thirty students made appointments for the experiment. Of these, two reported homosexual problems and were referred for a general clinic intake. A third volunteer was rejected because he was under the care of a psychiatrist at the time. Three *S*s dropped out of the experiment during the first week and were replaced. Two had been assigned to the Self-reinforcement therapy group and a third to the Nonspecific therapy group.

In addition, the criterion test battery was administered to 12 "normal" *S*s. These were male students from Introduction to Psychology classes who signed up for an experiment and received points toward the course grade for serving.

Design

A 3 × 4 factorial design was employed in the analysis of the experiment. Three therapy groups consisted of the experimental therapy group, labeled Self-Reinforcement (SR), a Nonspecific therapy control group (NS) and a No Therapy control group (NT). Four therapists each saw two *S*s in each of the three therapy groups. Data for the Normal Group were handled in separate analyses.

Screening

The screening interview conducted with each *S* consisted of the following: (*a*) A screening questionnaire, followed by a brief interview, was used to determine that the client did indeed feel he had a problem, that uncontrollable environmental restrictions were not the cause, and that the client was otherwise functioning adequately. (*b*) A position within the factorial design was randomly assigned to each *S*, with the restriction that the experimenter doing the screening did not assign *S*s to himself as therapist. (*c*) The *S*s assigned to SR constructed a desensitization type hierarchy from 30 standard items describing heterosexual social interactions. The items were typed on ¾ × 5 inch cards which *S*s were asked to place in rank order as to the amount of discomfort they would experience in each situation.

The *S*s were then asked to designate a point on the hierarchy at which they felt their discomfort would become serious enough that they would presently begin to avoid such situations. Two additional hierarchy points were then designated which divided items above and below this point into two smaller blocks, thus creating four hierarchy levels. The *S*s were asked to try to make these divisions at points where there would be a significant increase in discomfort, with the limitation that there be at least four items at each level.

For instance, for one *S*, the first hierarchy level included the item, "Taking a seat next to a girl in class," the second level included, "Being introduced to a girl while with a group of your friends," the third level included, "Calling a girl to ask her for a date," and the fourth level included, "Dancing with a girl on a date." The most intensive physically sexual items on the list involved kissing. All *S*s were told that the study would not be concerned with problems of more intense sexual behavior.

(*d*) The *S*s were provided with information sheets which they were asked to read before the first therapy session to give them an idea of the theoretical background of the experiment. The information sheet for the SR therapy group explained the concepts of reinforcement and self-reinforcement and the use of hierarchies and teaching machine techniques. The information sheet for the NS therapy group gave the rationale that the experiment was an attempt to conduct short-term therapy in a more efficient manner. Some general principles of nondirective therapy were included. The information sheet for the NT group gave the rationale that the experiment was examining the effect which volunteering for therapy and the consequent commitment to change would have on an individual's own approach to the problem.

(*e*) A battery of tests was administered to all *S*s at the screening session. The taped Situation Test to be described below was given during the session proper and the paper and pencil tests were given to each *S* to be taken in the waiting room.

Test Battery

The Situation Test was made up of two alternate forms each consisting of 10 social situations presented orally on tape. The items were presented by a male voice which described a situation involving a girl (e.g., "As you are leaving a cafeteria, a girl taps you on the back and says . . ."). A female voice then read a line of dialogue to which the *S*s were asked to respond aloud (e.g., "I think you left this book."). The *S*s were instructed to respond as they would in a real-life conversation and their responses were recorded on a second tape recorder. The experimenter left the room during the test. The two forms of the Situation Test were equated for mean ranked discomfort level. Twenty male undergraduates from Introduction to psychology classes had ranked the original pool of 20 mimeographed items as they felt they would be ordered by male peers with the proposed problem.

Seven different scales were derived from the experimental *S*s' responses to the taped Situation Test. The *S*s rated their own subjective anxiety for each item on a 7-point scale from "none" to "extreme." Estimates of the parallel forms reliability of this and the other scales derived from the Situation Test were obtained from the 12 normal *S*s who took both forms of the test in a balanced sequence, within the same testing session. The parallel reliability for *S*s' anxiety ratings was $r = .87$ ($p < .01$).

The recorded responses were independently rated by three pairs of undergraduate girls on three dimensions: anxiety, adequacy of response, and likability. Rated anxiety and adequacy scores for each protocol consisted of the total points summed over the 10 items each of which was rated on a 7-point scale. Likability was rated on a single continuous 50-point scale for the overall impression derived from the 10 responses on each protocol (Stoler, 1963). The sets of responses for pretesting and posttesting for all experimental *S*s plus responses to both forms of the test by the normal *S*s, a total of 72 protocols, were retaped in a random order on seven tapes. These tapes, which consisted of 10 or 11 sets of responses, were then rated by each rater in a separate order. Interrater reliability was obtained by having each rater rate one tape twice (first and last in their sequence). The second rating was used in obtaining mean scores for the two raters for each testing. Inter-

Table 1: Reliabilities of Dependent Measures from Situation Test (Pearson r*s)*

Measures	Parallel Forms[a]	Intrascorer[b]		Interscorer[c]
S anxiety	.87*	—	—	—
Rated Anxiety	.82*	.46	.77*	.47*
Rated adequacy	.67*	.94*	.85*	.69*
Rated likability	.72*	.58*	.93*	.65*
Anxiety signs	.05	—	—	—
Log latency	.74*	—	—	—
Number of words	.85*	—	—	—

[a] Based on normal *S* group, $N = 12$.
[b] Based on random selection of 10 *S*s' data.
[c] Based on two ratings of all *S*s' data, $N = 72$.
* $p < .01$.

rater reliabilities were obtained from correlations between the pairs of raters. The reliability data for these three ratings are summarized in Table 1.

In addition, the recorded responses were scored for average number of words per response, average log latency of response, and number of anxiety signs. Anxiety signs were scored one point for each response such as: a failure to respond, stuttering of a word, repetition of words or phrases, halting within a sentence, unfinished sentences or mispronunciations. The resulting total was divided by the average number of words per response and the resulting proportions were given an arc-sine transformation in order to approximate more closely a normal distribution.

A Situation Questionnaire consisted of the 30 heirarchy items used in the SR therapy presented in a random order. The Ss rated the amount of discomfort they would feel in each situation on a 7-point scale. The Manifest Anxiety Scale (MAS; Taylor, 1953) and Fear Survey Schedule (FSS), Form III (a revised version of the Fear Survey Schedule developed by Wolpe and Lang, 1964) were administered as measures of generalized anxiety. The specific FSS item, "Being with a member of the opposite sex," was also analyzed separately.

The Adjective Check List (ACL; Gough & Heilbrun, 1965) was given and scored as a self-concept measure. The number of positive adjectives checked was divided by a number of positive plus negative items checked. Four male graduate students in clinical psychology indicated whether they thought each adjective would be indicative of a positive or negative self-concept if used by a male college student to describe himself. Complete agreement between these judges determine the valence of the adjectives. Only adjectives which obtained complete agreement were scored (123 positive plus 138 negative out of a total of 300 adjectives). The obtained proportions were transformed by an arc-sine function to more closely approximate a normal distribution.

Procedure for Therapy Sessions: Self-Reinforcement Therapy Group

In the first session the therapist handled questions and reiterated some of the principles involved. The therapist then explained to *S* that he was to work systematically up the hierarchy by attempting to get into situations at given levels and then evaluate his performance and reward himself with self-approval for each situation. The *S*s were instructed to make records each night of each situation encountered during the day on forms supplied by the therapist. The forms required a brief description of the situation, including date, time, and what transpired, the equivalent hierarchy item number, the hierarchy level, and the number of points awarded. Amount of self-reinforcement was systematized by a point system. Zero points were to be given when the situation resulted in *S*'s overt avoidance or escape. One point was to be given for getting into the situation with minimal performance of the situation's requirements. Two points were to be given for any performance beyond this minimum, and three points were to be given for any situation in which *S* felt he did particularly well.

The therapist and client recorded sample goals for 1–3-point rewards for each of the hierarchy items. Goals were established using the individual *S*'s internalized standards for his own behavior, rather than possible external reinforcements which the *S* might desire from the situation or the amount of comfort he might experience. For instance for the item, "Calling up a girl for a date," a 2-point goal for one *S* was "extending the conversation to other topics." Goals such as "getting the date" or "feeling relaxed on the phone" were discouraged by the therapist.

In the first session, *S* was requested to focus on the lowest level of the hierarchy for the following week. The *S*s were encouraged to seek out these situations in particular during the week, although they were also to record situations at other levels as they occurred. Hierarchy items were to be considered as examples of classes of situations involving similar interpersonal relationships.

In subsequent sessions, *S*s described each of the situations which they had recorded during the week and reported the points given to themselves. The therapist reinforced the giving of 2 or 3 points for situations with verbal approval. For situations in which *Ss* gave themselves 0 or 1 point, the therapist asked them how they might have changed their behavior to increase their self-evaluation. Therapists did not suggest new kinds of behavior. Increases in the number of points given were encouraged by the therapist. The therapist recorded the number of points given, the equivalent item number, and hierarchy level. The hierarchy level on which *S*s were instructed to focus increased in a standard manner: Level 1 the first week, Level 2 the second week, Level 3 for the third and fourth weeks, and Level 4 the fifth week.

Procedure for Therapy Sessions: Nonspecific Therapy Group

For this group, therapists were instructed to employ a basically non-directive therapy technique which could include reflection and clarification of feeling, low-level interpretations and questioning for information. Interview content was unrestricted except that therapists were instructed not to suggest any specific behavior which *S* should carry out and not to make any direct positive or negative evaluations of the client's behavior. Therapy sessions were ½ hour long.

Procedure for Therapy Sessions: No Therapy Group

Procedure for this group involved weekly sessions where *S*s were asked to report on how they conceptualized their problem, how this conceptualization had changed over the previous week, what they had done during the week to work on the problem, and what their plans for the following week were. Therapists asked general questions and took notes on the answers. They encouraged *S*s to think through and work on the problem on their own but made no specific suggestions and gave no evaluation of what *S*s were doing.

Posttesting Session

All *S*s saw the experimenter who did the screening for posttesting within 1 week after the final therapy session. The same battery of tests was readministered with the addition of a Posttherapy Questionnaire. The first 16 items of this questionnaire made up a brief form of the Barrett-Lennard Relationship Inventory (Barrett-Lennard, 1962, as revised in Spotts, 1965). Four items were selected from each of the inventory subscales. The rest of the questionnaire consisted of questions concerning *S*s' attitude toward the experiment, their progress, and their estimation of their own improvement. Statements were presented and *S*s were required to indicate their degree of agreement or disagreement on a 6-point scale. They were also asked to indicate the number of dates during treatment and whether this was a change in frequency.

Follow-up

A follow-up study was conducted in the period 7–9 months after the end of the original study. All *Ss* who could be located were contacted and asked to come in to retake the test battery plus a follow-up questionnaire concerning their dating behavior and attitudes.

Therapists

The therapists were four third-year graduate students in clinical psychology, all of whom had had at least one summer of clinical experience plus one semester of therapy training in a practicum. Two of these students (one of whom was the first author) also conducted the screening interviews. No *S* was seen by the same person for screening and therapy. Therapists met for two 1-hour sessions prior to the experiment in which instructions were reviewed and examples of situations, goals, point giving, etc., were discussed. Therapists were asked to assume the attitude that all groups should show improvement and to attempt to convey this attitude to all *S*s.

RESULTS

Alternate Taped Situation Test Forms

To avoid possible practice effects, two equivalent forms of the Taped Situation Test were employed. The order of presentation of these two forms was reversed for half the *S*s in order to assess mean changes for all *S*s. The *S*s within the same cell in the 3×4 factorial design were treated as replications under the assumption that the two forms of the test were in fact equivalent. As a partial check on this assumption, Therapy Group $\times$ Test Form analyses of variance were performed for all 24 *S*s on pretesting, posttesting, and difference scores for all Taped Situation Test variables. The only significant test form effect was found for difference scores in average number of words per response. The form sequence BA led to a greater average increase in number of words than sequence AB, $F = 4.82$, $df = 1/18$, $p < .05$. Since this was the only significant finding out of 18 analyses, and since even a tendency toward and effect on the other variables would only increase the within cells error variance, Therapy Group $\times$ Therapist analyses were considered appropriate.

Comparison of Pretreatment Experimental Subjects with Normal Group

To test whether the experimental *S*s did indeed form a deviant, more anxious sample of the male college population, *t* tests were performed comparing the pretherapy scores of the experimental *S*s with the scores of the normal group. The results are presented in Table 2. All variables, except the rater's adequacy ratings and the average number of words per response on the Situation Test, significantly differentiated the two groups. The two nonsignificant results were also in the predicted direction.

Table 2: Comparison of All Treated Ss at Pretesting with Normal Ss

Variable	Normal *S*s *M*	Normal *S*s *SD*	Experimental *S*s *M*	Experimental *S*s *SD*	*t*
Situation Questionnaire	71.8	16.50	121.3	21.62	6.79***
*S*s' anxiety ratings	23.8	6.78	37.3	7.98	4.87***
Raters' anxiety ratings	35.9	11.61	44.2	5.91	2.24*
Log latency	.288	.123	.687	.140	7.98***
Anxiety signs	.12	.132	.35	.383	2.58*
Adequacy ratings	46.9	7.58	45.8	4.10	<1.00
Number of words	10.1	4.10	9.2	3.87	<1.00
Taylor Manifest Anxiety Scale	15.8	7.24	23.3	8.10	2.64*
Fear Survey Schedule	199.0	14.70	228.1	63.54	2.08*
Gough Adjective Check List	2.21	.194	1.77	.400	4.31**

Note.—For normal *S*s, $N = 12$; for experimental *S*s, $N = 23$.
* $p < .05$.
** $p < .01$.
*** $p < .001$.

Analysis of Improvement Measures[2]

Table 3 summarizes the results of the improvement scores between pretesting and posttesting. Since no significant therapist or Therapist × Therapy interaction effects were found, only therapy group *F*s are shown. All differences were scored so that a positive number indicates improvement. Thus, a decrease in latency, a decrease in ratings of anxiety and an increase in ratings of adequacy are all shown as positive numbers. For those variables which yielded a significant positive correlation between pretesting and difference scores, the differences were divided by the pretesting scores and the analyses of variance were performed using the resulting proportions. This was done for the subjective anxiety ratings made by the *S*s (Table 3, Line 1; $r = .63$, $N = 23$, $p < .01$), the anxiety ratings of the taped responses (Table 3, Line 2; $r = .43$), and the Situation Questionnaire scores (Table 3, Line 8; $r = .34$, $N = 23$, $p < .05$).

Analyses of the Situation Test variables yielded significant results for two of the variables. Although the *F* value for *S*s' anxiety ratings did not reach significance, subsequent *t* tests supported the specific hypothesis that the SR group would show significantly greater improvement than either of the control groups (Table 3, Line 1). Similarly, the analyses of variance of the average number of words scale (Table 3, Line 7) did not yield a significant

[2] One *S* dropped out of the SR group after two therapy sessions. Analysis of variance used a least squares solution (Ferguson, 1959, p. 259) for the unequal *N* problem.

Table 3: Summary of Comparisons of Treatment Groups on All Dependent Measures

Line No.	Variable	Treatment Mean Change Scores			*t*-Test Values		
		SR	*NS*	*NT*	*SR–NS*	*SR–NT*	*NS–NT*
1	Situation Test: Subjective anxiety	.33**	.16	.13	1.87**	2.13*	1.17
2	Situation Test: Rated anxiety	.11	.07	.19*	.46	−.88	1.34
3	Situation Test: Rated adequacy	4.17	2.20	2.50	.69	.58	.11
4	Situation Test: Rated likability	19.1*	7.4	8.9	1.21	.52	.69
5	Situation Test: Anxiety signs	.19	.06	−.11	.62	1.48	.85
6	Situation Test: Log latency	.09	−.02	.08	1.74	.17	1.57
7	Situation Test: Number of words	4.03**	1.60	.05	1.79*	2.93**	1.14
8	Situation Questionnaire	.42**	.19*	.09	2.42*	3.43**	1.01
9	Fear Survey Schedule	10.1	21.3	24.0	−.60	−.69	.14
10	Fear of opposite sex	1.43**	1.00*	−.13	.86	3.12**	2.26*
11	Manifest Anxiety Scale	5.14*	−1.50	.88	3.00**	1.93*	1.07
12	Adjective Check List	.45**	.21	.17	1.49	1.89*	.31

Note.—SR = Self-Reinforcement; NS = Nonspecific; NT = No Therapy.
* $p < .05$; For treatment means columns, * refers to significance of *t* tests of mean change vs. zero change.
** $p < .01$.

therapy group effect but subsequent *t* tests supported the hypothesis that the SR group would show a significantly greater increase in output in social situations than either of the other groups. As shown in Table 3, the SR group also had the greatest increase in rated adequacy (Line 3) and likability (Line 4) and the greatest decrease in overt anxiety signs (Line 5) and latency of response (Line 6). None of these last four differences reached significance, however.

The therapy groups varied significantly on the Situations Questionnaire scores (Table 3, Line 8). The SR group reported a significantly greater decrease in discomfort in the 30 situations than either the NS or NT groups as shown by the *t* test.

On the Fear Survey Schedule no significant differences were found between the Therapy groups (Table 3, Line 9). However, for the single item most relevant to the problem investigated (Being with a member of the opposite sex), a significant groups effect was found (Table 3, Line 10). Both the SR and NS groups reported greater decreases in rated fear than the NT group. The SR group reported a greater decrease than the NS group, but this difference was not significant.

Differences in generalization of anxiety reduction were found on the Manifest Anxiety Scale (Table 3, Line 11). A significant groups effect was found on general anxiety reduction and significant *t*-test differences were found between the SR group and the two control conditions which did not differ significantly from each other.

The Adjective Check List was scored as a self-concept measure under the hypothesis that the SR group procedure should raise the frequency of positive self-concept statements to a greater degree than the other two procedures. Only partial support was found for this hypothesis. The SR group obtained the greatest increase in positive self-concept adjectives checked. However, the overall group effect was not significant and of the *t* test for this hypothesis, only the difference between the SR and NT groups proved to be significant.

The Posttherapy Questionnaire consisted of a collection of items covering several areas. Two items concerned the number of dates which the *S*s had during the experiment as a measure of overt behavioral change. The SR group reported a greater frequency of dates than either of the two groups which did not differ from each other (Mann-Whitney *U* test, $p < .05$). The *S*s also indicated whether their dating during the experiment was an increase, about the same, or a decrease as compared with their usual dating. A comparison of the SR versus the combined NS and NT groups on their indication of an increase versus no change or a decrease in dating yielded a significant $\chi^2 = 3.84$, $df = 1$, $p < .05$, the SR group more often indicating an increase in dating.

The remaining items required *S*s to respond on a 6-point scale, as to the strength of their agreement or disagreement with a series of statements. Nine of these statements concerned feelings of improvement or change in attitude during the experiment (Table 4). One-way analyses of variance of agreement scores yielded significant therapy group effects for items concerning more interaction with girls (Line 1), more anticipated interactions with girls (Line 2), more independent self-evaluation (Line 4), more self-confidence with girls (Line 5), and a general statement of feeling helped by the experiment (Line 9). On all but the last item *t* tests demonstrated significantly greater agreement by SR group *S*s than by either of the other groups. The SR and NT groups did not differ significantly on the item concerning feelings of being helped by the experiment.

About one half of the questionnaire items concerned the quality of the relationship with the therapist. Sixteen items were selected from a revised

Table 4: Summary of Treatment Comparisons on Posttherapy Questionnaire Items

Line No.	Item	*M*			Treatment Effects	*t*-Test Values		
		SR	*NS*	*NT*	*F*[a]	*SR–NS*	*SR–NT*	*NS–NT*
1	20 Interacts more with girls	4.7	3.4	2.8	4.48*	2.08*	3.05**	<1.00
2	21 Probably will interact more in future	4.4	1.9	2.9	8.19**	4.17**	2.54**	1.66
3	22 More self-confident with girls	4.0	1.9	2.6	4.03*	2.91*	1.88*	−1.03
4	23 More insight into problem	3.6	2.3	3.1	1.56	1.78**	<1.00	−1.18
5	24 Can evaluate self more independently	4.1	2.4	3.0	4.67*	3.14**	2.03*	−1.11
6	25 Did better with girls than had expected	3.4	2.0	3.0	2.17	2.08*	<1.00	−1.45
7	26 More aware of feeling about self	3.0	2.0	3.3	1.94	1.50	<1.00	−1.87
8	32 Experiment was helpful	4.0	2.4	3.5	4.29*	2.93**	<1.00	−2.03
9	33 More insight into self	3.3	2.6	3.4	<1.00	<1.00	<1.00	<1.00

Note.—SR = Self-Reinforcement; NS = Nonspecific; NT = No Therapy.
[a] $df = 2/20$.
* $p < .05$.
** $p < .01$.

version of the Barrett-Lennard Relationship Inventory. Four items were drawn from each of the original four subscales of positive regard, empathic understanding, congruence, and unconditionality of regard. Total scores with a possible range of 0–80 were derived from each *S*, the 5-point item scale being reversed for negatively stated items. A two-way analysis of variance for therapy and therapist effects yielded no significant effects. Nor were any subsequent *t* tests between therapy groups significant. Means for the three groups were 54.9 for SR, 60.6 for NS, and 55.5 for NT. There was no evidence from this data that relationship factors were responsible for any greater improvement on the part of the SR group. In fact, this group rated the therapists as least positive in the relationships.

The remaining nine items of the Posttherapy Questionnaire concerned attitudes toward the experimental procedures and purpose of the experiment. No significant results were found in one-way analyses of these data.

SR Group Records

The SR group procedure was aimed at increasing (*a*) the number of interactions with the opposite sex, (*b*) the level of involvement in these interactions as operationalized by the hierarchy, and (*c*) the amount of positive self-reinforcement resulting from these interactions. The average number of interactions recorded by the *S*s for the 5 weeks of recording were, in order, 13.2, 9.7, 8.0, 8.9, and 6.7. The general downward trend over weeks was the reverse of what was expected but may be accounted for by several factors. Initial enthusiasm and ease of accessibility may account for the greater number of situations in the early weeks. Later on, *S*s tended to seek out only the higher, more difficult, and less frequent situations and in some cases failed to report some situations low on the hierarchy which then seemed less important.

The averages of each *S*'s mean item level on the 30-point hierarchies for all *S*s in the SR group were 10.0, 14.5, 16.2, 17.6, and 17.3 for the 5 weeks of recording. An analysis of variance of the individual *S* means yielded a significant weeks effect, $F = 2.79$, $df = 4/30$, $p < .05$. A trend analysis of these data yielded a significant linear component over weeks, $F = 9.06$, $df = 1/30$, $p < .01$. The SR group *S*s did make progress up the hierarchy during the experiment.

The averages of each *S*'s mean number of points awarded to himself for the situation were 2.39, 2.63, 2.68, 2.81, and 2.77 for the 5 weeks. An analysis of variance of the mean number of points per situation yielded a weeks effect which did not reach significance, $F = 2.02$, $df = 4/30$, $p < .10$. A trend analysis of these data yielded a significant linear component, $F = 7.21$, $df = 1/30$, $p < .05$. The SR group did increase in amount of self-reinforcement during the experiment as defined by the mean number of points per situation which they awarded themselves.

Follow up Treatment Differences

Sixteen of the original 23 *S*s were located and retested during the follow-up period (6 SR, 4 NS, and 6 NT). The NS and NT *S*s were grouped into one combined control group for follow-up comparisons. Pretesting to follow-up differences were compared for the resulting two groups on the various dependent variables. The SR group showed significantly greater improvement at the follow-up period on their self-report measures: (*a*) Situation Questionnaire, $t = 2.57$, $p < .05$, (*b*) *S*'s anxiety ratings on the taped situation test, $t = 1.99$, $df = 14$, $p < .05$ and (*c*) Taylor Manifest Anxiety Scale scores, $t = 2.02$, $df = 14$, $p < .05$. On the follow-up questionnaire SR

*S*s more strongly endorsed the items "I understand myself better now," $t = 1.84$, $df = 14$, $p < .05$, and "I feel I can evaluate my behavior in social situations more adequately now," $t = 2.02$, $df = 14$, $p < .05$. No significant differences were found on items concerning dating, though the SR group reported a mean frequency of dates twice as great as the combined control group (twice/month vs. once/month).

DISCUSSION

Using a population whose severity of pathology lay somewhere between the normal experiment volunteer and the patient who spontaneously seeks psychotherapy, this experiment has demonstrated greater improvement for the experimental therapy group (SR) than for either of the control groups on a variety of measures. In terms of Lang's (1964) analysis of fear into three modes of expression, greater reduction in anxiety has been shown in (*a*) several measures of verbal report of discomfort in heterosexual social situations, and (*b*) an approximation to direct measurement of overt-motor change (i.e., reports of more dates with girls and increased verbal output in the Situation Test). The third, somatic, mode was not tapped in the present study. In addition, generalization of improvement was demonstrated by greater reduction in Taylor Manifest Anxiety Scale scores by the SR group and a greater increase in positive self-concept was suggested by Gough Adjective Check List scores. While a number of the significant differences disappeared in the analyses of the follow-up data, a sufficient sample of the dependent measures, particularly those involving self-report, continued to show the superiority of the experimental therapy to warrant serious considerations of this approach to behavior modification.

Since the strategy of this research involved an initial combining of several elements in the experimental therapy, the control groups did not allow for a clear-cut identification of the active factors in the SR therapy. The control groups did seem to demonstrate that improvement was not due to factors such as commitment to change or a positive relationship with the therapist. Therefore, at this stage the elements of the SR therapy need to be further analyzed, both for theoretical reasons and to specify future control conditions.

The SR therapy was based on the assumption that overt behavior and experienced anxiety can be modified by the manipulation of cognitive states, that is, covert self-reactions. This assumption is essentially the one made in traditional insight psychotherapy. The difference, at least in intent, was the concentration on a specific category of cognitive response (i.e., self-evaluation or self-reinforcement) in a systematic manner, employing learning techniques to manipulate overt verbalizations of these responses.

The therapy was designed to shape positive self-reinforcement in such a way as to increase its probability of occurrence in the presence of the discriminative stimuli arising from the performance of the desired behavioral response, that is, approach to heterosexual social situations. In turn, the increased self-reinforcement was assumed to increase the probability of the desired approach response on future occasions. The therapist acted, in theory, almost as if the patient were two organisms: one socially responding and one self-evaluating. Alternatively, he acted as if he were attempting to shape a sequence of two chained responses: that is, a social approach response and a self-evaluating response.

According to this analysis, if *S*'s positive self-reinforcing behavior can be enhanced, then the positive change in social behavior should be self-sustaining, independent of the therapist. The problem then is to elicit the original positive self-evaluations. Several procedures were aimed at this goal. Individual situations were differentiated and arranged into a hierarchy. Marston (1965b) suggested that an individual's self-concept in a particular area may be tied to a single self-descriptive label. By differentiating among these situations, *S* is aided in evaluating his behavior in each situation individually. The formation of a hierarchy also is a means of differentiating situations on a dimension of difficulty, and of encouraging *S*'s behaving in a graded series of problem situations.

Explicit behavioral goals were set up with each individual *S* in accordance with his own criteria for varying degrees of success in each situation. The setting of minimal goals for each situation was stressed to *S*. Kanfer and Marston (1963a) demonstrated increased self-reinforcement with instructions facilitating lower criteria. Covert self-evaluation is assumed to be a function of many cues in an ongoing interaction. The experimenters instructed and encouraged *S*s to use only the carrying out of various behavioral acts as their goals and bases for self-evaluation. Goals such as not feeling nervous or getting a positive reaction from another person were discouraged. The stimuli to which *S* was to respond were delimited to more clearly observable behavior. To some extent this can be seen as altering the perceived stimulus context in which *S*'s self-evaluations are made. Relearning in this context might be expected to later generalize to other contexts such as perception of feedback from others.

The mechanism of generalization of a behavior change brought about in therapy continues to be a difficult problem. Most patients are not monosymptomatic, though one symptom may be focal. Do we need to treat each symptom or each area of behavior deficit? One of the hopes of the SR approach is that self-evaluation responses have a very flat generalization gradient. As has been indicated earlier, many patients suffer from overgeneralized *negative* self-evaluation. It is possible that *positive* self-evaluation will also generalize broadly, and, in combination with the patient's training in the use of response hierarchies, serve as a mediating mechanism for the patient to shape other response clusters.

Finally, a comment about anxiety. The patients reported experiencing anxiety and the experimenters used reported reduction in anxiety as a major measure of improvement. Yet the patients were explicitly told to avoid using absence of anxiety as a criterion for SR, and the above analysis of the SR therapy approach avoided use of the concept of anxiety. Therefore, an additional, untested assumption of the approach must be stated: negative self-evaluation is a primary cue for anxiety; reduction of the former will reduce the latter. A corollary of this would be that positive self-evaluation is a cue for responses which are incompatible with anxiety. At this stage of development, it is not possible to go further than this oversimplified statement of the relationship. The positive results of this study seem to confirm the assumption, but much work is needed to determine whether reduction of anxiety could have occurred without any emphasis on or apparent change in self-evaluation responses.

This analysis of the SR therapy points to several needed controls for future research. These can be stated in the form of the questions: "Is effective therapy due to: (*a*) instruction and reinforcement of use of SR, (*b*) use of hierarchical approach to anxiety-producing situations, (*c*) the statement of explicit behavioral goals in each situation, (*d*) the de-emphasis of external evaluation and/or anxiety reduction as immediate behavior change goals?" Correlational analyses in the present study provided inadequate separate evaluation of these elements, and future research must experimentally perform the separation.

SUMMARY

Male college students who reported anxiety in social situations involving females were seen in one of three therapy conditions. The experimental therapy (SR) involved increasing *S*s' rate and accuracy of positive self-reinforcement using a hierarchy of situations which *S*s sought out between sessions. One control treatment (NS) used nondirective techniques. The second control (NT) involved instructions to *S*s to work on their own and report weekly. Pretesting and posttesting difference scores yielded greatest improvement for the SR group on (*a*) self-reports of anxiety and overt behavior; (*b*) verbal output in a test simulating social interaction; and (*c*) generalization to scores on the Manifest Anxiety Scale and Adjective Check List.

30

SELF-DIRECTED PROGRAM FOR WEIGHT CONTROL

A PILOT STUDY

Mary B. Harris[1]

Attempts to deal with the undesirable behavior of overeating have been spectacularly unsuccessful. Although a great number of causal agents or correlates have been postulated, such as depression (Simon, 1963), anxiety (Cauffman & Pauley, 1961), power orientation (Suczek, 1957), a variety of other personality problems (Bruch, 1957; Kaplan & Kaplan, 1957, who list 28 suggested meanings of obesity; Shipman & Plesset, 1963), insufficient exercise (Mayer, 1955), presence of night-eating syndrome (Stunkard, 1959a), lack of correlation between report of hunger and gastric motility (Stunkard, 1959b), obesity of parents (Cappon, 1958), more dependence on external stimuli such as flavors and time of day to regulate hunger (Schachter, 1967), and no doubt many others, no clear causal relationships have been substantially detailed. An equally large variety of treatments have been tried, ranging from such nonacademic means as low-calorie products, exercise salons, yoga, and reducing clubs to hypnosis (Erickson, 1960), dietary instruction (Young, Moore, Berresford, Einset, & Waldner, 1955), appetite depressants and other drugs (Silverstone & Solomon, 1965), general medical advice (Stunkard, 1958), psychoanalysis and other forms of psychotherapy (Bruch, 1957) group discussion of physical and emotional factors (Harmon, Purkonen, & Rasmussen, 1958), aversion-relief therapy (Thorpe, Schmidt, Brown, & Castell, 1964), recording all eating (Ferster, Nurnberger, & Levitt,

Mary B. Harris, "Self-Directed Program for Weight Control: A Pilot Study," *Journal of Abnormal Psychology, 74,* 1969, 263–270.

[1] The author wishes to express her appreciation to Albert Bandura for his generous assistance with all phases of the study.

1962; Stollak, 1966), self-control (Ferster et al., 1962; Goldiamond, 1965), aversive counterconditioning with shock (Stollak, 1966; Wolpe, 1958), operant conditioning with shock (Meyer & Crisp, 1964), and aversive counterconditioning with nausea (Cautela, 1966b).

In general, the reported attempts to treat overweight people fall into two categories: case histories of techniques which proved successful with one or a very few patients (Cautela, 1966b; Erickson, 1960; Ferster et al., 1962; Goldiamond, 1965; Meyer & Crisp, 1964; Thorpe et al., 1964; Wolpe, 1958) and survey studies of patients in a medical setting, most of which have reported a general lack of success in effecting any long-range weight reduction (Franklin & Rynearson, 1960; Harmon et al., 1958; Shipman & Plesset, 1963; Silverstone & Solomon, 1965; Young et al., 1955). An experimental study by Stollak, using aversive counterconditioning therapy with electric shock and adequate control groups, reported the same poor results (a mean net loss of less than 5 lb.). The inadequacy of treatment has been nicely summarized by Stunkard (1958)—"most obese persons will not stay in treatment for obesity. Of those who stay in treatment, most will not lose weight and of those who do lose weight, most will regain it [p. 79]." The evidence to disconfirm this description has not yet appeared.

An examination of the contingencies governing addictive behavior in general and overeating in particular shows several reasons why this type of behavior should be so resistant to change. Addictive behaviors such as overeating provide immediate positive reinforcement for the individual, while the reinforcement for refraining from eating is usually extremely delayed. Moreover, the aversive consequences of overeating are typically delayed for weeks or even years. As Eysenck (1961b) has pointed out, therapies based on pairing aversive reinforcement with the performance of the undesirable behavior are likely to be ineffective in the long run, because the fear of the negative consequences will tend to be extinguished when the behavior is performed without the negative reinforcement following. In addition, there are two other variables which make overeating behavior particularly resistant to alteration. Both Ferster et al. (1962) and Goldiamond (1965c) have pointed out that eating behavior occurs in a very wide range of situations and is under the control of many stimuli other than those physiological ones causing hunger. A second factor, one unique to overeating among the addictions, is that one cannot be delivered from temptation. Drugs, cigarettes, sexual perversions, and alcohol can all be given up completely and the stimuli associated with them can be avoided; however, everyone must eat at least two or three times a day, and it is impossible to avoid exposure to situations and performance of behaviors one wishes to avoid. Thus the control of eating shares elements with the control of other undesirable appetitive behaviors but is further complicated by the facts that the stimuli for eating are ubiquitous and that some eating behaviors must be performed several times a day.

The study to be discussed attempted to use some of the specific procedures and methods of analysis which have been found useful in controlling both overeating and other undesirable behaviors. Many of these techniques, particularly those of Ferster et al. (1962) and Goldiamond (1965c) place a very strong emphasis on the development of self-control through altering the stimulus conditions under which the behavior occurs and generating self-produced consequences for the behavior. A second major influence was the use of aversive conditioning, both operant (Meyer & Crisp, 1964) and classical (Stollak, 1966; Wolpe, 1958), particularly the nausea conditioning of Cautela (1966b). For the present study, nausea has several advantages over electric shock. It is completely under the individual's control, can be used in any situation, and is a response directly antagonistic to eating. In addition, a group setting was used in this research, primarily because of convenience, but also to take advantage of any slight increase in motivation which group discussion and support might generate.

Because long-term control of eating has been so refractory to change, it was felt that there was little to be gained by employing an attention-placebo control group in addition to a no-treatment control group. For the same reason it was decided to study the efficacy of a treatment approach combining several different components rather than comparing different techniques. The study was thus designed as a broad program to produce change by use of all the procedures which might assist an individual in attaining control of his own eating behavior by gradually approximating the eating pattern he eventually wanted to maintain. Drugs, lists of forbidden foods, or rigid rules of only three meals per day were not used, as they were felt to be useless in the maintenance of permanent habits. Although the procedures used were often geared to the individual's specific problems with eating, the type of approach should prove amenable to extension to dealing with other types of addictive behaviors.

METHOD

Subjects

The *S*s for this study were both men and women who had answered an advertisement in the Stanford University newspaper, who were at least 15 lb. overweight, and who were not being medically treated for overweight or any serious illness. Two individuals who spontaneously began to discuss their psychiatric problems in a 10-minute interview with *E* were not included in the study. From the pool of satisfactory *S*s, two sections of three men and five women each who had the same available time for meetings were selected, along with a random group of three men and five women from the remaining potential *S*s to serve as a control group.

Control Group

The members of the control group were truthfully told that the experimental groups would not be meeting during their available hours. They were then asked if they would attempt to lose weight on their own and if they would consent to be reweighed at the conclusion of the experiment. All *S*s agreed. They were then weighed without shoes on a commercial bathroom scale, to the nearest half pound, given a calorie chart, and reminded that the only way to loose weight was to change their eating habits permanently.

Treatment Procedure

The two experimental sections of eight *S*s each met with *E* twice a week for approximately 2 months until the end of the school quarter. At the beginning of every meeting *S*s were weighed individually without shoes on a commercial bathroom scale to the nearest half pound. The *S*s were all given calorie charts and asked to keep a record of their normal eating habits for 1 week and of their daily intake, including place and time, for the next several months. At the first meeting and approximately every 3 weeks thereafter *S*s completed a brief questionnaire consisting of eight rating scales. Four of the scales concerned their levels of tension and depression both generally and with specific reference to eating; three scales concerned temptations to eat rich foods, large meals, and snacks; and one concerned time thinking about food. One purpose of this questionnaire was to ascertain whether any mood changes would accompany or result from the process of weight reduction, as is suggested by such theories as "obesity as a depressive equivalent" (Simon, 1963). Another purpose of the rating scale was to see whether changes in the temptation to eat would accompany changes in eating behavior.

Three very general aspects of the program were discussed thoroughly with *S*s. It was stressed that the program was designed to enable each individual to develop permanent eating habits he could maintain indefinitely. For this reason no arbitrary restrictions were placed on diet, and the individual was urged to consider what type of permanent eating pattern he would like to maintain. Along with the emphasis on establishing permanent habits there was an emphasis on awareness of what one was eating, especially caloric content and food value, and of the reasons for eating and the situation in which the eating occurred. A third general aspect of the treatment program was its emphasis on making only gradual changes. It was felt that making drastic changes, although perhaps producing greater immediate loss, would make it too difficult to maintain the changes indefinitely. The *S*s were urged to make only small changes which they were sure they could maintain and which were in the direction of the permanent eating pattern they desired to establish.

Techniques

Three general types of techniques for approaching their goal of altered eating habits were recommended to *S*s during the first 2 months of the program. First, *S*s were told about the concepts of positive and negative reinforcement, and it was explained to them how eating behavior was controlled by immediate positive reinforcement and only very delayed negative reinforcement. All *S*s were asked to consider the positive outcomes maintaining their eating and to hand in a list of the aversive consequences causing their desire to lose weight. In group discussions suggestions were made as to methods useful for making reward for refraining from eating more immediate and for making aversive consequences come immediately after beginning to eat; among the suggestions were the reciting of the list of reasons for losing weight when tempted to overeat, the viewing of an unattractive picture of oneself in a bathing suit when tempted, self-rewards of money, movies, clothes, etc. for every day or week of good eating habits or for every pound lost. It was emphasized that food should not be used as a reward.

The second group of techniques concerned the stimulus control of eating behavior and attempted to limit the situations which were associated with eating. The *S*s were asked to analyze the stimuli governing their eating behavior and were given suggestions about limiting the number of situations in which they eat and of stimuli connected with eating. Among these suggestions were many concerning limitations of place and time of eating—for example, try to eat sitting in only one chair at the same table or in as few places as possible; never eat while standing or in the office, bedroom, living room, etc.; try to eat meals and planned snacks only at certain definite times during the day. Other suggestions concerned the limitation of the availability of other reinforcements for eating and of tempting foods—for example, don't eat while reading, watching television, studying, etc.; try to avoid walking past candy machines, snack bars, etc. The *S*s were also informed of some Schachter's research (Schachter, 1967) demonstrating the control of eating behavior by external rather than internal stimuli in overweight people.

The third general group of suggestions dealt with the actual behaviors involved in eating. It was pointed out that many overweight people, particularly people on diets, eat much more rapidly than people of normal weight, and that it takes at least 15 minutes after beginning to eat before one begins to feel the effects of the food. It was thus suggested that *S*s try to break up the chain of eating by not putting any more food on the fork until they had finished chewing and swallowing the last bite, that they chew their food very slowly and with great attention to taste and texture like a gourmet, that they practice taking short breaks of not eating during a meal, and that they begin to try out all of these suggestions only near the end of a meal when they are not so hungry that these behaviors would become aversive. It was also recommended that they attempt to practice leaving a little bit of every food on their plate, rather than automatically eating it all.

Throughout the presentation and discussion of all these techniques for controlling eating habits, it was emphasized that these were all methods for self-control of these behaviors. Although each technique should prove to be useful in some cases, it was recognized that certain techniques would be differentially useful for certain individuals; for this reason, each *S* was asked to try out all techniques which he felt might be appropriate for regulating his own behaviors and to try to commit himself to one small change at a time in the direction of his permanent eating habits. After the above meetings were completed, so that *S*s had learned principles and techniques of reinforcement and self-control of eating behaviors, they were given a paper summarizing these principles and techniques. A list of low calorie foods and beverages suggested for cooking and eating was also given to them.

Two additional aspects of the treatment procedure were the discussion of nutrition and training in relaxation. A nutritionist spoke to *S*s about diet in general, answered many questions about the nutritional and caloric values of various foods, and made brief verbal and written comments to *S*s about the nutritional adequacy of their individual eating records. The *S*s were also given training in relaxation exercises by listening to a tape and reading a manual designed by *E* to accompany the tape. The relaxation exercises were presented as a alternative to eating in dealing with tension, depression, and boredom.

Differential Treatment of Subgroups

After a period of approximately 2½ months and following a change of schedule for those *S*s who were university students, each of the two earlier experimental sections was subdivided into an aversive conditioning subgroup and a continuation subgroup. As two participants had withdrawn from the program, only the remaining 14 *S*s were subdivided. The division was made into two subgroups such that each had four from one original section and three from the other, each had three males and four females, three good friends were put in one subgroup, each had about the same number of those who showed regular attendance in earlier meetings, and each had approximately the same mean weight loss for men and for women up to that time. A random selection was then made as to which of the two subgroups would be designated the continuation subgroup and which the aversive counterconditioning subgroup. Two hours per week were chosen at times when the continuation *S*s were free, and these *S*s were told that they could attend group meetings at one or both of these times. At these meetings, discussion centered around current problems *S*s were having with eating and included suggestions and support from the other group members. The aversion counterconditioning *S*s, on the other hand, did not have further group meetings, although a few of these *S*s attended one or two of the continuation subgroup meetings. Instead, the aversive counterconditioning was carried out in individual meetings with *E*, which were held approximately weekly.

Aversive Counterconditioning

The procedures used in conditioning were based on a report by Cautela (1966b). The *S*s who were not able to relax sufficiently after the group instructions in relaxation were given further individual instruction until they were able to experience a moderate degree of relaxation. Each *E* was then given a thorough explanation of and rationale for aversive counterconditioning including the fact that the response was completely under his control and that the nausea conditioning would only be applied to certain foods in certain situations in which he was sure he did not want to eat. As work with two *S*s in a preliminary study had demonstrated that nausea conditioning could also be effectively applied to reduce the positive valence of such behaviors as eating all the food on ones plate or eating more than one cookie, these were also mentioned as possibilities. Each *S* then chose a specific food in a specific situation where he desired to refrain from eating and was asked to describe the situation to *E* in great detail. The *S* was also asked to recall the last time he felt nauseous and vomited and to describe to *E* the sensations associated with nausea. Surprisingly, these varied a great deal among *S*s.

During the actual nausea conditioning session, *S* sat comfortably in a chair with eyes closed and tried to visualize and imagine as vividly as possible the scene *E* described to him. The *E* then described in detail the situation *S* had chosen and described *S*'s eating the food, feeling more and more nauseous and sick with every bite, and then vomiting. On alternate trials, *S* was described as about to eat the food, realizing how he didn't really want it, deciding not to eat the food, and then relaxing and feeling very happy. All but one *S* reported that their imagery and feelings of nausea were extremely vivid. One *S* (who had lost 20 lb.) reported at the next meeting that he did not want to undergo nausea conditioning again, because he had found it unpleasant. All the other *S*s reported that they felt the experience was very effective. Usually two aversive and two relief trials were given in each session. Some *S*s chose different situations for each aversive counterconditioning session; some practiced aversive counterconditioning at home; some did neither or both. Due to the approaching end of the academic year and because some *S*s required lengthier instruction in relaxation exercises than others and some were unable to meet with *E* each week, each *S* had only one to three sessions of aversive counterconditioning.

Final Weighing

A final meeting was held approximately 4 months after the study began in order to get a final weight for all experimental and control *S*s. All *S*s who could not attend the meeting were contacted and final weights were obtained for all but the two *S*s who had previously stopped participating and one control *S* who repeatedly broke appointments and finally could not be located. At the time of the final weighing, the experimental program was discussed with control *S*s, and they were given copies of the paper on suggestions for weight reduction, the list of low calorie foods, and the manual of relaxation exercises.

RESULTS

The weights for individual experimental and control *S*s are reported in Table 1. All 14 *S*s who remained in the study as well as the two who dropped out lost weight, with the difference between pretest and posttest weights being highly significant ($t = 5.19$, $p < .001$). These losses are represented graphically in Figure 1.

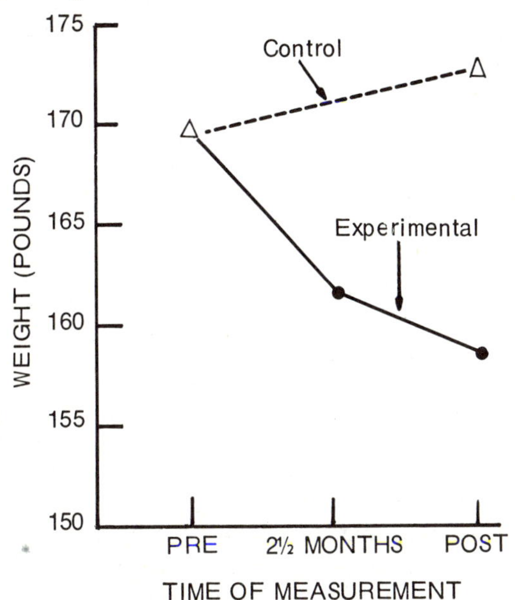

FIGURE 1. Mean weights for experimental and control *S*s.

Table 1: Weight Losses for Individual Experimental and Control Subjects

	Original Weight	Loss at 2½ Mo.	Final Weight	Total Change	Percentage of Change
Aversion counter-conditioning subgroup					
Male	196.5	−15.5	176.0	−20.5	−10
Male	197.0	−20.5	171.0	−26.0	−13
Male	198.0	−3.5	194.5	−3.5	−2
Female	135.0	−3.5	124.5	−10.5	−8
Female	143.0	−2.5	137.5	−5.5	−4
Female	159.0	−6.0	152.0	−7.0	−4
Female	135.0	−5.0	130.0	−5.0	−4
Mean for males	197.2	−13.2	180.5	−16.7	−8
Mean for females	143.0	−4.3	136.0	−7.0	−5
Mean for subgroup	166.2	−8.1	155.1	−11.1	−7
Continuation subgroup					
Male	190.0	−8.0	175.0	−14.5	−8
Male	218.5	−11.5	208.0	−10.5	−5
Male	214.0	−14.0	193.0	−21.0	−10
Female	155.5	−7.5	146.5	−9.0	−6
Female	143.0	+.5	137.0	−6.0	−5
Female	152.0	−7.0	145.5	−6.5	−4
Female	129.5	−2.5	127.5	−2.0	−2
Mean for males	207.5	−11.2	192.2	−15.3	−7
Mean for females	145.0	−4.1	139.1	−5.9	−4
Mean for subgroup	171.7	−6.9	161.9	−9.9	−6
Mean for treatment males	202.4	−12.2	186.4	−16.0	−8
Mean for treatment females	144.0	−4.3	137.6	−6.5	−5
Mean for treatment group	169.0	−7.5	158.5	−10.5	−6
Control *S*s					
Male	181.0		179.5	−1.5	−1
Male	178.5		166.5	−12.0	−7
Male	238.0		254.5	16.5	7
Female	149.0		144.0	−5.0	−3
Female	147.0		159.0	12.0	8
Female	143.0		155.0	12.0	8
Female	146.5		150.0	3.5	2
Mean for control males	199.2		200.2	1.0	.5
Mean for control females	146.4		152.0	5.6	4
Mean for control group	169.0		172.6	3.6	2

Tables 2 and 3 show the results of analyses of variance for pounds lost and percentage weight loss, respectively, for all experimental *S*s versus the controls. The effect of the experimental treatment is highly significant using both measures ($p < .001$), and the effect of sex is significant at the $p < .05$ level for pounds lost and at the $.05 < p < .10$ level for percentage weight loss. Clearly, the sample is too small to allow definite conclusions to be reached

Table 2: Summary of Analysis of Variance for Pounds Lost

Source	*SS*	*df*	*MS*	*F*
Sex	322.32	1	322.32	5.51*
Treatment	938.15	1	938.15	16.04**
Interaction	27.86	1	27.86	<1
Within	994.41	17	58.49	
Total	2282.74	20		

* $p < .05$.
** $p < .001$.

Table 3: Summary of Analysis of Variance for Percentage Weight Loss

Source	*SS*	*df*	*MS*	*F*
Sex	67.06	1	67.06	4.03*
Treatment	304.02	1	304.02	18.25**
Interaction	.58	1	.58	<1
Within	283.29	17	16.66	
Total	654.95	20		

* $.10 > p > .05$.
** $p < .001$.

about whether men are likely to lose more weight than women independent of original weight. A t test on the difference between the additional weight losses of the aversive conditioning and continuation *S*s during the last month and a half, when aversive conditioning *S*s were receiving the extra treatment, revealed no significant differences ($t = .201$) between the two experimental subgroups.

The questionnaire data generally did not show large changes in the mood indexes over time. Only the data from those 12 *S*s who had taken the questionnaire both in late January and in mid April were analyzed, as fewer *S*s completed questionnaires in May and June. General level of tension or depression as well as tension or depression specifically related to eating showed only nonsignificant decreases from beginning to end of the experiment and no relationship to amount of weight loss. Both the temptation to eat large meals ($t = 2.34$, $p < .05$) and a general index of temptation to overeat ($t = 2.22$, $p < .05$) showed significant decreases over the time course of the experiment, but the correlation between percentage weight loss and decrease in temptation was not significant ($r = .186$). The study thus provides no evidence that dieting necessarily causes large mood changes, although there is some evidence that this program can reduce the temptation to overeat over a 3-month period.

DISCUSSION

The minimal requirement for a weight reduction routine is that it enable people to lose weight and keep it off for a moderate amount of time without causing serious disruption of the individual's daily life or health. More desirable attributes would be the production of permanent weight loss with minimal expense of time or money and with the new eating pattern becoming both habitual and satisfying, so that the individual is not constantly troubled by desires to eat. It is clear that the program described in this study does satisfy the minimal requirements. All *S*s showed a decrease in weight, a loss which was significantly greater than zero and than the slight gain shown by control *S*s. Expense in money was nil and time spent attending meetings varied from about 10 to 20 hours.

Several of the less essential but desirable features are also found in this program. All *S*s expressed satisfaction with the program and stated that they had found it extremely helpful. The low dropout rate of 12.5% compares very favorably with those reported in the literature, such as 39% not returning after one visit (Stunkard, 1959c), 33% not answering questionnaires after 6 months (Franklin & Rynearson, 1960), 66% dropping out within 1 year (Silverstone & Solomon, 1965), 27% after one meeting (Shipman & Plesset, 1963). Of the *S*s who received aversive conditioning, only one was not enthusiastic about the technique. This was the only instance of any *S* objecting to any aspect of the procedure; part of the success of the program may have been that *S*s were free to choose the techniques and eating patterns which suited them best rather than being forced to conform to rigid rules.

The questionnaire data show no significant mood changes as a result of the program, although the changes are in the direction of greater happiness and relaxation. The only changes which were significant were those indicating a lesser desire to overeat at meals and a decrease in general temptation to overeat at meals, eat sweets, and eat between meals. It seems likely that 3 months is not a sufficient time for large changes in affective values of eating to occur. It is also possible that questions dealing with eating behaviors rather than attitudes would reveal more significant changes.

The data appear to indicate that the program may be more effective for males than females, a difference also reported in a study by Stunkard (1959c). Although the possibility of physiological differences is not ruled out, the variables of awareness and motivation probably contribute to the sex differences found. In general, the men participating in this study were less aware of the caloric and nutritional values of various foods and of what their own eating habits were than were the women; moreover it is possible that the commitment to a group weight-reduction program represents a greater degree of motivation for men than for women, who often have a long history of going on diets with "the girls." A larger study will be necessary to discover the extent and causes of these sex differences, which were not quite significant when percentage weight lost rather than pounds lost was used as the measure.

The most crucial test of a weight reduction program or indeed of any therapy program is the permanence of its changes. Although long-term data are very difficult to obtain on members of a fluctuating university population, some data are available on *S*s who participated in a preliminary study of many of the techniques used in this final program. Twelve female *S*s originally began the pilot study; two dropped out very early, one for medical reasons and pregnancy. Eight of the *S*s met with *E* in two groups; two of the *S*s met individually with *E* and received aversive conditioning. All *S*s learned about stimulus control procedures. Each *S* kept daily eating records before and during the period of the experiment. Most of the *S*s met regularly with *E* for only 2 to 3 months, although follow-up data were gathered on all available *S*s about 6 to 7 months after the start of the study. All but one *S* lost weight after 2 to 3 months with the mean short-term and also long-term loss for all pilot *S*s being 6 lb. Thus it does appear, for this preliminary study, that some of the effects of this program do last for at least 6 or 7 months. Other long-term data are provided by *E*, who lost about 27 lb., regained about 12 lb., and has lost about 7 of those, 12 months after the beginning of the original study. However, in view of the extremely poor long-term results of other weight reduction programs, it is clear that no conclusion can be drawn about the permanence of these changes.

It is possible that several variables may have contributed to the success of this particular study besides the planned experimental procedures. The modeling effect of *E*, who went from fat to moderate with the pretest *S*s and from moderate to thin with *S*s in the final study, was commented upon by many of the *S*s. Many of the *S*s stated that participating in a research project where data they provided were important increased their motivation. The majority of these *S*s, moreover, were college educated, which may have made it easier for them to assimilate such concepts as reinforcement, stimulus control, and caloric values.

It is also possible that certain of the variables in this program, such as the group interaction, might make no additional contribution beyond that of the other procedures. It is possible that certain procedures, such as eating only when sitting down at the table, might be effective for all *S*s whereas others, such as rewarding oneself monetarily for every day of good eating habits, might be of no use to any *S*. A much more controlled study in which various techniques and combinations of procedures are isolated would be necessary to discover their differential effects. In this study no additional effect of a very few sessions of aversive conditioning was found, although most *S*s reported that it had reduced or eliminated their desires for those foods and the two pretest *S*s given aversive conditioning continued to lose weight at least over a period of 6 months. It is conceivable that aversive conditioning, both classical and operant, will turn out to be a useful tool for

*S*s who do have cravings for certain foods or for eating everything set before them, although it may well be useless for *S*s whose problem is lack of awareness of their eating habits and caloric values. One might expect the effects of aversive counterconditioning used as an adjunct to such a program as the one described in this study to be much more enduring than the effects of aversive counterconditioning sessions alone. In short, the study was designed to see if any program for long-term weight reduction through change of eating habits could be achieved; future studies will be necessary to discover the contributions of specific variables, and the permanence of the weight losses achieved.

SUMMARY

A treatment program was designed to enable *S*s to lose weight through the use of self-monitored techniques for changing their eating behaviors. All *S*s who participated in the program achieved a stable loss in weight, and their mean loss was significantly greater than the change shown by a group of similarly motivated control *S*s. No additional effects due to a few sessions of aversive counterconditioning were demonstrated, and no general mood changes accompanied the weight loss. The *S*s did report a decreased temptation to overeat. It was suggested that similar programs or gradual habit change through self-control of stimulus conditions and reinforcement contingencies might be applied to the treatment of other addictive behaviors, which are also very refractory to change.

31

MODIFICATION OF SMOKING BEHAVIOR[1]

D. C. Ober[2]

One of the primary problems faced by researchers interested in psychotherapy has been the selection of the appropriate criteria by which to evaluate the effects of varying treatments. One solution to this problem, offered by Frank (1959), is to focus on "target behaviors." In this manner, samples may be obtained of *S*s who are homogeneous with respect to a given well-defined behavior. The goals of treatment then become the modification of those maladaptive target behaviors in a specific direction. The criteria for evaluating therapeutic effectiveness are specified behavioral changes.

This research was concerned with cigarette smoking, which, as Koenig and Masters (1965) note, fulfills the criteria for a target behavior, that is, it is both maladaptive (considering the related health hazards) and publicly observable. In addition to offering a well-defined behavioral target, excessive cigarette smoking represents a pressing problem in its own right.

D. C. Ober, "Modification of Smoking Behavior," *Journal of Consulting and Clinical Psychology, 32*, 1968, 543–549.

[1] This article is based upon a dissertation submitted in partial fulfillment of requirements for the Ph.D. at the University of Illinois. Gratitude is expressed to the dissertation committee chairman, Leonard Ullmann, and to the other committee members, William Gilbert, Merle Ohlsen, Donald Shannon, and Jerry Wiggins for their valuable suggestions and critical reading of the manuscript. The portable electric stimulators utilized in this research were purchased through United States Public Health Grant M6191.

[2] At the time this paper was written, the late D. C. Ober was at the University of Missouri at St. Louis. All correspondence should be directed to Alan Krasnoff, University of Missouri at St. Louis, 8001 Natural Bridge Road, St. Louis, Missouri 63121.

Little has been done in applying experimental controls to determine effectiveness of treatment for excessive cigarette smoking (e.g., Dale, 1964; Dalzell-Ward, 1964; Ejrup, 1964a, 1964b; Hess, 1964; McGuire & Vallance, 1964; Povorinsky, 1962; Ross, 1964). Some notable exceptions are the work by Horn, Courts, Taylor, and Solomon (1959), Greene (1964), and Koenig and Masters (1965). Compared to an untreated control group, Horn et al. (1959) found that discussion of the remote effects of smoking and discussion of the pros and cons of smoking resulted in statistically significant reduction in the number of cigarettes smoked. Greene (1964) attempted to reduce the rate of smoking of mental retardates by the use of white noise, superimposed upon continuous music, as a negative reinforcer. Increased smoking rates in experimental and control groups were attributed to the barely audible clicking of relays used in the recording of responses. Koenig and Masters (1965) found no treatment differences between the desensitization, aversion techniques applied in the experimental setting, and supportive-counseling conditions, while significant therapist differences were found.

Cigarette smoking, as well as overeating, alcoholism, and sexual deviation, may be viewed as instances in which certain appropriate behaviors are lacking. Self-control behaviors are among the appropriate behaviors often lacking. These behaviors are needed to overcome the time lapse between the reinforcement of immediate gratification (e.g., "lighting-up," food, liquor, sex) and the ultimate aversive consequences of that behavior (e.g. health dangers, obesity, Korsakoff's syndrome, social censure, etc.). That is, the chain of smoking behaviors, from the first desire for a cigarette to the reinforcement derived from smoking that cigarette, must be broken in order to avoid the ultimate aversive consequences. Self-control behaviors, imposed prior to the reinforcement derived from smoking, serve to interrupt this chain. Thus, treatment of excessive cigarette smoking might best be accomplished through the development of self-control behaviors.

The present study was designed to evaluate the relative effectiveness of three therapeutic approaches to the development of such self-control in excessive cigarette smoking. Two of these approaches were derived from learning theories; the third was based on neoanalytic theory. Each treatment approach was administered by two therapists, making a total of six treatment groups in all. A seventh group was composed of *S*s who received no treatment.

The first treatment approach, the operant self-control program, was based on the premise that *S* controls himself in the same manner as an external source would control him, that is, through the manipulation of the variables of which behavior is a function (Skinner, 1953). With the aversion program, self-control behaviors were initiated and maintained by the reinforcement of avoidance or termination of an aversive stimuli associated with the response of cigarette smoking. Traditional implications for the development of self-control over smoking may be as varied as hypotheses used to explain the persistence of the behavior. In an attempt to standardize treatments across therapists and *S*s for the purposes of research, the exemplar of the third treatment approach was Eric Berne's (1964) *Games People Play.* A smoking games program was developed and based on Berne's system of transactional game analysis. Transactional analysis has its roots in psychoanalytic theory and can be considered evocative (to use Jerome Frank's term), as compared to the other two procedures.

Predictions

PREDICTION 1. At the termination of treatment, no differential effects will be found between the operant self-control condition and the aversive condition (for those *S*s who remained in treatment). However, the evocative and control conditions will be, respectively, less effective in the termination of smoking than either of the other two treatment conditions. This prediction was based on the relative success of both self-control and aversive techniques as applied to other target behaviors. Transactional game analysis was predicted to be least effective since insight approaches have generally been unsuccessful with behavioral "excesses" (e.g., drinking, obesity) and since time restrictions supposedly prohibited development of the relationship which is presumed to serve as the vehicle for cure (Fenichel, 1945; Munroe, 1955; Rogers, 1951).

PREDICTION 2. No therapist differences are expected in this research, since the treatment conditions are highly standardized. Findings reported by Ullmann, Forsman, Kenny, McInnis, Unikel, and Zeisset (1965), indicate that providing therapists with specified and systematic procedures for each treatment condition may be influential in minimizing therapist differences.

PREDICTION 3. The effects of the operant self-control condition will be more enduring than those of the aversion condition. This prediction was based on the consideration that generalization decrement here would be minimized since *S*s would analyze and practice self-control behaviors in their own environmental situations. At termination of the experiment, the aversion condition should also prove effective. However, extinction of newly acquired avoidance responses has been shown to be particularly rapid in this form of learning (Estes, 1944; Eysenck & Rachman, 1965).

PREDICTION 4. An important dependent variable to be considered is the number of *S*s who complete the course of treatment in each of the three conditions under study. It is predicted that the defector rate will be highest for the aversion condition, since this is the least pleasurable of the three forms of treatment.

METHOD

Subjects

Forty-one male and 19 female students at the University of Illinois served as *S*s in this research. All *S*s were recruited through an article placed in the student newspaper and through questionnaires placed in the Student

Union Building. Sixty *S*s were selected from a total volunteer group of 79 students on the basis of the following criteria: (*a*) all smoked in excess of 20 cigarettes a day; (*b*) all inhaled; (*c*) all had smoked for more than 1 year; (*d*) all desired to stop smoking. Fifteen *S*s were then randomly assigned to each of four groups: operant, aversive, transactional analysis, and control. Within each treatment condition *S*s were randomly assigned to therapists. Arrangements were made for the no-treatment control group to receive treatment subsequent to the termination of the experiment.

Analysis of variance on data of age, number of cigarettes smoked per day, and total number of years smoked revealed no significant differences among the four groups (Ober, 1967, Tables 1, 2, & 3, pp. 47–49).

After *S*s had been randomly assigned to treatment conditions, a brief structured interview and inventory were administered. No significant differences between groups in *S*s' attitudes and expectations were found (Ober, 1967, Table 4, p. 50).

Therapists

Two advanced clinical psychology graduate students at the University of Illinois served as therapists in this study.[3] Both had had extensive individual experience and both had previously worked with groups. Each therapist treated groups of 69 *S*s under each of the three treatment conditions. Following termination of treatment, the therapists rated each client on a 5-point scale for likability, responsiveness to treatment, appropriateness of length and type of treatment, degree of improvement in other areas, indication of necessity for further treatment (prognosis), and therapist comfort in working with the client.

Procedure

The *S*s were seen for ten 50-minute sessions over a period of 4 weeks. The first meeting was the same for all treatment groups. At this time the therapist introduced himself as a person knowledgeable about smoking and the problems related to breaking the habit. Methods for day-by-day recordings of cigarette smoking were explained and utilized by all treatment groups. At the initial pretreatment group session *S*s were also asked for the names, addresses, and telephone numbers of at least two people who would be familiar with their smoking habits. Treatment was begun at the second group meeting. The data on smoking between the first meeting and the beginning of treatment at Session 2 served as the base line of smoking behavior.

Analysis of main effects was based on *S*s' daily records of smoking

[3] Thanks are given to Donald Meichenbaum and Daniel O'Leary who served as therapists for this research.

beginning with the initial meeting which preceded the onset of formal treatment. Since data on cigarette consumption were not available at follow up for the control group, an own-control design was employed to determine the effects of treatment.

At the conclusion of the ninth treatment session, *S*s were asked to fill out a Posttreatment Data Sheet to obtain their evaluation of treatment effectiveness and therapist helpfulness.

At 1-week intervals for 4 weeks following the termination of treatment, *S*s received a letter containing a stamped, addressed postcard. The letter requested *S*s to indicate on each card their present rate of smoking and return these cards immediately.

Treatment Programs

Uniformities–The *S*s in all experimental conditions were presented with treatment manuals of comparable length (Ober, 1967, Appendixes D, E, & F). All three treatment manuals used technical language but always with sufficient explanation of that language. The aversion treatment group received a lighter-sized, aversive stimulator (habit breaker). To control for the effects of calling attention to their smoking with this device, the operant and transactional groups were presented with small cards. The *S*s in these treatments were instructed to read the card before smoking a cigarette. The card for the operant self-control group read, "I have the self-control not to smoke this cigarette." The card for the transactional analysis group read, "I don't have to play the smoking game."

Self-Control Program–The operant self-control program itself was based in large measure on Mertens' *The Manual for the Alcoholic*[4] and represented an adaptation and extension of that program. In addition, the work of Ferster, Nurnberger, and Levitt (1962) was also drawn upon. Detailed explanations were presented for the analysis of behaviors in terms of their controlling stimuli. Topics dealt with by the program included basic principles of a learning approach to smoking, the ultimate aversive consequences of smoking, the use of incompatible responses, physical or environmental restraints, shaping, chaining, etc. During the first treatment session the self-control manual was distributed, and the rationale of treatment as presented in the introductory chapters of the manual was discussed. Each *S* was instructed to read and apply the principles included in the manual as well as to look at the above-mentioned card each time he desired a cigarette. From that point all sessions were concerned with analysis of behavior and application of the self-control principles. Attempts were made to focus on specific examples of application of the program brought up by group members.

[4] G. C. Mertens, The manual for the alcoholic, unpublished manuscript, 1963.

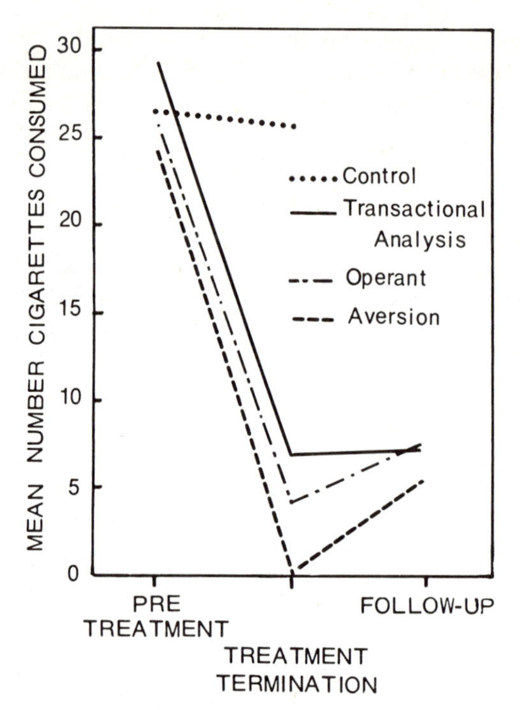

FIGURE 1. The mean smoking rate for the three experimental and the control conditions at each measurement point.

Aversion Program–In this condition *S*s were presented with pocket-sized aversive stimulators with which each *S* could administer a shock to himself. The level of the shock administered by the habit breaker[5] was altered at the beginning of each meeting so that *S* experienced the shock as "painful." Checking the level of the shock at the initiation of each session guarded against adaptation to the electrical charge which otherwise might have occurred. The operation and rationale of the treatment was presented in manual form during the first treatment session. Topics dealt with by the program included basic principles of a learning approach to smoking, aversion therapy and treatment for cigarette smoking, and examples of how to use the habit breaker for aversive conditioning, establishing incompatible responses, chaining, shaping behavior, and response suppression. Each *S* was instructed to administer a shock *as soon* as he craved a cigarette. He was further instructed to repeat the shock on every occasion he started to desire a cigarette. This procedure was to be continued until *S* could no longer postpone his desire for a cigarette. The importance of strict adherence to the instructions was stressed.

[5] Habit breakers may be purchased from John Batbie, 924 Commercial Avenue, South San Francisco, California.

Transactional Analysis Program–Using Berne's (1964) basic paradigm, a number of smoking games were devised and examined. Some of these smoking games included "I should stop smoking," "See, I'm independent," "I don't inhale all the time," "Wooden leg," "Everybody has to die sometime," and "Why don't you—yes, but." Emphasis was placed on the fact that smoking was a symptom of an underlying conflict. One goal of therapy was the identification of the underlying interpersonal conflict which made smoking reinforcing through the application of transactional game analysis to smoking behavior. Gaining insight and/or understanding into these games and the reasons for playing them was presented as crucial in dealing with the underlying conflict. Once the conflict had been ferreted out and dealt with, the individual was presumably free to behave in a more adult manner. This latter involved assuming responsibility for his actions and obtaining self-control over smoking. Some topics dealt with in the manual included basic principles of a transactional analysis, why games are played, structural analysis, transactional analysis of a game, and examples of smoking games.

RESULTS

Records from nine *S*s were dropped from the analyses because it was believed that more than four absences invalidated effective assessment of the three treatments. The data from one additional *S* were discarded because follow-up information could not be obtained. The final number of *S*s for Therapists 1 and 2, respectively, were six and five in the operant conditions, five and seven in the aversion treatments, and six each for the two transactional analysis groups. The mean smoking rate, including control data, is graphically represented in Figure 1.

PREDICTIONS 1, 2, AND 3: TREATMENT, THERAPIST, AND FOLLOW-UP EFFECTS

An analysis of variance for therapists by types of treatments by treatment alone was calculated (Winer, 1962). No effects differentiating therapists ($F > 1$) or types of treatment ($F > 1$) were found. But treatment, independent of what kind, was found to be highly effective ($F = 110.32$, $df = 2/58$, $p < .01$). No interactions reached statistically significant levels. These results are in line with Prediction 2, that there would be no differences in therapists. Contrary to Prediction 3, the different types of treatments were statistically indistinguishable at all measurement points. A collapsed one-way analysis of variance was performed allowing the generation of an error term for individual comparisons (Winer, 1962). Individual comparisons between

Table 1: Individual Comparisons between Pretreatment, Treatment Termination, and Follow-up Means in Smoking Rate

Comparisons	*q*	*df*
Pretreatment—treatment termination	19.89**	3/68
Pretreatment—follow-up	17.55**	2/68
Treatment termination—follow-up	2.34*	2/68

* $p > .05$.
** $p < .01$.

collapsed experimental group means are presented in Table 1. A studentized range statistic (q) was used for these comparisons (Winer, 1962).

These results indicate that a significant reduction in smoking rate occurred over the interval from pretreatment to treatment termination. The smoking rate at treatment termination and the follow-up point did not differ statistically, which suggests that the effects of all treatments were maintained over the treatment termination–follow-up interval. This finding is contrary to Prediction 3.

Prediction 4: Differential Defector Rate

An irregular analysis of variance was computed on *S*s' attendance at treatment sessions. All 15 *S*s originally assigned to each treatment were included in this analysis, regardless of how many sessions they attended. No treatment, therapist, or interactional differences of statistical significance were found (Ober, 1967, Table 16, p. 65). Attendance was uniformly regular (or irregular) across treatments and therapists.

Posttreatment Questionnaire: Subjects

When analysis of variance techniques were applied to the Posttreatment Questionnaire, 14 out of 24 items evidenced no group, therapist, or interactional differences of statistical significance (Ober, 1967, Table 17, p. 66). Clear-cut differences between the therapists were found, indicating that the two therapists differed with respect to how closely *S*s thought they followed the transactional program and the degree to which the aversion treatment was viewed as helpful in other areas. On the eight remaining items the Therapist × Condition interaction was significant, and no straightforward differences were found. There were no significant differences across treatments or therapists for increased nail biting, eating, sweating palms, memory difficulty, attentional difficulties, and sexual drive.

Posttreatment Questionnaire: Therapists

At the termination of treatment, there were no treatment, therapist, or interactional differences in therapists' ratings of *S*s as to *S*'s likability and responsiveness to treatment, length and appropriateness of treatment, need for further treatment for smoking, and therapist comfort in working with *S* (Ober, 1967, Table 18, p. 67). Two items, however, did reach statistical significance. Therapist 1 rated his operant and transactional groups as significantly less "improved in other areas" than his aversion group. Therapist 2 perceived all three of his groups as more in need of further treatment (in areas other than smoking) than did Therapist 1.

DISCUSSION

The results of this research indicate that self-control can be established over smoking behavior. The failure to find significant differences among treatments is similar to Koenig and Masters (1965) and may have been the result of several factors. To the extent of random assignment to treatment or control groups, all *S*s were equal on motivation or other variables. All *S*s receiving treatment were seen in groups. The first question requiring further investigation is the role, if any, that group processes played in the success of treatment. Next, all treatment *S*s recorded their smoking behavior and reported it to a therapist. This procedure in itself may well be therapeutic, and a group of *S*s restricted to such a regimen may well be included in future research. In a similar fashion, the cards placed on the cigarette packs provided an additional stimulus between the craving for a cigarette and smoking.

Beyond such considerations, all *S*s were receiving "treatment" of a nonspecific nature, which in itself may have accounted for the obtained results (e.g., Frank, 1961; Goldstein, 1962; Rosenthal & Frank, 1956; Stevenson, 1961).

The games presented in the transactional analysis program were generated solely by armchair consideration of smoking behaviors and the interpersonal situations in which smoking occurs. Since these games were apparently effective in helping *S*s alter their smoking habits, the transactional game analyst faces a dilemma. If game analysts accept this research as validation of a transactional treatment approach, they must also accept the fact that these "games" may be generated without benefit of the type of research in which they have been engaging.

It might be noted that self-report measures of cigarette smoking were the sole dependent variable measure used in other research on smoking. Through contacts with the two people whom *S*s had indicated would be familiar with their smoking habits, an additional check on the veracity of the *S*s' self-report was available. The correlation obtained between self-report and friends' report was .94 ($p < .001$). This is in contrast to the correlation obtained by Goldstein (1966) between peer-reports and self-reports. Goldstein's correlation was .44 for frequency of smoking ($p < .05$). However, Goldstein's results were based on a class of 25 high school girls, aged 15–18. The *S*s in this research were college students for whom the aspects of participating in a scientific study were stressed.

To aid people effectively it seems essential that they attend treatment sessions. Both Eysenck (1961b) and Phillips (1956) have indicated the importance of defector rate in the assessment of treatment efficiency. Breger and McGaugh (1965) critically allude to the failure of behavior therapists to use control groups and report dropout rate from therapy. Feldman (1966) levels this same criticism at practitioners of aversion therapy. Thus while the importance of defection rate has been stressed, little appears in the literature regarding differential defector rates from various forms of treatment. The results presented here indicate that attendance was uniformly regular (or irregular) across treatments and therapists. It appears that fears of defection from unpleasant forms of treatment, such as aversion techniques as used here, may be unwarranted. However, all *S*s knew they were participating in psychological research.

SUMMARY

Operant ($N = 11$), aversion ($N = 12$), and transactional analysis ($N = 12$) approaches to the development of self-control in excessive cigarette smoking were compared with each other and with a no-treatment control group ($N = 15$). 10 group treatment sessions were administered to *S*s randomly assigned to each of the treatment groups. At termination of treatment and at the end of a 1-month follow-up period, the smoking rates of all treatment conditions were significantly lower than the no-treatment control group ($p < .001$). No significant treatment, therapist, or interactional differences were found. No indications of symptom substitution were noted.

32

COVERT SENSITIZATION WITH ALCOHOLICS

A CONTROLLED REPLICATION

Beatrice Ashem and Lawrence Donner[1]

In the search for short-term, effective treatment of alcoholics many novel approaches making use of learning principles have been developed over the past decade. Among these have been conditioning techniques, which have used electric shock, Antabuse, and a variety of drugs to induce aversive responses. However, results have shown that while in the experimental room these techniques work well, when the subject (*S*) returned to his usual environment he did not always show the same avoidance behavior.

A possible explanation may be that the treatment situation (i.e., the experimental room, electrodes around his finger, etc.) is too dissimilar from the *S*'s usual environment. Furthermore, according to Cautela (1965) and Franks (1966), many investigators have not used the most efficacious classical conditioning paradigm, forward conditioning, but instead used the weaker model, backward conditioning, with the unconditioned stimulus (UCS) preceding the conditioned stimulus (CS).

It seems fairly evident that a technique which has greater generality is needed. One novel approach toward achieving such an end has been described by Gold and Neufeld (1965) in the treatment of homosexuality. This behavioral technique consisted of having the *S* visualize a stimulus con-

Reprinted by permission of the authors and Pergamon Press Ltd. from *Behaviour Research and Therapy*, 1968, *6*, 7–12.

[1] The authors wish to express their deep appreciation to R. A. Albahary, M.D., Director of the Alcoholic Unit, New Jersey Neuro-Psychiatric Institute, Princeton, without whose cooperation this study would not have been possible.

figuration in conjunction with an aversive response. Cautela (1967) describes a modification of the technique, covert sensitization, which appears to be very promising in the treatment of alcoholism. In effect, a phobic-type response is conditioned to alcohol. Specifically, an incompatible nauseous response was conditioned to a wide variety of stimuli which had previously led to drinking behavior in the *S*. Anant (1967), treating twenty-six alcoholics, reports treatment with this method produced total abstinence from alcohol for periods ranging from 8 to 15 months. No control group was used.

The present investigation was undertaken in an attempt to investigate, in a systematic and controlled manner, the feasibility and effectiveness of this procedure for hospitalized alcoholics.

METHOD

Subjects

The *S*s were twenty-three male patients at the New Jersey Neuro-Psychiatric Institute, Princeton, who had voluntarily entered for a 6-week course of treatment for alcoholism. The *S*s were selected according to the following criteria: 45 years of age or less, of average intelligence as measured by the Otis Intelligence Scale, free from any sign of gross psychological disturbance as assessed by the MMPI (no scores in the interpretable levels on the F scale and the psychotic scales, Pa, Sc, Ma), and whose family history suggested that a 6-month follow-up would be obtainable.

All *S*s had unsuccessfully engaged in either AA, clinic treatment, or private psychiatric care at one time prior to their present hospitalization. During participation in this study, all *S*s participated in the activities of the treatment unit, including group psychotherapy conducted by a resident psychiatrist.

Therapists

Two therapists, the authors, administered the treatment, one of whom (BA) had had some previous experience with systematic desensitization and reciprocal inhibition. Both were serving as interns at the New Jersey Neuro-Psychiatric Institute. In their approach to therapy both were described by their colleagues as warm and accepting. Each therapist treated *S*s in the two treatment groups.

In order to standardize treatment procedures the therapists practiced the treatment on each other, and then observed one another during treatment of a pilot *S*. Finally, each therapist used the treatment, independently, on pilot *S*s.

Experimental Design

The basic design of the experiment consisted of three conditions:

1. Systematic Conditioning: Forward Classical Conditioning (FCC)
2. Pseudo-Conditioning: Backward Classical Conditioning (BCC)
3. No Contact (Control)

The dependent variable was abstinence from drinking 6 months following treatment as measured by a follow-up questionnaire. To ensure the validity of the questionnaire it had to be answered identically by both the patient and his nearest contact, i.e., wife or parent.

Procedure

Subjects were matched into triplets on the basis of IQ, age, drinking experience, and then were randomly assigned to one of these three groups. The mean ages of *S*s assigned to FCC, BCC, and Control groups were 35, 39, and 36 respectively; mean IQ was 109, 103, and 101, respectively; mean years of drinking were 18, 20, and 18, respectively. The *S*s in the control group received no treatment, and following the initial screening tests were not seen again.

Originally 9 *S*s were assigned to each group. However, one *S* was lost from the FCC group, 2 from the BCC group, and one from the control due to: excessive sensitivity to the UCS (uncontrollable vomiting both in and out of the experimental session at the mention of alcohol), inability to visualize the stimuli, voluntary and involuntary departure from hospital. Eight *S*s in the FCC group and seven in the BCC group completed the treatments.

Following group administration of the screening battery of tests and questionnaire, *S*s who were to receive treatment were seen by the therapist for a short interview, during which they were told briefly of the treatment procedures. The treatment was described as a learning experience designed to counteract the bad habit of drinking that they had acquired. They were further told that a new technique had recently been used successfully in the treatment of alcoholics. The purpose of the treatment was to make drinking an extremely unpleasant experience. They were also told that they would be taught deep muscle relaxation, the "rationale" being that in the future relaxation would serve as an alternative mode of response to conditions which might lead to drinking behavior, i.e., tension and anxiety.

Both treatment groups were interviewed in regard to situations in which they drank, and descriptions of these situations were later used to form hierarchies unique to the individual. Information was also obtained concerning areas most aversive to them. The construction of hierarchies followed the procedure described by Cautela (1967). On the second con-

Table 1: Treatment Procedure

Session		Undisturbed Relaxation
1	15 min interview followed by 15 min relaxation training	3 min
2	10 min relaxation training followed by 10 min (3) aversive conditioning	3 min
3	5 min relaxation training followed by 20 min (7) aversive conditioning	3 min
4	25 min (8) aversive conditioning followed by 5 min (2) pushing away alcohol and relaxing	3 min
5	25 min (8) aversive conditioning followed by 5 min (2) pushing away alcohol and relaxing	3 min
6	15 min (5) aversive conditioning followed by 15 min (5) pushing away alcohol and relaxing	3 min
7	15 min (5) aversive conditioning followed by 15 min (5) pushing away alcohol and relaxing	3 min
8	5 min (2) pushing away alcohol and relaxing 25 min (8) well-being and adequacy feelings associated with sobriety	3 min
9	20 min (10) well-being and adequacy feelings associated with sobriety	3 min

Note: Numbers in parenthesis indicate the approximate number of scene presentations for each time period.

tact, training in deep muscle relaxation was begun, using an abbreviated form of Jacobson's technique.

The treatment program consisted of nine sessions which ranged in time from 30 to 40 minutes. Table 1 gives the specific treatment procedure, session by session. This was closely adhered to by both therapists.

Forward Classical Conditioning Group–Following initial relaxation, and while the *S* was in a relaxed position upon a cot, he was presented with a series of drinking scenes, one at a time. He was told to imagine the scene as if it was happening at that moment. The following example is typical of the scenes used:

> You have just gotten home from work; you are sitting in your easy chain in the living room. The TV is blaring out the news; there is a can of beer on the end table next to you. You can see the beer; you are reaching for it now. You have it in your hand and you're opening it. You want a drink very much. You are raising it to your mouth; you can almost taste it already. It is against your lips. You are drinking it now . . .

Immediately after the *S* had signalled experiencing the taste of alcohol the aversive stimulus was presented. The *S* was told that he felt extremely uncomfortable.

> The beer is warm; your stomach feels queasy. There is a heaviness in your throat. You are beginning to feel very sick. Your last meal is beginning to turn over in your stomach. The beer is beginning to come up. You begin to gag; you can't control your gagging. You feel the undigested food coming up; you are very nauseous. The food is in your mouth; you can feel it forcing its way out of your mouth. You can no longer keep it down. You are vomiting over your beer—into your beer—over your shirt. It is disgusting; the smell is foul. You can't stop.

Following this the *S* was told to stop imagining the scene and let it pass.

During the initial training period the *S*s varied in their ability to visualize the stimulus. As imaginal ability increased it became unnecessary to evoke the more remote associations to vomiting. In the event that vomit was not experienced as nauseous, or adaptation to its effects occurred, other stimuli reported as repugnant or fear-provoking, as seeing a dead soldier, incurring a brain injury, and so forth, were used in subsequent sessions.

As treatment sessions progressed, alternate responses to drinking became associated with relaxation. At first the *S* was merely relaxed at the end of the aversive conditioning session and told to associate pleasant thoughts with relaxation. Later relaxation was made contingent upon a visual image of pushing the alcohol away, taking a non-alcoholic drink, and finally behavior and performance incompatible with drinking, such as going to A.A., performing some desired positive task, and so forth. Feelings of adequacy and well-being were also associated with being relaxed and the performance of the above alternate responses.

Backward Classical Conditioning Group–Treatment for this group was identical to that of the FCC group, except that the visceral image preceded the image of alcohol. This was accomplished by telling *S*s, "You have just eaten; the feed isn't agreeing with you. You are experiencing a good deal of discomfort. You are beginning to feel sick. The food won't stay down," etc. As soon as the *S* showed overt signs of discomfort he was told that he was vomiting; vomiting over the beer that he was drinking. When this was successfully visualized, the *S* was told to stop imagining the scene; to let it pass.

Prior to treatment it had been assumed that this reversed order of the usual CS-UCS presentation would negate the effectiveness of the treatment.

RESULTS AND DISCUSSION

At the outset of treatment it became apparent that the BCC group was not, in effect, receiving pseudo-treatment. That is, while the first presentation

Table 2: Fisher's Exact Probability Test of Alcoholics Drinking and Non-Drinking

	Non-drinking	Drinking
Control	0	8
Treatment	6	9

under the backward conditioning paradigm was, in fact, backward conditioning, the patients very quickly made an automatic association between the CS (alcohol) and the UCS (nausea) on subsequent presentations. This was clearly evident from the *S*s' overt behavior and verbalizations directly following treatment sessions. Thus, both treatment groups were combined and compared with the Control groups.

For purposes of statistical analysis it was assumed that *S*s for whom no follow-up could be obtained were drinking. Table 2 shows the obtained results. Fisher's Exact Probability test was applied to the data. The resulting probability values ($p < .05$) indicated that the treatment groups significantly differed from the controls in the predicted direction.

The results clearly show a significant difference between treatment and control *S*s in drinking behavior at the 6-month follow-up. Whereas, 40 percent of the treated *S*s were not drinking, the corresponding figure for the control was zero.

These findings are encouraging in light of the fact that the 23 *S*s involved in the study had been drinking for an average of 18.5 years. All had had clinic treatment, private psychiatric care or A.A. participation before seeking help at the state hospital.

The study supports case-report findings of Anant (1967) and Cautela (1967) suggesting that covert sensitization is an effective treatment technique for modifying drinking behavior in alcoholics. Moreover, it is stressed that this modification was brought about in a relatively short period, i.e., treatment had been time-limited to nine 35–minute contacts over 3 weeks.

The obvious question which arises is why this procedure should be effective. The crucial variable involved in covert sensitization, unlike that in desensitization of fear responses, appears to be the induction of phobic-type responses to alcohol. The following quote from one of the treated *S*s illustrates the degree to which autonomic responses of an aversive nature were conditioned:

> . . . around Christmas I wanted to buy my wife a bottle of Southern Comfort. As I approached the liquor store I broke out in a sweat and could hardly open the door. When I finally got in I could hardly talk, for my throat was dry and choking and my stomach was flipping.

It is quite apparent that in order that a phobic-type response be conditioned, *S*s must not be allowed to drink during the early part of treatment. At this time the approach response is still strong to alcohol, and the aversive nauseous response weak. Drinking at this point would most likely extinguish any aversive response which had been conditioned. With increased sessions, however, the aversive response occurred almost immediately and automatically at the mention of alcohol. Exposure to alcohol at this time, like exposure to a phobic object, resulted in immediate discomfort and thus reinforced the aversive response. In addition, *S*s were conditioned to relax when they stopped thinking about alcohol or when they engaged in a response which was incompatible with drinking. In this way not only was a negative habit weakened but a positive habit was established.

In order for long-lasting effects to accrue, the association between alcohol and the aversive response must become an intrinsic part of the behavioral repertoire of the *S*. Relatively little is known of the power of the internalized versus the external stimulus presentation to control behavior. Luria (1961) has presented some evidence which suggests that the regulation of non-verbal behavior by speech is effective only when the external verbal command becomes internalized.

As with any innovative technique further investigation is necessary. Such factors as experience, sex of therapist, ability of *S* to visualize and relax need to be explored.

SUMMARY

Covert sensitization was used to condition a phobic-type response to alcohol for the treatment of maladaptive drinking behavior. A 6-month follow up showed significant differences between treated alcoholics and matched controls. It was concluded that covert sensitization was an effective short-term treatment for the modification of drinking behavior.

PART VII

Some Reflections on Self-Control

33

SELF-REGULATION

RESEARCH, ISSUES, AND SPECULATIONS

Frederick H. Kanfer

A major criticism of early learning approaches to psychiatric problems has been the superficiality of any technique aimed exclusively at behavior change. It has been argued by dynamic therapists that only reorganization of the personality, removal of unconscious blocks, or exposure of unconscious wishes can bring about lasting changes. Symptom removal or learning of more effective behaviors has been viewed solely as incidental by-products of change in more fundamental psychological processes. The criticism appeared especially cogent because early instances of behavioral approaches concentrated on symptoms which consisted of overt motoric responses and were easily controlled by direct environmental manipulations. These therapeutic approaches have been most dramatic in use with institutionalized psychotics and children. Due to the extensive control available with these populations, consequences of symptomatic behaviors can be relatively easily changed and a wide range of reinforcers can be used in acquisition and maintenance of new behaviors. In adult neurotics, the greater independence of the problematic behaviors from the controlling social environment has posed problems in definition of the target behavior, in arranging more favorable response-reinforcement contingencies, and in providing effective reinforcers (Kanfer & Saslow, 1965). These problems seemed especially difficult with patients whose symptomatic behaviors consisted mainly of private responses which are usually covert, unshared, often inaccessible, and not under direct environmental control. Furthermore, these behaviors constitute what have been called "mental events" and, on methodological and philosophical grounds, they were excluded from the early behavioristic systems.

The challenge to a behavioristic approach in clinical psychology lies in demanding that a good theory of human behavior provide engineering principles which cover *all* human functions, or handle the full range of problematic behaviors which have been tackled by traditional psychotherapies. The clinician recognizes in his daily contact with patients that a person's habitual patterns of response to his own past experiences, to his biological functions, to the variables controlling his behavior, and to his potential for dealing with his environment and himself are powerful determinants of his actions. Knowledge of the relationships governing the genesis and operations of these classes of "self-responses" is an essential requirement, if clinical practice is ultimately to be based on a science of psychology. While technological advances can be made on an essentially pragmatic basis, a science of human behavior and its derived engineering principles cannot ignore or exclude the domain of behaviors which govern the individual's actions in relation to himself and are only initiated or distantly maintained by his social and physical environment.

The importance of self-reinforcement in psychotherapy has been noted even in the earliest learning formulations of the therapeutic process (e.g., Shaw, 1946; Shoben, 1949). For these authors, the lifting of repression and subsequent insight pave the way for constructive planning which is regulated by the patient's self-reinforcement. Recent developments in behavior therapy give evidence of the growing awareness of the necessity for inclusion of "self-reactions" in the treatment of behavior problems. Homme (1965b) has proposed the term "coverant" for a class of operant responses whose main distinguishing characteristic is their relative inaccessibility to observation. These responses cover events commonly described as thinking, imagining, fantasying, etc. Homme (1966) suggests their amenability to control by the same general principles as hold for other operants. The use of self-controlling procedures in the treatment of behavior problems has been discussed by Goldiamond (1965c) which illustrates the feasibility of applying similar methods in the modification of one's own behavior as in the modification of the behavior of another. In extending aversion therapy procedures, Cautela (1966b) has substituted covert CS and US presentations with obese and alcoholic patients. Davison (1968a) has reported use of self-controlled counter-conditioning sessions in the treatment of a sexual problem. Techniques in which the patient assumes some part of the therapist's role are not an innovation of behavior therapy. The importance of self-regulation in achieving happiness has been stressed by ancient philosophers and moralists and is encountered in many religions. Behavior therapists differ not in applications of these general techniques but in their efforts to incorporate them into a theoretically consistent model of behavior modification and to provide the patient with supplementary behaviors which make self-regulation easier. Kanfer and Phillips (1966) have described a group of procedures, under the term *instigation therapy*, which have in common the general method of helping the patient to exercise control over his own environment and to modify his own behavior. The usual steps in these techniques involve training the patient in self-observation, in evaluating and categorizing his behavior, in planning to rearrange his environment or his own acts on the basis of learning procedures, and in providing self-reinforcement for maintaining improvements. The many advantages of these techniques are described elsewhere (Kanfer & Phillips, 1966).

Ultimately, most patients leave therapeutic supervision. It is apparent that training in self-control can help not only to shorten the therapeutic process but also to maintain and extend the changes initiated in therapy. Training in self-reinforcement for appropriate new behaviors has been used by the author in the context of clinical interviews as well as in systematically programmed training by eliciting self-evaluative responses to the patient's taped report of social interactions, followed by reinforcement from the therapist. The procedure has been found useful for adult patients and for children who live in an unfriendly or solitary environment and who cannot rely on external feedback for evaluation of their own behavior. It has also been used to supplement efforts at self-control of symptomatic behaviors, and to maintain planned programs in patients with serious behavior deficits.

The introduction of instigation therapy techniques among behavior therapies proceeds toward closer integration of interviewing and conditioning methods and expands the scope of learning-theory derived methods. The systematic use of training in self-control for "autotherapy" may be easier when data accumulate about the characteristics of people who can benefit most from such procedures, and about specific techniques which can provide more economical training for patients than is provided in the experimental efforts reported so far.

An experimental analysis of self-control also helps to foster interest in the study of specific techniques by which a person can learn to arrange his own behavior to maximize the attainment of socially sanctioned reinforcers. The contemporary cultural attitude implies that self-control is an active, conscious, and unitary process, and that its function is to inhibit socially undesirable behavior. In literature and in religious writings it is often regarded as man's noblest character trait and the explicit assumption is made of man's dual nature, the good and evil. When "loss" of self-control is pictured as the person's submission to ever-present irrational and evil urges, then it is reasonable to emphasize treatment methods which aim mainly at reestablishment of control, inhibition over desires and impulses, and training in the tolerance of hardships and deprivations. Such "control-restoration" methods may sacrifice more effective treatments.

It is likely that the same view also serves to maintain many pathological behaviors. A patient who justifies his deviant behaviors repeatedly by saying: "I cannot control myself," or "I do not know what makes me do it," is often viewed as mentally ill, deviant, or at least temporarily incapacitated in controlling his actions. The practical consequences of these attitudes is that many of the patient's previously punished deviant behaviors are now tolerated with sympathy. Social expectations of the patient are modified and responsibility for his actions may be assumed by social agents. The most common examples encountered in the clinic are of the juvenile delinquent who verbalizes his lack of control for the purpose of self-justification and avoidance of punishment, or the neurotic whose demands for support and special treatment are based on his plea that he cannot control his fears, his hypochondriacal concerns, or his depressive thoughts. The views expressed here suggest a therapeutic strategy which includes rejection of the patient's statements about his inability to control himself as an explanation of his problems, and incorporation of training in specific self-controlling and appropriate self-reinforcing behaviors, or use of environmental intervention as part of the treatment program.

Another potential use of the self-reinforcement (SR) and self-control procedures described in the preceding section lies in their adaptability for diagnostic purposes. Patterson[1] has used the SR procedure with patients to obtain data on their rate of SR as a pre- and posttherapy measure. With a standardized procedure SR+ and SR— frequencies, the discrepancies between those rates, their resistance to change under controlled procedures, and the extent of their generalization to related standardized tasks may yield useful samples of patients' self-attitudes. While the experimental methods reported above are crude procedures, they do suggest the possibility of a battery of tests for assessing self-responses which hold greater promise for standardization and quantification than current projective tests covering a similar range of behaviors.

SOME ISSUES AND SPECULATIONS

The crucial problems of observing and changing the psychological processes involved in the control of human behavior when they proceed in the same individual upon whom control is to be exerted involve many philosophical, methodological, and substantive questions. An underlying philosophical issue which has been extensively debated since the advent of behaviorism concerns the separation of behaviorism as a philosophical doctrine, closely related to the physicalism of Carnap and the Vienna circle, and behaviorism as a set of rules for scientific methodology. The rich inheritance of our cultural past and the constant contrast between a model of human functioning based strictly on a behavioristic philosophy and the commonsense dualistic models

[1] Personal communication, 1966.

encountered in our daily lives make it difficult for the clinician and the researcher to operate professionally in one framework and to discard this framework in all other roles in daily living as parents, citizens, lovers, friends, and so on. Consequently, the multiple impacts of patients, competent nonpsychological professionals, and institutional or agency policies, as well as the coarse experiences and descriptions which the patient presents to the clinician, make it even harder to maintain an "artificial" appearing behaviorial orientation (and language) in the clinic than in the laboratory.

A further dilemma of the behavioral scientist and engineer lies in the fact that the objects of his observations are organisms whose behavior is somewhat known to him by his own experiences. Chemists or physicists are not likely to succumb to the temptation of placing themselves in the position of their subject matter, since intentions, goals, or fears are rarely assigned to chemical or physical objects under study. The interchangeability of *E* and *S* would appear to give the psychologist enormous advantages over his fellow scientists. The assumption that "After all, we are all pretty much alike" (Bakan, 1956) has apparently not served as a catalyst but rather as a diversion along the path toward a theory of human behavior. Perhaps, the advantage of *E*'s capacity for anticipating *S* behaviors needs to be more clearly confined to the domain of hypothesis-formulation (the "context of discovery") and more rigorously excluded from data collection and data processing activities (the "context of verification").

The errors of introspectionism and phenomenology have been to assume (1) verbal reports are based on observation of existing inner mental events, and (2) that these events are faithfully depicted by the reports. Behaviorism attempts to tackle the same phenomena by observations of behavior and by assuming that the genesis and change of behaviors which constitute "consciousness" are ultimately determined by the social community. The specific content of covert responses is traced back to originally overt responses and corresponding experiences of the individual, eventually leading to self-observations. These self-observations are given the status of data language similar to that of responses observed in another person. This position has been widely criticized. The clearest basis for the objections has been presented by Malcolm (1964), who calls the treatment of first-person-present-tense sentences the Achilles' heel of behaviorism. Malcolm asserts that statements about one's feelings, plan, or other *self-testimony* are not based on self-observations, nor are they verifiable against physical events or circumstances other than the person's own testimony. Consequently, "self-testimony is largely *autonomous*, not replaceable even in principle by observations of functional relations between physical variables." (Malcolm, 1964, p. 154). Behaviorism is found lacking because it regards man as "*solely an object*."

Chomsky and his group attack behaviorism on somewhat similar grounds for its failure to grant some preprogrammed proclivity for ordering language and thoughts. A nativistic assumption fits better some of the remarkable capacity of the child to acquire competence not in speaking specific sets of utterances but a well-articulated language, by transformation of abstract rules for speech-part relationships (Chomsky, 1965; Katz, 1966). Recent information-processing and computer-simulation models also propose that complex "structural" characteristics of psychological functions can explain universalities in covert processes in a way which differs radically from the simplistic S-R view that "subjectivity" and the content of covert responses can be accounted for by a combination of learning and social variables, acting within the limits of the biologically given universality of capacity for various behaviors.

These problems in agreement on the degree to which human thought processes and other covert behaviors are genetically determined present major obstacles to research in self-regulation.

Firmly established views about the nature of voluntary behaviors, free will, conscious awareness, and similarly complex and partly covert intra-individual processes have bolstered the historical bias for acceptance of a different model for human behavior than for that of infrahuman organisms, not on a basis of greater complexity but on the assumption of emergent phenomena mainly associated with man's use of language. There are many current efforts to extend the behavioristic formulation to areas of problem-solving (e.g., Goldiamond, 1966; Skinner, 1966), to self-perception (D. J. Bem, 1965, 1967), verbal conditioning (Kanfer, 1968; Krasner, 1962; Verplanck, 1962), awareness (Maltzman, 1966), and other areas. Nevertheless, the role and mechanisms of covert behaviors and the general problem of handling events in which the same person is actor and object of action in momentarily shifting roles have not yet been resolved in a satisfactory way. It would seem to be the burden of those who urge the behavioristic model to continue their efforts to encompass these phenomena and to demonstrate their ultimate origin in the social-verbal environment, molded by the particular structural and functional characteristics of the human biological organism. They must show that environmental influences can, and do, originate and modify subjective experiences. Without incorporation of these phenomena into the behavioristic model it is quite probable that the days of even a methodological behaviorism are numbered. It is the author's belief that the study and understanding of self-regulatory processes occupy a central position in this area of controversy.

The clinical utility of behavioristic models may be limited to pragmatics. Current behavior modification clinicians appear to operate at two levels. New methods for observation of behaviors and for modifying specific target behaviors seem to derive well from learning methods and principles. In creating new procedures for treatment (and for diagnosis) an expanded store of techniques is becoming available for application to increasingly diverse problems. However, in decisions about selecting the target for therapy, in predictions of the probable effectiveness of procedures and in hundreds of momentary judgments about the patient and his response to various methods, clinicians of all persuasions shift to the commonsense model, drawn from their personal histories and other nonpsychological resources. While this compromise does retain the "human element" in treatment, it is important to recognize it as a compromise. Perhaps this facet of clinical work represents the art component encountered in any applied science. Even if the therapist's basis for application of his techniques is not fully understood, knowledge of the patient's capacity for self-regulation and of means by which it can be modified would still contribute toward more effective and economic procedures for behavior modification.

The specific task in the study of self-regulation concerns demonstration of the processes by which a person can modify his own behavior, with accounts of conditions which initiate the modification efforts, of the methods and mechanisms used for the modification, and of the cessation of modifying efforts.

If such terms as self-regulation or self-control are used, it is necessary to specify the limits of the types of behaviors which would fall into these categories. This requirement raises first the question about the continuous versus temporary nature of self-regulatory processes. Reflection suggests that the simple definition of self-control as either (1) the omission of behavior which would lead to attainment of rewards or avoidance of punishment, or (2) the commission of acts which have known aversive consequences, appears to be inadequate because it would cover thousands of easily observed examples in daily life in which behavior seems to be under such control without any apparent intentional or special intervention by the person himself. Further, there appears to be a cultural definition inherent in the use of the term "self-control." In many instances occurrence or nonoccurrence of the same response will consensually not be accepted as examples of self-control, depending upon the circumstances. For example, it is trivial to consider as an instance of self-control a healthy adult's failure to wet his pants. But the same behavior in a 3-year-old child might be used as such an example. Thus, the *non-occurrence* of many behaviors which may have had earlier functions in procuring reinforcing events is not sufficient evidence for self-regulation.

It appears that the process of self-regulation must have at its origin strong motivational components which are related to the physical or social environment of the person. In continuous daily adult behavior, there are points at which self-regulatory processes begin, and the cues for the onset of such processes need to be examined. On a speculative basis it is proposed that self-regulatory processes begin when self-monitoring of behavior reveals a departure from a band or range of consensually acceptable behaviors in a situation which may have ultimate aversive consequences. To explain the nature of this self-monitoring process one can take recourse to early learning when a mother, teacher, or other adult functions as monitor for young children by interfering only when a particular behavioral sequence shows some properties which are either excessive or deficient with regard to the band of behaviors appropriate for that situation. Such training in self-monitoring is facilitated when the trainer labels the cues for detecting deviations and assists in rectification of the behavior by direct training or by permitting the child to observe corrections. To some extent, a useful model may be one that is similar to the feedback circuitry involved in quality control analysis. At first the feedback loop affects only the mother of a child and brings into play corrective behaviors by the mother. Eventually direct feedback to the child is established and the necessity for mother's labelling and corrective responses no longer exists. Such a hypothesis would propose that self-regulation is *not* a continuous process, but is invoked as a self-correcting procedure only when discrepancies, cues of impending danger, or conflicting motivational states activate the monitoring system.

The implication of this approach is to deny the existence of a unitary and continuously acting inhibitory mechanism. Rather, it is suggested that the onset of self-controlling responses depends on the individual's learning history and on situational cues. The notion is also rejected that self-control is an internalized personality trait which affects the person's pattern of moral behaviors, guilt, shame, or other secondary social controlling techniques. The latter may be conceptualized as related but independent of self-controlling processes, based on separate developmental histories. Our line of thought suggests that self-regulatory behaviors are not always socially effective or desirable. Only if the person has had experiences under conditions similar to the current one and is familiar with the cultural expectations for the range of appropriate behaviors will his self-controlling behavior be adequate. A simple example is that of a foreigner who makes a faux pas, recognizes its deviational quality because of social signals from spectators, proceeds to modify his own behavior but often does so only to aggravate the situation because of his lack of socially prescribed standards for it. Similarly, self-control by administration of aversive stimuli may have only detrimental social effects.

We propose then that learning to monitor one's behavior is an essential prerequisite for the proper application of self-regulation and self-control. As a corollary, it would be expected that adequate self-control is encountered to a greater extent in individuals who have had better training in self-observation and self-monitoring, and who can activate the self-regulatory process when called for. The deviations from the culturally determined and commonly agreed behavioral band may be in terms of physical response characteristics, functional consequences, rate of the behavior, or any other characteristic.

Our view of self-regulation leads us to consider self-control as a special case of self-regulation. While self-regulatory behaviors generally result in some modification of one's own behavior or of the environmental setting, self-control is characterized as a special case in which there is some underlying motive for *nonexecution* of a response sequence which, under other circumstances, would be predicted to have a high probability of occurrence. Self-control always involves a situation in which there is potentiality of execution of highly probable behaviors, but instead a response of lower probability occurs. The interest is in the variables which effect the reduction of the occurrence of the probabilities of such behaviors. Self-regulation also includes instances in which simple adjustments occur, shifting the relative probabilities of a set of behaviors. These changes may follow self-monitoring or any event which leads the person to change his behavior toward greater effectiveness. For example, poor results from use of a paint brush may result in use of a different brush, washing it, or abandonment of the project. Such a behavioral episode involves self-regulation as defined here, but not self-control.

A number of cues for the onset of self-monitoring behaviors seem to be available. Among these are: (1) Intervention by others, e.g., the threat of punishment, or focus on one's own behavior by an external event. A mother's critical comment or a boss's low performance rating for a specific job are examples in this class. (2) The presence of extreme activation levels, either excessively high or low may serve as cues for self-monitoring. For instance, physiological feedback of hyperactivity, excitement, emotional states, boredom, depressed behavior, may serve such cue functions for self-monitoring. (3) The failure of predicted consequences to occur as the result of one's own behavior may occasion self-monitoring. Such cues are illustrated by a person's failure to achieve anticipated physical consequences, e.g., operation of an unfamiliar car does not lead to starting the engine, telling a joke in a social setting does not lead to laughter, a verbal response fails to exert control over a physical or social stimulus object. (4) The availability of several different roles or response sets, as encountered in most "choice" behaviors, can trigger self-monitoring.

A separate and somewhat subordinate question concerns the particular mechanisms which are available to the individual in a culture for control over problematic behaviors, once these behaviors are recognized and labeled as problematic by the individual. The description of these mechanisms constitutes the main content of research in self-control. Demonstrations of the regulation of behaviors by "conscience," "guilt," or other devices for establishing self-control represent technical descriptions of methods for achieving the desired end, i.e., for modifying the probability of occurrence of a highly probable response without use of direct external contingency relationships between the response and its immediate social consequences. It is also in this area that some motivational constructs, such as self-reward and self-punishment mechanisms, are required in order to invoke learning principles applying to motivated behaviors. Controls initiated by the person may involve the utilization of secondary positive *or* negative reinforcers. They may involve manipulation of the environment or of other response probabilities in the person's repertoire, or the utilization of verbal behaviors for the purpose of rearranging contingencies under his own control. It is this area in which expanded knowledge may bring both improved conceptual models of human functioning and more effective methods for behavior modification.

REFERENCES

Agras, W. S. Transfer during systematic desensitization therapy. *Behaviour Research and Therapy,* 1967, *5*, 193–199.

Amrine, M. The 1965 congressional inquiry into testing: A commentary. *American Psychologist*, 1965, *20*, 859–871.

Anant, S. S. A note on the treatment of alcoholics by a verbal aversion technique. *Canadian Psychologist*, 1967, *8A*, 19–22.

Arellano, A., & MacLean, P. D. *Electroencephalography and Clinical Neurophysiology*, 1949, *1*, 251.

Arkowitz, H. Desensitizations as a self-control procedure: A case report. Unpublished manuscript, University of Oregon, 1969.

Aronfreed, J. The origin of self-criticism. *Psychological Review*, 1964, *71*, 193–218.

Aronfreed, J., & Reber, A. Internalized behavioral suppression and the timing of social punishment. *Journal of Personality and Social Psychology*, 1965, *1*, 3–16.

Aronson, E., & Carlsmith, J. M. The effect of severity of threat on the devaluation of forbidden behavior. *Journal of Abnormal Social Psychology*, 1963, *66*, 584–588.

Ashem, B., & Donner, L. Covert sensitization with alcoholics: A controlled replication. *Behaviour Research and Therapy*, 1968, *6*, 7–12.

Ausubel, D. P. Relationships between shame and guilt in the socializing process. *Psychological Review,* 1955, *62*, 378–390.

Ax, A. F. Physiological differentiation of emotional states. *Psychosomatic Medicine*, 1953, *15*, 433–442.

Ayllon, T., & Azrin, N. H. Reinforcement and instructions with mental patients. *Journal of the Experimental Analysis of Behavior*, 1964, *7*, 327–331.

Bakan, D. Clinical psychology and logic. *American Psychologist*, 1956, *11*, 655–662.

Bandura, A. Psychotherapy as a learning process. *Psychological Bulletin*, 1961, *58*, 143–159.

Bandura, A. Social learning through imitation. In M. R. Jones (Ed.), *Nebraska symposium on motivation*. Lincoln: University of Nebraska Press, 1962.

Bandura, A. *Principles of behavior modification*. New York: Holt, Rinehart and Winston, 1969.

Bandura, A., Grusec, J. E., & Menlove, F. L. Some social determinants of self-monitoring reinforcement systems. *Journal of Personality and Social Psychology*, 1967, *5*, 449–455.

Bandura, A., & Kupers, C. J. Transmission of patterns of self-reinforcement through modeling. *Journal of Abnormal and Social Psychology*, 1964, *69*, 1–9.

Bandura, A., & Perloff, B. Relative efficacy of self-monitored and externally imposed reinforcement systems. *Journal of Personality and Social Psychology*, 1967, *7*, 111–116.

Bandura, A., Ross, D., & Ross, S. A. Transmission of aggression through imitation of aggressive models. *Journal of Abnormal and Social Psychology*, 1961, *63*, 575–582.

Bandura, A., Ross, D., & Ross, S. A. A comparative test of the status envy, social power, and secondary reinforcement theories of identification learning. *Journal of Abnormal and Social Psychology*, 1963, *67*, 527–534.

Bandura, A., & Walters, R. H. *Social learning and personality development*. New York: Holt, Rinehart and Winston, 1963.

Bandura, A., & Whalen, C. K. The influence of antecedent reinforcement and divergent modeling cues on patterns of self-reward. *Journal of Personality and Social Psychology*, 1966, *3*, 373–382.

Barlow, D. H., Leitenberg, H., & Agras, W. S. Experimental control of sexual deviation through manipulation of the noxious scene in covert sensitization. *Journal of Abnormal Psychology*, 1969, *74*, 596–601.

Barrett-Lennard, G. T. Dimensions of therapist response as causal factors in therapeutic change. *Psychological Monographs*, 1962, *76* (43, Whole No. 562).

Barron, F. The disposition towards originality. *Journal of Abnormal and Social Psychology*, 1955, *51*, 478–485.

Behanan, K. T. *Yoga: A scientific evaluation*. New York: Macmillan, 1937.

Bem, D. J. An experimental analysis of self-persuasion. *Journal of Experimental and Social Psychology*, 1965, *1*, 199–218.

Bem, D. J. Self-perception: An alternative interpretation of cognitive dissonance phenomena. *Psychological Review*, 1967, *74*, 183–200.

Bem, S. L. Verbal Self-control: The establishment of effective self-instruction. *Journal of Experimental Psychology*, 1967, *74*, 485–491.

Benedict, R. *The chrysanthemum and the sword: Patterns of Japanese culture.* Boston: Houghton Mifflin, 1946.

Berne, E. *Games people play.* New York: Grove, 1964.

Bijou, S. W., & Baer, D. M. *Child development I: A systematic and empirical theory.* New York: Appleton, 1961.

Birge, J. S. Verbal responses in transfer. Unpublished doctoral dissertation, Yale University, 1941.

Blakemore, C. B., Thorpe, J. G., Barker, J. C., Conway, C. C., & Levin, N. I. The application of faradic aversion conditioning in a case of transvestism. *Behaviour Research Therapy*, 1963, *1*, 29–34.

Bond, I. K., & Hutchison, H. C. Application of reciprocal inhibition therapy to exhibitionism. *Canadian Medical Association Journal*, 1960, *83*, 23–25.

Bonvallet, M., Dell, P., & Hiebel, G. Tonus sympathique et activite electrique corticale. *Electroencephalography and Clinical Neurophysiology*, 1954, *6*, 119–144.

Boomer, D. S., & Goodrich, D. W. Speech disturbance and judged anxiety. *Journal of Consulting Psychology*, 1961, *25*, 160–164.

Brady, J. P. Brevital-relaxation treatment of frigidity. *Behaviour Research and Therapy*, 1966, *4*, 71–77.

Brady, J. P. Comments on methohexitone-aided desensitization. *Behaviour Research and Therapy*, 1967, *5*, 259–260.

Breger, L., & McGaugh, J. L. Critique and reformulation of "learning-theory" approaches to psychotherapy and neurosis. *Psychological Bulletin*, 1965, *63*, 338–358.

Brehm, J. W., & Cohen, A. R. *Explorations in cognitive dissonance.* New York: Wiley, 1962.

Brener, J. Heart rate as an avoidance response. *Psychological Record*, 1966, *16*, 329–336.

Brogden, W. J. Animal studies of learning. In S. S. Stevens (Ed.) *Handbook of experimental psychology.* New York: Wiley, 1951.

Bruch, H. *The importance of overweight.* New York: Norton, 1957.

Bruner, J. S., Goodnow, J. J., & Austin, G. A. *A study of thinking.* New York: Wiley, 1956.

Cannon, W. B. *Bodily changes in pain, hunger, fear and rage.* (2nd ed.) New York: Appleton, 1929.

Cantril, H., & Hunt, W. A. Emotional effects produced by the injection of adrenalin. *American Journal of Psychology*, 1932, *44*, 300–307.

Cappon, D. Obesity. *Canadian Medical Association Journal*, 1958, *79*, 568–573.

Carlson, L. D. Temperature. *Annual Review of Physiology*, 1962, *24*, 85–101.

Cauffman, W. J., & Pauley, W. G. Obesity and emotional status. *Pennsylvania Medical Journal*, 1961, *64*, 505–507.

Cautela, J. R. The problem of backward conditioning. *Journal of Psychology*, 1965, *60*, 135–144.

Cautela, J. R. A behavior therapy approach to pervasive anxiety. *Behaviour Research and Therapy*, 1966, *4*, 99–109. (a)

Cautela, J. R. Treatment of compulsive behavior by covert sensitization. *Psychological Record*, 1966, *16*, 33–41. (b)

Cautela, J. R. Covert sensitization. *Psychological Reports*, 1967, *20*, 459–468.

Cautela, J. R. Behavior therapy and self-control: Techniques and implications. In C. M. Franks (Ed.) *Behavior therapy: Assessment and status*. New York: McGraw-Hill, 1969.

Cautela, J. R. Covert reinforcement. *Behavior Therapy*, 1970, *1*, 33–50.

Chomsky, N. *Aspects of the theory of syntax*. Cambridge, Mass.: MIT Press, 1965.

Clark, D. R. The treatment of monosymptomatic phobia by systematic desensitization. *Behaviour Research and Therapy*, 1963, *1*, 63–68.

Cloward, R. A., & Ohlin, L. E. *Delinquency and opportunity: A theory of delinquent gangs*. New York: Free Press, 1960.

Cobb, S. *Emotions and clinical medicine*. New York: Norton, 1950.

Cooke, G. The efficacy of two desensitization procedures: An analogue study. *Behaviour Research and Therapy*, 1966, *4*, 17–24.

Cooks, G. Evaluation of the efficacy of the components of reciprocal inhibition. *Journal of Abnormal Psychology*, 1968, *73*, 464–467.

Coué, E. *The practice of autosuggestion*. New York: Doubleday, 1922.

Creative Education Foundation. Compendium of research on creative imagination. Buffalo, N. Y.: S. J. Parnes, 1958.

Crider, D., Shapiro, D., & Tursky, B. Reinforcement of spontaneous electrodermal activity. *Journal of Comparative and Physiological Psychology*, 1966, *61*, 20–27.

Dale, C. L. A report on the 5-day plan to help adult smokers stop smoking. In, *Can we help them stop?* Illinois: American Cancer Society, Illinois Division, 1964.

Dalzell-Ward, A. J. The development of anti-smoking clinics in the United Kingdom. In, *Can we help them stop?* Illinois: American Cancer Society, Illinois Division, 1964.

Davids, A. H., & Eriksen, C. W. The relationship of manifest anxiety to association productivity and intellectual attainment. *Journal of Consulting Psychology*, 1955, *19*, 219–222.

Davis, L. W., & Husband, R. W. A study of hypnotic susceptibility in relation to personality traits. *Journal of Abnormal and Social Psychology*, 1931, *26*, 175–182.

Davison, G. C. Relative contributions of differential relaxation and graded exposure to *in vivo* desensitization of a neurotic fear. *Proceedings of the 73rd Annual Convention of the American Psychological Association*, 1965, *1*, 209–210.

Davison, G. C. Anxiety under total curarization: Implications for the role of muscular relaxation in the desensitization of neurotic fears. *Journal of Nervous and Mental Disease*, 1967, *143*, 443–448.

Davison, G. C. Elimination of a sadistic fantasy by a client-controlled counterconditioning technique: A case study. *Journal of Abnormal Psychology*, 1968, *73*, 84–90. (a)

Davison, G. C. Systematic desensitization as a counterconditioning process. *Journal of Abnormal Psychology*, 1968, *73*, 91–99. (b)

Davidson, G. C. Appraisal of behavior modification techniques with adults in institutional settings. In C. M. Franks (Ed.), *Behavior therapies: Assessment and appraisal.* New York: McGraw-Hill, 1969. (a)

Davison, G. C. Self-control through "imaginal aversive contingency" and "one-downmanship": Enabling the powerless to accommodate unreasonableness. In J. D. Krumboltz & C. E. Thoresen (Eds.). *Behavioral counseling: Cases and techniques.* New York: Holt, Rinehart and Winston, 1969. (b)

Davison, G. C., Goldfried, M. R., & Krasner, L. A postdoctoral program in behavior modification: Theory and practice. *American Psychologist*, 1970, *25*, 767–772.

Davison, G. C., & Valins, S. On self-produced and drug-produced relaxation. *Behavior Research and Therapy*, 1968, *6*, 401–402.

Davison, G. C., & Valins, S. Maintenance of self-attributed and drug-attributed behavior change. *Journal of Personality and Social Psychology*, 1969, *11*, 25–33.

Deese, J. *The Psychology of learning.* New York: McGraw-Hill, 1958.

Dollard, J., & Miller, N. E. *Personality and psychotherapy.* New York: McGraw-Hill, 1950.

Dunsmure, J., Jr. *Edinburgh Medical Journal*, 1874, *20*, 173.

D'Zurilla, T. J. Persuasion and praise as techniques for modifying verbal behavior in a "real-life" group setting. *Journal of Abnormal Psychology*, 1966, *71*, 369–376.

D'Zurilla, T. J. Reducing heterosexual anxiety. In J. D. Krumboltz and C. E. Thoresen (Eds.) *Behavioral counseling: Cases and techniques.* New York: Holt, Rinehart and Winston, 1969.

D'Zurilla, T. J., & Goldfried, M. R. Cognitive processes, problem-solving, and effective behavior. In M. R. Goldfried & M. Merbaum (Eds.) *Behavior change through self-control.* New York: Holt, Rinehart, and Winston, 1973.

D'Zurilla, T. J., & Goldfried, M. R. Problem solving and behavior modification. *Journal of Abnormal Psychology*, 1971, *78*, 107–126.

Eaton, J. W., & Weil, R. J. *Culture and mental disorders.* New York: Free Press, 1955.

Edwards, A. L. *Experimental design in psychological research.* New York: Holt, Rinehart and Winston, 1950.

Edwards, A. L. *Experimental design in psychological research.* New York: Holt, Rinehart and Winston, 1960.

Efron, R. *Brain*, 1956, *79*, 267.

Efron, R. The unconditioned inhibition of uncinate fits. *Brain*, 1957, *80*, 251–262.

Einstein, A., & Infeld, L. *The evolution of physics.* New York: Simon and Schuster, 1938.

Ejrup, B. The role of nicotine in smoking pleasure. In, *Can we help them stop?* Illinois: American Cancer Society, Illinois Division, 1964. (a)

Ejrup, B. Treatment of tobacco addiction: Experiences in tobacco withdrawal clinics. In, *Can we help them stop?* Illinois: American Cancer Society Illinois Division, 1964. (b)

Ellis, A. New approaches to psychotherapy techniques. *Journal of Clinical Psychology Monograph Supplement*, No. 11. Brandon, Vt.: *Journal of Clinical Psychology*, 1955. (a)

Ellis, A. Psychotherapy techniques for use with psychotics. *American Journal of Psychotherapy*, 1955, *9*, 452–476. (b)

Ellis, A. An operational reformulation of some of the basic principles of psychoanalysis. *Psychoanalytic Review*, 1956, *43*, 163–180. (a)

Ellis, A. The effectiveness of psychotherapy with individuals who have severe homosexual problems. *Journal of Consulting Psychology*, 1956, *20*, 191–195. (b)

Ellis, A. Rational psychotherapy and individual psychology. *Journal of Individual Psychology*, 1957, *13*, 38–44. (a)

Ellis, A. Outcome of employing three techniques of psychotherapy. *Journal of Clinical Psychology*, 1957, *13*, 344–350. (b)

Ellis, A. Rational psychotherapy. *Journal of General Psychology*, 1958, *59*, 35–49.

Ellis, A. A homosexual treated with rational psychotherapy. *Journal of Clinical Psychology*, 1959, *15*, 338–343.

Ellis, A. The treatment of a psychopath with rational psychotherapy. *Journal of Psychology*, 1961, *51*, 141–150.

Ellis, A. *Reason and emotion in psychotherapy*. New York: Lyle Stuart, 1962.

Engel, B. T., & Hanson, S. P. Operant conditioning of heart rate slowing. *Psychophysiology*, 1966, *3*, 176–187.

Erickson, M. A. The utilization of patient behavior in the hypnotherapy of obesity: Three case reports. *American Journal of Clinical Hypnosis*, 1960, *3*, 112–116.

Estes, W. K. An experimental study of punishment. *Psychological Monographs*, 1944, *57* (3, Whole No. 263).

Estes, W. K. The statistical approach to learning theory. In S. Koch (Ed.), *Psychology: A study of science*. Vol. 2. New York: McGraw-Hill, 1959.

Eysenck, H. J. The effects of psychotherapy: An evaluation. *Journal of Consulting Psychology*, 1952, *16*, 319–324.

Eysenck, H. J. The effects of psychotherapy. In H. J. Eysenck (Ed.), *Handbook of abnormal psychology*. New York: Basic Books, 1961. (a)

Eysenck, H. J. (Ed.) *Handbook of abnormal psychology*. New York: Basic Books, 1961. (b)

Eysenck, H. J. and Furneaux, W. D. Primary and secondary suggestibility: An experimental and statistical study. *Journal of Experimental Psychology*, 1945, *35*, 485–503.

Eysenck, H. J., & Rachman, S. *The causes and cures of neuroses*. San Diego: Knapp, 1965.

Feldman, M. P. Aversion therapy for sexual deviations. *Psychological Bulletin*, 1966, *65*, 56–79.

Fenichel, O. *The psychoanalytic theory of neurosis.* New York: Norton, 1945.

Ferguson, G. A. *Statistical analysis in psychology and education.* New York: McGraw-Hill, 1959.

Ferster, C. B. Reinforcement and punishment in the control of human behavior by social agencies. *Psychiatric Research Report*, 1958, *10*, 101–118.

Ferster, C. B., Nurnberger, J. I., & Levitt, E. E. The control of eating. *Journal of Mathetics*, 1962, *1*, 87–109.

Ferster, C. B., & Skinner, B. F. *Schedules of reinforcement.* New York: Appleton, 1957.

Festinger, L. A theory of social comparison processes. *Human Relations*, 1954, *7*, 117–140.

Fisher, V. E., & Marrow, J. Experimental study of moods. *Character & Personality*, 1934, *2*, 201–208.

Foulds, G. A. Temperamental differences in maze performance. Part 1: Characteristic differences among psychoneurotics. *British Journal of Psychology*, 1951, *42*, 209–217.

Fowler, R. L., & Kimmel, H. D. Operant conditioning of the GSR. *Journal of Experimental Psychology*, 1962, *63*, 563–567.

Frank, J. D. Problems of controls in psychotherapy. In E. A. Rubinstein & M. B. Parloff (Eds.), *Research in psychotherapy.* Washington, D. C.: American Psychological Association, 1959.

Frank, J. D. *Persuasion and healing.* Baltimore: Johns Hopkins, 1961.

Franklin, R. E., & Rynearson, E. H. An evaluation of the effectiveness of dietary instruction for the obese. *Staff Meetings of the Mayo Clinic*, 1960, *35*, 123–131.

Franks, C. M. Alcohol, alcoholism and conditioning. A review of the literature and some theoretical considerations. *Journal of Mental Science*, 1958, *104*, 14–33.

Franks, C. M. Conditioning and conditioned aversion therapies in the treatment of alcoholics. *International Journal of Addiction*, 1966, *1*, 61–98.

Frazier, T. W. Avoidance conditioning of heart rate in humans. *Psychophysiology*, 1966, *3*, 188–202.

Freud, S. *Collected Papers.* London: Hogarth Press, 1924–1950.

Freud, S. *Basic Writings.* New York: Modern Library, 1938.

Friedman, D. A new technique for the systematic desensitization of phobic symptoms. *Behavior Research and Therapy*, 1966, *4*, 139–140.

Galvin, E. P., & McGavack, T. H. *Obesity, its cause, classification and care.* New York: Hoeber-Harper, 1957.

Geer, J. H. The development of a scale to measure fear. *Behaviour Research and Therapy*, 1965, *3*, 45–53.

Geer, J. H. Effect of fear arousal upon task performance and verbal behavior. *Journal of Abnormal Psychology*, 1966, *71*, 119–123.

Gelder, M. G., Marks, I. M., Wolff, H. H., & Clarke, M. Desensitization and psychotherapy in the treatment of phobic states: A controlled inquiry. *British Journal of Psychiatry*, 1967, *113*, 53–73.

Gelfand, D. M. The influence of self-esteem on rate of verbal conditioning and social matching behavior. *Journal of Abnormal and Social Psychology*, 1962, *65*, 259–265.

Gelhorn, E. Motion and emotion: The role of proprioception in the physiology and pathology of the emotions. *Psychological Review*, 1964, *71*, 457–472.

Gerry, R., DeVeau, L., & Chorness, M. A review of some recent research in the field of creativity and the examination of an experimental creativity workshop. Training Analysis and Development Division. Lackland AFB, Tex., 1957.

Gilkinson, H. Social fears as reported by students in college speech classes. *Speech Monograph*, 1942, *9*, 141–160.

Gold, S., & Neufeld, I. L. A learning approach to the treatment of homosexuality. *Behaviour Research and Therapy*, 1965, *2*, 201–204.

Goldfried, M. R. Systematic desensitization as training in self-control. *Journal of Consulting and Clinical Psychology*, 1971, *37*, 228–235.

Goldfried, M. R. Reduction of generalized anxiety through a variant of systematic desensitization. In M. R. Goldfried & M. Merbaum (Eds.), *Behavior change through self-control*. New York: Holt, Rinehart and Winston, 1973.

Goldfried, M. R., & Merbaum, M. (Eds.) *Behavior change through self-control*. New York: Holt, Rinehart and Winston, 1973.

Goldfried, M. R., & D'Zurilla, T. J. A behavioral-analytic model for assessing competence. In C. D. Spielberger (Ed.) *Current topics in clinical and community psychology. Vol. I*. New York: Academic Press, 1969.

Goldfried, M. R., & Pomeranz, D. M. Role of assessment in behavior modification. *Psychological Reports*, 1968, *23*, 75–87.

Goldiamond, I. Justified and unjustified alarm over behavioral control. In O. Milton (Ed.), *Behavior disorders: Perspectives and trends*. Philadelphia: Lippincott, 1965. (a)

Goldiamond, I. Stuttering and fluency as manipulatable operant response classes. In L. Krasner and L. P. Ullmann (Eds.), *Research in behavior modification*, New York: Holt, Rinehart and Winston, 1965. (b)

Goldiamond, I. Self-control procedures in personal behavior problems. *Psychological Reports*, 1965, *17*, 851–868. (c)

Goldiamond, I. Perception, language, and conceptualization rules. In B. Kleinmuntz (Ed.) *Problem Solving: Research, method, and theory*. New York: Wiley, 1966.

Goldiamond, I., Dyrud, J., & Miller, M. Practice as research in professional psychology. *Canadian Psychologist*, 1965, *6a*, 110–128.

Goldman, R., Jaffa, M., & Schachter, S. Yom Kippur, Air France, dormitory food, and the eating behavior of obese and normal persons. *Journal of Personality and Sound Psychology*, 1968, *10*, 117–123.

Goldstein, A. P. Patient's expectancies and non-specific therapy as a basis for (un)spontaneous remission. *Journal of Clinical Psychology*, 1960, *16*, 399–403.

Goldstein, A. P. *Therapist-patient expectancies in psychotherapy.* New York: Pergamon, 1962.

Goldstein, K. M. Note: A comparison of self-reports and peer-reports of smoking and drinking behavior. *Psychological Reports*, 1966, *18*, 702.

Goodrich, F. W., Jr., and Thomas, H. A clinical study of natural childbirth. *American Journal of Obstetrics and Gynecology*, 1948, *56*, 875–883.

Gordon, J. E. (Ed.) *Handbook of clinical and experimental hypnosis.* New York: Macmillan, 1967.

Gore, W. J., & Dyson, J. W. (Eds.) *The making of decisions: A reader in administrative behavior.* London: Free Press, 1964.

Gough, H. G. *Manual for the California Psychological Inventory.* Palo Alto, Calif.: Consulting Psychologists Press, 1957.

Gough, H. G., & Heilbrun, A. B., Jr. *The Adjective Check List manual.* Palo Alto, Calif.: Consulting Psychologists Press, 1965.

Gowers, W. *Epilepsy and other chronic convulsive diseases.* London, 1881.

Gray, B. B., England, G., & Mohoney, J. L. Treatment of benign vocal nodules by reciprocal inhibition. *Behaviour Research and Therapy*, 1965, *3*, 187–193.

Greene, R. S. Modification of smoking behavior by free operant conditioning methods. *Psychological Record*, 1964, *14*, 171–178.

Guthrie, E. R. *The psychology of learning.* New York: Harper & Row, 1935.

Hall, J. F. *The psychology of learning.* Philadelphia: Lippincott, 1966.

Hammond, E. C. The effects of smoking. *Scientific American*, 1962, *207*, 39–51.

Harmon, A. R., Purkonen, R. A., & Rasmussen, L. P. Obesity: A physical and emotional problem. *Nursing Outlook*, 1958, *6*, 452–456.

Harris, M. B. Self-directed program for weight control: A pilot study. *Journal of Abnormal Psychology*, 1969, *74*, 263–270.

Hartmann, H. *Ego Psychology and the problem of adaptation.* (Trans, by D. Rapaport) New York: International University Press, 1958.

Hess, C. B. New York City's stop smoking program. In, *Can we help them stop?* Illinois: American Cancer Society, Illinois Division, 1964.

Hnatiow, M., & Lang, P. J. Learned stabilization of cardiac rate. *Psychophysiology*, 1965, *1*, 330–336.

Holland, J. G., & Skinner, B. F. *The analysis of behavior.* New York: McGraw-Hill, 1961.

Holz, W. C., & Azrin, N. H. A comparison of several procedures for eliminating behavior. *Journal of the Experimental Analysis of Behavior*, 1963, *6*, 399–406.

Homme, L. E. Control of the relaxation operant. Unpublished manuscript, 1965. (a)

Homme, L. E. Control of coverants: The operants of the mind. *Psychological Record*, 1965, *15*, 501–511. (b)

Homme, L. E. Contiguity theory and contingency management. *Psychological Record*, 1966, *16*, 233–241.

Honigfeld, G. Non-specific factors in treatment. I. Review of placebo reactions and placebo reactors. *Diseases of the Nervous System*, 1964, *25*, 145–156.

Horn, D., Courts, F., Taylor, R., & Solomon, E. Cigarette smoking among high school students. *American Journal of Public Health*, 1959, *49*, 1497–1511.

Hudgins, C. V. *Journal of General Psychology*, 1933, *8*, 3.

Hughes, C. C., Tremblay, M., Rapoport, R. N., & Leighton, A. H. *People of cove and woodlot: Communities from the viewpoint of social psychiatry*. New York: Basic Books, 1960.

Hull, C. L. Quantitative aspects of the evolution of concepts. *Psychological Monographs*, 1920, *28*, 85 pps.

Hull, C. L., Knowledge and purpose as habit mechanisms. *Psychological Review*, 1930, *37*, 511–525.

Hull, C. L. Goal attraction and directing ideas conceived as habit phenomena. *Psychological Review*, 1931, *38*, 487–506.

Hull, C. L. *Hypnosis and suggestibility*. New York: Appleton, 1933.

Hull, C. L. The concept of the habit-family hierarchy and maze learning. *Psychological Review*, 1934, *41*, 33–52; 134–152.

Hull, C. L. The mechanism of the assembly of behavior segments in novel combinations suitable for problem solution. *Psychological Review*, 1935, *42*, 219–245.

Hull, C. L. The problem of stimulus equivalence in behavior theory. *Psychological Review*, 1939, *46*, 9–30.

Hunt, J. McV., Cole, M. W., & Reis, E. E. Situational cues distinguishing anger, fear, and sorrow. *American Journal of Psychology*, 1958, *71*, 136–151.

Husek, T. R., & Alexander, S. The effectiveness of the anxiety differential in examination stress situations. *Educational Psychological Measurement*, 1963, *23*, 309–318.

Jackson, J. H. On a case of fits resembling those artificially produced in guinea-pigs. *Transactions of the Medical Society of London*, 1887, *10*, 78.

Jacobson, E. *Progressive relaxation*. Chicago: University of Chicago Press, 1938.

Jakubczak, L. F., & Walters, R. H. Suggestibility as dependency behavior. *Journal of Abnormal and Social Psychology*, 1959, *59*, 102–107.

Jasper, H., & Shagass, C. Conditioning the occipital alpha rhythm in man. *Journal of Experimental Psychology*, 1941, *28*, 373. (a)

Jasper, H., & Shagass, C. Conscious time judgments related to conditioned time intervals and voluntary control of the alpha rhythm. *Journal of Experimental Psychology*, 1941, *28*, 503. (b)

James, W. *The principles of psychology*. New York: Holt, 1890.

Johnson, S. B. Self-reinforcement vs. external reinforcement in behavior modification with children. *Developmental Psychology*, 1970, *3*, 147–148.

Johnson, W. *People in quandries*. New York: Harper, 1946.

Johnson, W. B. Euphoric and depressed moods in normal subjects. *Character and Personality*, 1937, *6*, 79–98.

Johnson, W. G. Some applications of Homme's coverant control therapy: Two case reports. *Behavior Therapy*, 1971, *2*, 240–248.

Kahn, M., & Baker, B. Desensitization with minimal therapist contact. *Journal of Abnormal Psychology*, 1968, *73*, 198–200.

Kamano, D. K. Selective review of effects of discontinuation of drug-treatment: Some implications and problems. *Psychological Reports*, 1966, *19*, 743–749.

Kanfer, F. H. Verbal conditioning: A review of its current status. In T. R. Dixon & D. L. Horton (Eds.), *Verbal behavior and its relation to general S-R theory*. Englewood Cliffs, N. J.: Prentice-Hall, 1968.

Kanfer, F. H. Self-regulation: Research, issues, and speculations, In C. Neuringer & J. L. Michael (Eds.), *Behavior modification in clinical psychology*. New York: Appleton, 1970.

Kanfer, F. H., Bradley, M. M., & Marston, A. R. Self-reinforcement as a function of degree of learning. *Psychological Reports*, 1962, *10*, 885–886.

Kanfer, F. H., & Goldfoot, D. A. Self-control and tolerance of noxious stimulation. *Psychological Reports*, 1966, *18*, 79–85.

Kanfer, F. H., & Marston, A. R. Conditioning of self-reinforcing responses: An analogue to self-confidence training. *Psychological Reports*, 1963, *13*, 63–70. (a)

Kanfer, F. H., & Marston, A. R. Determinants of self-reinforcement in human learning. *Journal of Experimental Psychology*, 1963, *66*, 245–254. (b)

Kanfer, F. H., & Phillips, J. S. Behavior therapy: A panacea for all ills or a passing fancy. *Archives of General Psychiatry*, 1965, *15*, 114–128.

Kanfer, F. H., & Phillips, J. S. *Learning foundations of behavior therapy*. New York: Wiley, 1970.

Kanfer, F. H., & Saslow, G. Behavioral analysis: An alternative to diagnostic classification. *Archives of General Psychiatry*, 1966, *12*, 529–538.

Kanfer, F. H., & Seidner, M. L. Self-control: Factors enhancing tolerance of noxious stimulation. *Journal of Personality and Social Psychology*, 1972, in press.

Kantor, J. R. *Principles of psychology*. Vol. 1. Bloomington: Principia Press, 1924.

Kantor, J. R. *Principles of psychology*. Vol. 2. Bloomington: Principia Press, 1926.

Kaplan, H. I., & Kaplan, H. S. The psychosomatic concept of obesity. *Journal of Nervous and Mental Disorders*, 1957, *125*, 181–201.

Kaplan, B., & Plaut, T. F. A. Personality in a communal society: An analysis of the mental health of the Hutterites. Lawrence, Kans.: *University of Kansas Publications, Social Science Studies*, 1956.

Karst, T. O., & Trexler, L. D. Initial study using fixed-role and rational-emotive therapy in treating public-speaking anxiety. *Journal of Consulting and Clinical Psychology*, 1970, *34*, 360–366.

Katz, J. A. *Philosophy of language*. New York: Harper & Row, 1966.

Kelly, G. A. *The psychology of personal constructs*. New York: Norton, 1955. 2 vols.

Kendler, H. H., & Kendler, T. S. Vertical and horizontal processes in problem solving. *Psychological Review*, 1962, *69*, 1–16.

Keutzer, C. S. Behavior modification of smoking: The experimental investigation of diverse techniques. *Behaviour Research and Therapy*, 1968, *6*, 137–157.

Kiesler, D. J. Some myths of psychotherapy research and the search for a paradigm. *Psychological Bulletin*, 1966, *65*, 110–136.

Kimble, G. A. *Hilgard and Marquis' conditioning and learning.* New York: Appleton, 1961.

Kimmel, E., & Kimmel, H. D. A replication of operant conditioning of the GSR. *Journal of Experimental Psychology*, 1963, *65*, 212–213.

Kleinmuntz, B. (Ed.) *Problem solving: Research, method, and theory.* New York: Wiley, 1966.

Kline, M. V., & Guze, H. Self-hypnosis in childbirth: A clinical evaluation of a patient conditioning program. *Journal of Clinical and Experimental Hypnosis*, 1955, *3*, 142–147.

Koenig, K. P., & Masters, J. Experimental treatment of habitual smoking. *Behaviour Research and Therapy*, 1965, *3*, 235–243.

Kopel, S. Self-control: Some new perspectives. Unpublished manuscript, University of Oregon, 1972.

Korzybski, A. *Science and sanity.* Lancaster, Pa.: Lancaster Press, 1933.

Krasner, L. The therapist as a social reinforcement machine. In H. H. Strupp & L. Luborsky (Eds.), *Research in psychotherapy*, Vol. 2, Washington, D. C.: American Psychological Association, 1962.

Krog, J., Folkow, B., Fox, R. H., & Andersen, K. L. Hand circulation in the cold of Lapps and North Norwegian fishermen. *Journal of Applied Physiology*, 1960, *15*, 654–658.

Kunckle, E. C. Phasic pains induced by cold. *Journal of Applied Physiology*, 1949, *1*, 811–824.

Kushner, M., & Sandler, J. Aversion therapy and the concept of punishment. *Behaviour Research and Therapy*, 1966, *4*, 179–186.

Lacey, J. I. Psychophysiological approaches to the evaluation of psychotherapeutic process and outcome. In E. Rubinstein & M. B. Parloff (Eds.), *Research in psychotherapy.* Washington, D. C.: American Psychological Association, 1959.

Lacey, J. I. Somatic response patterning and stress: Some revisions of activation theory. In M. H. Appley & R. Trumbull (Eds.), *Psychological stress: Issues in research.* New York: Appleton, 1967.

Lacey, J. I., Kagan, J., & Moss, H. The visceral level: Situational determinants and behavioral correlates of autonomic response patterns. *Symposium on the expression of emotions in man.* 1963, *9*, 161–196.

Lacey, J. I., & Lacey, B. C. The relationship of resting autonomic activity to motor impulsivity. In H. C. Solomon, S. Cobb, & W. Penfield (Eds.), *The brain and human behavior.* Vol. 36. Baltimore: Williams & Wilkins, 1958.

Lamaze, F. *Painless childbirth: Psychoprophylactic method.* London: Burke Publishing Co., 1958.

Landis, C., & Hunt, W. A. Adrenalin and emotion. *Psychological Review*, 1932, *39*, 467–485.

Lang, P. J. Experimental studies in desensitization psychotherapy. In J. Wolpe,

A. Salter, & L. J. Reyna (Eds.), *The conditioning therapies*. New York: Holt, Rinehart and Winston, 1964.

Lang, P. J. Fear reduction and fear behavior: Problems in treating a construct. In J. M. Shlien (Ed.) *Research in Psychotherapy*. Vol. III. Washington, D. C.: American Psychological Association, 1968.

Lang, P. J. The mechanics of desensitization and the laboratory study of human fear. In C. M. Franks (Ed.) *Behavior therapy: Assessment and status*. New York: McGraw-Hill, 1969.

Lang, P. J., & Lazovik, A. D. Experimental desensitization of a phobia. *Journal of Abnormal and Social Psychology*, 1963, *66*, 519–525.

Lang, P. J., Lazovik, A. D., & Reynolds, D. J. Desensitization, suggestibility, and pseudotherapy. *Journal of Abnormal Psychology*, 1965, *70*, 395–402.

Lang, P. J., Sroufe, L. A., & Hastings, J. Effects of feedback and instructional set on the control of cardiac rate variability. *Journal of Experimental Psychology*, 1967, *75*, 425–431.

Lashley, K. S. An examination of the "contiguity theory" as applied to discriminative learning. *Journal of Genetic Psychology*, 1942, *26*, 241–265.

Laufberger, V. *Comptes rendus de la Société de Biologie*, 1950, *144*, 467.

Lazarus, A. A. Some clinical applications of autohypnosis. *Medical Proceedings, South Africa*, 1958, *4*, 848–850.

Lazarus, A. A. The results of behavior therapy in 126 cases of severe neurosis. *Behaviour Research and Therapy*, 1963, *1*, 69–79.

Lazarus, A. A., & Rachman, S. The use of systematic desensitization in psychotherapy. In H. J. Eysenck (Ed.), *Behavior therapy and the neurosis*. London: Pergamon, 1960.

Lazarus, R. S. *Psychological stress and the coping process*. New York: McGraw-Hill, 1966.

Lazarus, R. S. Cognitive and personality factors underlying threat and coping. In M. H. Appley & R. Trumbull (Eds.), *Psychological Stress*. New York: Appleton, 1967.

Leitenberg, H., Agras, W. S., Barlow, D. H., & Oliveau, D. C. Contribution of selective positive reinforcement and therapeutic instructions to systematic desensitization therapy. *Journal of Abnormal Psychology*, 1969, *74*, 113–118.

Levin, H., & Baldwin, A. L. Pride and shame in children. In M. R. Jones (Ed.), *Nebraska symposium on motivation*. Lincoln: University of Nebraska Press, 1959.

Lewis, T. Observations upon the reaction of the vessels of the human skin to cold. *Heart*, 1929, *15*, 177–189.

Liebert, R. M., & Allen, M. K. The effects of rule structure and reward magnitude on the acquisition and adoption of self-reward criteria. *Psychological Reports*, 1967, *21*, 445–452.

Lindzey, G. (Ed.) *Handbook of social psychology*. Cambridge, Mass.: Addison-Wesley, 1954.

Lippmann, W. *Public opinion.* New York: Macmillan, 1930.

London, P. *Behavior control.* New York: Harper & Row, 1969.

Lundin, R. W. *Personality: An experimental approach.* New York: Macmillan, 1961.

Luria, A. R. *The Role of speech in the regulation of normal and abnormal behavior.* New York: Pergamon, 1961.

Lysons, D. *Practical Essays upon Intermitting Fevers.* Bath, 1772.

MacCulloch, M. J., Feldman, M. P., Orford, J. F., & MacCulloch, M. L. Anticipatory avoidance learning in the treatment of alcoholism: A record of therapeutic failure. *Behaviour Research and Therapy*, 1966, *4*, 187–196.

MacCulloch, M. J., Feldman, M. P., & Pinschof, J. M. The application of anticipatory avoidance learning to the treatment of homosexuality: Avoidance response latencies and pulse rate changes. *Behaviour Research and Therapy*, 1965, *3*, 21–44.

Mahl, G. F. Disturbances and silences in the patient's speech in psychotherapy. *Journal of Abnormal and Social Psychology*, 1956, *53*, 1–15.

Mahoney, M. J. Toward an experimental analysis of coverant control. *Behavior Therapy*, 1970, *1*, 510–521.

Mahoney, M. J. Research issues in self-management. *Behavior Therapy*, 1972, *3*, 45–63.

Mahrer, A. R. The role of expectancy in delayed reinforcement. *Journal of Experimental Psychology*, 1956, *52*, 101–106.

Malcolm, N. Behaviorism as a philosophy of psychology. In T. W. Wann (Ed.), *Behaviorism and phenomenology*. Chicago: University of Chicago Press, 1964.

Maltzman, I. Awareness: Cognitive psychology vs. behaviorism. *Journal of Experimental Research in Personality*, 1966, *1*, 161–165.

Mandler, G. Emotion. In R. Brown *et al.* (Ed.), *New directions in psychology.* New York: Holt, Rinehart and Winston, 1962.

Marañon, G. Contribution a l'etude de l'action émotive de l'adrénaline. *Review Francaise Endocrinology*, 1924, *2*, 301–325.

Marcia, J. E., Rubin, B. M., & Efran, J. S. Systematic desensitization: Expectancy change or counterconditioning? *Journal of Abnormal Psychology,* 1969, *74*, 382–397.

Marks, I. M., & Gelder, M. G. A controlled retrospective study of behavior therapy in phobic patients. *British Journal of Psychiatry*, 1965, *111*, 561–573.

Marks, I. M., Rachman, S., & Gelder, M. G. Methods for the assessment of aversion treatment in fetishism with masochism. *Behaviour Research and Therapy*, 1965, *3*, 253–258.

Marston, A. R. Variables affecting incidence of self-reinforcement. *Psychological Reports*, 1964, *14*, 879–884.

Marston, A. R. Imitation, self-reinforcement, and reinforcement of another person. *Journal of Personality and Social Psychology*, 1965, *2*, 255–261. (a)

Marston, A. R. Self-reinforcement: The relevance of a concept in analogue research to psychotherapy. *Psychotherapy: Theory, research and practice,* 1965, *2,* 3–5. (b)

Marston, A. R., & Feldman, S. E. Toward use of self-control in behavior modification. Unpublished manuscript, University of Southern California, 1971.

Marston, A. R., & Kanfer, F. H. Human reinforcement: Experimenter and subject controlled. *Journal of Experimental Psychology,* 1963, *66,* 91–94.

Mayer, J. Exercise does keep the weight down. *Atlantic Monthly,* 1955, *196,* 63–66.

McClelland, D. C., Atkinson, J. W., Clark, R. A., & Lowell, E. L. *The achievement motive.* New York: Appleton, 1953.

McDougall, W., *Outline of abnormal psychology.* New York: Scribner's, 1926.

McGuire, R. J., & Vallance, M. Aversion therapy by electric shock: A simple technique. *British Medical Journal,* 1964, *1,* 151–153.

Mead, M. *Sex and temperament in three savage tribes.* New York: Morrow, 1935.

Mead, M. Some anthropological considerations concerning guilt. In M. L. Reymert (Ed.), *Feelings and emotions.* New York: McGraw-Hill, 1950.

Meadow, A., & Parnes, S. J. Evaluation of training in creative problem-solving. *Journal of Applied Psychology,* 1959, *43,* 189–194.

Mednick, S. A. The association basis of the creative process. *Psychological Review,* 1962, *69,* 220–232.

Meichenbaum, D. H. Cognitive factors in behavior modification: Modifying what people say to themselves. Unpublished manuscript, University of Waterloo, 1970.

Meichenbaum, D. H., Gilmore, J. B., & Fedoravicius, A. Group insight versus group desensitization in treating speech anxiety. *Journal of Consulting and Clinical Psychology,* 1971, *36,* 410–421.

Meichenbaum, D. H., & Goodman, J. Training impulsive children to talk to themselves: A means of developing self-control. *Journal of Abnormal Psychology,* 1971, *77,* 115–126.

Merton, R. K. *Social theory and social structure* (rev. ed.). New York: Free Press, 1957.

Meyer, V., & Crisp, A. H. Aversion therapy in two cases of obesity. *Behaviour Research and Therapy,* 1964, *2,* 143–147.

Migler, B., & Wolpe, J. Automated self-desensitization: A case report. *Behaviour Research and Therapy,* 1967, *5,* 133–135.

Miller, M. M. Treatment of chronic alcoholism by hypnotic aversion. *Journal of the American Medical Association,* 1959, *171,* 1492–1495.

Miller, N. E. A reply to "sign-gestalt or conditioned reflex?" *Psychological Review,* 1935, *42,* 280–292.

Miller, N. E. Some animal experiments pertinent to the problem of combining psychotherapy with drug therapy. *Comprehensive Psychiatry,* 1966, *7,* 1–12.

Miller, N. E., & Dollard, J. *Social learning and imitation.* New Haven: Yale University Press, 1941.

Miller, R. E., Murphy, J. V., & Mirsky, I. A. Persistent effect of chlorpromazine on extinction of an avoidance response. *Archives of Neurology and Psychiatry*, 1957, *78*, 526–530.

Mischel, W. *Personality and assessment*. New York: Wiley, 1968.

Mischel, W., & Liebert, R. M. Effects of discrepancies between observed and imposed reward criteria on their acquisition and transmission. *Journal of Personality and Social Psychology*, 1966, *3*, 45–53.

Mischel, W., & Metzner, R. Preference for delayed reward as a function of age, intelligence, and length of delay interval. *Journal of Abnormal and Social Psychology*, 1962, *64*, 425–431.

Mitchell, W., Falconer, M. A., & Hill, D. *Lancet*, 1954, *2*, 626.

Moll, A. *Hypnotism*. (5th rev. ed.) New York: Scribner's, 1904.

Morgan, C. T. *Physiological psychology*. New York: McGraw-Hill, 1965.

Morrell, F., & Jasper, H. H. *Electroencephalography and Clinical Neurophysiology*, 1956, *8*, 201.

Morrell, F., & Ross, M. H. *Archives of Neurology and Psychiatry*, 1953, *70*, 611.

Mowrer, O. H. *Learning theory and the symbolic processes*. New York: Wiley, 1960.

Munroe, R. *Schools of psychoanalytic thought*. New York: Dryden Press, 1955.

Murdock, G. P. *Our primitive contemporaries*. New York: Macmillan, 1934.

Nelson, F. Effects of chlorpromazine on fear extinction. *Journal of Comparative and Physiological Psychology*, 1967, *64*, 496–498.

Nicholson, N. C. Notes on muscular work during hypnosis. *Johns Hopkins Hospital Bulletin*, 1920, *31*, 89.

Nisbett, R. E., & Schachter, S. Cognitive manipulation of pain. *Journal of Experimental Social Psychology*, 1966, *2*, 227–236.

Nolan, J. D. Self-control procedures in the modification of smoking behavior. *Journal of Consulting and Clinical Psychology*, 1968, *32*, 92–93.

Ober, D. C. The modification of smoking behavior. Unpublished doctoral dissertation. University of Illinois, 1967.

Ober, D. C. Modification of smoking behavior. *Journal of Consulting and Clinical Psychology*, 1968, *32*, 543–549.

O'Leary, K. D. The effects of self-instruction on immoral behavior. *Journal of Experimental Child Psychology*, 1968, *6*, 297–301.

Orne, M. T. Die Leistungsfähigkeit in Hypnose und im Wachzustand. *Psychol. Rdsch.*, 1954, *5*, 291–297.

Orne, M. T. The nature of hypnosis: Artifact and essence. *Journal of Abnormal and Social Psychology*, 1959, *58*, 277–299.

Orne, M. T. On the social psychology of the psychological experiment with particular reference to demand characteristics and their implications. *American Psychologist*, 1962, *17*, 776–783.

Osborn, A. F. *Applied imagination*. New York: Scribner's, 1957.

Osborn, A. F. *Applied imagination* (3rd ed.) New York: Scribner's, 1963.

Osgood, C. E. *Method and theory in experimental psychology*. New York: Oxford, 1953.

Parnes, S. J. *Description of the University of Buffalo Creative Problem Solving Course.* Creative Education Office, University of Buffalo, 1958.

Parnes, S. J. Can creativity be increased? *Personnel Administration,* 1962, *25,* 2–9.

Parnes, S. J. *Creative behavior guidebook.* New York: Scribner's, 1967.

Parnes, S. J., & Meadow, A. Effects of "brainstorming" instructions on creative problem solving by trained and untrained subjects. *Journal of Educational Psychology,* 1959, *50,* 171–176.

Paul, G. L. *Insight versus desensitization in psychotherapy.* Stanford: Stanford University Press, 1966.

Paul, G. L. Insight versus desensitization in psychotherapy two years after termination. *Journal of Consulting Psychology,* 1967, *31,* 333–348.

Paul, G. L. Outcome of systematic desensitization II: Controlled investigations of individual treatment, technique variations, and current status. In C. M. Franks (Ed.), *Behavior therapy: Assessment and status.* New York: McGraw-Hill, 1969. (a)

Paul, G. L. Physiological effects of relaxation training and hypnotic suggestion. *Journal of Abnormal Psychology,* 1969, *74,* 425–437. (b)

Paul, G. L., & Shannon, D. T. Treatment of anxiety through systematic desensitization in therapy groups. *Journal of Abnormal Psychology,* 1966, *71,* 124–135.

Pavlov, I. P. *Conditioned reflexes.* London, Humphrey Milford: Oxford University Press, 1927.

Pavlov, I. P. *Lectures on conditioned reflexes,* Vol. 1. New York: International Publishers, 1928.

Peterson, D. R. *The clinical study of social behavior.* New York: Appleton, 1968.

Phillips, E. L. *Psychotherapy: A modern theory and practice.* Englewood Cliffs, N. J.: Prentice-Hall, 1956.

Piers, G., & Singer, M. B. *Shame and guilt.* Springfield, Ill.: Thomas, 1953.

Pope, B., Siegman, A. W., Blass, T., & Raher, J. Anxiety and depression in speech. Unpublished manuscript, Psychiatric Institute, University of Maryland, 1968.

Popov, C. *Comptes Rendus de l'Academie de Science,* 1954, *239,* 1859.

Popov, C. *Comptes Rendus de l'Academie de Science,* 1955, *240,* 1268. (a)

Popov, C. *Comptes Rendus de l'Academie de Science,* 1955, *240,* 1929. (b)

Popov, C. *Comptes Rendus de l'Academie de Science,* 1955, *241,* 249. (c)

Popov, C. *Comptes Rendus de l'Academie de Science,* 1955, *241,* 335. (d)

Popov, C. *Comptes Rendus de l'Academie de Science,* 1955, *241,* 1414. (e)

Popov, N. A. *Comptes Rendus de la Société de Biologie,* 1950, *144,* 906. (a)

Popov, N. A. *Comptes Rendus de la Société de Biologie,* 1950, *144,* 1667. (b)

Popov, N. A., & Popov, C. *Comptes Rendus de l'Academie de Science,* 1953, *237,* 930. (a)

Popov, N. A., & Popov, C. *Comptes Rendus de l'Academie de Science,* 1953, *237,* 1439. (b)

Popov, N. A., & Popov, C. *Comptes Rendus de l'Academie de Science*, 1954, *238*, 1912. (a)

Popov, N. A., & Popov, C. *Comptes Rendus de l'Academie de Science*, 1954, *238*, 2026. (b)

Popov, N. A., & Popov, C. *Comptes Rendus de l'Academie de Science*, 1954, *238*, 2118. (c)

Popov, N. A., & Popov, C. *Comptes Rendus de l'Academie de Science*, 1954, *239*, 1243. (d)

Povorinsky, Y. A. Psychotherapy of smoking. In R. B. Winn (Ed.) *Psychotherapy in the Soviet Union.* New York: Grove, 1962.

Premack, D. Reinforcement theory. In David Levine (Ed.), *Nebraska symposium on motivation.* Lincoln: University of Nebraska Press, 1965.

Premack, D. Toward empirical behavior laws: I. Positive reinforcement. *Psychological Review*, 1959, *66,* 219–233.

Rachman, S. Studies in desensitization—I: The separate effects of relaxation and desensitization. *Behaviour Research and Therapy*, 1965, *3*, 245–251.

Rapaport, D. The theory of ego autonomy: A generalization. *Bulletin of the Menninger Clinic*, 1958, *22*, 13–35.

Rapaport, D. The structure of psychoanalytic theory. *Psychological Issues*, 1960, *2*, No. 6.

Rapaport, D., Gill, M., & Schafer, R. *Diagnostic psychological testing.* Chicago: Chicago Yearbook Publishers, 1945–1946. 2 vols.

Razran, G. The observable unconscious and inferable conscious in current Soviet psychophysiology. *Psychological Review*, 1961, *68*, 81–147.

Read, G. D. *Childbirth without fear.* New York: Harper & Row, 1944.

Reed, J. L. Comments on the use of methohexitone sodium as a means of inducing relaxation. *Behaviour Research and Therapy*, 1966, *4*, 323.

Rehm, L. P., & Marston, A. R. Reduction of social anxiety through modification of self-reinforcement: An instigation therapy technique. *Journal of Consulting and Clinical Psychology*, 1968, *32*, 565–574.

Rice, D. G. Operant conditioning and associated electromyogram responses. *Journal of Experimental Psychology*, 1966. *71*, 908–912.

Riesman, D. *The lonely crowd.* New Haven: Yale University Press, 1950.

Rimm, D. C., & Litvak, S. B. Self-verbalization and emotional arousal. *Journal of Abnormal Psychology*, 1969, *74*, 181–187.

Rogers, C. R. *Client-centered therapy.* Boston: Houghton-Mifflin, 1951.

Rogers, C. R., & Skinner, B. F. Some issues concerning the control of human behavior. *Science*, 1956, *124*, 1057–1066.

Rosenbaum, M. E., & Tucker, I. F. The competence of the model and the learning of imitation and nonimitation. *Journal of Experimental Psychology,* 1962, *63*, 183–190.

Rosenthal, D., & Frank, J. D. Psychotherapy and the placebo effect. *Psychological Bulletin*, 1956, *53*, 294–302.

Ross, C. A. Report on smoking withdrawal. In *Can we help them stop?* Illinois: American Cancer Society, Illinois Division, 1964.

Rotter, J. B. Generalized expectancies for internal versus external control of reinforcement. *Psychological Monographs*, 1966, *80* (1, Whole No. 609).

Roush, E. S. Strength and endurance in the waking and hypnotic state. *Journal of Applied Physiology*, 1951, *3*, 404–410.

Ruckmick, C. A. *The psychology of feeling and emotion.* New York: McGraw-Hill, 1936.

Salter, A. Three techniques of autohypnosis. *Journal of General Psychology*, 1941, *24*, 423–438.

Salter, A. *Conditioned reflex therapy*. New York: Creative Age Press, 1949.

Schachter, J. Pain, fear, and anger in hypertensives and normotensives: A psychophysiologic study. *Psychosomatic Medicine*, 1957, *19*, 17–29.

Schachter, S. *The psychology of affiliation*. Stanford, Calif.: Stanford University Press, 1959.

Schachter, S. The interaction of cognitive and physiological determinants of emotional state. In C. D. Spielberger (Ed.), *Anxiety and behavior*. New York: Academic Press, 1966.

Schachter, S. Cognitive effects on bodily functioning: Studies of obesity and eating. In D. C. Glass (Ed.), *Neurophysiology and emotion,* New York: Rockefeller University Press and Russell Sage Foundation, 1967.

Schachter, S., & Gross, L. P. Manipulated time and eating behavior. *Journal of Personality and Social Psychology*, 1968, *10*, 98–106.

Schachter, S., & Singer, J. E. Cognitive, social, and physiological determinants of emotional state. *Psychological Review*, 1962, *69*, 379–399.

Schachter, S., & Wheeler, L. Epinephrine, chlorpromazine, and amusement. *Journal of Abnormal and Social Psychology*. 1962, *65*, 121–128.

Schultz, J. H., & Luthe, W. *Autogenic training*. New York: Grune & Stratton, 1959.

Sears, R. R., Rau, L., & Alpert, R. *Identification and child rearing*. Stanford: Stanford University Press, 1965.

Shaftel, F. R., & Shaftel, G. *Role-playing for social values: Decision-making in the social studies*. Englewood Cliffs, N. J.: Prentice-Hall, 1967.

Shagass, C. Conditioning the human occipital alpha rhythm to a voluntary stimulus. A quantitative study. *Journal of Experimental Psychology*, 1942, *31*, 367–379.

Shagass, C., & Johnson, E. P. The course of acquisition of a conditioned response of the occipital alpha rhythm. *Journal of Experimental Psychology*, 1943, *33*, 201–209.

Shaw, F. A stimulus-response analysis of repression and insight in psychotherapy. *Psychological Review*, 1946, *53*, 36–42.

Shearn, D. W. Operant conditioning of heart rate. *Science*, 1962, *137*, 530–531.

Shipman, W. G., & Plesset, M. R. Anxiety and depression in obese dieters. *Archives of General Psychiatry*, 1963, *8*, 530–535.

Shoben, E. J., Jr. Psychotherapy as a problem in learning theory. *Psychological Bulletin*, 1949, *46*, 366–392.

Shor, R. E., & Orne, M. T. *Harvard Group Scale of Hypnotic Susceptibility*. Palo Alto, Calif.: Consulting Psychologists Press, 1962.

Silverstone, J. T., & Solomon, T. The long-term management of obesity in general practice. *British Journal of Clinical Practice*, 1965, *19*, 395–398.

Simon, H. A. A behavioral model of rational choice. *Quarterly Journal of Economics*, 1955, *69*, 99–118.

Simon, H. A. *Administrative behavior: A study of decision-making processes in administration organization.* (2nd Ed.) New York: Free Press, 1957.

Simon, R. I. Obesity as a depressive equivalent. *American Medical Association Journal*, 1963, *183*, 208–210.

Skinner, B. F. *The behavior of organisms.* New York: Appleton, 1938.

Skinner, B. F. *Science and human behavior.* New York: Macmillan, 1953.

Skinner, B. F. *Verbal behavior.* New York: Appleton, 1957.

Skinner, B. F. *Cumulative record.* New York: Appleton, 1959.

Skinner, B. F. An operant analysis of problem solving. In B. Kleinmuntz (Ed.), *Problem solving: Research, method and theory.* New York: Wiley, 1966.

Skinner, B. F. *Beyond freedom and dignity.* New York: Knopf, 1971.

Slack, C. W. *Social science is no damn good.* (Proposed title) Princeton: Van Nostrand, in press.

Snyder, C., & Noble, M. Operant conditioning of vasoconstriction. Paper presented at the meeting of the Midwestern Psychological Association, Chicago, April–May, 1966.

Sparks, L. *Self-hypnosis: A conditioned-response technique.* New York: Grune & Stratton, 1962.

Spotts, J. E. Some effects of exposure to a psychotherapy rating task in teachers of emotionally disturbed adolescents. Unpublished doctoral dissertation, University of Wisconsin, 1965.

Staats, A. W. An integrated–functional learning approach to complex human behavior. In B. Kleinmuntz (Ed.), *Problem solving: Research, method and theory.* New York: Wiley, 1966.

Stampfl, T. G., & Levis, D. J. Essentials of implosive therapy: A learning-theory-based psychodynamic behavioral therapy. *Journal of Abnormal Psychology*, 1967, *72*, 496–503.

Stauffer, S. A., Suchman, E. A., DeVinney, L. C., Star, S. A. & Williams, R. M., Jr. *The American soldier.* Vol. I. Princeton: Princeton University Press, 1949.

Stevenson, I. Processes of "spontaneous" recovery from the psychoneuroses. *American Journal of Psychiatry*, 1961, *117*, 1057–1064.

Stoler, N. Client likeability: A variable in the study of psychotherapy. *Journal of Consulting Psychology*, 1963, *27*, 175–178.

Stollak, G. E. Weight loss obtained under various experimental procedures. Paper presented at the meeting of the Midwestern Psychological Association, Chicago, May 1966.

Stuart, R. B. Behavioral control of overeating. *Behaviour Research and Therapy,* 1967, *5*, 357–365.

Stukat, K. G. *Suggestibility: A factorial and experimental analysis.* Stockholm: Almqvist & Wiksell, 1958.

Stunkard, A. J. The management of obesity. *New York State Journal of Medicine*, 1958, *58*, 79–87.

Stunkard, A. J. Eating patterns and obesity. *Psychiatric Quarterly*, 1959, *33*, 284–295. (a)

Stunkard, A. J. Obesity and the denial of hunger. *Psychosomatic Medicine*, 1959, *21*, 281–289. (b)

Stunkard, A. J. The results of treatment for obesity. *Archives of Internal Medicine*, 1959, *103*, 79–85. (c)

Suczek, R. F. The personality of obese women. *American Journal of Clinical Nutrition*, 1957, *5*, 197–202.

Sulzer, E. S. Reinforcement and the therapeutic contract. *Journal of Consulting Psychology*, 1962, *9*, 271–276.

Sushinsky, L. W., & Bootzin, R. R. Cognitive desensitization as a model of systematic desensitization. *Behaviour Research and Therapy*, 1970, *8*, 29–33.

Tallman, I. An experimental study of normlessness. Unpublished doctoral dissertation, Stanford University, 1962.

Taylor, D. W., Berry, P. C., & Block, C. H. Does group participation when using brainstorming facilitate or inhibit creative thinking. Department of Industrial Administration and Department of Psychology, Yale University, 1957. (Tech. Rep. No. 1, Contract Nonr 609 (20) NR 150–166.).

Taylor, D. W., & McNemar, O. W. Problem solving and thinking. *Annual Review of Psychology*, 1955, *6*, 455–482.

Taylor, J. A. A personality scale of manifest anxiety. *Journal of Abnormal and Social Psychology*, 1953, *48*, 285–290.

Teichner, W. H. Delayed cold-induced vasodilation and behavior. *Journal of Experimental Psychology*, 1965, *69*, 426–432.

Thorpe, J. G., Schmidt, E., Brown, P. T., & Castell, D. Aversion relief therapy: A new method for general application. *Behaviour Research and Therapy,* 1964, *2*, 71–82.

Thorpe, J. G., Schmidt, E., & Castell, D. A comparison of positive and negative (aversive) conditioning in the treatment of homosexuality. *Behaviour Research and Therapy*, 1963, *1*, 357–362.

Thurstone, L. L. *The nature of intelligence*. New York: Harcourt, 1924.

Tolman, E. C. *Purposive behavior in animals and men*, New York: Appleton, 1932.

Tooley, J. T., & Pratt, S. An experimental procedure for the extinction of smoking behavior. *Psychological Record*, 1967, *17*, 209–218.

Travis, L. E., & Egan, J. P. Conditioning of the electrical response of the cortex. *Journal of Experimental Psychology*, 1938, *22*, 524–531.

True, G. H. Creativity as a function of idea fluency, practicability, and specific training. Dissertation Abstracts, 1957, *17*, 401–402.

Ullmann, L. P., Forsman, R. G., Kenny, J. W., McInnis, T. L., Jr., Unikel, I. P., & Zeisset, R. M. Selective reinforcement of schizophrenics' interview responses. *Behaviour Research and Therapy*, 1965, *2*, 205–212.

Upper, D., & Meredith, L. A stimulus control approach to the modification of smoking behavior. Paper presented at the meeting of the American Psychological Association, Miami, September 1970.

Valins, S. Cognitive effects of false heart-rate feedback. *Journal of Personality and Social Psychology*, 1966, *4*, 400–408.

Valins, S., & Ray, A. A. Effects of cognitive desensitization on avoidance behavior. *Journal of Personality and Social Psychology*, 1967, *7*, 345–350.

Velten, E., Jr. *The induction of elation and depression through the reading of structural sets of mood-statements.* (Doctoral Dissertation, University of Southern California) Ann Arbor, Mich.: University Microfilms, 1967, No. 67–13, 045. Dissertation Abstracts, *28*, No. 4.

Velten, E., Jr. A laboratory task for induction of mood states. *Behaviour Research and Therapy*, 1968, *6*, 473–482.

Velvovski, I. Z., Platonov, K. I., Ploticher, V. A., & Csougom, E. A. *Painless childbirth through psychoprophylaxis.* Moscow: Foreign Languages Publication House, 1960.

Verplanck, W. Unaware of where's awareness: Some verbal operants-notates, nonents, and notants. In E. E. Jones (Ed.), *Behavior and awareness.* Durham, N. C.: Duke University Press, 1962.

Watson, D., & Friend, R. Measurement of social-evaluative anxiety. *Journal of Consulting and Clinical Psychology*, 1969, *33*, 448–457.

Watson, J. B. Psychology as a behaviorist views it. *Psychological Review*, 1913, *20*, 158–177.

Watson, J. B., & Rayner, R. 1920. Conditioned emotional reactions. *Journal of Experimental Psychology*, 1920, *3*, 1–14.

Wechsler, D. *Manual for the Wechsler Adult Intelligence Scale.* New York: Psychological Corp., 1955.

Weil, G., & Goldfried, M. R. Treatment of insomnia in an eleven-year-old child through self-relaxation. Unpublished manuscript, SUNY at Stony Brook, 1972.

Weitzenhoffer, A. M. *Hypnotism: An objective study in suggestibility.* New York: Wiley, 1957.

Wells, W. R. Experiments in waking hypnosis for instructional purposes. *Journal of Abnormal and Social Psychology*, 1924, *18*, 389–404.

White, R. W. *The abnormal personality.* New York: Ronald, 1964.

Whiting, J. W. M. Sorcery, sin, and the superego. In M. R. Jones (Ed.) *Nebraska symposium of motivation.* Lincoln: University of Nebraska Press, 1959.

Whiting, J. W. M., & Mowrer, O. H. Habit progression and regression—a laboratory study of some factors relevant to human socialization. *Journal of Comparative Psychology*, 1943, *36*, 229–253.

Williams, G. W. The effect of hypnosis on muscular fatigue. *Journal of Abnormal and Social Psychology*, 1929, *24*, 318–329.

Williams, G. W. A comparative study of voluntary and hypnotic catalepsy. *American Journal of Psychology*, 1930, *42*, 83–95.

Wilson, C., & Alexis, M. Basic framework for decisions. *Journal of the Academy of Management*, 1962, *5*, 150–164.

Wilson, S. A. K. *British Medical Journal*, 1930, *2*, 1.

Wilson, S. A. K. In Bumke and Foester (Ed.), *Handbuch der neurologie*. Vol. 17. 1935.

Winer, B. J. *Statistical principles in experimental design.* New York: McGraw-Hill, 1962.

Wolff, S., & Hardy, J. D. Studies on pain: Observations on pain due to local cooling and factors involved in the cold pressor response. *Journal of Clinical Investigation*, 1941, *20*, 521–533.

Wolff, S., & Wolff, H. G. *Human gastric function.* New York: Oxford, 1947.

Wolpe, J. *Psychotherapy by reciprocal inhibition.* Stanford: Stanford University Press, 1958.

Wolpe, J. Discussion of experimental studies in desensitization. In J. Wolpe, A. Salter, & L. J. Reyna (Eds.), *The conditioning therapies.* New York: Holt, Rinehart and Winston, 1964.

Wolpe, J., & Lang, P. J. A fear survey schedule for use in behavior therapy. *Behaviour Research and Therapy*, 1964, *2*, 27–30.

Wolpe, J., & Lazarus, A. A. *Behavior therapy techniques*, New York: Pergamon Press, 1966.

Woodworth, R. S., & Schlosberg, H. *Experimental psychology.* (Rev. ed.) New York: Holt, Rinehart and Winston, 1954.

Yahia, C., & Ulin, P. R. Preliminary experience with a psychophysical program of preparation for childbirth. *American Journal of Obstetrics and Gynecology*, 1965, *93*, 942–949.

Young, C. M., Moore, N. S., Berresford, K., Einset, B. McK., & Waldner, B. G. The problem of the obese patient. *Journal of the American Dietetic Association*, 1955, *31*, 1111–1115.

Young, P. C. Is rapport an essential characteristic of hypnosis? *Journal of Abnormal and Social Psychology*, 1927, *22*, 130–139.

Youtz, R. P. Psychological background of principles and procedures. In A. F. Osborn (Ed.) *Applied Imagination.* Buffalo: Creative Educational Foundation, 1955. (Mimeo.)

Zeisset, R. M. Desensitization and relaxation in the modification of psychiatric patients' interview behavior. *Journal of Abnormal Psychology*, 1968, *73*, 18–24.

Zuckerman, M. The development of an affect adjective checklist for the measurement of anxiety. *Journal of Consulting Psychology*, 1960, *24*, 457–462.

Zuckerman, M., Lubin, B., and Robbins, S. Validation of the Multiple Affect Adjective Check List in clinical situations. *Journal of Consulting Psychology*, 1965, *29*, 594–595.

NAME INDEX

Agras, W. S., 22–23, 250–252
Alexander, S., 334
Alexis, M., 190
Allen, M. K., 29
Alpert, R., 160
Amrine, M., 90
Anant, S. S., 22, 388, 392
Andersen, K. L., 131
Arellano, A., 322
Arkowitz, H., 16
Aronfreed, J., 306
Aronson, E., 76
Ashem, B., 22–23, 231–232, 387–393
Atkinson, J. W., 96
Austin, G. A., 193–194
Ausubel, D. P., 71
Ax, A. F., 55, 167
Ayllon, T., 28, 277
Azrin, N. H., 28, 270, 277

Baer, D. M., 13, 305
Bakan, D., 401
Baker, B., 15
Baldwin, A. L., 71
Bandura, A., 8, 10, 12, 21, 23–24, 29–30, 32, 70–77, 138–161, 252, 306, 348
Barker, J. C., 288
Barlow, D. H., 22–23, 251–252
Barrett-Lennard, G. T., 354
Barron, F., 96
Behanan, K. T., 236, 247
Bem, D. J., 128, 402
Bem, S. L., 26
Benedict, R., 71
Berne, E., 378, 383
Berresford, K., 364–365
Berry, P. C., 92
Bijou, S. W., 13, 305
Birge, J. S., 43
Blakemore, C. B., 288
Blass, T., 334
Block, C. H., 92
Bond, I. K., 255
Bonvallet, M., 167
Boomer, D. S., 334
Bootzin, R. R., 21
Bradley, M. M., 139, 348
Brady, J. P., 128, 251
Breger, L., 186, 386
Brehm, J. W., 76
Brener, J., 163
Brogden, W. J., 287
Brown, P. T., 364–365
Bruch, H., 195, 364
Bruner, J. S., 193–194

Cannon, W. B., 54
Cantril, H., 56
Cappon, D., 195–196, 364
Carlsmith, J. M., 76
Carlson, L. D., 131
Castell, D., 224, 288, 364–365
Cauffman, W. J., 364
Cautela, J. R., 22, 31, 224–234, 255, 287–296, 306, 316, 365–366, 370, 387–389, 392, 398
Chomsky, N., 401–402
Chorness, M., 93
Clark, D. R., 346
Clark, R. A., 96
Clarke, M., 346
Cloward, R. A., 73
Cobb, S., 171–172
Cohen, A. R., 76
Cole, M. W., 55, 57
Conway, C. C., 288
Cooke, G., 248, 250, 304
Coué, E., 332
Courts, F., 378
Creative Education Foundation, 92–93
Crider, D., 163
Crisp, A. H., 288, 365-366
Csougom, E. A., 16

Dale, C. L., 378
Dalzell-Ward, A. J., 378
Davids, A. H., 334
Davis, L. W., 236, 246
Davison, G. C., 18, 21–23, 106, 109, 115–129, 248, 250–251, 304, 306, 398
De Veau, L., 92–93
De Vinney, L. C., 125
Deese, J., 287
Dell, P., 167
Dollard, J., 3, 9–10, 12, 18–19, 26–27, 37–53, 140, 184, 188, 332, 336
Donner, L., 22–23, 231–232, 387–393
Dunsmure, J., Jr., 325-326
Dyrud, J., 269, 285
Dyson, J. W., 186
D'Zurilla, T. J., 16, 27, 183–194, 248, 251, 254, 304–316

Eaton, J. W., 77, 150
Edwards, A. L., 97, 339
Efran, J. S., 251
Efron, R., 15, 317-327
Egan, J. P., 324-325
Einset, B. McK., 364–365
Einstein, A., 43
Ejrup, B., 378
Ellis, A., 18–19, 81, 91, 171–182, 259–267, 331–332, 336
Engel, B. T., 167
England, G., 251, 304, 306
Erickson, M. A., 364–365
Eriksen, C. W., 334
Estes, W. K., 303, 379
Eysenck, H. J., 81–82, 331, 365, 379, 386

Falconer, M. A., 326
Fedoravicius, A., 19, 331–347
Feldman, M. P., 232–233, 386
Feldman, S. E., 13
Fenichel, O., 174, 379
Ferguson, G. A., 356
Ferster, C. B., 25, 138, 195–212, 217, 272, 293, 306, 364–366, 381
Festinger, L., 57, 140
Fisher, V. E., 85
Folkow, B., 131
Forsman, R. G., 379
Foulds, G. A., 85
Fowler, R. L., 162
Fox, R. H., 131
Frank, J. D., 126, 377, 385
Franklin, R. E., 365
Franks, C. M., 287, 387
Frazier, T. W., 163
Freud, S., 5–7, 174, 336
Friedman, D., 128
Friend, R., 334, 346
Furneaux, W. D., 82

Galvin, E. P., 195
Geer, J. H., 333–334
Gelder, M. G., 224, 346
Gelfand, D. M., 141
Gelhorn, E., 167
Gerry, R., 92–93
Gilkinson, H., 334
Gill, M., 92
Gilmore, J. B., 19, 331–347
Gold, S., 22, 289, 387
Goldiamond, I., 25–26, 217, 255, 268–286, 305–306, 365–366, 398, 402
Goldfoot, D. A., 17, 130–137, 306
Goldfried, M. R., 3–34, 183–194, 248–256, 297–304
Goldman, R., 25
Goldstein, A. P., 338, 385
Goldstein, K. M., 386
Goodman, J., 26
Goodnow, J. J., 193–194
Goodrich, D. W., 334
Goodrich, F. W., Jr., 17
Gordon, J. E., 81
Gore, W. J., 186
Gough, H. G., 96, 100, 352
Gowers, W., 318, 324, 326
Gray, B. B., 251, 304, 306
Greene, R. S., 378
Gross, L. P., 25
Grusec, J. E., 151, 160
Guthrie, E. R., 9, 303
Guze, H., 17

Hall, J. F., 226
Hammond, E. C., 218
Hanson, S. P., 167
Hardy, J. D., 131
Harmon, A. R., 364–365
Harris, M. B., 22, 25, 364–376
Hartmann, H., 6–7
Hastings, J., 163, 165
Heilbrun, A. B., Jr., 352
Hess, C. B., 378
Hiebel, G., 167
Hill, D., 326
Hnatiow, M., 163–164
Holland, J. G., 217, 271
Holz, W. C., 270
Homme, L. E., 19, 23–24, 26, 31–32, 213–223, 255, 306, 316, 398
Honigfeld, G., 126
Horn, D., 378
Hudgins, C. V., 324–325
Hughes, C. C., 150
Hull, C. L., 40, 42, 53, 235, 242, 245–246
Hunt, J. McV., 55, 57
Hunt, W. A., 56
Husband, R. W., 236, 246
Husek, T. R., 334
Hutchison, H. C., 255

Infeld, L., 43

Jackson, J. H., 326
Jacobson, E., 14–15, 162
Jaffa, M., 25
Jakubczak, L. F., 140
James, W., 54
Jasper, H., 324
Jasper, H. H., 325
Johnson, E. P., 324
Johnson, S. B., 30
Johnson, W., 332
Johnson, W. B., 85
Johnson, W. G., 19, 27

Kagan, J., 167
Kahn, M., 15
Kamano, D. K., 117
Kanfer, F. H., 11–12, 17, 28–30, 32, 130–137, 139, 255, 304, 306, 348, 362, 397–406
Kantor, J. R., 213
Kaplan, B., 77
Kaplan, H. I., 364
Kaplan, H. S., 364
Karst, T. O., 19
Katz, J. A. 402
Kelly, G. A., 332, 336
Kendler, H. H., 193
Kendler, T. S., 193
Kenny, J. W., 379
Keutzer, C. S., 22, 24
Kiesler, D. J., 331
Kimble, G. A., 162, 287
Kimmel, E., 162
Kimmel, H. D., 162
Kleinmuntz, B., 186
Kline, M. V., 17
Koenig, K. P., 377–378, 385
Kopel, S., 13
Korzybski, A., 332
Krasner, L., 18, 402
Krog, J., 131
Kunckle, E. C., 131
Kupers, C. J., 29, 152, 160, 348
Kushner, M., 226

Lacey, B. C., 167
Lacey, J. I., 163, 167
Lamaze, F., 16
Landis, C., 56
Lang, P. J., 14–15, 106, 114, 162–167, 248–250, 252, 297–298, 331, 346, 352, 361
Lashley, K. S., 39
Laufberger, V., 324-325
Lazarus, A. A., 16, 254, 298–300, 306, 315, 336–337, 346
Lazarus, R. S., 345
Lazovik, A. D., 106, 114, 248, 250, 346
Leighton, A. H., 150
Leitenberg, H., 22–23, 251–252
Levin, H., 71
Levin, N. I., 288
Levis, D. J., 303
Levitt, E. E., 25, 195–212, 217, 272, 293, 306, 364–366, 381
Lewis, T., 131
Liebert, R. M., 29–30, 152
Lindzey, G., 92
Lippman, W., 43
Litvak, S. B., 19
London, P., 33–34
Lowell, E. L., 96
Lubin, B., 85
Lundin, R. W., 284

Luria, A. R., 26, 393
Luthe, W., 14–16, 81, 162
Lysons, D., 318, 324, 326

MacCulloch, M. J., 232–233
MacCulloch, M. L., 232
Maclean, P. D., 322
Mahl, G. F., 334
Mahoney, M. J., 23, 33
Mahrer, A. R., 75
Malcolm, N., 401
Maltzman, I., 402
Mandler, G., 81
Marañon, G., 56
Marcia, J. E., 251
Marks, I. M., 224, 346
Marrow, J., 85
Marston, A. R., 13, 28–31, 139, 151, 348–363
Masters, J., 377–378, 385
Mayer, J., 364
McClelland, D. C., 96
McDougall, W., 101
McGaugh, J. L., 186, 386
McGavack, T. H., 195
McGuire, R. J., 288, 378
McInnes, T. L., Jr., 379
McNemar, O. W., 92
Mead, M., 71, 77
Meadow, A., 27–28, 92–100
Mednick, S. A., 190
Meichenbaum, D. H., 19, 26, 331–347
Menlove, F. L., 151, 160
Merbaum, M., 3–34, 255
Meredith, L., 25
Merton, R. K., 73
Metzner, R., 75
Meyer, V., 288, 365–366
Migler, B., 15
Miller, M., 269, 285
Miller, M. M., 22
Miller, N. E., 3, 9–10, 12, 18–19, 26–27, 37–53, 117, 140, 184, 188, 332
Miller, R. E., 118
Mirsky, I. A., 118
Mischel, W., 29–30, 33, 75, 152
Mitchell, W., 326
Mohoney, J. L., 251, 304, 306
Moll, A., 101
Moore, N. S., 364–365
Morgan, C. T., 162
Morrell, F., 325
Moss, H., 167
Mowrer, O. H., 71, 188, 193
Munroe, R., 379
Murdock, G. P., 42
Murphy, J. V., 118

Nelson, F., 118
Neufeld, I. L., 22, 289, 387
Nicholson, N. C., 101–102
Nisbett, R. E., 21, 107, 116–117
Noble, M., 163
Nolan, J. D., 25
Nurnberger, J. I., 25, 195–212, 217, 272, 293, 306, 364–366, 381

Ober, D. C., 25, 377–386
Ohlin, L. E., 73
O'Leary, K. D., 26
Oliveau, D. C., 251–252
Orford, J. F., 232–233
Orne, M. T., 17, 82, 84, 101–105
Osborn, A. F., 92–93, 186, 188–189
Osgood, C. E., 82, 84, 249–250

Parnes, S. J., 27–28, 92–100, 186–189
Paul, G. L., 14, 248, 250, 252–253, 297–298, 331–332, 334–338
Pauley, W. G., 364
Pavlov, I. P., 49, 318, 327
Perloff, B., 29–30, 152–161
Peterson, D. R., 33
Phillips, E. L., 81, 91, 331–332, 386
Phillips, J. S., 11–12, 304, 348, 399
Piers, G., 71–72
Pinschof, J. M., 232
Platonov, K. I., 16
Plaut, T. F. A., 77
Plesset, M. R., 364–365, 374
Ploticher, V. A., 16
Pomeranz, D. M., 33, 193
Pope, B., 334
Popov, C., 320, 325
Popov, N. A., 320, 325
Povorinsky, Y. A., 378
Pratt, S., 22
Premack, D., 19, 31–32, 215–216
Purkonen, R. A., 364–365

Rachman, S., 224, 250, 336, 379
Raher, J., 334
Rapaport, D., 5–7, 92
Rapoport, R. N., 150
Rasmussen, L. P., 364–365
Rau, L., 160
Ray, A. A., 20–21, 106–115, 251
Rayner, R., 287
Razran, G., 163
Read, G. D., 16
Reber, A., 306
Reed, J. L., 128
Rehm, L. P., 30–31, 348–363
Reis, E. E., 55, 57
Reynolds, D. J., 106, 248, 250
Rice, D. G., 162
Riesman, D., 71
Rimm, D. C., 19
Robins, S., 85
Rogers, C. R., 4, 271, 379
Rosenbaum, M. E., 140
Rosenthal, D., 385
Ross, C. A., 378
Ross, D., 140, 149
Ross, M. H., 325
Ross, S. A., 140, 149
Rotter, J. B., 126, 187
Roush, E. S., 102
Rubin, B. M., 251
Ruckmick, C. A., 55
Rynearson, E. H., 365

Salter, A., 16, 235–247
Sandler, J., 226
Saslow, G., 397
Schachter, J., 55
Schachter, S., 15, 18–21, 25, 54–57, 107, 115–117, 167, 249, 332, 345, 363, 368
Schafer, R., 92
Schlosberg, H., 287
Schmidt, E., 224, 288, 364–365
Schultz, J. H., 14–16, 81, 162
Sears, R. R., 160
Seidner, M. L., 17
Shaftel, F. R., 188
Shaftel, G., 188
Shagass, C., 324–325
Shannon, D. T., 250, 252, 297, 336–337
Shapiro, D., 163
Shaw, F., 398
Shearn, D. W., 163
Shipman, W. G., 364–365, 374
Shoben, E. J., Jr., 398

Shor, R. E., 82
Siegman, A. W., 334
Silverstone, J. T., 364–365, 374
Simon, H. A., 186–187, 190–191
Simon, R. I., 364, 367
Singer, J. E., 15, 18–21, 54–57, 107, 115–117, 167, 249, 332, 345
Singer, M. B., 71-72
Skinner, B. F., 4, 10–11, 24, 26, 33, 58–69, 130, 138, 184–186, 195, 213–215, 217, 270–271, 305, 348, 378, 402
Slack, C. W., 216
Snyder, C., 163
Solomon, E., 378
Solomon, T., 364–365, 374
Sparks, L., 81
Spotts, J. E., 354
Sroufe, L. A., 163, 165
Staats, A. W., 193
Stampfl, T. G., 303
Star, S. A., 125
Stevenson, I., 385
Stoler, N., 351
Stollak, G. E., 365–366
Stauffer, S. A., 125
Stuart, R. B., 22, 25
Stukat, K. G., 82
Stunkard, A. J., 195, 211, 364–365, 374
Suchman, E. A., 125
Suczek, R. F., 364
Sulzer, E. S., 269
Sushinsky, L. W., 21

Tallman, I.,, 75
Taylor, D. W., 92
Taylor, J. A., 352
Taylor, R., 378
Teichner, W. H., 131
Thomas, H., 17
Thorpe, J. G., 224, 288, 364–365
Thurstone, L. L., 188
Tolman, E. C., 45
Tooley, J. T., 22
Travis, L. E., 324-325
Tremblay, M., 150
Trexler, L. D., 19
True, G. H., 93
Tucker, I. F., 140
Tursky, B., 163

Ulin, P. R., 17
Ullmann, L. P., 379
Unikel, I. P., 379
Upper, D., 25

Valins, S., 20–21, 106–129, 248, 251
Vallance, M., 288, 378
Velten, E., Jr., 18–19, 81–91
Velvovski, I. Z., 16
Verplanck, W., 402

Waldner, B. G., 364–365
Walters, R. H., 29, 70–77, 140, 306
Watson, D., 334, 346
Watson, J. B., 8, 287
Wechsler, D., 94
Weil, G., 16
Weil, R. J., 77, 150
Weitzenhoffer, A. M., 82
Wells, W. R., 235, 244
Whalen, C. K., 138–152, 160
Wheeler, L., 167
White, R. W., 117
Whiting, J. M. W., 71
Williams, G. W., 102
Williams, R. M., Jr., 125
Wilson, C., 190
Wilson, S. A. K., 317, 326
Winer, B. J., 383
Wolff, H. G., 55
Wolff, H. H., 346
Wolff, S., 55, 131
Wolpe, J., 15, 81, 106, 224–225, 248–249, 254, 287, 297–300, 306, 315, 331, 336–337, 346, 352, 365–366
Woodworth, R. S., 287

Yahia, C., 17
Young, C. M., 364–365
Young, P. C., 235, 237
Youtz, R. P., 92

Zeisset, R. M., 251, 297, 304, 379
Zuckerman, M., 85, 334

SUBJECT INDEX

A

Adjective Checklist for Anxiety, 334–335, 339–340, 352, 356–358, 361–363
Aggression, 12
Alcoholism, 22, 211, 224–227, 231–233, 287–292, 295, 387–393, 398
Anger, 55
Anxiety, 14–15, 24
  generalized, 15–16, 297–304
  heterosexual, 16, 305–316, 348–363
  speech, 331–347
Anxiety differential, 334, 339–340
Anxiety-reducing techniques, 15, 20, 24, 297–316, 348–363
  See also Autogenic training; Autohypnosis; Rational-emotive therapy; Relaxation, self-administered; Systematic desensitization
Apparatus Test, 94
Assertive training, 224
Attribution theory (*see* Cognitive relabeling)
Autogenic training, 14
Autohypnosis, 16, 235–247
  dieting, aid in, 245
  fractional technique, 241–244, 247
  insomnia, treatment, 245
  memorized trance instructions, 240–241, 247
  nailbiting, treatment, 245
  noxious stimuli, tolerance, 245
  post-hypnotic suggestion, 236–240, 245, 247
  smoking, cessation, 245
  stuttering, treatment, 245
  See also Autosuggestion
Autonomic responses, control, 15
  cardio-vascular system, 14, 163–167
  electric shock, use of, 163
  epileptic seizures, 15
  GSR, 162
  See also Cardiac feedback; Feedback
Autosuggestion, 13–22, 81–91, 235–236
  See also Autohypnosis
Aversion therapy, 224–225, 232–233, 287–289
  See also Covert sensitization; Self-administered aversive conditioning
Aversive conditioning, self-administered (*see* Self-administered aversive conditioning)
Avoidance behavior, 106–115, 224

B

Barrett-Lennard Relationship Inventory, 354, 359
Behavior change, self vs. drug induced, 116–129
Behavior therapy, rationale, 3–4
  client-centered therapy, vs., 4
Behavioral rehearsal, 16, 24
Behaviorism, theoretical considerations, 397–406
Brainstorming, 28, 92–93

C

California Psychological Inventory, 94, 96, 100
Cardiac feedback, 15, 20, 107–111, 113–115, 163–167
  See also Autonomic responses, control
Cheating, 26–27, 75–76
Cognitive processes, 12, 183
Cognitive relabeling, 13, 17–24
  coverants, 19
  cue-producing responses, 18–19
  emotional states, 20, 107, 114–115
  noxious stimulation, tolerance, 21
  rational-emotive therapy, 18–19
  See also Language
Commitment for change, 12–13, 68–69, 403–405
Competence (*see* Effective behavior)
Compulsive behavior, 211, 224, 287–296

Conditioned inhibitors, 317–327
Contingency management, 218, 220–221
See also Self-reinforcement
Control of behavior by groups, 58–59, 69
Control, techniques of, aversive conditioning, 65–66, 224–225, 232–233, 287–296
covert sensitization, 224–233, 287–296
deprivation and satiation, 64
doing something else, 61, 68
drugs, 66, 287
manipulation of emotional conditions, 64–65
operant conditioning, 66–67
physical aid, 61–62
physical restraint, 61–62
punishment, 67–68
stimulus control, 9, 24–26, 63–64, 271–272, 274, 277, 279–280
Controlled response, 61–62, 130
Controlling response, 61–62, 130
Coping, 24, 27, 186, 188
See also Effective behavior; Problem-solving behavior
Coverants, 19, 27, 213–214, 398
smoking, control, 218–220
stuttering, control, 222
eating behavior, control, 220–221
definition, 214–215
difficulties in control, 215, 217
enhancing positive thinking, 217, 222
faulty labeling, 215
reinforcement, 214–215
Covert operant (*see* Coverants)
Covert reinforcement (*see* Reinforcement, covert)
Covert sensitization, 22, 224–233, 287–296
See also Aversion therapy; Self-administered aversive conditioning
alcoholism, 22, 225–227, 231–233, 289–292, 295, 387–393
compulsive behavior, 224–225, 287–296
delinquent behavior, 230–231
homosexuality, 22, 225, 289, 388
obesity, 22, 225, 227–229, 233, 289, 293–295
Creative Ability, AC Test, 94–95, 97–99
Creative thinking, 27–28, 59, 92–100, 186–187, 189
Cue-producing responses, 9, 12, 18–19, 27, 40–52
abstraction, 40
foresight, 44–45
language, 45–48
perception, 40
reasoning, 48–52
trial and error, 48–51
Cue value, 39–52
Cues, 9, 17, 404–405
acquired equivalence, 41–44
discriminative, 40–41, 43
external, 40
generalized, 41–43, 46, 48
internal, 40
response-produced, 17, 40–43

D

Delinquent behavior, 230–231
Depression, 83–91
Desensitization (*see* Systematic desensitization)
Drive, primary, 37–38

E

Eating behavior, control, 12, 22, 24–25, 220–221, 364–376
aversive conditoning, 22, 197–199, 288, 366, 370–371, 374–375, 398
controlling chains of responses, 196, 200, 205–207
covert sensitization, 225, 227–229, 293–295
food deprivation, 196, 199–201
maintenance, 196, 209–211
prepotent repertoires, 196–198, 207–209
stimulus control, 25, 202, 204–205, 271–272, 368
stimulus manipulation, 196–197, 201–202, 366
temporal control, 203
verbal conditioning, 198
Effective behavior, definition, 183
problem-solving, 183–194
Elation, 83–91
Emotional states, 54–57, 171–172
autosuggestion, 81–91
cognitive determinants, 55–57, 172–174
labeling, 54–55, 57
physiological determinants, 54–57
Epileptic seizures, 14–15, 317–327
Extinction, 303–304

F

Fear of Negative Evaluation Scale, 335–336, 342–343
Fear of snakes, 107–115
Fear Survey Schedule, 298, 333, 352, 356–357
Feedback, 11, 20
autonomic system, 15, 20, 107–108, 110–111, 113–115, 163–167
muscular system, 167
Foresight, 44–45

G

Generalization
innate, 38–39
response-mediated, 39, 41–43, 48
Guilford Unusual Uses Test, 94–95, 97–99

H

Harvard Group Scale of Hypnotic Susceptibility, 82
Hierarchy, innate, 37–39, 46
Homosexuality, 12, 14, 22–23, 224–225, 227–230, 259–267, 288–289
Hypnosis, 17, 81, 101–105
See also Autohypnosis

I

Imagery, 40
Impulsivity, control, 26
Imitative learning (*see* Modeling)
Implosion, 303
Insomnia, 16, 245
Instigation therapy, 304, 399
Instincts, 38
Instrumental behavior, 9–11

J-L

James-Lange theory of emotion, 54–55
Language, 45–48
See also Cognitive relabeling; Verbal self-direction

M

Manifest Anxiety Scale, 352, 356–358, 360–361, 363
Marital problems, 24, 26, 269, 273–278
Minnesota Multiphasic Personality Inventory, 388
Modeling, 29–30, 138–151
Modeling in children, 139–151
adult vs. peer models, 140–144, 146–148
imitative verbal responses, 148–149
reinforcement, vs., 29–30
rule structure, 29
same-sex vs. opposite-sex, 140, 144–146, 148–149
standards for self-reinforcement, 142–144, 148–151
Motivation, hypnotic trance, 101–105
Multiple Affect Adjective Checklist, 84–87, 89

N

Nailbiting, 243
Natural childbirth, 16–17
See also Psychoprophylactic method
Need achievement, 94–96, 98–100

O

Obesity, 12, 22, 25, 195-212, 220-221, 225, 227–229, 233, 289, 293–295, 364–376
See also Eating behavior
Otis Intelligence Scale, 388

P

Pain tolerance, 14, 16
drug-induced vs. self-attributed, 118–129
external distraction, 17, 131–137
obstetrics, 16–17
verbal responses, negative, 131–137
verbal responses, competing, 131–137
Pedophilia, 22–23
Perception, 40
Personal Report of Confidence of a Speaker, 334–336, 342–343
Phobias (*see* Avoidance behavior)
Premack's differential probability hypothesis, 215–216
Premack's Indifference Principle, 216
Problem-solving behavior, 27–28
definition, 185, 188–189
self-control, 11, 185–186
training, 27–28, 92–100, 186
trial and error learning, vs., 185
See also Effective behavior
Problematic situations, 27, 184
Psychoprophylactic method, 16
See also Natural childbirth
Psychosomatic symptoms, 265–266

R

Rational-emotive therapy, 18–19, 259–267, 332
description, 171–182, 260–261
homosexuality, treatment, 259–267
internalized sentences, 173–175, 179
irrational ideas, societal, 173–177, 179
neurosis, definition, 173–175, 178
neurosis, etiology, 175–176
neurosis, treatment, 175, 178–182
psychosomatic symptoms, treatment, 265–266
speech anxiety, treatment, 331–347

Rational psychotherapy (*see* Rational-emotive therapy)
Reasoning, 48–52
Relaxation techniques, 13, 248, 250–254
Relaxation, self-administered, 14–22, 255, 289
Reinforcement, covert, 31
Reinforcement, conditioned, 152
Reinforcement, self (*see* Self-reinforcement)
Reinforcement, token (*see* Token reinforcement)
Reward-cost theory, 160
Role playing (*see* Behavioral rehearsal)

S

Self-administered aversive conditioning, 14, 22–24
  See also Aversion therapy; Covert sensitization
Self-control, behavioral view, 4, 7–11, 32–34, 59–61, 69, 185
  commitment for change, 12–13
  creative thinking, vs., 10
  devaluation of unattainable goal, 75–76
  definition, 11–13, 60–61, 399–400, 403, 405
  emotional–physiological reactions, 13–24
  instrumental responses, 9, 13, 24–32
  mechanisms, 13–32
  mediational, 10–12, 17–18
  non-directive view, 4
  non-mediational, 10–11
  psychoanalytic theory, 4–7, 211
  training, 15–17, 27, 185–186, 248–256, 399–400, 403–404
Self-denial, 75–77, 139–140
Self-monitoring, 10, 403–405
Self-reinforcement, 10, 14, 24, 28–32, 76–77, 398
  contingency management, 31–32, 76–77
  covert reinforcement, 31
  external reinforcement, vs., 30, 152–161
  heterosexual anxiety, treatment, 348–363
  modeling, 29–30, 138–151
  sex differences, 158–160
  social comparison, 153, 160–161
  self-administered rewards, 28, 139, 152–153, 155, 158–161, 348–349
  standards, 153, 155–161
  token rewards, 28, 154–159
Self-study, 3–4
Semantic therapy, 81, 91
Sexual behavior, deviant, 12, 14, 22–23, 225, 259–267, 289, 388, 398
  See also Homosexuality; Pedophilia
Situation Questionnaire, 352, 356–357, 360
Situation Test, 351–352, 355, 357, 360
Smoking behavior, 12, 22–25, 218–220
  autohypnosis, 245
  aversive conditioning, 22–23, 378–379, 381–390
  operant self-control, 378–379, 381–390
  stimulus control, 24–25
  transactional game analysis, 378–379, 381–390
Social Anxiety Scale, 334
Social Avoidance and Distress Scale, 334–336, 342–344
Social control, 70–77
  discriminative training, 74–75
  fear, 71–72
  guilt, 71–72
  internal vs. external sanctions, 70
  shame, 71–72
  social restrictions and demands, 72–74
Stimulus change, 273–274
Stimulus control, 9, 24–26, 63–64, 271–272, 274, 277, 279–280
Study habits, 24, 26, 271–272, 281–284
Stuttering, 222, 245, 269
Systematic desensitization, 15, 224, 248–256
  anxiety, treatment, 15–16, 249–250, 297–316
  cardiac feedback, 107, 114, 251
  cognitive factors, 107, 114–115, 251–252
  coping skill, 15, 24, 250, 252
  drug-induced relaxation, 128–129, 251
  in vivo treatment, 16, 250–251, 253, 255, 299, 301–304, 306–312, 316
  mediational interpretation, 249–252, 254, 256
  phobias, treatment, 106–107, 248
  reciprocal inhibition interpretation, 248–249
  speech anxiety, treatment, 331–347
  symptom substitution, 250
  technique modifications, 252–256, 297–304

T

Thematic Apperception Test, 93–96, 98–99
Therapist Orientation Sheet, 332, 336
Token reinforcement, 28
Trial and error, 48–51, 185

V-W

Verbal self-direction, 18–19, 24, 26–28
  See also Language
Vicarious learning (*see* Modeling)
Wechsler Adult Intelligence Scale, 93–94
Will power, 4–5, 69